SEATTLE
ACCESS

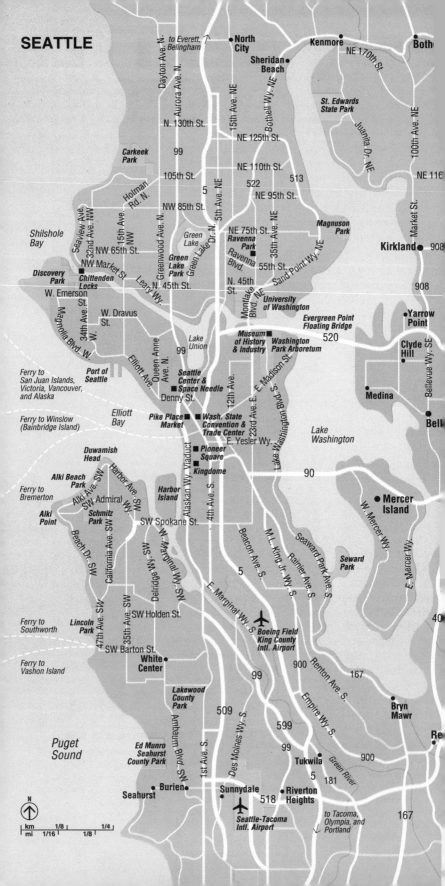

Orientation

Seattle, it seems, has always wanted to be something other than what it really is: a city struggling for a permanent identity. In November 1851, when founder Arthur Denny and his party of 23 adults and children from Illinois anchored in a rainstorm off what is now West Seattle, they dubbed their new home New York-Alki, Chinook jargon for "New York By-and-By." This bit of wishful thinking only seemed probable more than a century later, when Seattle's skyline had grown so tall and dense that it was finally regulated in 1989. Later, Seattle compared itself with San Francisco and assumed a pretentious nickname designed to overcome its historically low self-esteem: The Emerald City. With all due respect to *The Wizard of Oz,* few locals are so starry-eyed as to liken this town to that magical kingdom (although folks here, as in Dorothy's Emerald City, have lately been known to stop and congratulate each other on their home and its climate).

Only in the 1980s, when national media and wallet-waving tourists began to descend upon Seattle, did this city become more fully aware and protective of its envy-inducing virtues—the sharp peaks of the Cascade and Olympic mountains buckling it in on east and west, the neighboring saltwater Puget Sound aswim with giant octopuses and killer whales, an innovative and enthusiastic arts community, and the sparkling towers of white terra-cotta that literally punctuate downtown Seattle's reputation for cleanliness. Even the drizzle of winter . . . and spring . . . and fall . . . and sometimes summer earned cachet as a measurement of hardiness: There is no room here for weather whiners.

In 1983 *Esquire* magazine called Seattle "a mystical zone of indifference, a place so remote, so utterly far away from everything that your private demons will get lost trying to find you." By then, of course, this town in the upper left-hand corner of the country was already being "discovered." Attracted by low unemployment and exponential growth in the high-tech industries, as well as by the sense that Seattle could burgeon without completely jettisoning small-town values, new residents flocked to the city, as likely from Saigon as from Boston or Los Angeles. The area's population grew by 18 percent during the 1980s (twice the national average), and newcomers couldn't shut the entry gates fast enough behind them to completely safeguard what they'd found. A backlash of proprietary natives, spurred on by the *Seattle Times'* longtime columnist and curmudgeon, Emmett Watson, tried to counter the hype with half-truths and a few pointed prevarications regarding Seattle's resolute smugness, its notorious rainfall, and its general backwardness. "Plainly," Watson stated, "only a fool would want to live in Seattle, fools like me. . . ." But the influx could not be stemmed. Housing prices shot up, and some folks started to fret that air pollution, not just fog or rain clouds, was obscuring the city's noble vistas. By

M. BLUM

Space Needle

1990 Jonathan Raban (a Brit who now lives in Seattle), in his odyssey *Hunting Mister Heartbreak: A Discovery of America,* worried that Seattle had taken on the dangerous luster of a promised city.

But at least Seattle's promise wasn't hollow. There remains a youthful brashness to this place, a wild beauty that can certainly turn heads. In *Another Roadside Attraction,* Tom Robbins, a resident of nearby La Conner, Washington, describes the Puget Sound basin as having "a blurry beauty (as if the Creator started to erase it but had second thoughts)." And though Seattle hates to be called mellow, life among its 518,000 residents is ranked calmer than normal, which would help explain why ferries—rather than more expeditious bridges—still bring commuters across Puget Sound.

You, too, should take your time enjoying the city. But keep in mind that the Seattle you've heard about through the press is probably a mythologized spin on reality—all clear skies and leaping salmon, with a Birkenstock-wearing populace that builds mountain cabins in its spare time. A truly accurate read demands an understanding of Seattle's history and dreams, a more studied effort than Dorothy and Toto ever made of their Emerald City.

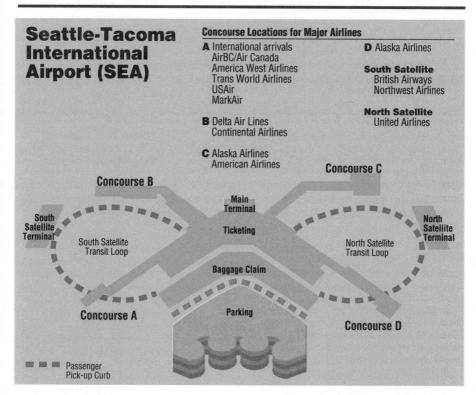

Seattle-Tacoma International Airport (SEA)

Concourse Locations for Major Airlines

A International arrivals
AirBC/Air Canada
America West Airlines
Trans World Airlines
USAir
MarkAir

B Delta Air Lines
Continental Airlines

C Alaska Airlines
American Airlines

D Alaska Airlines

South Satellite
British Airways
Northwest Airlines

North Satellite
United Airlines

Concourse B
Concourse C
Main Terminal
South Satellite Terminal
North Satellite Terminal
Ticketing
South Satellite Transit Loop
North Satellite Transit Loop
Baggage Claim
Concourse A
Parking
Concourse D
◼ ◼ ◼ Passenger Pick-up Curb

Area code 206 unless otherwise noted.

Getting to Seattle

Airport

Seattle-Tacoma International Airport (SEA)

This sprawling airport—known as Sea-Tac to locals—sits 13 miles south of Seattle, about a half-hour drive away, except during peak traffic periods (between 3PM and 6PM on most days) when it's wisest to launch out at least an hour before your plane departs. The airport is most easily reached by well-marked exits off either Interstate 5, running north and south, or Interstate 405 (becoming Freeway 518) from the east. Long-term and short-term parking are available within easy walking distance of the main terminal. A subway connects the main terminal with two satellite terminals; it's efficient, but just to be on the safe side, allow an extra 15 minutes to reach the outlying gates.

Emergencies	433.5400
Customs	553.4676
Immigration	553.5956
Information	431.4444
Interpreters	433.5367
Lost and Found	433.5312
Parking	431.4444

Lost or damaged baggage: See airline representatives in the baggage-claim area.

Rental Cars

Alamo	433.0182
Avis	433.5231
Budget	682.2277
Dollar	433.8131
Enterprise	243.4257
General	241.0866
National	433.5501
Penny	246.9828
Sears	224.7888
Thrifty	246.7565

Gray Line Airport Express picks up passengers at 11 downtown hotels daily from 5AM to 11:30PM. Departure times are every half-hour to every hour, depending on the stop. Trips from the airport back to town leave every half-hour from 6AM to midnight. The ride lasts about 50 minutes. The one-way adult fare is $7; round-trip is $12; and children pay less either way. Call 626.6088 for more information.

Metro Transit runs its No. 194 bus to Sea-Tac, a half-hour trip that leaves from the downtown bus tunnel about every 30 minutes. The No. 174 bus, departing from Second Avenue in downtown, also goes out to the airport every half-hour (a 45-minute excursion). For more information, call 553.3000.

Shuttle Express is a good deal, operating 24-hour door-to-door service for $16 (one way) in Seattle, $21 on the east side of Lake Washington. Reservations are essential when traveling to Sea-Tac but are not required on the way into town. One warning: the company's policy is to get you to the airport *at least* an hour in advance of your flight. To make reservations, call 622.1424 or 800/487.7433.

Taxis traveling between downtown and the airport charge about $25 one way.

The Metro Transit buses, Shuttle Express, and taxis (call for service from one of the sidewalk "hot line" phones) leave from outside the baggage-claim area on the main terminal's lower level.

Getting around Seattle

When roaming downtown, whether on foot, by bus, or in a car, just remember this helpful phrase: **Jesus Christ Made Seattle Under Protest (JCMSUP).** Starting at Jefferson Street and continuing north to Pine Street, you'll find two streets for each first letter in that ditty: Jefferson and James; Cherry and Columbia; Marion and Madison; Spring and Seneca; University and Union; Pike and Pine. To further simplify things, most north-south roads are "Avenues" and their compass directions are listed after their name or number (for example: 3825 Whitman Avenue North). Thoroughfares traveling west to east are "Streets," and their compass directions appear before their name or number (as in 118 NW 78th Street). Aberrations are the occasional "Ways," which usually run diagonally to the city grid. If you're lost, remember that Seattle is shaped like an hourglass, with downtown smack in the middle. Puget Sound is always west of the city, and Mount Rainier punches up to the east—that is, when you can spot it through the "blurry beauty" of overcast skies.

Automobiles

Residents of Seattle voted back in the late 1960s to pump money into more freeways, rather than into mass transit—a big mistake. Today, even the most reserved Seattleites have begun to honk their car horns downtown, as the cumulative swell of bicycle couriers, buses, cabs, and pedestrians forces motorists to play dodge between red lights. Beware especially of the human sargasso at Pike Place Market, where amblers always enjoy the right-of-way. Even some outlying routes, such as 45th Street between Wallingford and the University District, Broadway on Capitol Hill, and Lake City Way rounding Lake Washington's upper reaches, crawl on weekday afternoons. And it's a wonder there haven't been riots in front of the Fremont Bridge, where decks lift to allow pleasure boats passage through the Lake Washington Ship Canal while overheating cars are forced to wait.

Freeway traffic snarls here don't yet rival Los Angeles, but they're close: the average daily commuter takes just less than half an hour to drive into downtown, and even that sounds zippy to some folks living east of Lake Washington. The average speed during rush time is 22 mph, and peak-period delays are only expected to worsen. Particularly congested is the drive on the two floating bridges that cross Lake Washington. Express lanes relieve some of the pressure north of downtown along I-5; and High-Occupancy Vehicle (HOV) lanes (for cars carrying more than two or three persons, with restrictions varying according to area) are available on both I-5 and westbound on the 520 freeway. Highway 99, or Aurora Avenue, remains a decent alternative to I-5. In general, however, you're better off avoiding freeways and highways in Seattle from 6AM to 9AM and 3PM to 6PM.

Buses

Negotiating the streets of Seattle aboard **Metro Transit** buses is easy, though you should carry a book to read for any long trip, because transferring from route to route often demands a lengthy detour through downtown. Service is free in the commercial core (bounded by the Waterfront on the west, I-5 on the east, Jackson Street to the south, and Battery Street to the north). But beyond that, a two-zone system charges 85¢ within the city ($1.10 at peak times, Monday through Friday from 6AM to 9AM and 3PM to 6PM) and $1.10 if you travel beyond the city limits ($1.60 at peak times). When to pay is simple: Heading out of downtown, pay when you get off; heading in, pay when you board. Drivers don't carry change, so have the correct amount in hand or overpay in dollar bills. The buses are generally clean, comfortable, and—though every rider can list exceptions—on time. About 70 percent are wheelchair accessible, and some even sport exterior bicycle mounts (you'll see them on the fronts of buses; the drivers usually like to hook your bike up for you). In typical Seattle fashion, riders tend toward xenophobia (watch how they avoid sitting next to one another whenever possible), but drivers can be quite garrulous, launching into tour monologues as they pilot through the city or, during particularly bad winter slowdowns, engaging their passengers in a chorus or two of "Let It Snow."

An L-shaped bus tunnel, designed to shave a whopping five minutes off the time necessary to travel through the congested downtown traffic, was completed beneath the commercial core in 1990. Five entrances are available between the Washington State Convention and Trade Center, at Ninth Avenue and Pine Street, and the International District. Bus stops (identifiable by their yellow-and-white signs) are usually posted with current timetables, but schedules are also available aboard the buses and at most public locations around town, including libraries and shopping malls. Call Metro Transit's help line (553.3000) for trip-planning information 24 hours a day.

Ferries

Perhaps the most memorable sound in Seattle is the moan of ferry horns on a fog-cloaked eve. The **Washington State Ferry System** is the nation's largest, carrying some 18 million passengers a year over nine routes. The busiest run on weekdays is between Bainbridge Island and downtown Seattle, a 25-minute commuter chug. On weekends, and especially during the summer, the **Edmonds-Kingston Ferry** is shoehorned full of tourists, and it's not uncommon to wait three hours for car space on ferries bound for popular Victoria, British Columbia. Walk-ons stand a better chance than drivers of catching their boat of choice. Most passengers pay a round-trip fare up front, and costs vary according to distance. Food and beverages on the boats are mediocre at best, so you may want to pack something to snack on. Credit cards are not accepted, and travelers headed for Canada must have a passport or other proper identification. Schedules change from winter to summer; call

464.6400 or 800/843.3779 for current departure times and rates.

Monorail

The sleek, Buck Rogers-ish monorail contraptions weren't invented in Seattle, but almost. In 1911 the *Seattle Times* looked forward to a day when "wooden monorail lines, like high fences, will go straggling across country, carrying their burden of cars that will develop a speed of about 20 miles an hour." It took 51 more years and the opening of Seattle's Century 21 Exposition before this town had such a line, however, and some folks wonder why it still exists. Despite suggestions that its rails be extended to the airport or that it otherwise supplement existing mass-transit systems, the **Alweg Monorail** (its official moniker) still runs only a 90-second, 1.2-mile route from downtown's **Westlake Center** to the old World's Fair grounds, now known as **Seattle Center**. It's great for children, who love the train's smooth and uninterrupted ride. Adults pay 80¢ one way, $1.60 round-trip; kids 5 to 12 go for 60¢ ($1.20 round-trip), and children under 5 ride free. Seniors and disabled riders pay 25¢ one way, 50¢ round-trip. Trains depart every 15 minutes from 9AM to midnight during the summer; in winter they run until 9PM on weeknights and until midnight on Friday and Saturday. Call 684.7200 for more information.

Parking

Free parking options in the city are relegated to the rim areas—at the southern end of the Waterfront near Jackson Street, for instance, or on Elliott Avenue bordering Myrtle Edwards Park. Closer to downtown, it's hard to find a meter offering more than half an hour's time, and many others (marked in yellow) are off-limits except to delivery vehicles.

Downtown parking facilities may charge up to $7.50 per day; less-expensive lots are found on the fringes, along Alaskan Way on the Waterfront, in the International District, and near First and Bell streets. Beware of parking infractions: An overtime parking ticket costs about $20 in Seattle. If you're caught in a truck-loading zone, the charge is a little higher, and parking illegally in a handicapped-only spot will cost you about $50.

Taxis

Unlike their East Coast counterparts, Seattle cabs almost never stop for people hailing from the sidewalk. Dispatchers control most of the 2,300 cabs running the streets of King County, not anxious patrons. If you want a cab, they tend to cluster around the bigger downtown hotels (especially the Four Seasons Olympic Hotel and the Westin), as well as at the King Street train station. Otherwise, pick up the phone; one will arrive in, oh, 10 or 30 minutes. Or maybe not. (This is laid-back Seattle, after all.) Taxis are a fairly cheap means of transport here, and the meter doesn't start running until you're picked up. Companies include: **Broadway Cab** (622.4800), **Checker Deluxe Cab** (622.1234), **Farwest Taxi** (329.7700), and **Yellow Cab** (622.6500). **STITA** (246.9999) is a cooperative cab enterprise offering transportation between downtown and the airport.

Tours

The city's most familiar tour may be **Underground Seattle,** an hour-long excursion beneath the streets of historic **Pioneer Square.** A mammoth fire in 1889 burned most of this district to the ground. When it was rebuilt, the decision was made to raise this land farther above water level than it had been, improving drainage and expanding the city's buildable acreage. To allow for regrading, structures adopted double sets of entrances—one at the original ground level and another that was one story up, where sidewalks eventually would be laid.

This all seemed fine at first, but as it turned out, the streets were raised throughout Pioneer Square long before the sidewalks could be elevated to meet them. Victorian ladies and gents, therefore, had to scale tall ladders (eight to 30 feet high) just to cross from one side of the street to the other. Strolling in the neighborhood at night was a particular hazard, given the shortage of streetlamps.

Engineers finally made the roads and the sidewalks even, but they did so without destroying the lower-level pedestrian ways. The remaining "underground city" was condemned in the early 1900s, but for many years after, it was the province of Seattle's criminal element. Not until the 1970s did a local historian and author, the late **Bill Speidel,** win the permits he needed to conduct public tours of those all-but-forgotten corridors. Docents today have a somewhat corny spiel, and the mustiness below ground can be daunting, but for history buffs this trip is worth it. Tours leave from **Doc Maynard's Public House** (610 First Avenue) and last about an hour-and-a-half; they're available from late morning until mid-afternoon most days of the year. Reservations are recommended; call Underground Tour at 682.4646.

Chinatown Discovery Tours (236.0657) will escort you through Seattle's International District, taking in such attractions as a fortune-cookie factory and an herb dispensary, and breaking for a dim sum lunch. **Gray Line** (626.5208) offers a variety of sightseeing excursions, including runs along the Waterfront, out to Mount Rainier, and deep into "Twin Peaks" country (Snoqualmie Falls and the pocket-edition town of North Bend). **Gray Line Water Sightseeing** (441.1887) books tours around Seattle Harbor. **Seattle Harbor Tours** (623.1445) schedules cruises through the Hiram Chittenden Locks and around historic Elliott Bay. And the Seattle Architectural Foundation and the American Institute of Architects (local chapter) cosponsor **Viewpoint Tours,** a guided series that explores the historic architecture of various neighborhoods, from May through November (448.0106).

Brochures for most tour companies can be found at the **Seattle-King County Convention and Visitors Bureau** (520 Pike Street, Suite 1300; 461.5800) or the tourist information booth in the **Washington State Convention and Trade Center** (800 Convention Place; 461.5840).

Walking

Long city blocks, some daunting hills, and the polar separation of Seattle's two principal tourist meccas, Pioneer Square and Pike Place Market, make downtown an area best consumed by nibbling rather than gorging. There's an interesting diversity of architecture and street life, but early city founders—dismissing aesthetics in favor of a higher building profile—relegated green spaces to the neighborhoods, leaving little open pedestrian space in downtown. The result is urban canyons between Cherry and Pike streets. Don't feel guilty about taking buses from one point of interest to another. Neighborhoods offer more consistently intriguing strolls, particularly along Broadway on Capitol Hill, along Market Street in Ballard, and down University Avenue in the University District. On the suburban Eastside, only downtown Kirkland boasts enough sites within a small area to be walkable.

FYI

Climate

The predictions of Seattle-area meteorologists are often studies in equivocation, with the ultimate waffle being "partial sunshine, followed by partial low-cloudiness, and maybe some rain turning to showers in the afternoon." Look out your window for an accurate assessment, but remember that the weather you're experiencing now may be quite different from what's going on only two miles away. Warm offshore currents, mountains, and cold fronts from the north conspire to give Seattle an unpredictable but fairly moderate overall climate.

July and August are usually the warmest months of the year, with an average daily high of 74°F, an average relative humidity of 50 percent, and usually no more than an inch or so of rain a month. January is the coldest, with the record low experienced by Seattle on 31 January 1950, when the mercury plummeted to 0°F. Snow and ice are infrequent, but when they come, it can turn the city into a huge frozen sculpture and stop traffic dead in its tracks.

Drinking

Washington state's legal drinking age is 21. Bars usually stay open until 1:30AM, and wine and beer are available at most supermarkets and groceries. Hard liquor, however, must be purchased at one of the many state-regulated liquor stores.

Entertainment

Two clearinghouses offer tickets to a variety of performing arts and venues. **Ticket/Ticket** deals in half-price, cash-only, day-of-show buys from two locations: Broadway Market on Capitol Hill and Pike Place Market (they're both open Tuesday through Sunday; call 324.2744 for more information). **TicketMaster** sells advance admissions at several cash-only centers around town but also offers a charge-by-phone service (call 628.0888). In addition, some theaters (including the **Bathhouse**

Theatre, the **Empty Space Theater**, and the **New City Theater**) schedule special "pay-as-you-can" performances, and many offer reduced-price preview tickets. Broad-ranging and up-to-date calendars of events can be found in *Seattle Weekly*, the *Seattle Times'* Friday "Tempo" section, "What's Happening" in the Friday *Seattle Post-Intelligencer*, and *Eastsideweek.*

Money
Banks are generally open from 9:30AM to 5PM, with some also operating on Saturday mornings. Most of the larger downtown institutions will exchange foreign currency and traveler's checks. Better rates, however, may be available Monday through Friday at **American Express** (600 Stewart Street) or at **Thomas Cook Currency Services** (906 Third Avenue). In a pinch, **Check Mart** (1206 First Avenue) exchanges Canadian money *only* on Saturday from 9AM to 7PM, and Sunday 11AM to 7PM.

Publications
The city's two daily newspapers—the *Seattle Post-Intelligencer* (also called the *P-I*) and the *Seattle Times*—have been in the velvet grip of a Joint Operating Agreement (JOA) since 1983, ending an often vituperative rivalry. Both publishers now produce separate papers Monday through Saturday, but only a single *Times*-dominated "jumbo" edition on Sunday. The Hearst-owned morning *P-I* is strong on news and sports but unimaginative in its feature sections. The more successful afternoon *Times* is owned primarily by the local Blethen family (with a minority share held by Knight-Ridder). Although it has claimed several Pulitzer prizes for news coverage, the *Times* is still better known for its feature writing. The Eastside's principal broadsheet is the homey *Journal American,* owned by a Hawaiian chain, which is chockablock with upscale-neighborhood stories.

Seattle Weekly, published on Tuesday, has shed its scrappy "alternative" image over the years, becoming successful and mainstream, but the tabloid continues to attract readers with its arts coverage, essays, and opinionated calendar of events. A free sister publication, *Eastsideweek* (available on Wednesday), covers communities east of Lake Washington with a slightly more irreverent eye.

Slick bimonthly newcomer *Seattle* magazine claims a scattershot of topics, from politics to gardening and history, while *Pacific Northwest* attracts primarily out-of-towners with its nine-times-a-year editorial menu of travel, food, and pretty pictures. *The Rocket* concentrates monthly on the local pop-music scene, and *Reflex* is an often-quirky tab focusing on trends and politics affecting the arts.

Puget Sound Business Journal (PSBJ) and the *Daily Journal of Commerce* both keep track of local financial transactions, but the weekly *PSBJ* is usually more readable. *Media Inc.* concentrates on developments in local print, broadcast, and advertising realms, while *Washington CEO* is a monthly magazine of features about the state's financial movers. *Seattle Skanner, The Medium,* and *The Facts* all serve the black community. *Seattle's*

Child features a wealth of activities and health materials directed at young families. *Seattle Gay News* reports on subjects of interest to local gays and lesbians. *Seattle Chinese Post* now publishes an English-language edition, *Northwest Asian Weekly.* The *North American Post* is the Northwest's single Japanese-language paper, and *Hispanic News* is a bilingual weekly.

Smoking
Health-conscious Seattleites tolerate smokers even less willingly than they do Californians. Restaurants that don't outright ban lighting up have usually set aside separate smoking sections. Bars and taverns tend to be more lenient, but it's the rare place that permits cigars or pipes. And smoking is banned in all city-owned buildings.

Street Smarts
The Seattle police force patrols the streets by motorcycle, car, mountain bike, horse, and on foot, which is reassuring to all but jaywalkers (more than 3,500 jaywalking tickets are issued here annually). Pickpockets are rare, but they do turn up in crowded areas such as Pike Place Market, along Broadway on Capitol Hill, and in shopping malls. Panhandlers can be a problem, too. Though they are essentially harmless, one could go broke tossing change into all the upside-down chapeaus. Seattle isn't known for its violent crime (theft is the principal threat here), but some cabdrivers refuse to venture into the comparatively poor Central District, fearing at least robbery or assault. As with any large city, be more careful at night, especially in the downtown area.

Telephones
Local pay-phone calls (including those from Seattle to Bainbridge Island and the Eastside) cost 25¢. To reach directory assistance for Seattle and the rest of western Washington, you must now dial 206/555.1212. Note: Hotels generally lard premiums onto your calls, so it may prove a worthwhile savings to dial from the public phone booths.

Tipping
A 15-percent tip is standard in restaurants and taxis, and $1 per bag is sufficient for hotel porters. Concierges anticipate tips based on the quality of their service and a guest's individual largess. Twenty dollars for a week's worth of consistently good advice would be a healthy "thanks" in Seattle, although some guests prefer to give $1 per service.

Seattle is the country's 14th most populous urban area, according to Census Bureau data. New York, Los Angeles, Chicago, Dallas, Houston, Miami, and Atlanta are all larger, but between 1980 and 1990, Seattle rose ahead of Baltimore, St. Louis, and Minneapolis. The region is expected to surpass Cleveland in the 1990s. The Seattle urban area was only the 20th largest in 1970 and the 17th largest in 1980. (Note: The census takers lump Seattle together with Tacoma, Everett, and Bremerton when assessing its population.)

Phone Book

Emergencies
Ambulance/Fire/Police **911**
AAA of Washington 448.5353
AIDS Hotline..296.4999
Animal Control (Lost Pets) 386.7387
Arson Hotline.................................800/552.7766
Auto Impound.......................................684.5444
Auto Theft...684.8940
Battered Women Crisis Hotline 522.9472
Child Protective Services Crisis Hotline ...721.4306
Coast Guard 24-Hour Emergency 800/592.9911
Crime Prevention 684.7555
Crisis Clinic..461.3207
Domestic Violence Hotline..............800/562.6025
Drunk Driver Reporting...................800/223.7865
FBI..622.0460
Locksmith (AAA 24-hour)......................325.1515
Missing Persons....................................633.1009

Poison Center 526.2121
Rape Relief 632.7273
Suicide Prevention 800/422.2552
Visitor Information
American Youth Hostels 622.5443
Amtrak...800/872.7245
Better Business Bureau.........................448.8888
Convention and Visitors Bureau..............461.5800
Customs..553.4676
Gray Line 624.5077
Greyhound Bus......................................624.3456
Metro Transit...553.3000
Northwest Ski Report 634.0071
Passports 442.7941
Time...206/976.1616
(a long-distance call even from Seattle)
Traveler's Aid..461.3888
Washington State Ferries........................464.6400
Weather...526.6087

How To Read This Guide

SEATTLE ACCESS® is arranged by neighborhood so you can see at a glance where you are and what is around you. The numbers next to the entries in the following chapters correspond to the numbers on the maps. The text is color-coded according to the kind of place described:

Restaurants/Clubs: Red   Hotels: Blue

Shops/ 🌳 Outdoors: Green   Sights/Culture: Black

Rating the Restaurants and Hotels

The restaurant star ratings take into account the quality, service, atmosphere, and uniqueness of the restaurant. An expensive restaurant doesn't necessarily ensure an enjoyable evening; however, a small, relatively unknown spot could have good food, professional service, and a lovely atmosphere. Therefore, on a purely subjective basis, stars are used to judge the overall dining value (see the star ratings at right). Keep in mind that chefs and owners often change, which sometimes drastically affects the quality of a restaurant. The ratings in this guidebook are based on information available at press time.

The price ratings, as categorized at right, apply to restaurants and hotels. These figures describe general price-range relationships among other restaurants and hotels in the area. The restaurant price ratings are based on the average cost of an entrée for one person, excluding tax and tip. Hotel price ratings reflect the base price of a standard room for two people for one night during the peak season.

Restaurants

★ Good

★★ Very Good

★★★ Excellent

★★★★ An Extraordinary Experience

$ The Price Is Right   (less than $10)

$$ Reasonable   ($10-$15)

$$$ Expensive   ($15-$20)

$$$$ Big Bucks   ($20 and up)

Hotels

$ The Price Is Right   (less than $80)

$$ Reasonable   ($80-$120)

$$$ Expensive   ($120-$180)

$$$$ Big Bucks   ($180 and up)

Map Key

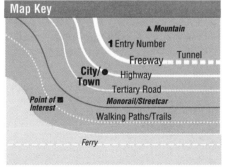

▲ *Mountain*

1 Entry Number

Freeway   Tunnel

City/ ● Highway
Town

Tertiary Road

Point of ▪
Interest   *Monorail/Streetcar*

Walking Paths/Trails

Ferry

Pioneer Square/ International District

In the middle of a parched summer in 1889, when Seattle had been an incorporated city for only 20 years, its business district—what's known now as Pioneer Square—started burning beyond control. A roiling column of purplish smoke could be seen from Tacoma, 32 miles to the south.

The conflagration had begun in a woodworker's basement, where a pot of glue boiled over a gas stove and into a mess of turpentine-soaked wood shavings. Whole city blocks were consumed by flames in less than 30

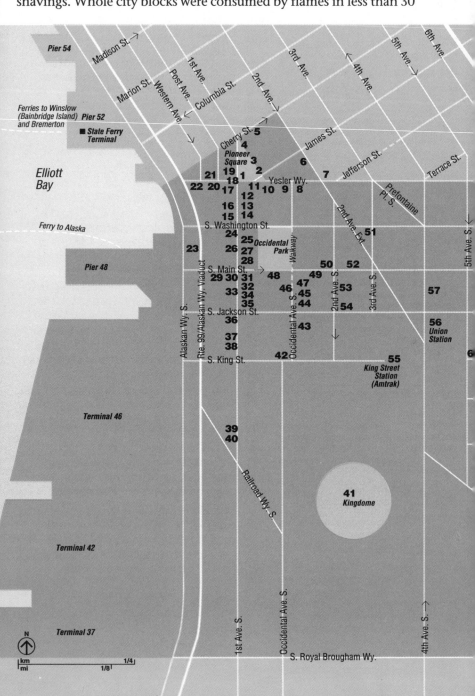

minutes because hydrant pressure was too weak to combat the disaster. **Fire Chief Josiah Collins** was away at the time, and the young acting chief was not up to this battle, so **Mayor Robert Moran** took over, dynamiting buildings in front of the fire and arranging bucket brigades to pull water from nearby gullies. Still, these efforts weren't enough. Thirty central city blocks totaling 64 acres were leveled before the **Great Fire of 1889** fizzled amidst tidelands where the **Kingdome** stadium stands today. Amazingly, not a single person is known to have perished in the blaze.

No sooner did the smoke dissipate than civic boosters were talking up the calamity as a boon for Seattle, a second chance to become a showplace and commercial capital. Sure enough, thanks in large measure to **James J. Hill** designating Seattle as the western terminus for his **Great Northern Railroad**, the town was back in business less than two years later—more populous and optimistic than ever, and this time requiring that all new downtown buildings be shaped smartly of brick, stone, and iron.

Today's Pioneer Square is vastly unlike what it was before the fire. For one thing, much of the land is higher. Ever since claims were first staked on **Elliott Bay** in 1852, city engineers had resorted to dredging and landfilling to both expand Seattle's commercial acreage and lift it above water level. Ship ballast was used, as was dirt graded down from precipitous hills behind the original town. After the fire, Pioneer Square was filled in with much of the excess earth, burying the first stories of many post-fire edifices (and creating what is now known as **Underground Seattle**). From the beginning of the Alaskan Gold Rush in 1897, which transformed Seattle into a wealthy embarkation point, until after the turn of the century, Pioneer Square celebrated a commercial heyday.

But as the city developed northward, this part of town was left to honky-tonk taverns, bawdy houses, and transient hotels. Opium dens and, later, Prohibition speakeasies sprang up in the shadowy tunnels created by regrading. During the Depression the area became so decrepit that in 1966 the proposal was made to level it to make room for more parking lots and new offices.

Architects and preservationists were incensed. So was well-known local newspaper columnist **Emmett Watson**. "I swear, my friends," Watson lamented in print, "progress is going to be the death of this city yet!" But death didn't assail Pioneer Square after all. Banks initiated incentive loan programs to revive the neighborhood, and businesses moved in to restore its sturdy buildings. Today, approximately 88 acres of offices, restaurants, art galleries, and specialty stores form what was the city's first historic district.

The International District (or "I.D.," as locals say), bordering Pioneer Square on the east and encompassing the city's Chinese and Japanese enclaves, has a similarly troubled but far different heritage. Seattle's original **Chinatown** was actually centered at Second Avenue and Washington Street, smack in what was then the middle of the city. Its Chinese inhabitants had ventured to **Puget Sound** to work on railroads and in lumber mills or mines. Later, they developed successful cigar-making and dry-goods businesses. But by the mid-1880s, as unemployment rose in the Northwest, some white laborers came to resent the Chinese and their "cheap labor." In February 1886 mobs of Seattle Sinophobes (including, it's said, many police officers) invaded Chinatown and herded almost all of the city's 350 to 400 Chinese toward steamships bound for San Francisco. Martial law was declared to halt the expulsion, but at least half of Seattle's Chinese left anyway, fearful of the consequences should they remain. Only well after the Great Fire of 1889 did the Chinese begin returning to Seattle, and by then new Japanese immigrants had filled up much of the labor vacuum.

Chinatown relocated to the blocks around King and Jackson streets in the early 1900s, after a regrading project made the district more hospitable. The Japanese, meanwhile, settled in an area just north of there, which they called **Nihonmachi**. By 1910 Nihonmachi housed more than 6,000 Japanese. But World War II took a toll on both communities. Many Japanese were interned in camps all over the West. Low-income housing subsequently invaded the south end of downtown and condemnation proceedings were brought against a number of older Asian-owned structures. But in the 1970s, a concerted effort went into revitalizing the I.D., and much there has since been renovated. Families started to move back in, the Kingdome stadium was opened, parks were laid out, and new businesses—especially the Asian restaurants—now attract residents from all over town, many of whom never have figured out how to order dim sum or sushi.

1 Pioneer Place Park The spiritual hub of Pioneer Square was once a disregarded and clumsy intersection called **Yesler's Corner**. Only after the fire of 1889 did it attain notoriety. Some visitors avoid this cobblestoned triangle because of the panhandlers and pigeons, but it's an ideal spot for people-watching or studying the surrounding architecture.

The drinking fountain and the bust of **Chief Sealth** you see here were designed by **James A. Wehn** and installed in 1909. Although the original is long gone, a western red cedar totem pole has stood on this spot since 1899. Carved by **Tlingit Indians** on southeast Alaska's **Tongass Island**, the original totem pole had been chopped down and taken as a souvenir by an excursion party from Seattle.

After an arsonist scarred but did not quite destroy the monolith in 1938, it was shipped back to the Last Frontier, where native totem carvers (apparently unperturbed by Seattle's filching of the original) crafted the replica now protruding from Pioneer Place Park.

A cast-iron-and-glass pergola was erected at the park's southern tip in 1909 (and rehabilitated in 1970) to serve as a shelter for pedestrians waiting to board passing trolleys. The pergola also marked the entrance to Seattle's first public restroom (opened in 1909)—a lavish underground hideaway of Alaskan marble and skylights that offered shoe shines and a newspaper stand until plumbing problems forced its closure in 1939. The facility still exists, but it's accessible now only through a manhole.

So far the city has refused efforts to reopen the restroom. ♦ First Ave (between Yesler Way and Cherry St)

2 Pioneer Building The **American Institute of Architects (AIA)** applauded this structure's value early on. In 1892, two years after it was completed, the AIA labeled it "the finest building west of Chicago." Commissioned by Seattle pioneer and entrepreneur **Henry Yesler** (whose first home sat on the same property), and designed by Massachusetts emigrant **Elmer H. Fisher,** the Pioneer is a paradigm of this neighborhood's architecture. (Fisher would go on to create some 50 other buildings in and around Pioneer Square, lending it a homogenous but hardly disagreeable look.) Its style is Romanesque Revival, as developed and refined by visionary architects such as **Henry Hobson Richardson** and **Louis Sullivan.** A rusticated stone base and Roman archway give way to progressively different window treatments in the upper stories. The Pioneer was originally endowed with a pyramid-topped central tower, but that was taken down (along with other towers and cornices in the district) as a precautionary measure after an earthquake rumbled up from **Olympia** to clobber Seattle in 1949. Don't miss the building's Italian red-marble interior and atrium. ♦ 606 First Ave

2 Doc Maynard's Public House ★$ This restored pub is high on atmosphere (check out the magnificent carved bar), and on a sunny day, its outdoor tables invite you to take a seat and wet your whistle. The menu is pedestrian, running from sandwiches to bar munchies, but Doc's does offer a lively repertoire of rock and R&B bands on Friday and Saturday nights. It's also the jumping-off point to tours of **Underground Seattle,** a long-buried maze of corridors that were once the sidewalks and first floors of Pioneer Square. (See page 7 for tour details.) ♦ American ♦ Cover charged Friday and Saturday. M-F 9:30AM-4PM, 8PM-2AM, Sa 9:30AM-5PM, 8PM-2AM, Su 9:30AM-5PM Sept-May; M-F 9:30AM-6PM, 8PM-2AM, Sa 9:30AM-5PM, 8PM-2AM, Su 9:30AM-5PM June-Aug. 610 First Ave. 682.4649

3 Romio's Pizza ★★$ Seattle is certainly not short on pizza joints, but few can beat the crust of this and four other Romio's branches around town (in Magnolia, Greenwood, Eastlake, and Belltown). Ingredients are liberally apportioned and the crusts are thick and chewy. The Gasp! is the house specialty, a wake-up call of garlic, artichoke hearts, and sun-dried tomatoes. Misguided thrill-seekers and daredevils will want to order this pie with the special garlic crust. For more tender palates, there's the soothing Zorba, which is kind of like a flat and open gyro sandwich,

with beef, onion, feta cheese, green olives, and homemade *tzatziki* sauce. Home deliveries are available, too. ♦ Pizza/Takeout ♦ M-Th 11AM-8PM; F-Sa 11AM-1AM; Su noon-5PM. 616 First Ave. 621.8500. Also at: 3242 Eastlake Ave East. 322.4453; 2001 W. Dravus St. 284.5420; 8523 Greenwood Ave North. 782.9005; 917 Howell St. 622.6878

3 Old Timer's Cafe $ The wood-and-brass decor are Pioneer Square clichés, and the boxcar narrowness of this tavern ensures it will seem crowded, even when only a few people have stepped inside. The draw is the nightly performances by local blues and jazz musicians.

The food served here is of a Southern bent, including gumbo, barbecue ribs, catfish, and mustard greens. ♦ Southern ♦ Cover. Daily 11AM-2AM. 620 First Ave. 623.9800

4 Lowman Building The only French Renaissance Eclectic-style tower at Pioneer Place, finished in 1900, is quite a standout from the parade of Romanesque piles. The principal designer was **August Heide,** an import from back east who worked primarily in the nearby town of Everett. ♦ 105 Cherry St (at First Ave)

Art by the Foot

Strolling through Pioneer Square is especially popular on the first Thursday of every month, when most of the area's art galleries, plus many of its specialty clothing stores and crafts shops, stay open late to show off their new displays. It's a chance to cover a lot of ground without the interference of businesspeople crowding the streets. Some art lovers miss the old days (actually, it wasn't that long ago), when galleries poured wine for **First Thursday** visitors, but at least there are enough restaurants and taverns in Pioneer Square that you won't be without a place to sit beside friends and discuss the nuances of your evening's artgrazing.

First Thursday's actual hours vary, beginning around 5:30PM and lasting until at least 8PM. Start at any gallery in Pioneer Square. There's no central number for First Thursday information, but contact one of the more prominent galleries, such as **Linda Farris Gallery** (623.1110) or **Foster/White Gallery** (622.2833), if you have questions.

Early Indian names for the area now called Seattle included the far less mellifluous Duwamps and Mulckmukum. And Pioneer Square was called Djidjilaletch, after the Duwamish Indian winter village once located there.

5 Seattle Mystery Bookshop Proprietor **Bill Farley** carries an abundance of new and used works, paperback and hardcover, including some detective and spy novels that just don't seem to turn up elsewhere in town. Sherlock Holmes stories and books by Puget Sound crime novelists (such as **Earl Emerson, J.A. Jance, Robert Ferrigno,** and **Aaron Elkins**) garner their own bookcases. Mailings alert regular patrons to signings by well-known authors. ♦ M-Sa 11AM-6PM. 117 Cherry St. 587.5737

6 Second & James Parking Garage In an earlier era, one of the city's first and finest hotels occupied this triangular block, now home to a ship-prow-shaped parking garage. The **Occidental Hotel** opened in the 1860s with 30 rooms. But in 1865, as the Civil War was being negotiated to an end, an entrepreneur named **John Collins** arrived in Seattle, unstrapped $3,000 in gold dust from his waist, and purchased a one-third interest in the ivory-hued hostelry. Collins would go on to write Seattle's first charter, serve on its first city council, develop coal fields on the east side of Lake Washington, and start the **Seattle Gas Light Company,** as well as serve a term as mayor. His hotel was no less ambitious.

While Collins was sitting in the first **Washington Legislature** (1883-84), he had the Occidental completely rebuilt in ostentatious style, proclaiming (with undue hyperbole) that his was now the "leading hotel in the Northwest." Guest capacity was expanded to 400. Collins even added an elevator. But then came the Great Fire of 1889. Collins tried to save his hotel by buying up the surrounding clapboard structures and blowing them to smithereens, thus crippling the blaze before it could reach his business— but the transactions couldn't be made fast enough, and the Occidental went up with most of the rest of old Seattle. Collins went on to build a third Occidental, which he later renamed the **Seattle Hotel;** it stood on this site until the early 1960s. ♦ Second Ave (between Yesler Way and James St)

7 Smith Tower When it opened on 4 July 1914, this was the tallest building (pictured at right) outside of Manhattan—42 floors, 522 feet—and for 48 years thereafter, it remained the highest west of the Mississippi River. (The local record was finally topped in 1962 by the **Space Needle,** at 605 feet, but it was broken officially in 1969 by the **Seattle-First National Bank Tower,** now the **1001 Fourth Avenue Building,** at 50 stories or 609 feet.) Constructed by order of **Lyman C. Smith,** the armaments entrepreneur-turned-typewriter baron, Smith Tower was also this city's first fireproof steel structure, decorated with terracotta facing and cornices.

Smith was an upstate New Yorker. Visiting Seattle in 1909 to do some real-estate speculation, he saw it as ripe ground on which to demonstrate the depth of his success, and thereby commissioned the firm of **Gaggin & Gaggin** to build a skyscraper that would anchor downtown Seattle once and for all near its starting place. (A forlorn hope: commercial construction moved farther and farther north, fashionably away from the "old city.") Smith also wanted a building that wouldn't be exceeded in height during his lifetime. That wish came true: L.C. died before Smith Tower was completed.

His "two-stepped" legacy, perhaps inspired by Gotham's magnificent **Woolworth Building,** remains Seattle's best-loved, if not loftiest, construction. An observation deck on the 35th floor provides a marvelous panorama of downtown; and on the same floor can be found the teak-ceilinged **Chinese Room,** which Smith conceived especially for his daughter's marriage and where weddings are still held. The West Coast's only manually operated elevators (complete

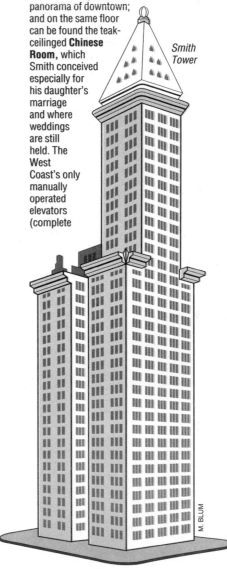

Smith Tower

M. BLUM

with original-style levers) are also to be found in this building. And don't miss the enchanting carved Indian heads above the first-floor elevator doors. ♦ Yesler Way and Second Ave

Within Smith Tower:

G&G Cigar Store No, this pungent place was not named, as many have supposed, after the firm that designed Smith Tower—**Gaggin & Gaggin.** In fact, the tobacco shop was established elsewhere in 1895 and relocated to Smith Tower only after its completion. Its moniker comes from former owners **Gifford and Good.** The cigar selection is rather limited; but with a wooden Indian statue in the window and aging paraphernalia throughout, G&G rates high in the historical gem category. ♦ M-F 8AM-5:30PM. 504 Second Ave. 623.6721

8 Interurban Building (Smith Tower Annex) The exceptional brick masonry, stone carving, and terracotta trim make this oft-overlooked office building another excellent example of Pioneer Square's Romanesque-Victorian style. Fenestration carefully orchestrated from floor to floor gives rhythm and a fine scale to the architecture. The corner entrance is ornamented with a lion's head. Not surprisingly, the architect who designed this 1890 building, **John Parkinson,** was an **Elmer Fisher** contemporary, who later employed Fisher as a designer in Los Angeles. Until 1920, this was the **Interurban Railway Depot.** And during World War II, **Boeing** had its headquarters here. ♦ 102-108 Occidental Ave South

9 Madame & Co. This is one of the classier vintage-clothing outlets in town; you'll be lucky to find anything here made after Amelia Earhart disappeared. The pieces are in fine condition, including some 19th-century apparel kept out of harm's way in the back, and there's usually a good pick of antique wedding dresses. ♦ Tu-Sa noon-6PM. 117 Yesler Way. 621.1728

10 Merchant's Cafe ★$ The city's oldest tavern (opened in 1890) is also one of its most democratic: down-and-outers creak stools right next to newcomers, but somehow every discussion winds around to "the way Seattle used to be." On summer days black-clad university students gather at sidewalk tables to smoke, eat burgers and other pub grub, and ponder the existential value of TV celebrity Arsenio Hall.

More wild and uproarious tales and outright whoppers have been swapped in this joint than beer has been spilled on its wooden floors. Klondike gold miners dropped by here in the late 1890s to swill 5¢ beers or sample wares in the high-class brothel upstairs. Before there was a Merchant's Cafe, a wooden drugstore occupied this spot, upstairs from which was a gallery displaying work by **E.M. Sammis,** Seattle's first resident photographer. Yet Merchant's, with its wonderful decorative glass and sputtering neon sign out front, seems well rooted in its place, like the evergreens that once stood here. The trees are gone, but Merchant's Cafe won't be so easily toppled. ♦ American ♦ M-F 11AM-2AM; Sa 10AM-2AM; Su 10AM-10PM. 109 Yesler Way. 624.1515

11 Rocky Mountain Chocolate Factory You've never seen so many candy-coated apples in one place. Just walking by this store is probably fattening, but oh, the smells! ♦ Daily 10:30AM-6PM. 105 Yesler Way. 682.2392

12 Cow Chip Cookies Only very hungry or metabolically advantaged snackers should consider tackling one of the gooey, mammoth munchies served at this chain outlet. Scientific researchers studying the effects of sugar overload are also welcome. ♦ M-Sa 9AM-6PM. 102 First Ave South. 292.9808

13 Greetings Trend Shop If you've been in the market for a salmon snout to strap over your nose, try this kooky shop. Other diverting kitsch includes wild-looking earrings, Gary Larson cartoon cups, and T-shirts so obnoxious the censorious gatekeepers at Disneyland won't let you into the park wearing one. ♦ Daily 10AM-6PM. 106 First Ave South. 624.7713

King Street train station provided the final scene in a particularly bizarre double murder in 1906. The first casualty was one Franz Edmond Creffield, unabashed debaucher and leader of a pseudo-religious cult in Oregon (the Bride of Christ Church), whose followers—almost all women—made a practice of rolling on floors and baying at the moon. On 7 May 1906, during a hiatus in Seattle, Creffield was shot in the head on the corner of First Avenue and Cherry Street. The killer was George Mitchell, brother of one of Creffield's flock, Esther Mitchell. Shortly after his release from jail, Esther Mitchell said good-bye to her brother at the King Street Station. As George turned to leave, Esther drew a gun and executed him in the same way he had Creffield. She was committed to an insane asylum for three years.

Restaurants/Clubs: Red   **Hotels:** Blue
Shops/ 🌳 Outdoors: Green   **Sights/Culture:** Black

14 Delmar Building (State Hotel) Pioneer Square preservationists saved some of the city's classic neon signs and painted billboards. One of the most endearing still hangs from the former State Hotel, an excellent brick-and-terracotta pile that went up in 1890 and was once a popular stop for gold-seekers coming back from Alaska and lumberers rolling into Seattle on a toot. "Rooms 75 Cents," it reads. Penny-pinchers will be disappointed to learn that the hotel went out of business in 1962. ♦ 114-116 First Ave South

Within the Delmar Building:

The New Orleans Creole Restaurant ★$ Internationally recognized jazz bands are generally showcased here on weekends, but this restaurant-cum-honky-tonk is hardly quiet during the remainder of the week. Monday nights feature Dixieland bands, Tuesday is Cajun night, and Wednesday is designated for contemporary jazz. Ragtime, zydeco, and R&B artists all make periodic showings. The food is good but not memorable. Gumbo and crawfish are distinctive picks; the catfish can be oily. An adjoining dark-wood bar is the only place in town where mint juleps ("The South's revenge for losing the war," as one wit put it) are regularly featured on the drinks roster. ♦ Cajun/Creole ♦ Cover charge on Friday and Saturday nights. M-Th, Su 11AM-11PM; F-Sa 11AM-2AM. Music starts at 9PM Friday and Saturday, 7PM other nights. 114 First Ave South. 622.2563

15 Maynard Building One of the more sophisticated Chicago School structures in the area, the Maynard illustrates the wide-ranging possibilities within the Romanesque Revival style. Compared to the bombast of **Elmer Fisher's** Pioneer Building, the Maynard, designed by **Albert Wickersham** in 1892, is a whisper of refined detail.

The exterior's handsome sandstone is from Bellingham Bay, to the north of Seattle, while the gray brick was railroaded over from St. Louis. Window designs in the upper stories show an expressiveness similar to **Louis Sullivan's**. In the lobby, the frame of an elevator shaft flaunts a brilliant bouquet of cast iron, and the staircase shows exquisite wood detailing. For years, the Maynard held

forth as a banking center; since its 1975 rehabilitation, however, the building has been occupied by many different businesses. ♦ 117 First Ave South

Within the Maynard Building:

Flora & Fauna Books Charles Darwin, had he lived long enough to discover this cloistered basement establishment, might never have left it. It's easy to imagine the bearded old gent wandering the packed stacks, flipping pages, continually finding new natural history or life sciences titles. Maybe Darwin's ghost will show up someday. But the question must be raised: Is there enough afterlife after life to read 25,000 books? ♦ M-Sa 10AM-6PM. 121 First Ave South. 623.4727

16 Colour Box A spirited 21-and-older club, Colour Box specializes in alternative rock and industrial dance. Just the names of some of the groups appearing here (from **Liquid American** to **Running with Scissors**) are enough to draw you in. Beer specials are available before the shows. ♦ Cover. Daily 3PM-2AM. 113 First Ave South. 340.4101

17 Yesler Building President Benjamin Harrison, during a flag-waving tour of the Northwest in 1891, pontificated from the balcony of this small, granite-based structure, which stands where **Henry Yesler** once had a dance hall. Erected in 1890, this **Elmer Fisher** creation was also damaged during the 1949 quake, although not irreparably. ♦ 95 Yesler Way

17 WE Hats Remember trying on all the old boxed hats stored away in your grandparents' attic? The same feeling is captured here, where walls are adorned with wacky and delightful chapeaus, and salespeople don't care if you try on 68 styles before deciding you really don't look that good in headwear. Then again, a well-made fedora or a duckbill cap could be just the adornment your face has always needed. Many of the works on sale are made in the shop upstairs. Special orders are fine. ♦ M-Th 10AM-6:30PM; F-Sa 10AM-midnight; Su 11:30AM-5:30PM. 105 First Ave South. 623.3409

18 Yesler Way No road in Seattle is more familiar than this one, even to people who've never been remotely near **Puget Sound.** Arriving in Seattle in April 1852, pioneer **Henry Yesler** was embraced by the town's few inhabitants when he announced his desire to build a sawmill in what is now West Seattle, but the enterprise was deemed too important to be located so far away. Locals instead ceded Yesler a ribbon of property running from the Waterfront to his claim of 320 forested acres. (Yesler's land was uphill from town, so oxen could drag timber down for milling.)

The strip—layered at one time with small, greased logs—was first called **Mill Street,** but it eventually assumed the diminutive nickname **Skid Road.** Then, in the early 20th century, it was known as the Deadline, or simply the Line. "Bawdy houses and low theaters were expected to stay south of the Line," explains **Murray Morgan** in his enthusiastic history *Skid Road.* But the nickname Skid Road predominated. After World War II, when businesses all but abandoned Pioneer Square, the whole quarter came to be known as Skid Road. So did other equally down-at-heel urban districts around the country, though the label was often changed to "Skid Row." ♦ Between Alaskan Way and Interstate 5

19 Mutual Life Building Additions can often detract from an architect's vision, but in this case they seem to have amplified and enhanced the look of this grand box, which sits where Seattle's first "restaurant," **Henry Yesler's** cookhouse, once did business. Most critics agree that the basement and first floor were designed by **Elmer Fisher** and finished around 1892. Upper stories, completed in 1897, are slightly contrasting creations from the partnership of **Robertson and Blackwell.** Another 30-foot hip was added to the west side in 1904, and a 1983 renovation cleaned up the old elevator cars, gave the exterior a swabbing of postmodern hues, and modernized the lobby. ♦ 605 First Ave

Within the Mutual Life Building:

Flying Shuttle The front windows of this shop are filled with lots of handwoven clothing and offbeat jewelry—great for browsing from the sidewalk. ♦ M-Sa 10:30AM-5:30PM; Su noon-5PM. 607 First Ave. 343.9762

Magic Mouse This must be where all stuffed animals pray they'll wind up, and hundreds of them do, especially teddy bears. The store's high-quality selection also includes wooden train sets, art supplies, award-winning children's books, and more than enough bathtub gizmos to occupy the kids. ♦ M-Sa 10AM-9PM; Su 10AM-6PM. 603 First Ave. 682.8097

20 Connections West Ltd. The temperature outside may be cool, but inside, a hot wind from the American Southwest has blown in Zapotec-woven fetish pillows, polychromatic fish sculptures, and a variety of bright-hued crockery—art to cure sun deprivation. ♦ M-Sa 11AM-6PM; Su noon-5PM. 87 Yesler Way. 223.0102

21 Trattoria Mitchelli ★★$ Owner **Dany Mitchell** defies Seattle's reputation for rolling up its sidewalks before 10PM. Late-movie crowds, Pioneer Square's after-theater clientele, couples meeting on the sly, and a jolly assortment of famished insomniacs end up at this festive, noisy joint at all hours of the night. Crave a heaping plate of ravioli in butter and garlic at 2AM? A tasty Italian breakfast frittata at 3AM? Step this way, your table's waiting. Plentifully apportioned lunches and early dinners are also served, but people-watching before "The Tonight Show" lacks for color. The service is often tardy, but who notices after midnight? ♦ Italian ♦ M 7AM-11PM; Tu-F 7AM-4AM; Sa 8AM-4AM; Su 8AM-11PM. 84 Yesler Way. 623.3885

Where to Spot Fowl Play

Northwesterners seem generally fascinated by the peregrinations of birds, and Seattle residents are no different. On almost any weekend you'll see clutches of watchers bouncing high-tech binoculars on their chests or toting cameras mounted with lenses big enough to subdue a charging elk. Bird-watching is best here in winter, when migrating species make the long flap down from the north in pursuit of warmer climes. But early and late summer aren't without their viewing opportunities.

The local **Audubon Society** recommends that bird-watchers scope out **Lincoln Park** in West Seattle, Magnolia's **Discovery Park** (where more than 150 bird species have been sighted, including red-tailed hawks, goldfinches, and ospreys), the **University of Washington** campus, and the **Washington Park Arboretum** (a stopping point—by last count—for some 200 species). Endangered peregrine falcons have been spotted in north **Ballard,** and another threatened species—purple martins—have been known to nest in downtown, amazingly enough on the skybridge of the **Bon Marché** department store. **Green Lake,** while certainly one of the best locations in summer to espy the "red-breasted Coppertone slatherer" and the "oggle-eyed people peeper," is most attractive for birders in the winter. Mergansers, mallards, and other ducks swoop down from November through January to grab bread crumbs and negotiate the frequent colloquies of visiting Canadian geese. Bald eagles are also known to perch in trees above Green Lake, but they actually nest in Discovery Park and **Seward Park** on the west bank of **Lake Washington.**

As is common with other port cities, sea gulls are the ubiquitous winged creatures in Seattle. Their screeches can be as memorable as the blow of a ferry horn, and their calligraphy of flight as familiar as the march of rain clouds.

If you have time for a day trip, about an hour's drive to the south, amidst the docklands near Tacoma's Lincoln Avenue bridge, is the **Gog-le-hi-te Wetland,** a man-made estuary inhabited by more than a hundred varieties of birds.

> The longest and steepest escalator west of the Mississippi is in the Seattle bus tunnel's Pioneer Square Station at Yesler Way and Third Avenue.

22 Al Boccalino ★★★$$$ Gone is **Luigi DeNunzio,** the former co-owner and effervescent front man who, for so long, made it a pleasure just to walk through this restaurant's door (he recently walked out that same portal to create **La Buca,** on Cherry Street). Chef **Tim Roth** continues, however, to use the robust recipes that DeNunzio brought over from his Italian hometown. The *gamberoni agli spinaci* (prawns with garlic and spinach) is especially tasty. Intimate rooms and brick walls make this an ideal setting for romance. ◆ Italian ◆ M, Sa 5:30-10PM; Tu-F 11:30AM-2PM, 5:30-10PM. 1 Yesler Way. Reservations recommended. 622.7688

23 OK Hotel Cafe/Gallery $ For a déclassé joint hutched away on the noisy backside of this block, in the dread shadow of the Alaskan Way viaduct, the OK has scored a lot of good press. It went through a cafe-of-the-moment phase in the late 1980s, when wanna-be style-mavens hung out there for hours, eating breakfast or just filling themselves to bursting with coffee. Paintings by local artists were hung on the cafe walls, and an adjoining gallery featured underground cartoons and the like.

But what really made the cafe's rep were its live performances, which were open to all ages. Acoustic singers and/or songwriters, free-jazz improvisers, storytellers, and poets—all of them took spins across the OK's stage. Hard-core punk bands, however, were the most popular. They played seven nights a week for more than two years to crowds of "moshers"—dancers jumping in wild pogo-stick fashion. To say the least, the scene was electric.

Then in early 1992, a mosher suffered a mild concussion, and safety suddenly became an issue. The club's owner ended the punk-music format (but continues to schedule other music acts), and there was talk that the OK would start serving beer and wine, putting an end to its all-ages reputation. A new booking agent wants to re-create the OK as a home not only to experimental music (he envisions it as a local version of New York's popular Knitting Factory) but also as a stage for performance acts. At press time, no liquor license had been awarded to the OK. ◆ American ◆ Admission to gallery only. Gallery 10AM-6PM. Cafe M-Th 7AM-midnight; F 7AM-4AM; Sa 8:30AM-4AM; Su 8:30AM-3AM. 212 Alaskan Way South. 621.7903

24 J&M Cafe ★$ Pioneer Square's most popular saloon has the longest lines, and no amount of fast-talking will get you past the Gibraltar-proportioned door sentries. This isn't to say that the J&M is a Seattle must-do. Its hamburgers and nachos are worth every

well-rubbed cent you fork out for them; but the beer selection is skimpy, and the ambient noise level inside almost requires you to use sign language to actually communicate. The cafe prospers on its hip rep and the fact that it does have one of the snazziest wooden bars this side of San Francisco. The building and tavern date back to 1900. ◆ American ◆ Daily 11:30AM-2AM. 201 First Ave South. 624.1670

25 Northwest Gallery of Fine Woodworking For people who thrill to the feel of soft, smooth wood, this place is a guilty indulgence. The gallery showcases local woodcraft and does so in a simple, well-lighted, inviting space without the hype or the pressuring salespeople. Imagine how the elegant chairs, desks, dressers, and assorted boxes might look in your home. Just don't gander at the price tags. ◆ M-Sa 10:30AM-5:30PM; Su noon-5PM. 202 First Ave South. 625.0542

25 Sound Winds/Air Arts Tiny but whimsical, this shop only *looks* like it sells kites. Actually, it specializes in a bright collection of wind socks and banners. ◆ M-Sa 10:30AM-5:30PM; Su noon-5PM. 206 First Ave South. 622.4386

26 Central Tavern and Cafe What kind of place would tout itself as Seattle's only second-class tavern? It's got to have a sense of humor, and the Central—dating back to 1889 and looking not quite every year of its age—has that. It also has live music from 9PM seven nights a week, mostly rock, blues, and R&B. ◆ Cover. Daily 11AM-2AM. 207 First Ave South. 622.0209

26 Larry's Greenfront Claustrophobes beware! When one of this club's regular blues bands gets its riffs kicking on a Friday or Saturday night, your personal space is destined to be violated—constantly. Dancing here is great fun for people who love to rub their vital body parts with strangers'. Table service is legendarily slow but getting your own beer on a crowded band night is no easier. ◆ Cover. 7AM-1:30AM. 209 First Ave South. 624.7665

27 FireWorks Gallery Local artists play show-and-sell at this popular shop. Playful bowls and lighthearted jewelry are the specialties of the house, but there are also more serious pieces of furniture to be had. Many a hard-to-shop-for giftee has received a present from FireWorks. ◆ M-Sa 10AM-5PM, Su 11AM-5PM Jan-May; M-Sa 10AM-6:30PM, Su 11AM-5:30PM June-Dec. 210 First Ave South. 682.8707

28 Grand Central Arcade What a long, strange trip this site has taken to the present. It first came to prominence in the 1870s, when arms-magnate **Phil Remington**

acquired it and several other nearby blocks on speculation. He was subsequently bought out by his entrepreneurial son-in-law, **Watson C. Squire,** who in 1879 opened the three-story **Squire's Opera House**—Seattle's first *real* theater—on the Grand Central property. **President Rutherford B. Hayes,** visiting the West Coast in 1880 (which no sitting president had done before), was given a warm reception at Squire's, but he had to shake some 2,000 hands before being released for the evening.

Two years later Squire remodeled the top two floors into the **Brunswick Hotel.** Of course, the Great Fire of '89 burned it down to its foundations (an estimated $9 million loss), but Squire was one of the first business leaders in town to announce his intentions to rebuild. In 1890 his new **Squire-Latimer Building** was completed on the same site. The facility supplied central heating and lighting to many other establishments in the district and reportedly made a profit doing so. Yet when the Alaskan Gold Rush took off in 1897, Squire again decided his property should be a hotel, this time called the **Grand Central.**

Meanwhile, however, Squire had embroiled himself in politics. When Seattle's anti-Chinese riots broke out in 1886, it was Washington Territorial *Governor* Squire who declared martial law until the violence was concluded. After Washington earned statehood in 1889, Squire was appointed one of its first U.S. senators. The Grand Central hotel was ultimately less successful. It declined with the rest of the old city and, during the Great Depression, became a flophouse. Only after 1970, when the **Pioneer Square National Historic District** was founded, did the hotel again receive attention. In fact, it was one of the Square's first major restoration projects, and now bustles with two levels of mall shops. ♦ Daily 7AM-6PM. 214 First Ave South. 623.7417

Within the Grand Central Arcade:

David Ishii Bookseller Would that everyone could adopt the laid-back demeanor of antiquarian proprietor David Ishii. At just about any time of the business day, it seems, you can walk by his used bookstore and see him slouched in a chair, reading his own dusty merchandise. Sometimes all the mellowness just makes you want to scream! But no, be dignified when you walk into this small, cluttered shop looking for an obscure volume on fly-fishing or baseball, Ishii's two passions and specialties (other subjects are stocked capriciously). And by all means, *be quiet.* You wouldn't want to disturb the owner when he's concentrating, now would you? ♦ M-Sa 10AM-6PM; Su 10AM-5PM. First floor. 622.4719

Millstream This place goes way overboard in promoting the natural attributes of Seattle and the Pacific Northwest. Walls of ferry and whale pictures? Salmon sculptures? And a trickling fountain just to establish the proper peaceful mood? Get real! Yet there's a strangely endearing quality to Millstream that even a jaded native can appreciate. Rumor has it, however, that Millstream is moving, so call ahead. ♦ M-Sa 10AM-6PM; Su noon-4PM. First floor. 233.9719

Grand Central Baking Co. ★$ The bakery on one side of Grand Central's chandelier-festooned main foyer is famous for its rustic breads and cinnamon rolls. Across the way, an affiliated deli does its best work with hearty soups and well-endowed salads (the sandwiches can be somewhat lackluster). Seating is available in the foyer. ♦ Bakery/Deli ♦ M-F 7AM-6PM; Sa-Su 9AM-5PM. First floor. 622.3644

The Paper Cat This is among the best resources in town when you're on the lookout for greeting cards, comical postcards (yuppies take a clobbering in these racks), or rubber stamps. Not everything here follows the cat theme, but there's enough to give this shop purr-sonality. ♦ M-Sa 9AM-6:30PM; Su 11AM-5PM. First floor. 623.3636

Megan Mary Olander Florist Fresh blooms abound, but it's even more interesting to see how many delicate and beautiful arrangements have been made of dried flowers. Lots of money could be spent here, but the sales staff is also very good at working within minuscule budgets. ♦ M-F 8:30AM-6PM; Sa 10AM-5PM. First floor. 623.6660

The Blacksmith Shop An ideal anachronism for an area steeped in history, this establishment rings all day long with the pounding of metal upon metal. Owner **Mike Linn** has been in this business for 20 years, making household items (sold through a neighboring retail outlet) and large custom pieces such as iron gates. A sign out front, however, makes it clear that this blacksmith "does not do horseshoes"—just in case you wanted to know. ◆ Daily 11AM-5PM. Basement. 623.4085

29 Ragazzi Upscale, custom-made women's wear by Seattle designers beckons the clothes hound. ◆ Tu-Sa 11AM-5PM. 85 S. Main St. 682.6977

30 Bread of Life Mission Victorian in style, with projecting bays but flat fenestrated detailing, this building was originally the location of Seattle's first store, put up in 1890 by pioneer **David "Doc" Swinton Maynard,** a Clevelander who'd come west hoping to cash in on the fish trade to gold-seekers in California. The building is now one of several help centers for elderly and disadvantaged residents of the Pioneer Square neighborhood. ◆ 301 First Ave South

31 Earl D. Layman Street Clock Time doesn't stand still, and neither has this fine pedestal timepiece. It used to decorate the sidewalk at the corner of Fourth Avenue and Pike Street, in front of Young's Credit Jewelers, but it was moved in 1984 and dedicated to the city's first historic preservation officer (who held office from 1973 to 1982). ◆ Corner of First Ave South and S. Main St

31 The Elliott Bay Book Company Opened in 1973, in what used to be the **Globe Hotel** (and before that was the site of Seattle's first hospital), this is the city's second-largest vendor of literature, after **University Bookstore,** in the University District. But of the two, Elliott Bay certainly enjoys the greater intellectual cachet, thanks in part to its very popular series of readings by well-known authors. (**Amy Tan, Don DeLillo, Ron Hansen,** and **David McCullough** all read here in the not-too-distant past.) The store even publishes its own quarterly paper, *Book Notes,* full of staff reviews.

History, current affairs, cooking, poetry, fiction, and mystery—all are well represented here. Travel books have their very own level;

works for children occupy a separate and substantial chamber. Staffers are knowledgeable and wonderfully responsive. If there's anything to quibble about, it's shortages in the architectural history and nature-lit departments. Author readings and/or signings are held several times a week, always at 7:30PM. Tickets to the readings are free, but seats are limited. ◆ M-Sa 10AM-11PM; Su noon-6PM. 101 S. Main St. 624.6600

Inside the Elliott Bay Book Company:

Elliott Bay Cafe ★★$ Could anything be more civil than buying a new book and then trotting downstairs to read it in this brick-and-book-lined retreat? The food runs the gamut, from sandwiches to rather overpriced (or is it just undersized?) desserts; beer and wine are available, as are steaming cups of coffee, just the right brace for a dive into the latest Gore Vidal doorstop. ◆ American ◆ M-F 7AM-10PM; Sa 10AM-11PM; Su 11AM-5PM. 682.6664

32 Bowie & Company, Inc., Booksellers The only way this newish shop (illustrated above) could survive next door to **Elliott Bay Book Company** is by attracting a completely different audience; and that's what Bowie does, with its shelves of barely thumbed first editions and cases of incunabula. Prices range from under $10 to several thousand dollars. Old maps and postcards are also available, as are mail-order catalogs. ◆ M-Sa 10AM-6PM; Su noon-6PM. 314 First Ave South. 624.4100

32 Grand Central Mercantile If you're one of those cooks who believes that the proper accessories will magically transform you into James Beard, then the Grand Central Mercantile can outfit you in style. Test your connoisseur's skill: can you actually give purpose to all the walls of oddball knickknacks? ◆ M-Sa 10AM-6PM; Su 11AM-6PM. 316 First Ave South. 623.8894

Restaurants/Clubs: Red   Hotels: Blue
Shops/ 🌳 Outdoors: Green   **Sights/Culture: Black**

33 Countrysport Only a fishing fanatic would think that so many different types of flies could exist. Just goes to show that aquatic beings can be as picky as humans about what they'll consume. Countrysport also packs a healthy selection of antique tackle boxes, sporting attire, and books on fishing. ♦ Tu-F 9:30AM-5:30PM; Sa 10AM-6PM. 317 First Ave South. 622.5357

34 The Wood Shop Keepers of this shop like to play with their own toys, which is always a good sign. At least one salesperson has been seen delighting young customers with a dog hand-puppet. Shelves of teddy bears and other sturdy toys charm even adults. The goods come from around the world. Check out the Russian stacking dolls (painted like Boris Yeltsin, Mikhail Gorbachev, and other previous Soviet rulers) if they're still available. ♦ M-Sa 10AM-5:30PM; Su noon-5PM. 320 First Ave South. 624.1763

35 Bud's Jazz Records Don't be afraid to open the metal gate and descend the narrow staircase from Jackson Street—there's nobody down here but a lot of ghosts. Well, in a manner of speaking, anyway. Chicago emigré and jazz aficionado **Bud Young** has created what must be the largest selection of jazz CDs, tapes, and records this side of the Windy City, some 150,000 titles.

Whole afternoons could be spent in Bud's cavelike and cluttered atmosphere, flipping through racks of John Lee Hooker, Dizzy Gillespie, Stanley Turrentine, Robert Johnson, Lightning Hopkins, and an eclectic lineup of other musicians who created the basis of contemporary jazz. Music searches are accepted and jazz trivia questions are happily fielded by employees. ♦ M-Sa 11AM-7PM; Su noon-6PM. 102 S. Jackson St. 628.0445

36 Pacific Marine Schwabacher Building An honest-to-goodness cornerstone of Seattle's development, Schwabacher's was the city's original hardware company. This exquisite brick structure from 1905, by

Leonard Mendel and English-born architect **Charles Bebb** (who later established a partnership with renowned Seattle designer **Carl Gould**), only punctuates Schwabacher's success and stature in the community. Notice especially the terracotta frieze around the front door, at the southwest corner of First Avenue South and South Jackson Street. Details like this used to be commonplace, decoration to doll up relatively plain-faced commercial buildings. Now, however, the Schwabacher Building is a frequently photographed oddity. ♦ 401 First Ave South

37 Il Terrazo Carmine ★★★$$$ There's so much deliberate sophistication here you can cut it with a knife . . . if you aren't already using that particular utensil to slice off pieces of Il Terrazo's marvelous venison medaillons. The veal *piccata* has a large count of local fans, but anyone would happily survive with the savory ravioli. Floor-to-ceiling drapes block out the sun and prying eyes, but on pleasant summer days, the patio out back is available (the nearby Alaskan Way Viaduct, however, often casts too much noise this way to allow for intimate conversation). ♦ Italian ♦ M-Th 11:30AM-3PM, 5:30-10PM; F 11:30AM-3PM, 5:30-11PM; Sa 5:30-11PM. 411 First Ave South. Reservations recommended. 467.7797

38 A La Francaise One of the best French bakeries in town (with another, larger location near the University District), A La Francaise has an intimate atmosphere, despite its position on the edge of industrial Seattle, and loaves of French bread that may not make it home untasted. ♦ Bakery ♦ M-F 6:30AM-5:30PM. 417 First Ave South. 624.0322. Also at: 2609 NE University Village Mall. 524.9300

39 Franglor's ★★$ Although this wonderful Creole restaurant moved several years ago from a knothole in the International District to the southern tip of downtown, Franglor's still couldn't exactly be called spacious. Nor would anyone label its countertop or dark-recessed, plastic-clothed tables elegant. But the food draws a crowd of expatriate Southerners and others (like **Mayor Norm Rice**) who long for spicy servings of jambalaya, catfish, and short ribs in gravy. The sausage-filled gumbo is a bit on the thin side but still excellent. And a jukebox rocks with Cajun and country tunes.

Hot days are a problem, since there's no air-conditioning here and fans just don't do the trick. Beware of game nights at the nearby Kingdome sports arena, when parking congestion may cause you to leave your car closer to the real New Orleans than to this little bit of New Orleans in Seattle. ♦ Cajun/Creole ♦ Tu-Sa 11:30AM-9PM. 547 First Ave South. 682.1578

40 Triangle Hotel Building C. Alfred
Breitung was born in Austria and trained as
an architect in Europe before coming to
Seattle in 1900. Like many other young
designers, Breitung was attracted to Puget
Sound's turn-of-the-century prosperity and
the reputations of people such as **Elmer
Fisher.** His name is now familiar because of
several large constructions in Seattle,
including the **Home of the Good Shepherd**
building in Wallingford. But the Triangle Hotel
was certainly one of his more unusual
commissions. When it was completed in
1907 the building housed an eight-room
hotel on the second floor, said to be the West
Coast's smallest such hostelry; it is now full
of offices. ♦ 551 First Ave South

41 Kingdome Newcomers are overwhelmed by
some of the statistics regarding this sports
stadium: it claims the largest single-span
concrete roof on the planet, seven acres in
size, with no posts to interfere with spectator
viewing; the top of the dome is 250 feet from
the Kingdome floor; the concrete used in its
construction weighs some 105,600 tons;
and what may still be the record for park
attendance was set in 1980, when Seattle's
Boeing aircraft company brought 103,152
people to the 'Dome for its Christmas
celebration.

Almost from the moment this round building
opened in 1976, though, Seattleites have
criticized it. "Ugly" is one of the nicer epithets
used. Many liken it to a huge orange-juice
squeezer. A newspaper columnist suggested
that its roof be painted beige, its exterior
walls be horizontally banded with green,
cream, brown, and beige hues, and the city
rent it to McDonald's as a huge advertisement
for Big Macs. Many other residents wish the
city would rip off the Kingdome's roof or
replace it with something retractable, in order
that sunshine may fall on the **Seattle
Mariners'** baseball games. (The city so far
contends that a movable roof assembly is
"cost-prohibitive.") The stadium capacity
varies depending upon the type of event: for
Seahawks' football games, it seats 64,800;
for Mariners' baseball games, 59,600; and for
concerts, about 80,000. No matter what event
goes on inside, the Kingdome creates
problems outside when cars spill from its
huge parking lots onto the tree-lined streets
of Pioneer Square. Tours of the 650-foot-
diameter stadium take at least an hour

(reservations aren't necessary; just show up
at Gate D). ♦ Tours M-Sa 11AM, 1PM, 3PM
mid Apr-mid Sept. S. King St (at Second Ave
South). 296.3663, game tickets 296.3111

**42 F.X. McRory's Steak, Chop and Oyster
House** ★$$ McRory's leads a split
existence. On the one hand, it wants to be
thought of as a high-class establishment,
with grilled meats, succulent bivalves, and
substantial dinner salads that earn critical
raves. On the other hand, McRory's dearly
loves being a party place, full of beer-sucking
bruisers and callipygous coeds who drop by
after game nights at the 'Dome. The latter
identity better matches the food, which, while
tasty, is not awe-inspiring. And don't wait for
a table in the dining room. Eat in the high-
ceilinged bar, with its full-mirrored wall of
liquor bottles and its **Leroy Neimann** art.
There's a good selection of Northwest
microbrews and an outdoor seating area for
bright afternoons. ♦ American ♦ Daily
11:30AM-3PM, 5PM-midnight. Bar open
daily 11:30AM-1AM. 419 Occidental Ave
South. 623.4800

43 Great Winds Kite Shop It almost hurts
your eyes to browse here, what with so many
kites, wind socks, and kite-flying accoutre-
ments in almost as many brilliant colors.
♦ M-Sa 10AM-5:30PM; Su noon-5:30PM.
402 Occidental Ave South. 624.6886

44 Occidental Avenue Interurban railcars
clanked and wobbled down Occidental
Avenue at the turn of the century, bound from
Seattle for Tacoma and back. Exclusive parlor
cars for spendthrift passengers willing to
shell out 85¢, rather than the regular fare of
60¢, brought up the rear. **First Avenue** (then
known as **Front Street**) was this city's oldest
thoroughfare, but aged photographs show
commercial Occidental Avenue being just as
busy during Pioneer Square's post-fire
renaissance. Both streets eventually fell on
hard times, but after the district earned
national landmark status, Occidental
Avenue's revitalization was a top priority.
Cobblestones were retained, two blocks were
closed to cars, and plane trees were planted
from Jackson Street to Yesler Way to lend the
new mall, called **Occidental Park,** a leisurely
Parisian boulevard atmosphere.

Today, food and art vendors gather here on
weekends, and starry-eyed couples are often
seen strolling the stones, hand-in-hand.
There's a handsome, old-fashioned shelter at
the corner of Occidental Avenue and Main
Street where you can hitch a ride on a
streetcar running from the Waterfront up to
the I.D. And a shady plaza between Main and
Washington streets contains totem poles and
a horse trough that can be converted to a
drinking fountain simply by cupping your
hand over it. Sadly, many tourists and even

more Seattleites avoid this plaza, fearful of its ubiquitous panhandlers; and the mall's northernmost block, between Washington Street and Yesler Way, has never quite overcome the shabbiness of pre-1970 Pioneer Square. ♦ Occidental Ave South (between S. Jackson and S. Main Sts)

44 Pacific Northwest Brewing Company ★$$ Seattle is a pub-lover's town, but this joint—with its shiny brass beer tanks and high ambient noise levels—is not the norm. (Wouldn't you know it was created by a New Yorker?) Bratwurst steamed in ale, the fish cakes, and a spicy gumbo are the choice dishes. Crowds are biggest at lunch and after Kingdome events. ♦ American ♦ Daily 11:30AM-10PM. 322 Occidental Ave South. 621.7002

45 Torrefazione Italia Quiet, filled with cozy small tables and books on Italian art, and serving potent cups of coffee in colorful earthenware, this is one of the most pleasant places in town to wait for a friend. ♦ Coffeehouse ♦ M-F 7AM-5:30PM; Sa 10AM-5:30PM. 320 Occidental Ave South. 624.5773

46 Davidson Galleries A changing selection of works by local and international artists is on display, along with a special collection of 19th- and early 20th-century American paintings. ♦ Tu-Sa 11AM-5:30PM; Su 1-5PM. 313 Occidental Ave South. 624.7684

46 Foster/White Gallery Established Northwest talents, such as **Morris Graves** and **Mark Tobey,** are represented here. Some **Pilchuck** glasswork is also on display. ♦ M-Sa 10AM-5:30PM; Su noon-5PM. 311½ Occidental Ave South. 622.2833

47 The Sunday Funnies What looks like a children's store is really for comic-loving adults who want cups decorated with **Garfield** and T-shirts that bear the nostalgic likeness of **Popeye.** Most of the material is Disney-inspired. ♦ M-Sa 11AM-6PM; Su noon-5PM. 312 Occidental Ave South. 621.8265

Seattle may have outgrown Pioneer Square (the original center of the city) long ago, but the handsome Pioneer Building, on First Avenue between Yesler Way and Cherry Street, is still the datum point from which all city elevations are measured.

48 Klondike Gold Rush National Historical Park On 17 July 1897 the *Portland* arrived almost empty in Seattle. But after word spread that the steamship was carrying two tons of gold found in Alaska, a full complement of passengers signed up for the return voyage—men who thought they could make a profit from Alaska's biggest gold rush, and women of questionable virtue who knew they could mine the pockets of any men who actually struck it rich.

This gold rush couldn't have come at a more propitious time for Seattle. Like the rest of the nation, the town was still trying to overcome the hard times that followed the infamous Panic of 1893, so it took full advantage of its position as a principal jumping-off point for prospectors, or sourdoughs, as they were called then. Hotels sprang up almost overnight in Pioneer Square to accommodate the thousands of men funneling through Puget Sound on their way north, and a number of mining schools opened here. Local outfitters, capitalizing on a Canadian law that required gold-seekers to pack along a year's worth of goods, grew rich from the hundreds of dollars each would-be miner had to spend on such provisions. The chamber of commerce even hired a hucksterish former editor of the *Seattle Post-Intelligencer,* **Erastus Brainerd,** to cement commercial links between this city and the Klondike. Magazines such as *Frank Leslie's Popular Monthly* bought right into Brainerd's game. "The eyes of the civilized world today are turned upon two points—namely the gold fields of Alaska and the City of Seattle," *Leslie's* wrote. A government assay office was established on Seattle's Ninth Avenue in 1898. During its first four years of business, it ran more than $174 million over its scales.

The Klondike Gold Rush National Historical Park is a highfalutin name for a colorful storefront museum (the *real* park is actually divided between Alaska and the Yukon). Through old photographs, walking tours of Pioneer Square, and films, the museum does basically what Erastus Brainerd did so well a century ago: proves that Seattle was indeed "the gateway to the Klondike." ♦ Free. Daily 9AM-5PM. 117 S. Main St. 442.7220

49 Artworks Gallery You'll love the eclectic agglomeration of polychromatic design subjects, everything from painted tablecloths to handmade paper and bright ceramic chicken sculptures. ♦ M-Sa 11AM-6PM. 155 S. Main St. 625.0932

50 Waterfall Garden Filled with crashing waterfalls and benches perfect for lunch breaks, this corner plot is a soothing escape from the business world. Yet its very existence is rooted in business, specifically the **United Parcel Service.** UPS grew from a packaging and delivery enterprise that opened in a basement under this spot in 1907. The company's principal founder, **James Emmett Casey,** was a Nevada boy who delivered his first parcel on behalf of a Seattle department store in 1899. ◆ Second Ave South and S. Main St

51 Washington Court Building What the late historian **Bill Speidel** called "the most glorious and sumptuously furnished palace of sin in the city" once operated from this unpretentious, four-story brick Victorian. The madam was **Lou Graham,** a strong-willed businesswoman who took this site in about 1888, rebuilt after the Great Fire, and for another dozen years entertained well-to-do gents and their scions. So successful was her business, writes historian **Paul Dorpat,** that "Graham and her ladies . . . helped keep the city solvent through the hard times of the mid-1890s." Some would say the building's occupancy has gone downhill since: it's now rented mostly by lawyers. ◆ 221 S. Washington St

52 Comedy Underground National acts, as well as local Seinfeld-wanna-bes, show up at this joint tucked beneath **Swannies** bar and restaurant. Monday and Tuesday nights are "open-mike dates" for amateurs, with other stand-up comics booked later in the week. ◆ Cover. Shows M-Th 8PM; F-Sa 8PM, 11PM. 222 S. Main St. Reservations recommended. 622.0209

53 Cafe Huê ★$ Created by husband-and-wife escapees from war-torn Vietnam, Cafe Huê (pronounced *way*) is a reflection of that country's colonial cultural division. Viet dishes are sometimes served with French touches, such as the escargot seasoned with ginger. Chef **Kieutuy Nguyen** was trained in Saigon by a French baker, so it's no wonder that desserts here (including the wonderful Parisian éclairs, amandines, and traditional napoleons) are so plentiful and rich. Spring rolls and soups are not to be missed (try the filling crab soup). Everything is presented with artistry. Service is fast and efficient, and there's no high-turnover mentality here (like at some Asian noodle houses). Despite its proximity to the Kingdome, Cafe Huê doesn't usually suffer from overcrowding on game nights. ◆ Vietnamese/French ◆ M-F 11AM-10PM; Sa-Su noon-10PM. 312 Second Ave South. 625.9833

54 Linda Farris Gallery Fairly inconspicuous on its corner, this place has a reputation for displaying some of Seattle's vanguard talent, as well as the occasional **Warhol** and **Rauschenberg.** ◆ Tu-Sa 11AM-5:30PM. 320 Second Ave South. 623.1110

55 King Street Station Still operating as a railroad depot, this neoclassical station (pictured above) was built in 1906 for **James J. Hill** and his **Great Northern Railroad.** In 1910, 62 passenger trains pulled up on the tracks adjacent to this depot every day, disgorging 3,500 passengers. Now, only a handful of **Amtrak** trains arrive here each day. Minnesota architects **Reed and Stem,** who did the design, would go on in 1913 to create Grand Central Station for New York. The building's brick exterior has hardly changed since day one, but the interior has been sadly modernized. Notice the clock tower; it was modeled after the Piazza San Marco campanile in Venice, Italy. ◆ Third Avenue South and S. Jackson St

56 Union Station Eastern railroad scion **Edward Henry Harriman** opened this barrel-vaulted stopping point for his **Union Pacific Railroad** in 1911, above the tidelands of Jackson Street. The last passenger train pulled away from here 60 years later. Ever since, the depot (designed by San Francisco architect **D.J. Patterson**) has been used for antiques shows and a range of catered events. In the 1970s a proposal was made to revitalize it as a "multiuse transportation center," but that didn't fly any better than a later idea to integrate it into a new city hall complex. The southernmost entry to downtown's bus tunnel is located next door to Union Station. ◆ Fourth Ave South and S. Jackson St. 622.3214

57 Chau's Chinese Restaurant ★$ The standard Cantonese dishes are okay, but this place really earns its nickel in its seafood. Try steamed oysters in garlic sauce or the Dungeness crab, and don't be shy about ordering geoduck. It's not available everywhere you go, nor is it always so well prepared as it is here. ◆ Cantonese ◆ M-F 11AM-11:30PM; Sa 4PM-midnight; Su 4-10:30PM. 310 Fourth Ave South. 621.0006

58 Nippon Kan Theater A reminder of Seattle's historic **Japantown,** opened in 1909 as the **Astor Hotel** and later a performance hall for Kabuki theater, this redbrick building was renovated in 1981 and is now best known for its **Japanese Performing Arts Series,** which runs October through May.

Restaurants/Clubs: Red   Hotels: Blue
Shops/ 🌿 Outdoors: Green   Sights/Culture: Black

♦ Box office daily 9AM-5PM. 628 S. Washington St. 467.6807

59 Maneki ★$ It looks rather shabby outside, notched into the ground floor of what used to be the **Northern Pacific Hotel** (built for rail passengers in 1914 by Seattle architect **John Graham, Sr.**, who later designed downtown's stately **Dexter Horton Building**), but the Maneki boasts what may be Seattle's first sushi bar. The selections are fresh and tasty. ♦ Japanese ♦ Tu-Su 5:30-10:30PM. 304 Sixth Ave South. 622.2631

60 Danny Woo International District Community Garden On one side, facing south, these one-and-a-half acres provide an excellent panorama of the old south end, from Smith Tower past Union Station. On the opposite side, however, at the top of the slope, Interstate 5 charges by in a smelly roar. Surprisingly, it's possible at most points in this garden to enjoy the former without enduring the latter. Established in 1975 and expanded five years later, the site contains about 120 individual growing areas, each managed by an elderly resident of Chinatown. But passersby are invited to climb the garden's graveled paths, sniff the fragrance of the many fruit trees, and admire a giant stone lantern at the hilltop, given by the Japanese city of Kobe to Seattle during this country's 1976 bicentennial. Benches are available for afternoon reading. A few transients hang about, but they're less obtrusive than in Pioneer Square. ♦ Above Sixth Ave South and S. Main St

61 Linyen ★★$$ The lemon chicken brings much of the clientele to this efficient, well-windowed location in the heart of Chinatown. And the specials, which may include clams in black-bean sauce, pot stickers, and spicy chicken entrées, are likewise delicious. The regular light-style Cantonese menu, however, is not nearly so enthralling. ♦ Chinese ♦ M-Sa 2:30PM-1:30AM; Su 2:30PM-midnight. 424 Seventh Ave South. Reservations recommended. 622.8181

62 Wing Luke Museum Wing Luke was Seattle's first Chinese-American city councilman, elected in 1962, as well as the first Asian-American elected to public office in the continental United States. He died in a plane crash in 1965, but his interest in meshing the Asian-American experience into Northwest history lives on in this small cultural center, which is full of old photographs, antiques, and Asian artifacts. ♦ Admission; free on Thursday. Tu-W, F 11AM-4:30PM; Th 11AM-7PM; Sa-Su noon-4PM. 407 Seventh Ave South. 623.5124

63 Han II ★$ There's nothing like having barbecued meats prepared at your tableside, and this upscale Korean restaurant puts on a good show for the eyes, as well as the palate.

Try the short ribs, arranged in a sizzling heap in the middle of your table, or the spicy octopus—the portions are generous. Chicken, pork, and beef are served with a side of pungent *kimchi* (pickled cabbage), a couple of tempura prawns, salad, and rice. ♦ Korean ♦ M-Sa 11AM-11PM; Su noon-11PM. 409 Maynard Ave South. Reservations recommended. 587.0464

64 Phnom Penh Noodle House ★$ It takes some thought to really appreciate Phnom Penh, since its menu boils down to seven variations of rice-noodle soup. But each bowl has distinctive characteristics that appeal especially to the local Cambodian population, members of which will almost inevitably be waiting in line for a table ahead of you. A second Phnom Penh location, called **A Pot of Phnom Penh Restaurant & Karaoke,** is located near Beacon Hill. ♦ Cambodian ♦ M-Tu, Th-Su 8:30AM-6PM. 414 Maynard Ave South. 682.5690

65 Hing Hay Park The colorful, traditional Chinese pavilion is a gift from the people of Taipei, Taiwan. The huge dragon mural that decorated the old **Bush Hotel's** backside was designed by **John Woo.** Together with trees and maybe a little rare sunshine, the urban-scaled Hing Hay becomes one of the I.D.'s nicest places to relax. ♦ Maynard Ave South and S. King St

66 Saigon Gourmet ★$ The idea seems so obvious, it's a wonder more places don't adopt it: charge low prices for meals, and people will flock to your doorstep. This place recently changed its name from **Hien Vuong,** but it doesn't seem to have altered its standards or prices. You can walk out of here having dropped no more than $10 on a lunch for two. And you'll even remember what you ate, especially if you ordered the shrimp rolls with peanut dipping sauce or the Cambodian soup. For able experimenters, there's grated papaya with shredded beef jerky. ♦ Vietnamese ♦ M-Sa 11AM-8:30PM; Su 11AM-7PM. 502 King St. 624.2611

67 Uwajimaya It looks as big, efficient, and clean as any other supermarket; and, yes, you're supposed to buy those fish in the tank *live* and ready to be sliced and served as sushi. Uwajimaya (illustrated above) is a great cultural experience, even if you don't purchase any of the innumerable fresh vegetables, porcelain pieces, or appliances on sale. This may be the largest Japanese store on the West Coast; it's certainly the hub

of Seattle's Japanese community. Founded in 1928 by **Fujimatsu Moriguchi**, the business moved into this huge location in 1970 but is still in the hands of Moriguchi's family. A variety of Asian cooking classes are available.
♦ Daily 9AM-8PM. 519 Sixth Ave South. 624.6248

68 Adams/Freedman Building Elaborate facades, with cast-stone canopies at the entrances and an intriguing hierarchical arrangement of windows, make this one of the neighborhood's more elegant structures. Raised in 1910 as a hotel, it's been rehabbed with apartments and commercial space.
♦ 515 Maynard Ave South

Within the Adams/Freedman Building:

Choy Herbs A native of Hong Kong, **Kai Chiu Choy** has been in this country since 1974, dispensing herbal medicine in a state where such a specialty is neither generally recognized by physicians nor licensed. Choy's diagnoses include taking a patient's pulse, looking at his or her tongue, and carefully examining the face and eyes for signs of internal disorders. (The eyes, it seems, are more than windows on the soul; according to Choy, they reveal kidney or liver problems.) ♦ M-Sa 11AM-5PM. 624.8341

69 Honey Court Seafood Restaurant ★$$ Octogenarian **Luk Sing Hing** applied an endearment for her late husband as the name for this much-written-about restaurant. Surely he would have approved of the 160-plus menu items here. Cantonese and Hong Kong styles are integrated to produce inexpensive curries of chicken or beef with rice, as well as the favored plates of barbecued pork over vermicelli noodles with scallions and slivered ginger. ♦ Chinese ♦ M-Th 11AM-2AM; F-Sa 11AM-3AM; Su 11AM-1AM. 516 Maynard Ave South. 292.8828

70 International District Children's Park If your offspring need a break from foot-touring, give them some time out at this quiet corner with its long, curving slide and a bronze dragon sculpture designed by Seattle artist **George Tsutakawa**. ♦ Between Seventh Ave South and S. Lane St

During the Great Fire of 1889, Judge C.H. Hanford, conducting a murder trial at Pioneer Square's old courthouse while flames were spreading in the nearby streets, refused to adjourn and release his jury, as they were about to be sequestered. Only when smoke finally billowed through his courtroom windows and a witness on the stand became too flustered to answer questions did Judge Hanford let the jurors flee—those, at least, whom he didn't impress into service to save the courthouse from being destroyed.

My favorite places are the outstanding pre-1930 buildings in Seattle's downtown and some of its parks and boulevards, proposed by the **Olmsted Brothers** in the first decade of the century:

Northern Life Tower (now called the **Seattle Tower**) is a wonderful 1928 Art Deco skyscraper by **Albertson, Richardson, and Wilson**. It's a mountain of multicolored brick over a steel frame, with terracotta trim recalling the snowcapped peaks of Mount Rainier. Three stylized evergreen trees crown the tower. Be sure to see the extraordinary lobby. The ornamentation was inspired by Northwest Coast Indian art and by the Chinese, Japanese, Hawaiian, and Mayan cultures, which were associated with trade routes along the Pacific Rim.

The **Arctic Club Dome** room in the **Arctic Building** was built in 1916 for a private club and is now owned and used by the City of Seattle. The club's former dining room is a great opalescent glass-domed space rich with Renaissance plasterwork that represents fruits and vegetables. Note the great terracotta walrus heads on the exterior of the building.

Pioneer Building in Pioneer Square. Many are familiar with the exterior of this brick and stone Romanesque building, but few venture past the entrance and up to the first floor. Here, this 1890 "skyscraper" opens up into two light-filled courtyards that rise six floors to a skylit roof.

The **Stimson-Green Mansion** is not open to the general public but is accessible by appointment during business hours. This home is a beautifully preserved 1901 English-style manor house designed by **Kirtland Cutter**.

For students of the American Arts and Crafts movement, a visit to the **Sorrento Hotel** lobby will reward you with a fine Rookwood tile fireplace. Or drop by the **John Leary House** (now the Episcopal Diocese headquarters) on 10th Avenue East just north of **St. Mark's Cathedral**. The Rookwood tile fireplaces and bathroom wall tiles here are wonderful, as is the Renaissance great hall. The Tiffany glass windows that originally hung in this hall are now on display in the **Burke Museum** on the **University of Washington** campus.

The **Suzzallo Library** at the center of the University of Washington's north and south quadrangles was modeled after King's College Chapel at Cambridge, England, and a peek into the main reading room on the second floor is a must. The north quadrangle becomes a sea of cherry blossoms during late February or early March.

One of my favorite drives is through the **Washington Park Arboretum** south of the University of Washington and along **Lake Washington Boulevard**, which borders Lake Washington, all the way south to **Seward Park**. En route, stop a while for a walk through the **Japanese Tea Garden** or **Azalea Way** in the arboretum. Drive into the residential neighborhood of **Washington Park** to experience the cathedral-like canopy of American elm trees along 36th Avenue. This street and the chestnut-lined boulevard of 17th Avenue NE just north of the university campus, known as **Greek Row,** are two of Seattle's loveliest tree-lined streets.

Another outstanding city drive is to **Kerry Viewpoint** on West Highland Drive, with **Mount Rainier** as its backdrop. It is worth walking farther west past the early Seattle mansions. Then, around Seventh Avenue West, the road turns north. Newly repaired balusters and reconstructed lighting fixtures frame views of **Puget Sound** and the **Olympic Mountains.** The stairways and concrete retaining walls that comprise this portion of the boulevard are themselves works of art.

VIEWPOINTS is an architectural tour program that offers residents and tourists an opportunity to explore and discover the best of design in the city. A diverse group of tours in Seattle's downtown and city neighborhoods offers history, old and new architecture, public art, and opportunities to meet and learn about the design industry from professionals. For more information, write to the Seattle Architectural Foundation, 1932 First Avenue, Seattle, WA 98101; or call 206/448.0106.

John Doerper
Food Editor, *Seattle* magazine

I like taking my laptop computer to **Gas Works Park** on a rainy day and finding a quiet place in the old machine shed where I can sit and work and look out over **Lake Union** at all the boat activity.

Westlake Mall is an urban open space gone postmodernist crazy—lots of concrete and glass, no grass, few flowers and shrubs. From the third floor, you can take the monorail to **Seattle Center.** If you're staying at a downtown hotel, the monorail is a great way to get to the **Opera House** (also in Seattle Center) in style.

Cool off from the concrete glare of Westlake Mall by stepping through the walk-through fountain nearby, a two-sided artificial waterfall. You'll hardly get wet, but you'll cool down considerably.

Forget about football games; the real attraction at **Husky Stadium** is the pregame tailgate picnic. Be sure to get an invitation from someone holding season tickets and get there early; that way you can park inside the gate—the only place to picnic properly.

Sit out on the deck at Lake Union's **Cucina! Cucina!** on a warm afternoon, sip a microbrew, and watch the floatplanes buzz in right over your head. Afterward, head down to the **Center for Wooden Boats,** check out a skiff, and row around **Lake Union.** You could also take a floatplane to the San Juan Islands, Victoria, or Vancouver. Or, if you feel really crazy, charter a plane to fly to a mountain lake in the Cascade or Olympic mountains.

Pick up sexually suggestive (and often very explicit) muffins or cakes at **Marzi Tarts** or a few more-

practical sexual gifts (you won't believe the variety) at the **Rubbertree** in Wallingford.

Take a boat ride through the **Hiram M. Chittenden Locks,** which connect Lake Union to Puget Sound.

The **Comet Tavern** on Capitol Hill isn't fancy—rather the opposite—but serves good microbrews. It's the last holdout for authentic Seattle atmosphere—grungy, friendly, and very '60s.

You'll be surprised at how many palm trees grow in Seattle. The courtyard at the **Sorrento Hotel** is encircled by palms; I've spotted palm trees outside a motel along **Aurora Avenue;** and they thrive in the gardens bordering the **Chittenden Locks.** Visiting the palms is a favorite pursuit of homesick Californians.

Step back in time at the **Luna Park Cafe** in West Seattle—not only is the food straight from the '50s and '60s, but so are the jukeboxes and the prices you pay for listening to oldies: a dime per song, a quarter for three.

Whenever I want to do some authentic ethnic shopping, I head for **White Center,** just south of West Seattle. Chinese restaurants here vie with Cambodian cafes, Vietnamese pool halls, and Mexican *tortillerías* and *panaderías.* It's as authentic as it gets in mostly Anglo-Saxon-Scandinavian Seattle.

While **Pike Place Market** isn't what it used to be, it's still a great place for take-out food. I like loading up on smoked salmon, cream cheese, lox, sushi, *dolmathes, hum baos,* or whatever, then walking down to the Waterfront, finding a picnic table, and settling down for a feast. If you're too tired to hike back up the hill, hire a horse-drawn carriage.

The **Seattle Aquarium** is where I enjoy looking at my favorite sushi in the round. Visiting the aquarium always gives me an appetite.

My friends and I hang out at **Elliott's Oyster House & Seafood Restaurant** on Pier 56. Not only does the place have the freshest oysters, but the selection is great. And the shuckers are fast—a necessary requirement given the way we slurp oysters.

The geoduck is a very large clam of rather phallic appearance, which is why even some native Seattleites have never eaten one—despite the fact that it tastes very good. Look for geoduck in sushi bars or Chinese restaurants. My favorite is served in the **Sea Garden** restaurant in the International District.

Seattle Pen is a little shop hidden away in a downtown office building (look it up in the phone book and call for directions) that has one of the best selections of fountain pens anywhere. It's a mecca for me and other "pensters."

Visit the old **Seattle Art Museum** in Volunteer Park, with its truly incredible collection of Asian art.

You haven't seen Seattle until you've visited its pubs and alehouses. My friends and I frequent **Murphy's Pub, Cooper's Northwest Alehouse,** and **Latona Pub,** near Green Lake.

Business District

"Downtown" Seattle is a geographical ambiguity. Technically, the center of town is at University Street and Fourth Avenue. But the city's heart, if anywhere, is split between **Pike Place Market** and **Pioneer Square.** What lies between the two sites is a high-tide area bounded on the south by Yesler Way, on the north by Virginia Street, and on the west and east by Second Avenue and Interstate 5. Seattle's financial, shopping, and entertainment districts moved here after the Great Fire of 1889 destroyed the original city center. But is that downtown? To say so suggests a public attention and even affection that this commercial district sadly does not enjoy, perhaps because it has long sought to impress rather than to please, or because it didn't evolve from a mixed-use retail-residential base.

Walt Crowley, a local TV commentator and longtime civic activist, pointed out some years ago that Seattle "is really a confederacy of neighborhoods. People don't identify so much with downtown as they do with the specific area in which they live. In Portland [Oregon], downtown is everybody's neighborhood. But in Seattle, everybody's neighborhood is their downtown."

Seattleites venture downtown to work, of course. And they come here to shop for obscure presents and to show out-of-town visitors the sights. Unfortunately, however, efforts to stem urban sprawl and keep the inner city alive by transforming old hotels or commercial buildings into condominium hives have seen only limited success in the face of high crime rates, noisy and disruptive construction projects, and knuckle-gnawing traffic jams.

Downtown's post-fire move north from Pioneer Square can be tracked in the age and character of its architecture. The downtown area first crawled up Second Avenue, dropping enough banks in its wake to create the closest thing Seattle had to a real financial district. With the **Alaska-Yukon-Pacific (AYP) Exposition** of 1909 (Seattle's "coming out party," held where the **University of Washington** stands today), the town was introduced to the efficacy of urban planning, which has since had a somewhat fitful relationship with this "Queen City of the Northwest." (Comprehensive development here tends to bow before the winds of expense and business opposition.) A building boom during World War I brought many of the magnificent terracotta structures that still stand on Second and Third avenues (for more about these buildings see "Terracotta Town" on page 32). After development of the boxy, modern **Seattle-First National Bank Tower,** a great fence of high rises ascended north along Fourth Avenue, and the area declared itself Seattle's new financial district.

Explore the central Business District on a weekday, when street musicians perform, espresso carts steam, and people-watching is at its best. Weekend activities gravitate to the Waterfront and Pioneer Square, with some spillover into **Westlake Center,** while the rest of downtown goes pretty much into a siesta mode.

---

1 Old Public Safety Building Young Seattle took a long time to erect a city hall to match its optimism and ambition. (For that matter, the city still lacks such a centerpiece, tolerating instead that glass-walled Kennedy-era monstrosity on Fourth Avenue known as the **Municipal Building.**) But in the 20th century's diapered days, local burghers hired architect **Clayton Wilson** to erect a new administration building on this triangular block. Comparisons with New York's **Flatiron Building** are inevitable, but Wilson did better than copy. His five-story structure with a penthouse, faced with brick and sandstone and boasting a curved copper roofline, was properly formal without being

Denny
Park

Denny Wy.

Bell St.

Blanchard St.

Lenora St.

8th Ave.

7th Ave.

6th Ave.

5th Ave.

4th Ave.

Virginia St.

Terry Ave.

9th Ave.

Stewart St.

Howell St.

Yale Ave.

Minor Ave.

Boren Ave.

Melrose Ave. E.

Bellevue Ave. E.

Westlake Ave.

60

Olive Wy.

61

63
62

59

58

53

57

Monorail
Terminal

54

55

64

Pike St.

Pine St.

52

51

50

49

48

47

Washington State
Convention and
Trade Center

39

38

56

46
45

44

43

Union St.

42

41

36

40

35

34

37

Minor Ave.

Boren Ave.

Terry Ave.

9th Ave.

8th Ave.

7th Ave.

6th Ave.

5th Ave.

I-5

25

24

Pike Pl.

Pike
Place
Market

31

32

33

University St.

30

Seneca St.

Spring St.

22

23

27 26

29 28

4th Ave.

3rd Ave.

2nd Ave.

1st Ave.

Post Ave.

Western Ave.

21

20

19

Madison St.

14

Marion St.

15

18

17

16

Columbia St.

13

12

Waterfront
Park

Pier 56

Rte. 99/Alaskan Wy. Viaduct

9

11

Cherry St.

James St.

Pier 55

Pier 54

8 7 10

Pier 53

Alaskan Wy.

Ferries to Winslow
(Bainbridge Island)
and Bremerton

Seattle
Ferry Terminal

Waterfront
Streetcar

6 5

4

3

Jefferson St.

2

Yesler Wy.

1

Pioneer
Square

Elliott
Bay

N

km
mi

1/8

1/4

1/4

1/2

Occidental Ave. S.

Occidental
Park

pretentious. City government moved in immediately but only seven years later it had to relocate again to larger digs in the **King County Courthouse** on Third Avenue. The Public Safety Building subsequently housed a hospital, a jail, and a police station. Still later, after abuse as a parking garage and as an unofficial sanctuary for the homeless, it was converted back into office space. ♦ 400 Yesler Way

2 City Hall Park Seattle's city hall, a rickety hodgepodge of wooden additions derisively nicknamed Katzenjammer Castle, stood on this tiny treed triangle until 1909. When that was leveled, **Mayor George Dilling** established this historic but now rather seedy site as the city's first downtown park, originally known as **Court House Park**.
♦ Jefferson St and Yesler Way

3 King County Courthouse From the 1890s until 1916 the county's center of legal activity was several blocks east of the intersection of Third Avenue and James Street. Where **Harborview Hospital** now perches atop its bluff, an old "cruel castle" of a courthouse then loomed, its imposing pillared mass lifting to a dome visible from all over town. Lawyers found the building inconveniently placed; they were often heard panting invectives as they sprinted uphill to reach their litigation, giving rise to the knoll's nickname of Profanity Hill. The current King County Courthouse was designed by **A. Warren Gould,** another of early Seattle's prolific designers. His concept broke away from the old notion of a monumental temple of justice, calling instead for a 22-story, H-shaped skyscraper with a pyramid-topped tower in the center. Only six stories were erected initially, with another five being added in 1930 under the direction of **Henry Bittman** and **John L. McCauley.** The tower and additional floors were never built.
♦ Third Ave and James St

4 521 Cafe $ Midday during a workweek, the 521 Cafe looks like an annex to the King County Courthouse across the street. Judges, lawyers, cops, and more than a few quavering defendants are staples of the clientele, supplemented by other city employees and a few down-on-their-luck types looking decidedly uncomfortable amidst all the designer suits. Burgers are the signature fare at this home-cooking joint, served best with grilled onions. But it's a hard choice sometimes between that and the meat-loaf special, and the milk shakes are sublime. Try to grab one of the two people-watching tables in the windows up front.
♦ American ♦ M-F 6:30AM-4:30PM. 521 Third Ave. 623.2233

5 Greg Kucera Gallery For a dinky location, this gallery has a standout rep for importing some of the country's top talent, as well as for promoting almost-unknown locals. Works shown here are generally thought-provoking, verging toward controversial in themed exhibits. ♦ Tu-Sa 10:30AM-5:30PM. 608 Second Ave. 624.0770

6 Ruby Montana's Pinto Pony Who would have thought that the kitschware of the 1950s and 1960s—all those trinkets that you were embarrassed to see decorating your grandparents' mantel—would someday become so chic? Lava lamps, Jetson-esque vinyl couches, and a huge selection of comical salt-and-pepper shakers can all be found here. The array of retro-cultural effluvia salvaged from the Jazz Age to the Information Age is amazing—anyone for a mountable moose head? ♦ Daily 10AM-6PM. 603 Second Ave. 621.7669

7 Alaska Building Opened in 1904, this 14-story structure (designed by the St. Louis firm of **Eames & Young**) was the first in Seattle to employ steel-frame construction. That technology, developed in Chicago office towers as early as the 1880s, allowed exterior masonry to be ornamental rather than strictly load-bearing. Thus, buildings could be made bigger and taller without becoming as heavy as the Romanesque piles of Pioneer Square. The penthouse here was once home to the **Alaska Club,** a social circle for Last Frontier emigrants, many of whom came south after the 1897 gold rush. ♦ 618 Second Ave

8 Bakeman's Restaurant $ Tucked beneath the historic **Hoge Building** (site of the city's first residence and famous for a pride of lion heads along its cornice; see illustration above), Bakeman's is a no-frills lunchtime fave among office drudges. Sandwiches (especially the turkey and meat-loaf varieties) are thick enough to defy easy gripping, and the soups attract a lot of acclaim. ♦ American ♦ M-F 7AM-7:30PM. 122 Cherry St. 622.3375

Restaurants/Clubs: Red   **Hotels:** Blue
Shops/ 🌱 Outdoors: Green   **Sights/Culture:** Black

9 Chamber of Commerce Building A Byzantine or Italian Romanesque basilica notched into the hustle of contemporary downtown? Leave it to the local chamber of commerce to plumb ostentatious associations. This 1924 design was allegedly inspired by a trip to Europe that the principal architect, **Harlan Thomas,** took to view 12th-century Lombardy churches. The chamber moved out of its poseur cathedral years ago and the structure is now occupied in large part by the architectural group **TRA,** which rehabilitated the building in 1970 and is the direct descendant of **Schack, Young & Myers,** the firm that assisted Thomas in the structure's conception. A sculptural frieze called *Primitive & Modern Industries* by **Morgan Padelford** extends to either side of the main entrance and refers to aspects of Northwest history. ◆ 219 Columbia St

10 Cherry Street Parking Garage While it isn't usually on the city tour, this arch-windowed structure was showman **John Cort's Grand Opera House,** the "finest theater in the city" when it opened in 1900. Where cars now puff and park, Seattleites used to gather along two huge balconies to take in turn-of-the-century culture. (Note what looks like the vestige of a grand entrance.) ◆ Third Ave and Cherry St

11 Arctic Building The tusks of the 25 terracotta walrus heads (see the illustration on page 33) that stud the handsome facade here are not the same ones that garnered public attention in 1917, when the prestigious old **Arctic Club** first opened this classically decorated building. It seems the originals were removed during the 1950s, owing to public fear that they'd break off and spear passing pedestrians. Not until the early 1980s and a loving restoration of this **A. Warren Gould** edifice did the walruses get their tusks back, this time cast of a special epoxy. Unfortunately, the life-size polar bear that formerly crowned the Arctic's Third Avenue entrance was not replaced. Inside, the recently restored **Dome Room,** a gold-leafed space once used as a restaurant for Arctic Club members and now rented for special events, is worth a peek. ◆ 700 Third Ave

12 McCormick's Fish House and Bar ★★$$$ The offerings here are pretty reliable and their quality consistent, which tends to attract an older, more conservative, but loyal clientele. Younger drop-ins usually come from city hall or one of the other government beehives nearby and wind up in McCormick's convivial bar. The menu features simple preparations of seafood, with selections changed daily. Service is almost always efficient. ◆ Seafood ◆ M-Th 11AM-11PM; F 11AM-midnight; Sa 5PM-midnight; Su 5-11PM. 722 Fourth Ave. Reservations recommended. 682.3900

13 Columbia Seafirst Center As much as Seattleites love to hate this 76-story cloud-ripper (pictured at right), and as much as it is radically out of scale with the rest of downtown, Columbia Seafirst Center does at least prove that T.S. Eliot was wrong when he predicted that cities of the future would display nothing of consequence but a hundred thousand miles of asphalt and a million lost golf balls. You can't fail to notice this exclamation point of steel and glass, the tallest building in town since 1985.

Chester L. Lindsey Architects achieved an unusual vertical and monumental sense by sheathing the center in black glass; a lighter face would have revealed individual floor levels and thus perceptually diminished the building. Alternating concave and convex exterior surfaces, as well as the skyscraper's stairstepped arrangement, create more complex light patterns than would be possible on a straight-sided tower. Stay away from the lower-level shopping floors, as they're dingy, overchromed, and generally suburban-ugly. An observation deck on the 73rd floor, however, provides a broad panorama of the city. For the privilege of gazing at the spectacular view, you'll pay about $3.50 per adult, $1.75 for children. ◆ Admission to the observation deck. M-F 8:30AM-4:30PM. Columbia St (between Fourth and Fifth Aves). 386.5151

14 First United Methodist Church Interstate 5 orphaned this church from **First Hill,** to the east, the neighborhood it had served for most of this century. Now it stands out as a handsomely domed anachronism amid the cornfield of central city skyscrapers. Designed by **James Schack** and **Daniel R. Huntington** (the latter of whom served for many years as city architect), this 1907 building combines Roman and Palladian Renaissance qualities, a departure from the Gothic cathedral designs then so popular in America. In addition to its religious activities, the church also serves as a lecture hall. ◆ Services Su 9AM, 11AM. 811 Fifth Ave. 626.7278

Terracotta Town

Granted it was a raging fire that destroyed early Seattle in 1889, but this very same fire also had a lot to do with how the city's architecture developed over the following five decades. Just trace the growth northward from **Pioneer Square.** Starting at **Smith Tower,** the handsome but weighty Romanesque Revival style of brick and stone gives way to paler, more gracefully ornamented terracotta towers that were believed (correctly) to be more structurally sound than their precursors. These buildings were also a kind of insurance policy for Seattle: terra-cotta, it had been proved, was more fire-resistant than many other building materials. Perhaps more significant, however, is that for most of this century these towers would characterize Seattle as a great white city on the water.

Terra-cotta became an accepted building material for Chicago's large-scale projects shortly after that city suffered its own skyline-devastating blaze in 1871. The enriched clay eventually became the facing of choice among early American skyscraper builders, including architects such as **Louis Sullivan** and **Daniel Burnham** who discovered they could use it to create higher and slimmer towers. They achieved this by assembling steel skeletons to bear most of a building's weight, and then sheathing the structure with a lighter skin of terra-cotta (which weighs about 70 pounds per cubic foot, compared to 170 pounds for granite).

Terra-cotta could also be modeled easily into an infinite variety of shapes before it was hardened by firing—a bottom-line plus during a period when the expense of traditional ornamental stonework was on the rise. As architect **Frank Lloyd Wright** later remarked, terra-cotta "takes the impression of human imagination. . . . It is in the architect's hand what wax is in the sculptor's hand." The material allowed designers to more fully express themselves in the sort of Beaux Arts embellishments popular during the early 20th century. Gargoyles, cartouches, French nymphs, or a ribbon of walrus heads could all be produced cheaply and quickly and in numerous shades to enhance a structure.

Of course, the Northwest's damp climate forced special requirements on terracotta manufacturing. More porous versions might have been fine for California, but here the clay renderings had to be highly glazed, a fact that contributed greatly not only to their waterproofing but also to their general longevity. (The **Capitol Theater** in Yakima, Washington, for instance, was hit by a fire some years back that destroyed the interior but left the distinguished terracotta facade standing until civic leaders could mount a complete restoration.)

One of the earliest architects erecting terracotta-sheathed edifices in Seattle was **Charles H. Bebb,** an Englishman who'd worked in Chicago with Louis Sullivan's firm. In about 1890 he moved to Seattle to serve as an engineer for an early terracotta company owned, at least in part, by pioneer **Arthur Denny.** Bebb formed his own architectural practice in 1898, subsequently linking up with **Leonard L. Mendel** and the talented New Yorker **Carl F. Gould** to create some of Seattle's most significant terracotta structures. They were joined in their taste for terra-cotta by local architects **John Graham, Sr.; Henry Bittman; A. Warren Gould;** and theater designer **B. Marcus Priteca,** an experimental stylist who created molds for classical ornamental motifs that became catalog items and eventually detailed buildings all down the West Coast.

Not until 1930 did the demand for terra-cotta suffer a decline, brought on by the Depression, escalating production costs, and changes in architectural taste. By then, however, Seattle—as well as Portland, Oregon, and San Francisco—all displayed a rich diversity of terracotta works. Unfortunately, some of the finest examples have been victims of the wrecking ball (including the old **Rhodes Building** and the **Orpheum Theater,** both once in downtown Seattle), but others are still standing and are definitely worth seeing. A few of the more interesting examples are listed below.

Alaska Building (1904; Eames & Young) Downtown's first steel-girdered high rise.
♦ 618 Second Avenue

Arctic Building (1917; A. Warren Gould) Ivory colored terra-cotta "with confectioner's touches of aquamarine and rose," as one architectural guide puts it. The walrus heads lining the edifice (see the opposite page) speak well of the artistic possibilities in this clay construction. ♦ 700 Third Avenue

Coliseum Theater (1916; B. Marcus Priteca) For all its decline over the last two decades, this is still one of downtown's most beautifully detailed buildings. ♦ 1506 Fifth Avenue

Corona Hotel (1903; Bebb & Gould) This structure's stylistic debt goes to Louis Sullivan, who inspired its woven floral ornamentation of unglazed terra-cotta. ♦ 608 Second Avenue

Dexter Horton Building (1922; John Graham, Sr.) Like the Arctic Building before it, this tower is ivory-hued—a nationally popular color at the time. But it's more sternly businesslike in conception, with giant Doric columns of granite on the north side that express the original height of its lobby. ♦ 710 Second Avenue

Fischer Studio Building (1912, Bebb & Mendel; 1914, Bebb & Gould) Built in two stages. In 1914 Bebb and his new partner Gould added five stories onto the original three and integrated the facade into a continuous whole. The seventh and eighth floors, blank on the exterior except for some Venetian-inspired detail, were built to house a Renaissance Revival-style music hall. ♦ 1519 Third Avenue

Four Seasons Olympic Hotel (1929; George B. Post) Designed by an important New York architect, with Bebb & Gould administering the construction. Brick clad with terracotta ornaments. ♦ 410 Seneca Street

Medical-Dental Building (1925; Kreutzer & Albertson, John Graham, Sr.) Graham designed this as a physical and spiritual extension of his 1919 **Frederick & Nelson** department store. But while the drama of the former F&N is apparent at all heights, most of the Medical-Dental's interest doesn't begin until the 14th floor, where Venetian filigrees and a series of setback penthouses and towers are located. ♦ 505 Olive Way

Sailors Union of the Pacific (1954; T. Bohannon and K. Better) A particularly late and simplistic example of terracotta design. ♦ 2505 First Avenue

Seafirst Bank (1908; J.J. Baillargeon) A former department store, this building has a great arched entrance, lion heads decorating the lower corners, and fine shell-patterned window frames adorning the ground level. ♦ 1100 Second Avenue

Securities Building (1912; John Graham, Sr.) Greco-Roman design executed in terra-cotta. Pay attention especially to the ornamentation, including playful green cartouches, along Third Avenue. ♦ 1904 Third Avenue

Smith Tower (1912; Gaggin & Gaggin) The light weight of terra-cotta allowed this early skyscraper to be built taller than was previously possible. ♦ 506 Second Avenue

Terminal Sales Building (1923; Henry Bittman) Tan brick and terracotta facing, with English Gothic ornament that stands out pleasantly against its Art Deco profile. ♦ 1934 First Avenue

Woolworth Building (circa 1935; Harold B. Hamhill) Built using Woolworth's standard design, this Moderne-style structure was the only new terracotta building constructed in downtown Seattle during the 1930s and 1940s (those who study these things, at least, haven't found any that were built earlier). ♦ 301 Pike Street

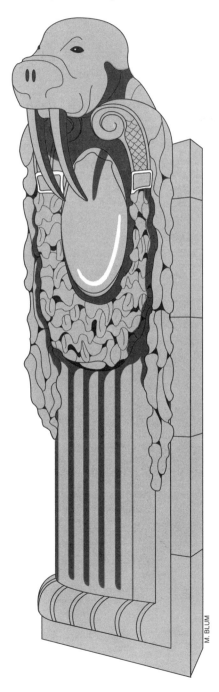

The Arctic Building's walrus heads (like the one pictured here) had their tusks removed about 30 years ago for fear they'd fall off and mortally wound passersby. During a 1980s restoration, however, the walruses got their tusks back.

M. BLUM

15 Rainier Club The architect, **Kirtland Cutter,** is not so well known here as in his adopted hometown of Spokane, Washington (where he designed, for instance, the eclectic old **Davenport Hotel**). Yet the formerly males-only Rainier Club, opened in 1904, is indeed one of the most startling and handsome juxtapositions to the skyscrapers of Seattle's central Business District. The club was to be a haven for the city's meritocracy, a place for them to gather and chat over cigars and brandy. Cutter modeled the Rainier after English men's clubs (a separate "guest" entrance for women was tucked away on the Marion Street facade), with rustic brickwork and curvilinear gables drawn from Jacobean, or late English Renaissance, style. In 1929 the prestigious partnership of **Charles Bebb** and **Carl Gould** added 54 feet to the south end of the building, all in character with Cutter's original. The membership here is no longer restricted to males. Yet from the outside, little has changed: many new Seattleites don't even know what goes on inside these brick walls, for there's no sign outside announcing the building's use. ◆ 810 Fourth Ave

16 Spade & Archer Connoisseurs of detective and crime fiction will want to track down this eccentric hideaway of collectible books in the field. ◆ By appointment only. 810 Third Ave, suite 440. 682.7064

![Metropolitan Grill logo]

17 Metropolitan Grill ★★$$$$ Proving that not all Seattleites are worried about their fat and cholesterol intakes, the Metropolitan turns out thick, mesquite-grilled steaks accompanied by baked potatoes or pasta. The clam chowder is worth a try, as are the onion rings, the burgers, and the Hawaiian mahimahi. An adjacent big-windowed bar is comfortable until 5PM, when financial district habitués start washing in. "The Met" is also popular with Japanese business-people, who can request a special translated menu. ◆ American ◆ M-F 11AM-3:30PM, 5-11PM; Sa 5-11PM; Su 5-10PM. Bar open daily 11AM-11PM. 818 Second Ave. Reservations recommended. 624.3287

18 Rosellini and McHugh's Nine-10 Restaurant ★★$$$ Seattle, burgeoning now with all kinds of first-rate restaurants, nonetheless has few restaurant institutions. One of them, however, is bonhomous **Victor Rosellini,** who's spent almost half a century greeting diners at his various establishments (**Rosellini's Six-10, Rosellini's Four-10**—

both long gone). Matriculated from the restaurants of San Francisco, he is credited as the person who introduced Seattle to white tablecloths, wine lists, and the like. The Nine-10 grillhouse pairs him up with **Mick McHugh,** a former protégé who over the last 20 years has given this city some of its liveliest dining houses-cum-saloons (including **F.X. McRory's** in Pioneer Square).

The menu includes recipes from Rosellini's former enterprises (anybody for crab and shrimp salad or a sourdough burger?), as well as Italian entrées such as spaghettini with Italian meatballs. Politicos, business wheels, and the newspaper columnists who court them represent the typical crowd here. ◆ Continental/Italian ◆ M-F 11AM-midnight; Sa 5PM-midnight. 910 Second Ave. Reservations recommended. 292.0910

19 1001 Fourth Avenue Plaza When this modernist bronze monolith (pictured at right) was completed in 1969, professional journals hailed it as among the most technologically advanced buildings of its time. The late **Don Winkelmann,** a partner in the **NBBJ Group** who was responsible for the design, rhapsodized for the *Seattle Times:* "You see a jet move across the horizon above this building and [the] two are compatible. It all fits with rockets to the moon." Many Seattleites took a dimmer view of the 50-story corporate headquarters for **Seattle-First National Bank.** They joked that it was the box that the Space Needle came in. Others criticized it as an ugly dark birthmark on the predominantly white terracotta hand of Seattle, and they didn't like the fact that it so overwhelmed the beloved **Smith Tower,** only 42 stories tall. But time has quieted the cavil, as did a 1986 revitalization that added small shops and a glass-enclosed **Wintergarden,** making the building more people-friendly. English sculptor **Henry Moore's** bronze *Three-Piece Sculpture: Vertebrae* is the most prominent feature of the plaza. ◆ 1001 Fourth Ave (between Madison and Spring Sts)

20 Seattle Public Library This plain-visaged International Style building from 1959 replaced one of the most imposing among

10 libraries in the Seattle area paid for by iron-and-steel-magnate **Andrew Carnegie.** (Only one other of the bunch faced the wrecking ball; eight more are still scattered in various neighborhoods, from Auburn to Fremont and Ballard.) The city's earliest library collection was housed in **Henry Yesler's** mansion at Third Avenue and James Street (now the site of the King County Courthouse); but when that burned down in 1901, taking 25,000 volumes with it, the editor of the *Seattle Post-Intelligencer* convinced Carnegie to build the city a *real* book repository. The answer to that wish opened in 1906, a big muscle of gray Tenino sandstone columns and giant arched windows, designed by Chicago architect **P.J. Weber,** that might have pleased even Emperor Nero. Cramping and construction problems finally doomed the Carnegie building. The rooftop cafe above the present library is a good idea, but it can be noisy up there and other buildings block the view toward Puget Sound. ♦ M-Th 9AM-9PM, F-Sa 9AM-6PM June-Aug; M-Th 9AM-9PM, F-Sa 9AM-6PM, Su 1-5PM Sept-May. 1000 Fourth Ave. 386.5151

21 Stouffer Madison Hotel $$$ Despite its proximity to the Interstate-5 gully, this 554-room hotel manages to project a sense of quiet. Maybe it's the regal color scheme, or the muted lighting, or the marbles and rich woods that decorate the guest rooms. Perhaps it's the peaceful views from both sides (Elliott Bay on the west, the Cascade mountains on the east). Luxury addicts should book a room on the **Club Floors** (25th and 26th), which offer special check-in services, a complimentary Continental breakfast, and even a library. A 40-foot-long rooftop pool and Jacuzzi will work out the jet-lag kinks. Indoor parking (for a fee) and free in-town transportation are also available. And there's a soothing piano bar right off the lobby. ♦ 515 Madison St. 583.0300, 800/468.3571; fax 622.8635

Within the Stouffer Madison Hotel:

Prego ★$$$ One of the city's better restaurants with a view (from the 28th floor), Prego is a choice spot to steal a date away from prying eyes. It's known for its combinations of Northern Italian dishes and Northwest seafood. Try the black linguine with sautéed Maine lobster, shrimp, and scallops. ♦ Italian ♦ M-Th 11:30AM-2PM, 5:30-10PM; F 11:30AM-2PM, 5:30-11PM; Sa 5:30-11PM; Su 5:30-10PM. 583.0300

22 Hotel Vintage Park $$$ Well-known San Francisco hotelier **Bill Kimpton** has given the formerly disheveled **Kennedy Hotel** a brand new lobby, some elegant furnishings, and a too-quaint-for-words Washington wine theme (the 129 guest rooms are named in honor of wineries and vineyards from across the state). It's all part of Kimpton's usual "discount luxury" package. Rooms are decorated in splashy textiles but subtle colors, and if they offer some unnecessary accoutrements (direct-dial phones in the bathroom?), their general comfort, as well as the hotel's convenience to downtown amenities, is undeniable.

As at other Kimpton properties on the West Coast, complimentary local wines are poured each afternoon in the fireplaced lobby. When making reservations, try to get a room high up or on Spring Street, as Fifth Avenue is a funnel for honking rush-hour traffic. On-site parking and 24-hour room service are available. ♦ 1100 Fifth Ave. 624.8000, 800/624.4433; fax 623.0568

Within the Hotel Vintage Park:

Tulio Ristorante ★★$$ Early judgments of a restaurant are always dicey, but the imaginativeness of Tulio's Italian menu is impressive. Chef **Walter Pisano** (late of **Bravo Pagliacci** and **Gerard's Relais de Lyon**) serves an appetizer of homemade mozzarella balls with tomato and grilled eggplant. The smoked-salmon ravioli is a delicate mating of Northwest and Mediterranean, and you might want to start off with the garbanzo-bean soup. ♦ Italian ♦ M-Th 7-10AM, 11:30AM-2:30PM, 5-10PM; F 7-10AM, 11:30AM-2:30PM, 5-11PM; Sa 8AM-noon, 1-11PM; Su 8AM-noon, 1-10PM. 624.5500

23 Pacific Plaza Hotel $ An older property (built in 1929, refurbished in 1989), the Pacific Plaza is a surprise deal in the middle of "Big-Bucks Hotel Land." The rooms aren't luxurious, and they're often too small for families, but the hotel's central location (only five blocks from **Westlake Center**) is hard to beat at the price. ♦ 400 Spring St (at Fourth Ave). 623.3900, 800/426.1165; fax 623.2059

24 Holiday Inn Crowne Plaza $$ What it lacks in architectural character, this hotel tries to compensate for in its services. Upper-level rooms, dressed up in appealing reddish hues, have access to a special lounge and their own concierge, and receive free newspapers. Guests staying on some of the lower floors, unfortunately, find less-distinctive rooms. The lobby is comfortable and the staff helpful, but in a downtown full of historic establishments, the Crowne Plaza is ultimately too new to be all that interesting. ♦ Sixth Ave and Seneca St. 464.1980, 800/521.2762; fax 340.1617

25 Freeway Park How better to defy noisy freeway canyons than to cover them with something as peaceful as this five-acre park? Developed in 1976 under the direction of **Lawrence Halprin,** this $13.8 million greensward atop Interstate 5 features small ponds, flower beds, an engagingly irregular array of stairs leading from level to level, and a concrete abstraction of a waterfall that audibly separates the park from its hectic surroundings. Kick back with a good book and imagine the blood pressures escalating on the freeway below you. ♦ Sixth Ave and Seneca St

26 Financial Center The designer of this 1972 rough-concrete tower, with its appealing, punch-cardlike fenestration, was the same man who did the dark **Seattle-First National Bank Tower** three years before: **Don Winkelmann.** In the 1970s Winkelmann assumed a reputation as "Mr. Fourth Avenue" because of the towers he was lining up along that thoroughfare. Despite his influence on the Seattle cityscape, Winkelmann appreciated the old architecture here as much as he did his own. So taken was he with the nearby **Seattle Tower,** for instance, that he insisted his Financial Center not block any of its views. His solution, unfortunately, was to lay down a fairly lifeless plaza to one side of the center. ♦ 1215 Fourth Ave

In 1907 moralist William Hickman Moore was elected mayor of Seattle and began a campaign to eliminate saloons and other vices from the city's borders. But Moore was out of office and his reform efforts were out of favor by 1910, when city councilman Hiram C. Gill was elected mayor. Gill favored a wide-open town. In fact, *McClure's* magazine reported that 30 to 40 gambling places opened under Gill's administration. Seattle's police chief himself was taking kickbacks from prostitution—$10 per harlot each month.

Residents were perturbed by His Honor's attitudes and actions, but their rumblings were fairly quiet until two of the police chief's cronies erected a 500-room brothel on Beacon Hill. Less than a year after Gill's inauguration, he was booted from office . . . only to be voted back as a reform candidate in 1914.

"One of Seattle's oddities is that while residents here own more Birkenstocks per capita than anywhere else—a fact—it's a city of hills and a lousy place to get around in sandals."

Smart Money magazine

27 Seattle Tower Being surrounded by more contemporary skyscrapers only enhances the nobility of this 26-story Art Deco tower (pictured below), completed in 1929. Faced with earth- and rock-colored gradations of brickwork—darker at the bottom, becoming lighter as the building ascends—the tower was intended to remind viewers of Northwest mountains. Principal designer **Joseph Wilson** tapered the structure upwards to emphasize its verticality and made the most of setbacks to bring light to a maximum of offices. At one time, those setbacks were filled with more than 200 flood units, which simulated an aurora borealis across the building face. The Third Avenue lobby builds on the mountain theme, achieving a cavernlike ambience with its dark marble walls and gilt ceiling. Look for interior details such as Indian headdresses, stylized evergreens, and abstract Chinese characters. ♦ 1218 Third Ave

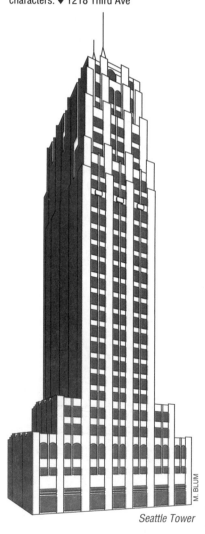

Seattle Tower

Restaurants/Clubs: Red   Hotels: Blue
Shops/ ♣ Outdoors: Green   Sights/Culture: Black

28 Washington Mutual Tower For a while, this tapered, 55-story eye-grabber was as popular in Seattle as the singer-cum-exhibitionist Madonna. The much-ballyhooed New York firm of **Kohn Pederson Fox** had bundled it up with historical references: a cruciform floor plan, for instance, harking back to Greek cross churches of the Renaissance, and a stepped-back profile that reminded critics of the Empire State Building. No one seemed to care that it barely related to the surrounding architecture and presented nothing better than a cliff face at sidewalk level. With an exterior of pink Brazilian granite, its playful pyramidal top (inspiring jokes about this being Seattle's largest pencil), and a lobby resplendent in mahogany, Washington Mutual seemed a significant and relieving departure from decades of almost featureless glass boxes. ♦ 1201 Third Ave

29 Brooklyn Cafe and Oyster Bar Lounge ★$$$ This place is packed into a splendidly refitted brick building that somehow survived the wrecking ball when land was being cleared to erect the Washington Mutual Tower. The interior finishings are quite handsome—lots of wood and shiny metals, plenty of big booths, and chic cafe tables surrounded by stools. But the menu—given to steaks and seafood—isn't yet innovative or consistent enough to make this a regular stop. Appetizers tend to be either too small or too expensive, or both. Service can be slow, but the valet parking is a relief in downtown. ♦ Steak/Seafood ♦ M-Th 11AM-3PM, 5-10PM; F 11AM-3PM, 5-10:30PM; Sa 4-10:30PM; Su 4:30-9PM. Bar open daily until 11PM. 1212 Second Ave. Reservations recommended. 224.7000

30 Cobb Building This august imposition of brick and terra-cotta, completed in 1910, is the last survivor of a once-grand midtown scheme. In 1861 Seattle pioneers **Arthur** and **Mary Denny** and **Charles** and **Mary Terry** dedicated this corner, along with the surrounding 10-acre knoll (all at that time on the outskirts of town), as the site of a territorial university. Thirty years later, school regents determined that their original clapboard-and-cupola institution was no longer sufficient, and moved the burgeoning **University of Washington** to its present site at the north end of **Lake Union**. The city then proposed to develop this knoll as a park. But the UW had other ideas. Regents signed a 50-year agreement with the **Metropolitan Building Company** to improve the acreage for commercial use.

The New York architectural firm of **Howells & Stokes** was engaged, and a comprehensive program was developed to raise uniform, 11-story facades along both sides of Fourth Avenue, with a central plaza and residential apartments on Fifth Avenue. Both the Cobb Building and the **White-Henry-Stuart Building,** on an opposite corner of Fourth Avenue and University Street, were completed before the plan began to deteriorate. Later neighboring structures, such as the **Olympic Hotel** and the **Skinner Building,** were compatible with the Howells & Stokes plan but deviated from its uniformity. In the 1960s a contrasting design scheme took control of the tract, and the White-Henry-Stuart Building was razed to make room for the popsicle-ish **Rainier Tower.** But the Cobb (believed to have been the first medical-dental office building on the West Coast) remains, and it is still very impressive. Note the Beaux Arts-inspired ornamentation, particularly the Indian heads attributed to sculptor **Victor G. Schneider.** ♦ 1305 Fourth Ave

31 Seattle Pendleton If consumption of woolwear has tapered off over the past 20 years owing to the increased use of synthetic materials, it has only made Oregon's **Pendleton Woolen Mills** more determined to promote its durable line of jackets, sweaters, scarves, and accessories beyond the Beaver State. Hard as it is to believe, this entire business evolved from the lowly Pendleton blanket, first crafted in eastern Oregon by one **Thomas Kay,** an Englishman who'd studied in the textile mills of Philadelphia and came out west in 1863 to "borrow" native blanket designs for his own products. ♦ M-Sa 9:30AM-6PM. 1313 Fourth Ave. 682.4430. Also at: Bellevue Square, Bellevue. 453.9040

32 Security Pacific Tower (Rainier Tower) First-time visitors are often caught staring up at this striking white high rise, alternately wondering how it balances on its 12-story pedestal and whether it might topple down upon them. Not to worry. The principal designer, **Minoru Yamasaki,** knew what he was doing. Born in Seattle, Yamasaki gifted his hometown with not only Security Pacific Tower, but another landmark: the **Pacific Science Center** complex at Seattle Center. His reputation spread beyond Puget Sound, for he designed the **Century Plaza Towers** in Los Angeles, the **World Trade Center** in New York, and corporate offices worldwide. In all his work, Yamasaki once said, he strove to offer "delight, serenity, and surprise." Certainly all three of those terms apply to this "upside-down pencil" of a skyscraper. Two levels of shops, collectively known as **Rainier Square,** anchor the pedestal. ♦ 1200 Fourth Ave

Within Rainier Square at the Security Pacific Tower:

Jeffrey Michael Supporting the menswear gospel according to *GQ,* this store carries lots of fine suits and stylish sports attire for the aspiring world-conqueror. ♦ M-F 10AM-7PM; Sa 10AM-6PM; Su noon-5PM. Lower level. 625.9891

Biagio Pricey but excellent leather accessories for the status-conscious shopper can be found here—the smells alone are worth a stop. ♦ M-Sa 10AM-6PM. Lower level. 623.3842

Littler Oxford-cloth suits, **Jaegar** clothes for women, and other dress-up accessories draw affluent shoppers with distinctly untrendy tastes. ♦ M-Sa 10AM-6PM. Lower level. 223.1331

Polo-Ralph Lauren This boutique carries a better selection of stylish **Lauren Collection** goods—all sporting that vital insignia—than is usually found in department stores. ♦ M-Sa 10AM-6PM. First floor. 587.0200

Bek's Bookstore Small and lacking in any but the most recent titles, Bek's at least offers a healthy selection of regional works and humor books. ♦ M-F 8:30AM-6PM; Sa 10AM-6PM. Upper level. 624.1328

Lynn McAllister Gallery Keep your elbows down and your shopping bags steady when walking around all the blown or crafted glass from Northwest artisans and other glassmakers. You wouldn't want to break anything, now would you? ♦ M-F 10AM-5:30PM; Sa 11AM-5:30PM. 624.6864

33 Four Seasons Olympic Hotel $$$$ Seattle newspapers printed special photo sections touting the Olympic's virtues when it opened in 1924. Men and women showed up in fancy cars and fancier dress, anxious to celebrate Seattle's newfound sophistication. The hotel's designers—**George B. Post, Carl Gould,** and **Charles Bebb**—had created an Italian palazzo, with a base of rusticated stone, a terracotta face, and details such as Roman arches and dentils. It was a landmark by which Seattle could steer its general prosperity.

After half a century, though, the declining hotel only narrowly escaped demolition. Sale to the Four Seasons chain and a 1982 rehabilitation by **NBBJ** brought grandeur back to both the interior and exterior. Public rooms, including the cavernous lobby, now showcase lots of marble, thick carpeting, comfortable armchairs, and giant potted plants. A balcony around the lobby features some delightful historical photos of the hotel. The 450 guest rooms are somewhat less ostentatious, but they're still large and come furnished with 1920s reproductions. Valet parking, 24-hour room service, and complimentary shoe shines all help to make you feel pampered.

Laura Ashley has a stylish outpost inside the hotel, peddling its demure line of dresses, blouses, nighties, and signature-print home decorations. **Shuckers** (★★$$), a clubby oyster bar on the Fourth Avenue side, is excellent for winding down after work. And

the Four Seasons' refurbishment added a large-windowed **Garden Court** (★★$$) above the University Street entrance, where you can enjoy a light lunch or high tea, or dance to swing bands on carefree weekend eves. ♦ 411 University St. 621.1700, 800/223.8772; fax 682.9633

Within the Four Seasons Olympic Hotel:

The Georgian Room ★★★$$$$ The decor of this ballroomlike space, with its chandeliers and tall windows, has often overwhelmed the cuisine—until lately, with the introduction of chef **Kerry Sear** into the kitchen. Blackened tomato lasagna and corn-pasta cakes with scallops in avocado butter? This isn't the same restaurant that used to draw mostly visiting potentates who never looked at the check. With Sear at the stove, even locals are rediscovering the Georgian Room. Breakfast and lunch are served, but it's dinner that shines. The best introduction to Sear's tastes is to order the three- or four-course chef's menu, which changes every two weeks. For about $20 extra, the sommelier will select wines appropriate to each course, adding further to the delights of your meal. ♦ Continental ♦ M-Th 6:30-11AM, 11:30AM-2PM, 5:30-10PM; F 6:30-11AM, 11:30AM-2PM, 5:30-10:30PM; Sa 6:30AM-noon, 5:30-10:30PM; Su 7-11AM, 11:30AM-2PM. Reservations recommended. 621.7889

34 Skinner Building What does this block-long, tile-roofed Mediterranean palazzo from 1926 have to do with the monumental **Old Faithful Inn** in Yellowstone National Park and the **Canyon Hotel** at the Grand Canyon? They were all designed by one **Robert C. Reamer.** Born in Ohio in 1873, Reamer started with an architectural firm in Detroit and moved from there to Cleveland, Chicago, San Diego, and Wyoming. He came to Seattle during World War I to become chief architect for the **Metropolitan Building Company** (see the **Cobb Building** on page 37). Considered at one time to be a supreme practitioner of his art—a Richardsonian in his architectural aesthetics and a romantic by inclination—Reamer has all but disappeared from Seattle history books. Yet his buildings (the Skinner as well as the **Meany Tower Hotel** in the University District, the **Seattle Times Building** on John Street, and the **1411 Fourth Avenue Building** downtown) are some of the most intriguing around. ♦ 1326 Fifth Ave

Within the Skinner Building:

Fifth Avenue Theater The Skinner's tame Wilkeson sandstone exterior hides Seattle's loveliest performance space, said to be patterned after the imperial throne room in Beijing's Forbidden City. **Gustav Liljestrom,** a Norwegian artist trained in China, was responsible for the interior of this former vaudeville house, which features a coiling dragon painted on the ceiling. The Fifth Avenue was restored in 1980 and now hosts Broadway shows. Don't miss a chance to venture inside. ♦ Box office M-F 9:30AM-5PM. 625.1900

35 Fox's Gem Shop A Diamond Jim sort of environment, Fox's is all glittering stones, a finely tailored clientele, and steep prices. There's lots of sterling silver jewelry and a boutique selection of **Tiffany** products. ♦ M-Sa 10AM-5:30PM. 1341 Fifth Ave. 623.2528

36 Eddie Bauer, Inc. It must have been Seattle's proximity to the wilderness that led it to offer the world not one but *two* significant chains selling outdoor gear: **REI (Recreational Equipment Inc.)** and Eddie Bauer. Of those, Bauer is the older and more colorfully rooted. Eddie Bauer was born to Russian immigrant parents on **Orcas Island,** northwest of Seattle, in 1900. Always enchanted with fishing and hunting, it was natural that he would move into sporting-goods sales for a career and then that he should be wildly successful at it. He finally opened his own store in Seattle in 1922, attracting customers with his demanding policies about quality and his interest in improving what was already on the market. It was the latter that led him to invent the down jacket.

While fishing on Washington's Olympic peninsula in 1934, Bauer almost froze to death because he'd failed to bring along an appropriate jacket. He started thinking about how to make both warmer and lighter outerwear and remembered a tale his uncle had told about surviving the Russo-Japanese War of 1904 by wearing goose-down quilted undergarments. Bauer took some of the down he was already importing from China for use in flyties and shuttlecocks, quilted a few jackets for himself, and when friends declared them a hit, patented both the jackets and their manufacturing process. There are now about 200 Eddie Bauer stores across the country.

Although bought out some years ago by **Spiegel Inc.,** the company still sells the well-known goose-down fashions, as well as sleeping bags, backpacking equipment, knives, sunglasses, and some of the coziest wool socks available anywhere. The downtown store is known for offering hefty price reductions on the Bauer line. ♦ M-Th

10AM-7PM; F 10AM-8PM; Sa 10AM-6PM; Su 11AM-6PM. Fifth Ave and Union St. 622.2766

37 Seattle Hilton $$ It's rather confusing that this hotel's lobby sits on the ninth floor rather than at ground level (to make way for a parking garage). But that may be the only unusual thing here. **Conrad Hilton's** progenies are the *USA Today* of hostelries—familiar wherever you go. Furnishings are tasteful, but hardly memorable, and color schemes in the 237 rooms are benign, reflecting the aesthetics of a 1980s redo. A view restaurant, the **Top of the Hilton** (★★$$$$) specializes in local seafood and attracts a wayward business clientele to its lounge. And an underground passage connects the hotel to both **Rainier Square** and the **Washington State Convention and Trade Center.** ♦ 1301 Sixth Ave. 624.0500, 800/542.7700; fax 682.9029

38 Eagles Auditorium When completed in 1925, architect **Henry Bittman's** Renaissance Revival-style home for the **Fraternal Order of Eagles** was among the country's most distinguished fraternal buildings. Underused and running to shabbiness now, the block is still a fine example of Seattle's ornate terracotta facades. In early 1993, **A Contemporary Theatre (ACT)** announced plans to move from its Lower Queen Anne digs into the Eagle by the spring of 1995. ♦ 1416 Seventh Ave

39 Washington State Convention and Trade Center Too chunky, gray, and cold to be appealing, this 370,000-square-foot convention center can at least accommodate the sort of large-scale get-togethers that Seattle couldn't easily host before. Reception rooms are designed for groups numbering 50 to 4,000 people. Indoor parking is available for some 900 cars. There's a Visitor's Center inside. ♦ Visitor's center M-F 8:30AM-5PM. 800 Convention Place. Convention Center 447.5000, Visitor's Center 461.5840

Fortune 500 companies that have their head-quarters in the Seattle area include Airborne Freight, Alaska Air Group, Boeing, Burlington Resources, Costco Wholesale, Microsoft, Nordstrom, Safeco, Safeco Life, Univar, United Pacific Life, Paccar, Washington Mutual Savings Bank, and Weyerhaeuser.

"Like any nouveau riche, Seattle is harder to love in her new finery than she was in her salad days. I grumble at her new greed, snarl at her misplaced snobbishness and then break down and admit: I love her still."

Eric Scigliano, *Seattle Weekly* columnist

40 Seattle Sheraton Hotel and Towers
$$$$ This modern hotel is a convenient retreat for businesspeople attending events at the **Washington State Convention and Trade Center,** just up Pike Street from here. An expansive lobby is decorated with **Dale Chihuly** glass art. Meeting rooms are plentiful. Most of the 840 guest rooms are cramped by comparison, lacking in all but the most essential components. Four VIP floors (31st through 34th) offer more elaborate rooms and a separate concierge. A health club and pool on the 35th floor are open to all overnight guests.

Banners (★★$$$), a casual, well-lighted restaurant off the lobby, offers a sumptuous buffet luncheon. **Gooey's** (named, they say, after that bizarre long-necked mollusk, the geoduck) is a rather small disco with a decent bar. Parking is available at a cost. ♦ 1400 Sixth Ave. 621.9000, 800/325.3535; fax 621.8441

Within the Seattle Sheraton Hotel and Towers:

Fuller's ★★$$$ For years, this has been a regular stop for East Coast restaurant critics. They'd go away clucking over the innovative young chefs (**Kathy Casey** first, then **Caprial Pence**) and write glowing reviews that would attract yet another batch of food scriveners, who would in turn spill purple prose from their pens, and be followed by yet more critics. But with Pence's departure after half a decade, Fuller's must suddenly fight to maintain its celebrity. The big stake is on the new chef, **Monique Barbeau,** a Canadian graduate of New York's Culinary Institute who prefers straightforward preparations using Northwest ingredients.

Under Barbeau, cod comes with a citrus glaze and wilted-cabbage salad. Salmon is accompanied by a very lightly smoked root-vegetable sauce. A five-onion soup, for which Fuller's had become justly recognized, was deemed too rich and supplanted by a spicy tomato bisque with warm scallop chutney. Lunches have been simplified for the rushing businessperson, with lots of warm and cold salads dominating the spring-summer menu. In a town where talented young chefs are starting to bunch up, Barbeau has a challenge ahead of her if she's to keep Fuller's on the must-try list. ♦ Northwestern ♦ M-F 11:30AM-2PM, 5:30-10PM; Sa 5:30-10PM. Reservations recommended. 447.5544

41 Banana Republic The exotic explorer theme may be pushed a bit too heavily (are you really happier buying clothes beneath a palm tree?), but this San Francisco-based company certainly knows how to make casual clothes that last. And they're not all in khaki or green anymore. ♦ M-Sa 10AM-7PM; Su 11AM-6PM. 508 Union St. 622.2303

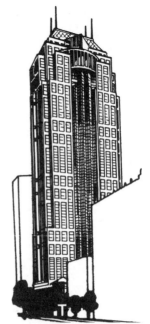

42 Pacific First Centre Although it's a hefty hunk of California glitz and post-postmodernist doodads staked into downtown Seattle, Pacific First (illustrated above) draws Seattleites with its nationally known retailers. The smaller shops here are also worth a browse. ♦ 1420 Fifth Ave

Within Pacific First Centre:

Ann Taylor In the same way that Brooks Brothers purveys timeless fashions for men, so Ann Taylor courts the women's trade. It's conservative and expensive but reliable. ♦ M-Sa 10AM-7PM. First floor. 623.4818

Design Concern With high-design office supplies and tableware, Japanese clocks, and a broad selection of obscure gadgets, this is a great place to shop for gifts. ♦ M-Th, Sa 10AM-6PM; F 10AM-7PM; Su noon-5PM. Second floor. 623.4444

Gucci The name has such a household quality and independent life that actually walking in here to shop for those trademark handbags and other fine leather goods is somehow disorienting. ♦ M-Th, Sa 10AM-6PM; F 10AM-7PM. Second floor. 682.7365

Boxer Bay When you weren't looking, men's skivvies became fashion statements, and Boxer Bay stepped in to make the most of that trend. In addition to silk drawers and Hugh Hefner-esque lounge attire, Boxer Bay sells comfy cotton robes and ties. ♦ M-Th, Sa 10AM-6PM; F 10AM-7PM; Su 11AM-5PM. Second floor. 625.9418

Restaurants/Clubs: Red	Hotels: Blue
Shops/ 🌴 Outdoors: Green	**Sights/Culture:** Black

Palomino ★★$$$ Leave your jeans and T-shirts in the closet. Like owner **Rich Komen's** other restaurants (**Cutter's Bayhouse** in Pike Place Market, **Triples** on Lake Union, and **Palisade** in Magnolia), this always-sparkling, highly stylized spot draws a beautiful mass of designer-suited gents and women in fancy dresses. **Dale Chihuly** glassworks sparkle in the directional lights.

The unwalled kitchen and open oven produce excellent king salmon, garlic chicken, and pork loin. Pizzas are thin-crusted and, sadly, also thinly covered. The bar crowds up rapidly after work, but the people-watching is even better here than in the dining area. There's a decent selection of microbrews on tap; have the knowledgeable bartenders help you try some new varieties. ♦ Mediterranean ♦ M-Th 5:30-10PM; F-Sa 5-11PM; Su 5-9:30PM. Bar open daily until about 11:30PM. Third floor. Reservations recommended. 623.1300

43 **Brooks Brothers** "BB" has had to make some changes in the last few years to maintain its commercial position, but this corner store (the only Brooks Brothers outpost north of San Francisco) doesn't seem to have lost a smidgen of traditional demeanor. A wealth of inventory, including some elegant women's lines, is presented in a refined manner; the salespeople are helpful but not intrusive, and the guys working the men's suits department might have learned their manners from valets to the Duke of Windsor. Annual sales in June and right after Christmas are worth waiting for. ♦ M-F 9AM-6PM; Sa 10AM-6PM. 1401 Fourth Ave. 624.4400

In the first two decades of the 20th century, cast-iron street clocks enjoyed unusual popularity in Seattle as an advertising tool for store owners, who would display the names of their shops on the clocks. Out of 24 street clocks that once stood on the downtown sidewalks, half of them remain. That's more street clocks than in any other city in the country (New York boasts a measly eight).

The "bubble" anchoring the flagpole at the top of Smith Tower was once a giant light directing ships into Elliott Bay.

44 **1411 Fourth Avenue Building** Textural details spun from Celtic motifs and Art Deco flourishes enliven the facade and lobby of this **Robert C. Reamer** office tower (pictured above), which opened in 1929. The stone facing represented a move away from the brick and terra-cotta that were so common to other structures in the neighborhood. Note the elegant entrance sign created by **Lloyd Lovegren** (who went on during the 1940s to design the **Lacey V. Morrow Bridge** across Lake Washington). ♦ Fourth Ave and Union St

Within the 1411 Fourth Avenue Building:

JoAnn's Cookies A must-try here are the chocolate-chip dippers—great disks made all the more dangerous to weight-conscious adults by their half-coatings of chocolate. ♦ M-F 6:30AM-6PM. 623.8853

45 **Fourth and Pike Building** Also known as the **Liggett Building,** this 1926 rise of cream-colored terra-cotta was one of the last commercial high rises built before the Great Depression brought downtown construction to a screeching halt. The impressive lobby here somehow survived relatively intact, while other downtown buildings were having theirs regretfully "modernized." ♦ 1424 Fourth Ave

Within the Fourth and Pike Building:

Dashasa Studio Jeweler **Daniel Shames** has a fondness for intensely colored opaque stones and crafts them into gorgeous pendants or rings. Pieces are hand-assembled to order and fairly affordable ($500 to $2,500). ♦ M-F 9AM-5PM; Sa-Su by appointment only. Suite 807. 623.0519

Seattle Pen

Seattle Pen This intimate shop sells only writing instruments, new ones and exquisitely kept older specimens. Repairs and engravings are available, too. ♦ M-F 9:30AM-5PM; Sa 9:30AM-1PM. Suite 527. 682.2640

46 Sharper Image A browser's delight and a gadgeteer's dream, this catalog-come-alive is full of high-tech sound equipment, full-body massage tables, adult toys, and fancy watches. ◆ M-Sa 10AM-6PM; Su noon-5PM. 1501 Fourth Ave. 343.9125

47 Coliseum Theater Believe it or not, this Italian Renaissance relic from 1916—somewhat the worse for wear now—was the first theater in the world designed specifically to show motion pictures. The owner was **Joe Gottstein,** an ambitious 23-year-old Seattle native who also built the popular **Longacres** horse track (regrettably torn down in 1992). Gottstein believed the public would flock to the movies if it could enjoy them amidst some class and comfort. So he commissioned **B. Marcus Priteca,** personal architect to vaudeville magnate **Alexander Pantages,** to create an opulent film palace. The resulting 1,700-seat Coliseum, with its terracotta facade detailed with grotesque masks, festoons of fruit, and bullock's heads, was a huge success.

But the passage of time and subsequent sales took their toll on this Priteca confection. A tremendous dome that once filled the space above the marquee was taken down, and a jarring neon sign was mounted in its place. Other theaters that opened in downtown drew away the Coliseum's business. For years, the theater languished in virtual disuse, waiting for another Joe Gottstein to dream it into a noble future. Recently, though, the **Banana Republic** outdoorwear chain purchased the landmark. The company plans to sink $5 million into its elegant renovation and reopen the theater as a Banana Republic flagship store in late 1993. ◆ Fifth Ave and Pike St

48 Nordstrom The department-store chain may have spread nationwide, but Seattleites still consider this locally owned store very much their own and the Nordy's label a symbol of cachet. Nordstrom went through some labor problems a few years back, thanks to its policy of cossetting customers. But that doesn't seem to have changed its helpful, verging on bend-over-backwards attitude. This is one place where returns are no big deal. In fact, unscrupulous people reportedly return things to Nordy's that they didn't even buy there and the merchandise is accepted without complaint. Salespeople are attentive without being cloying, and they're knowledgeable about current fashion trends. A personal-shopper service accommodates people who haven't time to browse through all the racks themselves.

Because Nordstrom grew out of shoe-store roots, the footwear department here is one of its largest. Women's clothes take up several floors and a series of departments, each with a character (and often age bracket) of its own. Men enjoy a large casuals section, a broad selection of ties, and suits for any occasion. Gifts and some gourmet foods can be found in the **Boardwalk** department. Several annual sales are much anticipated: the Nordstrom anniversary (July), and the two half-yearly sales for women (June and November) and for men (June and January). ◆ M-Sa 9:30AM-8PM; Su 11AM-6PM. Fifth Ave and Pine St. 628.2111

49 I. Magnin Good breeding breathes forth even from the rather sparse interior design of this exclusive womenswear store. Don't go looking for jeans here. There's a large cosmetics section, a leather department, and even pricier attire upstairs. Unfortunately, this store may close in 1993, so call ahead. ◆ M-Sa 10AM-6PM; Su noon-5PM. 601 Pine St. 682.6111

50 WestCoast Roosevelt Hotel $ When this 20-floor hotel (then the tallest in town) originally threw open its doors in 1930, the *Seattle Daily Times* could hardly contain its enthusiasm. The building's entryway received particular attention in the next afternoon's edition: "The ornately furnished lobby was virtually a tower of flowers as guests and well-wishers trooped into it last evening. Visitors were given the freedom of the house and were enabled to inspect the lounge, decorated in French moderne style and furnished in highly polished ebony and hardwood, and saunter up a winding staircase past the orchestra balcony to the mezzanine." Unfortunately, that lobby—with its strip skylight and several levels—was lost during a 1987 renovation. The present low-ceilinged space, though appointed pleasantly with light grays and glass block, was at one time the **Rough Rider Lounge,** sporting a disco dance floor where a baby grand piano now rests.

Designed by architect **John Graham, Sr.,** the hotel used to be a warren of 234 small rooms. The floors have since been redivided to allow for only 150 larger spaces, each decorated with subtle and comfortable furnishings. Superior-class rooms also boast Jacuzzis. The 19th floor (with a skylight enclosing the outdoor landing on that floor) is a town house for one of the building's owners. The top level has a single deluxe guest room, with what is perhaps the structure's best view of the city. ◆ 1531 Seventh Ave. 621.1200, 800/426.0670; fax 233.0335

Within the WestCoast Roosevelt Hotel:

Von's Grand City Cafe ★★$ A clubby restaurant that occupies the hotel's old main lobby space, Von's serves an assortment of sandwiches, fish, and steaks. But the cafe is best known for dispensing quality martinis—and lots of them. ◆ American ◆ Daily 6:30AM-11PM. 619 Pine St. 621.8667

51 Paramount Theater This and its smaller sister theater in Portland, Oregon, were modeled after the Paramount in New York City. Again, **B. Marcus Priteca** was the architect, but here, 13 years after construction of the Coliseum, he played a more reserved hand. The Paramount's monumental proportions—from its high-rise brick facade to its tall arched windows out front and its roofline decorations—were all meant to emphasize the theatricality and the fantasy of screen and stage drama. Where vaudeville performers used to trod the boards, the spotlights now fall mostly on rock musicians. You can get tickets at either the box office or through **Ticketmaster** (628.0888).

Like the Coliseum Theater, the Paramount also received some unexpected news recently: A group of deep-pocketed investors, headed by former Microsoft marketing exec and arts-management consultant **Ida Cole,** purchased the Paramount in early 1993, announcing that they would renovate and add to the theater, as well as replace low-income housing units in the upper stories with commercial spaces. As *Seattle Weekly* put it, "The effort will restore the Paramount as one of the grandest large theaters on the West Coast." ◆ Box office opens one hour prior to show time. 901 Pine St. Cash only. 682.1414

52 WestCoast Camlin Hotel $ Money to finish this brick-and-terracotta tower in 1926 was actually embezzled by a pair of hyper-ambitious bankers, **Adolph Linden** and **Edmund Campbell,** who were subsequently prosecuted and sent to Walla Walla State Penitentiary in eastern Washington. The architect was **Carl J. Linde** of Portland, Oregon, a onetime brewery designer from Wisconsin who had worked under noted Oregon architect **A.E. Doyle.** Most of Linde's efforts were concentrated on the hotel's Ninth Avenue facade. The basic style was Gothic, complete with lions' heads and other decorative gargoyles. Interestingly, the 11-story Camlin is only *half* a hotel. A second, 14-story establishment, to have been built just north of the existing hotel (where a parking lot now stands), never made it past the drawing board.

The Camlin was isolated to the northeast of downtown when it opened in 1926, but it has since been engulfed by the expanding city. A $2 million restoration in 1985 brought in double-paned windows, so that noise (even from the Paramount Theater across the street) isn't a problem in the large guest rooms, each of which is decorated in various shades of beige, with exposed pipe fixtures in the bathrooms and overstuffed chairs. Just

try to avoid the gloomier cabanas. ◆ 1619 Ninth Ave. 682.0100, 800/426.0670; fax 682.7415

Within the WestCoast Camlin Hotel:

The Cloud Room ★★$$ The restaurant turns out very acceptable meals (particularly pasta dishes), but the real attraction of the 11th floor is one of the city's most enjoyable and delightfully kitschy piano bars. ◆ Continental ◆ M-F 7-10:30AM, 11AM-2PM, 5-10:30PM; Sa-Su 7AM-1PM, 5-10:30PM. Lounge M-F 11AM-1:30AM; Sa-Su 5:30PM-1:30AM. 682.0100

53 Westlake Center Downtown's $250 million version of a suburban shopping mall is oversanitized, overlighted at night, and offers little in the way of a downtown park—a component that its creators, the Maryland-based **Rouse Company,** promised their center would go out of its way to provide. Overall, glitzy Westlake feels little connected to the architectural and social character of Seattle's nexus. And it seems aggressively unconnected to the town's history, even though it stands at what has long been an important hub, which, until 1931, held a glorious flatiron building called the **Hotel Plaza.** Yet in lieu of any real civic center, Westlake has succeeded in becoming a focus of activity. The third floor's carnival of food counters is always awash during weekday lunchtimes with workers from the surrounding office hives. A rather stark public plaza out front stays lively with T-shirt vendors, street musicians, hellfire-and-brimstone preachers, and a fountain that you can actually walk through. And it doesn't hurt business here any that the monorail from **Seattle Center** has its endpoint at Westlake, or that one of the downtown transit tunnel's five stations sits beneath the center. ◆ Fourth Ave and Pine St

Within Westlake Center:

Jessica McClintock Boutique Characters from a Barbara Cartland novel might shop at this store, which is filled with lots of frills and puffs of lace and flouncy skirts. ◆ M-F 9:30AM-9PM, Sa 9:30AM-7PM, Su 11AM-6PM 1 June-27 Dec; M-F 9:30AM-8PM, Sa 9:30AM-7PM, Su 11AM-6PM 28 Dec-31 May. Lower floor. 467.1048

Crabtree & Evelyn Somehow, even during the get-ahead '80s, this store never forgot how to relax. The shelves are full, with dozens of different soaps and jar after jar of bath scents, potpourri, sachets, and room fresheners. Combine a few of these tension-relieving nostrums with a good book and a glass of wine and you could poach in the tub for hours. ◆ M-F 9:30AM-9PM, Sa 9:30AM-7PM, Su 11AM-6PM 1 June-27 Dec; M-F 9:30AM-8PM, Sa 9:30AM-7PM, Su 11AM-6PM 28 Dec-31 May. First floor. 682.6776

FireWorks Gallery This downtown branch of the Pioneer Square store is even more devoted to artsy souvenirs and jewelry. ♦ M-F 9:30AM-9PM, Sa 9:30AM-7PM, Su 11AM-6PM 1 June-27 Dec; M-F 9:30AM-8PM, Sa 9:30AM-7PM, Su 11AM-6PM 28 Dec-31 May. First floor. 682.6462. Also at: 210 First Ave South. 682.8707

Williams-Sonoma The French porcelain, chrome gadgets, glassware, and cookbooks look so good in this pristine location that it's a shame to mess them up in your own kitchen. This is a great place for people who care as much about how their kitchenware looks as how it works. Look out for crowds here at Christmastime. ♦ M-F 9:30AM-9PM, Sa 9:30AM-7PM, Su 11AM-6PM 1 June-27 Dec; M-F 9:30AM-8PM, Sa 9:30AM-7PM, Su 11AM-6PM 28 Dec-31 May. First floor. 624.1422

Brentano's Efficiently run and impressively well stocked, this is one of downtown's best bookstores. Look for large selections of general fiction, mystery, science fiction, self-help books, travel, and history. The children's department could be beefed up some, but the magazine racks are amply stocked: if there were any more titles, Seattleites would never return to work from their lunch hours. ♦ M-F 9:30AM-9PM, Sa 9:30AM-7PM, Su 11AM-6PM 1 June-27 Dec; M-F 9:30AM-8PM, Sa 9:30AM-7PM, Su 11AM-6PM 28 Dec-31 May. Second floor. 467.9626

Purdy's Chocolates Ice-cream bars dipped in a coating of cocoa, hazelnut brittle to drive tastebuds loco, rich Easter rabbits all tied up with string—these are (no doubt) a few of your favorite things. ♦ M-F 9:30AM-9PM, Sa 9:30AM-7PM, Su 11AM-6PM 1 June-27 Dec; M-F 9:30AM-8PM, Sa 9:30AM-7PM, Su 11AM-6PM 28 Dec-31 May. Second floor. 682.8571

Victoria's Secret Sift through a variety of tasteful lingerie, suggestive nighties, sports bras, come-hither scents, and comfortable bathrobes. The prices are reasonable, and in case you wondered, guys, subscriptions to the catalog can now be ordered. ♦ M-F 9:30AM-9PM, Sa 9:30AM-7PM, Su 11AM-

6PM 1 June-27 Dec; M-F 9:30AM-8PM, Sa 9:30AM-7PM, Su 11AM-6PM 28 Dec-31 May. Second floor. 622.6035

BOSTON SOX

Boston Sox For those who appreciate wildly designed stockings, this is a near-Valhalla. ♦ M-F 9:30AM-9PM, Sa 9:30AM-7PM, Su 11AM-6PM 1 June-27 Dec; M-F 9:30AM-8PM, Sa 9:30AM-7PM, Su 11AM-6PM 28 Dec-31 May. Second floor. 625.1663

The Disney Store Frankly, the tie-ins between animated films and the huge lines of toys and clothing available here send shivers up some shoppers' spines. But how do you tell your kids that they can't have **Little Mermaid** T-shirts because you're philosophically opposed to shameless commercial pandering? ♦ M-F 9:30AM-9PM, Sa 9:30AM-7PM, Su 11AM-6PM 1 June-27 Dec; M-F 9:30AM-8PM, Sa 9:30AM-7PM, Su 11AM-6PM 28 Dec-31 May. Second floor. 622.3323

54 **Downtown Bus Tunnel** It's not exactly the London Underground, but Seattle's 1.3-mile transit tube isn't a gloomy bat cave, either. Buses passing through here are converted temporarily from diesel to electric power. Rails have already been laid to adapt this system to a future light-rail network. On a cold or rainy day, the heart of the shopping district is served by a mezzanine level just above the bus platform that connects the basement at **Westlake Center** with those at **Nordstrom** and the **Bon Marché. (Frederick & Nelson,** a Seattle shopping institution since 1890, was part of this commercial linkage until it went out of business in 1992.)

About $3 million was spent by Metro on public art for the five bus stations. At the Westlake stop, check out the multicolored terracotta tiles that carry leaf and vine patterns. The **Pioneer Square Station** features large clocks made from masonry remnants and a mural that captures aspects of Seattle history in tile. Origami designs spark up the **International District** bus terminal. ♦ M-F 5AM-7PM; Sa 10AM-6PM. Pine St (between Third and Fourth Aves). 553.3000

Restaurants/Clubs: Red   **Hotels:** Blue
Shops/ ♥ Outdoors: Green   **Sights/Culture:** Black

Grunge Rock Cleans Up

In recent years Seattle has enjoyed unprecedented and diverse success in pop music, adding a distinctive Northwest chord to the regional ferment that's igniting the industry. In fact, the Puget Sound area has become so popular and so closely associated with the new "grunge" style that some young musicians are moving here just in hopes of catching the wave. The music itself is a stupefying mix of shattering, electric-guitar fuzz; sloppy, barely cohesive rhythmic underpinnings; and, above all, an endless caterwauling about Generation X angst.

The rapping, scratching **Sir Mix-A-Lot,** who topped the pop charts for five weeks in 1992 with "Baby Got Back," led the assault, pulling in a string of gold and platinum albums and singles. But the really big news emerged from white underground rock bands such as **Nirvana** and **Soundgarden,** and the independent local label that spawned them, **Sub Pop.** Give those parties credit for creating what the press has come to call the "Seattle Sound."

In late 1991 Seattle-based Nirvana took the world utterly by surprise with their *Nevermind* album, which at release looked like just another noisy underground effort doomed to maximum sales of maybe 200,000. Instead it soared to the top of the album charts for weeks on end, beating out Michael Jackson and U2, and earning the group a cover spot on *Rolling Stone* magazine. Perhaps most astonishing was Nirvana's single, "Smells Like Teen Spirit," which scored Top-10 status. Many American critics claimed that Nirvana's album marked the triumph of punk rock—only 15 years too late.

As with any underground scene that has gone so far so fast, much of what remains of grunge music in Seattle is played by wanna-be copy cats and preening superstars who only occasionally deign to perform. On the up side, however, grunge has transformed Seattle's live music choices from virtually nil to something that might cautiously be described as cornucopialike—really. The best club

choices for catching an earful of grunge, or just a sense of what is happening in white-rock Seattle, include:

The Off-Ramp This is your best and most consistent club choice. The ambience is rough around the edges, with sweaty bodies packing into a "moshpit" (a frenzy of slam dancers) even as the lead guitarist hits the first power chord. Sightlines are generally very good, and proximity to performers—from **Psychotropic** to **Lacerations**—is appropriately intimate. ♦ Cover. Music daily 9:30PM-2AM. 109 Eastlake Avenue East. 628.0232

RKCNDY The bent here leans more toward beat-heavy dance rhythms, though bookings retain a decidedly ferocious edge, making RKCNDY (pronounced "rock candy") a good bet for seeing both local and national grunge antics. A bigger space than either of the other clubs mentioned here, RKCNDY is also more inclined to book marginally recognizable headliners such as **Ride.** Sightlines are excellent, on two levels, though the poured-concrete floor leaves much to be desired for a night of dancing or even just standing around. ♦ Cover. Music Tu-Sa 9:30PM-2AM. 1812 Yale Avenue North. 623.0470

Crocodile Cafe A popular admixture of restaurant, espresso stand, bar, and nightclub. Bookings are hardly exclusive to grunge; in fact, grunge groups make a showing here only now and then. Instead, the Crocodile offers a forum where Seattle's cutting-edge types may stray from the norm and try different material. **T-Bone Burnett** played here recently, and if **Mark Lanegan** (of the **Screaming Trees**) ever makes a solo appearance, you can bet it will be in this appreciative setting. ♦ Cover. Music W-Sa 9:30PM-2AM, with occasional performances on other nights. 2200 Second Avenue. 441.5611

Note that all of these joints schedule more than one band per evening, so headliners usually don't begin playing until about midnight.

55 Key Bank Tower (Olympic Tower) This 1929 Art Deco specimen doesn't seem like much until you gander over the polygonal crown and observe the restored terracotta facing. It was the creation of local architect **Henry Bittman.** ♦ Third Ave and Pine St

56 A.E. Doyle Building Built as a department store in 1915, this unobtrusive terracotta edifice, designed in the Venetian Renaissance palazzo style, was remodeled in 1973 and now carries the name of its original architect, a prominent figure in early 20th-century Portland, Oregon. ♦ Second Ave and Pine St

Within the A.E. Doyle Building:

M. Coy Books More selective than comprehensive in his selection of books, proprietor **Michael Coy** is usually on top of the latest best-sellers and new regional publications. General fiction is well

represented, and there's a mind-engaging array of nonfiction available, but the range within any particular genre (particularly mystery and science fiction) is fairly narrow. Fortunately, employees are helpful and ready to take special orders. A small coffee shop in the back contributes a relaxed and contemplative atmosphere. ♦ M-F 8AM-7PM; Sa 10AM-6PM; Su noon-5PM. 117 Pine St. 623.5354

57 The Bon Marché Upholding the tradition of department stores, "the Bon" wants to be everything to everybody. Clothes, cosmetics, china, shoe repair, furniture, candy, liquor—they're all under one roof. Merchandise is well selected and stocked, and prices are often more moderate than at similar stores in town. ♦ M-F 9:30AM-8PM; Sa 9:30AM-7PM; Su 11AM-6PM. Third Ave and Pine St. 344.2121

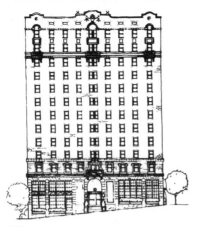

58 Mayflower Park Hotel $$ Rooms are furnished in antiques, but they're sometimes small—that's the trade-off for accommodations right in the heart of the downtown shopping district. Just be sure to ask for a room high up in this handsome 1927 tower (illustrated above), where you'll at least see a slice of the city past surrounding building walls. An antique-filled lobby provides access to a commodious, high-ceilinged bar and to neighboring **Westlake Center. Clippers** (★★$$), just off the lobby, serves three meals daily, but it is best for breakfast and lunch, when its big windows allow in plenty of natural light. ◆ 405 Olive Way. 623.8700, 800/426.5100; fax 382.6997

59 Times Square Building It was no coincidence that this flatiron structure and the irregular intersection to its immediate west came to be known as Times Square. First off, the building housed the *Seattle Times* newspaper from 1916 until 1931. Second, it bears a strong resemblance to Manhattan's Times Square. Constructed of terra-cotta and granite, with fine Beaux Arts detailing (note the elegant eagles decorating the roofline), it was one of the earliest downtown works by architect **Carl Gould.** A graduate of the Ecole des Beaux Arts in Paris who apprenticed with the famous New York firm of **McKim, Mead & White** before heading west for his health, Gould would eventually give Seattle a series of landmarks, including the original **Seattle Art Museum** on Capitol Hill and the **Suzzallo Library** at the University of Washington. ◆ Bounded by Fourth and Fifth Aves, Olive Way, and Stewart St

60 WestCoast Vance Hotel $ Built in 1926 by the **Vance Lumber Company** as a stopover for visiting lumber brokers and other dealmakers, the Vance was pretty seedy when the WestCoast chain decided to spend $7 million in 1990 on its restoration. The exterior was never meant to be breathtaking, but it does include fine terracotta detailing near street level and a nicely polished dark lobby. Rooms tend to be smaller than normal but still pleasant, with the best views of the Space Needle from above the fifth floor on the north side. ◆ 620 Stewart St. 441.4200, 800/663.1144; fax 441.8612

Within the WestCoast Vance Hotel:

Salute in Città ★$$ Although far less romantic than the funky original Salute, which is north of the University District, Città (city in Italian) makes the cut for its excellent and inexpensive designer pizzas. They're on the small side, but still ideal nighttime bar fare. ◆ Italian ◆ Daily 7AM-11PM. 728.1611. Also at: 3410 NE 55th St. 527.8600

61 Westin Hotel $$$ You can't miss this place: it's the one with the round twin pillars of guest rooms that look like corncobs. The circular design allows for a maximum number of the Westin's 865 rooms, all equipped with balconies. (The best vistas are from above the 20th floor.) Guests enjoy spacious and well-lighted accommodations but contrastingly plain furnishings. Room rates include a complimentary breakfast. The convention facilities are plentiful and spread over several levels. There's a large swimming pool and supervised exercise room, three lounges, and a trio of restaurants, the most casual of these being the **Market Cafe** (★$). ◆ 1900 Fifth Ave. 728.1000, 800/228.3000; fax 728.2259

Within the Westin Hotel:

The Palm Court ★★$$$ There's not much of a view (just out to concrete-filled Times Square), nor is this restaurant overwhelmed by greenery, as its name suggests, but the entrées here have proved to be excellent (the crab cakes and smoked-salmon chowder deserve culinary-museum positions). Evening selections include a piquant braised lamb shank with mushrooms, and roast chicken on a mattress of white beans. Desserts, particularly the chocolate variations, are extra, extra, extra rich. A nice touch: the menu includes wine suggestions with each dish. ◆ Continental ◆ M-Sa 11AM-2:30PM, 5:30-10:30PM. Reservations recommended. 728.1000

Nikko ★★$$$$ It is fitting that a showman and sushi chef such as Tokyo-trained **Toyama** should be performing on the corner where one of the city's gaudiest theaters, the **Orpheum,** stood for 40 years. But you don't need tickets to watch Toyama's act, just the willingness to let this fine chef take some command of your meal and prepare whatever's freshest—from tuna to fish liver and squid gut. ◆ Japanese ◆ M-F 11:30AM-2PM, 5:30-10PM; Sa-Su 5:30-10PM. Bar open daily 5-10:30PM. 322.4641

62 Dahlia Lounge ★★★★$$$ Among the notable chefs in town who've struck out from proven establishments to create their own places, one of the most successful has been former **Cafe Sport** wunderkind **Tom Douglas.** His Dahlia is a colorful place, with bright red walls and paper fish lamps that "swim" above the dining tables. The menu here sometimes tries too hard to be different (oysters in lemon-pepper vodka, anyone?), but Douglas' seafood dishes—nicely jazzed up with an Asian flair—are consistently delicious. ◆ Northwestern ◆ M-Th 11:30AM-2:30PM, 5:30-10PM; F 11:30AM-2:30PM, 5:30-11PM; Sa 5:30-11PM; Su 5-9PM. 1904 Fourth Ave. Reservations recommended. 682.4142

63 Annex Theatre This interesting fringe theater is run by ambitious, thoughtful twentysomethings. The experimental offerings can run to the dreadful, but there is almost always a spark to them. If you're looking for a sure bet, stop in for the late-night Friday improvs (11PM). ◆ Box office daily 6:45-8PM. 1916 Fourth Ave. 728.0933

64 Moore Theater and Hotel For many years pioneer **Arthur Denny** had reserved six acres here in hopes that Seattle might one day capture the Washington state capitol building (which was eventually built in Olympia). But in 1888 he filled this site instead with a first-class hotel—something the city desperately needed after the Great Fire of 1889. The national depression of 1893 stalled construction of this multitowered edifice, and it finally had to be completed a decade later by Seattle superdeveloper **James A. Moore.** (**President Teddy Roosevelt** was the first guest at Moore's new hotel when it opened in 1903.) Almost immediately, Moore had bigger dreams for this area. He wanted to enlarge his hotel and to erect the most artistic and beautiful theater in the West.

Sure enough, the hotel and an adjoining playhouse (both designed by prolific Seattle architect **E.W. Houghton**) went up in 1908. But in the meantime the hotel was razed to make possible the regrading of **Denny Hill.** James Moore fell on hard times not many years later and so did his theater. Its vaguely Egyptian Revival-style interior is still intact, but the likes of **Marie Dressler** and **John Barrymore** no longer perform here. Now the hall is used only sporadically, mostly for concerts. ◆ Box office hours vary, please call ahead. 1932 Second Ave. 443.1744

Bests

Peter Miller
Owner, Peter Miller Books

Pike Place Market is Seattle's soul. Get there early—the fruit and vegetable stands and the fish markets are all set up by 7:30AM. In season, the raspberries come in early in the morning, as do the chanterelles and the salmon. Find **Frank's Produce**—Roger will know what's fresh. Or **Verdi's,** where all the produce is homegrown. The bakeries are open then, for croissants, crumpets, muffins—always with good coffee.

Everyone asks, "Where is the best seafood?"; then off they go to some chain restaurant. Instead, I recommend: **Labuznik,** where **Peter Cipra** cooks every dinner. If the restaurant is full, I eat in the cafe. Try **Campagne.** Or just outside Pike Place Market, the **Queen City Grill.** All of these places know fish—what is in, what is out.

Have a beer or glass of wine at the **Virginia Inn,** still the best tavern in town.

Louis runs the finest Italian deli in the Northwest, **DeLaurenti's Specialty Foods.**

Richard Morrill
Geography Professor, University of Washington

What keeps me here in Seattle in the face of outside offers is what the University of Washington calls the "Mount Rainier Factor." The physical environment is a big part—the very setting of the city, with those inconvenient drawbridges, and the proximity of water and mountains. And although Seattle has pretensions to be a "world-class city," I also love its provincial healthiness.

The **Waterfront,** which is a workplace as well as a fun place.

University Book Store, but also many other good bookshops, new and used.

Coffee at **Starbucks,** and espresso everywhere.

The ferries—part of the state highway system, workaday as well as scenic.

Wondrous urban walks such as **Magnuson Park** past the wind chimes; around **Green Lake; Myrtle Edwards Park;** above the Sound at **Discovery Park;** and the **Washington Park Arboretum.**

The original **Nordstrom,** the **REI** co-op, and, in general, local clothing manufacturers and stores.

The arts-and-crafts fairs and the folk festivals.

Pike Place Market, as well as the local and rural farmers' markets.

The **Boeing plants** (such as the 747 plant near Everett), the **Microsoft** campus, and the spirit of entrepreneurship felt here.

The drawn-out spring, the glorious summer, and the early fall.

The fact that the city is not too dense or cosmopolitan, yet it's still big enough to support the arts.

Mount Rainier, but also years of further exploration in the **Cascade** and **Olympic mountains.**

The **University of Washington,** which is what really keeps me here.

Pike Place Market/ Waterfront

The market is a kinetic profusion of people, energy, and individual enterprise. Flowers for sale. Pottery. Pastries. Scarves. Cigars. Seascapes. T-shirts. Teacups. Wooden whistles that imitate the sound of ancient locomotives . . . *Woo wooooo.* Fish peddlers toss huge flounders above the heads of awed customers. A ragtag band coaxes a lively rendition of Jimmy Buffett's "Pencil-Thin Mustache" from time-distressed instruments. A hawker at the **Read All About It** newsstand shouts, *"P-I! Seattle Post-Intelligencer! Seattle Times! New Yo-o-o-rk Times! LA Times! We've got the Times!"* Shoppers jockey with automobiles for the right-of-way along Pike Place, with drivers almost invariably losing out. As many as 40,000 people visit this overgrown "mom 'n' pop store" every day.

There's no guarantee you'll find the finest, freshest produce here, but for urban color, Pike Place Market—the oldest continuously operating farmer's market in the country—is unbeatable. *New York Times* correspondent **Timothy Egan** calls it the Marrakech of the Northwest. Artist **Mark Tobey**, who haunted the market frequently, beginning in the 1920s, once described it as "a refuge, an oasis, a most human growth, the heart and soul of Seattle." This is a humble corner of an increasingly egotistical city, the apotheosis of the populist and anarchical, no more predictable nor less confusing than life itself. It is, to quote Egan again, a deeply loved "strip of commercial chaos."

The market's history began in 1907, when food wholesale houses formed a **Produce Row** along Western Avenue. Farmers who couldn't take a day or two off each week to sell their crops relied on wholesalers to do the job for them. But local growers suspected (quite rightly, in many cases) that these

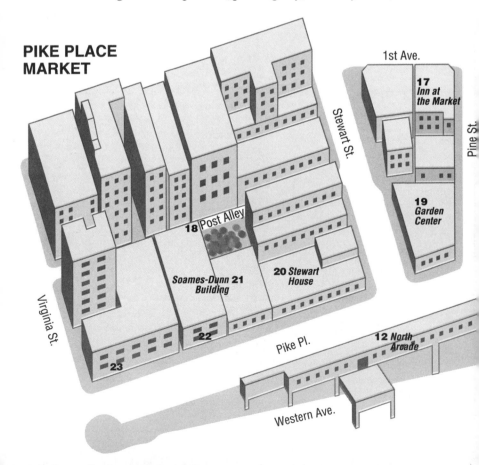

PIKE PLACE MARKET

1st Ave.

17 Inn at the Market

Stewart St.

Pine St.

18 Post Alley

19 Garden Center

Soames-Dunn **21** Building

20 Stewart House

Virginia St.

22

23

Pike Pl.

12 North Arcade

Western Ave.

middlemen were cheating them of a fair price for their goods and, at the same time, gouging customers with excessive fees.

The city's response to these complaints was to establish a *true* farmer's market. The location was based primarily on convenience (aggressive regrading had recently leveled the land at Pike Street's western end, and newly planked Western Avenue connected that site with the Waterfront), but it was a romantic coincidence that the selected land also may have been a centuries-old trading area for Native Americans. On opening day, 17 August 1907, fewer than a dozen produce wagons showed up here (and one of those, driven by a Japanese farmer, was ransacked), but thousands of Seattleites came eager to buy. The next week, 70 wagons ran the gauntlet of commission houses and took positions on the Pike Place curb. Fishmongers soon infiltrated the neighborhood, as did other small businesses. Stall sizes had to be reduced just to fit everybody in and canopies were built to keep commerce chugging along through the Seattle rains.

Several proposals (including one from the New York firm of **Howells & Stokes**, the architects of downtown's **Cobb Building**) called for Pike Place Market to grow into a grandiose commercial complex spilling down from its bluff into a railroad and marine terminal on the Waterfront. But voters preferred to keep the market small and personable: exuberant with Italians, Japanese, and Sephardic Jews hawking their goods; replete with characters such as **Horseradish Jerry**, who ground roots into relish, or the old-timers who droned tall tales of the Klondike Gold Rush. Within 10 years the market had become Seattle's funky equivalent of a community square.

The Depression of 1929 exacted its toll on Pike Place Market. So did World War II's internment of Japanese farmers; the decline of First Avenue, from a

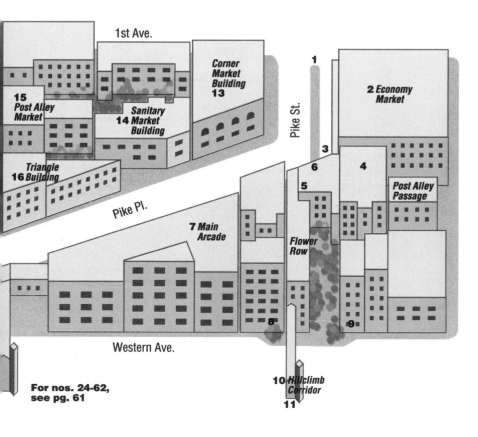

For nos. 24-62, see pg. 61

worker's mall to a strip of peep shows and honky-tonks; and the insurgence of supermarkets. By 1963, with the market and Seattle as a whole in wan condition, planners encouraged the city to bulldoze the center in favor of a parking and high-rise development. Only a concerted effort by preservationists, politicians, local architects (among them the persistent **Victor Steinbrueck**, who had designed the **Space Needle**), and eventually voters saved the heart and soul of Seattle. A seven-acre **Market Historical District** was established in 1974. There has been just one significant threat to this neighborhood since: in the early 1990s, it was revealed that a New York investment company had purchased substantial interest in the market without public knowledge. Goaded on by angry Seattleites, a King County court finally ruled the New Yorkers' claim invalid.

Regular guided tours will give you an overview of the market, but the best way to get a feel for it is to wander about its well-preserved edifices, exploring nooks and walking the uneven floors where buildings have been strung together. However, it would take years to fully appreciate all the attractions and rhythms of Pike Place Market; in fact, even most natives know it only in passing.

Pike Place Market (which is also referred to as the **Public Market**) is open every day from early May through December, and Monday through Saturday for the balance of the year. Individual shop hours vary, as do the seasonal schedules of businesses not contained completely within market buildings.

Since Pike Place Market achieved historic status, every one of its buildings has been renovated or reconstructed. The revitalization spirit has spilled over onto First and Western avenues, where some of the earliest commercial structures north of Pioneer Square were built. Unfortunately, less attention has been paid to Seattle's Waterfront. This was once the center of local commerce, a strip alive with the shouts of merchants and the jibs of the Mosquito Fleet, an early ferry service. But several decades ago the Waterfront was severed from the rest of downtown by the **Alaskan Way Viaduct** and—except for the estimable **Seattle Aquarium** and the too small **Waterfront Park**—has since been all but completely given over to fast-food joints and kitschy emporiums. Recent plans by the **Port of Seattle**, however, call for a maritime museum, new residential and hotel properties, and a lively short-term boat moorage, all of which may bring back some charm to Seattle's harbor. Keep your fingers crossed.

1 Market Information Booth Market maps and other visitor info are happily dispensed. Tours of the neighborhood begin here. ♦ Tu-Su 10AM-6PM. First Ave and Pike St. 682.7453

2 Economy Market Promoter and investor **Frank Goodwin** was an eccentric who played heavily with penny stocks, put together an early steam-powered automobile, and practiced a strict vegetarian diet that demanded two legumes for his evening repast. He also bought heavily into Pike Place real estate and was the man who finally brought the market in out of the rain in 1907, when he constructed the **Main Arcade.**

An amateur architect, Goodwin designed and built a multistory expansion of the market down Pike Place bluff to Western Avenue. In 1916 he obtained a lease on the **Bartell Building** (completed in 1900) at the corner of First Avenue and Pike Street, transforming it into today's Economy Market. Look for pieces of Goodwin's design work in this building's Doric columns and the plaster garlands of fruit and flowers. Preservation architect **George Bartholick** headed a rehabilitation of the Economy Market in 1978. The angled ramps in the atrium used to be trod by horses, which were checked through here on their way to the main market. ♦ Pike St and First Ave

Within the Economy Market:

Read All About It One of the two best-stocked newsstands in this city (the other top contender is **Bulldog News** in the University District), Read All About It packs a walloping diversity of American and international periodicals. Expect everything from *Popular Mechanics* and *Playboy* to *Tatler, HG, Ebony,* and *Ellery Queen's Mystery Magazine.* Looking for the *International Herald-Tribune* or the *Nome Nugget?* They're here, too. ◆ Daily 7AM-7PM. Main floor. 624.0140

Stamp Happy Pleasant hours could be spent merely testing out the available and often comic stamps, but buyers are also welcome. ◆ Daily 10AM-5:30PM. Main floor. 682.8575

Daily Dozen Doughnuts This is a dangerous place for congenital snackers. Snag a baker's dozen sack of miniature doughnuts—plain, covered with powdered sugar, or cinnamon. Then hope nobody witnesses your abject gluttony. ◆ Daily 8AM-5:30PM. Main floor. 467.7769

DeLaurenti's Specialty Foods Exotic Mediterranean canned goods, meats, and wines are shoehorned into a space barely big enough to contain them all, as an Italian deli should be. Though the history of DeLaurenti's is commonly traced back to owners **Pete** and **Mamie DeLaurenti** in the 1940s, Mamie's very Italian mother, **Angelina Mustelo,** had opened a small store on the market's lower level in 1928. ◆ Italian deli ◆ M-Sa 9AM-6PM. Main floor. 622.0141. Also at: 317 Bellevue Way NE, Bellevue. 454.7155

The Great Wind-Up Follow the noise of barking dogs, growling dragons, and hopping bunnies to this toy-filled corner shop. While children gather ideas for Christmas, adults will enjoy a tableful of windup kangaroos, chattering teeth, and mince-stepping eyeballs. ◆ M-Sa 10AM-5PM; Su noon-4PM. Atrium. 621.9370

You can identify a tourist in a snap by the way he or she pronounces the name of Seattle's least-understood, elephantine-appendaged shellfish: the geoduck. Repeat slowly: *goo*-ee-duck.

Sasquatch How appropriate that artist **Richard Beyer's** brooding, hand-carved sculpture should greet you to Seattle. Whether it is descended from prehistoric primates or was born whole from the vivid human imagination, Sasquatch (or **Bigfoot,** if you prefer) has become the Northwest's signature monster. Its appearances hark back to the tribal mythology of virtually every native people from coastal British Columbia to northern California. The name Sasquatch comes from *sas-kets,* a term used by Salish-speaking tribes of southwestern BC to describe the hairy, humanlike giants they said lived in the **Fraser River Valley** and communicated via whistles and shrill screams. More than 2,500 Sasquatch sightings have been recorded since the 1960s, most of them in Washington. ◆ Atrium

Tenzing Momo Any moment you expect the Dalai Lama to come sailing through the door of this herbal apothecary to buy a stick of incense or some bulk herbs. Fluid extracts, Chinese nostrums, ear-wax candles, books on witchcraft—Tenzing Momo (which, translated from Tibetan, means "illustrious dumpling") is holy ground for worshipers in the temple of natural health. ◆ M-F 10AM-5PM, Sa 10AM-5:30PM, Su 11AM-4PM; closed Jan-Oct. Atrium. 623.9837

3 Lower Post Alley This was once a major commercial route connecting the market with Western Avenue's **Produce Row,** the **Waterfront,** and **Pioneer Square.** Guttering beneath the main market sign and clock, the alley is now rather ignored, yet it is supposedly the only completely restored cobblestoned street in the Northwest. The glass-walled bridge above the alley's entrance off First Avenue was known historically as the **Bridge of Sighs.** Apparently, from here south, Post Alley used to be lined with bars, and sailors would stop in at each of them for a nip before shipping out of town. It's said that from the overpass women would watch their men amble slowly away. ◆ Between Pike and Union Sts

Along Lower Post Alley:

Il Bistro ★★$$$ Like a European cave or a wine cellar, Il Bistro is a quiet retreat trimmed in dark woods and arches. People

come here after work to decompress, sipping wine or whiskey in the jazz-filled bar, or chatting over dinner in this restaurant's more secluded reaches. Italian dishes got this place off the ground, and, while a variety of seafood plates have been introduced with varying degrees of success, pasta is still instrumental in keeping Il Bistro popular. Both the *tortellini alla panna* (tortellini with garlic, pine nuts, and tomatoes) and the *linguine carretiera* (linguine with seasonal mushrooms, hot pepper flakes, tomato, cream, and vodka) will satisfy your appetite. The cioppino is also a standout here.
♦ Italian ♦ M, Su 5:30-10PM; Tu-Th noon-3PM, 5:30-10PM; F-Sa noon-3PM, 5:30-11PM. Bar open daily until 2AM. 93-A Pike St. 682.3049

4 LaSalle Hotel This bay-windowed building beside the Public Market sign was Seattle's first bordello north of Yesler Way and survived to become the last of this city's big-time bawdy houses. Erected in 1909 as the **Outlook Hotel**, it was owned prior to World War II by a Japanese family who catered to frugal workers and the elderly. After the 1942 internment of Japanese living in Seattle, the hotel's lease was bought by one **Nellie Curtis** (née **Zella Nightengale**), who had run orderly disorderly houses across Canada before moving to Seattle in 1931. Small and birdlike, with a warm laugh but suffering from glaucoma, she drove Cadillacs, kept her money stuffed in drawers rather than banks, wore ermine shawls, and collected hats with the same superfluousness with which Imelda Marcos would later gather shoes. Nellie's original establishment in this city occupied a small hotel at the foot of First Avenue and Virginia Street, but the Outlook, which she renamed the LaSalle Hotel, was a quieter place and, after some remodeling, a far classier one. As **Alice Shorett** and **Murray Morgan** recall in their jolly history, *Pike Place Market: People, Politics, and Produce,* the LaSalle even had "enough rooms so that some could be used for legitimate hotel purposes, thus providing a cover for more profitable activities." Profitable, indeed.

Shortly after the LaSalle got under way, some of Nellie's girls went down to the Waterfront to meet incoming ships and hand out business cards: "LaSalle Hotel—Friends Easily Made." That night hundreds of libidinous wharf rats and sailors tried to anchor in one of the LaSalle's 57 berths, attracting attention not only from the local military but from reform **Mayor William Devin,** who ordered a prostitution crackdown. Nellie's fortunes went undisturbed.

It was only in 1949, after her nephew had botched a temporary management of the

LaSalle and Seattle had been shaken by its first major earthquake, that Nellie Curtis decided to sell the LaSalle. The buyers were a Japanese-American couple, **George** and **Sodeko Ikeda,** who had trouble convincing some of Nellie's old clients that there were no longer any "working girls" in the hostelry. "No girls?" puzzled one would-be Lothario. "Okay—but it's a hell of a way to run a whorehouse!" The Ikedas subsequently sued Nellie for overstating profits to be made from the LaSalle. Not only did she lose $7,500 in court, but she finally attracted the attention of the Internal Revenue Service. The LaSalle was rehabilitated in 1977 and now contains commercial space as well as low-income housing. ♦ Lower Post Alley (between Pike and Union Sts)

5 Market Clock Rising from the elbow that connects the **Economy Market** to the **Main Arcade,** this timepiece and the **Public Market Center** sign that surrounds it are supposed to be the oldest examples of public neon in Seattle, dating back to the 1920s or 1930s. The clock is a favorite among visiting photographers, and on New Year's Eve, crowds of happily tipsy Seattleites gather below it to celebrate at the stroke of midnight. ♦ Pike Pl and Pike St

6 Rachel, the Market Pig This overgrown piggy bank is the **Market Foundation's** friendliest fund-raiser. More than $33,500 has been dropped into her bowels since she took up her position below the Market Clock in 1986. ♦ Pike Pl and Pike St

7 Main Arcade Frank Goodwin's first market building, dating from 1907, reflects a simpler architectural style than he applied to his reworking of the **Economy Market.** Today this building is where you'll find about 50 percent of the market's fish and produce stalls, with many of the others located just across the street. Don't fail to observe the engraved floor tiles covering the arcade's main level, laid out as part of a fund-raising project in the mid-1980s. Seattleites paid $35 apiece to have their names imprinted on these tiles; **Ronald** and **Nancy Reagan** are also represented here, although they didn't pay one red cent for the privilege. Two floors (making up what used to be called **The Labyrinth**) descend from street level in this building and are known simply as **First Floor Down Under** and **Second Floor Down Under.** ♦ Pike Pl (between Pine and Pike Sts)

Within the Main Arcade:

The Athenian Inn $ Opened in 1909 as a Greek bakery/luncheonette, and later operated as a bar (it received one of Seattle's earliest liquor licenses, in 1933), the Athenian is among the market's most democratic restaurants. Fishers hunker up to the bar counter while designer-suited sales reps wait in line (often longer than is preferred) for tables overlooking the Sound. The menu hits all the local standards—from grilled oysters to fat burgers—with the breakfast fave being red-flannel hash. (The hash, with the rest of the breakfast menu, is available all day long.) The bar has 16 beers on tap but more than 300 brews total and is one of the few places left in Seattle where cigar smokers are still welcome. ◆ American/Greek ◆ M-Sa 6:30AM-7PM. Main floor. 624.7166

City Fish This busy stall was actually started by the city in 1918 to offer fresh and reasonably priced fish to Seattleites. Newspaper reports of overcharging led **Mayor Hiram Gill** to make his health commissioner responsible for setting up a market space stocked with dirt-cheap hatchery fish. Prices began at one-third to one-quarter of what was being charged elsewhere for fish. For four years, this operation was profitable, but as sales waned, the city sold out. **David Levy,** one of the first Sephardic Jews to arrive in Seattle, bought the stall in 1926 and quickly earned the nickname "Good Weight Dave" for keeping his thumb off the scale. The business, still in Levy family hands, continues to sell high-quality fish and now does overnight shipping to any location in the continental U.S. Look for the well-preserved **City Fish Market** sign on Pike Place. ◆ Daily 7:30AM-6PM. Main floor. 682.9329

Lowell's Restaurant $ This classic cafeteria and restaurant serves substantive, though not surprising, meals (try the fried oysters and the Monte Cristo or Reuben sandwiches). It was opened as a coffee shop in 1908 by brothers **Edward** and **William Manning,** veterans of the New England coffee and tea trade, who did something early on that much later would become a Seattle signature: they started selling roasted java beans in bulk. The Mannings eventually expanded their business down the West Coast, moving their headquarters to San Francisco in the 1920s and finally selling their Pike Place enterprise in 1957. **Reid Lowell,** a former manager for the Mannings, owned and operated the place for many years until he passed it along to his insurance agent, **Bill Chatalas,** in 1981. ◆ American/Seafood ◆ Daily 7AM-5PM. Main floor. 622.2036

Manzo Brothers One of the first farmers to sell produce at the market in 1909 was **Sosio Manzo,** an Italian immigrant who owned farmland south of the city. His descendants continue to operate this stall. ◆ M-Sa 7:30AM-6PM. Arcades 5 and 6, main floor. 624.2118

Market Spice Warning! Warning! Olfactory overload! More than a hundred flavors of tea, bulk coffee beans, and giant jars of seasonings can be found here, as well as tea-brewing paraphernalia and boxes of fine sweets. Head first to the free-tea dispenser, just beside the cashier's counter and usually filled with the popular Market Spice house blend (developed by the wife of a pharmacist in the 1970s). Then roam the aisles with an open mind . . . and an open nose. Mail orders are accepted. ◆ M-Sa 9AM-6PM; Su noon-5PM. Main floor. 622.6340

Maximilien-in-the-Market ★★$$$ You've got to admire the ego of a restaurant that showcases a review written entirely in French. Are you just to *assume* that the report is favorable, or should you simply allow yourself to be seduced by the old-fashioned charm and exceptional Puget Sound views here? Owned by **Francois** and **Julia Kissel,** this restaurant is proud of its "Frenchness," offering such minor but rewarding entrées as a boneless chicken baked with apples and sausage in cider, as well as fresh salmon and mussels. Yet that pride doesn't seem to stand in the way of consumer accommodation, which must explain why the Kissels also serve something as pedestrian, but well prepared here, as fish-and-chips. The bar is a fine redoubt from winter chills. ◆ French ◆ M-Sa 7:30AM-10PM; Su 9:30AM-4PM. Main floor. Reservations recommended. 682.7270

Pike Place Fish In 1947 the **Seattle City Council** forbade singing by market vendors—consistent with this town's outspoken preference for quiet. But wait until you hear the bellowing hawkers at Pike Place Fish, whose voices positively explode from beneath the Market Clock. Crowds gather to observe the iced beds of crab or gape as fishmongers hurl salmon over tourists' heads for weighing behind the counter. The store, founded in 1930, ships fresh fish anywhere in the U.S. ◆ Daily 6:30AM-7PM. Main floor. 682.7181, 800/542.7732; fax 682.4629

The Economy Market Atrium at Pike Place Market was home to Fagan's Grist Mill in the 1920s. It was there that the first version of dry pancake mix was sold commercially. Patents were later bought by the now-prosperous Albers company for $200.

PLACE PIGALLE

Place Pigalle ★★$$ Time was when this was essentially a bar, frequented by men (many of them descended from **Nellie Curtis'** cathouse) who wore their hats while they drank. Now it's one of the most pleasant dining spaces in the market: its floor covered in alternating black-and-white tiles, and its outlook on Puget Sound wondrously unobstructed. Lunch and dinner menus include what is seasonally fresh, leaning heavily toward seafood such as Dungeness crab, hazelnut-covered red snapper, and salmon in a brandy, Bing-cherry sauce. Pork medaillons in a saffron-almond sauce, and an open-faced chicken sandwich with chipolte pepper aioli are other worthy choices. The only disappointment here has been with the oyster stew, which, while rich and flavorful, can be poorly populated with bivalves. A porch is available for outdoor dining during the summer. ♦ Continental/Northwestern ♦ M-Th 11:30AM-10PM; F-Sa 11:30AM-11PM. Down the staircase behind Pike Place Fish. Reservations recommended. 624.1756

Golden Age Collectables This crowded corner store carries the city's largest selection of comics, everything from standards such as *Spiderman, Legends of the Dark Knight,* and the *Green Arrow* (the last now drawn by local talent **Mike Grell** and set in Seattle) to *Aliens, Swamp Thing, Bikini Confidential,* and some of the more obscure titles from the **Dark Horse** publishing house of Portland, Oregon. There's a wide array of vintage comics, too, plus science-fiction novels, models, sports cards, and binders full of classic, movie-star publicity stills. Unlike in comic-book outlets of old, at least half of the customers here are adults. Special orders are taken. ♦ M-F 9:30AM-6PM, Sa 11AM-5PM June-Aug; M-F 10AM-5PM, Sa 11AM-5PM Sept-May. First Floor Down Under. 622.9799

Market Magic Shop Puget Sound resident and practicing prestidigitator **Harry Anderson,** who portrayed a judge on TV's "Night Court," is supposed to shop here, but few people have ever spotted him. More common thrills are the impromptu performances by owners **Darrel Beckman** ("The Amazing Beckman") and **Sheila Lyon** ("Sheila the Magic Lady"), who always seem willing to open their bag of tricks. With professional paraphernalia and joke props, replicas of old Houdini posters, and juggling clubs, this is an ideal spot to conjure up an afternoon's escape—mental, if not physical. ♦ M-Sa 9AM-6PM; Su 10AM-5PM. First Floor Down Under. 624.4271

Old Seattle Paperworks With the feel of a richly cluttered attic, this is a narrow storehouse of old postcards for sale, classic black-and-whites from Seattle's early years, and piles of dusty *National Geographic* magazines like the ones your grandparents have held onto for half a century. ♦ Daily 11AM-5PM. First Floor Down Under. 623.2870

MisterE B∞ks

MisterE Books This store is tiny but caters nicely to both best-seller addicts and readers aspiring to collect first-edition mysteries, science fiction, and Westerns. Racks of old records take up one end of the space. ♦ M-Sa 10AM-5PM; Su 11AM-5PM. First Floor Down Under. 622.5182

Wisdom Marionettes Owner **Dan Wisdom** has made puppets for a quarter-century, since starting a marionette theater in Bakersfield, California, in 1967. He and his wife, **Adelle,** moved to Seattle in 1976, and for a time they had a shop in **Pioneer Square,** before Dan decided he preferred a cross-country solo act to supervising his string-wielding troupe. Their new market shop is a family affair, with Dan and Adelle's children and grandkids all pitching in to craft the soft-sculpture puppets, colorful marionettes, and hand puppets for sale. ♦ M-Sa 10:30AM-5PM. First Floor Down Under. 527.9124

Grandma's Attic One of several collectibles outlets on the arcade's lowest level, this one is filled with delicate, feminine vintage outfits and knickknacks. ♦ M-F 10:30AM-5PM; Sa 10AM-6PM; Su 10AM-5PM. Second Floor Down Under. 682.9281

Yesterdaze Intriguingly cluttered with well-kept old hats, ties, and jewelry but especially known for its period military clothing, Yesterdaze is a collector's idea of heaven on earth. ♦ M-Sa 11:00AM-5PM. Second Floor Down Under. No phone

8 Seattle Parrot Market and Reptile House Just follow the squawking to this "birdhouse." The owners have lodged almost every conceivable sort of parrot into their space. Their most exotic bird: the female electus parrot from the Solomon islands and

New Guinea. ♦ M-Sa 10AM-6PM; Su noon-5PM. 1500 Western Ave. 467.6133

9 Liberty Malt Supply Company/Pike Place Brewery Liberty Malt has sold fresh hops, malted barley, and home-brewing supplies since 1921. Only since 1979, however, has it been legal to brew beer on the premises. The first keg of **Pike Place Pale Ale** was wheeled up to nearby **Cutter's Bayhouse** in 1989. Since then, the brewery has been producing fine-quality beers in quantities of less than 10,000 gallons a year, carried by some of the better taverns in town. Tours are available seven days a week. Home-brewing starter kits, including a five-gallon bucket, carboy (or glass jug), siphon hose, malt extract, hops, and other ingredients, are for sale here. Beer-making classes are offered several times a year, covering basics as well as fermentation, bottling, and stylistic variations. Don't be afraid that your first batches might not turn out perfectly; only in ancient Babylonia were brewers of inferior beers thrown into the nearest river. ♦ M-F 11AM-6PM; Sa-Su 11AM-5PM. 1418 Western Ave (Liberty Malt Supply Company); 1432 Western Ave (Pike Place Brewery). 622.1880

KASALA

10 Kasala This glass-walled corner is a cheery showplace for contemporary and high-styled (but surprisingly comfortable) furniture that's appropriate for offices and most rooms of the house. There are lots of "techy" floor lamps and other European accessories. Salespeople are readily available but usually leave you alone to browse. ♦ Daily 10AM-6PM. 1505 Western Ave. 623.7795. Also at: 1014 116th Ave NE, Bellevue. 453.2823

11 Hillclimb Corridor In the market's early days, a wooden pedestrian overpass (built in 1912) connected Pike Place with Waterfront piers, an essential link. Many sellers at the market arrived by boat, often on craft belonging to the old **Mosquito Fleet,** an armada of 70 small steamers that hustled people and products to 350 ports on the Sound (and was flattened like its namesake under the weight of new bridge and highway construction in the mid-20th century). In 1973, after the market had won historical status, those rickety steps were replaced with these landscaped stairs down to the Waterfront and the **Seattle Aquarium,**

designed by **Calvin/Gorasht and Sanders.** The incline is steep (some refer to it as Cardiac Gulch), yet the Hillclimb has proved a magnet for both shops and shoppers. ♦ Between Western Ave and Alaskan Way

On the Hillclimb Corridor:

El Puerco Lloron ★$ It looks like a cafeteria decorated by cheesy Tijuana trinket collectors, but the handmade tortillas, tamales, and exceptional *chiles rellenos* more than make up for the decorative deficiencies. Beware of the salsas: it's always best to taste first before pouring them over your meal. ♦ Mexican ♦ M-Sa 11:30AM-9PM, Su noon-7PM Mar-Aug; M-Th 11:30AM-8PM, F-Sa 11:30AM-9PM, Su noon-7PM Sept-Feb. 624.0541

Procopio Treat yourself to a delicious homemade gelato sans artificial anything. For aspiring coffeeholics, flavors include cappuccino and mocha. ♦ M-Th 8AM-10PM; F-Sa 8AM-midnight; Su 10AM-6PM. 622.4280

THE GREAT NORTHWEST

The Great Northwest The Northwest is personified here: canopied beds, well-stuffed sofas, and rush-woven bench seats, all showing the knots and unique bulges of the Douglas fir trees from which they were shaped. Logs used by Seattle's **Chicken & Egg Productions** to make this furniture are peeled to their cambium layers and then cured in late summer sunshine until they achieve a palomino gleam. Knots are sanded and hand-rubbed with beeswax. The warmly natural, unmanicured results fit surprisingly well into even the most modern settings.

Profits from sales of this furniture go to funding child-abuse prevention efforts and school programs provided through the **Children's Trust Foundation** and **Cities in Schools.** And don't worry that forests are being devastated so you can have a place to dine with your in-laws; the firs used by Chicken & Egg are supposed to be culled only from overgrown stands. Also available are decorative accoutrements (dried flowers, small sculptures) and interior-design books supporting the natural look. ♦ M-Sa 10AM-6PM; Su 10AM-5PM. 1426 Alaskan Way. 623.6144

12 North Arcade This has become one of the slowest-moving pedestrian areas in the market, as everybody stops to look at the tables piled with handknit sweaters, homemade jellies and jams, and assortments of dried flowers. On warm days merchants even stretch out north along the sidewalk, selling some of the more interesting T-shirts available here, as well as jewelry and colorful "clubs" that are somehow kept in the air, even twirled, when batted between two other hand-held sticks. ◆ Pike Pl (between Pine and Virginia Sts)

13 Corner Market Building One of the things that most fascinates architects about Pike Place Market is that so little of the development here can be ascribed to professional designers. An exception is the formal 1912 Corner Market, which was conceived by **Harlan Thomas,** designer of the **Sorrento Hotel** and **Harborview Hospital** on First Hill and the **Byzantine Chamber of Commerce Building** on Columbia Street in downtown.

A three-story brick structure, the Corner Market is best recognized by its graceful arched top-level windows. The first tenant was **Three Girls Bakery,** which now operates in the **Sanitary Market Building.** Also housed here was the Northwest's first homegrown grocery chain: **Herman Eba** moved from the **Main Arcade** stall he'd occupied since 1910 to the Corner Market in 1929, and six years later adopted the business name **Tradewell,** a label that later became familiar to supermarket shoppers around the region. This was the first market landmark to be rehabilitated, which occurred in 1975. ◆ Pike Pl and Pike St

Within the Corner Market Building:

The Crumpet Shop A welcome alternative to the hegemony of coffeehouses in Seattle, this cozy tearoom prepares its own spongy crumpets, which are great topped with raspberry jam, marmalade, or even ricotta cheese. Lox or ham on open-faced crumpets are available at lunch, as are more conventional sandwiches. The space can be crowded with take-out patrons early on weekday mornings, but it's a comforting crowdedness—really. ◆ Teahouse ◆ M-Sa 7:30AM-5PM. First floor. 682.1598

![LEFT BANK BOOKS]

Left Bank Books It takes a while to acquaint yourself with the categorization (books written by men, for instance, are philosophically as well as physically divided from books by women), and the array of new and used volumes tends to be more funky than complete. But there's an endearing, antiquarian nature to this place, buttressed by its lack of computerization and its pack-rat mentality. In case you didn't guess already, the Left Bank's bent is toward liberal, sometimes revolutionary lit. George Bush and Pat Robertson will never set foot in here. ◆ Daily 10AM-9PM. First floor. 622.0195

Cafe Counter Intelligence $ It's hard not to appreciate this long, narrow joint, where the artwork along one wall may be a series of dinner plates decorated with desperado mug shots and where the countertop is a mosaic of tiny tiles spelling out the coffee shop's moniker. Noshes include toasted crumpets, seasonal fruits, sandwiches, and special soups. But the true culinary stars here are the coffee (in a dizzying array of permutations) and the milk shakes (especially the peppermint and the Dutch chocolate varieties). ◆ Cafe ◆ M, W-Su 9AM-5PM. Second floor. 622.6979

Chez Shea ★★★★$$$$ This romantic restaurant is especially good late at night, when candlelight is the principal illumination, torch songs are the featured entertainment, and the half-moon windows allow a softened perspective on the market below and the ferries gliding over Puget Sound. Sigh. . . . Four-course prix-fixe dinners offer a choice of entrées, surrounded by appetizers and a salad. Complaints leveled against some dishes have cited an overly complicated presentation and lack of substance, but recent visits suggest improvements have been made by chef **Martha McGinnis** and executive chef-owner **Sandy Shea.**

A dinner here might open with a savory filo tart decked in tomato and grated onion, followed by a sweet and moist corn pudding. Melt-on-the-tongue scallops sit in a crisp potato-string nest, and tender duck is served on a bed of stroganoff. The mixed greens pale by comparison, but they may be followed by the remarkably smooth French silk (chocolate) pie. The wine list represents both top West Coast and European vintages. ◆ Continental/Northwestern ◆ Tu-Su 5:30-10PM. Second floor. Reservations required. 467.9990

Pike Place Bar & Grill ★$ Sandee and Gordy Brock's joint is a market standard, not flashy but satisfying nonetheless. Newcomers usually wind up at the restaurant end, filling themselves with sandwiches (thumbs up, especially for the French dip) or satisfying pasta and fish specials. Seattleites gravitate to the noisier bar, where the same menu is available but you can also find the best views of the market. Piano players keep the bar's resident instrument well exercised. ◆ American ◆ Daily 11AM-11PM. Second floor. 624.1365

14 Sanitary Market Building The name derives from the fact that this was the first building in the market where horses were not allowed inside. It was four stories tall when put up in 1910, but the upper floors (which originally held garment shops) were destroyed by a fire 31 years later, one of several conflagrations to sweep through the market since its inception. City architect **Daniel R. Huntington** redesigned it in 1942 as a two-story edifice with rooftop parking. It was rehabilitated again in 1981 by the partnership of **Bassetti/Norton/Metler.**
♦ Pike Pl (between Pine and Pike Sts)

Within the Sanitary Market Building:

Jack's Fish Spot $ Behind the fresh shellfish tanks (the only ones in the market) is a walk-up seafood bar with a few stools. Try the cioppino or the fish-and-chips, both fresh. ♦ Seafood ♦ M-Sa 7:30AM-6PM; Su 8AM-5PM. Lower floor. 467.0514

Rasa Malaysia ★★$ This is the original in a popular chain of restaurants (sister outlets can be found in the University District; on Phinney Ridge; by Green Lake; and on Capitol Hill). The emphasis here is on noodles, usually served sautéed with very fresh veggies, peanut or another mildly spicy sauce, and a variety of fish, shrimp, or meat. Try a fruit smoothie or some of the fresh and not overly sweet lemonade. ♦ Malaysian/Takeout ♦ Daily 11AM-6PM. Lower floor. 624.8388. Also located at: 401 Broadway East, 328.8882; 7208 E. Green Lake Dr North, 523.8888; and 6012 Phinney Ave North, 781.8888

Three Girls Bakery ★$ Its roots are in the **Corner Market Building**, where it opened in 1912, but this bakery has since become an institution in the Sanitary Market Building. You can tell by the crowded lunch counter and the line weaving from its take-out window down the sidewalk. In addition to their baked goods, they feature a delicious assortment of sandwiches; the corned beef and the ham are savvy buys. ♦ Bakery ♦ M-Sa 7AM-6PM. Lower floor. 622.1045

Ace Loan This pawnshop is packed with wristwatches, cameras, and other hocked possessions. ♦ M-Sa 9AM-5PM. Upper floor. 682.5424

15 Post Alley Market Designed in 1983 by the partnership of **Bassetti/Norton/Metler,** this building is strictly functional (unlike some of the other nearby structures). Shops at the bottom give way to offices up top.
♦ Post Alley (between Pike and Pine Sts)

Within the Post Alley Market:

Made in Washington For people who can't live without Northwest slug souvenirs, locally made jams, and coffee cups that sport rigid whale-tail handles, *dis* is *da* place. ♦ M-Sa 9AM-6PM; Su 10AM-5PM. 467.0788

SBC 'Tis the rare Seattleite who would remember this, but **Jim Stewart** began selling roasted coffee in 1970, when he had an ice-cream parlor called the **Wet Whisker** in Coupeville, on Whidbey Island. He opened his first Seattle location with his brother, **Dave,** in 1971 at Pier 70 on the Waterfront. Ten years later, **Stewart Brothers Coffee** shop began business in **Bellevue Square.** By 1989, when Stewart Brothers Coffee became **SBC Coffee** (defined archly as "Seattle's Best Coffee"), Jim Stewart had several locations on both sides of Lake Washington, including a snazzy glass-walled stop in **Westlake Mall.**

This contemporary corner shop in Pike Place Market was designed by architects **Olson/Walker.** On warm days the alleyside wall opens and patrons spread onto sidewalks. Both bulk coffee beans and cups of espresso variations are available.
♦ Coffeehouse ♦ M-F 6:30AM-5PM; Sa-Su 7:30AM-5PM. 467.7700

Sisters ★$ During summer months its glass front opens to the elements so patrons sitting along the counter can eavesdrop on alley strollers (they, in turn, can listen in on your lunchtime confessionals). And year-round, Sisters is a bright and warm-hearted establishment, specializing in grilled European sandwiches on focaccia. The Corsica (Black Forest ham, artichoke hearts, fontina cheese, and tomato) and the Gesundheit (sun-dried tomato, cream cheese, avocado, and alfalfa sprouts) are no-fail faves. Black-bean chili and borscht are good winter warmers. Breakfasts of waffles and German rolls with selected deli meats and cheeses are served all day. ♦ European deli ♦ M-Sa 8AM-6PM; Su 11AM-5PM. 623.6723

In 1850 a ship sailing north from San Francisco, the *G.W. Kendall,* entered Puget Sound in the misguided belief that icebergs floated there. The plan was to break down the bergs and use the ice to keep drinks cool in saloons along the Barbary Coast. Instead, the *Kendall* returned home with a load of wood piling.

Restaurants/Clubs: Red   **Hotels:** Blue
Shops/ 🌳 Outdoors: Green   **Sights/Culture:** Black

57

16 Triangle Building When this building was constructed in 1908 as home to the **South Park Poultry Company,** shoppers used to browse here among the stripped chickens that hung from the ceiling. The structure was rehabilitated in 1977 by architect **Fred Bassetti,** along with the adjoining **Silver Oakum Building** to the north. ♦ Pike Pl and Pine St

Within the Triangle Building:

Cinnamon Works The signature cinnamon rolls here may be filling, but the chocolate-chocolate-chip cookies could become your secret weakness. ♦ Bakery ♦ Daily 7AM-5PM. First floor. 583.0085

Mr. D's Greek Deli Fast food, Aegean style, with *spanakopita,* juicy gyro sandwiches, and Greek pastries. ♦ Greek deli ♦ Daily 10AM-6PM. First floor. 622.4881

Mee Sum Pastries The service can be a bit surly, but it's a price worth paying for Mee Sum's fine Chinese pot stickers and *hum baos* (the curry-beef variety is especially good). ♦ Chinese bakery ♦ Daily 9AM-6PM. First floor. 682.6780

Copacabana Cafe ★$ The Copacabana was opened in 1963 by **Ramon Pelaez,** a writer, a former owner of Bolivia's largest radio station, and a political activist (**Franklin Roosevelt** once thanked him for leading Bolivian opposition to German Nazis), who in 1953 was jailed by a new leftist government and forced to dispense with his holdings. After 10 years in Chile, Pelaez came to Seattle to open a restaurant in the market, though he barely knew how to cook.

Ramon Pelaez died in 1979, but his daughter and son-in-law continue to run Seattle's only Bolivian restaurant, using many Pelaez family recipes. Look up one level as you stride the bricks of Pike Place and you're likely to spot the crowded, two-tables-wide deck that surrounds this place, which is a favorite summer dining option. Service here can be abysmal; don't be surprised if your beer order is forgotten or if you're given your check before receiving your lunch. But the food is worth missing a meeting or two. Best choices from the regular menu are the filling paella and the *pescado a la Española,* a delicate halibut steak in a sauce of onions and tomatoes. As an appetizer with beer, order the shrimp nachos. ♦ Bolivian ♦ M-Sa 11:30AM-9PM, Su 11:30AM-6PM Mar-Sept; daily 11:30AM-4PM Oct-Dec; closed Jan-Apr. Second floor. 622.6359

17 Inn at the Market $$ What finer location for a Seattle hotel than smack dab in the midst of its famous market district? And in most aspects, this 65-room hotel, wrapped about a surprisingly peaceful courtyard, will live up to your expectations. There's a well-respected restaurant, **Campagne,** located

right downstairs, a large deck overlooking the market and Elliott Bay, blessedly little chance that you'll be surrounded by conventioneers (thanks to a shortage of facilities in the hotel for their use), and a warm, European personality to the Inn that must not be undervalued.

Rooms (both for smokers and nonsmokers) are good sized, and they're decorated with sculptures and flowers. Though there is no kitchen in the hotel itself, Campagne graciously provides room service. Unfortunately, the same thing that makes the market a wonderful place to be—the noise and bustle—can also detract from the intimacy and comfort. Rooms on the west side have the best views, but there's disruptive noise for most of each day; those on the east, or First Avenue, side suffer traffic clatter. This is, subsequently, a hotel for lovers of the urban experience. ♦ 86 Pine St. 443.3600; fax 448.0631

Within the Inn at the Market:

Campagne ★★$$$ Romantically appointed, with Oriental rugs and a satisfying view of Elliott Bay, Campagne's Provençal menu enchants its patrons with salmon in a cognac-and-champagne butter sauce, lamb salad, and herb chicken filled with goat cheese. When complaints surface about Campagne, they usually have to do with brusque service. ♦ French ♦ Daily 5:30-10PM, with lighter fare available until midnight. Bar open daily until 2AM. Reservations recommended. Jacket required. 728.2800

Cafe Dilettante The five ways of sinning by gluttony, it's said, are "too soon, too expensively, too much, too eagerly, and making too much of a fuss." If so, many of the local fans of this establishment will be paying into eternity for their indulgent visits to Cafe Dilettante. Formulas for making the sweet temptations found here were passed down from **Julius Rudolph Franzen,** who created pastries for **Emperor Franz Josef** of Austria. Later, Rudolph served as master candy maker to **Nicholas II,** the last czar of Russia. Just before both his former bosses were assassinated (a propitious time, if ever he could have chosen one), Franzen immigrated to the U.S., where he educated his American brother-in-law, **Earl Davenport,** in the chocolatier's art. Now, Davenport's grandson produces some of the most tempting truffles, butter crèmes, and dragées (nut meats or dried fruits dredged through dipping chocolates) you'll ever try. ♦ M-Th, Su 11AM-7PM; F-Sa 11AM-10PM. 728.9144. Also at: 416 Broadway East. 329.6463

DeGraff Books This bookshop is cozy, with helpful salespeople and an intriguing assortment of recent issues, but sadly too small to carry much depth in any department. ♦ M-F 10:30AM-6PM; Sa 10AM-6PM; Su noon-5PM. 441.0688

18 Upper Post Alley Horse-drawn hearses once clattered down this uneven brick path to deposit corpses in the basement crematorium of the **Butterworth Mortuary,** now home to **Kell's Restaurant & Pub.** This is still the only part of Post Alley that accepts vehicular traffic. ♦ Between Stewart and Virginia Sts

Along Upper Post Alley:

The Glass Eye Gallery Mount St. Helens' volcanic eruption in 1980 proved a big boon to some of the Northwest's novelty glass makers. The Glass Eye co-owners **Rob Adamson** and **Dale Leman** caught on early to the possibilities (they're still riding the trend) and incorporated the peak's ashen and slightly iridescent detritus into their hand-blown glass pieces. Look here for dishware, blown fruit, and shapely vases. ♦ M-F 10AM-5PM; Sa 9:30AM-5PM; Su 11AM-4PM. 441.3221

Kell's Restaurant & Pub ★$$ You're likely to miss this hidden-away pub. But don't. Kell's is everything a pub should be: aged and full of smoke-darkened woods and sporting prints; it's a place where patrons aren't afraid to argue and maybe fight for their politics. Guinness is available on tap, or dip into a pint of one of the Northwest's assertive brews. The menu complements the Irish ambience with homemade stews and meat pies. And live Irish music is featured Wednesday through Saturday nights. In summer a small outdoor dining area is cordoned off in the alley. ♦ Irish ♦ Cover on Friday and Saturday nights. M-Sa 11:30AM-9:30PM. Bar open daily until 2AM. 728.1916

The Pink Door ★★$ Although some summer visitors know this place solely for its outdoor seating, the Pink Door does a fine job year-round of providing inexpensive Italian dishes in romantic surroundings. Service can be forgetful and sometimes you have to wield sharp elbows to find lunchtime seating, but the fettuccine with clam sauce and the lasagna are hard to beat. At night this high-ceilinged trattoria is illuminated by table candles. ♦ Italian ♦ Tu-Sa 11:30AM-2:30PM, 5:30-10PM. Bar open Tu-Th until 11:30PM; F-Sa until 1:30AM. 443.3241

19 Garden Center Built in 1908 to house an egg market, this building became the Garden Center in 1946. ♦ Pike Pl (between Stewart and Pine Sts)

Within the Garden Center:

Seattle Garden Center Potted plants decorate the sidewalk outside, and inside you'll find planters, tools, birdhouses, and more seed packets than most people would think to use in a lifetime. Polish up that green thumb. ♦ M-Sa 9AM-5:30PM; Su noon-4PM. 448.0431

Sur La Table Shirley Collins' hillside lodestone for butchers, bakers, and candy-stick makers represents the height of kitchen chic in Seattle. Even those who don't fancy themselves cooks can appreciate the shiny and variegated wealth of gadgets, dishware, picnic baskets, and kitchenware here. The staff is knowledgeable, and there's a wide assortment of pricey cookbooks to further expand your culinary expertise. Just watch out for weekends and lunch hours, when the cramped aisles seem to become all feet and elbows. ♦ M-Sa 9AM-6PM; Su 9:30AM-6PM. 84 Pine St. 448.2244, 800/243.0852

20 Stewart House A workingperson's hotel, built here in stages between 1902 and 1911, it was finally closed down in the 1970s for failure to meet city housing codes. A 1982 renovation by **Ibsen Nelsen & Associates** rehabilitated the original wooden structure and included a four-story brick-faced addition. Studios for disabled and elderly residents can be found above the street-level shops. ♦ Stewart St and Pike Pl

Within the Stewart House:

Cucina Fresca Stop by for exceptional pasta salads, entrées to warm in the oven or consume picnic-style, and other deli take-outs. ♦ Italian deli ♦ M-Sa 9:30AM-6PM; Su 11AM-5PM. 448.4758

Le Panier Warm, fragrant French breads are the main attraction, but, once you're inside, the pastries are no less an enticement. This is no place to be worried about your waistline. ♦ French bakery ♦ M-Sa 7AM-6PM. 441.3669

Market Tobacco Patch In a maverick style familiar to the West, owner **Bill Coulson** defies political correctness to maintain Seattle's premier pipe and cigar

---

Restaurants/Clubs: Red   **Hotels:** Blue
Shops/ �--- Outdoors: Green   **Sights/Culture:** Black

emporium. Pipe tobacco comes in a splendid variety, and Coulson keeps 60 to 80 types of cigars in stock—a tiny fraction of the 5,000 or so that can be found on the market. But the real treat here (for smokers, at least) is stepping inside the climate-controlled cigar humidor and inhaling deeply. ♦ M-Sa 8:30AM-5:30PM. 728.7291

21 Soames-Dunn Building Two adjoining structures from 1918, one of which held **Dunn's Seeds,** the other the headquarters of **Soames Paper Company,** which peddled paper bags to market merchants, were combined to make this building. A 1976 rehabilitation was accomplished by architect **Arne Bystrom.** ♦ Pike Pl (between Stewart and Virginia Sts)

Within the Soames-Dunn Building:

Emmett Watson's Oyster Bar ★$ Watson is a former semipro baseball player, now the city's curmudgeonly veteran columnist (he is with the *Seattle Times,* after an early stint slinging ink for the competing *Post-Intelligencer*). He was the newsman who first discovered and notified the world that **Ernest Hemingway's** 1961 death in Ketchum, Idaho, was a suicide. In more recent years he's led the so-called Lesser Seattle movement, endorsing slow or no growth for the city and railing against the local influx of Californians.

But while Watson's fame is clearly on the wane, this oft-crowded restaurant named in his honor has earned institution status for its consistently fresh and varied selection of oysters. Salmon soup and hearty helpings of fish-and-chips can also be had, if you'd rather not slurp from the shell. Wash your food down with something from the ample beer roster. One warning: niched beside a courtyard at the back of the Soames-Dunn Building, Emmett Watson's can be hard to find. Rather like Watson's column in the *Times.* ♦ Seafood ♦ M-Th 11:30AM-8PM; F-Sa 11:30AM-9PM; Su 11:30AM-4PM. 448.7721

The Soap Box Get indecent and indulgent with the bath oils and the rubber duckies that are sold here. ♦ M-Sa 9AM-6PM; Su 11AM-5PM. 441.5680

The Souk Foods and spices from the Middle East, Pakistan, India, and Africa stock these shelves. ♦ M-Sa 9:30AM-6PM; Su 11AM-5PM. 441.1666

Starbucks Judging from the old Turkish proverb, "Coffee should be black as Hell, strong as death, and sweet as love," the ancient Turks would be shocked to witness the local fate of their heady brew. The ol' black magic has all but disappeared from the coffee in the Seattle area, where ordering a cup of regular, "unmilked," unadorned java will fetch you the same kind

of bug-eyed stares offered to asylum escapees who scream obscenities at lampposts. The caffeine craze in Seattle can mostly be attributed to the Starbucks chain, which grew to ubiquity after this storefront opened in 1971. It's always crowded on weekends, when classical violinists regularly perform just outside the front door. ♦ Coffeehouse ♦ M-Th 7:30AM-6PM; F-Sa 7:30AM-7PM; Su 8:30AM-6PM. 448.8762

22 Louie's on the Pike While most market shops specialize, Louie's is a general-interest grocery—*the* place to shop if you're looking for something so pedestrian as a bottled soft drink or an ice-cream bar. There's also a decent deli counter inside. ♦ M-Sa 7:30AM-9PM; Su 9AM-7PM. 1926 Pike Pl. 443.1035

23 Pike & Western Wine Merchants The selection of French and German vintages here is well chosen. ♦ M-F 9:30AM-6:30PM; Sa 9:30AM-6PM; Su noon-5PM. 1934 Pike Pl. 441.1307

24 Victor Steinbrueck Park It's fitting that such a lively spot (designed in 1982 by both **Steinbrueck** and **Richard Haag**) should be dedicated to an architect who sought to maintain the vibrancy of Pike Place Market. This grassy viewpoint bustles on warm days with lunching business types, tourists pondering the passage of ferries on the Sound, and the usual Seattle complement of panhandlers. A pair of Northwest Indian totem poles designed by Quinault tribe member **Marvin Oliver** were carved with the assistance of **James Bender.** Too bad that right below the park rushes the interminably noisy Alaskan Way Viaduct. ♦ Western Ave (between Virginia and Lenora Sts)

25 Cutter's Bayhouse ★$$ People either love this place or they would sooner swear off *lattes* for life than dine here again. The problem isn't the food; like other stylish formula establishments owned by **Restaurants Unlimited** (**Triples** on Lake Union, **Palisade** in Magnolia, **Palomino** in downtown), this one shows skill in the kitchen. So what if the menu is all over the map—a little Chinese, some Cajun, a dash of Italian just to keep things cooking—as long as the pasta, seafood, and the garlicky focaccia remain impressive. The bar is somewhat overlighted, but nonetheless handles the crucial business of mixing and pouring cocktails with aplomb. No, the trouble here lies with the clientele: lots of competitive yuppie comers, lots of fatless body fanatics from the nearby **Seattle Club,** and everybody checking out each other's vital stats—comparing, contrasting, measuring, and weighing. ♦ Eclectic ♦ Daily 11AM-4PM, 5-11:30PM. Bar (serving light meals) open daily until 1:30AM. 2001 Western Ave. 448.4884

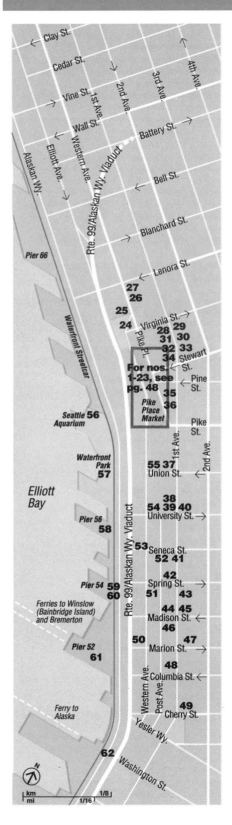

26 Cafe Sport ★★★$$$ Still riding a trend of popularity that rose during the '80s when **Tom Douglas** (now owner of **Dahlia Lounge**) was chef here, Cafe Sport is a white-tablecloth sort of place, with big picture windows that allow passersby to see you sitting down when they can't get a reservation here. Menus are based on seasonal foods, so don't get in the habit of ordering the same thing. If you can, try the *sake kasu cod*, the osso buco, or the lingcod in a spicy peanut and coconut sauce. Cafe Sport even does cheeseburgers well. ♦ Northwestern ♦ M-F 7-10AM, 11:30AM-2:30PM, 5-10PM; Sa 8:30AM-2:30PM, 5-10PM; Su 8:30AM-2:30PM, 5-9PM. 2020 Western Ave. Reservations recommended. 443.6000

♦

PHOENIX RISING GALLERY

♦

27 Phoenix Rising Gallery Simultaneously playful and pricey, Phoenix Rising is decorated with table after table of art-sculpted tea sets, jewelry, hand-carved trinket boxes, and "po-mo" clocks. There's also a small but choice assortment of blank greeting cards. ♦ M-Sa 10AM-6PM; Su 11AM-5PM. 2030 Western Ave. 728.2332

28 The Virginia Inn A favorite hangout for newspaper and magazine types, the "V.I." (originally the **Virginia Bar**) has anchored this corner of First Avenue and Virginia Street since about 1908. Unlike many similar pubs, the V.I. never closed during Prohibition but just converted temporarily into a card- and lunchroom. Knife-carved wooden booths hug a corner near the door, leaving the remaining floor space to a maze of little round tables and a long elegant bar that can barely be seen through the mass of revelers on weekdays after 5PM. The choice of craft beers and wines, while not extensive, is select. There's not much in the way of pub grub, although the platter of smoked salmon and bread provides a reasonable light lunch. Art on the brick walls changes frequently. The restrooms are worth a peek: *True Detective* motif in the men's john, and lip prints next door for women. ♦ Daily 11AM-2AM. 1937 First Ave. 728.1937

In 1992 a dozen grunge-style bands got together to record "Hey Joe," the first song ever released that was all about coffee.

The Word Out West

Seattle is a bibliophile's kind of town. Nationally, the average per-household expenditure for books is $57 a year. Here, it's almost double that: $106.91. Meanwhile, Seattle public libraries loan out more volumes per capita than any other system in the country. Noteworthy authors—from **Norman Mailer** to **Terry McMillan, Carlos Fuentes, Philip Roth, Jill Eisenstadt,** and **Robert B. Parker**—cycle through town for readings or book signings, and the **Seattle Arts and Lectures Series** schedules about half a dozen famous writers annually for lectures and special events (call 621.2230 for schedules and registration). And a number of nationally recognized authors—including **Mark Helprin, Jonathan Raban,** and **Pete Dexter**—have recently relocated to Puget Sound country.

Is Seattle's bookwormish tendency attributable to high local education levels? Or can it be traced simply to the number of inclement days that send waterlogged residents inside to the comfort of their reading lamps? Whatever the reason, the publishing industry has benefited. Counting the number of bookstores per person, Seattle ranks seventh in the nation (San Francisco tops the list).

A number of useful guidebooks and historical studies have evolved with Seattle's increasing popularity. The city is also rapidly becoming the setting of the moment for detective novelists. However, there is still nothing that can be pointed to as the quintessential Seattle Novel—nothing that acutely captures the spirit and essence of the city. The local literati await. For the time being, however, here are some must-reads on the city of Seattle.

Nonfiction

The Good Rain: Across Time and Terrain in the Pacific Northwest, by **Timothy Egan** (1990; Alfred A. Knopf). Prepare to enjoy an eminently readable and not-too-egregiously romanticized take on the Northwest's beauty and blemishes by the *New York Times'* local bureau chief.

Impressions of Imagination: Terra-Cotta Seattle, edited by **Lydia S. Aldredge** (1986; Allied Arts of Seattle). Spend a few hours flipping through this handsome, essay-filled encomium to Seattle's days as a white city on the Sound. It offers a wonderful architectural history.

Living By Water: Essays on Life, Land & Spirit, by **Brenda Peterson** (1991; Alaska Northwest). This book examines the sometimes soothing, sometimes antagonistic relationship between Northwesterners and their moisture-laden environment.

Meet Me at the Center, by **Don Duncan** (1992; Seattle Center Foundation). An entertaining former *Seattle Times* writer looks back at the 1962 World's Fair and forward to the future of the site that has become Seattle Center.

Out Here, by **Andrew Ward** (1991; Penguin). A Bainbridge Islander and lighthearted commentator with National Public Radio draws his sights on beggars, road-kill dogs, and other local exotica.

Seattle in the Twentieth Century, Volumes I and II, by **Richard C. Berner** (1991, 1992; Charles Press). These books aren't stirring reads, being so dense with facts that the artistry of writing has been squeezed thin. But if you want to find out the city's population in 1900 and 1910 or brush up on political machinations in early Seattle, these are the pages to start scanning. Volume I, "From Boomtown, Urban Turbulence, to Restoration," covers 1900 to 1920; Volume 2, "From Boom to Bust," dissects 1921 to 1940.

Seattle Emergency Espresso, by **Heather Doran Barbieri** (1992; Alaska Northwest). A handy drinking companion in a town that cares beans about coffee, *Seattle Emergency Espresso* designates the best and most convenient neighborhood java stops, plus the meaning of such local terminology as the "double tall skinny billiard ball" (a tall *latte* made with one percent or nonfat milk, without foamed milk on top).

Seattle Now and Then, Volumes I through III, by **Paul Dorpat** (1984-89; Tartu). Dorpat's work has terrific historical photos and a generosity of clever anecdotes, but there's sometimes just enough information about the city's past to make you regret there isn't more.

Skid Road, by **Murray Morgan** (1978; Comstock). Morgan's book is an irreverent, insightful, often embarrassingly candid parsing of Seattle history. No one who wants to know about this area's past should be without this book.

Fiction

Fish Story, by **Richard Hoyt** (1985; Viking). Private eye John Denson, connoisseur of screw-top wine and raw cauliflower, gets mixed up in a Native American fishing rights case that leads to the disappearance of a federal judge and the grisly discovery of various human body parts in Pioneer Place Park.

Picture Postcard, by **Fredrick D. Huebner** (1990; Random House). Lawyer Matt Riordan's efforts to locate a famous but long-missing Northwest painter take him back 50 years to a fateful houseboat party on Portage Bay and embroil him with more than a sufficient share of dangerous characters.

28 The Kaleenka ★$$ Seattleites may be most familiar with this Russian restaurant thanks to the popular food stands it sets up at city fairs such as **Bumbershoot** and the **Northwest Folklife Festival,** from which it purveys hot, hearty piroshkis (meat and cheese inside soft baked dough). But Kaleenka's sit-down menu is far more extensive and no less satisfying; it includes a terrific multivegetable borscht, chicken Kiev, and *galubtzi* (cabbage leaves filled with beef, pork, and rice and then baked in a sour cream and tomato sauce). ♦ Russian ♦ M-Th 11AM-9PM; F-Sa 11AM-10PM. 1933 First Ave. 728.1278

29 Peter Miller Books Specializing in architecture and design books (new as well as out-of-print), with such nifty accessories as build-it-yourself paper replicas of the Space Needle, this bookstore is a great place to while away an hour. There's even a catalog available. ♦ M-F 10AM-6PM; Sa 10AM-5:30PM; Su noon-5PM. 1930 First Ave. 441.4114

30 Labuznik ★★★$$$ Owner **Peter Cipra** defies current wisdom that says restaurants must continually change in order to remain interesting. For most of two decades, Labuznik has been a comforting holdout of traditional Central European cuisine (Cipra, himself, is from Czechoslovakia). The dinner-only menu is built around roast pork, veal chops, and rack of lamb, with side dishes of sweet-and-sour red cabbage, sauerkraut, and dumplings. The fish soup is usually remarkable. ♦ Central European ♦ Tu-Th 4:30-9PM; F-Sa 4:30-10PM. 1924 First Ave. Reservations recommended. 441.8899

31 Uno This is the second stylish clothing boutique owned by **Donald Fletcher** and his wife, **Roni Vincent-Fletcher** (who runs the women's store, **Duo,** just north on First Avenue). Donald has a fondness for distinctive attire that may show up best in Uno's layout of fine-print ties and racks of comfortable suits. The staff is friendly and willing to hunt down special colors or styles of garments. ♦ M-Sa 10AM-6PM; Su noon-5PM. 1927 First Ave. 728.9420

Restaurants/Clubs: Red   **Hotels:** Blue
Shops/ 🌳 Outdoors: Green   **Sights/Culture:** Black

31 Pensione Nichols $ While **Lindsey Nichols'** bed-and-breakfast has collected raves from such national sources as the *Atlantic* magazine, local attention has been far more stingy. Foreshadowing the Pensione has been the **Inn at the Market,** a more expensive and more expensively retailed hostelry. Also weighing against it may be the fact that Nichols' place occupies two floors in the 1906 Smith Block, which is directly over a porno-movie palace. In either case, the slight is unfortunate, for Nichols manages a secret uptown gem.

Prices are extremely reasonable for the location—a block off Pike Place and convenient to a superfluity of restaurants and shops. Guest rooms are brightly painted, cozy, and overlook either First Avenue or Elliott Bay; the latter are slightly quieter, but the former seem more intimate with their reduced outdoor illumination. A large third-floor sitting room embraces views of Elliott Bay and is replete with soft couches for reading or clandestine romancing. Guests (save for those in two second-floor suites) must share bath and restroom facilities, but those facilities are quite comfortable and well maintained. The Pensione's entrance may be easily missed: it's just a single doorway off the sidewalk, letting onto a cliff of stairs. Check in at the desk on the third level. ♦ 1923 First Ave. 441.7125

31 Cafe Sophie ★$ If the stone gargoyles, decorative angels, and cathedral ceilings inside give you an oddly sepulchral feeling, it's not without cause: Cafe Sophie's gaudy (and reportedly haunted) dining room was originally the chapel of a three-story funeral parlor built by undertaker **Edgar Ray Butter-worth.** Architect **John Graham, Sr.,** designed the stone-footed Victorian-Romanesque building—his first commercial structure in Seattle—in 1903, before venturing on to create such landmarks as the **Bon Marché** and the **Frederick & Nelson** stores downtown, as well as the **Seattle Yacht Club** in Montlake. Restaurateur **Shane Dennis** has shown a sense of humor in decorating this space with booths and dark green curtains (for an acutely intimate tête-à-tête) in the dining room and a red-walled library at the back that boasts splendid views of Elliott Bay.

Chef **Leonard Rede's** menu has been less interesting, but there are a few highlights: Northwest salmon cakes, served with a roasted-pepper sauce, black beans, and a small salad of bitter greens; tortellini with roasted walnuts and peppers; and galantine of duck, garnished with Bing cherries, served with a reduction of black muscat and nectarines. Don't fail to order dessert (maybe a mousse or the incredible chocolate hazelnut fallen soufflé), as that's often the most winning course. After that, sit back with a cup of the coffee and, pardon the expression, rest in peace. ◆ Northwestern ◆ M-Th 11AM-11PM; F 11AM-midnight; Sa 9AM-midnight; Su 9AM-11PM. 1921 First Ave. 441.6139

32 du jour $ The lowercase moniker should not suggest lower-class cuisine. Indeed, du jour serves some top-notch lunchables in cafeteria style, from thick, delicious sandwiches to hearty soups and a spread of tempting salads. (Try the chicken-pecan salad if it's available.) This is also a great find for lovers of morning baked goods. A dining area at the rear, aggressively white in its decor, provides agreeable views of the Sound. ◆ Deli ◆ M-F 7AM-6PM; Sa 8AM-5PM. 1919 First Ave. 441.3354

33 Fast Forward Owners **Jason Harler** and **Harry Green** focus on local designers of jewelry, eye-catching shirts, and dresses that can be tucked into a bag no larger than your fist. A small art gallery in the back (look for the steer skull with neon horns hanging over the doorway) schedules periodic shows. ◆ M-Sa 10AM-7PM; Su noon-6PM. 1918 First Ave. 728.8050

34 Zebra Club This menswear store carries sporty and lightweight street attire for those who favor the ultracasual "grunge" look. Local manufacturer **Shah Safari** is well represented on the racks. Ubiquitous video equipment heightens the youth-oriented tone. An espresso cart out front is particularly popular. ◆ M-Th, Sa 10AM-6PM; F 10AM-7PM; Su noon-5PM. 1901 First Ave. 448.7452

35 Local Brilliance There's playfulness in owner/designer **Renata Tatman's** affordable assortment of locally created womenswear, jewelry, belts, and other furnishings. Note especially the works of **Sara Campbell,** who matches styles from the 1920s through the

1940s with contemporary fibers and brocaded rayons. ◆ M-Sa 10:30AM-6PM; Su noon-5PM. 1535 First Ave. 343.5864

Retro Viva

36 Retro Viva The 20th century has been compressed, bled together, spilled over the ruins of itself, and then hung on the racks and arranged into the display cases here. What's old is you again, right? Vintage jewelry, jazzy bras, men's shirts, and hats that barely escaped the pages of early fashion mags—Retro Viva is full of well-priced attire for the funky fashion plate. ◆ M-Sa 10AM-6PM; Su noon-5PM. 1511 First Ave. 624.2529. Also at: 4515 University Way NE. 632.8886; 215 Broadway East. 328.7451

37 South Arcade The tower, a jarring, neon-highlighted contrast to the sedate Pike Place Market, was designed in 1985 by **Olson/Walker.** ◆ 1411 First Ave

Within the South Arcade:

Shorey Books The place is jumbled with used books housed on two floors and in many stuck-away warrens. Trying to find exactly what you're looking for at Shorey can be frustrating, especially when the texts are shelved two-deep. But chances are that something unexpected will attract your eye along the way. ◆ M-Sa 10AM-6PM; Su noon-5PM. 624.0221

World Class Chili ★$ Arguments about what chili should and shouldn't be could fill whole cookbooks and are guaranteed to fire up arguments among Texans. **Joe Canavan,** who collected recipes for years before he threw open the doors of this small joint, has decided to give purists and bean-lovers both something to sink their spoons into. The Texas-style bowl here leads the herd: dense with meat and chiles. Other versions mix beef and pork with chocolate and cinnamon, substitute chicken for red meat, or throw out the meat altogether in favor of lentils and veggies (sacrilege!). ◆ Chili ◆ M-Sa 11AM-6PM. 623.3678

38 Center on Contemporary Art (COCA) This gallery's controversial shows often strike back at traditionalists or ultraconservative values. An exhibition commenting on the anniversary of Columbus' New World voyages included ironic twists on Native American stereotypes. A collage by **Phil Young** featured a dark smear of paint with the legend "I do not speak . . . but I can write Jeep Cherokee" written underneath it. Black is the fashion color of choice at shows here. ◆ Tu-Sa 11AM-6PM. 1309 First Ave. 682.4568

39 Inside Owner **Pia Rochon** has filled this former COCA annex with an artist's trove: colorful glass pieces; wild screens; picture frames; wreaths crafted of bent sticks and dried flowers; and antique furnishings, from beds to end tables. Local designers and others are featured here. Drapes take the place of permanent walls and provide a rather exotic sense of mystery, like a dance of veils. ◆ M-Sa 10AM-5PM; Su 1-5PM. 1305 First Ave. 623.5646

40 Seattle Art Museum (SAM) Asked to explain the intent behind his firm's design of the new downtown Seattle Art Museum (pictured below), Philadelphia architect **Robert Venturi** said he wanted to create a "current urban art museum that is popular yet esoteric, closed but open, monumental yet inviting, an accommodating setting for the art, but a work of art itself." In other words, a little bit of everything: a sophisticated but unimposing juxtaposition of convex and concave curves, all faced in fluted limestone and terracotta ornament. Playful, billboardlike lettering along the roofline announces the building's name.

Working with zoning requirements that dictated view corridors to Puget Sound, Venturi, his partner **Denise Scott Brown,** and their associates created a waterfall of an outdoor staircase along the south wall that's almost mirrored by a processional stair inside, leading from the lobby to second-floor galleries and punctuated by sculptures of Chinese military guardians, camels, and rams. Brightly hued proscenium arches hang majestically over those inside stairs.

(The principal disappointment may be the contrast between this elaborate staircase and the narrow, twisting flights and elevators that continue your escalation within the building.) Loftlike galleries are pleasant, if spare, and broad, curving hallways are well lighted from view windows at either end.

The second-floor exhibition space hosts special shows. Native American, African, Chinese, and Near Eastern treasures occupy the next floor up. The fourth level contains a history of European and American works, with Northwest artists such as **Morris Graves, Jacob Lawrence,** and **Kenneth Callahan.** A cafe providing refreshments (open the same hours as the museum) is located on the mezzanine level.

The main entrance on First Avenue is enlivened by sculptor **Jonathan Borofsky's** *Hammering Man* (illustrated at right), a black, 48-foot-tall mechanical piece that took a spill during its installation and had to be repaired before final placement. Since the 1991 opening of SAM's new building, the original museum in **Volunteer Park,** a broad-shouldered 1933 Art Moderne creation from architect **Carl Gould,** has been under renovation to house Asian collections and a study center. ◆ Admission; discount for senior citizens and students; free for children age 12 and under, members, and on the first Tuesday of each month. Tu-W, F-Sa 10AM-5PM; Th 10AM-9PM; Su noon-5PM. 100 University St. 654.3100

41 Grand Pacific Hotel Displaying a stone and arched face that would have been more familiar in Pioneer Square than this far north on First Avenue, the Grand Pacific (or, as it was known upon opening in 1898, the **First Avenue Hotel**) was at no time a luxury inn. Miners, sailors, and businessmen of modest means were its tenants, many of the early ones blowing through town on their way to the Klondike Gold Rush. This doesn't mean, however, that the structure lacks class or style. With its Romanesque stone footing, arched windows along the third floor, and fine detailing over most of its brick upper facade, the Grand Pacific (now restored, joined internally to the neighboring **Colonial Hotel,** and divided into residential units) harkens back to a time when Seattle was just beginning to boom. ♦ 1115-1117 First Ave

42 Watermark Tower This sculpted 20-story edifice (designed by **Bumgardner Architects** in 1983) bursts upward from the preserved terracotta facade of the 1915 **Colman Building** (conceived by **Carl Gould** and **Charles Bebb**). Pay special attention to the dynamic entry arch on Spring Street. ♦ First Ave and Spring St

Within Watermark Tower:

McCormick & Schmick's ★★$$$
Waiters in black bow ties add an element of old-establishment class to this restaurant specializing in seafood and grilled meats. The lamb chops don't disappoint, nor do the salmon dishes. Enjoy a before-dinner cocktail in the comfortable, dark wood barroom. The Irish coffees served here are better than most. ♦ Seafood ♦ M-F 11:30AM-1AM; Sa-Su 4PM-1AM. 1103 First Ave. Reservations recommended. 623.5500

43 Millstream Larger sibling of the other Millstream store in Pioneer Square, this place likewise plays a sentimental riff off the Northwest's natural bounty, selling ferry photos, whale pictures, and lobster mobiles. ♦ M-Sa 10AM-5:30PM; Su 11AM-5PM. 1020 First Ave. 233.9719. Also at: 214 First Ave South. 583.0220

44 Alexis Hotel $$ Designed in 1901 by architect **Max Umbrecht,** this former **Globe Hotel** was rehabilitated in 1982 as part of a large-scale, private-money project that took in this along with several nearby edifices. It's now one of the most intimate hotels (only 54 rooms) in town, convenient to **Pike Place Market,** the **Seattle Art Museum,** and **Pioneer Square.**

Trapped between the revolting Alaskan Way Viaduct and noisy First Avenue, there are no views to speak of here, but a handful of balconied rooms face an interior courtyard and thus provide the most peace and quiet. Suites are outfitted with Jacuzzis, wood-burning fireplaces, and marble fixtures. Complimentary services include shoe shines, sherry in your room, a Continental breakfast, and a morning newspaper. Short-term memberships are available to the popular **Seattle Club,** an athletic facility near the market. "Discount luxury" hotel operator **Bill Kimpton,** who also owns the new **Hotel Vintage Park,** recently took over the Alexis, too. ♦ 1007 First Ave. 624.4844, 800/426.7033; fax 621.9009

Within the Alexis Hotel:

The Bookstore Bar This is a better taproom than it was a place for bibliophiles. Yet the Bookstore, with its shelves full of literary volumes, maintains some air of its previous incarnation. The atmosphere is conducive to political discussions and after-work jousts with colleagues, but there are too many windows to make this a proper trysting spot. Appetizers are brought over from the hotel's **Painted Table** restaurant, and there are microbrews on tap. ♦ M-Th 11:30AM-midnight; F-Su 11:30AM-2AM. 624.4844

The Painted Table ★★★$$$ After stints at Seattle's **Place Pigalle,** at the **One Eleven** (a small restaurant in Ketcham, Idaho), and as the co-chef at the **Cafe Alexis** when it occupied this corner of the Alexis Hotel, chef **Emily Moore** is trying hard to infuse energy and color into a location that's seen several restaurant failures in the past. Maybe she's trying a bit too hard, as some of her creations (like the polychromatic ceramic dinnerware they're served on) are more novel than they are transporting. Where she does shine, though, is with such things as crab cakes, most salmon entrées, and a risotto with wild mushrooms. And her chocolate desserts are sublime. The space is cavernous and hung with art, a pleasant room except for the jarring rock music that sometimes seeps in through the speakers. ♦ Northwestern ♦ M-Th 6-10AM, 11:30AM-2PM, 5:30-10PM; F 6-10AM, 11:30AM-2PM, 5:30-10:30PM; Sa 6:30AM-noon, 5:30-10:30PM; Su 7AM-noon, 5:30-10PM. Reservations recommended. 624.3646

Seattle's *Virginia V,* built in 1922 as part of Puget Sound's Mosquito Fleet and still chartered for celebratory cruises, is the last inland-water, passenger-carrying steamer operating west of the Mississippi.

Cajun Corner ★$ Just when you think you've got a handle on this joint, it changes its name and its raison d'être. Not many years ago, this was **The Mark Tobey,** catering to a literary crowd; later, it was transformed into the **Cajun Corner,** with plastic crocodiles dangling from the ceiling; then, just after Emily Moore took command of the **Painted Table** upstairs, she re-created this spot as the **Volcano Cafe,** with a promising menu that pulled from sources all over the volcanic Pacific Rim. But loyal fans apparently forced a Cajun comeback. For now, anyway.

Dark wood appointments, including a handsome vintage bar, suggest a comfort and old-world camaraderie that aren't backed up by the service (slow and careless) or the clientele (sparse, male-oriented, and still too young to be colorful). The menu has retreated sadly from its Moore-ish refinements to a bevy of bayou standbys: a decent but not outstanding gumbo; a shirt-splashing array of catfish, mussels, and rock shrimp in Creole rum sauce; a fine rendition of red beans and rice; and several sandwiches, among which the most memorable may be the stewed pork number. At press time, the Volcano's schedule of bands had been discontinued, but operators insisted that live music will be returning to the **Cajun Corner** (or whatever it's called that week). Parking around here can be a problem. ◆ Cajun ◆ M-Th 11:30AM-1AM; F-Sa 11:30AM-2AM; Su 5-11:30PM. 90 Madison St. 682.5019

The Legacy The collection of historic baskets, masks, and carvings from Northwest Indians and Eskimos is rounded out with some newer native merchandise. ◆ M-Sa 10AM-6PM. 624.6350

45 Warshal's Sporting Goods An anachronism on increasingly chic First Avenue, Warshal's has occupied this post-Great Fire edifice for half a century. Aside from its broad selection of hunting, fishing, and other equipment, Warshal's also carries photography and darkroom supplies. Look for frequent specials. ◆ M-Sa 9AM-5:30PM. 1000 First Ave. 624.7300

46 Old Federal Office Building Looking very much like a snow-capped mountain range, what with its brick facing topped by terracotta detailing, this memorable stepped-back Art Deco structure was one of the few projects raised in downtown during the Depression. The architect was **James A. Wetmore.** ◆ 909 First Ave

47 Henry M. Jackson Federal Office Building With its hipped and tiled roof, as well as a fenestration of interlocking, prefab concrete segments, this tower (designed by **Fred Bassetti,** along with **John Graham & Company**) gives off a sort of Mediterranean palazzo feel. The lobby appeals with its wood finishes, but the star of this building is its outdoor cascading hillside stairs, which include remnants of **Elmer Fisher's** 1889 Victorian **Burke Building,** torn down to make room for this 1974 tower.

Before the Burke Building took over this site, it held what was once this city's most ostentatious landmark: the **Frye Opera House,** mansard-roofed atop brick walls, featuring 1,400 seats and a stage punctured with seven trapdoors. The 1889 fire began at this intersection, in a woodworker's basement. Sculptor **Isamu Noguchi** contributed an abstract grouping of pink granite blocks, called *Landscape of Time,* to the Second Avenue plaza. ◆ Bounded by First and Second Aves and Marion and Madison Sts

48 Colman Building Scottish immigrant **James M. Colman's** namesake structure had trouble getting off the ground in more ways than one. A mechanic and a steam-mill operator, Colman first acquired this property by running a ship aground here long enough to earn legal title; he planned simply to build over the hull. But his original, very ornate design (conceived by architect **Stephen Meany** before the Great Fire of 1889) was stunted by Colman's business caution after the blaze. He went ahead with only the concept's first two stories, waiting to see what demand there was for more office and commercial space in the rapidly rebuilding city. Not until about 1904 did architect **August Tidemand** completely revamp floors one and two in brownstone style, and then add four more austere brick stories above those to form the basic edifice you see today. In 1930 Seattle architect **Arthur B. Loveless** performed another remodeling that incorporated several Art Deco elements into the glazed street canopy and lobby. ◆ 811 First Ave

49 Metsker Maps Joseph Conrad captured the appeal of maps best in his novel *Heart of Darkness,* when Marlowe explained: "Now, when I was a little chap, I had a passion for maps. I would look for hours at South America, or Africa, or Australia, and lose myself in all the glories of exploration." Marlowe might have begun many a voyage at Metsker, which sells hundreds of maps as well as guidebooks and assorted travel paraphernalia to satisfy the hunger of wanderlust. ◆ M-Tu, Th-F 9AM-5PM; W 9AM-6PM; Sa 11AM-5PM. 702 First Ave. 623.8747

Restaurants/Clubs: Red   **Hotels:** Blue
Shops/ 🌲 Outdoors: Green   **Sights/Culture:** Black

49 La Buca ★★$$ Another Italian restaurant—just what Seattle needs, right? But with a couple of familiar powerhouses behind it (**Luigi DeNunzio,** formerly of **Al Boccalino** in Pioneer Square, and **Raffaele Calise,** who helped create the popular **Salute** restaurants), this new one has a better-than-average chance of survival. Stuck below street level (the restaurant's name means "The Hole"), in an orange-walled space once occupied by the ancient **Skid Road Theater,** La Buca specializes in Southern Italian cuisine.

There's lots of chicken and veal, whole-wheat pasta, and calamari. Favorite dishes include the tenderloin of pork sautéed and served with red-pepper sauce and olives, and the *risotto di mare* (arborio rice bobbing with prawns, mussels, and clams, all accented with saffron). The kitchen also turns out some savory fish specials, particularly halibut. Forget the grilled and marinated prawns, though. And two cautions: main courses are served small, so don't pass up the first-course selection; and the ambient noise level can be high, so go somewhere else to make an intimate marriage proposal. ◆ Southern Italian ◆ M-Th 11:30AM-2:30PM, 5:30-11PM; F-Sa 5:30PM-midnight; Su 5:30-10:30PM. 102 Cherry St. Reservations recommended. 343.9517

50 Western Coffee Shop ★$ So narrow you couldn't get a respectable horse through here, **Niko** and **Jeanie Rondos'** charmingly campy coffee shop is an omnium-gatherum of little plastic cowboys, spurs, and black-and-whites from the Old West era. A counter up front (the best place to be) gives way to a handful of booths in back. The cooking technology here seems to have progressed little since "Bonanza." Yet even Hop Sing probably couldn't turn out such pleasantly filling grub as the Western's omelets, corned-beef hash, and chunky hash browns. For lunch do not, by any means, pass up the thick meat-loaf sandwiches. Creamy espresso milk shakes come with the metal shaker full of whatever wouldn't fit in your glass. It's crowded on weekends but worth the wait. ◆ Coffeehouse ◆ M-F 7AM-3PM; Sa 8AM-3PM; Su 9AM-3PM. 911 ½ Western Ave. 682.5001

Pier 54, now the Waterfront home of Ye Olde Curiosity Shop, is remembered by old-timers as the place where, in 1940, Two-Ton Tony Galento, a 350-pound boxer, climbed into a tank of seawater to wrestle a 75-pound octopus. Brokered by the late Seattle restaurateur Ivar Haglund, the bout ended in a draw. No word on whether Two-Ton Tony ever ate calamari again.

51 Italia ★★$ Like the blind men's fabled elephant, high-ceilinged Italia can be many things to many people, depending on their focus. It's part deli-cafeteria (with glorious pasta salads), part art gallery, and part sit-down restaurant, with occasional adventures as a lecture hall (art talks are given the second Thursday of every month).

Italia turns out superb king salmon with roasted-fennel salsa, cheese-filled tortellini with brown butter and sage, and great lunchtime pizzas covered in wild mushrooms, caramelized onions, and spinach, or with chicken, basil, tomatoes, and scallions. The fragrantly herbed focaccia and a couple of Northwest beers could easily satisfy you for a light dinner. Water, strangely, is served only by request. ◆ Italian ◆ M-F 7AM-10PM; Sa 10AM-10:30PM; Su 5-9PM. 1010 Western Ave. Reservations recommended. 623.1917

52 Tlaquepaque ★$$ Its obscure position (on an alley beneath an exit ramp from Highway 99) seems to have had little negative effect on this boisterous restaurant and cantina. Other places may open up nearby, yet Tlaquepaque still draws the crowds. The combo dinner platters (with mesquite chicken, *chile con queso,* roasted *camitas,* and a refreshing mango salsa) are prepared for two to five eaters, and they are the best bargain and an ideal way to sample the kitchen's depth. The bar provides the liveliest environment, with 'tenders specializing in margaritas (order them blended). A discount happy hour runs all day Sunday. ◆ Mexican ◆ M-Th, Su 11:30AM-11:30PM; F-Sa 11:30AM-2AM. 1122 Post Ave. Reservations recommended. 467.8226

In the Market for a Good Time?

Think of Pike Place Market as a separate village within a city, one that claims its own rules of conduct, its own traditions, its own unique style and pace. You really need a kindly old uncle or aunt to show you the ropes, but barring that option, here are a few tips for getting the most out of Seattle's spiritual nexus.

● Show up here early in the morning (between 7AM and 8AM) to see the farmers and craftspeople setting up their colorful stalls. If your goal is to find the best choice of fresh foodstuffs, come between 8AM and 11AM, before lunchers descend upon the market. And if you're hoping to score last-minute discounts on the day's still-unsold edibles, arrive at about 4:30PM.

● Vendors new to the market don't have enough seniority to earn display space on weekends, so they tend to bring their novel works to the market Monday through Friday. You'll find more familiar, longtime craftspeople here on weekends.

● Just as it is impolite in foreign countries to bargain for goods and then choose not to buy them, it also is considered gauche in the market to listen for any length of time to street musicians without contributing at least a few coins to their buckets or violin cases.

● Despite recent discussions about making Pike Place a car-free zone, the market just wouldn't be the same without the constant jockeying of humans and autos here. If you're happy to move at slug speed, stay on the crowded sidewalks. Otherwise, step right onto the brick-covered street and walk with the cars. Just keep a wary eye out for drivers wheeling in and out of the angled parking spaces.

● The odds of finding a parking spot around Pike Place are poor at best. Try, instead, the 550-space **Market Garage** just west of the **North Arcade,** off Western Avenue, which allows free parking with shopping validations from many market merchants. On-street parking is easiest to find heading north of the market, between Bell Street and Denny Way. Avoid parking lots along First Avenue, as they tend to be overpriced.

● Do not depend on market merchants to choose your produce. The best way to get the quality you pay for is to paw lightly over the foodstuffs yourself—no matter how much sellers try to discourage this practice.

● Two sets of public restrooms are available in the market. One is at the south end of the **Main Arcade,** downstairs from **Pike Place Fish.** The other can be found at the Main Arcade's north end, by descending the ramp adjacent to **City Fish.**

● One-hour tours of the market are scheduled on Saturday mornings, at either 9AM or 10:30AM, depending on the availability of guides. They set out from the **Market Information Booth,** at the corner of First Avenue and Pike Street. The charge is $5 per person and reservations are required. Call 682.7453 for weekly schedules and to sign up for an informative walk.

53 Current The high-style moderne furniture that turns up in these expansive showrooms is unquestionably elegant. All rooms are well represented, with a special focus on sconce lighting. The prices, unfortunately, can be quite steep. ◆ M-Sa 10AM-6PM; Su noon-5PM. 1201 Western Ave. 622.2433

54 Seattle Bagel Bakery Lines are long on weekends, as aspiring brunchers slip in for supplies of pumpernickel, onion, or salt bagels. Even with lox or cream cheese on top, the soft rings continue to command attention.

Along with **The Spot** in Wallingford, this is one of Seattle's top bagelries. ◆ Bakery ◆ Daily 7:30AM-5:30PM. 1302 Western Ave. 624.2187

55 Wild Ginger ★★★$$$ The *satay* bar here was the first of its kind in the nation and continues to be a main event. You can just hang out, enjoying the grilled chunks of chicken, beef, prawns, or veggies on skewers that are served with a zingy peanut or soy black vinegar sauce, or take a place in the dining room and order *satay* appetizers. The fragrant Wandering Sage soup is another house specialty. The seafood, particularly the scallops, is delicious, as are the beef curry and a sweetly flavored duck. Specials are influenced by cooking from around the Pacific Rim and are based on what's seasonally fresh. ◆ Asian ◆ M-Th 11:30AM-3PM, 5-11PM; F-Sa 11:30AM-3PM, 5PM-midnight; Su 5-11PM. Satay bar open daily until 2AM. 1400 Western Ave. 623.4450

56 Seattle Aquarium Designed by **Fred Bassetti and Company** in 1977, this Waterfront institution attracts visitors with its more-than-generous complement of tanks holding marine exotica, its "touching tank" where children can pet a starfish, and the playful clans of seals and sea otters that occupy its upper reaches. (Look for feeding-time notices: it's the best time to watch these jesters.) The aquarium's bowels are full with a glorious domed room where sharks, octopi, and myriad Puget Sound natives swim. Expect to spend at least two to three hours inside. ♦ Admission; discount for senior citizens, handicapped persons, children age three to five, King County residents, and groups of 10 or more; free for children age two and under. Daily 10AM-7PM Memorial Day-Labor Day; daily 10AM-5PM Labor Day-Memorial Day. Pier 59. 386.4320

57 Waterfront Park A soothing "boardwalk" hugging Elliott Bay, the elevated walkways here give you a better perspective on the city and the Sound. It's a good place for picnics, offering a superfluity of fish, hot dogs, and ice-cream parlors nearby. Long gone is adjacent **Pier 58,** where the first cargo of tea from the Orient arrived in 1896 and where the *Portland* steamer anchored in 1897 with the first news that gold had been discovered in the Klondike, but a plaque still recalls the beginning of Alaska's gold rush. The minipark was designed in 1974 by the **Bumgardner Partnership.** ♦ Pier 57

58 Elliott's Oyster House & Seafood Restaurant ★★$$$ Water views, fast service, and some of the best oysters in town are served here. ♦ Seafood ♦ M-Th, Su 11AM-10PM; F-Sa 11AM-11PM. Pier 56. 623.4340

59 Ye Olde Curiosity Shop A great mecca for tourist-trinket junkies, founded in 1899, this shop carries rubber slugs, souvenir Seattle T-shirts, Russian nesting dolls, seashells, scrimshaw, and shrunken heads—they're all here, alongside Barnum-esque oddities such as a bottled pig with eight legs, three eyes, three mouths, and a pair of tails. Most popular is Sylvester—the Desert Mystery, a mummified murder victim of about 45 (he was found in the Arizona sandflats in 1895 with a bullet through his stomach) who still bears a mustache and fingernails. ♦ M-Th, Su 9:30AM-6PM; F-Sa 9AM-9PM. Pier 54. 682.5844

60 Ivar's Acres of Clams and Fish Bar ★$ **Ivar Haglund,** who died just a few years back, was Seattle's quintessential promoter. He's remembered for his corny commercial slogan (Keep Clam), his guitar playing and storytelling, and the carp wind sock that he ran up the flagpole on **Smith Tower** when he owned that building, beginning in 1976. The several Ivar's restaurants he left behind (including **Ivar's Captain's Table,** 333 Elliott Avenue West) serve okay seafood; best choices are usually the clam nectar and the cod-and-chips. But the outdoor seating at this location—Haglund's first—can hardly be beat for Seattle charm. A sentimental statue of Haglund feeding gulls sits nearby. ♦ Seafood ♦ M-Th, Su 11AM-10PM; F-Sa 11AM-11PM. Pier 54. 624.6852

61 Colman Dock Elliott Bay's worst docking collision occurred here in April 1912, when the ocean liner *Alameda* charged right into this pier, toppling its previously elegant clock tower into the drink. The *Alameda* suffered barely a scratch. The clock from the tower was retrieved after the collision, and restored; you can see it inside. It wasn't the first time that Colman Dock was rebuilt, nor would it be the last. The original wharf went up by order of Scottish immigrant **James Colman** in 1882. The current, modern incarnation is its sixth and least interesting, dating back only to 1966. **Washington State Ferries** leave from here many times daily, bound for **Bainbridge** and **Vashon** islands (call 464.6400 for ferry schedules). ♦ Pier 52

62 Washington Street Public Boat Landing Built in 1920 from a design by city architect **Daniel R. Huntington,** this iron-and-steel pergola (pictured above)—much less ornate than the older Pioneer Place pergola only two blocks to the east—was intended to house Seattle's harbor master and be the entry point for visiting seamen. Now rehabilitated, it is more a curiosity than anything else, being located near **Pier 48** but away from other Waterfront landmarks. Watch for it on the Waterfront streetcar ride. ♦ Alaskan Way (at Washington St)

The world's first gas station opened on the Seattle Waterfront in 1907. It was the bright idea of John McLean, head of sales in Washington state for Standard Oil (Chevron) of California. He set up his station at the corner of Holgate Street and Western Avenue, next to Standard Oil's depot. As Adam Woog writes in *Sexless Oysters and Self-Tipping Hats: 100 Years of Invention in the Pacific Northwest,* "[McLean] and engineer Henry Harris then rigged a feed line leading from their main storage tank (housed at what was then called a 'bulk station') to a 30-gallon, six-foot-high galvanized tank equipped with a glass gauge and a valve-controlled dispensing hose. . . . The rest is petroleum history."

Bests

Mark Hinshaw
Architect/Urban Designer

The early 20th century elevators at **Smith Tower** are elegant, glass-enclosed vertiginous vehicles that are finer than anything ever done by architect John Portman.

The Pink Door—There's no advertising and no sign. This is Seattle's best-kept secret (they serve Italian food). Can you find it?

Cafe Septième might be found in Paris' seventh arrondissement, but it's here at Second Avenue and Battery Street, too. Clever little courtyard.

Fishermen's Terminal represents the *real* Seattle. Hundreds of fishing boats and not one T-shirt shop. Order mussels at **Chinook's.**

Bon Marché—Sorry, **Nordstrom,** your neighbor is classier.

Walt Crowley
Writer/Retired Activist/And the guy on the Left of "Point-Counterpoint" debates on KIRO-TV News

If you're a tourist based in a downtown hotel, here's a model day: Start with breakfast in **Pike Place Market** (at the **Athenian Inn, Lowell's,** or **Cafe Sport**) and walk around watching the farmers and craftspeople as they open their stalls for business. Descend the **Hillclimb Corridor** to visit the **Seattle Aquarium,** then walk or ride the streetcar south along the **Waterfront** to **Pioneer Square** to browse and shop. You could lunch there or hop back on the streetcar to the **International District** for more exotic fare.

After lunch, take the bus tunnel from downtown north to University Street. Hop off and walk half a block over to the new **Seattle Art Museum,** where you'll probably spend the rest of the day.

My favorite way to blow an afternoon includes lunch at the **Athenian Inn** or **Emmett Watson's Oyster Bar** (one of Pike Place Market's coziest crannies), or a quick curry beef *hum baos* from **Mee Sum Pastries,** a pint or two of Harp at **Kell's,** and a browse at **MisterE Books, Read All About It** newsstand, the **Old Seattle Paperworks,** or all of the above.

Now preserved as an unofficial cultural landmark, the **Blue Moon Tavern** has hosted radicals, poets, novelists, beatniks, hippies, academics, crackpots, and the occasional normal person since 1934. It's at 712 NE 45th Street, just off Interstate 5.

The **Two Bells Tavern**—**Patricia Ryan** and her crew cook the best hamburgers in town (served with the most delicious potato salad), and **Rolon Bert Garner** has turned this tiny tavern's walls into one of Seattle's most interesting art galleries. You'll find it at Bell Street and Fourth Avenue.

The **Virginia Inn**—Under the sensitive management of **Patrice Demonbynes,** old-timers and newcomers mingle here without friction or displacement. Located at Virginia Street and First Avenue.

An authentic (if modernized) hangout for commercial fishers working on the adjacent docks, **The Highliner** serves great fish-and-chips and a wide array of burgers and sandwiches. The nearby *Fisherman's Memorial,* sculpted by **Ron Petty,** is a powerful monument to the many men and women who never returned from the sea. The Highliner is at Fishermen's Terminal on Salmon Bay.

La Boheme—This Greenwood joint is a classic Seattle neighborhood tavern housed in a miniature chalet. In fact, it's my neighborhood tavern and it's already too crowded so I won't list the address.

America's original **Skid Road** in **Pioneer Square** is still a little raw around the edges, especially after dark—although this doesn't discourage the culture crowd from making the rounds of the area's many art galleries when they turn over their shows on the first Thursday of each month. Take the funky but informative **Underground Seattle** tour. The **Central Tavern** is my sentimental favorite for a beer, and it's a popular music venue at night. The nearby **Elliott Bay Book Company** has a literate staff, a huge selection of books, and a basement cafeteria where evening readings draw large audiences.

The **Seattle Aquarium,** a jewel on the Waterfront, features an underwater dome often inhabited by members of the world's largest species of octopus.

Consistently rated one of the nation's 10 best, Seattle's **Woodland Park Zoo** is a world leader in creating naturalistic habitats for its specimens. It now boasts two troops of lowland gorillas who are breeding like, well, gorillas.

Green Lake offers a pleasant two-mile-plus walk, jog, or skate around its perimeter. The adjacent **Bathhouse Theatre** is home to one of Seattle's best acting companies.

Historic Theaters—The Chinese-style **Fifth Avenue Theater** is the best preserved and features Broadway shows; the **Paramount** is the largest and grandest and hosts major pop acts. The **Moore** is the oldest (built in 1908) and boasts the best acoustics for everything from grunge bands to chamber music. The **Coliseum** (the first theater in America designed expressly to show movies) is protected as a historic landmark but will soon house a retail store. The **Eagles Auditorium** was the hub of Seattle's rock scene in the 1960s, but its future is unclear.

The **Museum of Flight**—Aerophiles must visit **Boeing's** original "Red Barn" factory. Scores of vintage aircraft such as a Boeing Model 80 trimotor biplane, one of the few flyable B-17s left, and a recently retired Lockheed SR-71 "Blackbird" are housed in a modern gallery or parked on the tarmac.

The **Space Needle**—This futuristic lingam has stood the test of time and taste since it was built for the 1962 World's Fair—despite the unfortunate addition of a banquet hall at the 100-foot level that makes the thing look like it dropped its drawers down around its ankles.

Belltown/Seattle Center

By whichever name you know it—Belltown or the **Denny Regrade** district—this area just north of downtown Seattle represents a forgotten heap of dreams, abandoned like old toys in the attic. During the late 19th century one of Seattle's original band of settlers, **William Bell**, hoped to create a vital commercial nexus here, but he died before his plans could amount to much. Between 1906 and 1911 city engineer **Reginald H. Thomson** ordered that 3,000-foot-high **Denny Hill**, which

Lake Union

Prospect St.

Ward St.

Aloha St.

← Valley St.

2 ← Roy St.

Mercer St. →

79

78

77

76

Ward St.

Aloha St.

Valley St.

74

73

75

Valley St.

80

Broad St.

Fairview Ave. N.

I-5

5th Ave. N.

Taylor Ave. N.

6th Ave. N.

Rte. 99/Aurora Ave. N.

Dexter Ave. N.

8th Ave. N.

9th Ave. N.

Westlake Ave. N.

Terry Ave. N.

Boren Ave. N.

Republican St.

Harrison St.

81

Fairview Ave. N.

Minor Ave. N.

Pontius Ave. N.

Yale Ave. N.

Eastlake Ave. N.

Melrose Ave. E.

Thomas St.

45

44

John St.

46 Denny Park

Denny Wy.

43

42

37

36

47

48

Wall St.

8th Ave.

34

7th Ave.

35

Battery St.

40

38

6th Ave.

33

Westlake Ave. N.

Boren Ave.

Terry Ave.

9th Ave.

Howell St.

41

39

Monorail

5th Ave.

31

32

16 17

18

4th Ave.

28

30

29

Olive Wy.

8th Ave.

7th Ave.

I-5

7 19

20 21

22

27

Bell St.

6 3

5 4

Blanchard St.

23

24 26

25

Pine St.

Lenora St.

2

Virginia St.

1

Stewart St.

3rd Ave.

Pike St.

2nd Ave.

6th Ave.

5th Ave.

4th Ave.

Spring St.

Madison St.

Rte. 99/Alaskan Wy. Viaduct

Waterfront Streetcar

Pike Place Market ■

Western Ave.

1st Ave.

University St.

used to loom up from the corner of Second Avenue and Virginia Street, be sluiced into **Elliott Bay**. The regrading was supposed to inspire business development by making the neighborhood flatter and thus easier to traverse. The hint, however, fell mostly upon deaf ears.

In 1911 internationally known engineer **Virgil Bogue** uncorked a plan that would have made the Belltown intersection of Fourth Avenue and Blanchard Street the new focus of downtown Seattle. A former assistant to landscape architect **Frederick Law Olmsted,** Bogue proposed the construction of a civic center that would stretch from this intersection all the way northeast to **Lake Union.** It would feature boulevards, federal buildings, a courthouse, a library, an art museum, a showy new city hall, and a 15-story memorial tower—amenities to recast dowdy Seattle as a major metropolitan player. Bogue was an urban visionary, but his plan didn't excite the city's business establishment, which feared a devaluation of their downtown property, and they encouraged voters to reject the civic-center proposal in 1912.

It wasn't until 1962, with construction of the **Century 21 Exposition** and the landmark **Space Needle** in Lower Queen Anne, that Belltown made the leap from historical dreaming to futuristic fantasizing. This **World's Fair** was "The Jetsons" incarnate, a spectacle that *Life* magazine called "out of this world." **Attorney General Robert Kennedy**, actors **John Wayne** and **Danny Kaye, Prince Philip** of England, and even **Lassie** showed up to take a gander. **Elvis Presley** arrived amid a wail of shrieking teenagers to shoot a not-so-good film called *It Happened at the World's Fair.*

This neighborhood still inspires dreams, but now they're more of the bohemian and artistic sort. Secondhand shops, bookstores, art galleries, and coffeehouses have sprung up in buildings vacated long ago by more conventional businesses, and Belltown is rapidly becoming the center of Seattle's dance-club scene, attracting a wide roster of rock and "grunge" bands. Restaurants, which once eschewed Belltown as just too far from the city's critical office mass, are likewise moving into this district, trailing fashion showrooms and condominium complexes. And while a recent spate of drug-related crimes at the south end of Belltown (near the corner of First Avenue and Virginia Street) has encouraged caution at dusk, the area's growth has not been stemmed.

Since the heyday of the 1962 World's Fair, the fairgrounds have become **Seattle Center,** the closest thing this city has to a genuine community center. Thousands of people crowd in here annually for events such as the **Northwest Folklife Festival** (held in May) and **Bumbershoot** (a music and arts celebration held in September). Parents bring their children to visit the museums; teens hang out with their friends at the amusement park, gobble pizza in **Center House,** and attend dances and karaoke competitions; and the Space Needle remains a popular upscale dating destination. Sporting events, ranging from national-league basketball (the **Seattle SuperSonics**) to high-school football, take place in the **Coliseum,** the **Arena,** and at **High School Memorial Stadium.** Several stages here deliver theater and musical productions, and there's a proposal in the works to create the world's first museum dedicated to the memory and music of local-boy-made-good **Jimi Hendrix.** William Bell would no doubt be proud to know that dreaming is still fashionable at this end of the city.

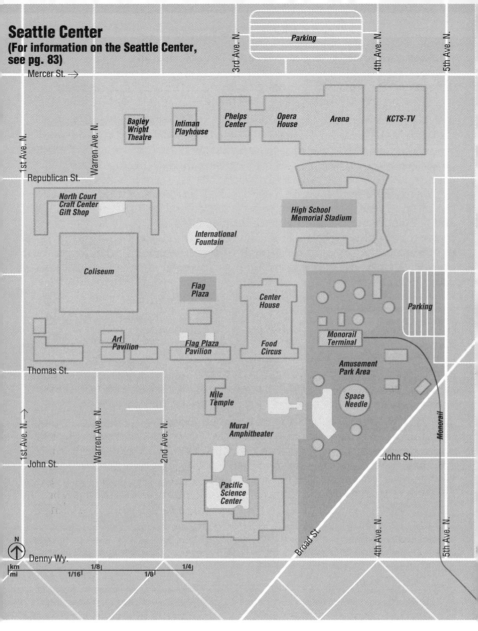

Seattle Center
(For information on the Seattle Center, see pg. 83)

Mercer St. →

3rd Ave. N.   4th Ave. N.   5th Ave. N.

Parking

Bagley Wright Theatre

Intiman Playhouse

Phelps Center

Opera House

Arena

KCTS-TV

1st Ave. N.   Warren Ave. N.

Republican St.

North Court Craft Center Gift Shop

High School Memorial Stadium

International Fountain

Coliseum

Flag Plaza

Center House

Parking

Monorail Terminal

Art Pavilion

Flag Plaza Pavilion

Food Circus

Amusement Park Area

Thomas St.

Nile Temple

Space Needle

Warren Ave. N.   2nd Ave. N.

Mural Amphitheater

1st Ave. N. →

John St.   John St.

4th Ave. N.   5th Ave. N.

Monorail

Pacific Science Center

N

Denny Wy.

km   1/8   1/4
mi   1/16   1/8

Broad St.

1 Gravity Bar ★$ This chic establishment has literally moved up in the world, from a slope just above **Pike Place Market** to the former and more spacious quarters of the *raison d'être* restaurant in the **Terminal Sales Building.** But the move seems not to have affected the Gravity's laid-back attitude or its menu. Healthy vibes positively exude from this joint, what with all the pine nuts, sun-dried tomatoes, tuna, and brown rice being dished around. Even chili garners a politically correct spin here, resulting in something like a black-bean soup served with corn bread. Only the daring or truly reckless order the Gravity's signature wheat-grass juice, which is rather like mowing a lawn with your gums. Stick to the carrot-based libations or the hot apple, lemon, and ginger drink instead. Founded in 1986 by local ceramic artist **Laurrien Gilman,** the Gravity Bar has an atmosphere and a clientele that are distinctly artsy.
♦ Vegetarian ♦ M-W 8AM-10PM; Th-Sa 8AM-11PM; Su 9AM-6PM. 113 Virginia St. 448.8826. Also at: 415 Broadway East. 325.7186

"They're backpacky, but nice."

The New Yorker, in a cartoon about residents of Seattle

2 Vogue This nightclub seems to attract lots of black outfits, women with rings in their noses, men with rings in their nipples, and bad-nightmare art. The small dance floor is filled with writhing limbs. You can tell things are really cooking when the waiters and waitresses start gyrating on the counter instead of bringing you a drink. ♦ Cover. Daily 7PM-2AM. 2018 First Ave. 443.0673

3 Jet City Take a neon-illumined trip down memory lane, complete with tables full of ashtrays and chromed toasters, walls covered in old movie posters and Marilyn Monroe images, and a smattering of bubblegum and pinball machines. This shop makes for terrific browsing and offers reasonable prices. ♦ Daily noon-6PM. 2200 First Ave. 728.7118

4 Queen City Grill ★★$$ The high-design interior clashes somewhat with the casual style craved by this restaurant, just off **Pike Place Market,** but it remains a comfortable setting. Much of the credit goes to co-owners **Peter Lamb** (also responsible for **Il Bistro** in the market) and **Steven Good,** as well as to chef **Paul Michael,** who does marvelously simple but wonderful things with grilled fish or meats and garlic. Now, if the portions would only grow to match the owners' ambitions. ♦ American ♦ M-Th 11:30AM-11PM; F 11:30AM-midnight; Sa 5PM-midnight. 2201 First Ave. 443.0975

5 Duo Walking south from this women's clothing store, you'll soon encounter a menswear mate to it, **Uno.** Not surprisingly, the shops are owned by a husband and wife, **Donald Fletcher** and **Roni Vincent-Fletcher.** Duo caters to women who wish to appear dressy and a bit daring without donning too many frills, wearing all black, or going completely into hock. ♦ M-Sa 10AM-6PM; Su noon-5PM. 2209 First Ave. 448.7011

6 Casa-U-Betcha ★★$ A gift from Portland, Oregon, where the first Casa was opened to raves in the mid-'80s, this ultrahip "tacoria" has two things going for it: the blue margaritas (stupid looking but quite tasty) and the blue margaritas, for they help you forget that what you're eating here bears only a passing resemblance to anything served south of the border. But you don't come here for traditional dishes, now do you? You come because, despite naysayers, Casa-U-Betcha is still a happenin' place full of happenin' people eddying up to the bar and the too-loud dining room to look for their beautiful happenin' *compadres.*

The food is filling, and an occasional stew or grilled meat is *muy bueno,* but on the whole, meals are just okay. People come here for the shiny decor, for the karaoke singing (Mondays and Sundays from 10PM on) or because they've never before had a Jell-O shooter made with tequila. (It sounds better than it is.) ♦ Southwestern/Mexican ♦ M-F 11:30AM-4PM, 5-11PM; Sa-Su 5-11PM. Bar open daily until 2AM. 2212 First Ave. 441.1026

7 Odd Fellows Hall/Austin A. Bell Building The connected brick structures you see here, plus the **Hull Building** kitty-corner across First Avenue, are about all that remain of an ambitious 19th-century scheme to develop Belltown as a commercial hot spot. The architect was **Elmer Fisher,** who put his substantial Romanesque Revival stamp all over **Pioneer Square,** but the larger promotion was the brainchild of pioneer **William Bell** and his son, **Austin Americus Bell.**

In 1883 William Bell erected the impressive four-story, mansard-roofed **Bell Hotel** (subsequently renamed the **Bellevue Hotel**) at the corner of Battery Street and what's now First Avenue. Four years later the elder Bell died from a "softening of the brain" that had brought on fits and confusion. Young Austin came north from his home in California, to attend the funeral and claim his inheritance. In 1888, while architect Fisher was working on a new hall for the Odd Fellows fraternal group two doors south of the Bellevue Hotel, Austin commissioned him to design a compatible apartment building that would fit between the hall and the hotel. This was to be Austin's first big mark on Seattle and though he'd suffered from periodic depression, he seemed enlivened by the project. He used to take people by the apartment property, explaining to them his dream. But in the spring of 1889, after a hearty breakfast and a stroll to his office, he wrote a shaky note to his wife and then shot himself in the head. He was 35, the same age his father had been when he carved out the clearing that would become Belltown. Friends claimed that Austin feared the mental deterioration that had consumed his father. In any case, his wife, Eva, completed Austin's handsome structure and named it in his honor.

The Bellevue Hotel has long since vanished, and the Odd Fellows Hall is now the **2320 First Avenue Building,** its upper stories warrened with offices. But the Austin A. Bell Building has been boarded up, a disheveled and desperate ghost of a tormented man's big, big dream. ♦ 2320 First Ave (between Bell and Battery Sts)

The Odd Fellows Hall (now the 2320 First Avenue Building) once played host to comedian W.C. Fields. Novelist Tom Robbins lived in the building in the mid-1980s; he says he was once visited there by Timothy Leary, who declared the place haunted.

DoWnuNder

8 Down Under The music at this sizable club is a blend of Top-40/MTV mainstays with a touch of hip hop. As always, much depends on the DJ. It's worth stopping by but shouldn't be the focus of anyone's evening. There's live music on Monday, jazz on Wednesday, and a fashion show of locally made clothes on Thursday. ♦ Cover. M 8PM-2AM; W-Th 9PM-2AM; F-Sa 9PM-4AM. 2407 First Ave. 728.4053

9 Cyclops ★★$$ If "funky" were considered a negative quality, people would never come within a mile of this place, cluttered inside and out with heaps and piles of kitschy detritus. Its walls glow purple, green, and yellow from a perverse series of paintings and torrents of bizarre music wash out of the sound system (Jewish klezmer music is a common choice). But some surprisingly good fare is on the menu: Italian, Russian, French, vegetarian—the proprietors aren't afraid to experiment and are seemingly incapable of botching anything. Their credo is: We *Never* Serve French Fries. So what if the help is a little surly? This food is worth the abuse. Cyclops' hours accommodate late-nighters. ♦ Continental/American ♦ M-Th 9AM-midnight; F 9AM-4AM; Sa 10AM-4AM; Su 10AM-midnight. 2416 Western Ave. 441.1677

10 Edgewater Inn $$ Rooms here literally hang out west over Puget Sound, affording marvelous scenery during the day and fresh salt air. At one time this hotel rented fishing poles to guests who wished to wet a line from their rooms (the **Beatles** were supposed to have indulged in this sport during an early visit here). But too many people made a mess while cleaning their catches, so the service was discontinued a few years ago when the hotel was remodeled. Water-side rooms are quietest, but city-view rooms are fine as well and cheaper. Parking is free, and the Edgewater contains a decent restaurant with a piano lounge, **Ernie's Bar & Grill** (★★$$). ♦ Pier 67. 728.7000; fax 441.4119

11 Pier 70 The **Ainsworth & Dunn Wharf** has stood at the north end of downtown Seattle's Waterfront for nearly a hundred years now. As a building it is a marvelous thing, with wide-plank flooring, rough-hewn log walls, and cavernous open spaces. (A history of this fine structure is mounted just inside the entrance.) As a place to shop, Pier 70 is considerably less interesting. ♦ Alaskan Way at Broad St

Within Pier 70:

Panos ★★$$ The original Panos was a lightning rod for lovers of Greek cuisine back in the 1980s, when it sat high atop Queen Anne Hill. Many foodies mourned owner **Panayotes Marinos'** decision to close shop and depart for Europe. But Marinos' return and his re-creation of Panos, in a bright new Waterfront location, left fans no less concerned: Would the food be as good as it was? Happily, the answer is a definitive yes.

As in the original restaurant, a rich moussaka is the primo menu pick, but the *keftedes* (spaghetti with meatballs and *mizithra* cheese) and *spanakopita* are not to be missed either. Even the soup with chicken, egg noodle, and lemon is far more interesting than its ingredients suggest. And the lightly fried squid rings may be the best in Seattle. The *aginares politikes,* a sort of soup with artichoke hearts, potato chunks, and carrots in an olive oil, lemon, and dill sauce, is too rich and not sufficiently complex. Overall the service is responsive, but the bouzouki music tends to blare, and both the wine and beer lists could be expanded and improved. ♦ Greek ♦ M-F 11:30AM-2:30PM, 5:30-10PM; Sa-Su 5:30-10PM. 2815 Alaskan Way. Reservations recommended. 441.5073

12 Waterfront Streetcar Seattle's original trolleys were stripped from service decades ago, but, for nostalgia's sake, Metro Transit imported these vintage machines out of Australia to make the clattering run from **Pier 70** through **Pioneer Square** to the **International District**. The 15- to 20-minute ride costs 85¢ for adults and children older than five, and $1.10 during weekday rush hour, 3PM to 6PM. ♦ Daily 7AM-9PM Mar-Sept; 7AM-6PM Oct-Feb. Alaskan Way at Broad St. 553.3000

13 Take It From Us ★$ Try the linguine salad with pine nuts and tomatoes, the sausage-and-peppers sandwich, the Greek potato salad with feta, and the corn chowder. There's even an appetizer bar, for the congenial grazer. Owned by **David** and **Sandra Brand** (he's a former senior writer for *Time* magazine, she's the real brains in the kitchen), this bright but

dinky cafe with mushroom photos all over the walls does a big lunch and carry-home trade. It's rather out of the way but worth discovering. Fax orders are accepted. ♦ Deli ♦ M-F 7:30AM-8PM. 2904 First Ave. 448.3442; fax 448.8827

14 Kaspar's by the Bay ★★$$ The fifth-story view toward Puget Sound is best appreciated at night, when interior candlelight softens the spartan ambience and Muzak rhythms. Owner/chef **Kaspar Donier,** who earned his kitchen bona fides at the Four Seasons in Vancouver, BC, backs up this outlook with a multicultural menu. Some of the dinner attractions include crab-and-salmon hash cakes topped with a mushroom sauce; seasonal asparagus spears in a marinade of olive oil, herbs, and garlic; and duck served in port wine and dried cherry sauce. The bar, lamentably jammed back by the kitchen door, leaves much to be desired, but its appetizer selection is not without distinction (try the pizzas, especially anything with chicken on top). ♦ Continental ♦ M 5-9PM; Tu-Th 11:30AM-2PM, 5-9PM; F 11:30AM-2PM, 5-10PM; Sa 5-10PM. 2701 First Ave. Reservations recommended. 441.4805

15 A-Jay's ★★$ Early risers should seek out this incredibly popular breakfast spot (beware of crowds, especially on Sundays), serving fluffy buttermilk pancakes in stacks of four, with real maple syrup on the side, and generously stuffed omelets all day long. The hash browns consist of great blocks of potato accented with onion. And in a city where it's near impossible to find old-fashioned black coffee, A-Jay's serves a pleasing cup. Early bird specials are available until 10AM. Lunches aren't such standouts, running to sandwiches and juicy burgers, but the service is always cheerful and the atmosphere unpretentious. ♦ American ♦ Daily 7AM-3PM. 2619 First Ave. 441.1511

16 Cafe Septième ★$ Welcome to Belltown central, a cozy atmospheric nosheria with excellent salads and sandwiches, hot entrées, desserts, and espresso, espresso, and more espresso. The fine coffees even come in handsome pottery bowls, the kind your mother told you never ever to drink from because it was rude. (Sorry, Mom.) The cafe is fine for reading but better for visiting with friends. Check out the wealth of magazines and newspapers scattered around. ♦ American ♦ M-F 7AM-midnight; Sa 9AM-midnight; Su 7AM-8:30PM. 2331 Second Ave. 448.1506

17 Rendezvous The primary battleground for the hearts and minds of Belltown, the bar here is worth a look, but in general steer clear of it unless trading triple scotches is your idea of a fun night out. Head instead straight for the **Jewelbox Theater** in back, surprisingly elegant (done up in what might be termed Cheesy Art Deco) and seductively comfortable. Entertainment includes an offbeat, highly imaginative, always interesting film series (Japanese monster flicks, jazz films, hippie movies, etc.) and a wildly uneven menu of live music, leaning toward down-on-the-world songs. ♦ Cover. W, F-Sa 9PM-2AM. 2320 Second Ave. 441.5823

18 2-11 Billiard Club Once upon a time this fine old establishment (with roots back to 1936) was located in downtown. But, to Belltown's eternal benefit, the club was forced to move north several years ago during construction of the **Metro Bus Tunnel.** Its regular clientele moved with it; they're the ones decorating the bar with their personal billiards equipment. Don't let this place intimidate you—pool-playing expertise is not registered at the door. The club's tables are adequate, although the cue sticks on hand are less so. The 2-11's best feature is its easy, laid-back atmosphere, conducive to hours of chasing the balls across a field of green felt. ♦ M-Sa 11AM-1:30AM; Su 3-11:30PM. 2304 Second Ave. 443.1211

19 Mama's Mexican Kitchen $ The atmosphere here is far more interesting than the food. Every inch of wall space is a witty adventure, overdecorated with Mexicana. Is there a stick of furniture at Mama's that matches any other? Probably not. Food comes in huge portions, with lots of taco and burrito plates and rice and beans on the side—a carbo-loader's fantasy. Little on the menu will blow you away, though. Come here when you desperately need a grease fix, or on a warm summer's night when you can fight for a table outside and eat basket upon basket of the saltless tortilla chips, washing it all down with Corona beer. ♦ Mexican ♦ Daily 11AM-10PM. 2234 Second Ave. 728.6262

Locals refer to Mount Rainier as "The Mountain," even though the city seems surrounded by noteworthy peaks. If someone says "The Mountain is out today," it doesn't mean that 14,410-foot-high Rainier has escaped its earthly tether, but that the frequent embrace of clouds has given way enough to see it.

20 **The Seattle Book Center** With mostly hard-cover stock for the collector, room after room of thoughtfully organized shelves wend across an upper floor. Walking through here is like reliving your childhood discovery of libraries: the possibilities seem endless, but you don't know exactly where to begin. The staff is friendly and helpful. ♦ M-Sa 10AM-5PM. 2231 Second Ave. 443.1533

21 **Hula's** Chockfull of 1950s and 1960s artifacts, this store has everything from pinball machines to radios, posters, and neon advertising signs. The prices are stiff, but the selection is good and the owner knowledgeable. ♦ M-F noon-6PM; Sa noon-8PM. 2222¾ Second Ave. 448.4767

21 **Dingo Gallery** Aficionados of World's Fair-era kitsch will find plenty artfully displayed here in about 10 rooms. The prices are not bad, but the real fun is soaking up the owner's impressive aesthetic in mounting and arranging each separate room. ♦ Tu-Sa 1-6PM. 2222½ Second Ave. 443.6935

21 **Signature Bound** The stock in this tiny bookstore is skimpy but well-chosen, running toward bohemian tastes of the '80s and '90s—selected classics, a smattering of science fiction, banned and obscure material, self-published 'zines, feminist tracts, and poetry. ♦ M-F noon-6:30PM; Sa 11AM-8PM. 2222 Second Ave. 441.3306

21 **Crocodile Cafe** ★$ During the day this cafe is an only periodically successful diner wanna-be. But at night the Crocodile turns into one of Seattle's most adventurous and intriguing rock clubs, booking cutting-edge acts from the city and around the country. Kitsch art crams every cranny and literally drips off both the ceiling and walls, even in the restroom. One of the more creative displays is the salad-fork mélange in the men's room. ♦ American ♦ Cover. Tu-F 7AM-2AM; Sa 8AM-2AM; Su 9AM-3PM. 2200 Second Ave. 448.2114; music information 441.5611

22 **Vonnie's, A Garden Cafe** ★$ This delightful garden-court bistro is surrounded by brick walls and focused on a gurgling fountain—a wonderful spot for Sunday brunch. Pasta and sandwiches may be the finest picks from the regular menu. The rotating menu of specials includes omelets and tender seafood. ♦ Continental/American ♦ Tu-W 11:30AM-2:30PM; Th-Sa 11:30AM-2:30PM, 5:30-9:30PM; Su 9AM-2:30PM. 120 Blanchard St. 441.1045

23 **Bethel Temple** Erected around 1915, this elegantly appointed terracotta edifice, designed by famed theater architect **B. Marcus Priteca**, originally housed the ritzy **Crystal Swimming Pool**. Where the corner of this structure now drops back to glass doorways and a lighted sign at Second Avenue and Blanchard Street, a huge metal dome used to rise over a pillared base. Model T's would drive up and disgorge youngsters here for an afternoon, or whole families would drop by for a dip. The only hint left to this building's early purpose may be the stylized green dolphins that decorate its roofline. It's now a Pentecostal church. ♦ 2033 Second Ave

24 **Bushell's Auctions** Owner **Mary Bushell** deals mostly in estate sellouts and private offerings, and some of the goods are real finds. There are lots of household items, including dishware and bedroom sets. Previews are scheduled noon to 5PM on Friday, and 8AM to 7PM on Monday; auctions are held Tuesday from 10AM to 3PM, with an evening auction once a month, also on Tuesday but at 7:30PM. ♦ 2006 Second Ave. 448.5833

25 **Caffé Mauro** One of the better finds for Seattle caffiends, Caffé Mauro anchors the most exposed corner of what used to be the nine-story **Calhoun Hotel** (constructed in 1918), now an apartment property called the **Palladian**. ♦ Coffeehouse ♦ M-F 8AM-6PM; Sa 9:30AM-5PM. 2000 Second Ave. 728.4901

26 **The Poor Italian Cafe** ★★$ This *caffè* serves very straightforward Italian food: hearty calamari and creamy pasta, including a rich ravioli guaranteed to commit criminal acts against your best dress shirt. Owner **Gregory Pesce** maintains a friendly, open environment. The wine list gets only a passing grade, but the service is cheery and the bread terrific. ♦ Italian ♦ M-F 11AM-10PM; Sa 4-11PM; Su 4-9PM. Virginia St and Second Ave. 441.4313

27 **Pacific Galleries** An auction house that specializes in liquidating estates. Like all such places, it's a crapshoot but sometimes a gold mine. ♦ Call ahead for dates and details. 2121 Third Ave. 441.9990

Restaurants/Clubs: Red **Hotels:** Blue
Shops/ 🌳 Outdoors: Green **Sights/Culture:** Black

28 Fourth and Blanchard Building
Affectionately known by locals as the Darth
Vader Building for its resemblance to the *Star
Wars* villain, this dark, 440-foot-tall glass
monolith was designed by the same folks who
brought you the **Columbia Seafirst Tower**
downtown (**Charles L. Lindsey Architects**).
It's all astonishing surfaces, with dramatic
angles at the top that make it eerily
reminiscent of New York architect **Philip
Johnson's** Pennzoil Place in Houston. ♦ 2101
Fourth Ave

29 Warwick Hotel $$$ Rather large to be
considered intimate and too small to feel so
corporate, the Warwick is an odd beast,
the eternal second choice. Rooms are
comfortable and large, with balconies that
offer decent downtown views. There's a pool
in the health club, albeit a shallow one, and
the Liaison piano lounge provides
entertainment nightly. Front-desk personnel
are friendly and efficient. A 24-hour courtesy
van will whisk you to downtown engage-
ments. Room rates, however, even the
reduced corporate tariffs, are steep for
accommodations so far from the heart of
downtown Seattle. ♦ 401 Lenora St.
443.4300; fax 448.1662

30 Alweg Monorail Walking Fifth Avenue just
north of Pine Street after dark, when the
ghostly monorail flashes by overhead, is one
of Seattle's finest urban experiences. The
monorail is really quiet, as billed, all alight
with peering faces. The slingshot-shaped
concrete supports make for a fine Hitchcock
scenario, with generous geometric lines and
shadows as far as the eye can see. Locals
who've pushed for the monorail's removal—
so a clear view of the **Space Needle** can be
opened along Fifth Avenue—don't appreciate
the drama of this silver-skinned dinosaur.
Film director **Alan Rudolph** did, however, and
he made plentiful use of it in his 1986 film
Trouble in Mind. Just be on your guard,
especially at night: Fifth Avenue beneath the
monorail is not heavily populated. ♦ Fee. Daily
9AM-midnight Memorial Day-Labor Day; M-
Th, Su 9AM-9PM, F-Sa 9AM-midnight off-
season. Westlake Center. 684.7200

31 Dimitriou's Jazz Alley Longtime jazz
producer **John Dimitriou** owns this club, a
genuine treasure for blues and jazz fans alike.
Some of the most significant names in the

genre have been booked here: **Harry Connick,
Jr.**, used to play at Jazz Alley before he was
famous, and **Diane Shuur** has been a regular
performer. **Charles Brown, Ray Brown,
Maynard Ferguson,** and **Betty Carter** are the
standard entertainment, seven days a week,
every week. The food here is nothing special,
but the room is excellent, with comfortable
seating. If you're a music fan, don't miss this
place. ♦ Cover. Tu-Su 7PM-midnight. Sixth
Ave and Lenora St. 441.9729

32 Sixth Avenue Inn $ One step above a motel
(some rooms even have brass beds, and
room service is available), the Sixth Avenue
Inn is reasonably priced and centrally located,
fairly convenient to both the downtown core
and **Seattle Center.** Street noise can be a
problem, especially on the Sixth Avenue side.
♦ 2000 Sixth Ave. 441.8300; fax 441.9903

33 Art/Not Terminal After four years in a
sizable space converted from a Trailways bus
station (hence the name), Art/Not Terminal
has finally moved into more presentable and
more noticeable digs. (So noticeable are they,
in fact, that only months after the move,
someone broke into the new space and made
off with many of the hanging pieces.)
Offerings change each month, though some
stay longer. Exhibits draw from the work of
about 200 member artists, including
sculptors, photographers, and painters. The
nonprofit gallery is good to its artists, taking
an uncharacteristically small percentage from
the sales, and customers can even work out
layaway plans with individual artists. New
show openings are scheduled the Saturday
immediately following the first Thursday of
each month, with live music and refreshments
on hand. ♦ M-Sa 11AM-6PM; Su noon-5PM.
2045 Westlake Ave. 233.0680

34 Thai Palace ★$ One of the best of its kind
in a town scattered with Thai restaurants, it's
certainly among the most reasonably priced.
Tucked inside a **Quality Inn,** the Thai Palace is
something of a secret as well. Don't worry if
you find it empty—that only means the
service is hyperefficient. The *pad thai* is very
good, as are the sizzling cod and the spinach
delight. A star system, meant to designate
which dishes are most spicy, is almost
completely insignificant. Order entrées with
three stars or more only if you want a meal
that'll fry your tongue, zero if you want it
merely mild. You take your chances with two
stars. ♦ Thai ♦ M-F 11AM-2:30PM, 5-10PM;
Sa-Su 5-10PM. 2224 Eighth Ave. 343.7846

Wet Side Story

An agglomeration of funky marinas, fishing boats, and scruffy light industry, **Lake Union** is Seattle's hardest- and longest-working waterway. Oh, sure, a few bits of upscale urban fluff have been thrown in for good measure: gentrified, kite-happy **Gasworks Park** at the north, for instance, and a sleek row of seafood restaurants on the south side. And on the boards is an ambitious and expensive plan to transform some 400 acres of land at the lower end of Lake Union into a parklike "urban village" called **Seattle Commons,** with docks and pavilions jutting out onto the waters. But basically, Lake Union remains inextricably linked to Seattle's blue-collar marine origins.

After the **Lake Washington Ship Canal** opened in 1917 to allow boat traffic access from Puget Sound, five- and six-masted schooners, barkentines, and other sailing craft would slip into these fresh waters for a winter's rest and cleaning. Ship moorages still dot these shores, and every summer the lake is strewn with fluttering sails, but nothing typifies Lake Union better than its houseboat community. There aren't many houseboat neighborhoods left in America, and even Seattle's has been decimated—from a peak of about a thousand units in the 1930s to maybe 450 today.

These houseboats used to be cheap, jerry-built abodes for feisty stevedores, lumberjacks, and Wobblies, with a few bohemian types—artists, students, leftist political organizers—filling out the population. It was a community awash with colorful characters such as the white-bearded **Robert Patten,** who moved to Seattle in 1900 at the age of 90 and settled on a Lake Union houseboat, wore a hat shaped like an umbrella every day of his life (no matter the weather), and was last heard from when he left here to start a new life in California at the formidable age of 99.

"Floating homes" ("houseboats" is considered by some an unflattering term) are no longer the province of impoverished workers or romantic

artists, however. In the 1940s you could buy a houseboat for $1,000, and old-timers recall bitter protest meetings when monthly moorage fees went from $15 to $17. But a massive cleanup of Lake Union in the 1960s, combined with increasing property values, led to a reappraisal; these days, floating homes have gone upscale. Many of them are architect-designed multistory wonders that can cost as much as (or more than) a brand-new home on solid ground, with high moorage fees tacked on top of that.

Many people think of these residences as antiquated, and efforts have been made over the years to eliminate them from the lake frontage. But there's still something special, something eminently freeing, about these gently bobbing domiciles that can't be experienced in a land-bound home. It's a romance captured well by newspaperman **H.E. Jamison,** who in the 1930s wrote about life on Lake Union for the now-defunct *Seattle Star:* "Come on folks, and sit with me on the front porch of my houseboat. . . . And let's heave a sigh for *les miserables* who live in a city of hills and lakes and salt water and yet have nothing better on which to feast their eyes when they return from their day's labors than the uninteresting walls of neighboring buildings. . . .

"It is night; to our left, and a little astern of us, a row of houseboats edges the shore. Each has at least one lighted window that stains the water a soft and shimmering yellow.

"A swell from [a stubby tug] rocks the house ever so gently—a slight shiver that suggests life. There's a gurgling and slapping of waves under the porch. . . . Somewhere a mooring chain creaks and groans. The lights reflected in the now disturbed water dance fantastically.

"Lights and shadows, shadows and lights, peace and contentment. An anodyne for frazzled nerves, a refuge from a troubled world—a moment of inertia in the movement of life. A reprieve, if you please, from the grim sentence that hangs over everyone's head."

35 The Doghouse $ All roads lead to this 24-hour coffee hole, a fact trumpeted by every piece of promotional flotsam in the joint. But nobody comes here for the food, which is mediocre and anything but heart-friendly (try the gut-busting chili burger with a toupee of onions and cheese). The real attractions are the surly waitresses, the god-awful piano bar, and the ludicrous menu that offers a portion of cottage cheese with fruit for more than $6 (don't ask why unless you want your head bitten off). But when you're feeling lonely and as if you haven't a friend on the face of the planet, there is no better place to go than the Doghouse. No one knows why—it's just one of those things. ♦ American ♦ Open daily 24 hours. 2230 Seventh Ave. 624.2741

36 Elephant Car Wash Sign Another tacky fave among locals, this blinking and revolving pink sign won the design contest held by the car-wash owners in 1956. It has since proliferated (several replicas now adorn Elephant Car Washes from here to Puyallup) and become almost as renowned a symbol of Seattle as the Space Needle. *Cosmopolitan* magazine even suggested that single women of the '90s should look out for this pink pachyderm, as the establishments it decorates tend to be hangouts for nice, eligible yuppie dudes. ♦ 616 Battery St

"Seattle, more than most cities, is wary of outsiders."
New York Times Magazine

37 Group Health Building (P-I Building)
This three-story block seems rather warehousy today, yet it was the winner in a national design competition. The New York firm of **Lockwood-Greene** was responsible for most of the architecture, although the landscaped top level was added in 1978 by Seattle's **Naramore, Bain, Brady & Johanson** (now the **NBBJ Group**). The *Seattle Post-Intelligencer* newspaper moved out of the building in the late 1980s, taking along the giant revolving globe that had capped the rounded tower at Sixth Avenue and Wall Street. The *P-I* now operates from a glass cliff on the Waterfront, while **Group Health Cooperative** has taken over this structure.
♦ 521 Wall St

38 Ditto Tavern A Belltown focus for the disgruntled, this tavern attracts those inclined to read, write, and recite poetry. It's charming enough, particularly with the manual typewriters scattered about and the writers busy at them. Poetry readings are held Sundays, beginning at 7PM. The second Monday of every month also features prose readings by aspiring novelists. Live alternative rock, with some jazz tossed into the mix, is scheduled most nights, beginning at 10PM. ♦ Cover for live music. Tu-Su 9PM-2AM. 2303 Fifth Ave. 441.3303

39 The Two Bells Tavern ★$ Belltown's great altar of burger worship is almost impossible to get into at lunchtime, when the suits mix with what remains of Seattle's boho culture in the booths and at the bar. Come for one of the Paul Bunyan-size decks of beef slotted inside a roll and drenched in fried onions, with a sidecar of chunky potato salad. It's messy but worth the dry-cleaning bill. The lemonade and the salads are also recommended. Small rock groups or solo singer-songwriters appear here on Monday nights, beginning at 10PM. All in all, it's a good place to see and be seen. ♦ American ♦ No cover. Daily 11AM-10PM. Bar open daily until 2AM. 2313 Fourth Ave. 441.3050

40 Engine House No. 2 A fire station has occupied the corner of Fourth Avenue and Battery Street since 1890, although the original wood building—**Engine House No. 4**—sat across Battery Street from where architect **Daniel R. Huntington's** frankly framed 1920 brick structure now stands. Unlike No. 4, which had to depend on horse-driven fire engines, the new No. 2 was the talk of the town during the Jazz Age for its "motor-powered apparatus." ♦ Fourth Ave and Battery St

---

"Seattle is an old Native American term for *latte*."
Comedienne **Elayne Boosler**

Restaurants/Clubs: Red Hotels: Blue
Shops/ 🌢 Outdoors: Green Sights/Culture: Black

41 Exotique Records The selection at this interesting, offbeat record store runs toward the adventurous and noisy in rock, jazz, electronic, and even classical. What the stock lacks in range, it makes up in depth. There is plenty to riffle through here, and if you are a fan of Big Black, Can, Loop, or Einstuerzende Neubaten, you will have much to talk about with the chatty if somewhat brusque owner. ♦ M-Sa 11AM-9PM; Su noon-6PM. 2400 Third Ave. 448.3452. Also at: 1311 NE 45th Ave. 632.5853

42 Taki's ★$ Though specializing in pizza and noodles, the lasagna here is also particularly good. Prices are very reasonable, and the room is a nice place to sit and visit—a great lunch spot. ♦ Italian ♦ M-Th 11AM-10PM; F-Sa 11AM-10:30PM. 425 Cedar St. 448.7750

43 Chief Seattle Fountain This bronze civic memorial to the city's namesake (who was originally called Chief Noah Sealth, not Seattle, by the way) was the first public artwork commissioned by the City of Seattle. With the **Alaska-Yukon-Pacific Expo** approaching in 1909, local business leaders had prevailed upon the city to set aside the triangle of property that would become **Tilikum Place.** There they proposed to commemorate the friendship between white settlers and Native Americans living on Elliott Bay. The symbol of that friendship would be a life-size rendition of Chief Seattle, who as leader of the Duwamish and Suquamish tribes had negotiated the treaty that gave over native title to what's now much of northwestern Washington state. The sculptor was **James A. Wehn,** who two years later would design the fountain and bust of Chief Seattle at **Pioneer Place Park** and go on to establish the sculpture department at the **University of Washington.**

Disputes between the artist and the city over which foundry should cast the work delayed the statue's unveiling, but it was finally put on view in 1912. For many years after that it stood green from advanced oxidation. In 1989 a local cabdriver took it upon himself to rectify the shameful situation and, using some solvents and a lot of elbow grease, completely cleaned Chief Seattle under cover of night. The first reaction from city officials was that the cabbie had wrecked this historic monument, and a warrant was issued for his arrest. He fled town before it could be determined that his actions had in fact been harmless. It's still a mystery what happened to that taxi jockey, but the statue does look rather nice now, don't you think? ♦ Tilikum Place (between Cedar St and Denny Way)

44 Chanterelle's ★★$$ This comfortable white-tablecloth spot, lying just beneath the monorail tracks, serves fresh and interesting nouvelle pastiches of French, Italian, and

Cajun fare, as well as excellent vegetarian selections. There's entertainment on weekends, beginning with new-age piano on Thursday, jazz on Friday, and jazz and R&B on Saturday. ♦ Continental/American ♦ M-Th 10AM-10PM; F-Sa 10AM-1AM. Music begins at 8PM. 112 Fifth Ave North. 441.5884

45 Oz One of Seattle's largest and longest-operating dance clubs, Oz caters to a predominantly twentysomething clientele. The fare runs to pop remixes, with occasional forays into alternative music and live shows. Some DJs are better than others. It's a mirror-globe heaven for one brand of weekend warrior. ID is required and the dress code is strictly enforced. ♦ Cover. W, F 9:30PM-2AM; Sa 9:30PM-4AM. 131 Taylor Ave North. No jeans, T-shirts, or sandals. 448.0888

46 Denny Park Pioneer **David Denny** donated the land on which this two-block-size oasis of trees was established in 1890. It is the city's oldest park. Previously, it had been **Seattle Cemetery.** ♦ Denny Way (between Dexter and Ninth Aves North)

47 13 Coins ★$ While other, swanker joints have failed (Seattle is notorious for restaurant closures), this culinary institution just keeps going and going. What's the secret? Probably a combination of the fact that it stays open 24 hours; has a huge menu of grilled meats, pasta, and fish entrées; and serves a dynamite Caesar salad. The portions are generous and the people-watching after 2AM is some of the best to be had here-abouts. ♦ American ♦ Open daily 24 hours. 125 Boren Ave North. 682.2513

48 Seattle Times Building The city's afternoon newspaper occupies a lesser-known building among those designed by architect **Robert C. Reamer** (who also did the **Skinner Building** and **1411 Fourth Avenue Building** in downtown). Completed in 1930 but added to since, this moderne-style headquarters is notable for the grillwork at its entrance and the understated sign cut along its facade. ♦ Fairview Ave North and John St

49 Cafe Lôc ★$ Good, basic, inexpensive Vietnamese fare is served quickly, unpretentiously, and abundantly. There's another outlet in **Seattle Center,** but, for its atmosphere and comparative tranquility, this one is much preferred. ♦ Vietnamese ♦ M-F

11AM-6PM June-Aug; M-F 11AM-8PM Sept-May. 407 Broad St. 441.6883. Also at: Center House. 728.9292

50 Seattle Center Site of the 1962 **Century 21 Exposition,** the center is now a motley aggregate of structures dotting 74 acres just north of Belltown (for a map of the center, see page 75). When it was built it evoked a gleaming, streamlined future. Americans saw in the World's Fair an optimism of upward mobility, a course paved with the mystifying gifts of science, from monorails to paper clothes and commuter helicopters. Now somewhat faded and worn, despite spot renovations over the years, Seattle Center stands as a glorious antique of the John F. Kennedy era, boasting an ambience at once modern, dated, silly, and thrilling.

Plans to completely modernize the center, including a fanciful $335 million Disney expansion scheme from the late '80s, have so far met with resistance. There is, however, a master plan that calls for some near-future improvements, including construction of a new home for the nationally admired **Seattle Children's Theater.** ♦ Admission for special events, Fun Forest rides, and theater performances. Open daily 24 hours. Between Denny Way and Mercer St, First and Fifth Aves North. 684.8582

Within the Seattle Center:

Space Needle "Back when we were in school, if you wanted attention, you put up your hand. That is what the Space Needle will do for the [1962 World's] Fair and Seattle." The speaker was **Joe Gandy,** used-car salesman turned president of the **Century 21 Expo.** His enthusiasm for the Needle (or "the Noodle," as locals say in jest) was not unfounded: In the three-plus decades since its erection, it has become the supreme symbol of Seattle, the city's equivalent to San Francisco's Golden Gate Bridge. If the Needle seems perfectly absurd at first, don't worry, it will grow on you.

This monument was the brainchild of World's Fair organizer **Eddie Carlson.** He scribbled his idea on a napkin one night, an image that looked like a flying saucer on a tripod. Architects **Victor Steinbrueck** and **John Ridley** gave it a kind of "Amazing Stories" reality. The Needle proved to be an enormous project. Just consider some of the stats: the foundation is 30 feet deep and weighs 5,850 tons. What you see aboveground weighs 3,700 tons. The legs are anchored by some 74 bolts, the dimensions of which are 4 inches by 32 feet. The tower claims 24 lightning rods and can endure winds of up to 150 miles per hour. It stands more than 600 feet high. The elevator takes 43 seconds to reach the peak (and is literally a breathtaking experience). The restaurant floor at 500 feet turns a single revolution every hour, thanks to a one-horsepower motor. And the view is magnificent from the **Observation Deck,** particularly on clear days. Locals may eschew the Space Needle after the first visit, but newcomers shouldn't miss the experience. ◆ Fee for rides to the Observation Deck. Daily 8AM-midnight Memorial Day-Labor Day; daily 9AM-midnight off-season. 443.2111

Within the Space Needle:

Space Needle Restaurant ★$$$ It's sad to say, but the casual Space Needle Restaurant and the swankier **Emerald Suite** (★$$$$) don't measure up to their lofty shared position on the same floor of the tower. It's understood, of course, that you're paying for the view, and it is a very fine view. But the cost is just too steep for the meals served here, which have a reputation for dipping to mediocre and rising only to very good. Both restaurants specialize in Northwestern fare, especially seafood. Diners ride the elevator free of charge. A dress code (no T-shirts, tennis shoes, or jeans) is enforced at the Emerald Suite. ◆ Northwestern ◆ Daily 8AM-3PM, 5-11PM Memorial Day-Labor Day; M-Sa 11AM-3PM, 5-11PM, Su 9AM-3PM, 5-11PM off-season. Reservations recommended. 443.2100

Fun Forest Amusement Park Seattle has enjoyed several amusement facilities in its time, at least one of which—**Luna Park** in West Seattle—could be considered a national classic. Fun Forest (originally called the **Gayway** in World's Fair days) doesn't even compare, although if you're a kid in the middle of your second Sno-Cone and your fifth disorienting mechanical whirl, "quality" may be a negotiable term. Adults will appreciate the old-fashioned carousel and classic bumper-car rides. Call ahead for hours and details on special offers. ◆ Daily noon-11PM Memorial Day-Labor Day; hours vary widely off-season. 728.1585

Alweg Monorail The **Seattle Center** marks this train's northern terminus. It travels from here south to **Westlake Center,** departing every 15 minutes. (See page 80 for more about the history of the monorail.) ◆ Fee. Daily 9AM-midnight Memorial Day-Labor Day; Th, Su 9AM-9PM, F-Sa 9AM-midnight off-season. 684.7200

Pacific Science Center It's an interesting stop for adults, but, with its hands-on exhibits and full slate of activities and programs (about dinosaurs, for instance, and whales), this place is even better for children. It's a sort of minicampus with six interconnected buildings. Designed for the World's Fair by well-known Seattle-born architect **Minoru Yamasaki,** along with **Naramore, Bain, Brady & Johanson,** it claims a wonderfully tranquil and inviting space outside, full of pools and soaring arches. ("It is as if Venice had just been built," crowed **Alistair Cooke** when the complex opened.) But the inside all too often feels cramped and constricted. There's a fine planetarium, a laser theater, and an **IMAX** theater. ◆ Admission. Daily 10AM-6PM. 443.2880

Pacific Arts Center Normally presenting work by children and teens (and with a full slate of activities for them as well), this is a surprisingly worthwhile stop for anyone who enjoys prowling art galleries and museums. Really. To paraphrase Art Linkletter, kids create the darndest things. ◆ Free. Tu-F 10AM-4PM; Sa-Su noon-5PM. 443.5437

Center House If much of Seattle Center reminds you of the 1960s, the Center House manages to lurch the aesthetic forward one decade, leaving you with a claustrophobic, somewhat dank space redolent of shut-up 1970s suburban malls. It's full mostly with overpriced fast-fooderies and knickknack shops. However, the **Seattle Children's Museum** (441.1768) is located on the fountain level and provides special multi-cultural programs as well as a permanent **Playcenter,** a supervised play area for the little ones. ◆ Daily 8AM-9PM (hours vary by merchant). 684.7200

International Fountain This is perhaps the ugliest water spout you can ever hope to see (**John Wayne,** looking it over in 1962, drawled, "What's that? An airplane crash?"), and therein lies its charm. A great pit is lined with poured cement and boulders, and a globe at the bottom center randomly spews liquid from 117 nozzles. (At night, this water may be set aglow with colored lights.) Meanwhile, an antiquated sound system valiantly pumps out wheezing strains of classical music. Is there a connection between the music and which nozzle will next let fly? Debate rages on.

Opera House Some of the finest cultural offerings to be found in Seattle cross the stages of this building along Mercer Street. The Opera House used to be Seattle's Civic Auditorium but was remodeled for the World's Fair by **B. Marcus Priteca** and **James Chiarelli.** It is now home to the **Seattle Opera, Seattle Symphony,** and **Seattle Youth Symphony.**

Pacific Northwest Ballet performs at what used to be the Exhibition Hall, recently remodeled and now called the **Phelps Center**. The **Intiman Playhouse** (out front of which stands **James Fitzgerald's** refurbished and graceful *Fountain of the Northwest*) is home to the theater company of the same name, and the **Bagley Wright Theater** hosts the **Seattle Repertory Theatre**. The quality of productions at these venues ranges widely, but they are all first-rate houses in their own right. ◆ Mercer St (between Warren and Fourth Aves North). Seattle Opera 389.7676; Seattle Symphony 443.4747; Pacific Northwest Ballet 441.9411; Seattle Youth Symphony 362.2300; Intiman Playhouse 626.0782; Bagley Wright Theater 443.2222

51 Champion Cellars The selection of wines here is both foreign and domestic, and staffers are helpful, knowledgeable, and bewilderingly happy to answer your every oddball query. Champion also sells imported beers, but the choice of these is much more limited. ◆ M-F 11AM-7PM; Sa 11AM-6PM. 108 Denny Way. 284.8306

52 Romper Room This funky dance club is unafraid to throw house, rave, industrial, and even good old grunge music into the stew. Live acoustic sets are scheduled on Monday night, and Tuesday is open-mike night. Look for occasional drink specials. There may be too much black-light ambience here for some dancers, but a pool table and art gallery in a side room provide a momentary escape from the fashion parade. ◆ Cover. Daily 4PM-2AM. 106 First Ave North. 284.5003

53 P-I Globe At least as tacky as the **Elephant Car Wash's** pink proboscidean is this revolving neonized world atop the *Seattle Post-Intelligencer's* Waterfront offices. It's easily visible from many points on **Elliott Bay** (including the ferry routes and harbor tours), as well as, suddenly and unexpectedly, from many parts of Belltown, Seattle Center, and the Queen Anne neighborhood. Locals come to rely so on the regularity of this landmark's spin that when mechanical or electrical problems cause a halt, you can almost see the psychological pall it casts. ◆ 101 Elliott Ave West

54 Myrtle Edwards Park Situated on the Waterfront just north of downtown and southwest of Seattle Center, this spot makes for one of the most spectacular city strolls. On nice days catch an unmatched view of the **Olympic Mountains, Mount Rainier,** the Seattle skyline, and more along the rolling greensward's two-mile-long walkway. On less-nice days (for which a rain slicker is heartily recommended) it offers moody sky and coal-gray churning waters. This is a favorite place for picnickers, rollerbladers, and lunchtime runners. ◆ Alaskan Way (between W. Bay and W. Thomas Sts)

55 Pottery Northwest Most of this building is devoted to rental studio space for local artisans. A small gallery toward the front lets you in on what residents are up to, which is often interesting, brightly colored work. Some classes are available here, too. ◆ Tu-Sa noon-5PM. 226 First Ave North. 285.4421

56 Le Tastevin ★★$$$ The menu vacillates between classic French and nouvelle Northwestern cuisines, surprising patrons with salmon in port sauce on the same menu as soft-shell crab and a fresh halibut with fruit puree. French traditionalists may declare this place a mere poseur to its rank, but for many, the culinary eclecticism staves off boredom.

The main dining room is bright and lively, pleasing for the evening's repast, but the bar is a much better resort at lunchtime. The prices are lower here and the food is no less interesting. Thanks to the tastebuds of **Emile Ninaud,** co-owner with **Jacques Boiroux,** Le Tastevin features an enormous list of superb, reasonably priced wines. ◆ French ◆ M-F 11AM-2PM, 5-10PM; Sa 5-11PM. 19 W. Harrison St. Reservations recommended. 283.0991

57 Espressly Yours This place is one for the books: an espresso shop sharing its space with an auto-body repair joint. Only in Seattle, right? The coffee here is not bad, and the hours are good for weekday early risers. ◆ Coffeehouse ◆ M-F 6:30AM-5PM. 418 Queen Anne Ave North. 282.0658

58 Wedgewood Court Hotel and Studios $ Studio apartments have been converted into hotel rooms with "kitchenettes" (full kitchens, really)—nothing fancy, but very functional. Longer-term rentals are available as well. The Wedgewood Court is located within two blocks of **Seattle Center** and a major grocery store, **QFC.** ◆ 505 First Ave North. 282.7357; fax 282.7619

59 Uptown Espresso One of the best cups of espresso available in Seattle (and that's saying a lot) is served with pizzazz, baked goods, and cutting-edge attitude. ◆ Coffeehouse ◆ M-Th, Su 6AM-10PM; F-Sa 6AM-11PM. 525 Queen Anne Ave North. 281.8669

60 Sorry Charlie's $ Food and drink are only the marginal reasons why people come here.

The real attraction is a piano bar, where singers and tin ears alike hold forth with enthusiasm. This was the original karaoke-type singing, before technology took over. And as with karaoke, piano sing-alongs always risk painful embarrassment both for listeners and crooners. ♦ American ♦ M-Sa 5:30AM-10PM; Su 5:30AM-8PM. Bars (regular and piano) open daily until 2AM. 529 Queen Anne Ave North. 283.3245

61 Park Avenue Records This may be the best record store in Seattle (though the used-CD selection is good, too). The used platters are stocked in magnificent profusion. To get exactly what you're looking for, you may have to return more than once, but the browsing is always a pleasure. Whether your taste runs to rock, jazz, country, or show tunes, there will be something here for you, usually at a reasonable price. (The selection of blues is the store's single failing.) One new treasure per visit is guaranteed. ♦ M-Sa 10AM-10PM; Su noon-8PM. 532 Queen Anne Ave North. 284.2390

62 Keystone Corner Cards Baseball and other sports card aficionados share a deep respect for this place. ♦ M-Sa 11:30AM-7PM. 534 Queen Anne Ave North. 285.9277

62 Titlewave The used-book selection is limited, but it's put together with excellent taste, which means you might spend less than 15 minutes browsing here but still turn up something you've wanted for a while. Unfortunately, the stock tends to be pricier than you'd expect. ♦ M 10:30AM-6PM; Tu-Th, Sa 10:30AM-7PM; F 10:30AM-10:30PM; Su noon-6PM. 7 Mercer St. 282.7687

62 T.S. McHugh's Restaurant & Pub ★$$ Owned by formula restaurateur **Mick McHugh,** T.S. McHugh's desperately wants to be a British pub. You can tell by the time-darkened faux facade and the rich wood appointments inside. Indeed, there's an old-world conviviality at the bar, where the counter staff chat up their customers and help them expand their knowledge of liquors and local microbrews. Pass on the dining room and stick instead to this bar. Order a hefty sandwich or burger here, gulp down a handful of the terrific curly fries, and sample the bartender's plentiful stash of beers. On Friday and Saturday night the atmosphere really gets thick when Irish musicians kick into gear, beginning at 9PM. ♦ American ♦ Daily 11:30AM-2AM. 21 Mercer St. 282.1910

63 Emerald Diner ★$ A burger joint with attitude for the '90s (they call it vegetarian-

friendly), this place boasts chrome and neon fixtures, shimmering color schemes, design angles so acute you don't want to bump against them, and neo- '50s and '60s kitsch decor. If you don't want a hamburger, try a nut-burger (they're actually better). The fries are fine and so are the desserts and break-fasts. There's live entertainment (from Brazilian bands to rock and gospel) on weekends, and Monday is open-mike night for musicians. ♦ American ♦ Cover charge for live performances. M-Th, Su 8AM-10PM; F-Sa 8AM-midnight. 105 W. Mercer St. 284.4618

64 A Contemporary Theatre (ACT) The fare fluctuates wildly at this equity house (just to be sure of what you'll get, ask around or see newspaper reviews before attending shows here). Expect primarily recent plays, with an annual holiday production of Dickens' *A Christmas Carol.* The season runs from May through December. ♦ Box office daily noon-6PM. 100 W. Roy St. 285.5110

65 Mediterranean Kitchen ★$ Vampires will want to keep clear of this garlic-heavy Middle Eastern restaurant, but budget diners should praise the Mediterranean's ratio of price per pound of food. It's unusual *not* to see patrons exiting here with a carton or more of leftovers, maybe the remains of the superb Farmer's Dish (tart lemon chicken on a hillock of rice) or a helping of lamb shank with couscous, carrots, and potatoes. Dinners come with a bowl of soup (lentil, if you're lucky) and a soothing romaine salad with mint leaves. Owner **Kamal Aboul-Hosn,** who also runs a Middle Eastern fast-foodery on Capitol Hill (**The Oven** on Broadway), offers several tempting appetizers (the *baba ghanouj* and *hummus* both deserve plaudits), but who other than the most ambitious gourmand can ever spare room for them? ♦ Middle Eastern ♦ M-Th 5-10PM; F-Sa 5-11PM; Su 4-10PM. 4 W. Roy St. 285.6713

66 Orestes' ★★$ Legends regarding this lumpy white monstrosity abound. It's supposed to have been built by an aspiring Mexican restaurateur who lived in it as a recluse after his venture failed. Nightclub entrepreneurs later tried unsuccessfully to make a go of it here, leaving the building empty for many years. Now specializing in Greek cuisine, with belly dancers as entertainment (consider yourself warned), Orestes' does a particularly outstanding job with stuffed grape leaves and tabbouleh. It's far more pleasant than its exterior promises. ♦ Greek ♦ Tu-Th, Su 11:30AM-10PM; F-Sa 11:30AM-11PM. 14 Roy St. 282.5514

Restaurants/Clubs: Red	**Hotels:** Blue
Shops/ 🌳 Outdoors: Green	**Sights/Culture:** Black

67 Cinema Espresso A fine little corner spot, this coffee shop is decked out in movie memorabilia and peopled by drifting screenwriters and actors just back from or about to go to LA. Usually not crowded, it's a good place to spend an afternoon reading a book. Desserts here are worth a shot. ♦ Coffeehouse ♦ M 6AM-10PM; Tu-Th 6AM-11PM; F 6AM-midnight; Sa 7:30AM-midnight; Su 7:30AM-10PM. 600 Queen Anne Ave North. 286.0866

68 Tower Books This stuffed-to-overflowing outlet of the national chain is up to snuff in fiction standards, with an especially large selection of science fiction and mysteries. There's also a large children's literature department and a huge magazine array. The weakest point may be in travel books. Browsers are welcome. ♦ Daily 9AM-midnight. 20 Mercer St. 283.6333

69 Jake O'Shaughnessey's ★$$ You'd think that both this joint and **The New Jake's** in Bellevue would be owned by the same folks. Not anymore. A few years back, restaurateurs **Mick McHugh** and **Tim Firnstahl** consummated the splitting up of their partnership by tossing a coin off the top of the **Space Needle** and dividing their empire accordingly. Among other properties, McHugh got The New Jake's, while Firnstahl was left with the Lower Queen Anne original, which had been slated for imminent demolition. Since then, however, the original Jake's has been given a reprieve (at least through the 1990s, they say), which may give it renewed energy.

The kitchen, serving Flintstone-ish helpings of beef and potatoes, with fish entrées taking up more and more of the menu, could surely use some new life and imagination. The dining room is easily eclipsed by the lively adjacent bar, known for its record-setting 774 bourbons and its wonderfully antique

appointments. Bartenders are courteous and knowledgeable and, despite their storied dedication to tradition (they *will not,* for instance, prepare Irish coffees using decaf), go out of their way to mix whatever bizarre combination you think you want to drink. And Jake's is one of the few locations in town where you can still purchase post-prandial cigars. ♦ American ♦ Daily 4:30-10PM. Bar open daily until midnight. 100 Mercer St. 285.1897

70 The Famous Pacific Dessert Company ★★★$ This late-night place is for sugar-lovers only and should be studiously avoided by anyone who is even contemplating a weight-loss program. The cafe features exquisite chocolate confections, fruit pies and tarts, espresso, and herbal teas. Table decor betrays a fascination with comic books. Rotating local art on the walls ranges from mediocre to very good (and whoever does the chalkboards is positively gifted). Warning: This place fills to overflowing after theater performances at **Seattle Center.** ♦ Dessert ♦ M 4:30-11PM; Tu-Th, Su noon-11PM; F-Sa noon-midnight. 127 Mercer St. 284.8100. Also at: 420 E. Denny Way. 328.1950; Crossroads Mall, Bellevue. 649.0306

71 Bamboo Garden ★$$ A decidedly odd vegetarian experience but one not to be missed, Bamboo Garden (aka the "fake-meat palace") lists items on its Hong Kong-style menu according to which meats they emulate, leaving you to wonder exactly what will arrive on your plate. Worry only about anything containing poseur "beef"—absolutely to be avoided. ♦ Vegetarian/Chinese ♦ Daily 11AM-10PM. 364 Roy St. 282.6616

72 Bahn Thai ★★$ Zestful but not overpowering Thai fare is served in an ornately overdecorated setting: a converted house. The curry of the day is usually an excellent choice, as is the chicken *satay.* Only dishes garnering more than two or three stars are hot. ♦ Thai ♦ M-F 11:30AM-3PM, 4:30-10PM; Sa-Su 4-10PM. 409 Roy St. 283.0444

73 Jillian's Billiard Club The concept of a billiards establishment where dressing up is as important as cueing up began in Boston during the 1980s and has since spread to three cities (Cleveland and Miami host the other two clubs). Jillian's offers 33 tables and a pedestrian munchies menu, along with beer, wine, champagne, and the ubiquitous espresso drinks. A bar at one end of the club provides a salutary windowed retreat. It's not your classic dark pool hall, like the **2-11 Billiard Club** in Belltown. Billiards lessons are available. ♦ M-Th, Su 11AM-2AM; F 11AM-4AM; Sa noon-4AM. 731 Westlake Ave North. 223.0300

74 Wawona Harking back to Seattle's maritime heritage is this tri-masted, 468-ton schooner built in 1897. For three decades, beginning in 1914, the *Wawona* sailed north to hunt for cod in the Bering Sea. Ironically, those fish that ended their lives on the *Wawona* actually helped extend this ship's own life, preserving the inner hull with their oils. In 1970 the *Wawona* was the first U.S. ship to be declared a national historic site. Every $1 donation goes toward the ship's upkeep. ♦ Daily 10AM-5PM. Northwest Seaport Dock (near the corner of Westlake Ave and Valley St, just west of the U.S. Naval Reserve station). 447.9800

75 Center for Wooden Boats A historical museum and boat-rental dock are rolled into one, with many vintage and replica craft on view. The center also offers classes in sailing, sail repair, boat-building, and other maritime skills. Rental costs range from $8 to $15 per hour. ♦ Museum/gift shop M, W-Su noon-6PM. Boat rentals daily 11AM-7PM Memorial Day-Labor Day; daily noon-6PM or when it gets dark (whichever comes first) off-season. 1010 Valley St. 382.2628

76 Chandler's Crabhouse and Fresh Fish Market ★$ One in a series of glitzy nosheries that round the southern end of **Lake Union** and attract a libidinally active clientele, Chandler's does its best with crab (no surprise here) in a multitude of variations. There's also a daily fresh-fish roster and a satisfying Sunday brunch. ♦ Seafood ♦ M-Th 11AM-3PM, 5-10PM; F-Sa 11AM-2PM, 5-11PM; Su 9AM-3PM, 5-10PM. 901 Fairview Ave North. 223.2722

76 Duke's Chowderhouse and Outrageous Canoe Club ★$ Stuck into the lower corner of the **Chandler's Cove** retail complex, this spot is rather hard to find. But the view of **Lake Union** can't be beat, even when the sun is bright enough to pierce your retinas, and the deck dining area makes a terrific after-work hangout. (The interior, by contrast, is often too noisy for a pleasant chat.) Fresh seafood is available daily, but the sandwiches and fries fit equally well with the yacht-club atmosphere. ♦ Seafood ♦ Daily 11:30AM-1AM. Bar open daily until 2AM. 901 Fairview Ave North. 382.9963

77 Cucina! Cucina! ★$$ Speaking the language of Rome isn't required at this restaurant-cum-stage; nobody can hear you, anyway. Being seen is the most important thing here, so dress smartly—crowds will be watching. This restaurant is big on pasta, focaccia, and designer pizzas (try the smoked-chicken pie), with deck seating out back where you can watch boats and pontoon planes on **Lake Union.** ♦ Italian ♦ M-Th 11:30AM-3PM, 5-11PM; F 11:30AM-3PM, 5PM-midnight; Sa 11:30AM-4PM, 5PM-midnight; Su noon-4PM, 5-10PM. Bar

open daily until 1:30AM. 901 Fairview Ave North. Reservations recommended. 447.2782. Also at: Bellevue Place, Bellevue. 637.1177

78 I Love Sushi ★★$ For years residents on the east side of **Lake Washington** could thumb their noses at Seattle because they had at least one thing the bigger city didn't: I Love Sushi in Bellevue, where chef **Tadashi Sato** creates tuna sashimi in the shape of a rose, an excellent *furumaki* of pink fish cake and mushrooms, and even a Dungeness crab sushi. But it was only a matter of time before Seattle caught up with this outpost location. **Hara-San,** one of the sushi masters from Bellevue, is in charge of the knives here, but the menu hasn't changed from the Eastside original. ♦ Japanese ♦ M-Th 11:30AM-10:30PM; F-Sa 11:30AM-11PM; Su 5-10PM. 1001 Fairview Ave North. 625.9604. Also at: 11818 NE Eighth St, Bellevue. 454.5706

79 Kamon on Lake Union ★$ Kamon advertises an array of American classics and sushi, but stick with the latter. The high-design, neonized sushi bar employs vigorous, efficient chefs who work nicely with fresh ingredients. The remainder of the restaurant provides a more pedestrian environment and certainly less entertainment. A sister restaurant, **Kamon of Kobe** (644.1970), is in Bellevue. ♦ Japanese ♦ M-Th 11:30AM-2:30PM, 5-10PM; F-Sa 11:30AM-2:30PM, 5-11PM; Su 5-10PM. 1177 Fairview Ave North. 622.4665

80 Lincoln Towing Another stop in the official "Outrageous, Never to be Sanctioned by the Chamber of Commerce" kitsch tour of Jet City features Lincoln Towing's pink, pedestaled pickup truck, accessorized with a gargantuan toe protruding from its roof. Get those cameras ready! ♦ Mercer St and Fairview Ave North

81 St. Spiridon Orthodox Church The city's first Russian Orthodox church was established in 1898, the same time Americans were rushing through Seattle on their way to goldfields in the old Russian outpost of Alaska. Tiny St. Spiridon, conceived by architect **Ivan Palmov** (who also designed **St. Nicholas Russian Orthodox Church** on Capitol Hill), came along much later—in 1938—yet it contains all of the arresting clichés of eastern churches. Drivers racing down Interstate 5 are often bewildered to see its white and blue onion domes towering to the west. ♦ Yale Ave North at Harrison St

---

"The days here are full of mist from Puget Sound and of depression. I find it hard to keep cheerful."

E.B. White, during his stay in Seattle, 1922-23

Bests

Timothy Egan

Seattle Correspondent, *New York Times;* Author, *The Good Rain: Across Time and Terrain in the Pacific Northwest*

Oyster-bar hopping, starting in **Pioneer Square** and ending up at the **Brooklyn Cafe and Oyster Bar Lounge**—the best place to sample Northwest beers.

Elliott Bay Book Company in Pioneer Square, where the walls resonate with well-selected words and strong coffee.

Hammering Man, the huge iron moving sculpture in front of the **Seattle Art Museum;** it's destined to take its place with the celebrated Space Needle as a quirky Seattle icon.

The first snow on the **Olympic Mountains,** across Puget Sound from Seattle, which usually shows up in early November after several weeks of rain—a magical appearance.

The **Virginia Inn,** near Pike Place Market, for good art and ale.

Husky Stadium, any Saturday in the fall, preferably when a team from California is the victim *du jour.*

Speight Jenkins

General Director, Seattle Opera

Seattle, in a strange sense, reminds me of both Paris and San Francisco: in all three cities it is almost impossible not to be suddenly confronted with the sight of something beautiful. In Paris it is often a building; in Seattle it is usually some natural wonder juxtaposed against a modern city.

Because music and art are of primary importance to me (irrespective of my career in the arts), I suggest you first go to the **Seattle Opera,** then to whichever of the major arts institutions in Seattle are performing—the **Seattle Symphony,** the **Pacific Northwest Ballet,** the **Seattle Repertory Theatre,** the **Intiman Theatre,** or the **Empty Space Theatre.**

The **Seattle Art Museum,** for unusual art superbly displayed and for the splendid architecture of the building, which opened in 1991.

Dinner at **Saleh al Lago** (on Green Lake) for excellent Northern Italian cuisine.

A trip for dinner or lunch or even just to see **The Herbfarm,** which is about a 45-minute drive east of Seattle beyond Issaquah on Interstate 90. There's space for 32 people, with three lunch and two dinner servings a week from April to January. Reservations are usually required months in advance.

Rover's, for splendid French cuisine.

After midnight, **Cutter's Bayhouse,** for light food and a busy, big-city ambience; earlier in the day, great views of Puget Sound.

For unusual Asiatic fare of great variety, try **Wild Ginger,** which is near Pike Place Market.

The salmon run at the **Hiram M. Chittenden Locks** in Ballard.

Pioneer Square from 10PM to 2AM, for young, somewhat bohemian bars and discos.

Running or walking around **Green Lake** (about three miles) for sight-seeing and people-watching.

The view from any ferry coming into Seattle.

Driving on any large street (John, Madison, Yesler, etc.) at the crest of either **First Hill** or **Capitol Hill,** for the startling beauty of **Elliott Bay.**

On a clear day, the view of Puget Sound and the Olympic Mountains from the old art museum in **Volunteer Park.**

Driving on **Magnolia Drive,** for the homes and the panorama of the city with Mount Rainier behind it.

The **University of Washington** campus is wonderful to walk around—the buildings are quite attractive.

The **Crêpe de Paris** cabaret show in **Rainier Square,** particularly if a show by **Scott Warrender** is playing.

Doug Kelbaugh

Chairman, Department of Architecture, University of Washington

Driving into town on Interstate 5, coming over the last hill with the sudden view of the downtown, arguably the most dramatic skyline west of Chicago; shooting under downtown in the express lanes with framed views of **Lake Union;** then flying high over the ship canal bridge and turning off to the majestic **University of Washington** campus.

Beer and oysters at **F.X. McCrory's** before a Mariners game; beer and buffalo wings at **Sneakers** after the game.

Touring the residential streets from **Washington Park** and **Denny-Blaine** to **Mount Baker,** with an eye out for **Ellsworth Storey** houses, the high watermark in the Craftsman Style, which left the city with more eye-catching treasures than any architectural flood before or since.

Shopping at **Peter Miller Books, Design Concern,** and **Current** for beautiful books, beautiful objects, and beautiful furniture—modernity and post-modernity at its retail best.

Biking fast along **Lake Washington Boulevard** from **Madrona** to **Seward Park,** with a rest stop at **Leschi.**

Pacific Northwest Ballet's annual *Nutcracker* with Maurice Sendak's sets and costumes, especially the Christmas tree and Chinese tiger.

Sunday brunch at the **Four Seasons Olympic Hotel,** most any event at the **Fifth Avenue** or **Paramount Theaters,** and dinner at **Wild Ginger.**

Bike frames at **Il Vecchio,** glass frames at **Market Optical** or **Collaizzo Opticians,** and picture frames at **Plasteel.**

Rowing through **Montlake Cut** to the **Washington Park Arboretum,** exploring unlikely habitats under the freeway.

km   1/2   1
mi   1/4   1/2   1

N

Union Bay

Fuhrman Ave. E.

Montlake
Montlake
Bridge

E. Hamlin St.

Portage
Bay

Foster
Island

E. Roanoke St.

Hwy. 520/Evergreen Point Floating Bridge

Eastlake Ave. E.

I-5

E. Lynn St.

24th Ave. E.

E. Blaine St.

Washington Park
Arboretum

Lake Washington Blvd. E.

Arboretum Dr. E.

Parkside Dr. E.

Broadmoor
Dr. E.

43rd Ave. E.

E. Garfield St.

McGilvra Blvd.

Louisa Boren
View Park

10th Ave. E.

E. Galer St.

Volunteer
Park

23rd Ave. E.

E. Prospect St.

E. Aloha St.

CAPITOL
HILL

**For nos 1-84,
see pg. 92**

E. Republican St.

E. Madison St.

MADISON
PARK

Bellevue Ave. E.

Belmont Ave. E.

E. John St.

E. Thomas St.

E. John St.

E. Denny Wy.

E. Denny Wy.

Florence
Ct.

31st Ave.

Broadway

12th Ave.

E. Pine St.

CENTRAL

E. Union St.

FIRST
HILL

15th Ave.

19th Ave.

23rd Ave.

34th Ave.

35th Ave.

Madrona Park
Bathing Beach

Madison St.

Boren Ave.

85

E. Cherry St.

MADRONA

James St. E.

E. Alder St.

E. Yesler Wy.

88

87

86

16th Ave. E.

90 Leschi
Park

91

Frink
Park

92

E. Jackson St.

89

Lake Washington
Lake Washington Blvd. S.

S. Dearborn St.

YESLER
TERRACE

12th Ave. S.

Airport Wy. S.

I-5

Hwy. 900/Rainier Ave. S.

I-90

I-90

Mercer
Island

S. Holgate St.

BEACON
HILL

93

94

Colman
Park

95

S. Lander St.

S. McClellan St.

4th Ave. S.

S. Spokane St.

S. Spokane St.

Beacon Ave. S.

Jefferson
Park
Golf
Course

Hwy. 900/M.L. King Jr. Wy.

34th Ave. S.

M.L. King Jr. Wy.

96 Stan Sayres
Memorial
Park

Industrial
Wy.

Genesee
Playfield

38th Ave. S.

S. Genesee St.

S. Columbia Wy.

Columbia
Park

100

99

MT. BAKER

42nd Ave. S.

51st Ave. S.

Lake Washington Blvd. S.

Andrews
Bay

97
Seward
Park

101
←

15th Ave. S.

98
↓

Capitol Hill/Madison Park/
Seward Park
In a city of exceptionally diverse neighborhoods, those areas lying just east of downtown, along the hilly ridge that separates Seattle's picket fence of skyscrapers from placid **Lake Washington**, are by far the most diverse. The wealth of old Seattle has been entrenched here since the pioneer days, but these streets have also often greeted penniless refugees, leather-clad punks with Jello-bright hair, and racers pumped up for **Seafair's** annual hydroplane competition.

The 1990 census identified two dozen distinct racial and/or ethnic groups in this enormous area. More, undoubtedly, wait to be discovered. While most residents are European-American, an estimated one-third are African-American and almost a quarter are Asian-American. Latinos and Native Americans also appear in significant numbers.

No central focal point exists here, and indeed the neighborhood boundaries are ill-defined; even city hall may find itself divided as to whether a given residence is located in, say, a neighborhood such as **Leschi** or **Madrona**. But this human diversity reaches an apex of complexity on central Capitol Hill, where one given block may include young singles, blue-collar Boeing families, male and female representatives of the city's politically powerful homosexual community, ambitious lawyers remodeling charming old homes, and émigrés from a half-dozen nations. Conservative politicians do not waste time courting these voters because even the wealthy seem relatively progressive, and liberal Democrats have ruled here since the glaciers receded. If there is a minority group in this part of town, it might be the white families with children that predominate throughout Seattle's other neighborhoods.

Outside of boisterous Broadway and a few neighborhood pubs, a stranger to Seattle will not find much nightlife on these tree-lined streets. But other diversions are stocked in quantity. Madison Park hosts an impressive enclave of stately and well-preserved mansions, an attribute rivaled only by a pair of historic districts on Capitol Hill, where Seattle's turn-of-the-century rainmakers came to erect their alcazars. City parks range from the traditionally styled **Volunteer Park** on Capitol Hill to the urban wilderness of Seward Park on Lake Washington. The lake itself draws flocks of citizens to its shores in warm months and is employed year-round for fishing and boating. **Washington Park Arboretum** will captivate both the casual stroller and the professional botanist. And these are just the largest greenswards; perhaps a dozen smaller (but no less charming) acreages are familiar only to their custodial neighborhoods.

1 Nellie Cornish Memorial Sculptures
They look like enormous pinwheels mounted atop sticks, but artist **Parks Anderson's** 1989 stylized windmills, jutting up from Lake Washington at the western end of the **Evergreen Point Floating Bridge** (Highway 520), actually honor longtime Seattle arts advocate **Nellie Cornish**, founder of Capitol Hill's **Cornish College of the Arts**. Each tower consists of four steel legs rising from a concrete base and topped with two bronze wind wheels, one over the other, that rotate in opposite directions amidst the wide vocabulary of Seattle's winds. Above these, and not visible except from boats that can get closer than cars to these sculptures, is a tiny bear, balanced whimsically on a golden ball, with another smaller ball perched on its nose. When the Northwest isn't experiencing a drought, fountains are turned on at the base of each sculpture, shooting eight-foot-tall sprays up the legs; they're lighted at night to create an eerie spectacle. ♦ West end of the Evergreen Point Floating Bridge

---

Restaurants/Clubs: Red   Hotels: Blue
Shops/ 🍷 Outdoors: Green   **Sights/Culture:** Black

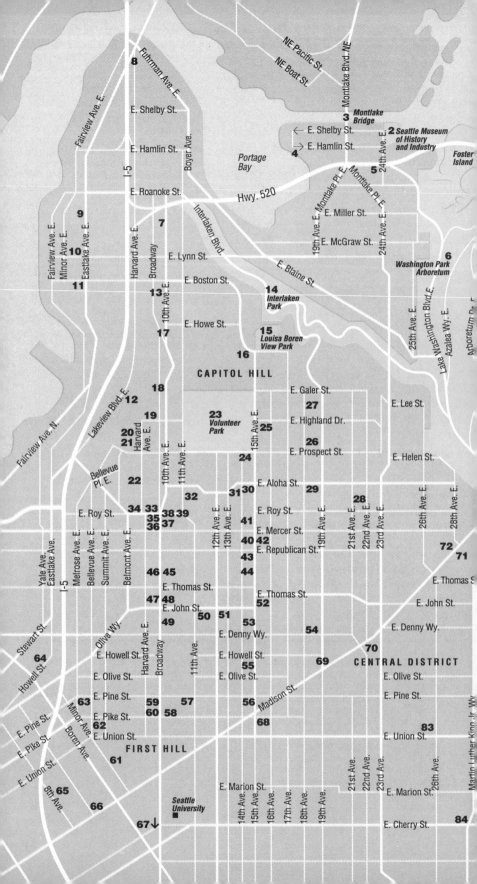

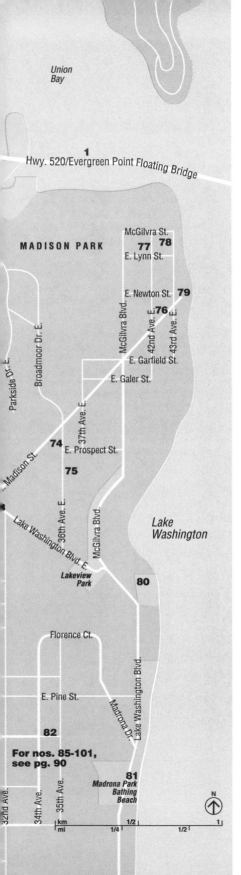

Union
Bay

1
Hwy. 520/Evergreen Point Floating Bridge

MADISON PARK

McGilvra St.
77 78
E. Lynn St.

E. Newton St. **79**
76

E. Garfield St.

E. Galer St.

E. Prospect St.
74
75

Parkside Dr. E.
Broadmoor Dr. E.
McGilvra Blvd.
42nd Ave. E.
43rd Ave. E.
37th Ave. E.
36th Ave. E.
McGilvra Blvd.
Madison St.
Lake Washington Blvd.

Lake
Washington

Lakeview
Park
80

Florence Ct.

E. Pine St.

Lake Washington Blvd.
Madrona Dr.

82

**For nos. 85-101,
see pg. 90**

32nd Ave.
34th Ave.
35th Ave.

81
Madrona Park
Bathing
Beach

N

| km | | 1/2 | | 1 |
| mi | 1/4 | | 1/2 | |

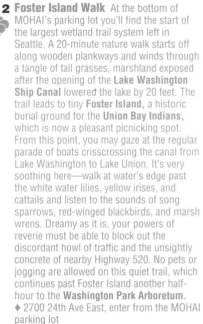

**2 Museum of History and Industry
(MOHAI)** Opened in 1952, the city's
premier repository of the past had a long
gestation period. Pioneer historians started
meeting in 1911 and began efforts to erect a
permanent museum shortly thereafter. But
sufficient funds weren't gathered until the
late '40s, and museum backers then ran into
trouble. After locating choice property on the
current site, they faced opposition from the
University of Washington, which owned the
land—or thought it did, anyway. It turned
out that a portion of the property was under
federal control; museum supporters lobbied
for its use and won.

MOHAI now chronicles the city's heritage
with displays of fire engines, a cable car, and
numerous artifacts from the lumber,
shipping, and fishing industries. Seattle is
the birthplace of the **Boeing Company,** so
it's no surprise to find a 1920s Boeing mail
plane here. The museum also boasts a rich
maritime collection—the model ships and
figureheads are popular with children—and
one of the state's most extensive arrays of
historic photographs from the region.
♦ Admission. Daily 10AM-5PM. 2700 24th
Ave East. Reservations are required to visit
the photo archives. 324.1125

2 Foster Island Walk At the bottom of
MOHAI's parking lot you'll find the start of
the largest wetland trail system left in
Seattle. A 20-minute nature walk starts off
along wooden plankways and winds through
a tangle of tall grasses, marshland exposed
after the opening of the **Lake Washington
Ship Canal** lowered the lake by 20 feet. The
trail leads to tiny **Foster Island,** a historic
burial ground for the **Union Bay Indians,**
which is now a pleasant picnicking spot.
From this point, you may gaze at the regular
parade of boats crisscrossing the canal from
Lake Washington to Lake Union. It's very
soothing here—walk at water's edge past
the white water lilies, yellow irises, and
cattails and listen to the sounds of song
sparrows, red-winged blackbirds, and marsh
wrens. Dreamy as it is, your powers of
reverie must be able to block out the
discordant howl of traffic and the unsightly
concrete of nearby Highway 520. No pets or
jogging are allowed on this quiet trail, which
continues past Foster Island another half-
hour to the **Washington Park Arboretum.**
♦ 2700 24th Ave East, enter from the MOHAI
parking lot

3 Montlake Bridge Built in 1925, with
distinctive Gothic-inspired towers (visually
linking it to the nearby **University of
Washington**), this span was designed by the
university's architect, **Carl Gould.** The need
for this bridge had only existed for eight
years, since the ship canal, finally linking
Puget Sound with Seattle's "inland sea,"
plowed through what had originally been
an isthmus here. An earlier, more easily

crossed canal (about a hundred yards south of the present **Montlake Cut,** and filled long ago) had been completed in 1884 but was used only for logs and the occasional canoe, being too narrow to carry ships.

Completion of the UW stadium in 1920 initiated interest in a bridge; in fact, in preparation for the stadium's first football game (between the UW and Dartmouth), a graduate manager at the school tied a row of barges together near this point to allow fans easy passage north from the Montlake neighborhood. Three elections later, this bridge was built. A pleasant walkway runs along the south side of the canal and beneath the Montlake Bridge. ♦ Montlake Blvd, just south of the University of Washington

4 Seattle Yacht Club This water-oriented city has a long list of yacht clubs—some spiffy, some not. This 3,000-member organization is the largest, the oldest (founded in 1892), and the hardest to get into (you must be nominated by a current member). It sponsors Seattle's traditional raft of events revolving around the opening day of yachting season, which is the first Saturday in May. The clubhouse was designed around 1920 by architect **John Graham, Sr.** Facilities also include four docks full of well-oiled teak and mahogany on **Portage Bay.** ♦ 325 E. Hamlin St. 325.1000

5 Cafe Lago ★★$$ The chefs at this cozy bistro pride themselves on their gnocchi, but the real prize here is the antipasti selection. Order the eggplant marinated in garlic and olive oil and the *coppa* ham. Arrive early, because Cafe Lago does not take reservations. ♦ Italian ♦ Tu-Th 11:30AM-2PM, 5-9PM; F-Su 5-10PM. 2305 24th Ave East. No credit cards. 329.8005

5 The Daily Grind Expansive and well-lighted, this corner coffee-teria is full with the scents of fresh-baked muffins and a raspberry coffee cake that may be even better than what your sainted mother made. It's great for extended planning sessions (nobody ever kicks you out of this place) and very early morning good-byes. ♦ Coffeehouse ♦ Daily 4AM-2PM. 2301 24th Ave East. 322.9885

"Seattle is a prim and proper, almost prissy, little city. It has a scrubbed-clean quality, a result, no doubt, of one rainstorm after another."

San Francisco Examiner

Arboretum

6 **Washington Park Arboretum** This 200-acre woodland, planned in 1936 and stretching south from Lake Washington's **Union Bay,** is arguably the city's jewel in a necklace of parks designed by the **Olmsted Brothers** landscaping firm of Massachusetts.

Like the Museum of History and Industry, the arboretum got off the ground slowly. After putting this area aside as parkland in 1904, the city developed Lake Washington Boulevard East, the narrow, curving thoroughfare that cuts through the park, as a scenic entryway to the 1909 **Alaska-Yukon-Pacific Exposition,** held on the UW grounds. But it didn't develop the park until the university agreed to manage it jointly. The arboretum first featured native plants (despite the Olmsteds' historical antipathy toward Northwest flora), but in the 1940s, it expanded to include species from all over the globe. More than 5,500 kinds of trees, shrubs, and flowers now flourish on the grounds.

Different parts of the park display unique characters and moods: toss a Frisbee across the broad, open meadows; stroll through the ornamental gardens, or enter into the serene, otherworldly atmosphere of the tea garden. A harmonious collaboration of natural elements and human stewardship prevails. Many plants carry identification tags, but the thickly wooded grounds have none of the fussy feeling familiar from some public gardens. There are several hours' worth of trails to explore. Dogs love to romp in this park, but the city's stuffy leash laws should at least be acknowledged, if not followed to the letter. Group tours begin at the visitors center and are offered every Sunday at 1PM and on every second Wednesday of the month at 10AM (except in December). ♦ Free. Daily 8AM-sunset. 2300 Arboretum Dr East. 543.8800

Within the Washington Park Arboretum:

Graham Visitors Center The park's focal point offers trail maps, botanical pamphlets, and a small gift shop and bookstore. The center schedules two large sales during the year, one of plants (in April) and another of bulbs (in October), when you may see normally serene local gardeners locked in combat for possession of a bewildered baby rhododendron. Just outside the front door, several hiking trails lead to wooded areas. ♦ M-F 10AM-4PM; Sa-Su noon-4PM. 543.8800

Winter Garden Plants that thrive in the mild Northwest climate and bloom between October and March are displayed here. Witch hazel and viburnum are prominent attractions. In early spring, the tall cornelian cherry shrubs burst forth with their small yellow flowers, set against an underplanting of Lenten roses.

Azalea Way This wide, grassy 3/4-mile path was the site of a raceway for harness horses in Seattle's pre-auto era but is now considered too fragile to withstand even joggers—take a walk here instead. Crowds gather along Azalea Way on weekends from April through June to see flowering cherry trees, azaleas, and dogwoods. Farther along, step into the **Rhododendron Glen,** where a pond reflects a riot of "rhodie" colors.

Japanese Tea Garden Many people consider this garden the highlight of the park. Designed in the Momoyama style in 1960 by Japanese architect **Juki Iida,** this three-and-a-half-acre garden is a tranquil world of Asian and Northwest plantings, rookeries, bridges, granite lanterns, waterfalls, and glassy pools. Believed to be one of the most authentic outside of Japan, construction of the garden required transporting more than 500 massive granite boulders, each wrapped in bamboo matting to prevent scratching, from high in Washington's **Cascade Mountains.** The original cypress-and-cedar teahouse, hand-constructed in Japan, was destroyed by fire in 1973, then rebuilt following the original plans. The teahouse offers monthly demonstrations in **Chado,** the highly ritualized Japanese tea ceremony. ♦ Admission. Daily 10AM-6PM Mar-25 Apr, Sept-24 Oct; daily 10AM-7PM 26 Apr-May; daily 10AM-8PM June-31 Aug; 10AM-4PM 25 Oct-30 Nov; closed Dec-Feb. 684.4725; for a schedule of tea ceremony demonstrations, call 324.1483

7 Rain City Grill ★$$ Plumbing the moist Northwest scene for every drop it's worth, this playfully decorated restaurant filled with colorful umbrellas does its best work with grilled fish but has also won plaudits for its salads. ♦ Northwestern ♦ M-Th 11:30AM-2PM, 5:30-9:30PM; F 11:30AM-2PM, 5:30-10PM; Sa 5:30-10PM; Su 5:30-9:30PM. 2359 10th Ave East. 325.5003

7 Roanoke Park Place Tavern For the just-over-21-and-frisky set down from Capitol Hill, this is a prime watering hole. It's lively and good for people-watching but definitely *not* the place to go if you're developing a panic attack about age. Burgers and beer represent the tav's two essential food groups, with double-decker nachos thrown in for abject health nuts. ♦ Daily noon-2AM. 2409 10th Ave East. 324.5882

8 Romio's Pizza ★★$ A late entry in the Romio's chain, this branch is pleasantly more spacious but also less homey than its brethren. It's hard, though, to diss a joint that serves pizza as fabuloso as this. ♦ Pizza/Takeout ♦ M-Th 11AM-11PM; F-Sa 11AM-midnight; Su 11AM-10:30PM. 3242 Eastlake Ave East. 322.4453. Also at: 2001 W. Dravus St. 284.5420; 8523 Greenwood Ave North. 782.9005; 917 Howell St. 622.6878; 616 First Ave. 621.8500

9 Tio's Bakery & Cafe ★$ Survey-takers a few years ago discovered that what Eastlake Avenue habitués found most lacking in this neighborhood was a decent bakery. And voilà! Tio's was born. It's more than a bakery, actually, offering renditions of paella, red snapper, and omelets for breakfast. But the entrées tend to be inviting in presentation and somewhat lackluster in taste. Come here instead for the coffee cakes, muffins, cinnamon rolls, and the breads used for sandwiches. Late-night visits (or early morning on extended-hour weekends) provide the most peaceful environment; Saturday and Sunday mornings hatch huge crowds, too many patrons really for the staff to handle with aplomb. ♦ Latin American/Bakery ♦ M-Tu 7AM-7PM; W-Th 7AM-midnight; F 7AM through Su 2PM. 2379 Eastlake Ave East. 325.0081

10 14 Carrot Cafe ★$ Previous owner **Julia Miller** sold the 14 Carrot in late 1991 to **Robert Christiansen,** but not much else has changed here. You still have to cool your heels outside the front door with a newspaper on weekends. And the menu still caters to veg-heads and red-meat haters: butternut-squash bisque, chicken and mushroom omelets, and sprouts, sprouts, and more sprouts. But on the whole, the 14 Carrot experience is merely satisfying. Too much adherence to the tried-and-true may yet be Christiansen's undoing. Once a magnet for the young and culinarily hip, this restaurant will have to provide both more adventurous and spicier meals in the future if it's to achieve acclaim again. ♦ Vegetarian ♦ Daily 7AM-3PM. 2305 Eastlake Ave East. 324.1442

The Big Snow of 1880 marked the worst winter this city ever experienced. Snow began to fall on 5 January and within a week was heaped in six-foot-high drifts. The *Seattle Post-Intelligencer* confessed that "we shall have to admit hereafter that snow does occasionally fall in this country. . . . The average citizen walks nowadays as though he were drunk." The 64-inch snow total from that week brought the city (including vital railroad lines) to a complete standstill.

Seattle on Celluloid

New York and Los Angeles are both overused (and increasingly expensive) backdrops for films, so directors are branching out, schlepping their cameras and their lights and their dealmakers to Northwest locales. Portland, Oregon, and especially Vancouver, British Columbia, already have been discovered by Hollywood, while Seattle—with enough lovely and quirky settings to turn any artist's eye—is just beginning to cash in on the trend, although the city already has a movie coordinator and is looking forward to the riches that may come from film fame. A few of the better-known theatrical films and television flicks shot in Seattle:

Black Widow (1987) pits determined investigator **Debra Winger** against murdering seductress **Theresa Russell**.

Cinderella Liberty (1973) shows a shabby-looking Seattle, a perfect backdrop for the troubled engagement between sailor **James Caan** and hooker **Marsha Mason**.

The Fabulous Baker Boys (1989) takes place in a jazzy Seattle, home to two piano-tickling brothers (**Jeff** and **Beau Bridges**) who have trouble keeping their hormones in check around singer **Michelle Pfeiffer.**

Frances (1983) is a haunting portrayal of Seattle native and later film star Frances Farmer (played by **Jessica Lange**), a woman who led a tragic life.

The Hand That Rocks the Cradle (1992) tells the story of an embittered widow (played by **Rebecca DeMornay**) who seeks revenge against thirtysomethings **Annabella Sciorra** and **Matt McCoy.** DeMornay pretends to be a kindhearted nanny while plotting to steal the couple's child.

Harry and the Hendersons (1987) is a light-hearted Sasquatch fantasy film starring **John Lithgow.**

House of Games (1987) stars **Joe Mantegna** as a gambler who fears he'll be murdered over a bad debt and winds up interesting a psychiatrist (**Lindsay Crouse**) in his big-stakes world. This dark-toned puzzle film marked playwright **David Mamet's** debut as a movie director.

It Happened at the World's Fair (1963) shows **Elvis Presley** eating dinner at the Space Needle and singing on the monorail.

McQ (1974) stars **John Wayne** in a late-career chasefest about a Dirty Harry-like cop who lives on a boat in Fremont.

The Night Strangler (1973) was a TV film that featured **Darren McGavin** as a rumpled reporter hot on the trail of a murderous member of the "living dead" beneath the streets of Pioneer Square.

An Officer and a Gentleman (1982) was shot in Seattle and Port Townsend. **Richard Gere** plays a loner and aspiring Navy pilot who tries not to fall in love with local factory worker **Debra Winger,** who in turn refuses to become pregnant in order to trap Gere into marriage. The other intense relationship in this fine story is between Gere and a strict sergeant played by **Lou Gossett, Jr.**

The Parallax View (1974) tells the tale of a senator's assassination. **Warren Beatty** portrays a local reporter in **Alan Pakula's** Space Needle-hanger.

Say Anything (1989) is about a straight-A student and closet beauty (**Ione Skye**) caught in an uncertain world inhabited by an unlikely but supportive kick-boxing swain (**John Cusack**) and a benevolent but ultimately dishonest father (**John Mahoney**). **Cameron Crowe** directed this film.

Singles (1992) stars **Campbell Scott, Bridget Fonda,** and **Matt Dillon**. Director **Cameron Crowe's** disarmingly sweet-spirited tale of twentysomething love is set contrastingly amidst Seattle's grunge-rock scene.

Sleepless in Seattle (1993) marks writer **Nora Ephron's** directorial debut. This romance story stars **Tom Hanks** and **Meg Ryan.**

Trouble in Mind (1985) is a not-quite-futuristic yarn with **Kris Kristofferson** as an ex-cop and ex-con trying to remake his life in "Rain City," a Seattle of the imagination, in which the old Seattle Art Museum building on Capitol Hill becomes the mansion of an arch-gangster.

Tugboat Annie (1933) stars **Marie Dressler** and **Wallace Berry.** The film was inspired by **Norman Reilly Raine's** popular "Tugboat Annie" stories of the 1930s, which were in turn inspired by the tale of **Thea Foss,** who, operating from Tacoma in the late 19th century, began what would become one of the country's largest tugboat empires.

Twin Peaks: Fire Walk with Me (1992) is director **David Lynch's** prequel to his weird but popular TV series.

11 Serafina ★★$$ The **Eastlake** neighborhood, anchored on the south by the historic **Lake Union Steam Plant** (slated for renovation as the new home of a biotech company) and snaking around the lake's northeastern edge, seems finally to be developing a fuller identity. A few taverns have always been present, plus the odd used-books outlet and some totally forgettable office buildings, but refined establishments such as Serafina should enhance Eastlake's profile as a destination rather than just a pass-through.

Replacing the late, lamented **Nick & Sully's,** Serafina bows in part to the trendy by offering small appetizers in the Spanish *tapas* style. (Order the *crostini* with Tuscan olive spread and goat cheese.) The food here, however, rises well above that with some of its entrées, including *salsiccia toscana* (sausage braised with caramelized onions and cabbage and served over polenta) and the *penne* pasta with smoked mozzarella in a tomato cream sauce. The smoked-chicken salad (with chèvre, peas, and a raspberry vinaigrette) is just as delicious.

Though invitingly well lighted, the restaurant is often crowded. Occasional live piano music can add romance to the scene, but be sure to avoid tables too near the instrument, lest you're compelled to yell just to be heard by your partner. Busy nights put too much of a strain on the still-underexperienced waitstaff. A wonderful wood deck is found out back, where diners at a handful of tables may imagine themselves in a garden setting far from the city. ♦ Italian ♦ M-Th 11:30AM-2:30PM, 5:30-10PM; F 11:30AM-2:30PM, 5:30-11PM; Sa 5:30-11PM; Su 5:30-10PM. 2043 Eastlake Ave East. Reservations recommended. 323.0807

12 Egan House This triangular oddity wedged into a wooded glen may well be the most unusual residence in Seattle. Built in 1958, the house is the work of **Robert Reichert,** a local architect well known for his unconventional designs. This building's form, write **Sally B. Woodbridge** and **Roger Montgomery** in *A Guide to Architecture in*

Washington State, "expresses its interior organization, in which levels, like graduated trays, diminish in size as they rise." Imagine, as you drive by, what it would be like to actually live inside Egan House. ♦ 1500 Lakeview Blvd East

13 Rocking Horse Inn $ Besides the fine hospitality, the main attraction here is the collection of rocking horses, the exact number of which has yet to be determined. Four rooms share two baths; one has a private balcony, and there's a hot tub out back. Owners **Donette Rotta** and **Robin McCabe** will sometimes permit kids and pets, but by prior arrangement only. ♦ 2011 10th Ave East. 322.0206

14 Interlaken Park This park is really just a serpentine, tree-lined street with a few shady footpaths frequented by neighbors and the occasional flasher. It was originally the route of a short-lived bicycle path, built during a Seattle bike craze around the turn of the century. **Interlaken Drive** now connects the **Washington Park Arboretum** and Lake Washington Boulevard East with **Capitol Hill,** before heading west into Highway 520 and Interstate 5. ♦ Interlaken Blvd (between Lake Washington Blvd and Delmar Dr East)

15 Louisa Boren View Park Pike Place Market hero **Victor Steinbrueck** designed this small park in 1975. Looking north, it commands views of Portage Bay, the University of Washington campus, Lake Washington, and the Cascade Mountains. The park was named after **Louisa Boren Denny,** the last survivor of the 1851 Alki Point settlers. The large untitled Cor-Ten steel sculpture, composed of 10 interlocking blocks rusted to an even brown color, was created by Portland, Oregon, artist **Lee Kelly.** ♦ 15th Ave East and E. Garfield St

16 Lake View Cemetery Before **Volunteer Park** could begin to grow in the 1890s, the city had to relocate one of its principal graveyards from what is known today as the park's north end. Regrettably, most of the resident dead there had already been moved before, in 1885, when Seattle decided to turn its pioneer cemetery into what is now **Denny Park,** south of **Lake Union.** Two years later **Leigh S.J. Hunt,** owner and editor of the *Seattle Post-Intelligencer,* convinced the city council that the graves should be moved yet a third time, just a few hundred feet north. This final site is now the Lake View Cemetery.

Perhaps no other graveyard in this city claims better outlooks than are available from here. Managers don't seem to mind casual visitors, but they're rattled by too much attention from the press and rankle at outright curiosity seekers. Nonetheless, there are some wonderful old tombstones here, dating back to the 1850s. People come from as far away as Japan and China to pay homage to the gravesite (near the cemetery's summit) of kung fu movie star **Bruce Lee,** a former Seattleite who died in 1973. Pioneer **David "Doc" Maynard,** who perished in 1873, is buried here beneath a tall California redwood and beside one of his two wives, **Catherine,** whose epitaph reads, "She did what she could." Nearby is found a rugged headstone under which lies **Chief Sealth's** daughter, **Princess Angeline,** in a coffin shaped like a canoe. Also interred near the northern end is **Edmond Creffield,** a turn-of-the-century cult leader who, newspapers reported, was "shot down like a dog" in Pioneer Square. He's buried next to his wife, **Maud Hurt Creffield,** beneath small gravestones that have been either abnormally weather-beaten or angrily abused over more than eight decades. ♦ 1554 15th Ave East. 322.1582

17 John Leary House When completed around 1904, this stone and half-timbered manse was one of the largest and most lavishly appointed houses in the city. The architect was Seattle's **J. Alfred Bodley.** The owner, **John Leary,** was born in 1837 in New Brunswick, Canada; arrived in Seattle in 1869; and founded the **West Coast Improvement Company,** which was primarily responsible for the development of Ballard. In 1882 Leary became principal owner of the *Seattle Post,* which he merged soon after with the competing *Intelligencer* to create what is still the city's morning daily, the *Seattle Post-Intelligencer.* He also opened and operated a nearby coal mine, was partly responsible for supplying Seattle with its first natural gas, and set up a waterworks system that brought in water from **Lake Washington** for the first time.

Still not content with his accomplishments, Leary was elected mayor of Seattle in 1884 and served two terms in that then-nonpaying office. It seemed John Leary could have anything he wanted. But he died in 1905 at the age of 68 before he could move into his dream house. The mansion is now home to the **Episcopal Diocesan Offices.** A stained-glass window designed for the house by New York's Tiffany Company is now at the UW's **Burke Museum.** ♦ 1551 10th Ave East

18 St. Mark's Episcopal Cathedral **Bakewell and Brown,** a noted San Francisco architectural firm, designed this graceful but somewhat chilly Episcopal temple for the Diocese of Olympia. Built between 1926 and 1930 in the neo-Byzantine style, the church has an interior that one critic described as "an immense masonry box."

St. Mark's also has a world-renowned Flentrop organ, acquired in 1965, which draws musicians from all over the world to perform in the cathedral's annual recital series. A major overhaul of the organ, which included checking and correcting the timbre and pitch of 3,744 pipes, was completed in 1992. ♦ Services Tu 8:30AM; W noon; Th 7AM; Su 8AM, 9AM, 11AM, 7PM. 1245 10th Ave East. 323.0300

19 Sam Hill House Designed by the Washington, DC, architectural firm of **Hornblower & Marshall,** this mansion was built in 1909 for the son-in-law of Great Northern Railroad magnate **James J. Hill.** The five-story fortress is a concrete variation of an 18th-century manor house, resembling in many respects Marie Antoinette's Petit Trianon at Versailles. Hill supposedly built it in order to be able to properly receive **Crown Prince Albert** of Belgium, who, despite two planned trips to Seattle, canceled both times. In 1917 **Sam Hill** commissioned Hornblower & Marshall to construct a similar building overlooking the Columbia River near Goldendale, Washington. That second version was supposed to be a plantation for Hill and his wife, **Mary** (after which the estate, **Maryhill,** was named), as well as the nexus for a new town run by Hill's fellow Quakers. The Hills, however, never did live there, and the Quakers weren't at all impressed with the site. The railroader wound up turning his Columbia River mansion into an art repository, what *Time* magazine in 1940 (the year it was completed) called "the loneliest museum in the world." The building now houses the **Pleetscheef Institute for the Decorative Arts.** ♦ 814 E. Highland Dr

20 C.J. Smith House The beautiful brick mansion, with lead-glass windows and an elegant low brick wall separating the front yard from the sidewalk, was built in 1907. The design, by Spokane architect **Kirtland K. Cutter** and his frequent partner **Karl Malmgren,** was influenced by the work of English architect **Richard Norman Shaw,** who was much in favor in America at the time. Born in 1854, **Charles Jackson Smith,** a native of Kentucky, was president of the **Dexter Horton National Bank,** a forerunner of today's **Seafirst Bank.** ♦ 1147 Harvard Ave East

21 Brownell-Bloedel House Architect **Carl Gould** departed from his usual style by sheathing this 1910 Georgian Revival residence in natural wood shingles. ♦ 1137 Harvard Ave East

22 R.D. Merrill House Built in 1910, this modified Georgian mansion, complete with formal garden and carriage house, is the only West Coast structure designed by famed New York architect **Charles A. Platt,** who is best known for his Freer Gallery in Washington, DC. Merrill was born in Michigan in 1869 to a lumber family from Maine. Continuing his family's westward inclinations, he moved to the Pacific Northwest in 1898 to manage the Washington and British Columbia properties of **Merrill and Ring,** a leading lumber firm of the era. ♦ 919 Harvard Ave East

23 Volunteer Park During the 1880s this 43-acre plot was known simply as **City Park**. But in 1901 it was renamed Volunteer Park to honor two companies of Seattle men who'd volunteered to fight in the Spanish-American War of 1898. In that same year a 20-million-gallon reservoir was carved from the park's southern flanks, and around 1906, a 75-foot-tall water tower (pictured below) was put up to increase water pressure in a bumper crop of mansions sprouting nearby. The **Olmsted Brothers** engineered the final refinements. As part of their comprehensive plan for the city, the landscape architects decided that this should become one of several "neat and smooth" central parks (as opposed to "wild" outlying ones such as **Seward Park**). Second-growth fir trees were felled and replaced by a more ordered regiment of blue spruce, flowering cherry trees, and Port Orford cedar. A carriage concourse was laid, fountains and a giant bandstand were built, and a semicircular concert grove was pruned out of the previous undergrowth.

With only a few exceptions, Volunteer Park looks much as it did when the Olmsteds completed their work on it. Fine clear-weather views of the Space Needle, Puget Sound, and the Olympic Mountains are available from this 445-foot elevation. Climb to the top of the brick-faced water tower (a tricky ascent, given its steep stairs) for an even better perspective. The park fills with people during summer theater performances and weekend festivals. Two outdoor tennis courts are well maintained but underused. A popular children's playground and wading pool lie in the northeastern corner.

Despite the ostensible tranquility, a few cautions should be exercised here. Behind the concrete bandstand, situated just north of the reservoir, sits a public restroom where various criminal activities have occurred despite frequent police patrols; scrupulous visitors might wisely avoid it after nightfall. It seems quite safe at all other hours, however. ♦ Daily dawn-dusk. E. Prospect St and 14th Ave East. 625.8901

Within Volunteer Park:

Conservatory The Volunteer Park Conservatory, constructed for $20,000 in 1912, was patterned after England's spectacular, three-story Crystal Palace exhibition hall, erected in 1851. Seattle's conservatory was actually chosen from a group of prefabricated building plans. Manufactured in New York, the components were shipped to Seattle and put together by parks department employees. Capitol Hill's landed gentry of the time readily embraced the Conservatory, calling it the finest structure of its kind west of Chicago and contributing plant specimens to its collection.

During the Great Depression, however, the Conservatory fell upon hard times, its humid environment rotting the Southern swamp cypress frames and rusting some of the iron supports. By the 1970s the greenhouse was beginning to list to one side and visitors weren't allowed on the premises during windy weather because panes of glass tended to pop out of their frames. A $500,000 restoration program in the early '80s re-created the building's graceful roof and sides using steel, cast iron, and Alaska cedar. During refurbishment, a colorful etched-glass canopy—*Homage in Green*—was installed over the entrance. Created by **Richard Spaulding,** a former artist-in-residence with the **Seattle Arts Commission,** *Homage* is enlivened with lilies, passion flowers, and convolvuluses (a kind of morning glory), all of which are familiar from Victorian designs. The sides of the canopy depict English designs from before 1900 and American designs from after that year. Inside, more than a quarter-million visitors each year study an incredible array of orchids, cacti, and tropical species in three crowded wings. Sadly, the abundant foliage permits no room for wheelchairs. The Conservatory's admirers periodically lobby the city for expansion, but the park's neighbors, fearing more traffic, object. ♦ Free. Daily 10AM-7PM 1 May-15 Sept; daily 10AM-4PM 16 Sept-30 Apr. 1400 E. Galer St. 684.4743

M. BLUM

Volunteer Park Water Tower

Monument to William H. Seward The weathered bronze statue immediately in front of the Conservatory is apparently a good likeness of the former U.S. Secretary of State and real-estate tycoon who bought Alaska from the Russians in 1867 for two cents an acre. New York artist **Richard Brooks** created this piece for placement at the **Alaska-Yukon-Pacific Expo** in 1909. It was moved "temporarily" to this site after the Exposition closed to await its final location in the soon-to-be-completed **Seward Park** on Lake Washington. The city, however, just never quite managed that final step.

Old Seattle Art Museum Since its completion in 1933, this Art Deco institution (designed by **Carl Gould** and replacing the park's old bandstand) was a partial gift to the city from **Dr. Richard Fuller,** philanthropist and president of the Seattle Fine Arts Society, along with his mother, **Mrs. Eugene Fuller.** While it exudes the repose and symmetricalness of Gould's Beaux Arts training, the museum was still a fresh expression at the time of its construction, a protomodern design with rounded corners, curved walls, and a foyer that flows gracefully toward side galleries and stairways. Until recent years the museum was the Pacific Northwest's premier showplace of the arts; that changed, however, with the 1991 opening of **Robert Venturi's** new Seattle Art Museum in downtown. Plans are to renovate this building to house Asian collections and a study center. Museum authorities expect the structure to reopen sometime in 1994. In the meantime, Gould's work is still worth observing as a symbol of Seattle's longstanding devotion to artistic pursuits. ♦ 625.8901

Black Sun One of the park's focal points is this massive black granite sculpture—nine feet in diameter—created in 1968 by artist **Isamu Noguchi** (who also did *Landscape of Time,* a collection of carved granite boulders at Second Avenue and Marion Street). Area residents call it either The Doughnut or The Black Hole. Not to discourage anyone, but if you choose to frame a photograph of the Space Needle through the sculpture's interior orifice, you won't be the first to do so. You'll find the sculpture across from the Old Seattle Art Museum.

24 The Parker House This vast Colonial Revival mansion was built in 1909 for **George H. Parker,** the West Coast fiscal agent for the **United Wireless Company.** Parker's $150,000 home, supported by Corinthian columns, boasted 5 covered porches, 12 bedrooms and 16 other rooms, 7 fireplaces, 5 bathrooms, hardwood floors, muraled walls, and an adjoining coach house. Parker, however, was not to enjoy his mansion for long. In 1910 he was convicted of stock-and-mail

fraud and given a two-year sentence at the federal prison on McNeil Island in south Puget Sound. ♦ 1409 E. Prospect St

25 Roberta's Bed & Breakfast $ This B&B (see picture above) offers five rooms (all but one claiming a private bath) with queen-size beds. The breakfast is a full, family-style affair but vegetarian. There are lots of books for the borrowing, and a fresh *New York Times* is available every day. Ask for the mountain-view room. It's a one-block walk from here to **Volunteer Park.** No off-street parking is available. ♦ 1147 16th Ave East. 329.3326

26 Capitol Hill Addition Many of the comparatively modest residences found just east of Volunteer Park were part of the Capitol Hill Addition, a residential development begun around 1905. Spearheading that project but backed by East Coast money, was **James A. Moore,** the real-estate promoter who would later build the **Moore Theater** in downtown and create the **University Heights** district. Moore already had an interest in this neighborhood; in 1901 he'd acquired a good portion of Capitol Hill, which the old *Seattle Argus* called the last of the "high-grade resident properties to be platted." Moore's wife, **Eugenia,** named this neighborhood after an exclusive section of her hometown, Denver.

Before opening his Capitol Hill Addition to occupancy, Moore spent $150,000 on improvements (cement sidewalks, street paving, sewers, and water), "a previously unheard-of procedure," wrote the *Seattle Times.* The subdivision attracted the construction of many Colonial Revival homes—a style now commonly referred to as the Classic Box—along a nearby streetcar line. This section may not compete with nearby Millionaires' Row or the Harvard-Belmont district for architectural eloquence, but its houses still delight with intricate details, such as squared-off corner bay windows, lead glass, and Moorish keyhole windows. It's worth walking these thoroughfares to observe Moore's early legacy. One of the finer examples of the Classic Box can be found at 747 16th Avenue East and is identified by its shallow ground-floor bays. ♦ Bounded by E. Galer St, E. Mercer St, 15th Ave East, and 23rd Ave East

27 Isaac Stevens School Early school district architect **James Stephen,** whose institutional artistry is also on display at **Summit Grade School** on First Hill, **Latona Elementary,** and **Interlake School**—now **Wallingford Center**—in Wallingford, designed this huge wooden Colonial Revival edifice in 1906. Children must feel over-whelmed when passing beneath its grand columned entrance every day. ♦ 1242 18th Ave East. 281.6760

28 Holy Names Academy Beaux Arts styling receives grand exposition in this domed Catholic girls' school, designed by **C. Alfred Breitung,** who also created the tiny **Triangle Hotel Building** in Pioneer Square and Wallingford's **Home of the Good Shepherd.** ♦ 728 21st Ave East. 323.4272

29 St. Joseph's Catholic Church Pay close attention to the tall, tapering belfry on this stripped-down Gothic house of worship, for it's there that you can find some relationship between this 1932 building and a still-more-impressive structure also designed by architect **Joseph Wilson:** the **Seattle Tower** in downtown. The covering on this church was apparently intended as something grander than cast concrete, but the Great Depression forced Wilson to simplify his dreams. Don't miss the stained-glass window on the entrance face. ♦ Services Sa 5PM; Su 9AM, 11AM, 5:30PM. 732 18th Ave East. 324.2522

30 Salisbury House $ A Victorian charmer owned and operated by sisters **Mary** and **Catheryn Wiese,** this bed-and-breakfast can accommodate eight guests in four rooms, all with private baths. Family-style, vegetarian breakfasts are served here, the library is comfy and well stocked, and **Volunteer Park** is two short blocks away. Off-street parking is not available. ♦ 750 16th Ave East. 328.8682

31 Thomas Bordeaux House "Millionaires' Row" is the name given to the tree-lined cluster of Xanadus extending south from Volunteer Park's East Prospect Street boundary along 14th Avenue East to East Roy Street. Seattle's most prominent families once found status as well as security here, as this mini-neighborhood was protected from mere mortals by a private gate at 14th and Roy. The gate is now gone, but the district retains much of its earlier elegance. Reflecting a trend in other affluent Seattle neighborhoods, however, many of the mansions have been converted from single-family residences to apartments.

The Bordeaux House was built by a Canadian who arrived here in 1852 and later ascended to the presidency of the **Mason County Logging Company** and the **Mumby Lumber and Shingle Company. Thomas Bordeaux** was also a director of the **First National Bank of Seattle.** His home, complete with a decorated tower, was built in 1903. Designed by Seattle architect **W.D. Kimball,** it reflects the half-timber style then in vogue. ♦ 806 14th Ave East

31 Shafer Mansion $$$ When he died in 1951, at the age of 79, the *Seattle Times* wrote that **Julius Shafer's** career was "a typical success story of a poor immigrant boy." Shafer, however, wasn't poor for long. Born in Austria, he came to the U.S. at age 12 and arrived in Seattle six years later, in 1890. He and his brother **Issle** had worked in Kansas and Texas, saved $700, and used that to start a secondhand clothing store in Seattle. The business prospered, and at the turn of the century, the Shafer brothers scored a fortune outfitting men bound for the Alaskan goldfields. In 1921 Julius Shafer retired from the rag trade to pursue real-estate interests, and two years later, he and his brother built the **Shafer Building,** a 10-story office tower that still stands in downtown at Sixth Avenue and Pine Street. Shafer later headed the **Hebrew Immigrant Aid Society** and assisted European refugees in resettling in this country.

As a reflection of his success, in 1914 Julius Shafer constructed this spacious and landscaped English manor on Millionaires' Row, overlooking Elliott Bay. Now a bed-and-breakfast, the mansion has 13 rooms, 10 of them with private baths. There's also a carriage house and a bridal suite. Current owner **Erv Olssen** has opened Shafer Mansion up to wedding and reception business, but that shouldn't detract from a pleasant stay here. After a buffet breakfast in the dining room, one that includes fruits and Danish pastries, repair to the formal library or take a one-block stroll to **Volunteer Park.** Off-street parking is available. ♦ 907 14th Ave East. 322.4654

31 Cobb House Built in 1910, this house—"a fusion of the spirit of the German Black Forest and the English Arts & Crafts movement," as *A Guide to Architecture in Washington State* so eloquently puts it—was designed by the prestigious early 20th century firm of **Charles Bebb** and **Leonard L. Mendel.** It has lovely lead-glass windows and a sizable second-floor balcony secluded by a parapet. The first owner was **C.H. Cobb,** a native of Maine, who moved west to California in 1876, then headed north to Seattle, where by the 1890s he had incorporated four logging and timber companies and the **Marysville and Arlington Railroad Company.** ♦ 1409 E. Aloha St

32 Landes House $ This turn-of-the-century establishment has a nice garden, a hot tub, off-street parking, and 10 guest rooms (some with decks). Resident owners **Tom Hanes** and **Dick Hurlocker** say business travelers appreciate the TBX central switchboard (it connects to the phones in all rooms). The breakfast is an expanded Continental. ♦ 712 11th Ave East. 329.8781

33 Harvard-Belmont Historic District This venerable Capitol Hill enclave was once home to many of Seattle's top industrialists, financiers, and business leaders, among them Great Northern Railroad heir **Sam Hill. Horace C. Henry,** another railroader, who'd moved to Seattle in 1890 from his native Vermont to build the original belt line around Lake Washington for the Northern Pacific Railroad, also lived here.

Most of the mansions in the district were built between 1905 and 1910, with the predominant architectural styles being Tudor, Colonial, and Georgian Revival. In the 1920s a second wave of building brought a number of elegant brick apartment complexes to the area, many of them designed by noted Seattle architect/builder **Fred Anhalt.** Unlike most of the city's old neighborhoods—which have largely succumbed to modern development —the Harvard-Belmont district has remained a gracious retreat of tree-lined streets, professionally tended gardens, and majestic residential and institutional buildings. It was entered in the **National Register of Historic Places** in 1982. ♦ Bounded by E. Highland Dr, E. Roy St, Broadway, and Belmont Ave East

33 Rainier Chapter House of the D.A.R. City architect **Daniel R. Huntington** designed the chapter house of the **Daughters of the American Revolution** in 1924 as a replica of George Washington's Mount Vernon estate. The building is rented out for parties, chamber-music concerts, and the like, and it is a favorite for wedding receptions. ♦ 800 E. Roy St. 323.0600

33 The Bacchus Restaurant ★★$ Where once a Greek restaurant thrived, might another do just as well? With the migration of the very popular **Byzantion** to Broadway, Bacchus swept in to fill the vacuum. Or to try to fill it, anyway. It's still too early to pass judgment on this place, but indications are that Bacchus, if not as uninhibited and adventurous as its namesake, can at least hold its own in Seattle's Greek pantheon. The *paidakia* (lamb chops broiled with lemon, olive oil, and garlic) is a fine treat, along with the panfried baby squid appetizer (lots of onions and chopped almonds for crunch and color). Try the *kefthethes,* meatballs served on pita and sprinkled with feta cheese; its easily broken globes of meat bring to mind a quote from gonzo food writer **John Thorne:**

"What is a meatball, after all, if not the triumph of quick wit over brute reality?" The Greek burger, buttermilk pancakes, and similarly shameful bows to naive American tastes could all be done without, but those are minor annoyances.

The atmosphere here may remind you of an old wine cellar, only one that has walls muraled over with an Alexander Pushkin folktale, painted by Russian artist **Vladimir Pavlovich Shkurin.** (They're left here from an earlier restaurant.) Service is efficient, if somewhat overly familiar, and it's surprisingly quiet. ♦ Greek ♦ M-Th 11AM-11PM; F 11AM-midnight; Sa 10AM-midnight; Su 10AM-11PM. 806 E. Roy St. 325.2888

33 Loveless Building Designed in an English cottage vein by Seattle architect **Arthur B. Loveless,** this graceful block of first-floor shops and second-floor apartments arranged around a concealed courtyard was built in 1931. In his book *Seattle Past to Present,* **Roger Sale** refers to the "enchanting Loveless Block, stores and apartments of an elegance that Arthur Loveless alone among traditional Seattle architects seemed to have." Loveless was a master of well-sited period revival designs. His houses are dotted over Capitol Hill, and in 1930, he remodeled the **Colman Building** on First Avenue in an Art Deco style. ♦ 711 Broadway East

34 Cornish College of the Arts This "quietly elegant building of Mediterranean persuasion," as it's described in *A Guide to Architecture in Washington State,* was designed in 1921 by the Seattle architectural firm of **Albertson, Wilson & Richardson. Nellie Cornish,** the piano-playing daughter of a Tennessee sheep farmer who moved to Seattle in 1900, founded the school without any initial support from the city. But with programs in art, music, theater, and dance, the Cornish institute has since played an important part in Seattle's cultural life. Renowned choreographer **Martha Graham** and painter **Mark Tobey** were members of the Cornish faculty. Nellie Cornish lived in an apartment on the top floor of this terracotta-ornamented edifice. ♦ 710 E. Roy St. 323.1400

35 Harvard Exit Taking over a building that once held a ladies' club, this is remembered as Seattle's first luxury art theater. It still schedules some of the better flicks passing through town. (Sorry, Mr. Stallone, you'll have to go elsewhere.) From the crowded entryway, pass through what once must have been an elegant drawing room or living room but is now a very comfortable, old-fashioned space to meet your moviegoing partners. Checkers are available for extended waits. Entries in the annual **Seattle International Film Festival** often play here. ♦ Box office opens one hour before show time. 807 E. Roy St. 323.8986

Grave Matters

Like any town worth its salt—not to mention its weight in garlic cloves and silver bullets—Seattle boasts a host of ghost stories. Here are some of the more popular tales of ghoulish gallivantings:

- **Pike Place Market**—normally as crowded and cheery as can be—seems to have more than its share of active ectoplasm. One legend involves the ghost of a 300-pound woman who, apparently during the market's more rickety days, fell through a ceiling there and landed on a table. Another is told about the spirit of an elderly Native American woman. Those who have seen her say she's stocky, beatific, and wrinkled. She wears a quilted shawl and her hair hangs in two long braids; she carries a couple of baskets and appears only in the evening, when the market is closing. By the way, it's believed that anyone who spots this Indian matron will die an unusual death, so watch out.

- The nearby **Butterworth Building,** halfway between Virginia and Stewart streets on First Avenue, was constructed in 1903. The builder was one of Seattle's best-known morticians, **Edgar Ray Butterworth,** which may help explain the structure's reported apparitional population.

  The Butterworth's bottom floor, now home to **Kell's Restaurant & Pub** on Post Alley, once held stables, a hearse garage, a cremation oven, and a vault for ashes of the dearly departed. The chapel, sitting parlor, visitation rooms, and choir loft were on the first floor, where **Cafe Sophie** does business today. Customers rode a hydraulic elevator—the first in Seattle—to the third story, where they could shop for caskets and where embalming and cosmetic work were practiced. (The mortuary moved from this building in 1923, relocating to Capitol Hill.)

  Mysterious mumbling has been heard in the bathrooms at Kell's, long after it has closed for an evening. But the best story comes from Cafe Sophie, where an electrician, working past midnight to rewire one of the restaurant's chandeliers, once encountered two shadowy gents sitting at a table, talking. He tried his best to ignore the reveling revenants, until they came over to help him steady a ladder. Then suddenly, a woman dressed in "an unearthly white linen dress" ventured into the dining room, provoking the other two ghosts to shout insults in her direction, until the terrified electrician rushed from the premises.

- The venerable **Arctic Building,** on Third Avenue in downtown, is supposedly inhabited by the specter of someone who leapt from one of its windows during the stock-market collapse of 1929.

- The building that once housed the **Burnley School of Professional Art** on Capitol Hill (now the south annex of **Seattle Central Community College**) has seen thousands of students in its day, and many of them swear they've encountered the school's poltergeist—an elderly man who walks the corridors with a heavy gait and sometimes unlocks doors or turns on coffee machines. Speculation has it that he's the ghost of a student from long-gone **Broadway High** (the original institution on the college site) who got into a fight during a basketball game in the school's third-floor gym and fell down a flight of stairs.

- The **United Methodist Church** on Capitol Hill, built at the turn of the century, has a couple of resident spirits: a woman in a flowing gown and a gaunt, white-bearded gentleman. Both have been seen by a variety of folks over the years. Some theorize that they are the **Reverend Daniel Bagley,** Seattle's first Methodist minister, and his wife.

- Whatever the reason, Seattle's ghosts especially seem to like moviehouses and theaters. The **University of Washington's Showboat Theater,** which has floated in Portage Bay since the 1930s, has been home to such diverse actors as **Lillian Gish** and **Kyle ("Twin Peaks") MacLachlan.** According to students and teachers, however, it's also the residence of a mysterious presence who performs harmless tricks like supplying cue lines and playing the onstage piano. Some says it's the ghost of **Glenn Hughes,** the father of the University of Washington School of Drama.

- Belltown's **Moore Theater** was built in 1907 as Seattle's first vaudeville house. (It's now used mainly for rock shows.) One night during its tenure as a movie palace in the 1970s, the Moore's owner-operators swore they encountered . . . well, something that sighed, smelled bad, and gave them a cold, tingling sensation. When they reluctantly reported it to their employees, the reaction was, "Oh, so you've seen it, too?"

- The **Neptune Theater,** a venerable repertory film house in the University District, is (according to persistent stories told by workers there) also the haunt of things not quite human. One is a lady with long, dark hair, swathed in white and surrounded by light, who likes to hang around in the organ loft. Another leaves behind the odor of fresh tobacco, and still another—the only one of the three who appears somewhat malevolent—loiters menacingly near the upstairs men's room.

35 Deluxe 1 Bar and Grill In his jolly but seminal guide to American groggeries, *The View from Nowhere*, Texas author **Jim Atkinson** applauds what he calls the "Bar Bar": a watering hole where folks can leap clear of responsibility and watchful eyes (they're often no better lighted than a wartime bunker), a spot to bend your elbow in hard-won isolation, "the only place left on earth where you can go and be Nowhere." Amidst the Broadway area's fervid grab for glitz and its increasing dependence on patrons from beyond Capitol Hill, the Deluxe has managed somehow to retain its Bar Bar credentials.

There are no bow ties behind the bar, no leather-skirted "waitrons" bringing you an Art Deco-designed menu. Warm a stool or pull up a chair and order a bacon, onion, and avocado burger that's guaranteed to put permanent frown lines in your doctor's forehead. Or try the pesto potato skins with a frosty pint of microbrewed beer. You don't have to go home yet, do you? In summer a retractable wall out front allows for a maximum of people-watching with a maximum of comfort. ◆ Daily 11AM-2AM. 625 Broadway East. 324.9697

35 Dancer's Series: Steps Hollywood may have its star-studded Walk of Fame, but Seattle claims a sidewalk attraction that may literally sweep you off your feet. Look down as you're strolling either side of busy Broadway between East Pine and East Roy streets. Periodically, you will spot arrangements of bronze footprints along with dance instructions by Seattle artist **Jack Mackie.** Mackie, with assistance from artist **Charles Greening,** created these eight street-level artworks to be used, not just observed. He even mixed a few steps of his own creation (the Busstop, for instance, and the Obeebo) in with the classic rumba, waltz, and tango. Mackie gave special symbolic treatment to the heels, imbedding parking tokens in those footprints outside a parking lot, and offering a simplified view of the skyline in a set near a bus stop. Don't be shy. Do your best to imitate Fred and Ginger. ◆ Broadway (between E. Pine and E. Roy Sts)

35 Cafe Cielo ★★$$ After at least two mediocre incarnations, this restaurant space seems to have finally attracted a winner. Owner **Larry Robinson** has brought in chef **Andy Burgess** from the old **Cafe Sport** in Bellevue to prepare a menu rich with *tapas* (try the roasted garlic with feta cheese and pita bread), pizzas, and a toothsome boneless and herby chicken breast served over polenta. The interior is cozy, with subdued lighting and an expansive view of boisterous Broadway street. ◆ Mediterranean ◆ M-F 11AM-2PM, 5PM-midnight; Sa-Su 10AM-2PM, 5PM-2AM. 611 Broadway East. Reservations recommended. 324.9084

36 Byzantion ★$ Here you'll find Greek food (and lots of it) from a recently relocated restaurant that's gained a reputation for the quality of its *spanakopita* and lamb dishes. At breakfast, try the feta-cheese omelet. ◆ Greek ◆ M-Th 11AM-11PM; F 11AM-midnight; Sa 9AM-midnight; Su 9AM-11PM. 601 Broadway East. 325.7580

37 Siam on Broadway ★$ Regulars don't even consider sticking around here to eat—there's generally a 10- to 20-minute wait for a table. Instead, they call ahead, then fly by to pick up steaming orders of garlicky orange beef, *phad thai*, panfried butterfish, or one of the effervescent soups. Unlike some Thai establishments in Seattle, the star ratings that reflect the "hotness" of a dish should be taken seriously at Siam; you'll pay for any negligence. ◆ Thai/Takeout ◆ M-Th 11:30AM-10PM; F 11:30AM-11PM; Sa 5-11PM; Su 5-10PM. 616 Broadway East. 324.0892

38 Orpheum With compact discs galore, from heavy metal rock to old jazz, this store is usually noisy (the owners must be conducting hearing tests to determine how loud music can be played before eardrums start to explode) but ideal for browsing after a movie at the Harvard Exit or on a lazy weekend afternoon. ◆ Daily 10AM-midnight. 618 Broadway East. 322.6370

39 Anhalt Apartments Dating to the late 1920s, these represent well the stylish but practical sort of brick apartment houses designed and constructed by developer/builder **Fred Anhalt.** Some apartments here have nine rooms, two baths, and a fireplace. To ensure soundproofing, Anhalt used double floors and double interior walls. The lovely landscaped courtyard and picturesque round-stair tower (an interesting and space-saving alternative to stairways) are Anhalt trademarks. ◆ 1005 E. Roy St

40 Matzoh Momma ★$ Seattle has nothing approaching the Jewish kosher delis of Detroit or New York, but Matzoh Momma may be the next best thing. Food is "kosher style," rather than authentically blessed by a rabbi. But some of it is still delicious. Try the chicken soup with matzoh balls or the Reuben sandwich. Every few months, the popular **Mazeltones** klezmer band will drop in to entertain at dinnertime. ◆ Jewish ◆ Daily 9AM-9PM. 509 15th Ave East. 324.6262

41 Capons ★$ Chicken is served here in a generosity of styles—whole, half, and in sandwiches and soups. The fowl is juicy and fresh, sometimes fresher than the steamed vegetables available on the side. Service is cafeteria style, and the atmosphere pleasant and casual. ◆ Chicken ◆ Daily 11AM-10PM. 605 15th Ave East. 323.4026. Also at: 1814 N 45th St. 547.3949; 4400 Wallingford Ave North. 547.7246

42 The Cause Célèbre Cafe It was Voltaire who, responding to word in his time that coffee might actually be poisonous, quipped, "I have been poisoning myself for 80 years and I am not yet dead." Cause Célèbre is one of the funkier establishments at which Seattle caffiends can find their preferred poison. The first floor of a former residence is decorated in American garage-sale style, with a deck for sunny days. This place is popular with the black-on-black-on-black fashion contingent. ♦ Coffeehouse ♦ M-Sa 9AM-9PM; Su 9AM-5PM. 524 15th Ave East. 323.1888

42 Olympia Pizza and Spaghetti House III ★$ Comfy booths, room for small parties, and killer pizza—all this and more can be found at Olympia. The House Special is the best-seller, but those who crave recognition as pizza authorities should sample a slice of the Greek Special. ♦ Pizza/Takeout ♦ M-Th 11:30AM-11PM; F-Sa 11:30AM-midnight; Su 3-11PM. 516 15th Ave East. 329.4500. Also at: 1500 Queen Anne Ave North. 285.5550; 4501 Interlake Ave North. 633.3655; 3213 W. McGraw St. 286.9000

42 City Peoples' Mercantile This small store somehow includes something for everybody. A well-stocked hardware department for the neighborhood wall-bangers is in the back; housewares, art supplies, and a trendy selection of clothing can be found closer to the entrance. The espresso cart out front provides nourishment and newspapers. Four women founded the Mercantile back in the 1970s and have since expanded their operations to include **City Peoples' Garden Store,** an upscale emporium for gardeners (2939 Madison Avenue; 324.0737). ♦ M-F 9AM-8PM; Sa 9AM-6PM; Su 10AM-6PM. 500 15th Ave East. 324.9510. Also at: 3517 Fremont Ave North. 632.1200

Longtime Seattleites seem surprisingly undaunted by the precipitation here. Many don't carry umbrellas on wet days, and chances are they don't even *own* one, preferring for some reason to make mad dashes from the car to the office and back. And is it wishful thinking or downright denial that leads locals to buy more sunglasses per capita than residents of any other city in the United States? Probably neither. More likely they stash their old pairs away during rainstorms and, after a while, forget where they put them.

Restaurants/Clubs: Red   Hotels: Blue
Shops/ Outdoors: Green   Sights/Culture: Black

43 Jalisco ★$ A small, family-run Mexican restaurant, Jalisco is patronized almost exclusively by Hill residents. The standard dishes—especially enchiladas and burritos—are well done, and waiters will cheerfully help you create a personalized combination plate. Or you could just order the delicious quesadillas. They serve great margaritas and a wide selection of Mexican beers, but entertainment is limited mostly to the clientele, who seem anxious to practice their dubious Spanish on the patient and extraordinarily efficient staff. ♦ Mexican ♦ Daily 11AM-10PM. 1467 E. Republican St. 325.9005. Also at: 122 First Ave North. 283.4242; 12336 31st Ave NE. 364.3978; 115 Park Lane. 822.3355

44 Horizon Books An older home has been converted to a used-book cavern, where intrepid literati wander labyrinthine passageways in search of affordable reading. Your best bet is to ask for directions upon entering the maze. The science-fiction section is out of this world. ♦ M-F 10AM-10PM; Sa-Su 10AM-9PM. 425 15th Ave East. 329.3586

45 Cafe Dilettante Formulas used to manufacture the confections sold here are said to have been passed down from **Julius Rudolph Franzen,** who created pastries for **Emperor Franz Josef** of Austria and later served as master candy maker to **Nicholas II,** last czar of Russia. A chocoholic's fantasy, Dilettante carries some of the most tempting truffles, butter crèmes, and dragées (nuts or dried fruits dredged through high-quality dipping chocolates) you will ever try to resist indulging in. On the menu as well are such things as Romanian borscht and sandwiches. (Note that Dilettante also operates an imperfect-chocolates outlet store at 2300 East Cherry Street; 328.1530.) ♦ M-Th, Su 10AM-midnight; F-Sa 10AM-1AM. 416 Broadway East. 329.6463

45 Bailey/Coy Books Covering a lot of area in a fairly confined space means that Bailey/Coy, for all its efforts, must be very selective. Look for current best-sellers, a wide selection of gay and lesbian studies, lots of magazines, and respectable depth in the gardening and fiction categories, but lesser representation elsewhere. ♦ M-Th 10AM-10PM; F-Sa 10AM-11PM; Su 11AM-8PM. 414 Broadway East. 323.8842

46 Broadway Market A former **Fred Meyer** store has been entirely gutted and revamped into one of Seattle's liveliest small market-places. Musicians often entertain in the main gallery. A parking garage is available on East Harrison Street. ♦ M-Sa 10AM-9PM; Su noon-6PM. 401 Broadway East. 322.1610

Within Broadway Market:

B&O Espresso Located right in the middle of the arcade, this fine coffee and dessert stop is one of two B&Os on Capitol Hill. ♦ Coffeehouse ♦ M-Th 8AM-10PM; F-Sa 8AM-10:30PM; Su 8AM-9PM. First floor. 329.3290. Also at: 204 Belmont Ave East. 322.5028

Bulldog News This shrunken sibling to the expansive University District store still carries a diverting array of magazine titles, from *Men's Journal* to *Working Woman* and *Cigar Aficionado*. ♦ M-F 9AM-11PM; Sa-Su 8AM-11PM. First floor. 322.6397. Also at: 4208 University Way NE. 632.6397

Gravity Bar ★$ This place is right out of *Star Wars*, chromey with high-tech lighting. As with its larger branch in downtown, this Gravity Bar specializes in healthy juices and things heavily into brown rice. The staff is too, too trendy. But you can do lots of sidewalk-watching from the tall windows. ♦ Vegetarian ♦ M-F 8AM-10PM; Sa 8AM-11PM; Su 9AM-5PM. First floor. 325.7186. Also at: 113 Virginia St. 448.8826

Rasa Malaysia ★★$ Another in a popular chain of take-out or eat-in spots, Rasa specializes in noodles, usually sautéed with fresh veggies; peanut or another mildly spicy sauce; and a variety of fish, shrimp, or meat. ♦ Malaysian/Takeout ♦ Daily 11AM-8:30PM. First floor. 328.8882. Also at: 7208 E. Green Lake Dr North. 523.8888; 6012 Phinney Ave North. 781.8888; Pike Place Market. 624.8388

Sergio's ★$ An extremely unprepos-sessing place (it actually takes some work to find it off an obscure hallway), Sergio's nonetheless serves pleasing burritos and tacos. The decor is modern mall, so order to go. ♦ Mexican/Takeout ♦ Daily 11AM-9PM. First floor. 328.6055

Hamburger Mary's ★$ A gift from Portland, Oregon, and San Francisco, Mary's naturally cooks up hamburgers in all their

thick and oozing glory. But don't ignore the omelets (choose from a bewildering assortment of ingredients), which provide genuine comfort food on inclement Northwest mornings. ♦ American ♦ M-Th 10AM-midnight; F 10AM-2AM; Sa 9AM-2AM; Su 9AM-midnight. Second floor. 325.6565

47 The Oven ★$ This is the fast-food affiliate of Lower Queen Anne's **Mediterranean Kitchen**. In large part, the menu here is the same (yes, the renowned Farmer's Dish is available), but there are also gyro sandwiches and beef or chicken *shawarma*. ♦ Middle Eastern/Takeout ♦ M-Th, Su 11AM-9PM; F-Sa 11AM-10PM. 213 Broadway East. 328.2951

47 Macheesmo Mouse ★$ Is there really such a thing as healthy fast food? Here you'll find south-of-the-border fare that's unfried, low fat, and low cholesterol. Tacos, enchiladas, and other entrées come with black beans, brown rice . . . and a calorie count. Burritos are your best bet. ♦ Mexican/Takeout ♦ M-Sa 11AM-10PM; Su noon-10PM. 211 Broadway East. 325.0072. Also at: 4129 University Way NE. 633.4658

48 TestaRossa ★★$ Thick and wonderfully flavorful Chicago-style pies are turned out by this second-floor pizza joint. The garlic, spinach, and mushroom pie is everyone's favorite. ♦ Pizza ♦ M-Th 11AM-11PM, F-Sa 11AM-midnight, Su 1-10PM Mar-Sept; M-W 11AM-10PM, Th 11AM-11PM, F-Sa 11AM-midnight, Su 1-10PM Oct-Feb. 210 Broadway East. 328.0878

48 Steve's Broadway News Steve Dunnington, formerly a mustachioed fixture at **Read All About It** in Pike Place Market, has brought his love of magazines and other periodicals to hyperkinetic Broadway. The usual mix is available here, as well as some oddball foreign papers. A connoisseur of tabloid journalism, Dunnington keeps the scandal sheets prominently displayed ("Devil Escapes From Alaskan Oil Well!"), for their humor potential. ♦ M-Th, Su 8AM-11PM; F-Sa 8AM-midnight. 204 Broadway East. 324.7323

48 Espresso Roma Head for Espresso Roma when you have the hankering to read all of *Billy Budd* in a public setting. Small and quiet, this is one coffeehouse where nobody's going to disturb you. Lots of students and wanna-be artists camp out here. ♦ Coffeehouse ♦ M-F 7AM-10PM; Sa-Su 9AM-10PM. 202 Broadway East. 324.1866. Also at: 4201 University Way NE. 632.6001

49 D'Afric ★★$ Chances are that, unless you know to look for this charming little Ethiopian restaurant behind a nondescript shopping arcade, you'll miss it in a march up Broad-way. A sandwich board on the sidewalk outside is hardly notice for all of the subtle treasures to be found within. Family owned,

D'Afric is gaining fame by word of mouth. In the traditional manner, helpings are served here on flavorful *injera*, the spongy flat bread that substitutes as an eating utensil in Ethiopian dining rooms. Meat dishes are generally spicy, with favorites including *yebeg wot* (beef and vegetables in a rich sauce) and the *yesiga tibs* (beef mixed with green chile peppers). *Shifinfin* comes highly recommended by the hostess and is described by the menu in purple tones, but is in truth a less-than-satisfying if well-spiced mound of the *injera*. Of the appetizers, the pureed yellow split peas are among the tastiest. Service here is friendly, efficient, and helpful. If you've never had East African cuisine, order the combination plate, which includes three main dishes and three side dishes of your choice. ♦ East African ♦ M-Sa noon-10:30PM; Su 2-10:30PM. 112 Broadway East. 328.5117

50 Hill House $ Owners **Ken Hayes** and **Eric Lagasca** offer three rooms, one of which has a private bath. The location is close to Broadway and to buses to both downtown and the **University of Washington.** Breakfast is an expanded Continental on weekdays, family style on weekends. ♦ 1113 E. John St. 720.7161

51 Prince of Wales $ Try to secure the attic suite here, with its westward deck view of the city, Puget Sound, and the Olympic Mountains. There are four rooms, two boasting a private bath; two rooms can accommodate up to three guests. Owners **Naomi Reed** and **Burt Brun** serve a full breakfast and will accept older, well-mannered children. The bus stops across the street, and it's only a one-mile walk to downtown's **Washington State Convention Center.** ♦ 133 13th Ave East. 325.9692

52 Group Health Cooperative Group Health's central facility is Seattle's largest hospital and the neighborhood's major employment center, spawning an attendant flock of shops and restaurants on 15th Avenue East. With 472,000 members in Washington and Idaho, it is the nation's 15th-largest HMO and the fifth-oldest such organization in the country. Park in the underground garage (about $2 for three hours). ♦ 200 15th Ave East. 326.3000

53 Kidd Valley ★$ Unlike some chain burger joints you may know, Kidd Valley succeeds at being both fun for children and culinarily satisfying for the adults who are along to make sure they clean off their plates. Hamburgers here are flavorful fistfuls of juicy meat and bun, best accompanied by the thick and not-too-greasy fries. The milk shakes are some of the best in town (order the chocolate or the root beer). Lines are common at the counter. ♦ American/Takeout ♦ 135 15th Ave East 328.8133. Also at: 4910 Green Lake Way. 547.0121; 14303 Aurora Ave North. 364.8493; 531 Queen Anne Ave North. 284.0184; 5502 25th Ave NE. 522.0890

53 Giorgina's ★$ This joint specializes in fresh, high-quality toppings and ingredients. The Quattro, a sausage-and-pepperoni extravaganza, is just the thing to avoid before having your cholesterol count taken across the street at Group Health hospital. Pasta, sandwiches, soups, and ice cream are also available. Sit at the sidewalk-view counter and watch heart-and-lung specialists sneaking out for a furtive cigarette. ♦ Pizza/Takeout ♦ Daily 11AM-10PM. 131 15th Ave East. 329.8118

54 The Corner House $ Of special note in the Corner House (illustrated above) are the beds, guaranteed to rival or surpass your own in comfort. There are only two rooms (each with a private bath), but the atmosphere is warm, eclectic. Owners **Julianne Nason** and **Oliver H. Osborn** serve a Continental breakfast and offer off-street parking. ♦ 102 18th Ave East. 328.2865

"Seattle is an old gold-mining stopover peopled by too many boring Canadians to have any real style. . . . The personality is that of a Boeing engineer—a guy who still wears wide-wale corduroy pants and a pullover sweater. . . . I suppose I might be missing the charm of the area, whatever it is. I say this because Seattle dwellers always talk about going back as if the burg were some sort of Mecca. The stay-put locals seem content enough in their pretty little environment. There must be drugs in the water."

San Francisco Examiner

The Gaslight Inn

55 The Gaslight Inn $ This is a good bed-and-breakfast choice if you want easy access to downtown: the No. 10 bus line stops right out front of the Gaslight (pictured above) and goes all the way down to the Waterfront. Antique furniture graces the dining room, parlor, living room, and library at this inn. A pool is heated for use during summer months but is closed during winter. Five of the nine rooms have private baths, one has a city-view deck, and another has a fireplace. A Continental breakfast is served. Month-in-advance reservations are appropriate in summer; a couple of weeks will suffice during winter months. ♦ 1727 15th Ave. 325.3654

56 The Globe Cafe & Bakery Soy-milk *lattes*? That's as bad as using decaf in Irish coffee. But the Globe's vegan tilt is balanced by a relaxed atmosphere and gingerbread that may be better than Mom's (not that anyone would ever tell her that). Toys are on hand for the young-uns. ♦ Coffeehouse ♦ M-F 7AM-10PM; Sa-Su 10AM-10PM. 1531 14th Ave East. 324.8815

57 REI Founded in 1938, **Recreational Equipment Inc.** has become a Seattle institution, as well as the nation's largest consumer cooperative, with more than one million active members worldwide. The main headquarters have moved south to suburban Kent and REI has grown to a nationwide chain of 34 stores, but this hallowed temple remains the heart and soul of the operation, at least for outdoorsy Seattle natives. Everything you'll need for your next expedition to the Himalayas or just a jog around the block is here: gear and clothing for backpacking, climbing, water sports, cycling, and skiing. There's even an adventure-travel arm to the business now, and the mail-order catalog goes all over the world. ♦ M-Tu 10AM-7PM; W-F 10AM-9PM; Sa 10AM-6PM; Su noon-5PM. 1525 11th Ave. 323.8333

58 Comet Tavern This pub is rather down-at-heels, and damn proud of it. The clientele is a Whitman sampler of politicos, aspiring artists, writers, and escapees from nearby Seattle University. There's lots of graffiti but zero video games. Bottom line: the Comet is an honest drinking joint. ♦ Daily noon-2AM. 922 E. Pike St. 323.9853

59 Egyptian Theater One of the city's classiest moviehouses is contained within an old Masonic temple that also serves as headquarters for the **Seattle International Film Festival,** held each May. Inside is **Cafe Cairo,** an espresso bar operated by **Craig Donarum,** who actually gave this city its first espresso cart. ♦ 805 E. Pine St. 323.4978

60 Neighbours It operates during the day as a fairly mediocre restaurant, but at night, Neighbours metamorphoses into a truly cavernous disco, catering mostly to a gay crowd. Very-late-night patrons may be treated to a galley of over-fried foods just to keep up their strength. ♦ Cover. M-Th, Su 11AM-2PM, 5-8PM. Dancing M-Th, Su 9PM-2AM; F-Sa 9PM-4AM. 1509 Broadway. 324.5358

Restaurants/Clubs: Red   **Hotels:** Blue
Shops/ 🌲 Outdoors: Green   **Sights/Culture:** Black

61 Stimson-Green Mansion As Seattle began to establish itself on the shores of Elliott Bay in the mid-19th century, the city's captains of industry all competed furiously to build grander mansions than those of their rivals. The first such examples graced **First Hill,** just east of downtown. This became Seattle's earliest status neighborhood, but its reign was brief, lasting only a generation or two before developments more remote from the city were settled. The baronial Stimson-Green house (illustrated above) is a fine reminder of those times.

Built between 1899 and 1901, from designs by architects **Kirtland K. Cutter** and **Karl Malmgren** (whose efforts in this case were heavily influenced by the European Arts & Crafts movement), the house was occupied from its completion until 1914 by the family of Ballard mill-owner **Charles D. Stimson.** From then until 1975, it was the property of the **Joshua Green** family (Green having been a prominent early Seattle banker). Since its designation as a historical site, the mansion's 35 rooms have been open for public touring. Weddings and large parties are also frequently hosted here. Fin de siècle opulence pervades the mansion; sneak back to the kitchen and giggle at the intricate, pre-electronic switchboard used to summon the servants. ♦ Free. M-F 9AM-3PM. 1204 Minor Ave. 624.0474

62 Summit Grade School/The Northwest School One of the finest among architect **James Stephen's** many Seattle schools, this 1905 wood structure is a catalog of brick-and-stucco facing, stepped parapets, and decorative ironwork, with an octagonal bell tower. The local school district closed this building in 1965, but more than a decade later it was bought and rehabilitated by operators of **The Northwest School,** a private institution for grades 6 through 12. ♦ 1415 Summit Ave. 682.7309

63 Cafe Sabika ★★$$ This bistro certainly deserves its rep for homey friendliness (it's not uncommon to hear the chef singing) and classic, elegant meals. Chef/owner **John Rios'** background in the food preparations of Provence has added an interesting dimension to his dishes, such as pork burritos, as well as skill to his work on entrées from tender beef Wellington to an exceptional duck linguine. ♦ Country French/Northern Italian ♦ Tu-Sa 5-11PM. 315 E. Pine St. 622.3272

64 Re-bar Probably the best danceteria in Seattle, Re-bar certainly boasts the liveliest disc jockeys (don't miss Queen Lucky if she's in town). The crowd is mixed, straights and gays, with mostly the latter on signature **Queer Disco Nights.** You'll hear lots of Diana Ross and industrial dance—the fare depends on the DJ. Live bands are scheduled irregularly. ♦ Cover. M-W, F-Su 9PM-2AM; Th 8PM-2AM. 1114 E. Howell St. 233.9873

65 Reiner's ★★★$$$ A chef worth watching is **Reiner Greubel,** formerly of New York's Plaza Hotel and the Seattle Westin, now with his own small but elegant restaurant. Choice picks are Greubel's tender veal and fish dishes. He also serves the finest tortellini pesto-cream soup you've ever sunk a spoon into. The service is somewhat tardy but very courteous. ♦ French ♦ Tu-F 11:30AM-2PM, 5:30-10PM; Sa 5:30-10:30PM. 1106 Eighth Ave. Reservations recommended. 624.2222

66 Sorrento Hotel $$ Built in 1908, in preparation for Seattle's grand **Alaska-Yukon-Pacific Expo,** the Mediterranean-style Sorrento boasted the city's first rooftop restaurant. (The architect was **Harlan Thomas.**) Restored now to its original elegance, the Sorrento is small by comparison with some local hotels, and guests sometimes complain that its dark-wood appointments look gloomy, but it boasts an unusual intimacy. Some of the guest rooms can be small (a few must satisfy with only narrow slices of view), but they're always comfortably appointed. Try to reserve a room with a westward perspective over Puget Sound. The lobby's **Fireside Lounge** has an appealing clublike atmosphere, and complimentary limousine service is available within the downtown area. ♦ 900 Madison St. 622.6400; fax 625.1059

Within the Sorrento Hotel:

The Hunt Club ★★★★$$$$ Longtime chef **Barbara Figueroa** took a rather dingy redoubt of Old Money Seattle and turned it into one of the city's most inventive, elegant, and written-about restaurants. A master experimenter and Wolfgang Puck protégé, she made the most of seasonal and local ingredients. Figueroa's departure from the Hunt Club in late 1992 (she went to open a new restaurant in San Francisco) left local foodies and critics both stunned and fearful: Would the Sorrento's dining room lose its edge? The new executive chef, **Christine Keff,** certainly thinks not. Keff, an alumnus of Seattle's **McCormick & Schmick's** restaurant and former apprentice to the legendary chef Seppi Renggli of the Four Seasons in New York, says she wants to put her own distinctive stamp on the Hunt Club kitchen. However, as of early 1993, she was following Figueroa's menu. Foodies are hoping for the best. ♦ Northwestern ♦ M-Th, Su 7AM-2:30PM, 5:30-10PM; F-Sa 7AM-2:30PM, 5:30-11PM. Reservations recommended. 622.6400

67 St. James Cathedral Imagine what this astonishing neobaroque church, with its twin 175-foot-tall towers, would look like with a copper dome above its entrance. That was its appearance from December 1907 until January 1916, when the canopy (and a lighted cross on top of that) collapsed beneath the weight of 30,000 pounds of snow. "A roar like the boom of a heavy gun brought priest and layman to the cathedral," wrote the *P-I.* "They saw a huge jagged hole where the massive dome had soared and poured great clouds of mortar dust and flying snow." Months later, the church was reopened with a flat roof that lessened the building's visual impact (it was designed by **Heins & LaFarge,** along with **John Graham, Sr.**) but actually improved interior acoustics. ♦ Services M-Sa 6:25AM, 8:15AM, 12:10PM, 5:30PM; Su 8AM, 10AM, noon, 5:30PM. Ninth Ave and Marion St. 622.3559

67 Trinity Parish Episcopal Church This handsome, rough-cut stone landmark is in the style of English-country parish churches. **John Graham, Sr.,** did the original design in 1891, then restored the building and gave it a new rectory after a terrible fire in 1901. ♦ Services Su 8AM, 10:30AM, 5:30PM. 609 Eighth Ave. 624.5337

68 Temple de Hirsch Sinai A stylized Jewish mountain with exquisite stained glass, this hardly seems like the work of the same man—**B. Marcus Priteca**—who many years earlier designed the downtown's **Coliseum** and **Paramount** theaters. But it is. The sanctuary was built in 1960. ♦ Services F 8:15PM; Sa 10:30AM. E. Pike St and 16th Ave. 323.8486

69 Mount Zion Baptist Church First settled by Italian farmers, the **Central District (CD)** became more urban and residential during World War II, as African-Americans from the Southern states arrived to work in Seattle's booming war-era economy. Much of the neighborhood has since fallen into disrepair, and vice and violence have crept in to spoil its reputation. But there's also a closeness felt by the residents here, people bravely fighting inner-city plagues. As elsewhere, the community's churches have helped hold things together. Most prominent is 102-year-old Mount Zion Baptist, where the 100-member choir transcends its normal function and has become nationally famous through several acclaimed gospel recordings. The church, which seats a thousand people, is packed to the rafters every Sunday. Its 2,000 members include several of the city's major politicos, and its pastor—the **Reverend Samuel McKinney**—is an assertive and familiar voice for African-Americans in Seattle. ♦ Services W 7PM; Su 8AM, 10:45AM. 1634 19th Ave. 322.6500

70 East Madison Street Notable as Seattle's only waterfront-to-waterfront street, East Madison stretches from Elliott Bay through the Central District to Lake Washington. Look at it as a core sample of local history and economics, taking in affluent neighborhoods, poverty-stricken pockets, new condominiums (especially in the area known as **Madison Valley,** from 23rd Avenue East to the lake), and old, single-family residences. ♦ Elliott Bay to Lake Washington

71 All the Best Even though it's just a shop full of pet digestibles and other supplies, All the Best typifies the quality of stores now opening along a once slumlike stretch in the Madison Valley area (halfway between **Madison Park** and downtown). This stretch has undergone extraordinary gentrification in recent years, giving it a recognizably upscale attitude. Owners of All the Best will hold forth ad nauseam on the sinful nature of grocery-store pet foods versus those they sell, which pack more natural ingredients. Indulgent pet owners will appreciate the diversity of neat toys and books in stock here, too. ♦ M-F 11AM-7PM; Sa 10AM-5PM; Su noon-5PM. 2713 E. Madison St. 329.8565

72 Rover's ★★★★$$$$ "If anyone had told me five years ago that French restaurants would not only stage a comeback but become the most significant dining trend of the '90s, I would have dismissed the notion as idiocy," writes *Esquire* restaurant columnist **John Mariani.** Chef **Thierry Rautureau's** small, semiformal, and exquisitely intimate establishment in a frame house has benefited more than many of Seattle's neo-French ilk. Perhaps that's because he's giving familiar Northwestern fare a French accent, rather than simply reproducing Gallic classics.

Rautureau specializes in generous servings of seafood, including Columbia River sturgeon and halibut, the latter served with an embarrassment-of-riches lobster sauce. Ellensburg lamb, rabbit, and game entrées also make appearances on the menu. The chef's talents may be sampled best by ordering the five-course prix-fixe dinner, which can also be substituted with vegetarian ingredients. Wines from the Northwest and France complement the meal. There are only about a dozen tables, plus a courtyard for warm-weather gustation. ♦ French ♦ Tu-Sa 5:30-9:30PM. 2808 E. Madison St. Reservations recommended. 325.7442

73 Lake Washington Boulevard The landscaping **Olmsted Brothers,** and their father before them, were great believers in contouring human developments to the land, making the improvement graceful rather than an imposition. The Olmsteds' comprehensive plan for Seattle included this scenic and meandering boulevard along the west side of Lake Washington, connecting **Seward Park** on the south with the **Alaska-Yukon-Pacific Exposition** grounds (now the UW campus) on the north. Today, some parts of this 1910 contoured drive have been bypassed by straighter Lakeside Avenue South (especially the famous curves through **Colman Park,** just south of the Lacey V. Morrow Floating Bridge/I-90). But you can still follow the old route; watch closely for signs. ♦ Lake Washington Blvd (between E. Calhoun St and S. Orcas St)

74 Alexander Pantages House Lying south of Madison Street and north of where Lake Washington Boulevard dips down to the lake from the **Washington Park Arboretum** is a wooded and palatial residential canton called **Washington Park.** Although it only began to develop after the 19th century, the neighborhood has the classic weight of a much older subdivision. One of the most impressive architectural statements made here is the home of impresario **Alexander Pantages,** who owned vaudeville theaters all over the West. His half-timbered mansion, designed in 1909 by **Wilson & Loveless,** carries overtones of California Mission Revival style. ♦ 1117 36th Ave East

75 Ames House Architects **Charles Bebb** and **Leonard L. Mendel** designed this stately Colonial Revival manse in 1907. It is now the residence of the **University of Washington** president. ♦ 808 36th Ave East

76 The Red Onion Tavern This is a classic neighborhood joint where the never-rowdy clientele grows younger as the night wears on; by closing time young singles predominate. Pool tables are bumpy here, and the pizza is filling but mediocre. However, a fireplace does much to promote lingering conversation. ♦ Daily 11AM-2AM. 4210 E. Madison St. 323.1611

The 39 inches of rain that Seattle receives in a year is in fact less than what falls on New York or Boston or Atlanta. Miami actually puts up with a whopping 60 inches annually.

76 Cactus ★★★$$ Popular Spanish-Mexican specialties are served here, with fish flown in from the Yucatán. But the primo draws are the *tapas*— invitingly displayed and spicy. Especially recommended is the shrimp served with a sauce of tomatoes and roasted almonds. The atmosphere can be rather dark unless you're out for romance. ♦ Southwestern ♦ M-Sa 11:30AM-2:30PM, 5:30-10PM; Su 5:30-9:30PM. 4220 E. Madison St. Reservations recommended. 324.4140

77 Madison Park Hardware Yes, there are lots of standard supplies here, plus a frosting of kitchen paraphernalia, toys, and baskets. But a bonus to visiting Madison Park Hardware is proprietor **Lola McKee,** the unofficial mayor and historian of Madison Park, who has become a tenacious advocate for preservation of this community's many charms. ♦ M-Sa 9AM-6PM. 1837 42nd Ave East. 322.5331

78 Sostanza ★★★$$$ The name translates from Italian to mean substance, and that's exactly what chef **Erin Rosella** delivers at her intimate, very European restaurant. Occupying a space formerly given over to the popular but cramped **Dominique's,** Sostanza was an immediate must-try when it opened in 1992. This was mostly owing to the local reputation of Rosella, whose family supplies fresh produce to many Seattle restaurants, and whose bona fides as a chef have been earned at **Saleh al Lago** and First Hill's late, lamented **Settebello.** Sostanza's informal foyer opens onto a busy kitchen and gives way to a pleasant dining room centered about a raised fireplace. Low lighting helps build a romantic atmosphere, one buttressed by seemingly unhurried service from a knowledgeable staff.

For such a well-known chef, Rosella is no supplicant to trendiness; dinners here are, as the business' name implies, *substantial*. A boneless breast of chicken comes pan roasted in brown butter. A grilled veal chop is stuffed with prosciutto and spinach and served with sautéed wild mushrooms. The salad of romaine hearts with Gorgonzola and slightly candied walnuts is a wonderful introduction to the meal, as are two appetizers: the peppered beef tenderloin carpaccio with Gorgonzola cream and a light fry of calamari and prawns. The wine list is hefty, too (if rather pricey). Try to be seated by the fireplace, and in the summer, repair to tables on the front patio. ♦ Italian ♦ Tu-Th, Su 5:30-9:30PM; F-Sa 5:30-10PM. 1927 43rd Ave East. 324.9701

79 Madison Park and Beach Not originally a component in the **Olmsted Brothers'** greenbelt scheme but linked to it by later planners, this is the northernmost in a continuous string of parks that lines **Lake Washington's** west bank south of the **Evergreen Point Floating Bridge.** Roped-off swimming areas and lighted tennis courts are available. On steamy summer noons, droves of coconut-scented narcissists pour into a hip-to-hip jam on the beach.

This stretch of lakefront was popularized first in 1890 by **Judge John J. McGilvra,** an aspiring real-estate mogul who had practiced law with Abraham Lincoln in Chicago before setting off west. The **Madison Street Cable Car Company** ran out here to a small amusement park that claimed a 500-seat pavilion, a boathouse, a ballpark, and a racetrack. Boat cruises around Lake Washington began from this spot, and summer vacationers came to mount big canvas tents on specially constructed platforms.

In preparation for the **Alaska-Yukon-Pacific Exposition,** $30,000 was expended on improvements to the amusement park, then called **White City.** A grandly arched entrance was put up, as were a new carousel, a circle swing, an alligator tank, a dancing pavilion, a curious and compact Japanese village, and a miniature railroad. Ferries left here bound for **Mercer Island** and other nascent **Eastside** communities. But the area suffered after the Expo ended, thanks to disputes among realtors and neglect of the streetcar route. In 1919 the city bought the streetcar line from central Seattle, along with Madison Park and its entertainment facilities. Twenty years later the city initiated a WPA landscaping program to take advantage of new waterfront left dry here after the ship canal lowered Lake Washington by 20 feet. ♦ East end of E. Madison St

80 Denny-Blaine Park Located on the bank of Lake Washington in the Washington Park neighborhood is a tranquil little public beach (aka Liberal Ladies Beach) frequented mostly by women and their female companions. There's no bathhouse and no lifeguard on duty. ♦ Near 40th Ave East at Lake Washington Blvd

81 Madrona Park Bathing Beach Change in the bathhouse and then wade out from the beach. But be careful. The water looks pristine here (thanks to a major civic cleanup of Lake Washington back in the 1960s), but it's painfully cold, even in summer. During lazier moods, seat yourself in one of the usually unoccupied lifeguard perches and people-watch amongst the joggers, dog-walkers, and picnickers. In clear weather, there is no better place in Seattle to view 14,411-foot **Mount Rainier,** which (although 50 miles away) dominates the southern horizon. Scientists suspect that Rainier may someday blow its stack, as Mount St. Helens did in 1980, but don't hold your breath. Clear skies will also reveal other snowy peaks in the **Cascade** mountain range to the east, and the sharp-eyed may spy 10,778-foot **Mount Baker** north of the lake. It would be easy to forget that you're relaxing near a city, were it not for the jagged profile of **Bellevue** across the lake. ♦ Lake Washington Blvd at E. Marion St

82 Hi-Spot Cafe ★$ An old-time coffeehouse in a Madrona home enjoys new vitality from owners **Amanda Wood** and **Michael Kingsley.** The meal of choice is breakfast (hearty omelets and terrific cinnamon rolls), but lunch fetches out sumptuous burgers. Even the BLT (a sandwich so often given short shrift) is done well here. Soups are vegetarian. ♦ American ♦ M, W-Su 8AM-2:30PM. 1410 34th Ave. 325.7905

83 Sam's Super Burgers ★$ This is a required stop on the hamburger lover's tour of Greater Seattle. The sandwiches are big, with lots of meat. The hot-links burgers purveyed by this unpretentious Central District joint are also good, but you probably won't have room for both of them at once. ♦ Soul food ♦ M-Sa noon-8PM. 2600 E. Union St. 329.4870

84 Catfish Corner ★★$ Talk about specialization: Catfish Corner does offer other things on its menu, but why consider them when the breaded catfish here is so superb? The potato salad is a bit too mustardy but still excellent. ♦ Soul food ♦ M-F 11AM-10PM; Sa noon-10PM; Su noon-7PM. 2726 E. Cherry St. 323.4330

85 Ezell's Fried Chicken ★★$ This is the take-out place that talk-show hostess **Oprah Winfrey** calls when she needs some chicken placed on the next airmail plane headed east.

Restaurants/Clubs: Red   Hotels: Blue
Shops/ 🍃 Outdoors: Green   **Sights/Culture: Black**

Thankfully, fame hasn't hurt the place.
♦ Fried Chicken/Takeout ♦ M-Th 10AM-10PM; F-Sa 10AM-11PM; Su 11AM-10PM. 501 23rd Ave. 324.4141

86 R&L Home of Good Barbeque ★★$ This establishment has been a Central District culinary landmark since **Robert** and **Louise Collins** opened the pit in 1952. Recommended are the alder-smoked pork ribs, the hot links, and the baked beans. ♦ Barbecue ♦ Tu-Th 11AM-10PM; F-Sa 11AM-11PM. 1816 E. Yesler Way. 322.0271

87 New Hong Kong Seafood Restaurant and B.B.Q. ★★$ Southeast Asians (mainly Vietnamese but also Cambodians, Laotians, and Thais) are beginning to put their mark on Seattle, as the Chinese and Japanese did a century ago. The result is a spin-off from the city's International District, around the intersection of South Jackson Street and 12th Avenue South. You need only glance at the native-language storefront signs to know that these places aim to solidify their support among various Asian nationalities before they worry about drawing a crowd from the city at large. With its 200-item menu featuring Chinese, Vietnamese, and Thai dishes, the New Hong Kong is one of the better new restaurants gaining a foothold in this area. Word is that it serves some of the best wonton soup in town. ♦ Southeast Asian ♦ Daily 10AM-10PM. 212 12th Ave South. 324.4091

88 Frye Art Museum Dominated by the 19th-century European salon paintings of patrons **Charles** and **Emma Frye,** the museum also includes Wyeth works and some by non-native Alaskan artists. The International Style building was designed in 1952 by **Paul Thiry** and is similar to his **Museum of History and Industry** in Montlake. ♦ Free. M-Sa 10AM-5PM; Su noon-5PM. 704 Terry Ave. 622.9250

89 Tabernacle Missionary Baptist Church Certainly one of the most exuberant black churches in Seattle, the Tabernacle Missionary has a congregation inspired by **Reverend Robert Manaway** to clap, sing, sway, and stamp its feet on a Sunday morn. The choir has all the energy (and some of the talent) of Aretha Franklin. Congregants call out affirmations of their faith: "Sing it, sister!" Even the smallest children get into the rhythm. ♦ Services W 8PM; Su 8AM, 11AM. 2801 S. Jackson St. 329.9794

90 Leschi Park The name comes from an 1850s Nisqually tribal leader, who liked to camp here and was accused by **Territorial Governor Isaac Stevens** of leading attacks against Seattle's white pioneers in what has come to be called the **Battle of Seattle.** It was a bloody uprising, resulting in pioneer deaths as well as the reciprocal slaughter of Native Americans who were on their way to reservations after the 1855-56 war. **Chief Leschi,** the focus of so much hatred, was tried for the deaths of two federal peace-keeping volunteers, and then shamefully hanged despite evidence of his innocence.

The Leschi neighborhood has ascended to its present affluent status only within recent decades, as indicated by the modern architecture of its homes and condos. Until the 1970s it was decidedly blue-collar and bohemian. At the turn of the century a trolley carried Seattleites (and three U.S. presidents) here to patronize an amusement park and opera house, both now long gone, and a cross-lake ferry docked at Leschi before the Interstate-90 floating bridge was opened in 1940. The **Olmsted**-designed park across the street from the marina is styled along the lines of the classic English garden and includes an ancient stone bridge over which the trolley once rumbled. Joggers and cyclists travel frequently over the 10 tree-lined and lightly trafficked miles between this greenbelt and **Seward Park** to the south. ♦ Lakeside Ave South and Leschi Pl

91 Leschi Lakecafe ★★$$ A busy bar (with 18 beers on tap) and a kitchen that does its best work with fresh- and saltwater fish, particularly salmon, are the main attractions here. Diners may select a Dungeness crab right out of the fish tank. In warm weather the alfresco tables are packed with the tanned and single. Fish-and-chips from the Lakecafe's adjacent **Koby's** take-out counter are delicious (some critics contend—sacrilege!—that they're even better than the greasefests dished up by **Spuds**'), but they're also overpriced. ♦ Seafood ♦ M-Sa 11:30AM-10PM; Su 10AM-10PM. 102 Lakeside Ave South. 328.2233

92 Daniel's Broiler ★★$$$$ As the name suggests, the emphasis here is on flame-cooked red meats and seafood. There's a terrific perspective of Mount Rainier and Lake Washington to the east. Chef **Russell Lowell** actually ventures out into the forests with bow

and arrow for duck, pheasant, and venison, his personal specialties. If you prefer seafood, try the swordfish. There's a second, more chichi Daniel's in Bellevue. ♦ Steak house ♦ Daily 5-11PM. 200 Lake Washington Blvd. 329.4191. Also at: 10500 NE Eighth Ave, Bellevue. 462.4662

93 Remo Borracchini's A lot of Seattleites wouldn't go anywhere other than this landmark Italian bakery to find special-occasion cakes. The confections can be tough to turn down: Remo's

chocolate Bavarian cream should really be listed as a controlled substance. This bakery also does pasta and breads, and sells Italian canned goods and wines. Remo isn't officially a restaurant, but it does offer tables for snackers and serves sandwiches, a rich lasagna, pizza, and baked items. ♦ Italian bakery ♦ Daily 6AM-7PM. 2307 Rainier Ave South. 325.1550

94 Mutual Fish Company Here's the best seafood store south of Pike Place Market. Owned and operated by the **Yoshimura** family since about the time the dinosaurs succumbed, Mutual Fish specializes in packing purchases for the trip home. ♦ M-Sa 8:30AM-5:30PM. 2335 Rainier Ave South. 322.4368

95 Evans House This is the compelling work of **Ellsworth Storey,** a Chicago native who arrived in Seattle in 1903 and set about building houses (some of them on specu-lation) in the developing neighborhoods along the west bank of Lake Washington, especially **Madrona** and **Mount Baker.** Apparently not interested in a large-scale practice, Storey stuck with residential design, an eminent example of which is this wood home. Note the strong diagonal emphasis. ♦ 2306 34th Ave South

96 Stan Sayres Memorial Park On the first weekend in August this park becomes—in more ways than one—"The Pits," the staging area for the annual **Seafair** unlimited hydroplane extravaganza. The race course is a long oval just off the park, with straight-aways paralleling the shoreline. The usually quiet park (formerly a slough) becomes a circus of noise, warm beer, provocatively exposed flesh, and confusion, with attendees angling for a variety of VIP and press passes that will permit close-up looks at the monster boats and their frenzied crews. Boaters cluster about an offshore log boom. For years, young Seattleites anxiously awaited this weekend, packing the shoreline and engaging in a variety of creative behaviors. That tradition seems to be on the wane, however, with Seafair officials giving priority to the "family values" crowd. Race-day attendance is noticeably slimmer, down from the half-million-people crowds attained in the 1970s and 1980s. But neighbors still complain about the traffic and the ear-splitting roar produced by the **Blue Angels** jet-fighter aerial-acrobatics team, which rattles pets, windows, and nerves for miles around. ♦ Lake Washington Blvd South and 42nd Ave South

97 Seward Park Instead of selling off almost all of the Lake Washington waterfront to the affluent, Seattle city founders might have preserved this waterway's entire circum-ference as a park for future generations. Had they been so prescient, Seward Park (and the shoreside greenbelt lying to the north) is a glimpse of what would be here today. This peninsula's 277 acres of mainly Douglas fir trees are true old-growth forest, of the sort fought over by loggers and environ-mentalists. A 2.5-mile paved roadway circles the park's outer shoreline, offering strollers, joggers, rollerbladers, and cyclists a quiet respite. Oddly, Seward Park never seems crowded.

A variety of pathways—some marked, some obscure—lace the woodlands, and a public fishing pier and swimming beach provide recreation on the northern end. Boaters will find a public ramp and the city's **Lakewood** docks a short distance north of here. According to the **Olmsteds'** comprehensive plan, this was intended to be a "wild" park, contrasting with more manicured garden spots such as **Volunteer Park.** In addition to picnic tables, barbecue pits, and a small amphitheater atop the hill, there is a state trout hatchery out at the end of the point and Japanese gardens, which, while quite pleasant, are obviously outclassed by those at the **Washington Park Arboretum.** A grouping of three traditional Japanese stone lanterns and an inscribed granite boulder stand sentinel at the park's entrance. These were placed here during the U.S. bicen-tennial in 1976 to commemorate the gift of one thousand cherry trees given by the citizens of Japan to the American people. Though shaped from Washington State granite, the lanterns were carved in Japan; the granite boulder carries an inscribed duplication of calligraphy painted by **Takeo**

Miki, the then-prime minister of Japan. Translated, it reads succinctly, "Congratulations on the bicentennial of the United States of America's independence."

Visitors with refined taste in music may wish to avoid the parking lot along the southern shoreline, where local youths meet in fair weather to compare the upper decibel ranges of their cars' stereo equipment. The offended are encouraged to complain to the city parks department (684.4082). ♦ S. Juneau St and Lake Washington Blvd South

98 Kubota Gardens The founder was a Japanese immigrant to Seattle, who started a 20-acre garden in 1929 in the midst of a swamp. Now a delight to the eye (not to mention the flora-loving nose), the gardens were purchased by the City of Seattle in 1987. A creek trickles through the lush greenery, feeding five ponds. Amongst the many rare plants are *tanysho* pines and weeping blue atlas cedars. ♦ Free. Renton Ave South and 55th Ave South. 725.4400

99 El Palacio ★★$ Any restaurant that has *menudo* on its menu at least wants to give a better-than-average impression of serving authentic Mexican cuisine. This place serves delicious *menudo* sausage, which in the old country is thought to be a hangover cure and is best left undiscussed as far as its preparation goes. El Palacio's seafoods are also exquisite: try the shrimp, either *camarones gigantes* (prawns) or the *camarones al mojo de ajo* (prawns with garlic and butter sauce). The tortillas here are homemade, of course. ♦ Mexican ♦ M-Sa 11:30AM-10PM; Su 11:30AM-9PM. 5212 Rainier Ave South. 725.9139

100 Pho Hòa ★★$ The menu gets no more expansive than *pho*, a good-anytime Vietnamese soup, but that's actually quite enough, thank you. The broth has a wide variety of spices and textures; diners select additional ingredients from a long list of meats and veggies. Pho Hòa's growing clientele is no longer restricted to Vietnamese-Americans, but you may still overhear old-timers replaying the fall of Saigon. ♦ Vietnamese ♦ Daily 9AM-8PM. 4406 Rainier Ave South. 723.1508

101 Museum of Flight Biplanes, military jets, early mail planes, a giant B-47—21 aircraft in all—dangle from the ceiling of this museum's glass-and-steel **Great Gallery**. Children, especially, love to wander among these relics; they can study a reproduction of Boeing's first seaplane and a real DC-13, or trace the history of flying in the adjacent **Red Barn**. A former wooden shipyard that **William Edward Boeing** bought to have his yacht built in, the Red Barn eventually became the Boeing Company's original 1910 airplane factory.

Although the Museum of Flight is often called Boeing's Museum of Flight, it is, in fact, an independent operation. Its immediate adjacency to the **Boeing Development Center** serves the museum's goal of making you feel at one with the world of flight. A gift shop is fully stocked with models, books, and leather bomber jackets. ♦ Admission; discounts for senior citizens and children. M-W, F-Su 10AM-5PM; Th 10AM-9PM. 9404 E. Marginal Way South. 764.5720

Bests

Dan Samson
Gourmet Ice Cream Guru/President,
Dankens Gourmet Ice Cream

Relaxing on **Lake Washington** in a boat filled with good friends, great wine, and fresh seafood, while gazing at the majesty of **Mount Rainier.**

Cheering for the **Washington Huskies** on a crisp, sunny fall afternoon with the incomparable view of sailboats and the Space Needle in the distance.

Strolling through **Pike Place Market** in the early morning hours sipping a *latte* and juggling bundles of fresh fish and fragrant flowers.

Snuggling by a crackling fire in the **Sorrento Hotel's Fireside Room.**

Surviving a "Sweat Express" workout taught by Karl Anderson at **Pro-Robics** (the country's best).

Browsing for endless hours at the **Elliott Bay Book Company** in Pioneer Square. Then, after choosing a good read, sitting in **Waterfall Garden.**

Cycling, walking, running, or driving through the **Washington Park Arboretum.**

Biting into a piping-hot "just out of the oven" cinnamon roll at the **Madison Park Bakery.**

Slurping a Frango milk shake at **Sommer Sparks** (the former Cafe Frango).

And, to save the best for last: indulging in one or more delectable Dankens Gourmet Ice Cream flavors while feasting on the breathtaking view atop **Magnolia Bluff.**

Gary Levy
Owner, City Fish Company

Pike Place Market.

Having a sandwich at the **Three Girls Bakery.**

Lunching at **Cutter's Bayhouse.**

Watching the salmon run at the **Hiram M. Chittenden Locks** in August and September.

Snoqualmie Falls in the spring—a really spectacular runoff.

Restaurants/Clubs: Red	Hotels: Blue
Shops/ ♠ Outdoors: Green	Sights/Culture: Black

Duwamish **4**
Head

Elliott
Bay

5

3

*Public
Fishing
Pier*

SW Massa-
chusetts St.

2 *Seacrest Park
& Boathouse*

Bonair Dr. SW

Sunset Ave. SW

Ferry Ave. SW

1

Harbor Ave. SW

Pier 2

Alki Ave. SW

41st Ave. SW

SW Walker St.

W. Marginal Wy. SW

Terminal 5

West Waterway

*Alki Beach
Park*

57th Ave. SW

Admiral Wy. SW

Fairmount Ave. SW

Admiral Wy. SW

60th Ave. SW

Admiral Wy.

SW Lander St.

65th Ave. SW

63rd Ave. SW

61st Ave. SW

SW Stevens St.

*Schmitz
Park*

47th Ave. SW

45th Ave. SW

California Ave. SW

42nd Ave. SW

SW Hanford St.

39th Ave. SW

36th Ave. SW

West Seattle Fwy.
SW Charlestown St.

59th Ave. SW

SW Charlestown St.

55th Ave. SW

52nd Ave. SW

49th Ave. SW

SW Andover St.

SW Dakota St.

SW Genesee St.

SW Avalon Wy.

SW Genesee
St.

*Delridge
Playfield*

*Schmitz
Viewpoint
Park*

SW Oregon St.

SW Alaska St.

SW Jacobson Rd.

Fauntleroy Ave. SW

37th Ave. SW

35th Ave. SW

*West Seattle
Golf Course*

Beach Dr. SW

SW Hudson St.

For nos. 6-39,
see pg. 119

Erskine Ave. SW

SW Brandon St.

*Fairmount
Playground*

40

26th Ave. SW

Delridge Wy. SW

23rd Ave. SW

*Puget
Sound*

Atlas Pl. SW

47th Ave. SW

45th Ave. SW

SW Juneau St.

SW Raymond St.

34th Ave. SW

48th Ave. SW

Fauntleroy Ave. SW

SW Morgan St.

21st Ave. SW

Sylvan Wy. SW

41
*Lowman
Beach Park*

Lincoln Park Wy.

42

Bainbridge Wy.

47 SW Myrtle St.

29th Ave. SW

SW Webster St.

43
*Lincoln
Park*

Kenyon
Pl. SW

California Ave. SW

SW Holden St.

39th Ave. SW

35th Ave. SW

SW Portland St.

*Hughes
Playground*

Delridge Wy. SW

SW Thistle St.

*Ferry to Vashon Island
and Southworth*

44

Fauntleroy Ave. SW

Fauntleroy Pl. SW

SW Trenton St.

46

km
mi

1/4

1/2

1/2

1

45

SW Barton St.

N

West Seattle

On balmy summer afternoons, Alki Beach in West Seattle is a polychromatic amalgam of people and vehicles and noise, noise, noise. Bathing beauties in bikinis sashay down the sand, boom boxes close at hand, while jocks polish up their already shiny cars and look on in hormonal delight. Skaters, cyclists, runners, strollers, and families with tethered German shepherds jockey for position along a bike path. On the inland side of Alki Avenue Southwest, a variety of restaurants provide everything from sit-down dinners to fast food. It's not exactly LA's Venice Beach, but then it's not generic Seattle—not by any stretch of the imagination.

The scenario stands in marked contrast to events that took place here in November 1851, when a schooner dropped off **Arthur Denny's** small cadre of pioneers at this same spot to develop what would become Seattle. The settlers built their first cabins in the primitive Alki wilds and established good relationships with the native Duwamish tribespeople before seeking shelter on **Elliott Bay**. It's difficult to say exactly what effect this abandonment of Alki had on future West Siders (as residents of West Seattle are known), but ever since, those who have lived here have very much prized their physical—if not also psychological—separation from the body of Seattle (the 1907 annexation of West Seattle to the rest of the city did not come without a fight).

Located southwest of downtown, across the **Duwamish River**, West Seattle is a collection of mostly residential areas distinguished by their views of downtown, Harbor Island, the Cascade and Olympic mountains, and three Puget Sound islands: Vashon, Blake, and Bainbridge. Downtown West Seattle, as it is occasionally, if facetiously, called, is best known simply as **The Junction** (it's centered at the confluence of California Avenue Southwest and Southwest Alaska Street). This central shopping area has had its ups and downs over the years; a number of businesses have made fleeting appearances, while several others have stood almost unchanged for more than half a century. Although the growing number of high-rise condominiums on Alki attracts young urbanites, property values in many parts of West Seattle remain affordable, and the area retains some of its historic working-class spirit. But Alki Beach—which many residents claim is the only *real* beach in Seattle—is the area's principal attraction, boasting a wide expanse of sand, a long cycling-jogging-rollerblading lane, a boat launch, and grassy areas dotted with picnic tables.

1 Salty's on Alki ★★$$ Owner **Gerald Kingen** compares his upscale restaurant to the Space Needle, claiming that no other place in the city commands as good a view. That's debatable, but from Salty's you can get a fine perspective on the downtown skyline and ferries cruising across the Sound; it's especially beautiful at night. The food is a little pricier here than at most West Seattle restaurants, but it's served with more flair. Alder-smoked salmon stuffed with Dungeness crab, and clams steamed with vegetables and white wine are two favorites. Noise, however, can be a problem. ◆ Seafood ◆ M-Th 11:30AM-2PM, 5-10PM; F 11:30AM-2PM, 5-10:30PM; Sa 4:30-10:30PM; Su 9:30AM-1:30PM, 4:30-10:30PM May-Aug. M-Th 11:30AM-2PM, 5-9:30PM; F 11:30AM-2PM, 5-10PM; Sa 4:30-10PM; Su 4:30-9:30PM Sept-Apr. 1936 Harbor Ave SW.

Reservations recommended. 937.1600. Also at: 28201 Redondo Beach Dr South, Federal Way. 946.0636

2 Seacrest Park and Boathouse This clean new park has watercrafts for rent, a simple coffee shop, and a fishing pier. Aluminum 16-foot-long fishing boats with six-horsepower motors rent for $10 an hour; 14-foot-long fiberglass rowboats rent for $10 a day; and fishing boats without motors rent for $14 a day. Even if you never get so much as a bite on your line, views from out on the water are spectacular here. ◆ M-Sa 11AM-2AM; Su noon-2AM. 1321 Alki Ave SW. 932.9970

Restaurants/Clubs: Red **Hotels:** Blue
Shops/ ♣ Outdoors: Green **Sights/Culture:** Black

3 Don Armeni Park Boat Ramp A popular place for boaters to enter Puget Sound, this ramp was named after a deputy sheriff, active in fishing derbies, who was shot and killed in the line of duty in 1954. ♦ Harbor Ave SW (between SW California and SW Maryland Sts)

4 Duwamish Head Thanks to its views of Elliott Bay and downtown, this headland has long been a prime point of interest. In the late 19th and early 20th centuries the broad shoulders of beach were frequented by summertime revelers and campers. In 1901 a former Klondike gold miner built something here called the **Coney Island Baths,** which offered "a good bath and swim and use of fresh running water." Suits could be rented if you failed to pack your own. Six years later, Duwamish Head became the site of the largest and showiest amusement park ever built in Seattle: **Luna Park.**

As with so many other amusement parks of the early 20th century, this one sat on the water—actually and symbolically on the very edge of things. Named after one of the gaudiest, most prosperous components of New York's Coney Island, it was a great fake of pasteboard assembled with nuts and bolts and 11,000 electric lights—a permanent carnival reclined on pilings driven into Puget Sound. For eight summers, from 1907 to 1913, locals came to ride the roller coaster, the giant Circle Swing, the Canals of Venice, the Cave of Mystery, and the Shoot-the-Chutes (with a lagoon built right atop the pilings). They gawked at the "Original Human Ostrich," the high divers, and the daredevil motorcycle riders on their loop-the-loop runs. They sat before "The Great Davenports," who performed "mid-air extravaganzas on the high wire," and they bought red lemonade, rode in hot-air balloons, and watched their own images distorted in a hall of mirrors.

Created by **Charles I.D. Looff,** a German who had installed the first carousel at Coney Island in 1876, Luna Park stretched over more than 10 acres, an imposing admixture of Atlantic City kitsch, Spanish Mission, and carnival gothic. This fantasyland wanted to be all things to all people, and unfortunately that's what finally got it in trouble. For along with the arcades and thrill rides, Luna Park also boasted "the longest bar on the bay," an easy target for reform-minded West Siders shocked by tales of drunkenness. The final straw came when Luna Park's manager was implicated in a scandal involving the construction of a 500-room brothel on Seattle's Beacon Hill. When Luna Park opened for the summer of 1913, Looff was gone. Luna Park didn't have a ninth season, although the natatorium (with its huge billboard exhorting, "Let's Swim!") remained in business until an arsonist set flame to the one-story frame building in 1931. All that's

here now is a popular beach and some apartment buildings. ♦ Alki Ave SW and Harbor Ave SW

5 Hamilton Viewpoint Generations of West Seattle teenagers have come to this lookout to, uh, "watch the submarine races." They couldn't help noticing also that it offers one of the most outstanding views of downtown Seattle across Elliott Bay. It's also a stop on Gray Line's **Grand City Tour** (call 626.5208 for more information). Two coin-operated telescopes are available for a closer look. ♦ California Ave SW and SW Donald St

6 Cherry Blossom Teriyaki $ Japanese cuisine, seafood, and, naturally, teriyaki dishes are the specialties of this small restaurant across the street from the beach. ♦ Japanese ♦ M-F 10AM-10PM; Sa-Su 9AM-10PM. 2620 Alki Ave SW. 933.0848

7 Alki Beach Park In late 1910 the city paid $75,000 for 2,500 feet of waterfront along **Alki Avenue,** between 57th and 65th avenues, and erected an imposing bathing and recreation pavilion (which is now long gone). Bands played to holiday crowds and as many as 20,000 people turned out here on Sundays. For many years Alki was the spot where teenagers showed off their cars and themselves. Laws passed in the late 1980s prohibited both cruising and amplified sound on the beach, cutting down considerably on the summer noise and traffic that had plagued local residents but hardly decreasing the park's popularity. Today, the park is a two-and-a-half mile stretch with a sandy strip that's the closest thing Seattle can claim to a Southern California beach. Volleyball courts on the sand are usually filled with players and lined with spectators when the sun shows its face. A bike path is active with skaters and runners. Picnic tables and shelters are available, and Alki is also one of the few local parks that allows beach fires, although only in designated concrete rings. There are no lifeguards on duty, so swim at your own risk. ♦ Open 24 hours; closed 11PM-6AM 15 Apr-1 Oct. Alki Ave SW

8 Alki Playground Facilities at this small playground about a block from the beach include a softball field, a soccer field, children's play equipment, and two lighted tennis courts. ♦ 58th Ave SW and SW Stevens St

9 Alki Community Center Located adjacent to Alki Elementary School and the Alki Playground, the center offers family roller-skating on Friday nights, as well as a game room (with a pool table) and a gym for basketball and volleyball. ♦ M-Th 2-10PM, F 10AM-10PM, Sa 9AM-5PM Oct to mid-Apr; M-Th 2-10PM, F 10AM-10PM, Sa 10AM-6PM mid-June to late Aug. 5817 SW Stevens St. 684.7430

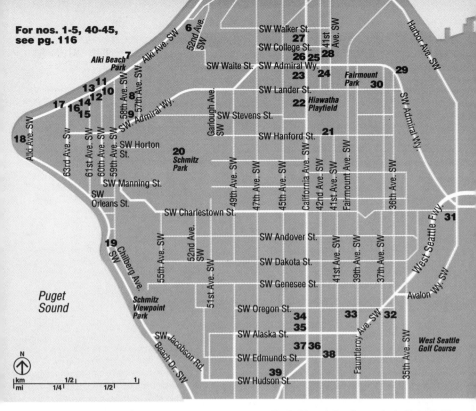

For nos. 1-5, 40-45,
see pg. 116

Alki Beach 7
Park

SW Walker St.
27
SW College St.
26 25 28
SW Waite St. SW Admiral Wy.
23 24
Fairmount
Park 30
SW Lander St.
22 Hiawatha
Playfield
SW Stevens St.

SW Hanford St. 21

13 11
12 10
17 16 14
15

9

SW Admiral Wy.

SW Horton
St.
20
Schmitz
Park

SW Manning St.

SW
Orleans St.

18

6th Ave. SW
52nd Ave. SW
41st Ave. SW

Harbor Ave. SW

29

31

SW Charlestown St.

SW Andover St.

SW Dakota St.

SW Genesee St.

19

Puget
Sound

Schmitz
Viewpoint
Park

Avalon Wy. SW

SW Oregon St. 34
33 32
SW Alaska St. 35
37 36
SW Edmunds St. 38
39
SW Hudson St.

West Seattle
Golf Course

N
km   1/2   1
mi 1/4   1/2

10 Spud Fish and Chips $ Two English guys, **Jack** and **Frank Alger,** opened a summer fish-and-chips stand at Alki in 1935. Fish-and-chips were then 10 cents per order, to go. Today, under the same ownership, Spud's is open year-round and seats as many as 82 people inside. The menu includes prawns, oysters, clams, and scallops, as well as chocolate-chip cookies and milk shakes. ♦ Seafood/Takeout ♦ Daily 11AM-10PM. 2666 Alki Ave SW. 938.0606. Also at: 6860 E. Green Lake Way North. 524.0565; 9702 Juanita Dr NE, Kirkland. 823.0607

11 Alki Bathhouse Art Studio The old bathhouse on Alki Beach has been opened to all local artists as a free studio (available on a first-come basis). It's staffed by volunteers and administered by the **Alki Community Center.** ♦ M, W 10AM-3PM. SW 60th St and Alki Ave SW. 684.7430

12 Alki Cafe $ A local fave for weekend breakfasts (omelets, fresh-baked bread, and cinnamon rolls), this long, narrow cafe also serves lunch and dinner. Try the linguine primavera or the filling cheese tortellini with chicken and rosemary. In 1992 cafe owner

Kevin Piper (who also owns the **Point Grill)** moved his bakery counter across the street and opened **Alki Bakery** (935.1352) in a former drugstore space. This is where they now turn out all of the bread and pastries served in the cafe. Besides baked goods, the storefront also dispenses espresso drinks. ♦ Continental ♦ M-Th, Su 8AM-9:30PM; F-Sa 8AM-10PM. 2726 Alki Ave SW. 935.0616

13 Statue of Liberty The **Boy Scouts of America** dedicated this three-foot-high replica of New York's harbor heroine to the City of Seattle in 1952. ♦ SW 61st Ave and Alki Ave SW

14 Pegasus Pizza & Pasta ★$ Though legends of flying horses have zero to do with West Seattle, the pizza here has itself become legendary. One of the best varieties is Tom's Special, with mushrooms, green peppers, onions, olives, feta and mozzarella cheeses, spinach, pepperoni, fresh garlic, diced tomatoes, and sunflower seeds. The Greek pizza (with feta and mozzarella cheeses, spinach, onions, and ground beef), the feta bread, and the spaghetti and ravioli are also worth a taste. On weekends the line of customers usually extends well outside the doorway. ♦ Italian ♦ M-F 4-11PM; Sa-Su noon-11PM. 2758 Alki Ave SW. 932.4849

14 Point Grill $ "Smoke 'em if you got 'em" is more than a casual comment here; it's a culinary edict. The Point smokes its own salmon, then serves it atop a fine Caesar salad. It also smokes ribs and chicken, then barbecues them. Also on the menu: pot roast and turkey dinners. ◆ Barbecue ◆ M-Th 11AM-9PM; Sa 10AM-10PM; Su 10AM-9PM. 2770 Alki Ave SW. 933.0118

15 Alki Homestead ★★$$ Many people love the funky ambience of this restaurant, which is located in a 1902 cabin that was fit together with logs salvaged off Alki Beach. The food is served family style, with the specialty of the house being panfried chicken with mashed potatoes, gravy, and green beans. The menu also includes steak, prime rib, and seafood. Cocktails are served in a spacious glassed-in porch. ◆ American ◆ W-Sa 5-10PM; Su 3-8:30PM. 2717 61st Ave SW. 935.5678

16 Sunfish Seafood $ Regular fish-and-chips or, for a little more (and the difference is worth paying), halibut-and-chips are served here. You can see the influence of the Greek brothers who own this place in the halibut shish kebab and calamari on the menu. Indoor and outdoor seating are both available. ◆ Seafood/Takeout ◆ Daily 11AM-9PM. 2800 Alki Ave SW. 938.4112

17 Monument to the Birthplace of Seattle A concrete pylon marks the place where **Arthur Denny** and his pioneering party landed in 1851. Presented to the city in 1905 by Denny's daughter, **Lenora**, the column was installed originally just across the street from its present location and beside the old **Stockade Hotel**. It was moved to the beachside in 1926. At the same time, a piece of Massachusetts' famed Plymouth Rock was embedded in the pylon's base and a plaque was added to commemorate the occasion. The Stockade Hotel, by the way, folded in 1936 owing to a combination of inadequate ferry service from downtown and the commercial blight of the Great Depression. Apartments now occupy the land on which it formerly sat. ◆ 63rd Ave SW and Alki Ave SW

18 Alki Point Light Station Alki Point marks the southern entrance to Seattle's harbor, **Elliott Bay.** There's been some kind of warning beacon for ships here since the mid-1870s, when **Hans Martin Hanson,** who bought the land from pioneer **Doc Maynard,** began lighting lanterns on the point every night. In the 1880s the U.S. Lighthouse Service erected a lens-lantern on a scaffold here. The present 37-foot-high octagonal tower (pictured above right) was completed in 1913. Its light was converted to electricity five years later, and in 1984 its operation became fully automatic. Today, the lighthouse stands surrounded by apartments and condominiums. The station is maintained by the U.S. Coast Guard and opens

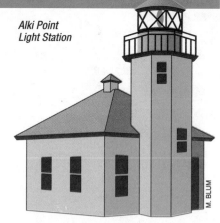

Alki Point Light Station

M. BLUM

for regular tours on weekends, though group tours can be arranged Wednesday through Friday. ◆ Tours W-F by appointment; Sa-Su noon-4PM. 3201 Alki Ave SW. 932.5800

19 Weather Watch Park The area's newest viewpoint is a small knoll between the apartments and cottages that line Beach Drive. Once a dock site for Puget Sound's ferry service from Seattle, the park was designed and built by local artist **Lezlie Jane** in 1991. ◆ Beach Dr SW and SW Carroll St

19 Dulce's $ This little cafe offers a great view through Weather Watch Park, as well as soup, salads, sandwiches, and delicious desserts and baked goods. ◆ Deli ◆ Tu-W 7AM-6PM; Th-Sa 7AM-9PM; Su 7AM-3PM. 4101 Beach Dr SW. 933.8400

20 Schmitz Park Donated to the city by wealthy West Siders **Ferdinand** and **Emma Schmitz** in 1908, on the condition that the land be forever maintained as nearly as possible in its natural state, Schmitz Park is now home to one of the last stands of old-growth forest—some of the trees are more than 800 years old—within the city limits. It is also a 50-acre nature preserve where narrow trails through the thick woods can be hard to follow. There are no picnic areas or playgrounds. ◆ Daily dawn-dusk. SW Stevens St and Admiral Way SW

21 West Seattle High School Built in 1917, this school was designed by **Edgar Blair,** an architect who made modifications on at least two **James Stephen** schools in Seattle (**Latona Elementary** in Wallingford and **John B. Allen Elementary** at Green Lake) and initiated steel framing in other local educational institutions. West Seattle High alumni include: restaurateur **Ivar Haglund** (class of 1923); songwriter **Earl Robinson** (1928); film star **Frances Farmer** (1931); mountaineer **Jim Whittaker** (1947); and actress **Dyan Cannon** (née Diane Friesen), who graduated in 1954. ◆ 4075 SW Stevens St. 281.6070

22 Parkside News Cafe $ Espresso, salads, and sandwiches are the specialties at this friendly place, which is across the street from a playground. Try the excellent hazelnut torte, the tiramisù, and the carrot cake. In keeping with the shop's name, a wide variety of magazines and newspapers are for sale. ♦ American ♦ M 6AM-10PM; Tu-Th 6AM-11PM; F 6AM-midnight; Sa 7AM-midnight; Su 7AM-10PM. 2735 California Ave SW. 932.2279

23 Alki Bicycle Company This store has been outfitting local cyclists—and renting bicycles to visitors—for years. (Its name reflects the shop's original location on **Alki Beach.**) Besides peddling bikes and all manner of accessories, Alki Bicycle also provides repair services, sells used bikes on

consignment, and offers Saturday morning classes in road safety. The **Alki Bicycle Club** operates out of this shop, with free Wednesday night rides and guided tours available to groups of five or more. Bike rentals are $7 to $9 per hour, with daily, weekend, and weekly rates available. ♦ M-F 10AM-7PM; Sa 10AM-6PM; Su noon-5PM. 2611 California Ave SW. 938.3322

24 Starbucks No Seattle neighborhood seems complete anymore without its own branch of this coffee chain, selling pastries, espresso drinks, coffee by the pound, and all the equipment you need to brew your own beans at home. ♦ Coffeehouse ♦ M-Th 6AM-9PM; F 6AM-10PM; Sa 7AM-9PM; Su 7AM-8PM. 4101 SW Admiral Way. 937.5010

Painting the Town

Historical murals are increasingly familiar sights in West Seattle, each of them part of a project designed to set this district apart and cement its position as the city's birthplace. Located in the Junction and Morgan business districts, these paintings reflect a variety of artistic styles, ranging from the paint-by-numbers look to trompe l'oeils, but most are lifelike images of West Seattle in the late 1800s and early 1900s.

After admiring murals in southwestern Washington and in Chemainus, British Columbia, where more than 25 murals serve as that town's primary tourist draw, **Earl Cruzen** determined that his neighborhood should adopt the popular public-art theme. Most of the nine murals painted in West Seattle since then have been funded by local donations, city matching funds, and contributions from building owners. Here's a brief guide to the works of art.

- *Streetcar Crossing,* the most spectacular of West Seattle's murals, depicts the Junction during the 1920s, when the old streetcar lines converged here. The work of **Eric Grohe,** this trompe l'oeil looks so realistic that local wits have suggested the city hang a traffic light in front of the painted streetcar tracks. You'll find it framed by a mock concrete arch on the south wall of the **Junction Feed & Seed Store** (4747 California Avenue SW).

- Part of the west side of **Morton's Drugs** (4707 California Avenue SW) is covered with a montage that includes images of onetime local attraction **Luna Park,** the old **West Seattle Cable Railway,** and turn-of-the-century ferries. Artist **William Garnett** of Portland, Oregon, completed the mural in 1989 and dubbed it *West Seattle Ferries.*

- A deep-blue nighttime scene of a horse-drawn wagon dashing away from the 1913 Junction Fire Station brightens the south side of the **Don Swanson Insurance Building** (4711 44th Avenue SW), across from where that fire station once stood. Seattleite **Don Barrie** painted the mural, titled *Midnight Call,* in 1990.

- *The First Duwamish Bridge,* a panorama of the old swing bridge that crosses the **Duwamish River,** is the work of Louisiana artists **Robert** and **Douglas Dafford.** Located on the north wall of the **Jacobson Building** (44th Avenue SW and SW Edmunds Street), it shows a trolley crossing the river, with the Cascade Mountains in a background of dreamy sunset shades of orange.

- A colorful 1937 view of the old **Morgan Street Market** was painted in 1990 by Nova Scotian artist **Bruce Rickett** on the west wall of **Olsen's Drugs** (6501 California Avenue SW). The original market stood across the street.

- Another artist from Nova Scotia, **Susan Tooke Crichton,** depicted a 1910 landing by the old steamships that hauled freight and passengers between Puget Sound's ports. *Mosquito Fleet Landing* can be seen on the east wall of the **Campbell Building,** which sits at the corner of California Avenue SW and SW Alaska Street in Junction.

- **Huling's Chevrolet** dealership (4755 Fauntleroy Way SW) is the site of another **Bruce Rickett** mural, this one a portrait of a 1919 Chevrolet and a woman painting.

- **School Bank Day,** a local project that helps teach children about saving money, is the subject of the mural on the north side of the **Washington Mutual Bank** building (California Avenue SW and SW Oregon Street). At the project's inception in 1923, only Washington Mutual was willing to take the pennies, nickels, and quarters that students wanted to deposit; the bank even offered interest on accounts exceeding a few dollars. British Columbian **Alan Wylie** was the artist.

- A local parade from the 1940s is portrayed in a mural on the wall of the **West Seattle Post Office** (4412 California Avenue SW).

25 Rock City Sports Bar & Grill Offering something for almost everyone, this sports bar has live Top-40 dance music on weekends, a big-screen TV, pool tables (with Tuesday tournaments), dart boards (with Wednesday tourneys), and karaoke singing on Thursday and Sunday nights. ♦ Cover varies, so call ahead. Daily 11AM-2AM. 2306 California Ave SW. 933.9500

25 Peace Cafe Though started as the second branch of Capitol Hill's popular **B&O Espresso,** this establishment was recently purchased by West Seattle residents **Madeleine Khass** and **Bashar Al-Nakhala.** They changed the name, says Khass, because "It's about time for peace in this world." But its savory cakes, pies, tortes, biscotti, and brownies still come from the B&O. Sample one over an espresso. Lunches offer falafel and *schwarma* sandwiches, along with more-American dishes. ♦ Middle Eastern ♦ M-Th 8AM-11PM; F 8AM-midnight; Sa 9AM-midnight; Su 9AM-11PM. 2352 California Ave SW. 935.1540

25 Admiral Benbow Inn $ This replica of an old English inn was modeled after the fictional hostelry where pirates planned their voyage in Robert Louis Stevenson's *Treasure Island.* The **Chart Room Lounge** is a replica of the fictional ship *Hispaniola.* The fare ranges from seafood to prime rib, but it isn't as interesting as the story promises. ♦ American ♦ M-Th 11AM-1AM; F-Sa 11AM-2AM. 4212 SW Admiral Way. 937.8348

26 Angelina's Trattoria ★$ Here is yet another in **Dany Mitchell's** stable of Seattle trattorias. Like the others (including **Stella's** in the University District and Pioneer Square's **Trattoria Mitchelli**), Angelina's serves rich Italian meals at reasonable prices. Entrées range from simple pastas of the day with marinara sauce to the more elaborate *fettuccine con pollo e nocciale* (pasta in a velouté sauce with roasted hazelnuts and chicken). ♦ Italian ♦ M-Th 6:30AM-11PM, F 6:30AM-midnight, Sa 8AM-midnight, Su 8AM-11PM June-Labor Day; M-Th 6:30AM-10PM, F 6:30AM-11PM, Sa 8AM-11PM, Su 8AM-10PM Labor Day-May. 2311 California Ave SW. 932.7311

26 Ristorante di Ragazzi ★$ Italian food is served in a comfortable setting with murals on the walls and deep-green wicker furniture. Ristorante di Ragazzi (which means "The

Boys' Restaurant") serves hearty pasta and great pizzas (try the pie with pesto and artichoke hearts). ♦ Italian ♦ M-F 11AM-2:30PM, 4:30-10:30PM; Sa-Su 4:30-10:30PM. 2329 California Ave SW. 935.1969

26 Admiral Theater The roots of this establishment were planted in the old **Portola Theater,** built on this site in 1919. In the '20s the Portola—along with the nearby Olympus and Apollo theaters—offered feature films, newsreels, and comedy shorts, all for a mere 20 cents per customer. An $18,000 pipe organ was added there in 1924, followed by talkies in 1929, and, in response to the Great Depression, in 1933 adult admission was dropped to 15 cents.

In 1942 the historic moviehouse was expanded and reopened amid great fanfare as the Admiral Theater. The owner was **John Danz,** who held a contest so West Seattle residents could name his picture palace. The architect was **B. Marcus Priteca,** famed designer for **Alexander Pantages'** nationwide theater chain, whose local work may be remembered best in the Coliseum and Paramount theaters in downtown Seattle. Priteca picked up on the theater's winning moniker, adding nautical allusions to the Admiral's facade (note the portholes, anchors, and a giant mast with crow's nest on the "upper deck," as well as the seahorses riding exit signs). Early usherettes even sported naval uniforms. A gala opening in 1942 drew 3,000 people to a showing of *Weekend in Havana,* starring Alice Faye, Carmen Miranda, and John Payne. In 1953 the Admiral put in "the first panoramic wide screen installed in a suburban theater."

Twenty years later the theater was converted to a "twin" with two 430-seat viewing rooms. But the Admiral closed in 1989, after several years of false hopes that its Canadian owners would restore its original majesty. A campaign by the **Southwest Seattle Historical Society** finally led locals to purchase the Admiral in 1991 and open it as a second-run movie palace offering five to six shows per week at about $1.75 a seat. ♦ 2347 California Ave SW. 938.3456

27 Pailin Thai Cuisine $ This new restaurant took the place of a longtime favorite seafood establishment. It's still getting its feet wet, though the food—especially the *phad thai*—was quick to distinguish itself. ♦ Thai ♦ M-F 11:30AM-10PM; Sa-Su 5-10PM. 2223 California Ave SW. 937.8807

28 West Seattle Library This attractive 1910 brick building was created by **W. Marbury Somervell** and **Joseph C. Cote,** who in the same year also designed two other Carnegie libraries: the **University Branch Library** on Roosevelt Way North and **Green Lake Public Library.** Free special programs are available for children and adults on top of the usual library services. ♦ M 10AM-9PM; Tu-W 2-9PM; F-Sa 10AM-6PM; Su 1-5PM. 2306 42nd St SW. 684.7444

29 Belvedere Viewpoint The totem pole here, carved by Boeing engineers **Michael Morgan** and **Robert Fleishman** and dedicated in 1966, is modeled after one that had been presented to the city in 1939 by **J.E. "Daddy" Standley,** owner of downtown's **Ye Olde Curiosity Shop.** (Standley's original, crafted by the Bella Bella tribe of British Columbia's Queen Charlotte Islands, had decayed beyond repair.) There are only a few parking spaces with a good view over Harbor Island to downtown. ♦ Admiral Way SW

30 Hainsworth House $ A 1906 Tudor mansion, the 18-room Hainsworth House offers excellent views of downtown Seattle, lovely landscaped grounds, and two guest rooms. The larger room, decorated in French country style, has an antique Austrian king-size bed, a private deck, a fireplace, and a full view of the city. The second has a partial view, a deck, and an antique oak bedroom set. Guests are treated to coffee half an hour before eating a full champagne (or sparkling cider) breakfast served by owners **Carl** and **Charlotte Muia.** No smoking is allowed, and visitors with animal allergies beware: there are two dogs on the premises. ♦ 2657 37th Ave SW. 938.1020

31 Luna Park Cafe ★$ Eat 1950s-style food beneath a black-velvet Elvis painting. A neon-laden, Seeburg jukebox (the remote selectors at each table actually work) spins 200 selections, including Elvis Presley (both the blimped-out and slender earlier versions), Frank Sinatra, Bob Marley, and Annette Funicello. It costs an amazing dime per play. A 1946 Wurlitzer 1015 Bubbler is a display jukebox only. Other kitschy decor, from the 1920s on, includes an impressive collection of children's lunch boxes along with old business signs.

The food here is basic but good. (Try the meat loaf on whole wheat or the Cobb salad—turkey, bacon, blue cheese, egg, Swiss cheese, tomato, and olives.) The milk shakes (root beer, coffee, fresh fruit, and more flavors) are much in demand on steamy days. The Luna Park name (taken from the amusement park that graced **Duwamish Head** between 1907 and 1913) isn't exactly appropriate to this place, but it does lend an air of gaiety. ♦ American ♦ M-Th, Su 7AM-10PM, F-Sa 7AM-11PM Oct-May; M-Th, Su 7AM-11PM; F-Sa 7AM-midnight June-Sept. 2918 Avalon Way SW. 935.7250

32 YMCA The main branch of the West Seattle Y is also the most deluxe. There's a swimming pool, a weight room with free weights and exercise machines, a gym for basketball and volleyball, a running track, two racquetball courts, and a spa. All facilities, except regularly scheduled classes, are available on a drop-in basis: $7.50 per day for adults, $3 for children 18 and younger, and $5 for seniors. ♦ M-F 5:30AM-10PM, Sa 8AM-5PM, Su 1-8PM late Aug to mid-June; M-F 5:30AM-10PM, Sa 8AM-5PM, Su 2-6PM mid-June to late Aug. 4515 36th Ave SW. 935.6000

33 West Seattle Bowl Generations of young West Siders spent many Friday nights during their "wonder years" at this bowling alley, although not necessarily rolling balls in the general direction of pins. For kids with lots of quarters and boffo hand-to-eye coordination, there are video games. A restaurant inside has changed hands and cuisines a few times over the years (a recent check found it serving Chinese dishes). ♦ Daily 9AM-midnight. 4505 39th Ave SW. 932.3731

34 Capers $ The deli in this kitchen and coffee shop serves terrific scones, muffins, and cobblers, as well as an estimable seafood salad and a daily quiche. It's popular with local workers at lunchtime. A variety of items for the kitchen and dining room, as well as Dilettante chocolates and coffee by the pound, are also available. ♦ Coffeehouse ♦ M-F 6:30AM-7PM; Sa 7AM-6PM; Su 7AM-5PM. 4521 California Ave SW. 932.0371

34 Coho Cafe ★★$$ It doesn't take an Einstein to figure out that salmon is a specialty here; even the logo carries a prize coho. (Try the salmon served with tarragon sauce.) However, chef/owner **Richard Davis** (formerly of **La Fleur** at Sand Point) prepares other seafood and fresh meats, as well, some creatively. Frequent diners rave about the Coho's hazelnut pork with cranberry chutney and the chicken breast with a shiitake mushroom sauce. ♦ Seafood ♦ Tu-Th, Su 5-9PM; F-Sa 5-10PM. 4533 California Ave SW. 935.5930

35 West Seattle Speedway and Hobby Behind the stacks of plastic and intricate wooden model kits, this shop boasts a 135-foot, Euro hill-climb slot-car track, one of only a few similar wooden tracks left in the city. Renting a car and speeding it over the boards is often a nostalgic journey for people in their 30s and 40s (there was a time in the 1960s when slot-car races were all the rage).

But this sport actually owes its historical debt to auto racers of the 1920s, who, before the advent of dragsters and mud racers, gunned Duesenbergs and Millers around 24 steeply banked board loops located across the U.S. None of those board tracks survived the Great Depression, but slot-car competitors can still imagine that they're Barney Oldfield, Tommy Milton, or another of the wooden-track giants. The shop sells slot cars, parts and accessories, and baseball cards. ♦ 4539 California Ave SW. 932.9620

35 Pegasus Book Exchange What is it about flying horses and West Seattle? This book-shop buys, sells, and trades used books. Its principal stock is in paperback fiction, but the owner also has an interest in metaphysics and will help you find anything in that category that isn't already available here. ♦ M-Sa 10AM-6PM; Su 11AM-4PM. 4553 California Ave SW. 937.5410

36 California and Alaska Street Brewery $ Despite this brewpub's silly name (indi-cating the cross streets of its location), it turns out some decent beers in a city that's known for them. The brewmaster is **Charles McElevy,** trained in Germany and formerly of the **Rainier Brewing Company** and Fremont's **Red Hook Brewery.** This tiny West Seattle brewery opened in October 1991. Beer names reflect the local geography: Junction Ale, Alki Ale, Fauntleroy Stout. The Alki Ale is red, with medium body. Hi-Yu Brown Ale (which means "Big Time" in Chinook jargon and also applies to an annual festival held in West Seattle since 1934) is rich, brown, and malty. Pub grub is limited, covering the short span betwixt chili and sandwiches. For entertainment, there are dart boards and board games. Beware the no-smoking policy. ♦ Tu 2-10PM; W-Th 2-11PM; F-Sa 2PM-midnight; Su 4-9PM. 4720 California Ave SW. 938.2476

37 Husky Delicatessen A local institution since 1933, this family-owned deli grew from an ice-cream parlor specializing in large chocolate-covered cones. It still attracts customers from all over Seattle with its homemade ice cream, as well as its cold cuts, salads, beers and wines, and truffles. ♦ Deli ♦ M 10AM-7PM; Tu-Su 10AM-10PM. 4721 California Ave SW. 937.2810

38 ArtsWest This nonprofit organization (formerly the **West Seattle Cultural Society**) has established a cultural center within **Jefferson Square,** a garish retail/residential complex named for the brick elementary school that stood at this site from 1912 until it was razed in 1985. The center offers educational theater, music, dance, and other arts programs. There's also an art gallery that displays local talent. ♦ Tu-Sa noon-5PM. 4720 42nd Ave SW. 938.0963

39 Villa Heidelberg $ A converted 1909 house (constructed and named by a German immigrant), this bed-and-breakfast inn has lead glass windows, beamed ceilings, a finely landscaped yard (from which the owners pick their decorative flowers), and a covered porch. Four guest rooms share two baths. One of the guest rooms offers an Olympic-view sun deck; another has a fireplace. Popovers are a treat at breakfast. ♦ 4845 45th Ave SW. 938.3658

40 Camp Long One of the city's few parks to offer overnight facilities, this 68-acre patch is open to organized groups for camping and wilderness-skills programs. It also features a rock wall for climbing practice and instruc-tion. The rustic lodge holds 35 people in the basement and 75 in its upper room (a popular spot for wedding ceremonies). Cabin rentals are $15 per night. Picnic shelters may also be reserved. Rock climbing instruction is $15 for a one-and-a-half-hour session, with a minimum class size of 15. Free nature walks are scheduled on Saturday, and there are educational programs for youngsters; call ahead for a rundown. ♦ Park ranger station Tu-Sa 8AM-5PM. 5200 35th Ave SW. 684.7434

41 Lowman Beach Named after a former Seattle parks commissioner, this tiny park offers not only access to the sand but a swing set and one tennis court. Locals gather here annually to watch Seattle's ceremonial Christmas ship make its December loop through Puget Sound. Pleasant strolls can be had down an access road into the lower portion of adjacent **Lincoln Park.** ♦ 48th Ave SW and Beach Dr SW

42 Cat's Eye Cafe $ Most of the sandwiches served at this deli feature cute feline names: the Kit Cat (sliced chicken, avocado, tomato, and sprouts), the Catalina (turkey with jack cheese), the Cat on a Hot Tin Roof (a classic Reuben), and the Cat in Heat (tuna melt with tomato). Hot focaccia sandwiches come filled with prosciutto ham, roast chicken, or tomato and mozzarella. Other menu items include pesto lasagna, quiche, chili, and salads. The cafe does a brisk business in espresso, and a wide variety of fresh-baked muffins, scones, and breads are available daily. Though seating inside is limited to stools along one wall of the deli, on sunny days there are picnic tables on the grass across the parking lot. ♦ Deli ♦ M-F 6:30AM-8PM; Sa 7AM-7PM; Su 8AM-6PM. 7301 Bainbridge Pl SW. 935.2229

43 Lincoln Park Designed by **Frederick Law Olmsted, Jr.,** and **John Charles Olmsted,** who developed Seattle's 1903 comprehensive plan, Lincoln Park holds 130 acres of wooded and waterfront trails, with picnic areas, tennis courts, softball fields, horseshoe pits, and children's playground equipment. As with most beach parks on Puget Sound, no lifeguards are on duty even during summer months. A bit of historical trivia: Lincoln Park received its name at the request of the local **Young Men's Republican Club,** which promised in the early 20th century to erect a statue of Honest Abe at the park entrance. The promise was never kept. ♦ Fauntleroy Ave SW and SW Kenyon St

Within Lincoln Park:

Colman Pool This heated, outdoor, Olympic-size pool is filled with both chlorinated freshwater and saltwater. It's open only during summer vacation for the Seattle School District (usually late June through the end of August). Access is limited to foot traffic through Lincoln Park; park roads are open only to park vehicles or for emergencies. ♦ Admission; discount for senior citizens, handicapped persons, and children 18 and younger. Daily noon-7PM late June-Sept. 684.7494

44 Fauntleroy Ferry Dock Washington State Ferries leaving this dock take passengers to **Vashon Island,** a 28-minute ride that's packed with commuters on weekday mornings and late afternoons. Vashon is a charming rural area that seems far removed from the rush of city life. Residents who work in town often farm as a hobby, but others have found work on the island itself in industries such as ski manufacturing (**K2 Corporation**), orchid growing, or food processing. ♦ 47th Ave SW and SW Henderson St. 464.6400, 800/542.0810

45 The Original Bakery Though this is a working bakery, specializing in gooey cinnamon rolls, birthday cakes, and bread, it also has a small seating area and serves espresso. ♦ Bakery ♦ Tu-F 7:30AM-6PM; Sa 7:30AM-5PM; Su 8AM-5PM. 9253 45th Ave SW. 938.5088

45 Georgie Cafe $$ This new restaurant offers a variety of Greek and Middle Eastern specialties, including *hummus* and gyros. An outdoor dining area is available above the restaurant on sunny days. Service is usually good, but complaints have been raised about improperly chilled wine. ♦ Greek/Middle Eastern ♦ M-Th 11AM-9:30PM; F 11AM-10PM; Sa-Su 9AM-10PM. 9214 45th Ave SW. 933.8413

46 Thai Thai ★$ Stuck far away in White Center, this place serves some of the most authentic and deliciously spiced Thai food in town. Soups and curries are especially recommended. ♦ Thai ♦ M-F 11:30AM-2:30PM, 5-9:30PM; Sa 5-9:30PM. 11205 16th Ave SW. 246.2246

47 High Point This intersection sits 518.05 feet above sea level, higher even than lofty Queen Anne Hill. ♦ 35th Ave SW and SW Myrtle St

Bests

Harvey Manning
Writer

Everywhere west of the **Cascade Mountains**—very little sunshine, lots of rain, and fog. One February we did not see the sun even once. And many a July we see it only for a dozen days. This freaks out the sun-worshipers and sends them south.

Seattle is a genuine city, well supplied with good arts and expensive restaurants, but a person can live out his life (as I do now) and never go into the city more than two or three times a year. Unlike in other areas, those of us who *like* rain and fog don't have to get our kicks in fancy restaurants.

Robert W. Prado
Owner, Marzi Tarts Erotic Bakery

Breakfast at Pike Place Market's **Sound View** cafe during the week.

Dinner at the revolving **Space Needle Restaurant**—such a grand view.

Watching the faces of first-time customers when they arrive at my store and see a cake with a pair of breasts or a big erect male body part. It's so amusing to hear adults titter like children.

Seldom being a driver, I find it encouraging when an auto stops traffic to let a pedestrian cross the street; that's Seattle for you.

The Puget Sound Council of Governments predicts that between 1988 and the year 2000 about $500 million worth of gasoline will be wasted by vehicles waiting on crowded roadways in the central Puget Sound region.

Restaurants/Clubs: Red   Hotels: Blue
Shops/ 🌳 Outdoors: Green   Sights/Culture: Black

Queen Anne/Magnolia

In 1853 Seattle pioneer **Thomas Mercer**, newly arrived from the East Coast, staked a claim to 320 heavily forested acres on what is now **Queen Anne Hill**. Looking out at Puget Sound and the Olympic Mountains, you can no doubt understand why Mercer called his new home Eden.

To much of Seattle's old guard, Queen Anne and adjacent Magnolia *did* represent Edenic escapes from the burgeoning city. After **First Hill** and **Capitol Hill**, it was to these neighborhoods that the wealthy retreated,

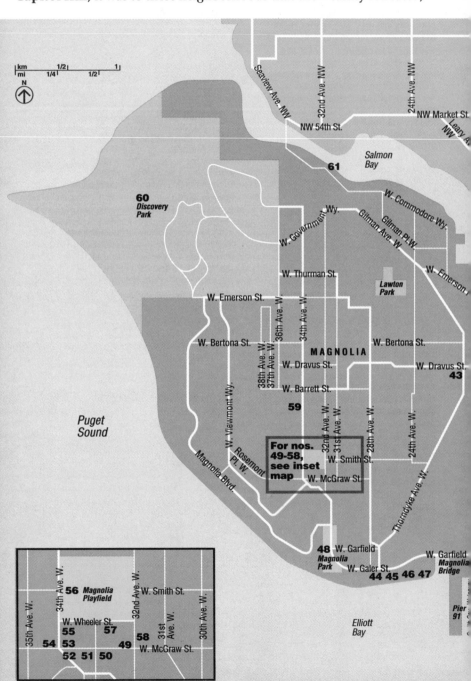

erecting their capitalist castles as the 20th century made its debut. Queen Anne, at a dizzying crest elevation of 457 feet, looked down its nose—both literally and figuratively—at the city's center. It was the second-highest point in the city, eclipsed only by the intersection of 35th Avenue Southwest and Southwest Myrtle Street in West Seattle, at 518 feet above sea level. "The Hill," as residents call it, adopted an air of elegance; so many of the homes on its south flank were designed in an Americanized spin on classic Queen Anne architectural style that by the 1880s the district had been dubbed **Queen Anne Town.** Even after it was conquered by cable-car lines and then

snatched within Seattle's city limits in 1891, the hill tried to remain parochial, a kind of feudal state protected on three sides by water (**Elliott Bay** to the south and west, **Lake Union** to the east, and the **Lake Washington Ship Canal** connecting those two to the north).

Most of the towered villas that inspired Queen Anne's name a century ago are now simply gone. Many of the other larger, older dwellings have been carved into duplexes and triplexes to make room for the neighborhood's growing population (30,000 in 1990). Hideous 500-foot-tall television towers—which, ironically, disturb TV and radio reception in the immediate neighborhood—have been thrust up against the sky here. And yet, Queen Anne still strives to rise above it all.

Magnolia is even more luxuriously isolated. Connected by only three streets and a bridge to Queen Anne and the rest of the city, this hamlet—discovered in 1865 after a United States Coast Survey misidentified a stand of madrona trees as magnolias—has until recently been dominated by single-family houses. Along with the properties bordering **Magnolia Bluff** and the waterfront homes hugging **Perkins Lane,** the area has been infiltrated over the past decade by a great many apartment and condo complexes. A clear indication of Magnolia's shifting profile is the main shopping district along West McGraw Street between 32nd and 35th avenues. More than half the businesses in **The Village,** as Magnolians call the area, have opened since the mid-'80s. Successful thirtysomething couples are moving in, drawn to Magnolia's manageable size (only about 16,000 residents so far), natural beauty, and relative calm.

1 Kinnear Park This 14-acre park of majestic trees, sloping lawns, and Sound-and-mountain views was donated to the city by Midwesterner **George Kinnear,** who first visited Seattle in 1874 and invested his money (accumulated pay from Civil War duty 10 years earlier) in local real estate. Kinnear returned to the Northwest for good in 1878 and helped form the **Home Guards,** an emergency peacekeeping force that tried to quash anti-Chinese rioting in Seattle during the mid-1880s. This park was once the terminus for a cable-car line. Unfortunately, in addition to its natural views, it also looks down on the **Port of Seattle** grain terminal, which is second only to the Kingdome among Seattle's few real eyesores. ♦ Seventh Ave West and W. Olympic Pl

2 Queen Anne Counterbalance The name for the steep ascent on Queen Anne Avenue north of Roy Street dates back to the late 1800s and early streetcar technology. While other cable-car lines in Seattle (the Yesler Way, James Street, and Madison Street operations) employed conventional underground mechanical power until 1940, the First Street car that ran through these parts had been converted as early as 1900 to draw its energy from overhead electrical wires—a fine system, in most respects. When it came to scaling the 20-percent incline of **Queen Anne Hill** near the conclusion of its run, the streetcar demanded assistance from a pair of special counterweight arrangements. Here's how it worked: two streetcars at a time could go up and down this hill, each linked via cable to a 16-ton "truck," which ran on tracks through a tunnel beneath the street. When that truck went downhill, it helped pull the heavier streetcar uphill. Going the other direction, the ascending truck restrained the descending streetcar. At eight miles per hour, it was slow going.

In a race up the Counterbalance on 5 March 1937, a more modern trackless trolley loaded with 92 passengers "embarrassed the Queen Anne streetcar, making the 2,150-foot hill in less than half the time required by the streetcar," reported the *Seattle Times* the next morning. The Counterbalance's last two cable cars were retired in 1943, but the pair of tunnels remain in place under Queen Anne Avenue. ♦ Queen Anne Ave North (between N. Roy and W. Galer Sts)

A C-700 seaplane carried the first international airmail from Vancouver, British Columbia, to Seattle's Lake Union on 3 March 1919. Eddie Hubbard was the pilot. His only passenger was aircraft company founder William E. Boeing, Sr.

3 Adriatica Cucina Mediterranea
★★★$$$ **Jim** and **Connie Malevitsis**
(along with a partner, long since departed)
opened this immensely popular restaurant in
1980. With its hillside location—you have to
climb a couple of flights just to reach the
front door—Adriatica looks out at the south
end of Lake Union and its twinkling lights
after dark. An upstairs bar offers a second
level of gorgeous views, as well as a more
casual atmosphere in the dining room.

The kitchen is the province of talented **Nancy
Flume,** a graduate of Seattle Central
Community College's acclaimed culinary-arts
program (which has turned out many of
Seattle's best chefs over the years). She and
Connie, herself an accomplished cook, have
collaborated most successfully on the menu.
No one in Seattle makes fried calamari better
than Adriatica, and the accompanying
skorthallia sauce has an international
following. The red-pepper prawns (angel-hair
pasta with prawns, cilantro, and roasted-red-
pepper cream) are wonderful, and many
people think the lamb loin chops are heads
and tails above any local comparisons. Jim,
an engaging and gregarious host, is always
happy to recommend a wine from his
carefully chosen list of fine European and
California labels. Trust him—Jim knows his
wines cold. ♦ Mediterranean ♦ M-Th, Su
5:30-9:45PM; F-Sa 5:30-10:45PM. 1107
Dexter Ave North. 285.5000

4 Triples ★★$$ Try to get past the fact that
this is a primary hunting ground for partner-
hungry yuppies. The kitchen turns out
consistently laudable preparations of local
seafood (especially salmon), plus worthy
pasta. Poultry and beef selections have
proved less interesting; the same can be said
about the sushi counter at the bar. Avoid this
restaurant during the lunchtime rush on
weekdays (it's all too popular with the
expense-account crowd) and especially on
Friday afternoon, when the testosterone level
is so high here it threatens to go ballistic.
Views of boat and pontoon-plane traffic on
Lake Union are dazzling, especially from the
outdoor porch, beside which sailboats are
often docked while their captains and crew
grab a quick gin and tonic. ♦ Northwestern
♦ M-Th 11:15AM-10PM; F 11:15AM-
10:30PM; Sa 5-10:30PM; Su 5-10PM.
Limited late-night menu served daily until
1AM. 1220 Westlake Ave North. Reservations
recommended. 284.2535

5 Latitude 47 Lunch and dinner are served
here, but it's the dance floor that's most
interesting. Small, mirrored, and circled by
TV sets playing rock videos, this arena is
often the warm-up stop in an evening's cruise
of wilder joints around Belltown or Pioneer
Square. Latin salsa cuts in on the Top-40
repertoire twice a week. ♦ Cover. M-Tu, Th-
Sa 9PM-1:30AM. Latin music W, Su 9:30PM-
1:30AM. 1232 Westlake Ave North. 284.1047

6 Arrowhead Cafe ★$ This triangular cafe
blends Southwestern specialties (don't miss
the spicy all-beef chili) with classics that have
been adapted to the Northwest setting.
Anybody for an oyster club sandwich?
Accompaniments are sometimes the biggest
surprise, including a toss of red onions with
several fruits. ♦ Southwestern ♦ M-Tu
11:30AM-9PM; W-Th 11:30AM-9:30PM;
F 11:30AM-10PM; Sa 8:30AM-10PM; Su
8:30AM-2PM. 1515 Westlake Ave North.
283.8768

7 The Williams House $ **Doug** and **Sue
Williams** opened this charming bed-and-
breakfast 10 years ago in a quiet residential
neighborhood on the east side of the hill. It
has five spacious guest rooms, most with
commanding views east and west. A winning
sun porch on the first floor faces south.
♦ 1505 Fourth Ave North. 285.0810

8 Bhy Kracke Park **Werner "Bhy" Kracke**
donated one-and-a-half acres of his property
to the city, along with $20,000 to develop the
land as a park, but the deal wasn't closed by
the time his casket was. In 1970 the city
bought the property from Kracke's heirs and
named the park in his memory. Visit here for
the views, sweeping from **Lake Union** and the
Cascade Mountains to the **Space Needle**.
The park is on several levels; follow the
winding paved path. You'll feel you've
discovered a little gem that most locals don't
know exists—and you'll be right. For parking,
look for the street sign signaling Comstock
Place and Bigelow Avenue North, ignore the
Dead End sign, and head east to the three-car
parking area just ahead. ♦ Bigelow Ave North
and Comstock Pl

9 Queen Anne High School Apartments
A successful conversion from institutional to
residential, this school closed its doors in
1981 and seven years later, reopened as an
apartment building. It now has 139
apartments—studios, one bedrooms, and
two bedrooms—on five floors, many of them
with expansive views; from a top-floor
apartment, for instance, you can see all the
way to Canada. Some of the studios have
sleeping lofts, and some of the two-bedroom
apartments come with private decks, two full
baths, and their own washer/dryer. Rents
range from $625 to $1,300 a month.

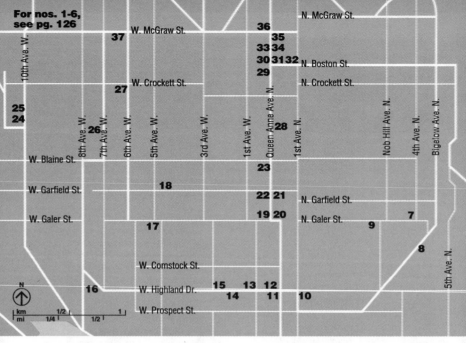

For nos. 1-6, see pg. 126

N. McGraw St.

W. McGraw St. 37 36 35

33 34

30 31 32 **N. Boston St.**

29

W. Crockett St. 27 **N. Crockett St.**

25
24

10th Ave. W. 8th Ave. W. 7th Ave. W. 6th Ave. W. 5th Ave. W. 3rd Ave. W. 1st Ave. W. Queen Anne Ave. N. 1st Ave. N. Nob Hill Ave. N. 4th Ave. N. Bigelow Ave. N.

26 28

W. Blaine St.

23

W. Garfield St. 18

22 21 **N. Garfield St.**

W. Galer St. 19 20 **N. Galer St.** 7

17 9

8

5th Ave. N.

W. Comstock St.

16 **W. Highland Dr.** 15 13 12

14 11 10

W. Prospect St.

N

km 1/2 1
mi 1/4 1/2

The school was designed in 1909 by **James Stephen,** the accomplished son of a Scottish cabinetmaker, who received his architectural training through a Chicago correspondence course and served as the Seattle School District's resident architect from 1899 to 1908. (Stephen also created **Summit Grade School** on First Hill, **Latona Elementary** and **Interlake School**—now **Wallingford Center**—in Wallingford, and many other educational facilities needed to service the city's growing population during its early boom years.) The building was converted by **Bumgardner Architects.** Despite its new use, Queen Anne High School is still the most visible landmark on the hill, especially when it's lit up at Christmastime. ♦ 201 Galer St. 285.8800

M. BLUM

10 Riddle House Proving the diversity of architectural vision along Highland Drive is this 1893 Queen Anne-Shingle style residence (pictured above), with its colonial allusions and great rounded bows of windows. The designer was **E.W. Houghton,** who 15 years later would put his finishing touches on the ambitious **Moore Theater** in downtown. ♦ 153 Highland Dr

11 Gable House This house of 14 gables was completed in 1905 by **Harry Whitney Treat,** a founder of investment and real-estate firms on Wall Street and an associate of **John D. Rockefeller.** Treat came to Seattle in 1904. His first act—a confirmation of his wealth and stature—was to commission the firm of **Charles Bebb** and **Leonard L. Mendel** (responsible for downtown's **Hoge Building** and the vast **University Heights Elementary School**) to design a Queen Anne residence that would accommodate his family of four, plus a domestic staff of 14, and would cost exactly $101,000.

Treat kept coaches and horses and a tallyho pulled by blooded steeds purchased from the New York Vanderbilts. Not content with his existing fortune, he bought hundreds of acres just north of Ballard, creating **Loyal Heights** (named after one of his two daughters) and establishing **Golden Gardens** park. An acquaintance of **Colonel William F. "Buffalo Bill" Cody,** Treat had Cody's entire Wild West troupe come to Queen Anne Hill to entertain his daughter on her ninth birthday. It was also in this house that Treat and Cody planned the acclaimed **Whitney Gallery of Western Art** in Cody, Wyoming. Originally, 61 rooms occupied the 18,000 square feet of living space here. But in 1974, Seattle's **Gary Gaffner** bought the 69-year-old mansion and began a four-year restoration project that included reconfiguring the floors to hold 15 private residential suites, each of which now rents for $800 to $1,900 a month. ♦ 1 W. Highland Dr

Restaurants/Clubs: Red	Hotels: Blue
Shops/ 🌳 Outdoors: Green	Sights/Culture: Black

12 Highland Drive Heading west from Queen Anne Avenue and about halfway up the hill, this elegant residential street reflects a variety of architectural styles in its mix of mansions and lovely brick apartment houses. For many years, beginning at the turn of the century, Highland Drive was *the* finest address in Seattle. One of the most prominent residents there was **Alden J. Blethen,** a bombastic former lawyer from Maine who'd entered journalism in the Midwest and lost a fortune there before moving to Seattle in 1896 to found the *Seattle Times.* So proud was Blethen of his pillared manse and the neighborhood in which it sat that for years he paid out of his own pocket to have Highland Drive gaslit every night.

Leisurely strolls are highly recommended along this route; at the end of Highland Drive notice the brick-in-concrete retaining walls at Seventh and Eighth avenues, designed by **W.R.B. Wilcox** in 1913. The steps, railings, and lights are all part of the design. ♦ Between Queen Anne Ave North and Seventh Ave West

12 Ballard-Howe Mansion This stately white house, built in 1906, was designed in the Colonial Revival style by **August Heide,** whose larger-scale work can be seen in the **Lowman Building** at Pioneer Place. It now contains apartments. ♦ 22 W. Highland Dr

13 Victoria Apartments Built in 1921, this large, Tudor-style brick apartment building, enclosing a lovely, expansive courtyard, was designed by prolific architect **John Graham, Sr.** The building was later refurbished as Seattle's first condominium complex. ♦ 100 W. Highland Dr

14 Kerry Park Albert Sperry Kerry, Sr., a Canadian born in 1866, moved to Seattle as a teenager and got into timber milling, first as a tallyman, later as owner of the **Kerry Timber Company.** On the side, he was instrumental in pushing the **Olympic Hotel** into existence and was something of a national figure in the world of golf; his wife, **Katherine,** sat on the **Seattle Symphony's** first board of directors. The wealthy pair donated this small, rectangular park to the city in 1927. From here the views of the Space Needle, downtown office spires, and Elliott Bay are stunning, day or night; the sight of Mount Rainier will take your breath away. Also worth appreciating: *Volumetric Space Frame,* a steel sculpture of giant framed holes created by local artist **Doris Chase** in 1969, and a seemingly out-of-place totem pole across from Kerry Park at 222 West Highland Drive. ♦ 211 W. Highland Dr

When they were built by the Port of Seattle in 1915, Piers 90 and 91 below Magnolia were the longest earth-filled piers in the world.

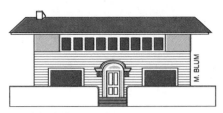

15 Black House Architect **Andrew Willatsen,** who worked in Frank Lloyd Wright's Chicago office, designed this precisely lined residence (illustrated above) that was built in 1912. According to **Sally B. Woodbridge** and **Roger Montgomery** in *A Guide to Architecture in Washington State,* the home's "strong Prairie School character is revealed by the low-pitched, broadly overhanging gable roof, the band of second-story windows tied to a belt course, and the large, boldly framed ground-floor windows." The arched front doorway is nice, too. ♦ 220 W. Highland Dr

16 Betty Bowen Viewpoint Isn't it romantic? Tony Bennett would be the ideal musical accompaniment on a visit to this spot at the end of Highland Drive. From here Puget Sound, the Olympic Mountains, and the dying blaze of sunsets can all be espied. If nobody's ever popped "The Question" here, somebody should. The overlook was designed in 1977 by **Victor Steinbrueck,** the architect and preservationist who brought the Space Needle to concrete reality and fought successfully to save Pike Place Market. ♦ Seventh Ave West and W. Highland Dr

17 West Queen Anne Elementary School This historic brick structure, with its whimsical medieval hints, was created in 1896 by the Seattle architectural firm of **Skillings and Corner** (responsible also for the **Old Main Building** at Bellingham's **Western Washington University**). It was used as a school until the 1980s, when it was converted into condominiums by local architect **Val Thomas** (who reserved the former gymnasium for himself). The building rests on lovely landscaped grounds in a neighborhood of residential grandeur. ♦ 515 W. Galer St

18 Queen Anne Branch Library It was opened on New Year's Day 1914 in a burst of festivity attended by more than a thousand people. *Seattle Times* owner **Alden J. Blethen** contributed $500 to help buy the land, with the city kicking in the remaining $6,500. Pennsylvania steel-and-iron-magnate **Andrew Carnegie** had donated the money for the building: $32,667. And a couple of heavy architectural guns had been brought out to develop the handsome library in a style that might best be labeled English Scholastic Gothic: **W. Marbury Somervell,** who, along with partner **Joseph C. Cote,** already had listed on his curriculum vitae the **Providence Hospital** in the Central Area and the **West Seattle Public Library;** and **Harlan Thomas,**

who's probably best remembered for downtown's 1924 **Chamber of Commerce** building on Columbia Street.

During the library's first year, it circulated 71,623 books. It became an active community center, and many organizations—the **Earwig Club** among them—held their meetings in the auditorium. Interior highlights include small-pane leaded-glass windows, oak-panel doors with bronze mortise handles and locks, and stained-glass entry windows. In 1978 a vividly colored art-glass mural, created by Seattle artist **Richard Spaulding,** was hung on the north wall. ♦ M, W-Th 1-9PM; Tu, Sa 10AM-6PM. 400 W. Garfield St. 386.4227

19 La Tazza di Caffe Coffee imported directly from Italy and unusually well-brewed *lattes* pack 'em in to this handsome coffee bar, which also serves four kinds of *panini,* including the tasty Fresca: fresh mozzarella, roma tomatoes, and fresh basil on focaccia bread. ♦ Coffeehouse ♦ M-F 6:30AM-7PM; Sa 7:30AM-7PM; Su 8AM-2PM. 1503 Queen Anne Ave North. 284.8984

20 Olympia Pizza & Spaghetti House ★$$ There are several Olympia pizzerias around town now, but this one, perched at the top of the **Counterbalance,** was the very first. Choose from a list of 30 pizzas, including the three house specialties: the Spiro (pepperoni, Canadian bacon, mushrooms, shrimp, olives, green peppers, cheese, and tomato sauce), the Olympia (sausage, fresh garlic, mushrooms, Canadian bacon, olives, onions, and fresh or cooked tomatoes), and the House Special (salami, pepperoni, sausage, Canadian bacon, green peppers, olives, cheese, mushrooms, and tomato sauce). Gourmands will want to know that Olympia also makes deliveries. ♦ Pizza/Takeout ♦ Daily 11:30AM-midnight. 1500 Queen Anne Ave North. 285.5550. Also at: 3213 W. McGraw St. 286.9000; 516 15th Ave East. 329.4500; 4501 Interlake Ave North. 633.3655

20 The 5-Spot ★★$ **Peter Levy,** the high-energy cofounder (along with **Jeremy Hardy**) of Wallingford's attitude-intensive **Beeliner Diner,** has stretched himself slightly more here to develop a menu strong on regional American cooking. Some representative dishes: salmon linguine from the Northwest; shrimp enchilada *con queso* from the Southwest; steaming bowls of smoked chicken and corn chowder, à la New England; and, from the Land of Dixie, "Hoppin John" cakes (seasoned black-eyed-pea pancakes topped with sour cream and

salsa). There's also a dynamite red-flannel hash served for breakfast and a different dinner special every day, purveyed from 5PM "till it's gone."

The kinetic energy and sass that make the Beeliner such a warm locale are sadly diluted in this much larger venue. But you've got to give Levy, a former dining-room manager at **McCormick and Schmick's** in downtown, heaps of credit for experimenting—there's little he won't try here at least once. Portions are plentiful and the **Counterbalance Room** bar, set off near the kitchen, is a surprisingly peaceful place, rarely crowded. Weekend mornings, there's a line out the door for the dining room. ♦ American ♦ M-Th, Su 8:30AM-10PM; F-Sa 8:30AM-11PM. 1502 Queen Anne Ave North. 285.7768

21 Pasta Bella ★$$ **David Rasti** opened this second Pasta Bella (the original is in Ballard) in the former **Après Vous Cafe** and has warmed up the space considerably, changing the dominant hue to a rich green. A very pleasant deck enhances warm-weather meals (try to ignore the monstrous TV tower next door). *Linguini amatriciana* (a sauce of fresh tomatoes, pancetta, chile, garlic, and wine), *linguini con vongole* (clams, garlic, wine, butter, and cheese), and *pollo piccata* (breast of chicken with capers, garlic, butter, and wine in a lemon cream sauce) are highly recommended. The selective wine list is 80-percent Italian, just as it should be. ♦ Italian ♦ M-F 11:30AM-10PM; Sa noon-10PM; Su 2-9PM. 1530 Queen Anne Ave North. Reservations recommended. 284.9827. Also at: 5909 15th St NW. 789.4933

22 Pepe's $ The hilltop's only Mexican restaurant serves great tostadas, enchiladas, and burritos, and the margaritas are rapidly winning fans. ♦ Mexican ♦ M-Th 11AM-10PM; F-Sa noon-11PM; Su noon-9PM. 1531 Queen Anne Ave North. 283.0788

23 Queen Anne Avenue Books Alice Osborne and **Randy Brownlee** opened this fine bookstore (selling new publications) in 1991. For its size, this shop is strong on fiction, but there's also a nice selection of travel books and magazines. Children's books can be found in back. ♦ M-Sa 10AM-8PM; Su 11AM-5PM. 1629 Queen Anne Ave North. 283.5624

24 Westside Stories This bookstore (selling mostly used works) is a welcome addition to the otherwise arid landscape of trafficky 10th Avenue West. While there are good selections in art, history, travel, and biography, the fiction department is particularly strong, reflecting owner **Beth Dunn's** interests. ♦ Tu-F 11AM-8PM; Sa 10AM-5PM; Su noon-5PM. 1901 10th Ave West. 285.2665

25 Cadiz Espresso $ **Jean Villagas** opened this intimate coffeehouse in 1992, filling it with wall decorations that are a legacy of her extensive travels. Villagas believes in expressive espresso; no coffee milk shakes here. Pastries are from Queen Anne neighbor **Sweet Success.** ♦ Coffeehouse ♦ M 6:30AM-1PM; Tu-F 6:30AM-1PM, 5-8PM; Sa 8AM-5PM; Su 9AM-5PM. 1905 ¹/₂ 10th Ave West. 282.0779

26 Queen Anne Hill Bed & Breakfast $ **Mary** and **Chuck McGrew** own a charming five-room B&B at the top, west side of Queen Anne Hill. Of the three upstairs guest rooms, one has a private deck from which glorious views of the Olympic Mountains and the sunsets are available; another claims its own bath. A shared bathroom, complete with claw-foot tub, is as big as a small guest room. There are two bright and cheerful downstairs bedrooms, as well. Common areas include a deck facing west, a cozy living room, and a small sun porch; you're even welcome in the kitchen. The plentiful art—from original works to posters—is a story in itself. ♦ 1835 Seventh Ave West. 284.9779

27 Sweet Success You can't miss this place; just look for the huge nostril looming above the doorway. The business was opened in early 1992 by **Julie Maitland,** a professional baker who apprenticed for five years at Patisserie Lanciani in New York. The specialty of the house is birthday and wedding cakes, and Maitland's pastries are turning up at coffeehouses and espresso stands in the area. ♦ Bakery ♦ M 6:30AM-3PM; Tu-F 6:30AM-4PM; Sa 8AM-4PM. 1955 Sixth Ave West. 283.0436

28 Queen Anne Thriftway Seattle's first—and many would say its best—upscale supermarket has an espresso counter and flower stand out front and a car-washing service in the parking lot. Inside, there's everything from an exceptionally good wine department, with depth in European, California, and Northwest labels, to an organic gourmet salad bar featuring endive and arugula. The bakery section features French breads, croissants, and other fresh comestibles from the justly celebrated **Boulangerie** on North 45th Street. The seafood department is likewise estimable, and the staff is helpful and friendly, even at 3AM. ♦ Open daily 24 hours. 1908 Queen Anne Ave North. 284.2530

29 Queen Anne Cafe $ Breakfast all day, 11 kinds of burgers, French dip and hot turkey sandwiches, onion rings, and shakes are featured at this hilltop institution. ♦ American ♦ Daily 6AM-10PM. 2121 Queen Anne Ave North. 285.2060

30 Starbucks The Microsoft of coffee companies, Starbucks deserves credit for starting the quality-coffee revolution in the Northwest. Limited, uncomfortable seating discourages lingering. Order your *caffè latte*—make it a *grande*—to go. ♦ Coffeehouse ♦ M-F 6AM-10PM; Sa 6:30AM-10PM; Su 7:30AM-8PM. 2201 Queen Anne Ave North. 285.3711

30 The Santa Fe Cafe's Blue Mesa Pam Gibbons' shop is the take-out arm of the popular **Santa Fe Cafe,** which specializes in authentic Southwestern cuisine. You can get everything here from *chile con queso* and Santa Fe crêpes (blue-corn crêpes filled with chicken breast, mushrooms, green chiles, and sliced almonds in a white Spanish sherry sauce) to *posole* stew (hominy, pork shoulder, and red chiles). The shop does full-service catering, too. ♦ Southwestern/Takeout ♦ M-W, Sa-Su 11AM-7PM; Th-F 11AM-8PM. 2205 Queen Anne Ave North. 282.6644

30 Teacup Enjoy a steeped cup of tea at **Mary Noe's** charming shop, then place your bulk-tea order from a list of more than a hundred selections. She sells fine English marmalades and other imported goodies, too. ♦ Teahouse ♦ M-Sa 9AM-8PM; Su 11AM-6PM. 2207 Queen Anne Ave North. 283.5931

30 McCarthy & Schiering Wine Merchants This is the second location for the friendly and knowledgeable team (the original shop is in Ravenna), who are as attentive to your request for a $10 chardonnay as they are to someone else's interest in a case of Batard-Montrachet. The owners recently built a state-of-the-art wine-cooling room, so you can order a case of Taittinger Blanc de blancs in the morning and pick it up chilled for the evening's dinner party. ♦ Tu-F 11AM-7PM; Sa 10AM-6PM. 2209 Queen Anne Ave North. 282.8500. Also at: 6500 Ravenna Ave NE. 524.0999

31 Standard Bakery Bite into one of the biggest apple fritters you've ever seen. ♦ Bakery ♦ M-Sa 6AM-6:30PM; Su 6:30AM-2PM. 2 Boston St. 283.6359

32 Maybe Monday Caffe ★$ The engaging **Emmon Pitaksakpong** owns this cheerful place, named after her response to the repeated query: "When are you going to open?" She specializes in good sandwiches and delicious house-made soups. ♦ American ♦ M-F 7AM-8PM; Sa-Su 8AM-5PM. 10 Boston St. 283.7118

33 The Broadway Clock Shop Certified master clockmaker **Brian Varner** moved his business from Capitol Hill some years ago

---

Restaurants/Clubs: Red   Hotels: Blue
Shops/ 🌿 Outdoors: Green   **Sights/Culture:** Black

but kept the original name. Browsing among the antique wall clocks and wonderful grandfather timepieces is like stepping back in, well, time. ♦ Tu-F noon-6PM; Sa 10AM-3PM. 2214 Queen Anne Ave North. 285.3130

34 Hanh's Southeast Asian Cafe ★$$ A cozy restaurant in a converted house, Hanh's is fluent in Chinese, Thai, and Vietnamese cuisine. Chicken roll-ups (chicken, vegetables, and herbs rolled in rice paper and dipped in peanut sauce or spicy vinegar), and seafood papaya (calamari, scallops, and prawns with green papaya) are house specialties. At presstime, rumor had it that Hanh's was closing to make way for **Pirosmani**. Call ahead. ♦ Asian ♦ M-Th, Su 5-9:30PM; F-Sa 5-10:30PM. 2220 Queen Anne Ave North. 285.3360

35 Ristorante Buongusto ★★$$ Hailing from Naples, the **Varchetta** brothers, **Salvio** and **Roberto**, and **Anna**, Salvio's wife, operate one of Seattle's best Italian restaurants on Queen Anne Hill. The space, a former house, is warm and inviting. Dinner highlights include the superb *gamberoni alla brace* (grilled jumbo prawns with garlic, olive oil, parsley, and red pepper), *agnello alla griglia* (grilled lamb chops), and *linguine alla pescatora* (linguine with shellfish and calamari in a fresh tomato sauce). Eggplant *parmigiana* and panfried calamari lead the list of appetizers. Choose from a strong selection of fine Italian wines. ♦ Italian ♦ M, Su 5-9:30PM; Tu-Th 11:30AM-2:30PM, 5-9:30PM; F 11:30AM-2:30PM, 5-10:30PM; Sa 5-10:30PM. 2232 Queen Anne Ave North. Reservations recommended. 284.9040

36 A&J Meats Long considered one of Seattle's leading meat markets (in the literal, as opposed to the barfly, sense), A&J also offers an entire menu of convenient pre-prepared dinner specialties: Bavarian Rouladen (rolled beefsteak stuffed with bacon, Italian salami, mushrooms, and Parmesan cheese), chicken Cordon Bleu, meatballs, chicken puff pastries, and more. There's a variety of fine sausages, too. ♦ Tu-F 11AM-7PM; Sa 9AM-6PM. 2401 Queen Anne Ave North. 284.3885

37 McGraw Street Bakery In less than 10 years **Jessica Reisman** has gone from baking a few batches of her patented mazurka cookies in her apartment to turning out more than 3,500 mazurkas a week in this operation, complete with its 70-year-old brick oven and a staff of 21. Adapted from a Polish recipe (mazurka is, in fact, the name of a Polish folk dance), these cookies—crumbly, fruit-filled squares similar to a Linzer torte—are made "from scratch using all-natural ingredients," according to their creator.

Reisman's 75 regular mazurka clients include Nordstrom espresso carts, some of the city's better supermarkets, and the Eastside's natural-food stores. The popular neighborhood hangout makes other baked goods as well, including cinnamon rolls; blueberry, bran, and apple cardamom muffins; cookies and brownies; and an outstanding apple walnut coffee cake. Linger over a pastry, a cup of good java, and the house copy of the *New York Times,* or pick up something to go. ♦ Bakery ♦ M-F 7AM-6PM; Sa-Su 8AM-6PM. 615 W. McGraw St. 284.6327

38 Canlis ★★★★$$$$ For more than 40 years **Peter Canlis'** restaurant—now in the capable hands of his son, **Chris**—has occupied a commanding position high above Lake Union at the south end of the George Washington (a.k.a. Aurora) Bridge. From the moment you walk in, you'll be in good hands. Relax, settle back, and let the kimono-clad waitresses—a Canlis tradition—pamper you. The place made its rep as a steak house, and many people, restaurant critics among them, still consider the cuts of beef here to be the very best in town.

Among the appetizers, the Dungeness crab legs with mustard sauce and the lobster bisque are worth a visit by themselves. The mahimahi broiled over Kiawe wood and the butterfly prawns with pork are highly recommended main courses. And the ever-popular Canlis salad ("with no apologies to Caesar," as the menu says) is prepared at your table; pick up the recipe at the reception desk on your way out. ♦ Steak House ♦ M-Sa 5:30-10:30PM. 2576 Aurora Ave North. 283.3313

39 Turret House Two blocks east of the Christian Science church, you'll come to an arresting residence: a multigabled, cedar-shake structure, complete with solarium, turret, and a widow's walk. In the 1970s this was home to the communeish and controversial **Love Israel** "family," one of whose members, **Logic Israel,** is the son of entertainer/author **Steve Allen.** ♦ W. Halladay St and Sixth Ave West

40 Seventh Church of Christ—Scientist Built in 1926, this impressive, if somewhat squat looking, red-tile-roofed structure anchors the northwest corner of Eighth Avenue West and Halladay Street. It was designed in neo-Byzantine/Early Christian Revival church style by the firm of **Thomas, Grainger & Thomas,** which a few years later created **Harborview Hospital** on First Hill. ♦ 2555 Eighth Ave West

41 Lofurno's ★$$ Phil Lofurno's lively place on 15th Avenue West (the dividing line between Magnolia and Queen Anne) is noted for good pasta, generous portions, and live jazz five nights a week. Upstairs, normally a banquet and private-party area, a big band plays on the first Thursday of every month. ♦ Italian ♦ W-Th, Su 5-10PM; F-Sa 5-11PM. 2060 15th Ave West. 283.7980

42 Panda's ★$ Like its much-praised older sibling in Wedgewood, Panda's of Magnolia is known for inexpensive, high-quality food and fast, friendly service. Soup noodles, dumplings, buns, and sauces are made fresh daily. The Orange Beef (tender beef slices with an orange sauce) and Happy Family (stir-fried scallops, shrimp, and breast of chicken) specials are outstanding. Sit at the counter and observe firsthand the skill in the kitchen. Delivery is free to Magnolia and Queen Anne residences. ◆ Chinese/Takeout ◆ M-Th 11AM-9:30PM; F-Sa 11AM-10:30PM; Su 4-9PM. 1625 W. Dravus St. 283.9030. Also at: 7347 35th St NE. 526.5115

43 Romio's Pizza ★$$ One of five Romio's in Seattle, this joint is just west of **Burlington Northern's** main railroad yard. It's a popular, busy stop, with a constant stream of deliveries going out the door. While all the pizzas are good, the Zorba (onions, tomatoes, Greek feta cheese, olives, and gyro meat with a house-made *tzatziki* sauce) and the G.A.S.P. (fresh garlic, artichoke hearts, sun-dried tomatoes, and pesto) are the most memorable. ◆ Pizza/Takeout ◆ M-Th 11AM-11PM; F 11AM-midnight; Sa noon-midnight; Su noon-11PM. 2001 W. Dravus St. 284.5420. Also at: 8523 Greenwood Ave North. 782.9005; 3242 Eastlake Ave East. 322.4453; 917 Howell St. 622.6878; 616 First Ave. 621.8500

44 Runions House Built in 1972 on a triangular site, this striking home was designed by Seattle architect **Ralph Anderson.** With its expanse of glass, wide eaves, decks, and fine integration with the natural environment, it represents a late flourishing of what's come to be known as Northwest Style architecture—a regional, mostly residential style that took root in the 1930s. At its best, Northwest Style was organic in nature and functional in form, drawing from modernism, common barn design, the early 20th-century Western Stick Style (itself derivative of florid Victorian architecture), and even Japanese design. Anderson, along with Seattleite **Paul Thiry** and Oregon architects **Pietro Belluschi** and **Van Evra Bailey,** helped to create the look. ◆ 2587 Magnolia Blvd West

45 Magnolia Boulevard Heading west across the **Magnolia Bridge,** you drop onto this scenic route (originally called **West Galer Street,** but it's the same road), with its distinctive madrona trees and views of Puget Sound and the Olympic Mountains. Continuing west on the boulevard lands you at Seattle's largest park, **Discovery Park.** ◆ Between W. Galer and W. Emerson Sts

46 Elliott Bay Marina Opened in 1991, this privately owned state-of-the-art marina, located at the base of Magnolia Bluff, can accommodate 1,200 boats. Within its first year, it was 85 percent full. An interesting mix of graceful old boats and sleek new yachts are moored here, some of them one hundred feet long. This is a select sight-seeing spot for boat-captain wanna-bes. ◆ 2601 W. Marina Place. 285.4817

At the Elliott Bay Marina:

Palisade ★★$$$ Rich **Komen,** the man behind **Restaurants Unlimited** (Triples, Palomino, Cutters Bayhouse) never does anything without a splash. You could practically see the ripples from his 1992 opening of the high-concept, $4 million Palisade restaurant fanning out among local food critics, drawing attention that a less theme-parkish place would never garner so easily. The 13,000-square-foot restaurant seats 300 patrons inside, another 30 out on the deck. The main dining room is a soaring space, complete with an elevated piano trellis and player piano.

To get to the dining room, you cross a 60-foot-long bridge over a 1,000-square-foot pool of circulating Elliott Bay seawater filled with Pacific Northwest finfish and shellfish. Cecil B. DeMille should have had interiors architect **Gary Dethlefs,** who created this environment, as a set designer. The view sweeps 180 degrees from the Port of Seattle grain terminal, past downtown, across Elliott Bay to West Seattle and Alki Point, and out to Puget Sound and the Olympic Mountains. *Whew!*

At Palisade, you can order many of the fish, poultry, and meat dishes in a variety of cooking methods: wood-fired oven, searing grill, wood-fired rotisserie, apple-wood broiler. Menu highlights include a shellfish chowder, Dungeness crab cakes (listed on the lunch menu only, but ask for them at dinner), wood-oven roasted black tiger prawns, and applewood-grilled salmon (king or silver). ◆ Northwestern ◆ M-Th 11:30AM-10PM; F-Sa 11:30AM-11PM; Su 10:30AM-10PM. Reservations recommended. 285.1000

Maggie Bluffs $ This cafeteria-style restaurant below Palisade specializes in pizza, burgers, and breakfasts. Prices are lower here than in the fancier digs above. Unfortunately, it is almost impossible to escape the TV at Maggie Bluffs; NFL football is not everyone's cup of coffee at Sunday breakfast, thank you very much. ◆ American ◆ M-Th 8AM-10PM; F-Sa 8AM-11PM; Su 8AM-9PM. 283.8322

Elliott Bay Yachting Center If you've always wanted to lease a yacht—sail or power, 27 feet to 50 feet—you've come to the right place. Various lease options are available, starting at $145 a month. Expert instruction is provided when you sign up. ♦ M-F 9AM-5:30PM; Sa 9AM-5PM; Su noon-5PM. 285.9499, 800/422.2019 (WA and OR only)

The Hanging Locker Anchor here for a fine assortment of deck shoes, good-quality long-sleeve cotton pullovers, shorts, jackets, and T-shirts for boat people. Landlubbers are welcome, too. ♦ M-F 11AM-6PM; Sa 11AM-5PM; Su 11AM-4PM. 285.1397

Marine Center A catalog store for boaters (the "oldest and largest on the West Coast," according to promo materials), this is a fascinating place to visit, even for terra firmanians. You'll find abundant marine paraphernalia, including nautical charts, teak shelving, and other hardware, radios, and assorted electronic gadgetry. ♦ M-F 9AM-6PM; Sa 9AM-5:30PM; Su 9AM-4PM. 285.1663

47 Smith Cove Park On the Elliott Bay waterfront between Pier 91 and the Elliott Bay Marina, this is a fine place to catch sea-level views of the harbor and watch the car-carrying ships docked at Pier 91. Two men played key roles in establishing this place. The first and more powerful was **James J. Hill,** "empire builder" of the **Great Northern Railroad.** After Hill muscled his tracks to Seattle in 1893, and before he completed the King Street rail station in 1906, he constructed giant double docks at **Smith Cove** to service the steamers *Minnesota* and *Dakota,* both carrying beautiful silk from the Orient to be loaded onto Great Northern trains in Seattle and shipped to East Coast markets. It was a lucrative trade until about 1940, when nylon replaced the demand for silk.

Smith Cove was taken over for a time by the U.S. Navy, but the Port of Seattle bought it back in the 1970s and created Smith Cove Park, which brings up the second man

memorialized by this spot: **Dr. Henry A. Smith,** who arrived from Ohio to build a log cabin here in 1853. A well-liked gentleman farmer, poet, and surgeon, known for anesthetizing patients through hypnotism and promoting the therapeutic use of dream analysis, Smith was King County's first school superintendent and a territorial legislator. He also supposedly translated Duwamish Indian **Chief Sealth's** famous 1854 caution to invading white men that their day of decline would come as surely as had the Native Americans'—a speech that took on controversy in the early 1990s when questions were raised about its authenticity. Smith died at his home here in 1915 at the age of 85, due to a chill he'd caught while planting tomatoes in his garden. A plaque was dedicated in his honor at the Smith Cove Park in 1978. ♦ 23rd Ave West and W. Marina Place

48 Magnolia Park Take a break, enjoy the breeze and the quiet, and gaze up at the trees or out to the water. This spot is excellent for picnics. Look for a small parking area on the boulevard's west side. ♦ W. Garfield St and Magnolia Blvd West

49 Magnolia's Bookstore Thanks to owner **Molly Cook,** Magnolia finally has a neighborhood bookstore to call its own. There's a good selection of general fiction and mysteries, along with travel, self-help, cooking, reference, and other categories. A surprising variety of alternative magazines greets you up front, with conventional 'zines found in the back of the store. ♦ M-F 9AM-7PM; Sa 9AM-6PM; Su noon-5PM. 3206 W. McGraw St. 283.1062

50 Olympia Pizza and Spaghetti House ★$ The fourth member of the Olympia family (the original is on Queen Anne Hill) opened in late 1992. The dough is fresh, the service fast, and the pizza great. Deliveries are available. ♦ Italian/Takeout ♦ Daily 11AM-midnight. 3213 W. McGraw St. 286.9000. Also at: 1500 Queen Anne Ave North. 285.5550; 516 15th Ave East. 329.4500; 4501 Interlake Ave North. 633.3655

Selling Seafood by the Seashore

When it comes to supplying savory salmon and other seafood delectables, Seattle is not only Washington's largest seaport, but Alaska's as well. The salmon, halibut, and sablefish caught in Alaskan waters generally pass through this city to be processed or shipped to international markets. Seattle also has easy access to seafood from around Washington state: mussels from Penn Cove on Whidbey Island, pink swimming scallops from the San Juan Islands, octopus from Puget Sound, Pacific oysters from the Hood Canal and Willapa Bay, Olympia and Kumamoto oysters from southern Puget Sound, and Dungeness crab from offshore waters. Oysters and salmon are the big favorites

here, and there are so many species of each of these available—all with different flavors and textures—that it can easily boggle the mind of the average landlubber. Here's a reference to the local catch.

Oysters

Four varieties of oysters are commonly found in Seattle-area restaurants and seafood markets, from the native Olympia to the often pricey European Flat. In general, these oysters are in season from late October through May or June—as long as the Puget Sound waters remain cold. Oysters prepare to spawn and turn milky and soft during warm weather, which is why they are usually not at their best during the summer months (but that's all right, since summertime is when salmon is most abundant in local waters). They're all best served raw on the half-shell.

European Flat Oyster Often erroneously called "belon," after the most famous French beds of this delectable mollusk, Euro-flats were recently introduced here. Primarily raised in the pristine waters off **San Juan Island** (especially in **Westcott Bay**), they have a delicate yet satisfying flavor. Supplies are limited and often more expensive than the other varieties raised hereabouts, so feast on them whenever they are available. (Some Seattle restaurants serve a related oyster, the **Chiloë,** in midsummer when local oysters are out of season.)

Kumamoto Oyster Deeply cupped, thus better preserving their tasty juices, the Kumamotos have a complex and subtle flavor. At their best they surpass the renowned Olympia oyster.

Olympia Oyster The tiny Olympia oysters' superb taste—one reason for their scarcity—more than compensates for their drab exterior. This is the Northwest's only native oyster; all other species were first raised from spawn shipped in from Asia or Europe.

Pacific Oyster Seattle's primary commercial variety is a plump, lusciously flavored bivalve, originally imported from Japan but now ubiquitous in Washington's inland waters. Fatter than other shellfish, they have a rich, satisfying flavor that's excellent raw or cooked. Pacific oysters are often named after the areas they're grown in, such as Samish Bay, Hood Canal, Shoalwater Bay, and Skookum Inlet.

Salmon

There are five species of salmon caught in Seattle's local waters. The earliest to migrate are the spring salmon, which are also the last to spawn. Sockeyes run in August, silver salmon in August and September, pinks in summer, and chums in fall. These dates are important to know, because most local salmon are caught just before they enter the rivers to spawn. Since it's often difficult to tell salmon apart in the markets, a few identification tips may prove helpful:

Chum Salmon They're similar in shape to silver salmon but have a more deeply forked tail with a rounded slender base. Sometimes sold as **"silverbrite,"** chum is low in oil and should be grilled or smoked. Don't miss the superb chum salmon caviar served at **Ray's Boathouse.**

Pink Salmon Large oval spots on the tail and back and small scales are the predominant features of these fish. Pink salmon get their name from the color of their flesh, which is low in oil (they're delicious when smoked).

Silver Salmon Also known as **coho,** they have dark spots on the back and upper tail, and are smaller and more slender than spring salmon. Silvers are commonly featured on local menus, since

they are farmed in Washington and caught in the wild. Farmed silver salmon are smaller than others but are still very flavorful, and they're especially good served with sauces made from fresh, tart berries.

Spring Salmon These fish (pictured below), also called **chinook** or **king,** have gray or brown spots on the upper body, tailfin, and head (other salmon don't have spotted heads). The flesh is rich in oil and often deep red in color, but it may be white or even streaked with white, red, and pink (particularly in the rainbow king variety). Whatever the color, spring salmon make for great eating.

Sockeye Salmon The bodies are slender (see the illustration below), with a few tiny specks on the back but none of the spots found on other salmon. These are the oiliest and most richly flavored of salmon. Their flesh is deep red. Consider yourself lucky if you find **Fraser River** sockeyes in a Seattle seafood market; they're brought in from British Columbia.

When buying salmon look for fish with red gills, a complete coat of scales, and bright, unclouded eyes. To avoid buying fish that has turned sour, smell the stomach cavity. The flesh should be firm, glossy, brightly colored, and resilient to the touch (meaning your finger shouldn't leave an impression when you poke it). Atlantic and silver salmon can be farmed, but try to buy wild fish whenever possible for their superior texture and flavor. **University Seafood & Poultry** (1317 Northeast 47th Street, 632.3900) and **Mutual Fish Company** (2335 Rainier Avenue South, 322.4368) sell the best seafood in town.

If you prefer to have your oysters shucked by a professional or want to have the catch of the day cleaned and cooked for you, Seattle offers a wide assortment of first-rate seafood restaurants. For example, **Elliott's Oyster House & Seafood Restaurant** on the Waterfront and **Shucker's** in the Four Seasons Olympic Hotel are renowned for their oysters on the half-shell. **Ray's Boathouse** on Shilshole specializes in salmon dishes, while its neighbor **Anthony's Homeport** features a superbly rich Yukon River king salmon in the spring. And for salmon and pasta entrées, don't miss **Saleh al Lago** at Green Lake.

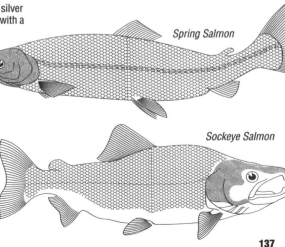

Spring Salmon

Sockeye Salmon

50 Caffè Appassionato ★$ **Tucker McHugh** (brother of successful theme restaurateur **Mick McHugh**) and **Phil Sancken** opened this charming place in 1991. Unusually handsome for a coffeehouse, Caffè Appassionato roasts its beans on site, so the coffee could hardly be fresher. *Caffè lattes* are consistently tasty, and the pastries, made off-premises by a "cottage-industry" baker, are also delicious.

Lightly grilled *panini*—including one variety with prosciutto, provolone, tomato, and fresh basil served on *schiachatta,* an Italian flat bread from Tuscany—make a satisfying lunch. An up-and-comer in a coffee-crazed town, Caffè Appassionato brand beans are making their way into Seattle restaurants. A second, slightly larger store operates in Bellevue. ♦ Coffeehouse ♦ M-Th 6AM-10PM; F-Sa 6AM-11PM; Su 7AM-7PM. 3217 W. McGraw St. 281.8040. Also at: Bellevue Square, Bellevue. 450.0886

51 Tora Japanese Restaurant ★$ Sushi is what draws most Magnolians to this cozy place, but try the *yakisoba,* as well. ♦ Japanese ♦ M-Sa 10AM-9PM. 3311 W. McGraw St. 285.4460

52 Szmania's ★★$$$ Owners **Ludger** and **Julie Szmania** have finally given Magnolia a restaurant of the first order. Chef Ludger uses regional ingredients but reveals his German roots in the signature sauerkraut "à la Szmania," with smoked pork loin and homemade sausages. The imaginative dinner menu also includes cinnamon-roasted chicken breast in white zinfandel sauce and superb grilled prawns with asparagus, olive oil, and basil on linguine. Some regulars opt to sit at the bar with a glass of wine and appetizers (try the blackened scallops and the risotto with mushrooms and Asiago cheese). An outside deck, unusual in these wet parts, has been rebuilt and expanded. ♦ German/Northwestern ♦ M-Th 11:30AM-9:30PM; F 11:30AM-10PM; Sa 11AM-10PM; Su 5:30-9PM. 3321 W. McGraw St. Reservations recommended. 284.7305

53 Starbucks This company will let no neighborhood be. At least its *lattes* are dependable, even if the atmosphere (harsh lighting and uncomfortable stools) stinks. You can even buy an espressomaker here. ♦ Coffeehouse ♦ M-F 6AM-9PM; Sa 6:30AM-9PM; Su 7AM-7PM. 3320 W. McGraw St. 298.3390

"It's cute. Why are they tearing it down?"

Fran Leibowitz, humorist, commenting on Seattle and the signs of its obsessive growth

---

Restaurants/Clubs: Red   Hotels: Blue
Shops/ 🌳 Outdoors: Green   Sights/Culture: Black

54 Loco Cafe ★$ As the name suggests, there's a friendly, playful attitude about this spot, opened in early 1992 by the youthful team of **Brigid McVeigh** and **Linda Hegg**. The customer mix reflects the changing neighborhood, with younger, freer spirits alongside Magnolia's old guard. You can order meat loaf here—*good* meat loaf, too—as well as prime rib, grilled or poached king salmon (with papaya salsa), and a vegetarian pesto pasta. The tasty omelets and the three-egg scramblers are served all day. ♦ American ♦ M, Sa-Su 7AM-2PM; Tu-F 7AM-9PM. 3416 W. McGraw St. 281.9233

55 Hot Cha Cha Interactive art reaches a boisterous high in this kinetic sculpture, created in 1987 by artist **Kenny Schneider** and located beside Fire Station No. 41. Seventy-seven identical stainless-steel firefighters, arranged in 11 rows, dance at a speed consistent with how fast you turn a wheel on the installation's side, a peculiar ode to hand-cranked motion pictures of the early 20th century. The piece's name is a humorous allusion both to the movement of Schneider's figurines and to the working environment of firefighters everywhere. ♦ 34th Ave West and W. McGraw St

56 Catherine Blaine Elementary School Built in 1952, the school was designed by Seattle architects **J. Lister Holmes and Associates,** with **Robert Dietz** and **Charles MacDonald.** "An outstanding example of the large public school in the full-fledged post-war Modern idiom," enthuses *A Guide to Architecture in Washington State,* "with natural lighting through sawtooth skylights, antiglare ceiling baffles, window walls, and modular construction." Some observers might find this place more mundane, but design buffs will nod knowingly at the project. ♦ 2550 34th Ave West

57 Eleganza Ltd. Despite its obscure location on an alleylike street, this nationally known porcelain gallery and importer of fine statuary is worth a visit. ♦ M-F 9AM-5:30PM; irregular hours on Saturday, please call ahead. 3217 W. Smith St (between 32nd and 33rd Aves). 283.0609

58 Village Pub ★$ Popular for lunch, this friendly public house draws all segments of the Magnolia community: long- and short-termers, old and young, well-to-do and just barely squeaking by. Though known for its juicy hamburgers and "snowshoe fries" (huge, wide, and flat), the Village also offers good fish-and-chips. ♦ American ♦ M-Sa 11AM-midnight. 2410 32nd Ave West. 285.9756

59 Magnolia Library Designed by Seattle architect **Paul Kirk,** this handsome modern institution occupies three lots acquired from the Catholic Diocese. Kirk used weathered cedar shingles and large plate-glass windows to "bring the beauty of the outside inside." Clerestory windows face north to admit the best light for reading. Even the furniture is noteworthy: handcrafted solid walnut chairs and tables made by Pennsylvania artist **George Nakashima.** Outside, a bronze sculpture by **Glen Alps** graces the courtyard wall; inside, you'll find a fused-glass screen by **Steven Fuller,** and two ceramic sculptures by **Ebba Rapp McLauchlan.**

The building was dedicated in July 1964, and two years later won awards from the American Institute of Architecture, the National Book Committee, and the American Library Association. Despite those laurels, the library has not won unanimous neighborhood approval; occasional complaints about the "raw shingles" and "big, bare windows" can still be heard. ◆ M-Tu, Th 1-9PM; W, Sa 10AM-6PM. 2801 34th Ave West. 386.4225

60 Discovery Park When **Captain George Vancouver** was exploring Puget Sound in 1792, he reportedly anchored nearby; the park is named after his ship, the *Discovery*. This is the largest park in Seattle, comprising 527 acres of richly varied terrain—woods, bluffs, beach, meadows, and trails. The farthest link in the 20-mile string of **Frederick L. Olmsted's** planned parklands was built north and west from **Seward Park** on Lake Washington during the early 20th century; it is a haven for Seattleites desperate to escape urban forests of concrete and steel.

Once the site of **Fort Lawton Army Base,** the land was declared surplus by the federal government in 1964. Eight years later, with considerable help from **U.S. Senator Henry M. Jackson** of Washington, the city acquired the property at no cost. Jackson's efforts didn't stop there, however. In 1968 the Department of Defense actually planned to build an Anti-Ballistic Missile (ABM) base on the Fort Lawton site. Only through Jackson's personal intercession with **Secretary of Defense Melvin Laird** was the missile-base plan deactivated.

Walking or jogging along the 2.5-mile loop trail will take you through a quiet forest, across colorful meadows, and up to windy bluffs with panoramic views west to the Sound and mountains. Follow signs for trails to the beach. Bald eagles are a common sight here (you'll know where they are by the crowds of people milling about with their faces craned to the sky). In 1982 a cougar also turned up in the park; mercifully, restraint and sensitivity prevailed, and the creature was captured without harm. Picnic possibilities are endless and playing fields abound. ◆ 3801 W. Government Way. 386.4236

Within Discovery Park:

Daybreak Star Indian Cultural Center Built in 1977 on a piece of parkland leased to the **United Indians of All Tribes Foundation** for 99 years, this dramatic timbered building was designed by **Arai Jackson** in collaboration with **Lawney Reyes.** The place is filled with interesting works of art by Native American artists, including: **John J. Hoover's** carved polychromed cedar panel, *Ancestor Spirit Boards; Buffalo Hunt,* a ceramic-tile mural by **Glenn LaFontaine;** and **Marvin Oliver's** painted and carved fir tree, *Raven/Eagle and Bear.* Daybreak Star also has a small gallery of rotating Native American art, and the center sponsors a variety of Native American activities. There's a well-equipped playground for energetic children and a spectacular viewpoint with picnic tables. ◆ Free. M-F 9AM-5PM; Sa-Su 10AM-5PM. 285.4425

61 Commodore Park Opposite the **Hiram M. Chittenden Locks** on the Lake Washington Ship Canal, the aptly named park is a secluded spot for picnicking while watching boats cruise by. Take a walk over the canal to the locks and fish ladder. ◆ W. Commodore Way and Gilman Ave West

Hoping to shed the raw wooliness of its frontier roots, in 1903 Seattle hired the Olmsted Brothers landscaping firm of Massachusetts to develop a comprehensive city plan. Like their firm's founder, the renowned Frederick Law Olmsted (who designed Boston's park systems and New York's Central Park), Frederick Law Olmsted, Jr., and his cousin, John Charles Olmsted, believed that the most beautiful cities integrated natural areas with commercial and residential ones. After surveying Seattle, John explained that one of his principal ideas for the town was to provide a park or playground within a mile of every home. Unfortunately, much of the best land here had already been scooped up by business and industry, and the city had to exercise its broad powers to acquire barely developed or undevelopable land wherever possible.

The pleasant result was a 20-mile string of parklands and boulevards that eventually reached north and west from Seward Park on Lake Washington to Discovery Park in Magnolia. Beacon Hill, Green Lake, Woodland and Volunteer parks, the University of Washington campus, and the Mount Baker neighborhood would all eventually be influenced by the Olmsteds' visions. "In the absence of the Olmsted plan," writes historian Richard C. Berner in *Seattle 1900-1920: From Boomtown, Urban Turbulence, to Restoration,* "the city would have no coherent blueprint for the future at all. Its growth would have been dictated entirely by commercial considerations."

Ballard

Although Scandinavians once dominated the population of this old fishing and lumbering district, and businesses continue to reflect its Nordic heritage, a scant 12 percent of Ballard's 40,000 current residents now claim Scandinavian descent. The new neighbors are young professionals (if still predominantly Caucasian) attracted to Ballard's abbreviated skyline, its classic main street, and its unpretentious style. And the fact that Ballard continues to offer reasonably priced housing only adds to its drawing power.

Located north of the **Lake Washington Ship Canal** and extending west to Puget Sound, the Ballard area hosted an early settlement of the **Shilshole Indians.** (*Shilshole*, meaning "tuck away a bit" in the Salish Indian dialect, aptly describes old Ballard's protected position on **Salmon Bay**.) Concealed

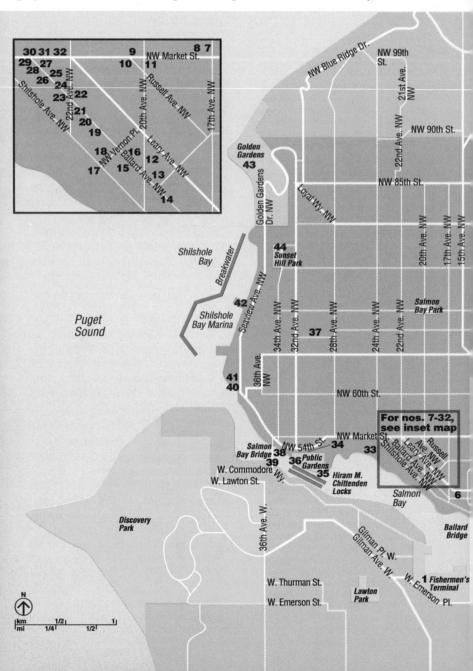

from raiding parties on Puget Sound, the village's location served the Shilsholes well, and their population grew to about one thousand. But the village was eventually discovered by other natives, and in the late 17th and early 18th centuries, repeated attacks by northern tribes, many of them down from Alaska, took a heavy toll. By the time the first white settlers arrived in the 1800s, the population of Shilshole Village had dwindled to a mere dozen families.

In 1852, **Ira Wilcox Utter,** an adventurous 27-year-old from Bridgewater, New York, filed a claim to become the first white settler at Salmon Bay, which was then an area of pristine beauty, with a virgin forest of giant thousand-year-old cedars. By 1870, 50 to 100 white settlers had staked claims in the Salmon Bay area; before the decade was over, the logging of the bay's shore—which was to change this place forever—had begun.

With a population of 1,636 in 1890, Ballard was the first community to incorporate as a city after Washington became the 42nd state in 1889. By 1892 the population had risen to 2,000. The city was named in honor of **Captain William Rankin Ballard,** who, along with lawyer **Thomas Burke** (who later became Chief Justice of the Washington Supreme Court) and **John Leary** (entrepreneur and one-time Seattle mayor), developed and sold off much of this canton. Ballard started out as an industrial community, with five shingle mills, three sawmills, a sash-and-door factory, a steel- and iron-works, a boiler works, three shipyards, a blacksmith shop, and a booming saloon district to service all of the workers. (By 1907 there were 20 saloons, bars, and wine rooms in this active town.)

Ballard sawmills provided much of the wood used to rebuild Seattle after the city's devastating fire in 1889. By 1902 daily output from the 12 local mills was three million shingles and 350,000 board feet of lumber. That year, the largest mill, owned by former Midwesterner **C.D. Stimson,** produced enough shingles to fill one thousand railroad cars, each holding 150,000 shingles. The mills also clouded the skies with a blizzard of what was termed Ballard snow—air pollution dense enough to produce a "vast wall of smoke which makes an impenetrable barrier between the city and Salmon Bay," in the words of one frustrated photographer.

The Ballard waterfront was equally bustling. Naturally shallow Salmon Bay had become a log-booming harbor. The commercial fishing fleet, comprising 25 vessels by the early 1900s, brought in tons of halibut, salmon, and cod. Large, oceangoing ships docked at nearby shipyards for hull repairs.

By 1906 Ballard was the seventh-largest town in Washington, with more than 10,000 residents. Such rapid growth brought inevitable problems, none more urgent than finding an adequate water supply. Annexation to Seattle, which was eager to expand northward, became a hot topic. And in November, after a bitter, divisive battle, citizens of Ballard narrowly approved the merger—996 to 874. The *Seattle Post-Intelligencer* suggested with arrogance that Ballard immediately be renamed Seattle Northwest, but that idea died thankfully on the page.

Separated geographically from the main burners of city development and choosing to maintain at least some of its image as a rarefied sanctuary for longtime Seattleites, Ballard continues to exist very much as a small town within larger metropolitan boundaries. Its attributes are appreciated without being flaunted. For instance, Ballard is still home to one of the largest fishing fleets in the world, a fact that rarely gets much play in the city media. While seeking to gentrify its older sections, Ballard has simultaneously tried to maintain its historic character. Locals describe their neighbors in the most generous of terms. "A typical native Ballardite," says one, "is a down-to-earth sort of person, careful with money but generous with friendship." Yet many urban Seattleites look at Ballard as remotely as they do Bainbridge Island—a destination so far from the mainstream that they rarely, if ever, choose to visit. No doubt Ballardites prefer things that way.

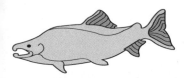
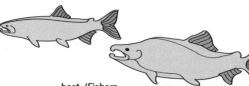

1 Fishermen's Terminal Owned and operated by the *Port of Seattle* since 1913, Fishermen's Terminal, located at the south end of the Ballard Bridge on Salmon Bay, is home base to more than 700 commercial fishing vessels, ranging in length from 30 feet to 300 feet. Here you find the trollers, gill-netters, seiners, long-liners, crabbers, and trawlers that make up the North Pacific fleet, which is one of the largest commercial fishing fleets in the world. Every year, Washington fishers harvest 2.3 billion pounds of fish and other seafood, more than half the total edible catch in the United States. The huge factory trawlers that moor at Fishermen's Terminal—some as long as a football field—catch 85 percent of the bottom fish taken by U.S. fishers. The moorage provides not only a good location for sightseers and photographers but opportunities to buy whole fish right off the boat. (Fishers aren't supposed to fillet what they sell here, but there's no harm in asking, now is there?) ♦ 1735 W. Thurman St. 728.3395

At Fishermen's Terminal:

Bulletin Board Advertising everything from a $450 Coast Guard-approved radar course to a Puget Sound seine permit selling for $8,000, the bulletin board posted inside the terminal building provides a fascinating peek at the nuts and bolts of commercial fishing life.

Chinook's ★★$$ As you might expect, fresh Northwest seafood is featured—along with a wall-to-wall view of the fishing boats—at this popular addition to the **Anthony's Homeport** restaurant fleet. The grilled Copper River salmon (which is not always available) is superb, and the mussels are fresh and flavorful. ♦ Seafood ♦ M-Th 11:30AM-10PM; F 11:30AM-11PM; Sa 7:30AM-11PM; Su

7:30AM-10PM. Reservations recommended. 283.4665

Bay Cafe $ Specialties are the three-egg house omelet, with Havarti cheese, bacon, fresh mushrooms, onion, and green pepper, and the grilled Alaskan halibut. If you're seated at a window booth, you'll be close enough to the fishing boats to read their registration numbers. ♦ American ♦ M-F 6:30AM-3PM; Sa-Su 7AM-3PM. 282.3435

Wild Salmon From Alaskan king salmon to Dungeness crab, the catch is as fresh as it gets at **David Leong's** superb seafood market, one of the best in Seattle. Wild Salmon will also ship anywhere in the U.S. The canned tuna here will make you forget all about the stuff you grew up on. ♦ M-Sa 10AM-6PM; Su 11AM-6PM. 283.3366

E.F. Kirsten Tobacconist Get a world-renowned Kirsten pipe and choose from a broad selection of pipe tobaccos in bulk, the unusual Mariner's Mixture and Dutch Harbor Blend among them. The cigar humidor is as big as a walk-in closet. You'll find a serious selection of kitchen (and other) knives, decks of cards, and flasks among the merchandise. ♦ M-F 7:30AM-7PM; Sa 9AM-7PM. 783.0700

Seattle Ship Clothing The heavy-duty outdoor gear sold here is designed for professional fishers. The **Stormy Seas Clothing** line was developed by commercial fisherman **Michael Jackson** after he had been swept overboard in Alaska's Bering Sea. ♦ M-F 8:30AM-5:30PM; Sa 10AM-4PM. 283.0830

Seattle Fishermen's Memorial The gathering point for the ceremonial blessing of the fleet, held annually in May, this memorial (pictured at right) was created by Seattle sculptor **Ron Petty** in honor of the 400 Seattle fishers lost at sea during this century; their names are inscribed on a plaque. Dedicated 8 October 1988, the memorial is a bronze and concrete sculpture, with a variety of North Pacific marine life sculpted at the base and a lone bronze fisherman perched at the top.

Seattle Fishermen's Memorial

2 Mike's Chili Parlor ★$ **Mike Semandaris** started out here in 1933 with a sidewalk stand. Now a popular tavern, Mike's was a location for filmmaker **Bud Yorkin's** 1985 movie *Twice in a Lifetime,* starring **Gene Hackman, Ellen Burstyn, Amy Madigan,** and **Ann-Margret.** The place is still owned by the Semandaris family, and the chili—with beans offered on the side for nonpurists—is still good. ♦ American ♦ M-Sa 11AM-midnight. 1447 NW Ballard Way. 782.2808

3 Bardahl Manufacturing Corp. Remember the notorious villains Blacky Carbon, Sticky Valves, and Gummy Rings? No? Well, those three reprobates, along with their partner-in-grime Dirty Sludge, made their television debut in a "Dragnet" parody advertising Bardahl, one of the world's best-selling motor-oil additives. The manufacturing company was founded in 1939 by **Ole Bardahl,** a native of Trondheim, Norway, who arrived in Seattle in 1922. Bardahl came up with the winning mixture (which he initially spelled "Bardol") after many experiments in his bathtub. By 1952 the company was an industry leader in automotive and industrial additives. Today, Bardahl Manufacturing produces more than a hundred oil and fuel additives, which are sold in 80 countries. The company's hydroplane, *Miss Bardahl,* has won five gold cups and six national championships, and has set numerous world records. The gigantic sign—ADD BARDAHL OIL—clearly visible from the Ballard Bridge, announces the company's location (and stature). ♦ 1400 NW 52nd St. 783.4851

4 Le Gourmand ★★★$$$ How surprising to find one of the city's finest restaurants in a nondescript building at the eastern edge of Ballard. Le Gourmand is a small, intimate room, with drapes drawn to protect diners from view (and from harsh sunlight). Ingredients are fresh and the menu is limited so owner/chef **Bruce Naftaly's** kitchen can concentrate on—and unfailingly deliver—excellence. Roast duckling with black currant sauce and a sautéed rabbit with chanterelles are a pair of aces in a deck of kings. ♦ French ♦ W-Sa 5:30-9:30PM. 425 NW Market St. Reservations recommended. 784.3463.

5 Pacific Bed & Breakfast A pioneer in her trade, **Irmgard Castleberry** started this lodgings reservation service in 1981. Her list has expanded to include 200 guest homes—mostly B&Bs, but also inns, cottages, condos, and vacation rentals—throughout the Northwest, including Victoria and Vancouver, British Columbia; rooms range from $45 to $200 a night. Pacific B&B is conscientious about matching guests with accommodations (and all establishments have been inspected and approved). You tell them what you

M. BLUM

want—short-term or long-term, waterfront, view, private bath, city or country, whatever—and they make an advance reservation for you. ♦ M-F 9AM-5PM. 701 NW 60th St. 784.0539

6 St. Charles Hotel Built in 1902, this place, with its projecting bays and a hundred feet of building frontage, was an imposing presence in early Ballard. Now painted an appalling lavender, the building is home to **Ballard Mini Storage.** ♦ 4714 Ballard Ave NW

7 Odd Fellows Building Built in 1911 by **Ole Woog,** the building was—and still is—used for dances and parties. Woog, who came to Ballard from Norway in 1894, also built 30 houses in the area. ♦ 1706 NW Market St

8 The Old Pequliar Ale House The only thing peculiar about this place is the spelling of its moniker. Before it went *veddy veddy* British, it was known as the **Valhalla Tavern**—a tad more in keeping with Ballard's Scandinavian heritage. There is a good selection of Northwest brews on tap. ♦ Daily 11AM-2AM. 1722 NW Market St. 782.8886

9 Carnegie Library Raised in 1904 with a $15,000 grant from the generous **Andrew Carnegie Foundation,** this was the first Carnegie Library built in King County. (A total of 10 were erected in the Seattle area.) The structure was designed by local architect **Henderson Ryan,** and it served bookish Ballardites for nearly 60 years, until it was replaced by a new and much less interesting facility in 1963. It is Seattle's oldest library building, and, like so many local treasures, it teeters on the endangered-species list, having narrowly escaped demolition more than once. Today, it hosts a mall filled with antique vendors, a fringe art gallery, and, of all things, a law firm. ♦ 2026 NW Market St

10 Old Ballard Firehouse Designed by the successful Seattle partnership of **Charles Bebb** and **Leonard L. Mendel,** Firehouse No. 18 was built in 1908. It served Ballard for 62 years before being replaced in the early 1970s by a new station just a few blocks away. Now a hot spot on the Ballard nightclub scene, the monumental Firehouse is a big space, with lots of room for dancing to the blues, country, reggae, and rock bands that play here nightly. ♦ Cover. M-F 11:30AM-midnight; Sa-Su 5:30PM-midnight. 5429 Russell Ave NW. 784.3516

11 Andre's Pizza ★★$$ The eponymous Andre is **Andre Goldberg,** a professional baker trained in his native France, who's been turning out superb pizza for years in an unassuming brick building just big enough for himself, his equipment, and a pickup counter; the food is takeout only. The pizza dough could very well be the best in town, and the toppings—you name the combos—include pesto, sun-dried tomatoes, and sausage

made on the premises. ♦ Pizza/Takeout ♦ Tu-Sa 5-9PM. 5402 20th Ave NW. 783.0479

12 Cors and Wegener Building Until Ballard's city hall building went up on Ballard Avenue in 1899, the Cors and Wegener, built in 1893, was the grandest edifice in town. The owners operated an elegant wine room on the ground floor in the 1890s and early 1900s, and the *Ballard News* occupied the second floor for years. One of the first of the old buildings to be renovated, it now houses apartments on the top floor and offices along the street level. ♦ 5000-5004 20th Ave NW

13 Owl Cafe Opened in 1898, this may be the oldest continuously operating tavern in Seattle. Blues is the specialty of the house, and you can hear it live six nights a week. ♦ Cover. M-Sa 11:30AM-2AM. 5140 Ballard Ave NW. 784.3640

14 Ballard Avenue Named a **Historic Landmark District** by the City of Seattle in 1976, this seven-block stretch—slanting southeast off Market Street toward Salmon Bay—represents the heart, if not also the soul, of Ballard. It contains many of the community's oldest buildings (and newest businesses). The majority went up between 1890 and 1930: brick, stone, and stucco constructions of no more than two or three stories in height. Thanks to the 1930s shift of commercial development north to Market Street, these buildings were still sitting here, just waiting to be revitalized, in the 1970s. Pick up a Historic Ballard Avenue Walking Tour brochure, available from most avenue merchants. The **Ballard Historical Society** also conducts guided excursions, sometimes with docents in 1890s attire (call 784.3086 for schedules and reservations; donation requested). ♦ Between 17th Ave NW and 24th Ave NW

15 New Melody Tavern This high-spirited folk venue schedules live music every night, ranging from Appalachian clogging to bluegrass and Cajun. An hour of dance instruction sometimes precedes the performance. ♦ Cover. Daily 5PM-2AM. 5213 Ballard Ave NW. 782.3480

16 The Junction Block Built in the late 1890s, this was once a three-story structure (now two), complete with elaborate turret, and one of the largest brick buildings on Ballard Avenue. It was a gathering place for locals, who held meetings and dances here. Attorney **H.E. Peck,** the last mayor Ballard elected as an independent town, had offices in the Junction. Today, the century-old building is home to *Northwest Yachting* magazine. ♦ 5202-5210 Ballard Ave NW

17 Salmon Bay Cafe ★$ Hearty breakfasts draw a devoted clientele every morning and a lined-up-out-the-door crowd on weekends. Among the many egg dishes, the Ballard omelet—bacon, cream cheese, green onion, tomato—and the crab, shrimp, and green-onion omelet topped with hollandaise stand out. You can also get eggs with Polish or Italian sausage or with steak. A side order of the huge french fries is a satisfying meal in itself. ♦ American ♦ M-F 6:30AM-2:45PM; Sa 7AM-2:45PM; Su 7AM-2PM. 5109 Shilshole Ave NW. 782.5539

18 C.D. Stimson Company Charles D. Stimson, the one-armed scion of a wealthy Michigan lumber family, railroaded out to Seattle just in time to help fight the Great Fire of 1889. The rebuilding of what's now **Pioneer Square** forced the nascent milling center there to move north to Lake Union and Ballard. With it went Stimson, who founded the huge **Stimson Mill Company** in Ballard, the anchor around which other mills would gather. C.D. Stimson himself became a wealthy man, building an elaborately landscaped home in the Highlands, an exclusive subdivision north of Seattle. This surprisingly modest single-story brick building, meanwhile, was designed in 1913 in a modern English style by noted Spokane architect **Kirtland K. Cutter** (who also created the **Rainier Club** in downtown). It still houses the Stimson offices, although that company is no longer in the lumber business. The one-two punch of declining markets and escalating tariffs sent Ballard's shingle-making industry into a tailspin in the early 20th century and eventually forced the Stimson mill to close. The Stimson operation now leases commercial real estate in the Seattle metropolitan area and operates a pleasure-boat marina on Salmon Bay. ♦ 2116 NW Vernon Pl

19 Cafe Illiterati ★$ Bobby Beeman opened this refreshingly idiosyncratic restaurant in 1991. His menu includes such specialties as hearty beef, chicken, and veggie dinner pies; stuffed tomatoes (ricotta and spinach sauté inside a baked Roma tomato); grilled pork sandwiches with provolone cheese, red onions, and roasted peppers; bread pudding French toast; and cappuccino eggs—three eggs steamed using the steam wand on an espresso machine, with fresh herbs and cheese. The deck out back, cats and all, is a most salutary place for weekend brunch. ♦ American ♦ M-F 10AM-9PM; Sa 9AM-9PM; Su 9AM-3PM. 5327 Ballard Ave NW. 782.0191

20 Jay White Law Offices This wood-frame structure is actually a combination of two pre-1890 houses, looking much like those that lined Ballard Avenue around 1900. In 1976 the **Historic Seattle Society** rescued the buildings from development in the International District and moved them over here to Ballard Avenue. A bordello reportedly occupied the houses at their original location. ♦ 5341 Ballard Ave NW

21 Guitar Emporium Owner **Robb Eagle's** merchandise ranges from fine inexpensive imported instruments to handmade acoustic masterpieces. He'll also recommend instructors—and offer encouragement—to would-be Segovias. ♦ M-Sa 11AM-7PM. 5349 Ballard Ave NW. 783.7607

22 Sunset Building This three-story brick-veneered construction, with arched windows and decorative cornice work, was built in 1901. In the 1940s a local public market occupied the street level. The residential **Sunset Hotel** still takes up the upper floors. ♦ 5400-5404 22nd Ave NW

Within the Sunset Building:

Jones Brothers Meats You're talking serious meat here. You can get everything from a 35-pound "pork package" (pork chops, ham, bacon, sausage, spareribs) to a side of beef—anywhere from 250 to 400 pounds. ♦ M-F 9AM-6PM; Sa 9AM-5PM. 5404 22nd Ave NW. 783.1258

23 Portland Building Erected in 1901, this two-story brick pile was home to various well-established businesses—Cascade Drug and J.C. Penney among them—before Ballard's commercial district moved to Market Street. Taverns anchored the corner storefront for 40 years until the Portland's renovation in 1985. Now, a seafood trading company, picture frame shop, and hair salon occupy the ground floor; studio apartments with ladder lofts can be found upstairs. ♦ 5403 Ballard Ave NW

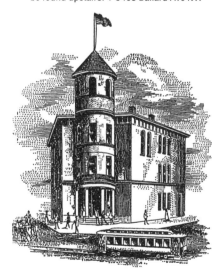

24 Ballard Centennial Bell Tower **Ballard City Hall** (pictured above), built in 1899, stood proudly on this corner for more than 60 years. The three-story structure, one of the first on Ballard Avenue, included the usual administrative warrens and a jail, as well as community meeting rooms and, on the top floor, a dance hall. There was also a bell

Ballard

tower, whose occupant—a 1,000-pound brass noisemaker—was saved when the building was torn down in 1965 after extensive earthquake damage. Thanks to efforts by former state senator **Ted Peterson,** who grew up hearing the bell, it has been returned to its original site and is now housed in a copper-capped cylindrical obelisk designed by architect **Thom Graham.** ♦ 22nd Ave NW and Ballard Ave NW

25 Julia's Park Place ★★$$ With two popular Julia's locations already in the family (one in Wallingford, and the original—recently sold—on Eastlake), **Julia Miller,** a social worker turned restaurateur, and her boatbuilder husband, **David** (they met when he was a customer at the Eastlake establishment, now the **14-Carrot Cafe**), opened Julia's Park Place in 1991. It's a handsome, spacious restaurant that turns out three meals a day of well-prepared natural foods. Salads are very good, especially the signature "Julia's Caesar," and the nutburgers (made of ground nuts) are surprisingly tasty. Penn Cove mussels and pasta, seafood marinara, and peppercorn steak top the dinner selections.

Julia's can be overpriced, but it is still one of Seattle's most popular breakfast stops, especially on weekends, when you may have to cool your heels in line for some time. If and when you finally get in, try the whole-wheat pancakes with blueberries and 100-percent-pure maple syrup. Pick up a peanut butter and mocha cookie at the espresso counter to go with your requisite *caffè latte.* ♦ West Coast Natural ♦ M, Su 7AM-3PM; Tu-Th 7AM-9PM; F-Sa 7AM-10PM. 5410 Ballard Ave NW. 783.2033. Also at: 1714 44th Ave. 633.1175

26 Burk's Cafe ★$$ The joys of gumbo and crayfish (in season) await at **Terry Burkhardt's** lively cafe. Spicy sausages, catfish, and exceptional pecan pie are likewise memorable draws. Try the mild pickled okra, available in a jar at every table. The building, put up in 1891 to hold Ballard's premier tavern, was remodeled in 1968 to revive its wooden-frame origins. A serene fenced courtyard buffers the dining room from the sidewalk. ♦ Creole/Cajun ♦ Tu-Sa 11AM-10PM. 5411 Ballard Ave NW. 782.0091

27 Ballard Computer One of the largest computer retailers on the West Coast, Ballard Computer sells laptops, PCs, notebooks, printers, software, books, cables and switch boxes, memory boards, templates, dust covers, and . . . well, you get the idea—the price list is 36 pages long. Salespeople are knowledgeable and actually seem to welcome questions, even over the phone. The service department is in a separate building. ♦ M-Sa 8AM-9PM; Su 10AM-7PM. 5424 Ballard Ave NW. 781.7000

28 Ballard Smoke Shop $ It's not a smoke shop at all (although it is smoky inside) but a simple, old-fashioned restaurant (with a separate entrance to the bar), where you can still get an eight-ounce New York steak for $10. Built in 1903, this is one of the last frame buildings left from Ballard's early days. Remodeled in the 1920s, the building is now Spanish-style white stucco with a red-tile roof. ♦ American ♦ Daily 6AM-10PM. Bar open daily until 11PM. 5443 Ballard Ave NW. 784.6611

29 Scandie's at Ballard $$ Since the demise of the splendid **Vaersgo** restaurant some years back, this may be the only place left in Ballard that specializes in Scandinavian cuisine. Look for such delicacies as *kokt torsk* (poached cod) and *friskadeller* (Swedish meatballs). ♦ Scandinavian ♦ M-Tu 10AM-5PM; W-F 10AM-9PM; Sa-Su 8AM-9PM. 2301 NW Market St. 783.5080

30 Johnsen's Scandinavian Foods Everything from *lefsa* to *rullepølse* to *kransekake* can be found here. Owners **Reidar** and **Ebba Olsen,** who took over Johnsen's in 1972, are justly proud of their homemade specialties, which include lamb sausage (outstanding—Reidar's been making sausages for 30 years), fish cakes, fish loaf, smoked salmon, and marzipan cake. There are also imported Scandinavian foods, such as dry soups from Norway, Swedish peas, and cloudberries. ♦ M-Th 9AM-5:30PM; F 9AM-6PM; Sa 9AM-5PM. 2248 NW Market St. 783.8288

31 American Eagles Inc. A paradise for serious hobbyists, this store packs in precisely detailed train sets and models of virtually every airplane that's ever caught an updraft. Armchair saber rattlers will revel in the army of miniature Desert Storm troops on sale here. ♦ M-W, Sa 10AM-6PM; Th-F 10AM-8PM. 2220 NW Market St. 782.8448

32 Ballard Building This four-story Second Renaissance Revival edifice—representing the only large-scale use of terra-cotta in Ballard—was erected in the early 1920s by the **Fraternal Order of Eagles.** Ballard's community hospital occupied the second floor from 1928 to 1954, with doctors' offices on the third floor. The second level now contains offices of the *Ballard News-Tribune,* a respectable weekly community paper that began life in 1891 as—of all odd things—the *News-Echo.* ♦ 2208 NW Market St

Within the Ballard Building:

The Backstage A showcase venue for national acts, this basement club features live blues, rock, jazz, and folk. Get here early for a good seat. ♦ Cover. Th-Sa (and some other nights, please call ahead) starting between 8PM and 9:30PM. Box office M-F noon-5PM. 2208 NW Market St. 781.2805; box office 789.1184

Lombardi's Cucina ★$$ Lombardi's occupies the former home of **Lafferty's Drugstore and Soda Fountain** (which moved—sans soda fountain, alas—to 5312 17th Avenue NW) in the southeast corner of the **Ballard Building.** This place serves honest Italian cuisine, with *gamberoni di scampi* and *cannelloni di mare* among the menu's highlights. There's a select list of good Italian wines, moderately priced, and pleasant outdoor seating in warm weather. ♦ Italian ♦ M-Th 11AM-10PM; F 11AM-11PM; Sa 9AM-11PM; Su 9AM-10PM. 2200 NW Market St. 783.0055

33 Yankee Diner ★$$ After a $2.5 million renovation of the former **Canal Restaurant,** this third Yankee Diner in the Seattle area opened in 1992 on the Salmon Bay waterfront. Emphasizing "home-style" cooking, the dinner menu features meat loaf, breaded veal cutlets, chicken-fried steak, the eponymous Yankee pot roast, and roast tom turkey. Fresh seafood and daily breakfast specials are available, too. ♦ American ♦ M-Th 7AM-10PM; F-Sa 7AM-11PM; Su 8AM-9PM. 5300 24th Ave NW. 783.1964. Also at: 1645 140th Ave NE, Bellevue. 643.1558; 4010 196th Ave SW, Lynnwood. 775.5485

34 Lockspot Cafe & Tavern $ You can't miss this place, sitting at the eastern edge of the **Chittenden Locks,** its sign boasting the World's Best Fish and Chips. The claim is open to debate, but the Lockspot does have a 60-year history in this location, having opened in the early 1930s to take advantage of traffic at the locks and along Seaview Avenue. There's a convenient takeout window for fish-and-chips aficionados on the fly. ♦ Seafood/Takeout ♦ Daily 5AM-2AM (even Christmas Day). 3005 NW 54th St. 789.4865

More than $10 million of locally grown marijuana was confiscated in King County in 1992.

35 Hiram M. Chittenden Locks Completed in 1917, after decades of indecisiveness, legal delays, and government red tape, the eight-mile-long **Lake Washington Ship Canal**—winding through Seattle's Ballard, Fremont, Wallingford, University, and Montlake districts—is a protected route connecting the saltwaters of Puget Sound and Shilshole Bay with the higher-elevation freshwaters of Salmon Bay, Lake Union, and Lake Washington. Attended by much fanfare, the Ballard locks were officially opened two months after completion of the canal, on 4 July, when the *Roosevelt,* flagship of **Admiral Robert Edwin Peary's** North Pole expedition, led a procession of ships through the canal. In 1956 the locks were named for Major Hiram M. Chittenden, who, as Seattle's district engineer of the Army Corps of Engineers from 1906 to 1908, had chosen and designed the site for this project. (Lock buildings, however, were created by renowned Seattle architect **Carl Gould.**)

In an average year, 100,000 crafts, both commercial and pleasure, and two million tons of cargo and logs now pass through the locks. People line up on weekend afternoons to watch the regatta rise and fall, rise and fall. The shorter of the two locks—150 feet long and 28 feet wide, with a wall 42 feet high—is used for small pleasure boats; larger vessels are "locked" through the bigger portal: 825 feet by 80 feet, with a 55-foot-high wall. Depending on tides and lake levels, the lift varies from six feet to 26 feet. Free guided tours leave from the Visitors Center daily at 1PM and 3:30PM. ♦ Daily 7AM-9PM. Visitors Center daily 10AM-7PM. 3015 NW 54th St. 783.7059

At the Hiram M. Chittenden Locks:

Fish Ladder In 1976 this $2.3 million 21-level fish ladder—connected by walkways to the locks—was opened on the south shore of the canal adjacent to **Commodore Park.** More than half a million salmon, steelhead, and trout scale the ladder annually, bound for spawning areas in the Cascade range. You can watch (and even cheer on) their progress from an interior viewing port. In the mid-1980s sea lions, recognizing a feast when they smelled one, caused quite a stir with their extended stay near the fish ladder. Officials were determined to send them packing, and locals were equally determined that the creatures—known collectively as Herschel—not be harmed. After defeating a number of human (and humane) efforts to discourage them, Herschel was sent to California; undaunted, some of the sea lions turned right around and swam back home to Seattle.

Carl S. English Jr. Ornamental Gardens These lovely seven acres of lawn, trees, shrubs, and flowers—one thousand plant species in all, including palm trees—were developed from a handful of plantings in 1916. A fine spot for picnicking, the gardens are named for the man who, as head of the Corps of Engineers' gardening staff, spent 34 years cultivating them.

36 Totem House $ This place opened in 1937 as an Indian artifact shop; the building is a replica of an Indian *haiat* house (resting place). The original owner sold the structure during World War II, and it became a fish-and-chips restaurant. Fish-and-chips is still a specialty here, as is the homemade clam chowder. ♦ Seafood ♦ Daily 11AM-9PM. 3058 NW 54th St. 784.2300

37 Nordic Heritage Museum Founded in 1979 in the former **Webster Elementary School** (built in 1907), this is the only museum in the United States that covers all five Scandinavian countries: Denmark, Finland, Iceland, Norway, and Sweden. Its emphasis is on the Nordic people who settled in the Pacific Northwest. Permanent exhibits include *Promise of the Northwest,* which describes life in early Washington, and *Ballard Story,* a richly detailed history of the community. The museum also offers Scandinavian language classes, lectures, and films, and sponsors ethnic festivals. Beware of the house grizzly. ♦ Admission; discount for children. Tu-Sa 10AM-4PM; Su noon-4PM. 3014 NW 67th St. 789.5707

38 Hiram's At The Locks ★★$$ Right next door to the Hiram M. Chittenden Locks, this restaurant overlooking the ship canal gives you a front-row seat for watching the passing boat parade. Hiram's uses grain-fed Midwestern beef for its top-sirloin and filet-mignon steaks. Seafood specialties include mesquite-grilled king salmon, Dungeness crab-shrimp-scallop cakes with a delicious roasted-red-pepper sauce, and the zesty pesto salmon sandwich. A lavish Sunday brunch, popular with locals, includes fresh fruit of many kinds, grilled or chilled salmon, made-to-order pasta dishes and omelets, and a weight-watcher's nightmare table of desserts. In warm weather the patio is a favorite spot for after-work drinks. The corrugated metal building was designed in 1977 by **Barnett Schorr & Co.**, which also refurbished the Legislative Building in Olympia. ♦ Seafood ♦ M-Th 11AM-10PM;

F-Sa 11:30AM-10:30PM; Su 9AM-9:30PM. 5300 34th Ave NW. Reservations recommended. 784.1733

39 Salmon Bay Bridge Built in 1914 by the **Great Northern Railroad** (now **Burlington Northern**) to avoid congestion along the Ballard waterfront and to handle the boat traffic from the soon-to-open **Government Locks,** this imposing bascule bridge over the ship canal can be raised quickly to allow passage for big ships (and high-masted sailboats). Normally suspended, the bridge is lowered only for approaching trains. ♦ Just west of the Hiram M. Chittenden Locks and Commodore Park

40 Ray's Boathouse ★★★$$ Begun in 1946 as a coffee shop at a charter-fishing boat dock, Ray's has passed through several incarnations on its way to becoming one of Seattle's best—some say *the* best—seafood restaurants. Destroyed by fire in 1987, Ray's reopened a year later without missing a beat (or losing a customer). The restaurant buys fresh regional foods from local fishers and growers. Thanks to executive chef **Wayne Ludvigsen,** Ray's steamed clams and pasta with smoked salmon have both won raves from Northwest food critics. So popular is the main-floor restaurant that you may want to head instead upstairs to the less-pricey, blond-wood-and-glass cafe level. Both floors look out on the water, the Olympic Mountains, and tremendous sunsets. ♦ Seafood ♦ Daily 11:30AM-midnight. 6049 Seaview Ave NW. Reservations recommended. 789.3770

41 Anthony's Homeport ★★$$ With its waterfront location and plentiful outdoor seating, Anthony's is a great place for views of Puget Sound and the Olympic Mountains, especially radiant at sunset. Fresh seafood is the order of the day, with cioppino a particular palate-pleaser. ♦ Seafood ♦ M-Th, Su 11AM-10PM; F-Sa 11AM-11PM. 6135 Seaview Ave NW. Reservations recommended. 783.0780. Also at: Des Moines Marina, Des Moines. 824.1947; Edmonds Marina, Edmonds. 771.4400; Homeport Marina, Kirkland. 822.0225

42 Shilshole Bay Marina In 1950 the waterfront at Shilshole was not a pretty sight, what with its derelict ferry dock, scattered boathouses, vacant, untended land, a shipyard in decline, and what one writer derisively described as an "expanse of beach with a perimeter road that kept slipping off into the water." Today, after a 30-year effort to build a breakwater (completed in the early 1980s), the marina is the preferred moorage of Seattle's sailboat fleet; the waiting list to win berth space there is a mile long. The boat ramp is a terrific place to waste an afternoon watching boat owners curse their craft onto or off of trailers. ♦ 7001 Seaview Ave NW. 728.3385

Within the Shilshole Bay Marina:

Charlie's Bar & Grill $ Come early for a quiet waterfront breakfast, or enjoy a late-afternoon/early-evening drink while gazing at the sailboats and the sunset. ♦ American ♦ M-Th, Su 7AM-10PM; F-Sa 7AM-11PM. 783.8338

Sharky's Beach Bar Dancing is the attraction here, with rock 'n' roll bands mounting the stage six days a week. ♦ Cover Th-Sa. Daily 3PM-2AM; live music M-Sa starting at 9:30PM. 784.5850

Wind Works Take a basic sailing course or (if you've passed the official qualifying course) rent a sailboat from this enterprise, one of Seattle's leading big-boat sailing schools. The instructors, all U.S. Coast Guard-licensed captains, teach on 28-foot to 54-foot craft. ♦ Daily 9AM-5PM. 784.9386

43 Golden Gardens That expanse of beach north from the marina—where Ballard families used to camp for weeks at a time during the summer—is now part of the immensely popular Golden Gardens park. **Harry Whitney Treat,** a New York invest-ments mogul and real-estate mover, established this park soon after he moved to Seattle in 1904. To enhance its popularity, Treat even built a special trolley line (the fare: three cents) from downtown Ballard, which was later incorporated into the Seattle transit system. Much of this 95-acre reserve is covered in woods and scratched with trails, but it is always the stretch of sand that receives the most attention. It's perfect for beachcombing, walking, or just looking out to Puget Sound and breathing in what is arguably this city's freshest air. Windsurfers test their mettle nearby, as the Sound is considered warmer than Lake Washington during the wintertime. Be warned, however, that hardly anyone else would call this water warm; it's only for the hearty.

Before the **Seattle Aquarium** was con-structed on the downtown waterfront in 1977, there was talk of building it at Golden Gardens. But the idea aroused such public opposition that it was quickly dropped. The enamel and welded-steel sculpture at the park's south end is called *Atala Kivlicktwok Okitun Dukik (The Golden Money Moon),* by **Lawrence Beck.** ♦ North of Seaview Ave NW and NW 80th St to NW 95th St

44 Sunset Hill Park From here, high above Golden Gardens, the unobstructed view is, in a word, spectacular. ♦ NW 75th St and 34th Ave NW

Restaurants/Clubs: Red   Hotels: Blue
Shops/ Outdoors: Green   **Sights/Culture: Black**

Norman B. Rice
Mayor of Seattle

Pike Place Market is eclectic, colorful, spicy, and diverse—a wonderful, exciting place for visitors and residents. The market has a rich history in Seattle; it is a place where farmers, fishers, and artisans come to sell their goods and services. The sights, smells, and sounds here are incomparable.

If you're a jazz enthusiast, **Dimitriou's Jazz Alley** in Belltown is a must for your itinerary—elegant dining followed by the sounds of local, national, or inter-national jazz artists.

Hiram M. Chittenden Locks, located in the Ballard community of Seattle and operated by the U.S. Corps of Engineers, is a favorite place to visit any time of the year. This impressive engineering structure started construction in 1912; the small locks opened in June 1916, and the large locks in July 1917. Whether having a picnic, browsing in the beautiful flower gardens, watching the salmon "climb the fish ladders" as they migrate back to their spawning grounds (the best time for this is April to May or October to November), seeing the fishing boats return from Alaska, or just oohing and aahing over the splendid boats and yachts for the opening of yachting season each May, this is an educational, fun place. It's where people meet, and where freshwater meets saltwater.

Bob Whitt
Insurance Sales, The Whitt Agency

Watching the sun set from **Golden Gardens** park. There's nothing like the Seattle Waterfront for great sunsets.

The deck at **Ray's Boathouse** is probably the best place to enjoy Seattle seafood while watching the action on the Waterfront.

Sailing on **Elliott Bay**—getting out on **Puget Sound** is by far one of the best activities the city of Seattle has to offer.

If you have enough time, the **San Juan Islands** offer the best getaway either by private boat, float plane, or state ferry. Destinations such as **Roche Harbor, Friday Harbor,** and **Sucia Island** share a diverse landscape and represent the best of what the Northwest has to offer.

Hiking on **Mount Rainier.** No visit to Seattle would be complete without a side trip to this incredible mountain.

"Seattle floats along on Mr. Toad's Wild Ride, stuck in the quicksand of consensus, unfocused, unclear about much except that it would be, well, nice to keep things the way they are."

Seattle Times

Fremont/Wallingford

Fremont and Wallingford today seem about as citified as neighborhoods can get without actually inviting skyscrapers into their midst, yet this area to the north and west of **Lake Union** was once considered suburban. Both neighborhoods runneth over with specialty shops and restaurants. Both steam with rush-hour traffic piloted by teeth-gritting drivers. While there are still many older single-family homes about, these two areas have been taken over in large part by apartments and duplexes servicing downtown professionals (mostly white and single), who can usually reach their offices from these parts in 20 minutes or less.

Fremont grew up a mill town, platted first as the **Denny-Hoyt Addition** in 1888. When its annexation to Seattle was granted in 1891, two of its three founders agreed to rename the neighborhood Fremont, after their Nebraska hometown (which, in turn, had been named in honor of western explorer and one-time presidential candidate **John C. Frémont**). The third founder accepted the right, instead, of naming **Aurora Avenue** after his Illinois birthplace; had he known what a haven of kitsch that roadway was to become, he might have insisted on some other namesake.

Wallingford was stitched together from the previous communities of **Latona** and **Edgewater**. It took its present moniker from a real-estate promoter who'd moved here from Maine and annexed itself to Seattle in the same year as Fremont. The area once supported dairies, a furrier, and a candy store that made Easter eggs to order. A train used to run along what's now the popular **Burke-Gilman Trail**, hustling Sunday pleasure-seekers all the way east to **Snoqualmie Falls**. Many of the homes built here were bungalows, a gable-and-shingle design rooted in the 1890s, when wealthy Californians applied the style to their vacation houses. (Bungalows are still this neighborhood's quintessential digs, but those that cost $1,000 during Franklin D. Roosevelt's presidency are now considered a bargain at $150,000.) Don't get the impression, though, that Wallingford was any kind of ritzy 'burb. It was instead a working-class district huddled around the **Seattle Gas Company** plant, which opened on Lake Union in 1907 and proceeded to shower the area with sparks and soot from the burning of coal.

Fremont's sawmill was permanently closed in 1932; Wallingford's gasworks shut down in 1956. During the 1960s and early 1970s, as the whole city went through some trying economic times, these **North End** districts were allowed to become somewhat shabby places that no one really dreamed of moving to. All that changed in the '80s, however, when Seattle began burgeoning and new interest was focused on the unintentionally well preserved character found in this part of town.

Both Wallingford and Fremont come off as confident and cool, almost folksy. But they have iconoclastic and defiant sides, as well. Fremont declared itself one of the city's earliest **Nuclear-Free Zones**. At various times in the past, Wallingforders have railed against the rattle-and-roll of streetcars along North 45th Street and demanded an end to seaplane noise from the nearby lake. They've raised a stink over garbage dumping and prohibited McDonald's from raising a set of golden arches at its local franchise. The annual **Seafair** children's parade passes through here in July, but so do protest marches of all stripes. In a tizzy over parking congestion caused by Wallingford's recent popularity, residents have won restrictions that on a Friday or Saturday night may make it near impossible for you to leave your car within a quarter-mile of your destination. And don't believe for a second that people here won't report violators or call towing companies on their own. This is no longer complacent suburbia, after all.

---

1 318 Tavern $ You may find yourself seduced by the 318's barbecued beef sandwich or beef stew, but your heart will long be faithful to the big, sloppy cheeseburgers and long, slender fries served here. Burgers made the 318 what it is—a narrow, dark, often crowded joint where patrons are known to insult duded-up business folks. Even the hired help can be surly as a wet alley cat. ◆ American ◆ M-Sa 11AM-2PM. 318 W. Nickerson St. 285.9763

The Unidentified Flying Objects (UFOs) Reporting and Information Service estimates that Seattleites report 20 to 100 UFO-type incidents per year.

2 Ponti Seafood Grill ★★$$$ The location— right on the south lip of the Lake Washington Ship Canal, with a direct watch on the tiny blue-and-orange Fremont Bridge—cries out for a restaurant with broad view windows. And that's exactly what **Jim** and **Connie Malevitsis** (owners also of **Adriatica**), along with **Richard** and **Sharon Malia** (ex-**Malia's Northwest**), tried to create in 1990: an upscale establishment where the outlooks would be coupled with fine foods for an altogether pleasing experience. For the most part, they

Ponti SEAFOOD GRILL

Restaurants/Clubs: Red   Hotels: Blue
Shops/ 🌳 Outdoors: Green   Sights/Culture: Black

succeeded in their task. Chef **Alvin Binuya** (previously at **Cafe Sport**) offers wonderfully fresh seafood in his salads, and the dishes are often influenced by Mediterranean or Asian cooking styles. But the kitchen is stingy to the point of ridiculousness when it comes to appetizers; a serving of peppered tuna, for instance, could hardly satisfy a squirrel, much less two mildly hungry humans. The owners apparently think diners are still living in the nouvelle cuisine world of the '80s. The wine list is on the expensive side, and service can be slow when the house is packed. In summer ask for seating on the porch, where the views are partial compensation for Ponti's few deficiencies. ♦ Northwestern/Seafood ♦ M-Th 11:30AM-2:30PM, 5:30-10PM; F-Sa 11:30AM-2:30PM, 5:30-11PM; Su 10AM-2:30PM, 5-10PM. 3014 Third Ave North. Reservations recommended. 284.3000

3 People Waiting for the Interurban Created by **Richard Beyer,** this sculpture portrays a motley clutch of people anticipating the approach of a bus or train or some other public transportation. Installed in 1978, *Interurban* has become a cynosure, a cast-aluminum tableau decorated appreciatively through the seasons by Fremonsters who enjoy its gentle reflection of everyday life. Beyer, who has lived in Seattle since 1957, is also responsible for a number of other art pieces around town, including the wooden *Sasquatch* at Pike Place Market and *The Itinerant,* which portrays a newspaper-draped man sleeping on a bench in Capitol Hill's Broadway district. ♦ Fremont Ave North and N 34th St

3 Frank and Dunya Unless you're looking for home furnishings and accessories—the more outrageous and colorful, the better—you're barking up the wrong tree at this storefront (named in honor of the owners' long-dead dogs). Canines are popular motifs in the statuary, jewelry, and hangings, but so are other members of the wild kingdom. This is the place to come to when you're in dire need of a two-legged drinking cup painted like a cow, or a huge green frog perfect for mounting on your dining-room wall. ♦ Tu-Sa 11AM-6PM; Su 11AM-5PM. 3418 Fremont Ave North. 547.6760

3 The Daily Planet Fremont is gaining a rep as the North End's vintage and retro capital, thanks to joints such as this one, dense with old lamps, fans, hats, clocks, mirrors, globes, and even a motorbike or two. ♦ M-Sa 10:30AM-6PM; Su by appointment only. 3416 Fremont Ave North. 633.0895

Restaurants/Clubs: Red   **Hotels:** Blue
Shops/ 🌲 Outdoors: Green   **Sights/Culture:** Black

4 Red Door Ale House $ One of several recently upscaled groggeries in Fremont, the Red Door is this neighborhood's best-known and most crowded after-work hangout. (Don't even *try* to get in on a Friday night.) The least claustrophobic seating can be found on a small back deck. Inside, try for a bar seat—no easy task. Twenty-two beers are on tap, and the small menu is strongest on steamed mussels, french fries, and burgers. ♦ Daily 11AM-2AM. 3401 Fremont Ave North. 547.7521

4 Spencer's Bistro ★★$ This new restaurant is so eager to please that it ditched one of its premier dishes just because a critic at *Seattle Weekly* said it "needed deep rethinking." Then it made a big deal of the change with notices plastered all over its front windows. Yikes! One would like to think the kitchen has more confidence than that in its food, some of which has been outstanding. Try the lemon-caper salmon, pan roasted with fresh dill, thyme, and basil. And be careful what you say about it, okay? ♦ French/Italian ♦ M, Su 10AM-4:30PM; Tu-Sa 10AM-4:30PM, 5-9PM. 3411 Fremont Ave North. 632.3602

4 Simply Desserts Some of the baked delights you've enjoyed at several of the more upscale movie theaters around town can now be savored with a cup of espresso from Simply Desserts' dinky outlet store. Highly recommended is the white-chocolate strawberry cake. ♦ Bakery/Coffeehouse ♦ M-Th noon-10PM; F-Sa noon-11:30PM; Su noon-6PM. 3421 Fremont Ave North. 633.2671

4 Fremont Sunday Market The idea of an open-air weekend market where crafts, food, and collectibles are sold has proved popular in other areas, including the Oregon towns of Portland and Ashland. But so far, Fremont's version hasn't been as interesting or successful. Thanks to some good word of mouth, however, it is slowly expanding. A weekday parking lot behind the Red Door Ale House fills up on Sundays with vendors of jewelry, pottery lamp stands, produce, and hot dogs. In classically lowbrow Fremont fashion, there are also people here selling reusable castoffs—old radios and books, used videotapes, clothes that haven't yet been worn out. Musicians provide entertainment, as do the shoppers themselves, a cross section of hippie holdouts and slumming stockbrokers. ♦ Su 10AM-5PM May-Christmas. 670 N 34th St. 283.2077

5 Fremont Antique Mall The entrance is at street level, but the goods—collectible toys and appliances, along with some larger antique furniture—are in the basement of the Fremont mall, built in 1901. Take a nostalgic browse. ♦ Daily 10AM-6PM. 3419 Fremont Pl. 548.9140

5 Manna Barbecue ★$ There's only one way to serve barbecue: smoked, juicy, and with no frills whatsoever. A restaurant's ambience isn't worth a heap of cow dung in the world of BBQ; in fact, anybody who's ever chowed down on authentic, slow-cooked, heartbreaking-to-the-point-of-tears West Texas barbecue knows that the best of the lot often comes from the worst-looking places. You may be a little suspicious at first of the fairly well kept Manna Barbecue, even though it does serve its grits on déclassé disposable dishware. But after you've had a bite to eat, you'll no doubt declare yourself converted.

Manna's pork (shoulder or ribs), beef ribs, turkey breast, and chicken come mesquite-roasted and tender enough to eat with a spoon. Unlike some traditional joints, where helpings are so huge you might as well ask for doggie bags right up front, Manna meats can be had in various à la carte quantities and two sizes of lunch sandwiches. Sauces come in mild or hot, neither of which is quite spicy enough to burn chrome from a bumper. Dinners are served with baked beans, corn bread, and grilled potatoes that some tasters say are as much "manna" as the meats sold at this comfortable joint. ♦ Barbecue/Takeout ♦ M-Sa 10:30AM-9PM. 3423 Fremont Ave North. 632.7060

5 Guess Where There's something classier than normal about this retro resource. Maybe it's the winged cherubs that decorate the front windows. Perhaps it's the statuary that looks as if it's waiting to decorate some dear departed's grave. Or could it be the wide array of vintage men's shoes and suits that your father always told you would come back in style and did? ♦ M, W noon-5:30PM; Tu, Th-Su noon-6PM. 615 N 35th St. 547.3793

5 Yoohoo $ Tables are covered in comic-book collages, the lights appear to be crafted from bulbs and old pizza trays, drinks are squeezed from fresh fruit, and calzones or waffles prove satisfying and

filling. Wear either all-black clothing or cat's-eye sunglasses to dine here. ♦ Vegetarian ♦ M-F 7:30AM-4:30PM; Sa 7AM-6PM; Su 9AM-6PM. 607 N 35th St. 633.3760

6 Still Life in Fremont ★$ This unpretentious coffeehouse may once have epitomized the hippieish, won't-buy-into-your-neuroses attitude of Fremont. But hey, the '60s are over. Nobody oohs or aahs these days over intellectual wanna-bes discussing Nietzsche at lunch. The Still Life, consequently, is rapidly earning anachronism status. It continues to serve some of the better cafe grub in town: pasta specials are usually terrific, soups are chunky, and sandwiches are thick and savory. The sidewalk seating is pleasant—much better than enduring the interior stagnation in summer. And it's a quiet locale for coffee drinking. Just leave your tie-dye at home. Jazz or folk music is sometimes performed on Thursday nights from 8PM to 10PM. ♦ Vegetarian ♦ M-Th, Su 7:30AM-9PM; F-Sa 7:30AM-11PM. 709 N 35th Ave. 547.9850

7 Fritzi Ritz This is a Marlene Dietrich fantasy of a vintage store, with feathered boas and sequined dresses on display. Well-preserved wing-tip shoes and fedoras wait for Fred Astaire to waltz through the door. ♦ M-F 11:30AM-5:30PM; Sa noon-5:30PM; Su noon-5PM. 3425 Fremont Pl North. 633.0929

7 Triangle Tavern ★★$ Some of the ancient pensioners who knew this place as the **Classic** (and still weave in here on occasion) may have trouble getting used to its recent refashioning. Odd-shaped tiles crawl up the support pillars; old phones dangle from the walls; the dining-room ceiling looks earthquake-distressed—deliberately. The Triangle is a hip spin on the traditional tav, "Cheers" by way of MTV. Lots of finger foods are featured on the typo-pocked menu, leaping from mediocre burgers to delightful two-person pizzas with soft crusts and a spinach lasagna layered with roasted-red-pepper pasta. The seafood fettuccine includes salmon, Penn Cove mussels, prawns, calamari, and lots of garlic. *Bruschettas du jour* (spicy Italian bread baked with different toppings) should be ordered straightaway, as they're invariably satisfying. Salads, including the Caesar, make a lesser showing. The broad pick of beers specializes in West Coast craft varieties. ♦ American ♦ Daily 11:30AM-2AM. 3507 Fremont Pl North. 632.0880

8 Deluxe Junk A stock of mid-20th century clothing (which rotates as it is seasonally appropriate), furniture, housewares, and stacks of kitschy doodads are all on display in a onetime funeral parlor. ♦ Daily 11:30AM-5:30PM. 3518 Fremont Pl North. 634.2733

9 The Redhook Ale Brewery Seattle's first microbrewery opened in Ballard in 1982. That was just at the beginning of the West Coast's craft beer craze, which benefited Redhook Brewery so greatly it was forced to move to a larger location after just a few years. The new site was actually a very old site in its own right: Fremont's 1905 **Seattle Electric Company** streetcar barn. Trolleys used to roll out of this building on their routes to Green Lake, Phinney Ridge, Wallingford, Ballard, and Meridian. But when the city converted from tracks to trackless trolleys in 1940, the Fremont barn went first to the U.S. Army as a wartime warehouse and later to a garbage company. Redhook owners **Paul Shipman** and **Gordon Bowker** ultimately bought the barn and commissioned architect **Skip Satterwhite** to turn it into their new brewery. Brewing began here in 1988. ♦ Free one-hour tours of the facility M-F 3PM; Sa-Su 1:30PM, 2:30PM, 3:30PM, 4:30PM. 3400 Phinney Ave North. 548.8000

Within the Redhook Ale Brewery:

Trolleyman Pub $ This taproom is a bit harshly decorated for a tavern—all white walls and neatly arranged tables. But a good-sized fireplace and a piano make things cozy in winter. As expected, all Redhook brews are on tap here, from the ESB to the Blackhook and the seasonal Winterhook Christmas Ale. The snack menu is small, highlighted by the black-bean burritos served with two cheeses, sour cream, and salsa. ♦ M-Th 8:30AM-11PM; F 8:30AM-midnight; Sa noon-midnight; Su noon-7PM. 548.8000

10 Fremont Public Library This was the last of 10 Carnegie-financed libraries raised in the Seattle area during the early 20th century. Money for construction—$35,000—had been promised from the **Carnegie Corporation** in 1917, but it wasn't until after World War I that building got under way on the site, and not until 1921 that it opened. **Daniel R. Huntington,** for many years Seattle's city architect, designed this excellent neighborhood library in an echo of California Mission style. ♦ M, Tu-W 2-9PM; Th 2-6PM; Sa 10AM-6PM. 731 N 35th St. 684.4084

11 Aurora Bridge Nobody uses its proper name—**George Washington Memorial Bridge**—and most don't even know it. (The bridge's 1932 dedication to the first U.S. President can only be found on a plaque at its south end, not on regular city maps.) And sometimes this span is referred to as **Suicide Bridge** because of the number of people (an average of three per year) who leap from its 135-foot height into **Lake Union** below. The sidewalk across is narrow; walk at your own risk and never on rainy days, when taking a bath in your clothes would leave you less soaked than the speeding traffic does. ♦ Aurora Ave, over Lake Union

12 Pacific Inn This pocket-edition pub benefits from its disproportionately large windows and assertively spiced fish-and-chips. ♦ M-F 11AM-2AM; Sa-Su noon-2AM. 3501 Stone Way North. 547.2967

13 Archie McPhee's Shop here for Halloween creepy-crawlies or things to surprise your spouse with in the shower—McPhee's has hundreds of spiders, fish, rubber slugs, and wacko party favors. The owner, **Mark Pahlow,** is a natural-history buff and a stickler for anatomical correctness in his plastic wildlife. Apparently he's had some trouble convincing his manufacturers to produce cockroaches that look exactly like they do in real life—gross! An adjacent espresso stop, **Archie McPhee's Tacky Tiki Hut,** provides warm refreshments. ♦ M-F 10AM-6PM; Sa 10AM-5PM; Su 11AM-5PM. 3510 Stone Way North. 547.2467

14 Stone Way Cafe ★$ All doctors and anyone on a serious diet regimen should please skip to the next review. This restaurant is intended only for people who don't dissect menus looking for "heart smart" entrées. Such foodophobics might stand agape before the Stone Way's outstanding plates of biscuits and gravy or corned-beef hash. And what about the weighty, onion-slathered hamburgers or the omelets stuffed shamelessly with meats and cheeses?

Owner **Charlene Iverson** usually has a few healthy soups cooking (don't miss the vegetable or navy bean varieties), and there are always muffins on hand, but the cooks here mostly serve truck-stop cuisine. Lines at the door are de rigueur on weekends. ♦ American ♦ M-F 6AM-2PM; Sa-Su 8AM-2PM. 3620 Stone Way North. 547.9958

15 Fremont Troll It's a Brothers Grimm nightmare brought forth in sculpture: a crook-nosed, long-haired, malevolent-looking troll that hides beneath the north end of the **Aurora Bridge.** Constructed in 1990 of ferroconcrete, with a real Volkswagen Bug squeezed in the creature's left hand, the 18-foot-high installation was a whimsical community project from the **Fremont Arts**

Council that was built with money from the **Seattle Neighborhood Matching Funds Program.** Adults and children seem equally ready to climb all over the thing. ♦ Heading east on N 34th St, turn left up the hill under the Aurora Bridge

16 B.F. Day Elementary School While other classic Seattle schools have been torn down or closed, B.F. Day Elementary (kindergarten through fifth grade) recently concluded a two-year restoration program that has returned it to the grandeur it enjoyed at its dedication in 1892. This brick structure was designed by **John B. Parkinson.** A draftsman under famed Pioneer Square architect **Elmer Fisher,** Parkinson opened an architectural office in Los Angeles at the turn of the century, where he later employed Fisher. B.F. Day is supposed to be the city's oldest school still in operation, and its history even predates Parkinson's building. Classes were held in private homes for some years before the structure for the school was built.
♦ 3921 Linden Ave North

17 Pizzeria Pagliacci ★$ There are four sit-down Pagliaccis scattered across Seattle, but this newest branch is takeout or delivery only. It's just as well. At home you can savor your meal without having to worry that people see you dribbling tomato sauce down your chin. The dough is fresh and the toppings are plentiful. The Pizza Centioli features an extra-thin crust coated with olive oil, fresh garlic, peppers, and mozzarella and fontina cheeses. The South Philly comes with Italian sausage, mushrooms, and onions. And if somebody asks you whether you'd like to buy the Brooklyn Bridge (pepperoni, Italian sausage, mushrooms, black olives, and green peppers), by all means say yes. Calzones and pasta are also on the menu. ♦ Pizza/Takeout ♦ M-F, Su 5-11PM; Sa 11AM-midnight. 4003 Stone Way North. 632.1058. Also at: 4529 University Way NE. 632.0421; 426 Broadway Ave E. 324.0730; 550 Queen Anne Ave North. 285.1232; SeaTac Mall. 839.8595

18 Buckaroo Tavern $ Most of the motorcycles have disappeared from out front, and more young white-collar businesspeople show up here now than was common just a few years back, but the "Fabulous Buckaroo" has hardly lapsed into benign respectability. Pool balls still slap against one another, voices rise in cursing contraltos, and nimbuses of cigarette and cigar smoke loom over the knife-scarred booths in the back. It is still possible to disappear here, to sink your elbows into the bar and drink beer for hours without the 'tenders asking you word one about your life or your investments or any current political campaigns.

Founded in 1938, the Buckaroo has so far warded off the forces of civil gentrification that prey so merrily on Fremont. The food—burgers, thick potato wedges, steaming bowls of chili mountained with cheddar and onions—hasn't yet become "cuisine." Distinctly nongourmet hot dogs go for 25¢ apiece on Monday nights from 6PM until they run out. Twenty tap beers, many of them microbrews, can be had, too, whether you're wearing leathers or not. ♦ Daily 11AM-2AM. 4201 Fremont Ave North. 634.3161

19 Swingside Cafe ★$ For years Fremonsters have desperately wanted to love this place, but several make-overs of the restaurant frustrated the gatherings of regulars. Only recently has the Swingside seemed to have settled down. The small, divided, and low-ceilinged dining room, fielded with baseball paraphernalia that must justify the cafe's name, doesn't invite parties of four or more; it's best to show up here with one close friend (who isn't adverse to repeating sentences several times to be heard above the din). Come in the morning, when you can linger with a newspaper over delicious *huevos rancheros* or buckwheat pancakes, generous helpings of toast, and black java that hasn't been adulterated by Seattle's espresso militancy. Wide-bodied omelets are whipped together in several worthy variations, but the best usually appear on the specials board; try the spicy Cajun omelet with sausage, chicken, and prawns. Lunch turns to barbecued chicken and sandwiches, with dinners built around pastas. Expect a line at the door but keep in mind that the wait is worthwhile.
♦ Mediterranean ♦ M-Sa 5:30-10PM; Su 9AM-2PM. 4262 Fremont Ave North. 633.4057

20 City Cafe $ Founded by a former manager of **Sorel's** (the popular Wallingford coffee stop), the City Cafe is a small place that's stuck into a lower corner of a new apartment building. Nonetheless, it's handsome and convivial. Expect generously sized coffee drinks, muffins, and sandwiches or soup at lunch. Dawdling is encouraged, with copies of *Vanity Fair* and the local dailies around to consume your wayward hours. ♦ Coffeehouse ♦ M-F 5:30AM-5PM; Sa-Su 8AM-1PM. 4459 Fremont Ave North. 633.2139

Restaurants/Clubs: Red   Hotels: Blue
Shops/ ♥ Outdoors: Green   **Sights/Culture:** Black

21 Blue Star Cafe & Pub ★★$ Owner **Steve Cohn,** for years a member of the board of **Consolidated Restaurants** (Metropolitan Grill, Hiram's At-The-Locks, Elliott's Oyster House & Seafood Restaurant), has caught the restaurateuring bug himself and opened this new tavern-cum-dinner house. He's applying what he has learned of the business. The Blue Star's interior—with rich wood booths and a handsome, mirrored bar—is refined enough to be the spawn of an upscale restaurant chain. From the day it opened in late 1992, this joint already seemed like it had been around awhile. And let's hope it is.

The cuisine falls somewhere between dress-up dining and pig-out tavern. Chef **Greg Tushar's** combination soups are usually delicious, even if they sound egregiously chichi (yam, pear, and cinnamon in one bowl?). The roasted lamb and garlic sandwich, skillet-fried chicken with mashed potatoes, and Caesar salad are all excellent choices; burgers, however, are merely passable. Save room for the peanut butter ice-cream pie drizzled with chocolate sauce and nuts—merely sniffing it increases your belt size. For lighter appetites, there are half-orders of fettuccine Alfredo or the fine black-bean chili, both with salad. Eighteen beers, mostly microbrews, are on tap, but the alehouse atmosphere is disrupted by a blanket no-smoking policy, even at the bar. ♦ American/Continental ♦ M-Th, Su 4-11PM; F-Sa 4PM-12:30AM. Bar open daily 3PM-closing. 4512 Stone Way North. 548.0345

22 Sorel's $ A former flower shop has become one of the neighborhood's friendliest coffee stops. Espresso drinks are rich and poured large, perhaps to match the size of the Danishes and scrumptious apple fritters available by the cash register. Several types of sandwiches can be ordered at lunch, but try the thick chili and the soups instead. In warm weather rack out with the Sunday paper and your coffee on an outside deck. Service is excellent. ♦ Coffeehouse ♦ M-F 6AM-4PM; Sa 7AM-3PM; Su 8AM-3PM. 4615 Stone Way Ave North. 547.7835

23 Olympia Pizza and Spaghetti ★$ Olympia is known for a variety of pizza pies so large that you're asked to order by number, not by name. Nonetheless, remember this name: the House Special (salami, pepperoni, sausage, Canadian bacon, green peppers, olives, cheese, mushrooms, and tomato sauce). This is a great place to take children. The original is on Queen Anne Avenue. ♦ Pizza/Takeout ♦ M-Th, Su 4-11PM; F-Sa 4PM-midnight. 4501 Interlake Ave North. 633.3655. Also at: 1500 Queen Anne Ave North. 285.5550; 516 15th Ave East. 329.4500; 3213 W. McGraw St. 286.9000

24 Musashi's ★$ This place has lots of fans, and, as luck will have it, they'll all be trying to get one of the few tables on the night you visit. Thankfully, Musashi's does a healthy take-out biz. A wide variety of excellent sushi is offered beside just a few other choices (try the teriyaki chicken if you're leery of raw fish). *Bento* box meals are available at lunch, including rice, a crab cake, sashimi, and a teriyaki chicken skewer. Cooks tend to throw extra items in for the restaurant's regulars. ♦ Japanese/Takeout ♦ Tu-Th 11:30AM-2:30PM, 5-9PM; F 11:30AM-2:30PM, 5-10PM; Sa 5-9:30PM. 1400 N 45th St. 633.0212

25 Tien Tsin $ Expect a few inconsistencies, but for the most part, the Mandarin-style dishes turned out here are both of fine quality and generously proportioned. Try the cashew or sweet-and-sour chicken. Lunch bargains are available. ♦ Chinese/Takeout ♦ M, W-Th 11:30AM-2PM, 5-9:45PM; F 11:30AM-2PM, 5-10:45PM; Sa 4-11PM; Su 4-10PM. 1401 N 45th St. 634.0223

26 Islabelle Caribbean Food ★$ Seattle falls way behind the Caribbean isles in terms of tropical pleasures, but **Lorenzo Lorenzo's** bright, modern storefront doesn't acknowledge the local inclemency. Reggae plays inside, while staffers sporting flowered togs cheer up locals wrapped tight against winter thaws. Have one of the filling but not-too-spicy dishes of halibut or chicken served with mounds of rice and black beans. Also recommended is the marinated-pork sandwich. Some folks opt for the Caribbean burger topped with salsa, but that's like visiting Jamaica without ever escaping the resort. Experiment. ♦ Caribbean/Takeout ♦ Tu-Sa 11AM-9PM; Su noon-9PM. 1501 N 45th St. 632.8011

26 Firehouse No. 11 Erected in 1913, this building is surprisingly unimposing, even given its drying tower, which was long ago blocked on the skyline behind taller structures. Architect **Daniel R. Huntington** covered the building with cedar shakes, shutters, and trellises that surrounded the accordion-style doors through which horse-drawn fire wagons once charged. The design was meant to blend in with Wallingford's growing predominance of bungalow homes. At one time both police and firefighters occupied this building, but since 1984 it has been home to a community health clinic. The Wallingford-Wilmot branch of the **Seattle Public Library** shares part of the ground floor, as well. ♦ N 45th St and Densmore Ave North

"People go out of their way to be polite in Seattle. Ask directions and likely as not a perfect stranger will offer to walk you to your destination."
Smart Money magazine

27 Guadalajara ★$ Easily and unjustly overlooked in Wallingford's proliferation of chic restaurants is this unassuming Mexican outpost. Although service in the dining room can be curt, the kitchen turns out fine and filling burritos and enchiladas. The tacos are so-so, but the Guadalajara nachos (chicken or beef), topped with guacamole and sour cream, are excellent. A chunky salsa of veggies marinated in pepper juice is some of the hottest around. And the bartenders usually have a heavy hand on the tequila bottle when mixing margaritas. ◆ Mexican ◆ M-Th, Sa 11AM-10PM; F 11AM-11PM; Su noon-9PM. 1715 N 45th St. 632.7858

27 Julia's in Wallingford ★★$$ Julia's onetime restaurant-of-the-moment status is actually starting to backfire on this upscale business. A number of former regulars have been heard to say "We just don't go to Julia's anymore." The problem could be that Seattle's dining scene offers too many other good choices. When there are complaints about the Wallingford outlet (another, **Julia's Park Place,** can be found in Ballard), they usually have to do with crowds or the rising cost of meals (no longer is Julia's a bargain). There also has been grumbling about the sometimes superior attitude of the waitstaff. Rarely, however, does fault lie with the health-conscious menu, which includes build-your-own omelets (20 possible ingredients), pancakes, and *huevos rancheros;* nutburgers and other sandwiches and soups hold sway at lunch, while Greek salads and pasta draw the dinner crowd. Bring a book or newspaper along to occupy the wait for a table on weekends. ◆ Vegetarian ◆ M-Sa 7AM-9PM; Su 7AM-2PM. 4401 Wallingford Ave North. 633.1175

27 The Store Next Door This Julia's annex (literally located right next door to the restaurant) serves the fresh-baked goods—breads, cinnamon rolls, and other pastries—that people know from the restaurant, only without the wait. It's a great early morning coffee stop but has only three tables for lingerers. ◆ Bakery ◆ M-F 7AM-6PM; Sa 8AM-5PM; Su 8AM-noon. 4405 Wallingford Ave North. 547.3203

27 Alfi News They carry both domestic and international newspapers, and a still-wider array of magazines—particularly bounteous in nature, sports, and home or craft publications. Clerks are sometimes slow to get new issues racked and allow back issues of the *New Yorker* and *New York* magazines to hang around long after their usefulness has waned. ◆ M-Th 8:30AM-10PM; F-Sa 8:30AM-11PM; Su 7:30AM-8PM. 4427 Wallingford Ave North. 632.9390. Also at: 113 Lake St South. 827.6486

28 Wallingford Center As long ago as 40 years, there were plans to condemn or relocate this three-story, neoclassical wooden behemoth to open up valuable commercial property. The neighborhood's population of children was in decline, and business leaders argued that soon there would simply not be enough of them left to justify the operation of what was then **Interlake Public School.** The school had originally been the community's pride and joy, one of Wallingford's first public buildings. It was created by the prolific architect **James Stephen,** who also designed **West Queen Anne Elementary** and **Latona Elementary School.** Sorry to say, the school district finally closed the building in 1981. But before commercial interests could aim a wrecking ball at the abandoned Interlake School, preservationists linked arms with community officials to gentrify the building into a warren for jewelry, clothing, and book stores—hence the stylish Wallingford Center. Outside, on the corner of North 45th Street and Wallingford Avenue North, look for *Wallingford Animal Storm,* a 1984 bronze and aluminum totem created by neighborhood resident **Ronald W. Petty.** A tribute to local wildlife, the Petty installation features raccoons, Canadian geese, cats, pigeons, and even slugs. ◆ 4400 Wallingford Ave North. 547.7246

Within the Wallingford Center:

Capons Rotisseria ★$ You'd better like chicken, because that's just about all that's served here—whole marinated rotisserie chickens, half chickens, chicken sandwiches, chicken potpie, and chicken soup. The fowl is fresh and juicy. Some feathers have been ruffled by limp servings, but for the most part, both the vegetables and salads are satisfying if only second-fiddle accompaniments to the birds. Service is cafeteria style, with an atmosphere that's pleasant and casual. ◆ Chicken/Takeout ◆ M-Sa 7AM-10PM; Su 8AM-10PM. Ground floor. 547.3949. Also at: 605 15th Ave East. 323.4026

Garden Spot Plentiful supplies of potted flowers and hanging plants, along with a wide range of pots, can be found here. In summer the courtyard outside is an excellent place to browse and sniff, but even the interior space seems warmed by an interest in nature. The staff is knowledgeable and helpful. ◆ M-F 9:30AM-8PM; Sa 9:30AM-7PM; Su 9:30AM-5PM. Ground floor. 547.5137

Simpatico ★$ There's a secluded, brick-walled wine bar in the back and out front lots of white-draped tables where flavorful pasta dishes are served. But eschew both those spaces and head instead for the expansive sunken patio when the weather allows. You can order a pizza (versions with chicken and pesto top the list) and a cold microbrew, then sit in the shade provided by umbrellas, listen to the burbling fountain, and try to solve the problems of the world. Moving mountains seems feasible in such a peaceful setting. ♦ Italian ♦ M-Th, Su 5-10PM; F-Sa 5-11PM. Ground floor. 632.1000

Spot Bagel Bakery Grand, doughy, and kosher bagels come in garlic, pumpernickel, pesto, jalapeño, and other flavors. Try any of them spread with herb cream cheese or layered with lox. Because the Spot is so popular, service can be slow. If you grow impatient, remember that Spot bagels are also available across North 45th Street at **Food Giant.** Another Spot can be spotted in the **Newmark Building** downtown. ♦ M-Th 6:30AM-8PM; F 6:30AM-9PM; Sa 7AM-9PM; Su 8AM-8PM. Ground floor. 633.7768. Also at: 1401 Second Ave. 625.1990

Second Story Bookstore Along with broad offerings in new general fiction and children's lit, Second Story has a rental library that makes it possible to read the latest best-sellers or rent recent books on tape without shelling out big bucks for the privilege. Armchairs in the back provide the proper setting for thinking over any purchases. ♦ M-F 10AM-8PM; Sa 10AM-6PM; Su 10AM-5PM. Second floor. 547.4605

Zanadia Among the nicely designed accessories for the kitchen and home, you'll find a wide array of glassware and some intriguing candlesticks. ♦ M-F 10AM-8PM; Sa 10AM-6PM; Su 10AM-5PM. 547.0884

29 Teahouse Kuan Yin $ Running distinctly against the grain in this coffee-lover's town is this quiet teahouse owned by world travelers **Frank Miller** and **Miranda Pirzada.** Miller, a former travel agent with a special interest in Asia, tasted teas all over Hong Kong before selecting the black, green, herbal, and oolongs that decorate his menu. Quiche, focaccia, and other light edibles supplement a cup of tea nicely. In a brilliant synergistic move, the Teahouse has a doorway connecting it to **Wide World Books.** Indulge yourself with any of these aromatic beverages while reading a book purchased next door. Staffers are always ready to educate you about tea qualities, but as to how long your brew should properly steep, there is no science. ♦ Teahouse ♦ M-Th, Su 10AM-10PM; F-Sa 10AM-midnight. 1911 N 45th St. 632.2055

29 Wide World Books Here you'll find shelf upon shelf of guidebooks and travel literature, plus staffers who've probably already been where you want to go and can help you make the most of your visit. The shop also features maps, some luggage, and a passport-photo service. ♦ M-F 10AM-7PM; Sa 10AM-6PM; Su noon-5PM. 1911 N 45th St. 634.3453

30 Ace Hardware Very organized, very well stocked, and very old-fashioned, this is the sort of small store your parents knew as kids. Tradition dies hard here: though the sign out front reads Ace Hardware, you can still write a check to the business' sweetly enduring former moniker, **Tweedy & Popp.** ♦ M-Sa 9AM-6PM; Su 10:30AM-5PM. 1916 N 45th St. 632.2290

Who invented the Happy Face, that lemon-yellow symbol of goodwill that was ubiquitous during the Vietnam War years and continues to make passersby smile . . . or cringe, depending on their kitsch threshold? A San Francisco button-store owner once tried to take the credit. Other wags say the noseless, browless, guileless character with the vapid grin has no single parent but rather a variety of folk sources. Seattle advertising exec David Stern contends, however, that he was actually responsible for making the Happy Face the world's third-most-recognizable symbol (the red octagonal traffic STOP sign is the most recognizable, while the circle with a bar through it that silently screams "don't, don't, don't" takes second place).

The legend goes like this: Stern was looking for an image to boost the profile of a University District savings and loan. Inspired by Dick Van Dyke singing "Put On a Happy Face" in the musical *Bye Bye Birdie,* he had thousands of Happy Face buttons made during the late 1960s. The S&L passed them around to war protesters, hospital patients, businesspeople—anybody who needed a lift. And the fetching smiles caught on. In a big way. "People took handfuls of them," Stern recalls, "and we didn't stop them."

Hundreds of thousands of Happy Faces have been printed since the 1960s—on T-shirts, bumper stickers, coffee mugs, foglight covers (check your button collection; you probably still have a Happy Face in there somewhere), all of which might make Stern smile broadly himself, if only he'd remembered to do one thing way back in the '60s. You see, Stern never thought to trademark the Happy Face.

30 Murphy's Pub Moving from cramped accommodations just up the street to a site that used to be occupied by a Radio Shack store, this Irish pub (shown above) has improved substantially. A careful revamping gave the facade the appropriate old-world charm, and dark furnishings inside lend the place an almost reverential history. The new location is more spacious, so you needn't go two out of three rounds anymore with the crowd just to place an order at the bar. Fifteen tap beers (primarily substantive microbrews and imports) and a trio of alcoholic ciders are on hand, accompanied by a limited menu that makes its biggest splashes with the enormous nacho platter and the cider stew. Dart boards can be found to one side of the bar. Wednesday is open-mike entertainment night, with live Irish music played (usually too loudly) on Fridays and Saturdays. ♦ Cover. Daily 11:30AM-2PM. 1928 N 45th St. 634.2110

31 Starbucks Local resentment ran high when this chain coffee-teria took over the former **Murphy's Pub** location. After all, Wallingforders prefer their shops unique, and Starbucks is as familiar in Seattle as rain. They also resented Starbucks' close commercial proximity to the much-loved **Boulangerie** bakery. But so far, this shop—large, compared with some of its brethren around town—has had no negative effects on the neighborhood. Stay tuned.
♦ Coffeehouse ♦ M-Th 6:30AM-9PM; F 6:30AM-10PM; Sa 7:30AM-10PM; Su 10AM-9PM. 2110 N 45th St. 548.9507

31 Beeliner Diner ★★$ This narrow, attitude-heavy dispensary of rapid service (based on an Eat It and Beat It policy) is brought to you by **Peter Levy** and **Jeremy Hardy,** the same pair who later created Queen Anne's **5-Spot Cafe.** Waitpersons joke with diners, chiding them lightly for not cleaning their plates or for sitting around to yammer while a line forms outside. Sit at the bar rather than pasting yourself into one of the vinyl booths, and you have the extra luxury of being harassed by the cooks, too. Orders yelled into the tiny kitchen sound like static trapped in a wireless radio for 40 years—"One bossy in a bowl!" (beef stew)—and the wine list lampoons America's current recherché supping habits by prominently offering "cheap white wine."

The regular menu sounds pedestrian, but the chicken-fried steak is spicier and made from better cuts of beef than you'll find at a roadhouse, and the hot turkey sandwich is really huge slabs of white meat reclined across homemade bread and doused with a buttery gravy. There are blue-plate specials daily, the best being Wednesday night's meat loaf. For a light meal, try the hot cabbage salad that's marinated in vinegar and sprinkled with blue cheese. Top it off with a slice of hot apple pie à la mode. Almost anything here is worth lying about in your diet diary. ♦ American/Takeout ♦ M-Th, Su 9AM-10PM; F-Sa 9AM-11PM. 2114 N 45th St. 547.6313

32 Boulangerie Repeatedly chosen by Seattleites as their favorite bakery, the Boulangerie specializes in crusty baguettes and other French loaves, plus such memorable sweets as the Tarte Normande, with Granny Smith apple slices arranged inside a nutty pastry. But it may appeal even more as a take-out coffee and pastry stop. Try the *pain au chocolate* (croissants filled with chocolate). ♦ Bakery ♦ Daily 7AM-7PM. 2200 N 45th St. 634.2211

Café **VIZCAYA**

32 Café Vizcaya ★★$$ Forget obsequious service. The laissez-faire demeanor of Vizcaya's waitstaff recalls that found in Spain and in some Latin American countries, where patrons are expected to take a larger hand in ensuring their own dining satisfaction. It actually lends authenticity to this dimly lit Spanish restaurant. So does the separate *tapas* menu. The Spanish make whole dinners of these often heavily spiced finger foods, so order several different small plates to share in a group and toast the experience with sherry. Seattleites tend to use these tasty morsels as appetizers, which is not inappropriate. Favorite *tapas* include the *gambas brava al ajillo,* prawns sautéed in a marinade of onion, garlic, paprika, cayenne, and olive oil; the more basic *crostini,* rounds of toasted bread with a variety of toppings, is accompanied by a cilantro pesto.

As far as entrées go, they're a balance of Spanish and citrus-accented Cuban dishes (the owner, **Barbara Soltero,** was born in

159

Cuba before moving to Vizcaya, Spain); there are also a few pasta holdovers from the former restaurant tenant in this space, **Paparazzi.** A marinated fillet of red snapper, baked over potato slices, comes in a white sauce with peppers, capers, olives, and plenty of onions. The *pollo asado* is a half-chicken marinated in lime juice, garlic, and pepper, then roasted and garnished with a delightful papaya-tomatillo salsa. Try also the roasted pork smothered in onions. Unfortunately, salads here are less inventive, and the bread served before your meal is cold and tends to be dry. But don't let such things dissuade you from what can be a thoroughly novel and romantic experience. ♦ Spanish/Cuban ♦ M-Th, Su 5-10PM; F-Sa 5-11PM. 2202 N 45th St. Reservations recommended. 547.7772

32 Twice Sold Tales Spun off a popular used-books outlet on Capitol Hill, this Twice Sold shop is most densely packed with general fiction, science fiction, and mystery novels. Former best-sellers crowd an extra-cheapo cart on the sidewalk outside. The owners' political leanings are reflected in newspaper clippings hanging on the front windows and walls. Money, but no credit, is given in exchange for books sold. ♦ M-Th, Su noon-8PM; F noon-10PM; Sa 10AM-10PM. 2210 N 45th St. 545.4226. Also at: 905 E. John St. 324.2421

33 Kabul ★★$$ Assuming control of a space that for too many years was filled by a rarely occupied Chinese-American restaurant, chef **Sultan Mahmoud Malikyar** has introduced the rich pleasures of Afghan cuisine (he learned from his father at Seattle's long-gone **Horseman** restaurant) into Wallingford's culinary melting pot. Kebabs are a safe introduction, especially the tender fillets of chicken marinated in turmeric, garlic, and cayenne. A hands-down favorite is the *qorma-i tarkari*—fresh vegetables and lamb tossed with dill, saffron, turmeric, and cumin. The *ashak* (flat dumplings stuffed with scallions, leeks, and cilantro and covered in a sauce of yogurt, garlic, and ground beef) posts as runner-up. For an appetizer, try the *burta,* which is crushed eggplant blended with yogurt, sour cream, garlic, cilantro, and mint. It's served with a somewhat dry but satisfying pita bread. The room is filled with small tables and pleasant sconce lighting. Service is friendly and efficient. ♦ Afghan ♦ M-Sa 5:30-10PM. 2301 NE 45th St. 545.9000

About 3,000 to 5,000 homeless people are out on Seattle's streets every day.

Restaurants/Clubs: Red   **Hotels:** Blue
Shops/ 🌳 Outdoors: Green   **Sights/Culture:** Black

160

33 Marzi Tarts Specializing in party cakes designed to look like male or female sex organs, this erotic bakery is not really as ribald as it sounds. ♦ Bakery ♦ M 11AM-6PM; Tu-Sa 10:30AM-6:30PM. 2323 N 45th St. 328.2253

34 Good Shepherd Center Built in 1906 from a design by architect **C. Alfred Breitung** (who designed other Seattle edifices such as the **Triangle Hotel Building** in Pioneer Square), this was originally a Catholic convent and residence, the **Home of the Good Shepherd.** The community later fought to protect the imposing four-story structure from being replaced by a shopping center. In more recent years it has become something of a political football, fought over by historic restoration forces and Wallingforders, who can't agree on its appropriate use. At last check, **Greenpeace,** private art and elementary schools, and the **Seattle Tilth Association** all occupied some portion of the building and grounds. The grounds and the Tilth gardens are well worth strolling. ♦ 4649 Sunnyside Ave North. 547.8127

35 Dick's Drive-In $ The long, pencil-thin fries here are best consumed from the grease-spotted bag in great gangly handfuls. Complete your feast with a thick chocolate shake. Better fast food can be had in this town, but there are few more interesting human-study environments than the parking lot at Dick's, where hyper-testosteronic high schoolers attempt to mingle with university students. The "scene" is especially entertaining just before closing time on Friday and Saturday nights. Other Dick's are found in Lake City, Crown Hill, and Broadway, with a sit-down joint available in Lower Queen Anne. ♦ Fast food ♦ Daily 10:30AM-2AM. 111 NE 45th St. 632.5125. Also at: 115 Broadway East. 323.1300; 9208 Holman Rd NW. 783.5233; 500 Queen Anne Ave North. 285.5155; 12325 30th Ave NE. 363.7777

36 Latona Elementary School You may eyeball this great wooden building from Interstate 5, just north of the North 45th Street overpass. If you have a chance, get closer for a better view. Dating back to 1906 (long after the community of Latona had been folded into Wallingford; Latona Elementary was probably named instead after bordering Latona Avenue NE), this is the only one of architect **James Stephen's** many Seattle schools to feature Queen Anne-style towers. ♦ NE 42nd St and Fifth Ave North

37 Gas Works Park Twenty-five years after the **Seattle Gas Company** plant belched its last coal dust in 1956, the gasworks at the north end of **Lake Union** reopened as a park for picnickers and kite enthusiasts, its industrial towers retained as totems of the pre-computer age. It's like something out of *Planet of the Apes.* Imagine Charlton Heston riding by here, as he horsebacked past a waterlogged Statue of Liberty in that movie, realizing just how much the world has changed.

Children now scamper over ground that was once so polluted it demanded intensive purifying before Seattleites were safe walking its rolls. Landscape architect **Richard Haag** (who had earlier remodeled the Century 21 fairgrounds into **Seattle Center**) was responsible for seeing aesthetic value in this industrial wasteland and saving the plant as a bizarre relic. His modifications were relatively minor—bright primary colors in some covered areas, a huge symbolic sundial (created by artist **Charles Greening** in 1979) that's mounted atop a knoll to the west, and outdoor dining tables on the beautified grounds. Visitors have an unobstructed view of boats chopping over the lake. ♦ Lake Union, off N. Northlake Way

Bests

Tom Cottrell
Owner, La Cantina Wine Merchants;
Wine Columnist, *The Journal American*

Strolling among the gracious old homes on **Capitol Hill,** especially along Harvard and Federal avenues; watching the sunset from the bench in back of **St. Mark's Cathedral;** then having dinner at **Aoki** and going to a movie at the **Harvard Exit.**

The elegance of the **Four Seasons Olympic Hotel**—a glass of wine in the **Garden Court** followed by dinner in the **Georgian Room.**

Dinner at **Wild Ginger.**

Seeing what's freshest at **Mutual Fish Company,** then plowing through our cookbook collection for a recipe.

Walking along the **Lake Washington Ship Canal,** west of the **Fremont Bridge.**

A warm summer evening, an hour before sunset, sipping champagne in a room at the **Inn at the Market,** then wandering downstairs for dinner under the stars in the courtyard at **Campagne.** A nightcap back in the room, with the lights of the Sound and the Public Market below, then breakfast (or lunch) the next day at **Cafe Sport.**

The *Fremont Troll* sculpture under the **Aurora Bridge,** the *People Waiting for the Interurban* sculpture in **Fremont,** the "doughnut" at **Volunteer Park,** and the "slabs" at **Myrtle Edwards Park.** I know the last two sculptures have names, but they'll always be slabs and a doughnut to me.

The view from **Kinnear Park** on Queen Anne Hill, especially in the evening.

Watching the boats make their way toward the **Hiram M. Chittenden Locks** at dusk from the dining room at **Ray's Boathouse.**

An autumn walk from the **Museum of History and Industry** through the **Washington Park Arboretum** to the **Japanese Tea Garden.**

A winter meal at **Sostanza** or **Al Boccalino,** both warm and comforting places.

Never being more than a block-and-a-half from the next espresso cart.

Saturday morning breakfast at **Maximilien-in-the-Market,** early; thus strengthened, shopping for dinner in **Pike Place Market.** Buying something for the kitchen at **Sur La Table** as a reward for getting up so early.

The Rockers Iko seafood stew served at the **Maple Leaf Sports Grill.**

A rainy day and lunch at **Place Pigalle**—or dinner as the summer sun parks behind the Olympic Mountains.

The water tower at **Volunteer Park;** can you still climb to the top?

Bellevue's downtown park.

For pepperoni pizza late at night—**Abruzzi;** for more than a person can eat—the **Northlake Tavern & Pizza House.**

Hamburgers at the original **Kidd Valley** on 25th Street NE.

The fountains at **Freeway Park.**

Tai Tung when you want a late-night meal; dim sum at **King Cafe.**

The **Intiman Theatre** and its courtyard just in front.

Buying a new book at the **Elliott Bay Book Company** and then plunging into it over coffee in the cafe downstairs.

The *spiedini misti* (lamb, sausage, and marinated chicken on two skewers) at **Cafe Juanita.**

A walk, a drive, or perhaps a picnic along **East Interlaken Boulevard** or **East Interlaken Drive.**

"Keeping Clam" at **Ivar's Acres of Clams and Fish Bar** on the Waterfront.

Best way to come back to the city: a ferry from **Bremerton** or **Winslow** at dusk. Second best way to come back to the city: driving from the south on Interstate 5 at night.

"A rust-brown smudge ballooned over Seattle, end to end, a thousand feet thick. Mac knew the locals were telling themselves that if they were getting headaches and their eyes were bloodshot and their noses ran, it must be something else. Seattleites had a stunning town, but it grew dirtier by the minute. It was only Northwest vanity that kept people calling it fog."

Earl Emerson, *Black Hearts and Slow Dancing*

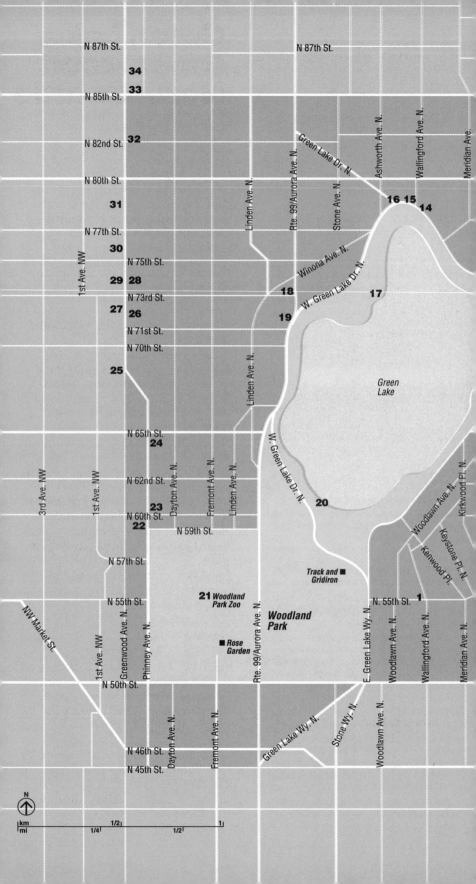

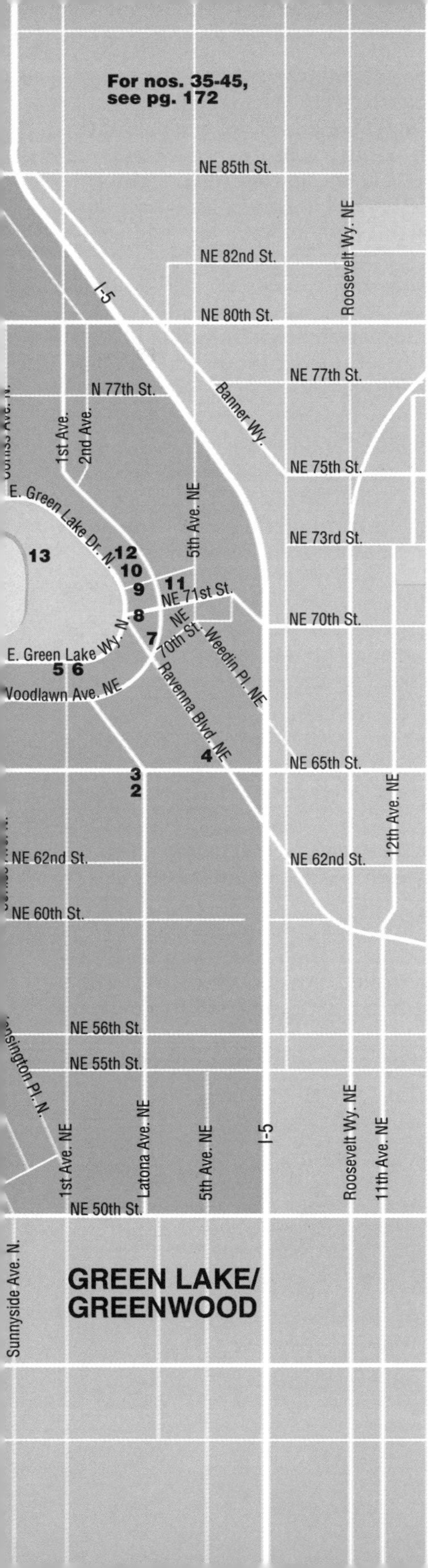

For nos. 35-45,
see pg. 172

Map labels:

NE 85th St.

NE 82nd St.

NE 80th St.

NE 77th St.

N 77th St.

NE 75th St.

Roosevelt Wy. NE

Banner Wy.

NE 73rd St.

E. Green Lake Dr. N.

1st Ave.
2nd Ave.

5th Ave. NE

13   12
     10
9   11
     NE 71st St.
8   NE
7   70th St.

NE 70th St.

E. Green Lake Wy. N.

Ravenna Blvd. NE

Weedin Pl. NE

5 6

Voodlawn Ave. N.

3
2

4

NE 65th St.

12th Ave. NE

NE 62nd St.   NE 62nd St.

NE 60th St.

NE 56th St.
NE 55th St.

ensington Pl. N.

1st Ave. NE
Latona Ave. NE
5th Ave. NE
I-5
Roosevelt Wy. NE
11th Ave. NE

NE 50th St.

Sunnyside Ave. N.

I-5

**GREEN LAKE/
GREENWOOD**

Green Lake/ Greenwood/ North Seattle

A quiet residential district, the Green Lake/Greenwood area is bordered by Ballard to the west, Wallingford and Fremont to the south, and the University District on the east. Its houses range from modest bungalows to some of the most desirable homes in Seattle— the large turn-of-the-century residences and modern dream houses atop **Phinney Ridge**, for instance, command views of both the Olympic and Cascade mountain ranges.

The centerpiece here is **Woodland Park**, located at the south end of Phinney Ridge, where you'll find the well-known **Woodland Park Zoo**, sports playgrounds, tennis courts, a rose garden, and acres of wooded trails and picnic areas. Bisecting the park is **Aurora Avenue (Highway 99)**, which in the early 1930s—following bitter public debate—was extended north from downtown Seattle. The benefits of this bit of progress are dubious; the highway leaves the park with what Washington writer **Ivan Doig** once called "a concrete gorge." The western half of Woodland Park contains the zoo, and most of the rest of its recreation-oriented facilities, including Green Lake, can be found in the eastern half.

Serving as Seattle's "Jogging Central," Green Lake—with two paths around it—is also *the* center of summertime fun in Seattle. Aside from running, there's plenty of kayaking, bicycling, rollerblading, windsurfing, pram-pushing, golfing, baseball playing, fishing, or just plain people-watching here. The city purchased the property around the lake in 1911, fulfilling the hopes of early developer

163

W.D. Wood that the Green Lake frontage be secured by the city for park purposes, and that the lake be made a water park. In 1908, as a part of their comprehensive planning for Seattle, the **Olmsted Brothers** of Massachusetts proposed lowering the level of this lake to create an elegant encircling boulevard. This was accomplished in 1911, and the seven-foot drop exposed hundreds of acres of land. Yet lowering this body of water also had an undesirable side effect: the elimination of creeks and springs in the natural drainage basin created stagnant waters. By 1921 Green Lake had become a smelly, algae-infested swamp famous for causing an annoying ailment known as **Green Lake Itch.** The health department was forced to close the lake to swimmers, but a massive cleanup in the early 1960s made it safe again. A controversial program to treat the algae with alum is currently under way. But many Seattleites still won't plunge into these seemingly beautiful waters, fearing uncomfortable microbial infestation.

Parallel to Aurora Avenue on the park's western edge—along the spine of Phinney Ridge—runs **Phinney Avenue**, which becomes **Greenwood Avenue** farther north. With its secondhand stores spanning the gamut from junky to sublime, the avenue is ripe territory for antique lovers. The Greenwood district, centered at the intersection of North 85th Street and Greenwood Avenue North, retains a funky charm that has endured nobly against encroaching gentrification. There aren't too many neighborhoods left, after all, where a trophy shop can still display in its window, without blushing, a poem on a plaque titled "I'm Proud to be a Norwegian."

A couple of small commercial areas service the Green Lake area year-round on the east and north sides of the lake, and seasonal businesses (such as roller-skate and windsurfing rentals) pop up in the summer. And remember, this is Seattle; on your stroll around the lake, you won't need to travel far before encountering an espresso stand.

A little farther afield is North Seattle. The city limits used to end at North 85th Street, but as Seattle has grown (the line now stands at North 145th Street), the various smaller communities embraced by the North Seattle rubric—**Lake Forest Park, Northgate, Broadview, Maple Leaf,** and **Wedgewood** among them—have developed in their own inimitable way. North Seattle is primarily home to auto dealerships, budget motels, strip malls, and modest housing, but even this unpromising mix has a particular flavor worth sampling.

1 Honey Bear Bakery ★$ Dropping by the Honey Bear for a cup of joe (pour your own) and a sourdough cinnamon roll is a regular ritual for many folks. Crowded and convivial, the no-smoking-allowed bakery has become a neighborhood institution in which to linger over conversation or grab a quick bite. The take-home breads are famous (at least locally), and don't overlook the enormous chocolate-chip cookies or the white-chocolate brownies. Dinner is a dicier matter, as specials can be far less flavorful than you would expect, especially anything containing brown rice. The black-bean chili, however, is a safe bet. ♦ Bakery ♦ M-F 6AM-7PM; Sa-Su 6AM-11PM. 2106 N 55th St. 545.7296

2 Cafe Los Gatos ★★$ This tiny restaurant features the subtle flavors of Central and South America. The food is sometimes spicy and always intriguing in its use of ingredients such as cilantro and cardamom. Nightly fish, meat, chicken, and vegetarian specials are available. Or try the pork stew, a rich sargasso of fruit and nuts with pork. Spirited dinners and friendly service make up for the dimly lit decor. Nut tarts are a good bet for dessert. A recent expansion and a license to serve beer and wine should entice patrons to linger here. ♦ Central/South American ♦ Tu-Th 5-9PM; F-Sa 5-10PM; closed the first Tuesday of every month. 6411 Latona Ave NE. Reservations recommended. 527.9765

3 Latona Pub ★$ This funky, friendly neighborhood tavern offers a good selection of wines and a frequently changing assortment of microbrews, including products from the **Rogue Brewery** in Ashland, Oregon, and from the **Maritime Pacific Brewing Co.** in Seattle—any one of which is worth sampling. Bartenders are happy to help you choose something that will educate your palate. The pub grub menu is limited, but salads are a good choice. In addition, there's something called the Haystack, a rewarding variation on nachos, with chips scattered about a bowl of room-temperature bean dip smothered in cheese.

The best place to sit is at the bar; the worst place is on a balcony overlooking the main floor, where the service is glacially slow and you'll feel cut off from the action. A variety of fine local musicians, usually playing folk or jazz, are on hand Thursday through Sunday evenings. A small cover is sometimes charged for the music, but if you're inside already, you can usually slide. A mailing list will keep you apprised of new brews. ♦ M-F 3PM-1AM; Sa 1PM-2AM; Su 2PM-midnight. Music Th-Sa 9PM; Su 8:30PM. 6423 Latona Ave NE. 525.2238

4 Boehm's on Ravenna It's somewhat off the beaten Green Lake path, but this shop is worth a visit. Old man Boehm, a Swiss immigrant, was a master candy-maker and a legendary mountain climber and skier; his original shop in the town of Issaquah has for years been a regular stop for travelers headed east across **Snoqualmie Pass.** This small retail outlet, a few blocks from the main Green Lake commercial district, caters mostly to fans of its splendid handmade chocolates, oversize muffins, buttercream-filled chocolates, and espresso drinks. But there are a few tables, in case eating and running is not an essential part of your day. ♦ M-F 6AM-6PM; Sa 8AM-5PM; Su 9AM-4PM. 559 NE Ravenna Blvd. 523.9380

Mail carriers don't hesitate to identify Seattle's most exclusive neighborhood: The Highlands. The houses there don't even have addresses. Letters and packages to residents are simply addressed "The Highlands, Seattle, Washington 98177."

Restaurants/Clubs: Red   Hotels: Blue
Shops/ 🌿 Outdoors: Green   Sights/Culture: Black

Saleh al Lago

5 Saleh al Lago ★★$$ You wouldn't think this sleek restaurant with its modern and minimal pastel decor, set in an otherwise ordinary block of shops, would have been praised as among Seattle's top Italian places. Especially when you learn further that the owner/chef is **Saleh Joudeh,** a Syrian. But Joudeh studied cooking (and medicine) in Italy; his imaginative blendings of various Mediterranean influences can make even plain-sounding fare remarkable. Fresh pasta and veal dishes are consistently delicious. Special praise goes to the chef's *ravioli al mondo mio* (with various sauces and fillings) and the garlicky calamari antipasto. Joudeh prefers his seafood dishes prepared simply, and in his capable hands, that's just fine. ♦ Italian/Mediterranean ♦ M-Sa 11:30AM-2PM, 5:30-10PM. 6804 E. Green Lake Way North. Reservations recommended. 522.7943

6 Spud Fish and Chips $ The ambience is a big zero, with horrendous on-site seating. Yet this is a choice spot to come on sunny days when all you want is to grab a quick lunch and burn off a few skin cells beside the lake. The fish is remarkably flaky and the fries are filling and salty. Everything's a bit on the greasy side, but that's the way you'd expect it here. ♦ Seafood ♦ Daily 11AM-10PM. 6860 E. Green Lake Way North. 524.0565

Gregg's Greenlake ⚙ Cycle

7 Gregg's Greenlake Cycle This is the biggest and busiest of several shops around Green Lake that rent bicycles, rollerblades, and skateboards for a nominal fee. By the way, these modes of transport are also for sale at Gregg's, and there's a helpful service department available when things go bewilderingly wrong. ♦ M-F 9:30AM-9PM; Sa-Su 9:30AM-6PM. 7007 Woodlawn Ave NE. 523.1822

8 Kyllo's Lakeside Deli ★$ A bustling cafe with good sandwiches and home-baked items caters to the let's-stop-after-our-walk-around-the-lake crowd. ♦ Deli ♦ M-F 6:30AM-6PM; Sa-Su 7:30AM-6PM. 315 NE 71st St. 522.9088

165

9 My Friends Cafe ★$ With good breakfasts and sandwiches at lunch, the menu at this cafe emphasizes fresh fruit and other healthy ingredients. ♦ American ♦ M-F 5:30AM-4:30PM; Sa-Su 7:30AM-4:30PM. 310 NE 72nd St. 523.8929

10 Lemon Grass Grill ★★$$ The Thai cuisine at this glossy restaurant is tamed down considerably for the American palate, which (depending on your own tastes) can be a plus or minus. Best picks include the *phad thai* or anything with green curry. The atmosphere is cool and pleasant. There's also a full page of inexpensive lunchtime specials on the menu. ♦ Thai ♦ M-Th 11:30AM-2:30PM, 5-10PM; F-Sa 11:30AM-2:30PM, 5-11PM; Su 5-10PM. 7200 E. Green Lake Dr North. Reservations recommended. 525.6510

10 Rasa Malaysia ★★$ The emphasis here is on noodles, usually served sautéed with very fresh vegetables; a variety of fish, shrimp, or meat; and mildly spicy sauces, such as peanut sauce. Fruit smoothies and not-too-sweet lemonade are the drinks of choice. ♦ Malaysian ♦ 7208 E. Green Lake Dr North. 523.8888. Also at: 6012 Phinney Ave North. 781.8888; 401 Broadway East. 328.8882; 1514 Pike Place. 624.8388

11 Rosita's ★$ Just a couple blocks off the lake, this place is commonly crowded and uncommonly efficient despite that fact. Try any of the combination plates or the *chiles rellenos.* The Super Nachos platter is a winning appetizer. A plus for parents: Rosita's is extremely kid-friendly. ♦ Mexican ♦ M-Th 11:30AM-10:30PM; F 11:30AM-11PM; Sa noon-10:30PM; Su 4-10PM. 7210 Woodlawn Ave NE. 523.3031

12 Green Lake Public Library Perched on a grassy knoll with bushes snuggled about its entrance, this well-maintained, proud-looking building shows Mediterranean and Chicago School influences. Opened in 1910, it is one of eight libraries still standing in the Seattle area (two, one in downtown and the other in Renton, were lost to wrecking balls); they were all built thanks to the largess of iron-and-steel-magnate **Andrew Carnegie.** Designers of this building were **W. Marbury Somervell** and **Joseph C. Cote,** who in the year of its opening would also see two of their other library projects open: the **University Branch Library** on Roosevelt Way North and the **West Seattle Public Library** on 42nd Avenue SW. Not surprisingly, these three structures bear some resemblance to one another. ♦ M-W 1-9PM; F-Sa 10AM-6PM. 7364 E. Green Lake Dr North. 684.7547

13 Green Lake Boat Rentals Rent a canoe, small boat, or paddle-wheel craft at this Parks Department concession. It also rents out windsurfing equipment, and windsurfing lessons are available. ♦ Daily 10AM-dusk, May-Sept. 7351 E. Green Lake Dr North. 527.0171

14 The Urban Bakery ★$ Long hours make this a convenient spot for exercise fanatics who squeeze in Green Lake walks or runs during busy days. It serves good espressos and iced *lattes.* Hearty sandwiches, soups, baked-on-the-premises pastries, and a full line of juices are also on hand. ♦ Bakery ♦ M-F 6AM-6PM; Sa-Su 8AM-7PM. 7850 E. Green Lake Dr North. 524.7951

15 Ed's Juice and Java ★$ Tiny but convivial, this joint features just what the name suggests. A variety of unusual concoctions are available in the juice department, such as carrot and wheatgrass; the coffee-based drinks are more conventional. ♦ Coffeehouse ♦ Daily 7AM-8PM. 7907 Wallingford Ave North. 524.7570

15 Secret Garden Bookshop The oldest and best bookstore in the Seattle area devoted exclusively to children, Secret Garden carries hundreds of titles, many on sale at bargain prices. There's a table of toys, an inviting reading area, a loose-brick floor that makes great crunching noises, and a helpful staff. Owner **Sher Smith** (a walking encyclopedia of kid's lit) sponsors weekly story times and regular author signings. ♦ M-W, F-Sa 10AM-6PM; Th 10AM-8PM; Su 1-5PM. 7900 E. Green Lake Dr North. 524.4556

16 Guido's Pizzeria ★$ Pizza by the slice or by the pie comes with a wider-than-normal range of toppings, such as fresh basil and sun-dried tomatoes. Crusts are made thin or Sicilian thick. Calzones, salads, a variety of juices and mineral waters, and of course—this being Seattle—espressos and *lattes* are also available. The pizzeria is minuscule and crowded, so most of the business is takeout. (Several picnic tables beckon from just across the street in **Green Lake Park.**) The cheerfully brash New York-style attitude of the employees is free. ♦ Italian ♦ Daily 8AM-11PM. 7902 E. Green Lake Way North. 522.5553. Also at: 2108 NE 65th Ave. 525.3042

16 Elliott Bay Bicycles This is a high-end shop for serious cyclists and an ideal place to rent bikes for a cruise around the lake. ♦ M-F 11AM-8PM; Sa 10AM-6PM; Su noon-5PM. 7904 E. Green Lake Dr North. 524.4270

16 Greenlake Jake's ★$ Good burgers and breakfasts can be ordered here and carried to the lake or enjoyed on site. (The mushroom burgers or the biscuits and gravy for breakfast are especially recommended.) Portions are traditionally copious. Blueberry-muffin lovers also come here for their fix. An outdoor eating area beats the sterile interior. ♦ American ♦ Daily 7AM-9PM. 7918 E. Green Lake Way North. 523.4747

Pillars of the Community

That tourists regard Seattle as home to a relative superfluity of totem poles is an odd quirk of taste and history. Native Americans of the Seattle area, after all, did not practice this detailed form of columnar art, but Seattleites took a shine to it way back in the 19th century. Ever since, totem poles have been imported, duplicated locally, or stolen for their aesthetic attributes rather than for their regional relevance. Poles scattered around town are generally the work of the Tlingit people of southeastern **Alaska,** the Haidas of the **Queen Charlotte Islands,** or the Kwakiutl and Tsimshian Indians of southwestern **British Columbia.** They symbolize this city's longstanding reputation as the Gateway to the North.

Totem poles originated as memorials, grave posts, and architectural supports. Their designs traditionally included creatures of nature mythologized into specific, powerful figures of lore known as the Raven, Frog, Coyote, and others, each with its own temperament and style of behavior. Their representations were stacked on a totem pole in a way that related parcels of Indian history or legends, with the top figure identifying the clan whose story was being told.

The 50-foot-tall western red cedar pole in **Pioneer Place Park** is Seattle's best-known totem. The original monolith, a Tlingit pole stolen by a Seattle expeditionary party during the 19th century, stood in that park from 1899 until it was damaged by dry rot and arson in 1938. What exists today is a replica, also carved by Tlingits. This totem symbolizes not one but three myths, the predominant one involving the cunning Raven (a figure depicted at the top of the totem at right), who stole the sun and the moon from Raven-at-the-Head-of-Nass and brought them to the world. (When you're looking at the pole in Pioneer Place Park, notice how the figure at the top still holds the moon in its beak.) In addition, this totem tells how intermarriages between Raven and Frog clanspeople, who have been transformed into humans, are complicated when their offspring are shaped like frogs. The Pioneer Park obelisk also recalls a sea voyage taken by Mink and Raven in the belly of Killer Whale. During the trip, the two passengers feast on their host's body until they reach its heart, at which point Killer Whale dies and washes ashore. The adventure leaves Raven with a sleek and oily sheen, while Mink has become dirty from rolling in rotten wood to clean himself.

In Pioneer Square's peaceful **Occidental Park** you can see a totem called **Sun and Raven,** a 32-foot pole carved by artist **Duane Pasco** for the 1974 Spokane World's Fair. Three other Pasco pieces—**Man Riding on Tail of Whale, Tsonoqua** (a mythical giant of the deep forest), and **Bear**—are also in the park. And at **Seattle Center,** near the Center House's southwest corner, you can see a 30-foot Pasco pole with four main figures: Hawk, Bear (holding a salmon), Raven, and Killer Whale.

The 35-foot-tall carved cedar pole at the intersection of Alaska Way South and South Washington Street was commissioned by the Port of Seattle to commemorate links between Seattle and Alaska. This 1975 piece, created at the **Alaska Indian Arts Center** in Haines, Alaska, includes several symbols of the 49th state. Eagle sits at the top, representing the main Tlingit tribe; below him is Brown Bear holding a coin, which symbolizes Alaska's great size and wealth, and Killer Whale, representing tenacity and strength; and at the pole's base is the figure "Strong Boy," which stands for Alaska's youth and vigor.

The more traditional of the two poles in **Victor Steinbrueck Park,** at the north end of **Pike Place Market,** does not depict a legend but includes mythical figures inspired by Haida Indian designs, all of which stand for qualities of strength and abundance. The other, a nontraditional unadorned totem pole, was apparently inspired by a pole found near Ketchikan, Alaska, that features **Abraham Lincoln;** Seattle's version is topped by two eight-foot-high figures of a farming couple standing back to back. These pieces were designed by both Quinault Indian artist **Martin Oliver** and Seattleite **James Bender.**

A 1937 example of the art, carved originally for a fish cannery in Waterfall, Alaska, by a Haida Indian, can be seen just east of the **Montlake Bridge** on East Shelby Street. After many years of greeting fishers returning to Alaska, this pole was carved and stored in a Seattle warehouse until it could be purchased and reassembled by philanthropic locals. The 40-foot-tall obelisk tells about a very old woman whose brother, a Haida chief, considered her worthless. When the chief moved his people, he ordered that his sibling be left behind without food or fire. She, however, called upon the spirits for help, and was rewarded with an eagle that brought her food each day. When a bear tried to steal the raptor's gifts, the woman appealed to the spirits, who sent someone to kill the thieving bruin.

Two other fine examples of totem art are located in Vancouver's **Stanley Park. Charles James** carved the turn-of-the-century house posts, both of which depict Thunderbird at the top (a photograph of one of the poles is featured on the cover of this guidebook). They were originally designed to serve as architectural supports for communal homes.

M. BLUM

167

17 Bathhouse Theatre Under the auspices of its irrepressible artistic director, **Arne Zaslove,** the Bathhouse produces six productions annually on a year-round schedule, specializing in innovative updates of classics. In addition it mounts numerous free public shows in Seattle parks throughout the summer. This building was originally erected in 1927 as—you guessed it—a brick bathhouse. In its first year of operation, 53,000 people used it for changing and showering; by 1958 the numbers had dropped to 10,000. When the bathhouse finally became a theater in 1970, it was at a time when showing a bit of skin was no longer socially unacceptable. Women and men now stroll around the lake and ride sailboards in swimsuits that would have shocked their ancestors. ◆ 7312 W. Greenlake Drive North. 524.9108

18 Beth's Cafe $ This greasiest of spoons, located between **Twin Teepees** and **Butch's Gun Shop,** attracts plenty of college students, who drop over here after pulling all-night study (or make-out) sessions to wolf down inexpensive 12-egg omelets (be prepared to share!), layered over a two-inch bed of hash browns, with toast. Half orders can be had by the less gluttonous. Breakfast is served all day. Burgers and enormous french fries carry on the stomach-busting tradition. It's a real scene. ◆ American ◆ Open daily 24 hours. 7311 Aurora Ave North. 782.5588

19 Twin Teepees Restaurant ★$ A classic of roadway kitsch on the west side of Green Lake, Twin Teepees is a 1934 mishmash of Native American design motifs. The structure was apparently prefabricated in California and then trucked up Highway 99 to this site. Inside, you'll find substantial breakfasts and other forms of good, solid American food. ◆ American ◆ Daily 8AM-9PM. 7201 Aurora Ave North. 783.9740

20 Green Lake Small Craft Center This concession, at the lake's southwest corner, offers year-round canoe and kayak instruction, as well as special programs. It's also home to the **Seattle Sailing Association,** which lends out its small boats for an annual fee. The lake is often active on weekday mornings with rowers embarking from this center. ◆ M-Sa 1:30-5PM. 5900 W. Green Lake Way North. 684.4074

Green Lake, which has an average depth of only 15 feet, is left over from a huge Ice Age lake that once stretched between the present cities of Everett and Olympia. Haller and Bitter lakes, in the northern part of Seattle, are also remnants of that ancient body of water.

21 Woodland Park Zoo Origins of this zoo and the surrounding park trace back to **Guy Phinney,** a flamboyant Englishman who made his fortune in Canadian real estate before moving to Seattle at the end of the 19th century. Phinney built a private park, **Woodland,** as part of his estate at the southern end of the ridge that bears his name. He included—among other amenities—a trolley line, a flower garden, a conservatory, picnic grounds, a zoo, a bathing beach, and a music pavilion. The city bought the land from him in 1900 for the then-extravagant sum of $100,000 and turned it into the present-day park.

After some rocky early years (for decades, elephants were maintained in a shed that had been condemned), Seattle's zoo is now rated among the nation's top 10. It has evolved recently from a typical iron-bars-and-concrete-cages holdall into a collection of exciting and innovative exhibits. Animals are free to wander in near-natural settings such as an African savanna (where you can peer from afar at giraffes and gazelles); an Asian elephant forest, including a replica of a Thai logging camp; a farmlike petting zoo for kids; and a lush, lowland gorilla enclosure, the largest of its kind in the world, in which you can get up close and personal (behind glass) with these fascinating creatures. A $9 million tropical rain-forest exhibit, complete with artificial vegetation (created by a technique pioneered in Hollywood) and authentic, digitally recorded sounds from a real rain forest piped in over hidden speakers, opened in late 1992. Now, if something can only be done to make life more comfortable for the penguins, imprisoned as they are in a small, stark enclosure. Older children will love the periodic exhibits of raptor flight, and parents shouldn't miss the memorial **Jimi Hendrix** rock at the African savanna—a tribute to one of Seattle's favorite native sons. The zoo offers lectures, summer musical performances, and educational series for youngsters. ◆ Admission; discount for senior citizens, disabled persons, and ages 3 to 5; free for children under 2. Daily 9:30AM-6PM 15 Mar-15 Oct; daily 9:30AM-4PM 16 Oct-14 Mar. 5500 Phinney Ave North. 625.2244

22 The Santa Fe Cafe ★★★$$ Sparse but elegant decor combines with consistently high-quality, innovative cuisine to create Phinney Ridge's classiest restaurant. A couple of the appetizers alone—an order of garlic custard, say, and a luscious artichoke ramekin—could make a meal. Green-chile stew, enchiladas, and green-chile burritos made with blue-corn tortillas are all tried-and-true entrées, should you still have room for more.

The owners, both from Albuquerque, New Mexico, import tons of red and green chiles from their home state to keep their dishes tasting just right. If your waitperson warns you that something like the red-chile burrito may be too hot for most palates (probably yours, too), take his or her word for it. Another Santa Fe branch is found in Ravenna, with a take-out spot, **Blue Mesa** (2205 Queen Anne Ave North, 282.6644), on Queen Anne Hill. ♦ Southwestern ♦ M-F 5-10PM; Sa 11AM-10PM; Su 9AM-2PM. 5901 Phinney Ave North. Reservations recommended. 783.9755. Also at: 2255 NE 65th St. 524.7736

23 Rasa Malaysia ★★$ This popular take-out or eat-in noodle house has outlets in the University District, Green Lake, and Capitol Hill. ♦ Malaysian ♦ M-F 6-9PM. 6012 Phinney Ave North. 781.8888. Also at: 401 Broadway East. 328.8882; 7208 E. Green Lake Dr North. 523.8888; 1514 Pike Place. 624.8388

24 Mae's Phinney Ridge Cafe ★$ In years past this was an unappetizing grease pit, but Mae (the name is actually the *nom de cuisine* of three women owners) has transformed it into a much more congenial nook for breakfast and lunch. Sandwiches, burgers, and cinnamon rolls are to die for here. Omelets are the top pick at breakfast, but for the truly famished, a cheese-shrouded mountain of hash browns is served as a main course. The **Moo Room** (formerly a bar) features a soda fountain, great milk shakes, a jukebox, and more cow-related art than you can shake a hoof at. Service can be slow, and the lines form quickly on weekends, but the wait isn't usually too long. ♦ American ♦ Daily 7AM-3PM. 6412 Phinney Ave North. 782.1222

25 Espresso Dental TV ads may caution consumers about coffee stains on their teeth, but that hasn't stopped dentist **Ron Wallach** and his massage therapist wife, **Sharing Lawrence,** from providing steaming **Starbucks'** coffee drinks for their patients to enjoy while they wait to have their teeth cleaned (the coffee is not available to the general public, regrettably). ♦ 6725 Green-wood Ave North. 284.2483

26 Terra Mar This shop features an eclectic assortment of handmade items—including masks, clothes, and artwork—by a wide variety of local and international folk artists. The emphasis is on unusual folk art and primitive designs. ♦ M-F 11AM-7PM; Sa-Su 10AM-6PM. 7200 Greenwood Ave North. 784.5350

27 2nd Hand Hube Furniture and kitschy stuff from the 1930s to the 1950s, some of it high-quality collectibles and some of it near-junk, is featured here. ♦ W-Su 11AM-5PM. 7217 Greenwood Ave North. 782.1335

27 The Couth Buzzard Every section, except for that containing mainstream fiction, could be beefed up, but that's not to say this dusty bookstore with the peculiar moniker has naught to offer bibliophiles. Indeed, it can be a most beguiling trove of unlikely and sometimes unheard-of finds in used hardbacks and paperbacks. Look for sidewalk sales out front. ♦ Tu-Th noon-8PM; F-Su 10AM-6PM. 7221 Greenwood Ave North. 789.8965

27 Greenwood Bakery ★$ Excellent made-on-the-spot pastries, breads, cookies, and other delectables are complemented by the good espresso drinks. ♦ Bakery ♦ Tu-Sa 6:30AM-9PM; Su 6:30AM-6PM. 7227 Greenwood Ave North. 783.7181

27 Ken's Market This better-than-average grocery store caters to an upscale crowd with its wealth of coffee beans, delicious deli sandwiches (try the meat loaf), and fresh pasta. The espresso drinks served here are just as good as those sold next door at **Greenwood Bakery,** and the service is faster. ♦ Daily 6AM-11PM. 7231 Greenwood Ave North. 784.3470. Also at: 2400 Sixth Ave West. 282.1100

28 George's Corner A charmingly eccentric shop full of goofy collectibles, George's makes an especially strong showing in cowboy paraphernalia. Indulge the Tom Mix or John Wayne inside you that is crying for release. ♦ Tu-Sa 11AM-5PM; Su noon-4PM. 7400 Greenwood Ave North. 781.0973

Restaurants/Clubs: Red
Shops/ 🌳 Outdoors: Green

Hotels: Blue
Sights/Culture: Black

169

Aurora—Another Roadside Distraction

Aurora Avenue North, a.k.a. **Highway 99,** used to be the main highway running north and south through Seattle. Today, it's a comparatively minor thoroughfare. At the city's heart, Aurora becomes an elevated highway running along the Waterfront; south of downtown, it's known as **Pacific Highway South.** But north of Seattle, rolling out into the suburban hinterlands of **Lynnwood,** now, that's a different kettle of kitsch. There, Aurora Avenue becomes the car culture equivalent of a Marrakech bazaar, bordered by a jumble of bleeding neon, strip malls and strip joints, questionable motels, taverns, used-car lots, and assorted other businesses— alternately cheerful and new or grim and shopworn, but always uniquely local.

"Aurora is the homely and affordable face of American capitalism. . . ." writes **Jonathan Raban,** a British author expatriated to Seattle. "Driving Aurora is like riffling at speed through the text of an eccentric illustrated encyclopedia. The entries rush past too rapidly to follow, and they couple promiscuously with each other: Something about pest control gets tangled up with something about foam rubber and chiropractors and The Love Pantry."

Aurora Avenue's kitsch evokes three essential aspects of American life: fast cars, quick bucks, and a high tolerance for personal weirdness. It exists less to identify a business for what it is than simply to attract your attention—and your money—in any way possible.

For example, the **Twin Teepees Restaurant** (7201 Aurora Avenue North) is a loony tribute to Native American culture. Built in 1937, it cheerfully mixes Northwest Coast and Plains Indian clichés with no particular regard for accuracy; case in point are the paintings that flank the entrance to the "teepees"— they look like bears, or maybe whales. You don't stop here because you've heard the food is to die for (it's not), but because you're curious to see what's inside those twin peaks.

Another kitsch-o-rama classic is an extremely ratty-looking life-size elephant that advertises the **Aurora Flower Shop** (8808 Aurora Avenue North) just north of the Twin Teepees. It was also built during the Great Depression, as were so many of these highway come-ons. Legend has it that a florist who once owned this shop kept the paunchy proboscidean in his backyard for years before hoisting it onto a pole above busy Highway 99.

Seal's Motel (12035 Aurora Avenue North) displays a seal balancing a ball on its nose. **Harvey's Tavern** (4356 Leary Way North) features—what else?—an elaborate blue-whiskered neon rabbit. The signs reel by, each more outlandish than the last until you reach some true showstoppers such as "DO BUGS, NOT DRUGS," which promotes an insect-killing enterprise.

Some of Aurora reflects the changing face of suburban America; the many signs in Korean, Vietnamese, Japanese, and Chinese represent the interests of Asian immigrants who are settling into residential areas off Highway 99. But you'll also find remnants of old-time Seattle. The **Denny Hill Fuel Company** (9000 Aurora Avenue North), which sells wood and other fuels, relocated to Aurora when Denny Hill, north of downtown, was regraded into nonexistence at the turn of the century; it looks as if not much has changed since. And in the time capsule called Aurora Avenue, that's not far from the truth.

29 74th Street Ale House ★★$ This former hard-drinker's dive has been reincarnated as a light, airy neighborhood tavern serving an excellent array of Northwest microbrews and standard-issue beer (16 taps in all), along with wine. The brains behind this operation are **Jeff Eagan,** formerly of **Roanoke Park Place Tavern** on Capitol Hill and the long-lamented **Mark Tobey** restaurant in downtown, and **Jeff Reich,** who runs the kitchen. The menu is brief but thoughtful. Try the big-fisted burgers (decked with grilled onions and peppers), the sausage sandwich, or the Reuben. The vegetarian sandwich, a neat orchestration of Montrachet and cream cheese, sun-dried tomatoes, artichoke hearts, and heaps of roasted garlic on country bread, is another fine choice. Some fans claim this alehouse serves Seattle's best chicken sandwich, but critics have found it to be rather dry and unexciting compared with other offerings here. Try the white clam chowder served on Friday. ♦ American ♦ M-Th, Su noon-midnight; F-Sa noon-2AM. 7401 Greenwood Ave North. 784.2955

29 Yanni's Lakeside Cafe ★★$ Huge portions of good Greek cooking are offered at this congenial neighborhood hangout. Try the gyro platter for lunch and any of the lamb dishes or moussaka for dinner. The appetizer plate of calamari can make a whole meal. Desserts have been less interesting. There's a simple, no-nonsense wine list. ♦ Greek ♦ M-Sa 4-10PM. 7419 Greenwood Ave North. 783.6945

30 Pelayo's Antiques This large, well-stocked store is at the upper end of the price continuum. Specialties are pine furniture, toys (such as elegant hobbyhorses), and crockery. ♦ Daily 11AM-6PM. 7601 Greenwood Ave North. 789.1999. Also at: 8421 Greenwood Ave North. 789.1333

31 Patty's Eggnest ★$ Often overlooked is this pleasure center of comfort foods such as Denver omelets, liver and onions, blueberry pancakes, and gyro sandwiches. Decor is nothing to write home about: tables smothered in checked cloths, and walls covered with black-and-white stills of local TV personalities you'd rather not see over breakfast. But proprietor **Patty Papadopoulos** (she's the one with the long black hair, slinging plates and instructing her waitstaff to keep the coffee pouring all around) remembers regulars and always greets them on their visits. That familiarity breeds loyalty. Breakfast is served all day. ♦ American ♦ Tu-F 7AM-3PM; Sa-Su 8AM-3PM. 7717 Greenwood Ave North. 784.5348

32 Arita Japanese Restaurant ★★$ A very pleasant family-run restaurant, Arita serves Japanese dishes only slightly altered for the standard American palate. The atmosphere

is calm and cool, with gentle music in the background and simple furnishings. There's no sushi bar, but the sashimi and sushi dinners are fresh and reasonably priced. ♦ Japanese ♦ M-Th 11:30AM-2PM, 5-9PM; F 11:30AM-2PM, 5-9:30PM; Sa 5-9:30PM. 8202 Greenwood Ave North. 784.2625

33 Phad Thai ★$ Greenwood has not escaped the explosive procreation of Thai restaurants that Seattle has witnessed over the last few years. Phad Thai is informal in decor and cheerful in service; employees have been known to take fussy children in hand for a kitchen tour, giving grateful parents a chance to eat. The food is fresh, well-presented, and cooked without MSG. Try the vegetable curry or the chicken in peanut sauce. ♦ Thai ♦ M-F 11:30AM-2:30PM, 5-9:30PM; Sa-Su 4-9:30PM. 8530 Greenwood Ave North. 784.1830

34 El Tapatio ★$ A venerable Greenwood institution, El Tapatio offers few culinary surprises, but it's cheerful, inexpensive, and informal. The standards are all available—taco combination plates, burritos, enchiladas—and come with heaping sides of rice and beans. Even the salsa served with tortilla chips as a warm-up has some bite. Kids

are welcome, too; they receive helium balloons and lots of attention. ♦ Mexican ♦ M-Th, Su 1-10PM; F-Sa 11:30AM-10:30PM. 8564 Greenwood Ave North. 782.7545

35 Carkeek Park Nicely bordering Puget Sound, this 198-acre greensward has been left mostly to wilderness. But a number of forest trails and picnic areas are still available. Crews of **Camp Fire Girls** conduct week-long summer camps out here. And couples run their dogs or enjoy lunch by the water. ♦ NE Carkeek Road and Ninth Ave NW

36 Bella Luna ★$ The northernmost in **Dany Mitchell's** local Italian chain, which also includes **Trattoria Mitchelli** in Pioneer Square, **Trattoria Angelina** in West Seattle, and **Stella's Trattoria** in the University District, is housed in a former pizza parlor. This warm restaurant serves hearty, unpretentious, consistent fare—pasta specials that change daily and good pizzas—plus a few welcome left-field contributions such as a garlicky spinach linguine with walnuts and red peppers. The wine list is simple but effective. The decor is spacious, featuring a fireplace for chilly days and a plant-bedecked atrium for sunny ones. ♦ Italian ♦ M-Th 11AM-10PM; F 11AM-11PM; Sa 8AM-11PM; Su 8AM-10PM. 14053 Greenwood Ave North. 367.5862

37 Tan Duc ★$ This quiet, friendly restaurant specializes in Chinese and Vietnamese food. Especially recommended are the Vietnamese "box dinners"—huge platters of barbecued shrimp, bean sprouts, cooked meats, vegetables, and other savories. Wrap these all up in a delicate rice-flour pancake, dip it in the sweet sauce, and chow down. (Noncondescending help from the staff is available for novices.) ♦ Chinese/Vietnamese ♦ Daily 9:30AM-9PM. 10009 Aurora Ave North. 525.0511

38 Doong Kong Lau ★★$ A better-than-average, usually busy Chinese place, Doong Kong Lau specializes in hot and spicy Hakka cuisine. The "hot pots"—the name is quite literal—come in a fine assortment of styles (vegetarian, seafood, pork, etc.), and the garlic eggplant should not be missed. ♦ Chinese ♦ Daily 11AM-11PM. 9710 Aurora Ave North. 526.8828

39 Larry's Market Welcome to Grocery Land, U.S.A., a pop-cultural spin on the classic American supermarket. **Larry McKinney** was a grocer's son who inherited his first store in the 1960s and has since expanded the family business into a chain. Like other Larry's, this one offers a deceptively industrial appearance—exposed ventilation pipes and rafters and metal racks supporting boxes of unpacked supplies. McKinney favors architecture as theater and design as chorus line. Sit back and enjoy the show. It's easy to forget that you're standing inside a business catering to the quotidian needs of a basically upper-middle-class and convenience-hungry clientele, a place where shelf after shelf of snack crackers and sushi and wine must be moved through the check stands as profitably and economically as possible. Function is only a subtitle here. Flowers are sold at the front door, and there's a deli counter inside with fresh salads galore and cheeses arranged in almost exhaustive variety. ◆ Open daily 24 hours. 10008 Aurora Ave North. 527.5333

40 Northgate Shopping Center Holding the dubious distinction of being the world's first regional shopping mall, Northgate was designed in the 1950s by architect **John**

Graham, Sr., who also invented the revolving restaurant and helped develop the **Space Needle** for the 1962 World's Fair. Oddly enough, considering Seattle's prevailing weather, it was originally uncovered; only later was a roof added. All the usual suspects can be found here: **Nordstrom, B. Dalton Bookseller, Lamonts,** and **The Tux Shop.** ◆ M-Sa 9:30AM-9:30PM; Su 11AM-6PM. Interstate 5 at Northgate Way NE. 362.4777

41 Maple Leaf Sports Grill ★★$ Don't let the name fool you; the fresh flowers on the tables are a dead tip-off that this is more than your typical brew-and-Bruins sports bar. The Maple Leaf is a true neighborhood hangout, serving an excellent assortment of beers and wines. The decor has lots of old wood and open space. Lunch and dinner items include one of the most succulent burgers in town and a changing array of imaginative yet unpretentious specials featuring fish, chicken, pasta, and other staples. ◆ American ◆ M-Sa 11:30AM-10PM. 8909 Roosevelt Way NE. 523.8449

42 Cooper's Northwest Alehouse ★★$
Technically not a brewpub (no beers are
prepared on the premises), this crowded and
cheery tavern nonetheless deserves special
mention as a mecca for Northwest microbrews. Twenty-one of its 22 tap brews are
West Coast specialties. The staff is
knowledgeable about the subtle distinctions
of each type, and small samples of untried
concoctions are accompanied by enthusiastic
debate over their relative merits and demerits.
Cooper's serves wine as well as some bar
food such as fish-and-chips, but people come
here for the beer. Darts tournaments are held
on a regular basis. ◆ M-F 3PM-2AM; Sa 1PM-
2AM; Su 1PM-midnight. 8065 Lake City Way
NE. 522.2923

43 Panda's ★$ Known for inexpensive high-
quality food and fast, friendly service, Panda's
makes its soup noodles, dumplings, buns,
and sauces fresh daily. The Orange Beef
(tender beef slices with an orange sauce), the
Happy Family (stir-fried scallops, shrimp, and
breast of chicken), and the *mu shu* pork are all

outstanding. Delivery is free to North Enders.
◆ Chinese ◆ M-Th 11AM-9:30PM; F-Sa 11AM-
10:30PM; Su 4-9PM. 7347 35th Ave NE.
526.5115. Also at: 1625 W. Dravus St.
283.9030

44 Wurdemann Mansion The main attraction
in **Lake Forest Park,** the Wurdemann Mansion
was once the home of **Adolph Linden,** who,
along with fellow banker **Edmund W.
Campbell,** embezzled the money to open
downtown's **Camlin Hotel** in 1926 (both
were later incarcerated at Walla Walla State
Penitentiary for the crime). Linden purchased
this two-story Georgian manse in 1924, 10
years after it had been erected by an eye
surgeon named **Harry Wurdemann** and just
after Linden took over as president of Puget
Sound Savings & Loan.

Wurdemann's place stood on five acres of
land at the entrance to the park, just off what
was then two-lane **Victory Way** (later rechris-
tened **Bothell Way**). The grounds were
planted with rose bushes, apple trees, and a
cherry orchard that had given the estate its
name, **Cherry Acres.** When Linden bought the
house (family records say it cost him $6,300),
he sank as much as $100,000 into ground and
building improvements. He dug a fine wading
pool in the side yard and encircled his
property with a fence made partly of white
wood latticework, partly of brick and iron. A
gate on Victory Way opened onto a driveway
that curved up to the white, pillared mansion,
then swept around to a porte cochere at the
rear. This grand entrance off Victory Way
eventually had to be locked up because
travelers continually mistook the Linden abode
for a roadhouse and would come knocking at
all hours in search of lodging. Linden and his
wife, **Esther,** decorated the house with
Oriental rugs and turned a pink, tapestry-lined
music room into a library to hold their
immense collection of books, including
Abraham Lincoln's personal Bible. After
decades of decrepitude, the Wurdemann
Mansion has been restored as the centerpiece
of a small, upscale housing community. The
mansion is now privately owned. ◆ Bothell
Way NE and NE Ballinger Way

45 Parker's A legendary North Seattle teen
hangout of the 1950s and 1960s, Parker's
has since been transformed into a more
sophisticated dinner-dance-and-music venue
for a variety of rock and pop artists. Acts range
from international legends, including **Ray
Charles,** to local country-and-western bands.
The dance floor is gigantic, and the cover
charge varies depending on the performance.
◆ Cover. Tu-Th 11AM-3PM, 5-9PM; F 11AM-
3PM, 4:30-10PM; Sa 4:30-10PM. Live music
Tu-Th 9PM-midnight; F-Sa 9:15PM-1:30AM;
Su 8PM-midnight. 17001 Aurora Ave North.
Reservations recommended. 542.9491

Froula Playground

NE 70th St.

NE 68th St.

I-5

NE 65th St.

34
35

32

NE 63rd St.

NE 62nd St.

12th Ave. NE

33
Cowen Park

36
Ravenna Park

NE 60th St.

NE 60th St.

31

Cowen Pl. NE

37

Latona Ave. NE

Ravenna Blvd. NE

NE 58th St.

27th Ave. NE

38

RAVENNA

NE 55th St.

25

Ravenna Ave.

NE 52nd St.

NE Blakeley St.

Burke-Gilman Trail

15th Ave. NE

17th Ave. NE

26

24

23

27

22

NE 50th St.

University Playfield

Latona Ave. NE

Roosevelt Wy. NE

12th Ave. NE

Brooklyn Ave. NE

21

11th Ave. NE

University Wy. NE

20th Ave. NE

25th Ave. NE

NE 47th St.

20

39

40

29

28

17

19
18

NE 45th St.

Hwy. 513

15

16

8th Ave. NE

9th Ave. NE

13

Burke Memorial Museum

Clark P

14

Stevens Wy.

NE 43rd St.

12

11

10

NE 42nd St.

5

9

8

NE 42nd St.

7

Pend Oreille Rd.

Montlake Blvd. NE

Walla Walla Rd.

NE 41st St.

6

Edmundson Pavilion

NE Campus Pkwy.

1

2

Husky Stadium

3

University of Washington

30
NE Northlake Wy.

NE 40th St.

4

Burke-Gilman Trail

NE Pacific St.

Stevens Wy.

Lake Washington Ship Canal Bridge

University Bridge

NE Boat St.

Pacific Pl. NE

Fuhrman Ave. E.

Columbia Rd.

San Juan Rd.

University of Washington Medical Center

Eastlake Ave. E.

N

Walla Walla Rd.

Portage Bay

Montlake Bridge

Waterfront Activities Center

km
mi

1/4   1/2

1/2   1

Union
Bay

University District/ Ravenna

Centered around the **University of Washington (UW)**, the University District has grown with the school, which opened its doors downtown in 1861, then relocated to this area just north of **Lake Union** in 1895. Around the beginning of the 20th century the "U District," as it's usually called, was sparsely populated, without paved streets, sewers, lights, or sidewalks. It could take half a day just to journey to downtown by streetcar (which is only what it seems to take nowadays on Seattle's clogged arterials). Residents called it "Brooklyn" back then, trusting that this neighborhood, like the more famous Brooklyn on the Atlantic, would thrive since it was adjacent to a big city.

In 1909 their faith was rewarded when Seattle located the **Alaska-Yukon-Pacific Exposition (AYP)** to the UW (pronounced "U Dub") campus. The city's first World's Fair was inspired by Portland, Oregon's 1905 **Lewis and Clark Exposition** (sibling rivalry was heated even in those days) and promoted by downtown business burghers who wished to attract East Coast attention and stimulate regional growth. University officials eagerly volunteered their land for the fair's site, hoping to reap a legacy of buildings and development for what was then a backwoods campus.

The AYP was a stunning success. It took two years to build, cost $10 million, drew 3.7 million visitors, turned a small profit ($62,676) despite the fact that liquor was banned in the district at the time, and stamped Seattle as a young city on the move. Exhibits showcased 26 countries and featured dozens of classical-style buildings set amid stately grounds laid out by the

175

Olmsted Brothers of Massachusetts, the nation's foremost landscape architecture firm and a principal player in Seattle's early planning. The AYP opened with **President William Howard Taft** pressing a golden telegraph key in Washington, DC, to switch on the fair's opening lights. (That same key would be used by **President John F. Kennedy** 53 years later to kick off the **Century 21 Exposition** in Seattle.) It lasted more than four months, drawing visitors to hundreds of industrial and educational exhibits, though one of the star attractions was actually a carnival area called the **Pay Streak.** There, visitors shelled out 5 to 25 cents to gaze at Prince Albert the Talking Horse, Philippine villagers in skimpy loincloths, simulated Civil War battles, and La Belle Zamona's belly dancers doing the hootchy-cootchy.

When the 1909 exposition was over, the neighborhood was left with sewers, water mains, and other modern amenities, while the university had been given a parklike campus and about 20 buildings. With the Olmsteds' help again, the AYP grounds were adapted to university use. In 1915 **Henry Suzzallo** took over as the university's president. In the next decade he doubled school enrollment to almost 6,000 (it's currently near 34,000),

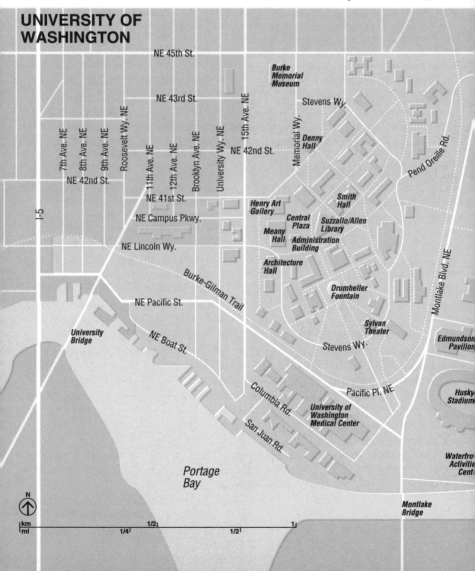

UNIVERSITY OF WASHINGTON

raised academic standards, and initiated a building program that produced dozens of spectacular Gothic buildings, most of which are still standing.

The school and its neighborhood have often been the center of controversy. In 1948 a state legislature-appointed commission held McCarthy-like hearings and scrutinized the campus for "un-American activity." In the dark days that followed, the Board of Regents dismissed three faculty members and three others were put on probation for their Communist Party associations. Then the tumultuous '60s arrived, fully engulfing the district in long hair, rock music, marijuana, and a countercultural lifestyle. Tensions ran high. In 1967 the **Black Student Union** took over part of the Administration Building. The next year, antiwar demonstrators bombed university structures. On 5 May 1970 some 10,000 people marched down Interstate 5 from the campus to downtown in protest over the deaths of four students at Kent State.

Today the University of Washington is one of the largest single-campus universities on the West Coast. Its 694-acre tract, hosting 16 schools and colleges, occupies nearly half of the neighborhood. Firmly lodged among

the top five universities nationwide for receiving annual federal grants and awards, UW has an annual budget exceeding $1 billion. A number of its component schools—including health sciences, engineering, and computer science—are ranked regularly among the nation's top 10 contenders.

The U District mirrors the school's diversity and energy. Streets are filled with bookstores, clothing shops, coffeehouses, and informal, inexpensive cafes. This area is a big reason why Seattle consistently ranks among the nation's highest in per-capita moviegoing, book purchasing, and espresso consumption. The district's spine, as well as its heart, is represented by **University Way** ("The Ave"). During the noon hour each day, more than a thousand pedestrians move through this lengthy corridor. The Ave also hosts the annual **University Street Fair**, a popular arts and crafts fest held in May, which brings long-haired hippies with necklaces for sale, street musicians, and the scent of patchouli oil back to these streets.

Colorful as it is, the U District isn't as interesting as it could be. Outside of the university campus, it's dominated by dull, modern apartment buildings. Though it is loaded with bargain-filled restaurants, few count among the city's finest. And there is a dearth of places that have good music or dancing. More seriously, the Ave is frequently besieged by panhandlers and drug dealers. Generally, however, this and other streets are safe to stroll after dark, which is a relief, because the district's flat topography invites walking.

Named for the large, lovely park that graces its center, Ravenna lies just north of the University District. It is a safe, well-tended, middle-class enclave where many UW professors and other staff members reside in 1920s and 1930s "bungaloids"—remodeled two-bedroom houses that have retained the neighborhood's original character. A decade or two ago mainly middle-aged and older people dwelt here, but many families with young children have moved in and the playgrounds are full again. As could be guessed, nightlife here is practically nonexistent, though several commendable restaurants have popped up.

1 Visitors Information Center An ideal starting point, this visitors center offers campus maps, a restaurant, lodging and bus info, and local events schedules. ♦ M-F 8AM-5PM. 4014 University Way NE. 543.9198

2 University of Washington The upper campus of the University of Washington (UW) is the classic evocation of academe: ivy-covered Gothic-style buildings grouped around formal, brick-paved quadrangles; majestic sycamores, maples, and oaks; and curved walkways leading through nicely landscaped grounds. There's no denying that this is a beautiful place to stroll (see the map of UW on the preceding page), whether you're dazzled by the architecture, the cherry trees in bloom, or the million-dollar views of **Lake Washington** and the **Cascade** peaks from the student dorms. The lower campus, marked by newer, 1950s concrete edifices, merits little attention by comparison. Today, the University of Washington keeps up a continuing enrollment of about 33,675; its most popular graduate schools are arts and sciences, engineering, medicine, law, and dentistry.

The main entrance is at the intersection of 17th Avenue NE and NE 45th Street, from which you travel along **Memorial Way** beneath a dramatic archway of sycamores to arrive on campus. At NE 41st Street, a pedestrian overpass crosses 15th Avenue NE to reach the university via **Central Plaza.** The entrance to a large parking garage (located below Central Plaza) can be found here, too. Another point of entry is on the eastern backside of campus, at 25th Street NE, about one-eighth of a mile north of **Husky Stadium.** ♦ 17th Ave NE and NE 45th St

On the University of Washington campus:

Central Plaza Commonly referred to as **Red Square** (attributable to its expanse of red bricks, not to any Bolshevik incidents), this campus crossroads was designed in 1972. The vast, almost treeless plaza is surrounded by stark, hard-surfaced buildings constructed in a mishmash arrangement of architectural styles. It's all overpowering and strikes many people as depressing and inhuman, but on sunny days this spot functions as a kind of Italian piazza, alive with students strumming guitars, throwing Frisbees, and enjoying sack lunches.

Suzzallo/Allen Library Certainly the most impressive building on campus, this ornate Tudor Gothic library was designed by **Carl Gould** and dates from about 1926. Founder of the UW architecture department, Gould laid out plans for 18 campus buildings (as well as Volunteer Park's old **Seattle Art Museum** and, with partner **Charles Bebb,** the **Times Square Building** in downtown). This library was the crowning achievement—and also the downfall—of **Henry Suzzallo,** former University president (1915-1926), who is often recalled as the UW's "modern father." Suzzallo wanted an ambitious, cathedral-like building, believing that "the library is the soul of the university." Washington **Governor Roland Hartley** didn't agree. He looked at the $900,000 invoice, dubbed it "Suzzallo's extravagance," and fired the respected educator, who went on to head the philanthropic **Carnegie Foundation.** Outside, observe three sculptures perched over the entrance: *Thought, Inspiration,* and *Mastery,* created by Tacoma artist **Allan Clark.** Inside, follow the curved staircase from the building's entrance to the mezzanine-level **Graduate Reading Room,** where vaulting and 36-foot-high stained-glass windows tower above. ♦ M-Th 7:30AM-midnight; F 7:30AM-6PM; Sa 9AM-5PM; Su noon-midnight (hours are more restricted during school breaks).

Smith Hall Twenty-eight gargoyles decorate the exterior of this 1940 building, which houses the history and geography departments. Designed by **Dudley Pratt,** a university faculty member, each gargoyle symbolizes something different. Six figures at the east entrance signify humankind's primitive needs, while those on the southeast corner depict concepts of weather. Those on the northeast corner stand for the power and war of Europe, the magic of Africa, and the knowledge of the Orient. A book-laden egghead in the grouping stands for the intelligent democracy of America. Groups on the north side depict Seattle's history.

Meany Hall Named in honor of a popular and longtime UW history professor, **Edmond S. Meany,** this performing-arts building contains a 1,200-seat theater, a 200-seat studio, and dance facilities. Excellent acoustics and intimate seating make it one of the city's premier venues for chamber music series, dance recitals, and concerts.
♦ 543.4880

Art around the Plaza The west facade of the Suzzallo Library hosts 18 terracotta figures of famous people, including Shakespeare, Beethoven, and Plato. The original design for Darwin featured a small ape thumbing its nose at the humans below, but the university president vetoed that concept. (Look closely at Darwin, and you'll see a hole at the bottom of the figure where the ape should be.) Hidden behind oak trees, the Gothic-style **Administration Building** on the south side of the plaza is ringed by 24 gargoyles and other figures, each one representing an academic discipline. The square contains *Broken Obelisk,* a two-ton, 26-foot steel work that resembles an upside-down pencil and is a rare sculpture by **Barnett Newman,** a New York painter known mostly for abstract color fields. The three campaniles that soar into the sky are visually striking but have a more quotidian purpose, as well: they are vents to disperse car exhaust fumes from the underground garage. A bronze statue of *George Washington* on the square's west side was sculpted in 1909 by **Lorado Taft** and unveiled for the AYP Expo.

Sam Spade may be San Francisco's most famous fictional private eye, but he got his start elsewhere. In Dashiell Hammett's renowned novel *The Maltese Falcon,* Spade explains that in 1927 "I was with one of the big detective agencies in Seattle."

Restaurants/Clubs: Red   **Hotels:** Blue
Shops/ 🍷 Outdoors: Green   **Sights/Culture:** Black

Henry Art Gallery This **Carl Gould-**designed museum boasts classical lines: Tudor Gothic architecture, striking decorative brickwork, and handsome skylit exhibition galleries. Opened in 1927, its construction was funded by **Horace C. Henry,** a local real estate-cum-railroad magnate, who also donated to it an art collection worth more than $400,000. The Henry blends past and present, so you might stumble upon a video exhibition just as easily as you would an exhibit of historical Western landscapes or modern Chinese painting. The permanent collection holds the 19th- and early 20th-century American and European paintings from Henry's original contribution.
♦ Donation requested. Tu-W, F-Su 10AM-5PM; Th 10AM-9PM. 543.2280

Denny Hall This turreted, châteauesque, French Renaissance structure was the first—and for some time the only—building on campus, and was built circa 1895. Given this classroom hall's original importance, its very ordinary location (with no expansive view over Lake Union) seems curious. But campus legend has it that officials argued for so long over the building's proper site that one exasperated regent finally stuck his umbrella into a fallen fir tree and said, "You fellows can put the building where you want it; I'm going to put it here." And there it's been ever since.

Thomas Burke Memorial Washington State Museum Exhibits in natural history, anthropology, and geology from Pacific Rim cultures span many epochs. High on the list of must-sees is the collection of Northwest Coast Indian artifacts. An Alaskan Arctic collection of basketry, ivory, beadwork, and masks (like the three pictured above) wins accolades. Children will enjoy dinosaur skeletons, other fossils, and totem poles. Note the stained-glass window portraying a peacock in the **Burke Room.** It's by master **Louis Comfort Tiffany** himself. The Burke museum was designed in 1962 by **James J.**

Chiarelli in honor of **Judge Thomas Burke,** an attorney who negotiated early Seattle land acquisitions for Great Northern Railroad builder **James J. Hill.** ◆ Donation requested. M-W, F-Su 10AM-5PM; Th 10AM-10PM. 543.5590

Within the Thomas Burke Memorial Washington State Museum:

The Boiserie ★★$ The Burke's basement contains the toniest and one of the most pleasant coffeehouses in Seattle. The high-ceilinged room features 18th-century French pine panels and artwork, antique wooden tables, classical music, and very tasty pastries. It's a favorite java joint for students between classes and also a resting spot for campus cops. Desserts are plentiful and delicious; the carrot cake comes from the **Broadway Baking Company.** The tree-shaded patio is ideal for lounging on warm days. ◆ Coffeehouse ◆ M-F 7AM-8PM; Sa-Su 9AM-5PM. 543.9854

Penthouse Theater Built in about 1940 as the nation's first theater intended specifically for theater-in-the-round presentations, the Penthouse provides the stage for some of the **UW School of Drama's** plays. A $3 million face-lift has left in place the original frescoes and seats. Tickets are available here at the box office or at the **UW Ticket Office** (4001 University Way NE, 543.4880), open Monday through Friday from 10:30AM to 6PM. ◆ Box office opens one hour before show time. 543.4880

Architecture Hall This is the only major structure built for the Alaska-Yukon-Pacific Expo (as a museum, originally) that is left standing. San Francisco's **John Galen Howard,** who in 1909 was campus architect for the **University of California, Berkeley,** created the eclectic Classical Style design. Today, the building houses UW's **Department of Urban Planning.**

Frosh Pond, Rainier Vista During the AYP Exposition, this body of water was a geyser basin. Afterward it became a spot where first-year students received honorary dunkings from sophomores. And today it's a decorative pool with a fountain that's especially appealing when surrounding roses are in bloom. Proud moms and dads snap Polaroids of students here. The walkway down to the **Montlake Bridge** was designed by the **Olmsted Brothers** in 1909 as a culminating viewpoint from which fairgoers could eyeball **Mount Rainier.**

Sylvan Theater The grassy glade, site of an annual UW summer Shakespeare series, is easily missed. Tucked away within a grove of trees, it contains a cool, shady amphitheater and the odd tableau of four white columns standing by themselves with nothing to support. These columns, shaped

of cedar poles, were transported—at the insistence of **Professor Edmond Meany**—from their positions at the entrance to the original downtown **Territorial University** building, when that old edifice was finally being torn down in 1908. Each of the four columns has a name—Loyalty, Industry, Faith, and Efficiency—the first letters spelling together LIFE.

Husky Stadium Football-crazed fans watch the Huskies (often called "The Dawgs" but never "Dogs") here in the Northwest's largest stadium, seating 72,500 people. The Wave was invented here in 1981 by a Husky marching-band director and a student cheerleader, **Robb Weller,** who has gone on to some TV fame since. The south section of the cantilevered steel balcony and roof was finally erected in 1987, after a calamitous construction accident. On the morning of 25 February 1987, steel support beams weakened and the entire south section crumbled into a massive pile of twisted metal. No one was hurt, but the scene was immortalized when a photographer, **John Stamets,** riding by on his bicycle, snapped a frame-by-frame account of the collapse and published it in a local newspaper.

Waterfront Activities Center Rent canoes or rowboats to cross **Union Bay** and then wander through the soft, lily-padded backwaters near the **Washington Park Arboretum** for a Monet-like experience. Audubon types might want to go north from the center, creeping along the shore to see blue herons, eagles, and other wild creatures in a protected reserve. ◆ M-F 10AM-sunset Feb-Oct. 543.9433

3 College Inn Guest House $ A renovated 25-room bed-and-breakfast, College Inn Guest House is popular with visiting professors and other university types on a small travel budget. Built as a hotel for the 1909 AYP, it is included on the **National Register of Historic Places.** Rooms are very plain, spare (no TV, no telephones) but clean and generally pleasant. Bathrooms can be found at the end of the hall. ◆ 4000 University Way NE. 633.4441.

4 The Last Exit on Brooklyn ★$ Seattle's oldest coffeehouse, the Last Exit opened in 1967 and prides itself on being part of the '60s time warp. Long hair and ragged jeans are de rigueur, bad folksingers turn up on Mondays for **Open Mike Night,** and communal tables guarantee conversations that start with "Far out." The hot apple pie à la mode is delicious, and the Last Exit takes its obligation to starving students seriously by serving six times the normal amount of peanut butter in a typical PB&J sandwich. ◆ American ◆ M-Th 7AM-midnight; F 7AM-2AM; Sa 11AM-2AM; Su 11AM-midnight. 3930 Brooklyn Ave NE. 545.9873

5 University Inn $ A recent $2.5 million addition has added a sleek touch to a small, friendly, already modern hotel (pictured above). There are 60 comfortable rooms—none with a view worth mentioning, however—and a small heated outdoor pool. ◆ 4140 Roosevelt Way NE. 632.5055; fax 547.4937

6 European Restaurant & Pastry Shop ★$ German-style food (Hungarian goulash, stuffed cabbage rolls, sausage sandwiches) is served in an Old World atmosphere. Most people, though, come here for the pastries, especially the Black Forest cherry cake. ◆ German ◆ M-Sa 7:30AM-11PM. 4108 University Way NE. 632.7893

7 Macheesmo Mouse ★$ Ideal for all the UW's body-obsessed students, this place actually serves "healthy" Mexican cuisine, along with a calorie count per dish. The meals (burritos are the safest bet, with tacos and enchiladas being acceptable) are nonfried, low fat, and low cholesterol. Unfortunately, the atmosphere is just too clean and bright for many Mexican meal aficionados. There's another Mouse on Capitol Hill. ◆ Mexican ◆ M-Th 10AM-10PM; F-Sa 10AM-9PM; Su noon-9PM. 4129 University Way NE. 633.4658. Also at: 211 Broadway East. 325.0072

8 Folk Art Gallery-La Tienda Begun in the early 1960s by an anthropology aficionado who brought back a carload of trinkets from Tijuana, this small shop has flowered into a folk art treasure trove. Gift-hunters can choose items from 80 countries: Chilean rain sticks, Guatemalan ceremonial *huipils* (woven ponchos), Balinese masks, and Indonesian shadow puppets. ◆ M-W, F-Sa 10AM-5:30PM; Th 10AM-9PM. 4138 University Way NE. 632.1796

8 Shultzy's Sausage $ The homemade sausages served here are ground and stuffed with Uncle Norm's recipe. This hole-in-the-wall won its 15 minutes of fame in 1992 when local football star **Lincoln Kennedy** set a record by eating 11 sausage sandwiches in 60 minutes. Lines form out the door for the spicy-hot Ragin' Cajun and milder Andouille choices. ◆ Sausage ◆ M-F 11AM-9PM; Sa 11AM-8PM; Su 11:30AM-7PM. 4142 University Way NE. 548.9461

9 Big Time Brewery and Alehouse ★$ This tavern-turned-brewpub offers four kinds of beer made on the premises, all flavorful, unpasteurized, and heavier than your standard-issue Bud. An 80-year-old back bar, hardwood floors, vintage signs, and a jukebox create a traditional American alehouse atmosphere. Large front windows allow for a maximum of people-watching. A small kitchen produces hefty sandwiches and very acceptable nachos. ◆ M-Th, Su 11:30AM-12:30AM; F-Sa 11:30AM-1AM. 4133 University Way NE. 545.4509

10 Magus Bookstore Unswept floors, books stacked precariously high, a guy who has a Ph.D. and speaks 11 languages working behind the counter—this is your quint-essential college used-book seller. Don't expect to find Judith Krantz among the piles of literature, philosophy, history, and art books. ◆ M-W 10AM-8PM; Th-F 10AM-10PM; Sa 11AM-6PM; Su noon-8PM. 1408 NE 42nd St. 633.1800

10 Cafe Allegro ★$ Reputed to have introduced Seattle to espresso during the 1960s and still a funkier, more traditional coffeehouse than most in Seattle (only recently did it condescend even to use the term *latte,* rather than the French equivalent *au lait*), this small, smoky, brick-lined cafe enjoys a remarkably loyal clientele. There's great coffee, ordinary pastries, and a staff that will let you curl up in a corner to read *War and Peace* in its entirety. The political graffiti in the bathrooms is not to be missed. ◆ Coffeehouse ◆ M-F 7AM-11PM; Sa 7:30AM-11PM; Su 8:30AM-11PM. 4214 University Way NE (in the alley around the corner from Magus Bookstore). 633.3030

11 Bulldog News The largest, most eclectic newsstand in the Northwest carries everything from the *New Yorker* and *National Review* to *Spy, Spin, Story,* British *Esquire, The Hockey News,* and *British Columbia Report.* Hundreds of alternative weeklies, out-of-town papers, and foreign periodicals are also on hand. Service can sometimes be indifferent to your requests. An espresso counter dispenses drinks to sidewalk patrons; watch out, the lines here can get long. ◆ Daily 8AM-11PM. 4208 University Way NE. 632.6397. Also at: 401 Broadway East. 328.2881

12 Ezell's Fried Chicken ★$ Better-than-average (some label it divine) fried chicken is served in these fast-food digs. It's said that **Oprah Winfrey** orders the chicken and the sweet-potato pie "to go" from her home in Chicago. ◆ American ◆ 4216 University Way NE. 548.1455

12 Hot Lips Pizza ★$ Try one of the exotics (clam, feta cheese, and broccoli toppings) or stick to the standard three-cheese model. Crusts are soft but hearty. ◆ Pizza ◆ M-F 11AM-9PM; Sa 11AM-8PM. 4222 University Way NE. 548.9354

13 University Book Store Banished from campus in 1925 when its location was deemed a fire hazard, the business landed here, the former site of a pool hall that was closed by state authorities to protect students from "distractions." The present store, now the largest bookstore in Seattle and one of the largest college bookstores in the nation, offers an extensive selection of general fiction, mysteries, science fiction, and travel books. The children's department is estimable, and textbooks and academic press offerings can be found in almost overwhelming proportions. There's free gift wrapping on the second floor and frequent sales of general-interest books. ◆ M-Sa 9AM-6PM; Th 9AM-9PM; Su noon-5PM. 4326 University Way NE. 634.3400. Also at: 990 102nd Ave NE, Bellevue. 646.3300

14 Toscana ★★$$ Sit down to a candlelit dinner with white tablecloths and imagine yourself in an intimate, no-name *ristorante* off the Via Veneto. The homemade pastas are light and zesty, the stuffed chicken and sautéed squid are expertly prepared, and the desserts are wonderful. ◆ Italian ◆ M, W-F 11:30AM-3PM, 5-11PM; Sa-Su 5-11PM. 1312½ NE 43rd St. 547.7679

15 Safeco Building At 23 stories in height, the tallest—and some would say the ugliest—structure in the district is corporate headquarters for an insurance company. More interesting, the company has assembled a $1 million, 600-piece collection of modern Northwest art and makes some of it public. Go into the lobby or up to the mezzanine to see rotating exhibitions of Pilchuck School glass and abstract paintings. The bronze fountain outside was created by famed local sculptor **George Tsutakawa. Naramore, Bain, Brady & Johanson** (precursors to today's **NBBJ Group**) designed the tower. ◆ M-F 8AM-4PM. 4333 Brooklyn Ave NE. 545.5000

16 Neptune Theater The most elaborate movie palace built outside of downtown when it was erected in 1921, the Neptune has seen better days. But it's one of the few repertory movie houses in town, showing popular revivals and Seattle's longest-running midnight flick, *The Rocky Horror Picture Show*. This cult classic, having run already at the Neptune for a decade and a half, plays every Saturday at midnight and draws hordes of fans dressed in character. ◆ 303 NE 45th St. 633.5545

17 Meany Tower Hotel $$ This is where the histories of Yellowstone National Park and the U District intersect. Meany architect **Robert C. Reamer** also designed those oversized mountain cabins known as the **Old Faithful Inn** and the **Canyon Hotel,** though you'd never know it to look at this 14-story Art Deco column, opened to great fanfare in 1931 as the district's first luxury hotel. The recently renovated lobby offers little of interest, and there's an almost militant use of peach tones everywhere, but Reamer (whose other credits include the **Skinner Building** and the **1411 Fourth Avenue Building** in downtown) shaped the Meany so that each of the 155 guest rooms provides a broad corner view. (Try to get one facing either south to the city or east across **Lake Washington.**) On the first floor, the **Meany Grill** (★$$) serves prime rib, steaks, and seafood in an undistinguished setting. The lounge has a big-screen TV and an oyster bar. ◆ 4507 Brooklyn Ave NE. 634.2000, 800/648.6440

18 Danken's Gourmet Ice Cream This rich, creamy ice cream is for serious junkies and gets lots of resultant publicity for owner **Dan Samson.** The Chocolate Decadence Bar, reputed to be a whopping 22-percent fat, won a nationwide contest in *People* magazine. The coffee ice cream is tops. ◆ Tu-Th, Su noon-11PM; F-Sa noon-midnight. 4507 University Way NE. 545.8596

19 New Seattle Massage A longtime district fave for relaxing, hands-on treatments, this salon offers Swedish, Shiatsu, and Sports styles. Call for an appointment. ◆ M-Sa 9AM-9PM; Su noon-9PM. 4519½ University Way NE. 632.5074

Restaurants/Clubs: Red   Hotels: Blue
Shops/ 🌳 Outdoors: Green   Sights/Culture: Black

Grounds for Celebration

Seattle "caffiends" are as fond of good coffee as the British are of tea, consuming an estimated 929,000 cups of java each day. The city's caffeine culture percolates with 200-plus licensed espresso carts and at least as many coffee bars and cafes. More than a dozen coffee roasters are headquartered here, including **Starbucks** (credited with starting the craze back in the 1970s, when it opened this area's first roasting company), and two others praised by the national media, **Torrefazione Italia** and **Caffé Mauro.** Drive-up espresso windows beckon from all over the city, and sidewalk stands are appended to everything from hardware stores to insurance companies. A local magazine, *Cafe Olé,* is dedicated to the coffee-loving life, and there's even an "espresso dentist" in Greenwood, where patients waiting to have their teeth examined can sip *caffè lattes.* Other towns have their own unifying symbols; Seattle's is the ubiquitous coffee cup.

Brewing the perfect Seattle espresso involves a certain amount of "rocket science" know-how. Technically, it can be made with any bean or roast, but residents of this city—who've become shamelessly snobbish about coffee over the last few years—favor high-quality beans, usually locally roasted. (At least 25 percent of the coffee gulped here is brewed from specialty blends, a much higher figure than the national norm.) And the espresso can't be made in diner-size volumes. A well-trained Seattle *barista* (that's Italian for espresso puller) will use impeccable technique to prepare only a cup or two at a time: water is heated and forced under pressure through finely ground (but not powdery) coffee, well tamped, in a stovetop or countertop espresso maker. The combination of water and pressure extracts the celluloids and oils that give the beverage its characteristic aroma, body, and flavor.

Just getting a cup of coffee in Seattle may demand the same sort of care. The typical connoisseur uses so many espresso variations that you have to be precise when placing an order. Fess up to any lack of knowledge; baristas are usually patient and helpful, and their assistance could mean the difference between a pleasant blend and a straight shot of sludge ending up in your cup. Note also that locals have created their own espresso-speak, names for beverages that you probably won't hear elsewhere. Among the more unusual: "Thunder Thighs" (a double-tall mocha made with whole milk and topped with extra whipped cream) and the "Yankee Dog with White Hat on a Leash" (an "Americano"—which is basically a watered-down espresso—with foam, to go). The fave, however, is still the *caffè latte,* one or more shots of espresso with steamed milk, for $2 or less. The drink has become so popular, in fact, that *Seattle Times* columnist **Jean Godden** now calls Seattle "LatteLand." Yuk.

Here are some of the best caffeine-driven hangouts where you can test your ordering prowess:

B&O Espresso is one of the city's original coffee-houses, home to the hippest crowd and some of the best desserts and espresso in Seattle. ♦ M-Th 7:30AM-noon; F-Su 7:30AM-1PM. 204 Belmont Avenue East. 322.5028

Cafe Allegro, according to the *New York Times,* was the first coffeehouse in the city to serve espresso. It is a smoky, intellectual retreat, redolent of the 1960s. The entrance is essentially in a **University District** alley. ♦ M-F 7:30AM-11PM; Sa 8AM-11PM; Su 8:30AM-11PM. 4214 University Way Northeast. 633.3030

Cafe Septième is a romantic cafe straight from Paris' Left Bank. ♦ M-F 7AM-midnight; Sa 9AM-midnight; Su 9AM-8PM. 2331 Second Avenue. 448.1506

Caffé Mauro is a pleasant corner establishment in the **Denny Regrade** district. ♦ M-F 8AM-6PM; Sa 9:30AM-5PM. 2000 Second Avenue. 728.4901

Gravity Bar will remind you of the *Star Wars* bar scene with its trendy clientele and futuristic decor. ♦ M-Th 8AM-10PM, F-Sa 8AM-11PM, Su 9AM-10PM, winter; M-Th 8AM-11PM, F-Sa 8AM-midnight, Su 9AM-11PM, summer. 415 Broadway East. 325.7186

SBC, which stands for either "Seattle's Best Coffee" or "Stewart Brothers Coffee," depending on whom you ask, operates a voyeuristic glass-house coffee bar in the middle of busy **Westlake Center** plaza. Other SBC stops can be found in **Pike Place Market** and on the **Eastside.** ♦ Daily 5AM-6PM. Fourth Avenue and Pine Street. 682.7182

Starbucks' tiny flagship store in **Pike Place Market** is where the caffeine craze was supposedly born. (More branches are scattered on both sides of **Lake Washington.**) ♦ M-Th 7:30AM-6PM; F-Sa 7:30AM-7PM; Su 8:30AM-6PM. 1912 Pike Place. 448.8762

Torrefazione Italia is a cozy **Pioneer Square** bar, where Italian artistry is an integral part of the sipping experience—from the music in the air to the charming Italian ceramic cups. ♦ M-F 7AM-5:30PM; Sa 10AM-5:30PM. 320 Occidental Avenue South. 624.5773

20 The Continental Greek Restaurant ★$ Old-timers play backgammon, the post-grad crowd sips retsina in an unhurried atmosphere, and parents of young children return time and again because owner **Demetre Lagos** works magic with unruly tots. The souvlakia sandwiches, Greek fries, and feta cheese omelets are all good. ♦ Greek ♦ Daily 7AM-11PM. 4549 University Way NE. 632.4700

20 University Bar & Grill ★$ This is a quiet location for drinking, adult conversation, and maybe even a romantic interlude or two. The menu's strength is in fettuccine dishes, but the restaurant's real raison d'être is its full bar, surprisingly a rarity in this neighborhood. Grab a front table for people-watching along the Ave or slip into the back room for privacy. Service is fast and friendly. ♦ Italian ♦ M-Sa 11:30AM-2AM; Su 9:30AM-2AM. 4553 University Way NE. 632.3275

20 University Seafood & Poultry Very fresh, high-quality gifts from the sea—Dungeness crabs, local oysters, salmon, halibut, caviar—are sold at this third-generation, family-owned business. The shop will pack and ship your fish or, if you prefer, put it in an airline-approved, odorless, leakproof carton good for 48 hours. ♦ M-F 10AM-6PM; Sa 9:30AM-5:30PM. 1317 NE 47th St. 632.3900

21 Greek Row Six blocks of stately, traditional, brick-faced fraternity and sorority houses set amid a long archway of tall, old trees will make you want to get out your college letter sweater and yell, "Sis boom bah!" Of the 31 frat houses and 18 sororities, the most interesting include the **Sigma Nu House** (built in 1926 and designed by architect **Ellsworth Storey**), showing Wrightian overtones (1616 NE 47th St); the **Alpha Tau Omega House** (completed in 1929 and designed by **Lionel Pries**), the work of a onetime teacher at the UW's Department of Architecture (1800 NE 47th St); and the **Phi Gamma Delta House** (built in 1927 and designed by **Mellor, Meigs & Howe,** with **J. Lister Holmes**), a Tudor Revival edifice (5404 17th Ave NE).

This Ivy League atmosphere was also the setting for the 1975 disappearance of **Georgann Hawkins,** an 18-year-old UW coed living at a nearby sorority house. She was among the victims of serial killer **Ted Bundy,** a good-looking, smooth-talking former UW psychology student who terrorized Seattle during the 1970s before he was caught and finally executed in Florida in 1989. Bundy confessed to more than a dozen murders in Washington, Oregon, and Utah, but detectives suspect he actually committed between three dozen and one hundred. ♦ Between NE 45th and 50th Sts, and 17th and 22nd Aves NE

22 Grand Illusion This independently owned theater regularly books daring material—experimental or political films. The screen is small and the viewing room is claustrophobic, but a blue velvet couch in the back row gets a thumbs-up for providing a great smooching spot. ♦ Box office opens a half-hour before show time. 1493 NE 50th St. 523.3935

23 Sala Thai ★★$ Consistently good Thai soups, curries, and coriander chicken are served at this unassuming restaurant. ♦ Thai ♦ M-F 11:30AM-3PM, 4:30-9PM; Sa-Su 4-9PM. 5004 University Way NE. 522.2297

24 University Heights Elementary School Established in 1902, the district's first primary school grew in the 1920s to become the largest of its kind in Seattle. Contending that major repairs were needed, the school district closed University Heights down several years back, despite widespread community protest. The wooden-framed structure, designed by **Charles Bebb** and **Leonard L. Mendel** (who together would later create the **Old Ballard Firehouse**), is now used by nonprofit organizations and community groups. ♦ 5031 University Way NE. 527.4278

25 Giggles Comedy Nite Club Stand-up comics with national credentials (including **Jerry Seinfeld, Ellen DeGeneres,** and **Pat Paulsen**) appear here. ♦ Cover. Tu-Sa 6PM-midnight. 5220 Roosevelt Way NE. Reservations recommended. 526.5653

26 University Branch Library Architects **W. Marbury Somervell** and **Joseph C. Cote** were busy in the year 1910. Not only were they putting the final touches on this building but also on two other Seattle libraries that opened that same year: the **Green Lake Public Library** and the **West Seattle Public Library.** Did Somervell and Cote find themselves overwhelmed by all this business? That could be the reason all three of these branches look eerily similar, all showing Mediterranean touches. Or perhaps virtual duplication was their intention from the get-go. There's no telling now, but in any case, this building, like its brethren, is a handsome legacy of an ambitious project. It is one of eight libraries still standing in the Seattle area that were built thanks to the largess of iron-and-steel-magnate **Andrew Carnegie.** ♦ M-Tu, Th 1-9PM; W, Sa 10AM-6PM. 5009 Roosevelt Way NE. 684.4063

27 Mamma Melina Ristorante ★★★$$
Excellent Neopolitan cuisine is served in an open, elegant room decorated with bright frescoes. The sounds of Puccini (sometimes too loud) flow through the air and Mamma herself may be in the kitchen. Reviewers rave over the lasagna, which is strewn with tiny meatballs, but you can't really go wrong with any of the dishes here. The spinach cannelloni, the veal dishes, and the appetizers all deserve stars. ♦ Italian ♦ M-Th 11:30AM-2PM, 5:30-9:30PM; F-Sa 11:30AM-2PM, 5:30-10PM. 4759 Roosevelt Way NE. 632.2271

27 Cinema Books A major find for cineasts, this specialty shop sells movie picture books, celebrity bios, screenplays, guidebooks to shows, technical and analytical treatises, and some film memorabilia (posters, stills, a hundred different Marilyn Monroe postcards). ♦ M-Sa 10AM-7PM. 4753 Roosevelt Way NE. 547.7667

27 Seven Gables Theater Once upon a time there was a single theater in Seattle that showed high-quality films. Called Seven Gables, it grew into a chain and then sold out to a California operator. But with nine theaters and 28 screens in town, Seven Gables has carried on the tradition of presenting first-rate movies in a city that shows it will support literary and non-commercial fare. Often used as a test market for independent productions, Seattle has "saved" several small films (among them *The Black Stallion, The Stunt Man,* and *Never Cry Wolf*) that Hollywood studios had written off. This theater is the chain's flagship and shows fine foreign films. Its viewing room is small, but you'll enjoy the antique-decorated lobby. ♦ 911 NE 50th St. 632.8820

28 Metro Cinemas With 10 screens, Dolby sound, and a mix of good-quality, first-run commercial and independent films, this theater is a sanctuary on a rainy afternoon. There's a soundproof room for infants. ♦ 4500 Ninth Ave NE. 633.0055

28 Stella's Trattoria ★$
There is better Italian food nearby, but this lively, bistrolike establishment is ideal for grabbing a quick bite before or after a movie at Metro Cinemas next door. Nighthawks, rejoice: one of Seattle's

rare all-night eating spots, Stella's is still hopping at 3AM. Pastas, fish, and breakfast are served after 11PM, when the full menu isn't available. This is one number in a small chain of restaurants that also includes **Trattoria Mitchelli** in Pioneer Square and **Angelina's** in West Seattle. ♦ Italian ♦ Daily 24 hours. 4500 Ninth Ave NE. 633.1100

29 Blue Moon Tavern Poet **Carolyn Kizer** once described this tav as "a grubby oasis just outside the university's one-mile-limit Sahara (the old no-drinking zone). Here, the jukebox roars, Audrey the waitress slaps down schooners of beer, and poets, pedants, painters, and other assorted wildlife make overtures to each other." She wrote that in 1956, but not much has changed. This fabled bar, supposedly frequented by the likes of **Ginsberg, Kerouac, Roethke,** and **Robbins** (the last of whom once planted a collect call to **Pablo Picasso** from the bar, and, yes, it was refused) still attracts free spirits and loosely wrapped crazies. In 1990 it was scheduled to be razed, but an 11th-hour campaign to save the bar prevailed. Sunday night, the tape deck plays only **Grateful Dead** music; Monday is **Opera Night.** ♦ Daily noon-2AM. 712 NE 45th St. No phone. (They must have ripped it out after the Robbins incident.)

30 Northlake Tavern & Pizza House ★★$
The principal wall decorations here are cartoons from the *Seattle Post-Intelligencer's* **David Horsey,** who seems to pass around his illustrations as another person might hand out business cards. (You'll see them at other restaurants he frequents, as well.) But there's nothing comic or cartoonish about the Northlake Tavern's commitment to pizza. Crusts (including a respectable whole-wheat variety) are chewy without threatening to yank out your wisdom teeth, and the kitchen help has nothing against mounding the toppings. Build your own pie from a 14-ingredient list, or just order the Italian Special (salami, Italian beef sausage, mushrooms, onions, and tomatoes). You can even order an uncooked pizza to pop in the oven later on. ♦ Pizza/Takeout ♦ M-Th, Su 11AM-11PM; F-Sa 11AM-1AM. 660 NE Northlake Way. 633.5317

Seattle was the first city in the United States to elect a woman as mayor; Bertha Knight Landes took office in 1926.

31 Salvatore Ristorante Italiano ★★★$$$
Specializing in Southern Italian cuisine, including veal you could cut with a plastic fork, Salvatore serves a varied selection of delicious pastas and features an extensive wine list with gentle prices to complement your meal. ♦ Italian ♦ M-Th 5-10PM; F-Sa 5-11PM. 6100 Roosevelt Way NE

32 Sunlight Cafe ★$ Meat eaters beware: The Sunlight serves only vegetarian meals, including soyburgers, tofu scrambles, and various stir-fry concoctions. Whole-wheat waffles, blueberry pancakes, and nutritious muffins draw healthy crowds on weekends. ♦ Vegetarian ♦ Daily 7AM-10PM. 6403 Roosevelt Way NE. 522.9060

33 Cowen Park Donated in 1907 by **Charles Cowen,** an Englishman reared in South Africa, this area was undeveloped until the city filled and flattened it with dirt from freeway construction in 1961. The result is an eight-acre patch of picnic grounds with a playfield used for softball. The park is used heavily by the neighborhood despite periodic incursions by transients. ♦ University Way NE and NE Ravenna Blvd

34 Bagel Oasis ★★$ Some of the best bagels in town are available here: big, soft, chewy, and often sold hot right out of the oven. Nosh on any of these with cream-cheese spreads and Port Chatham lox, or order them as part of a sandwich. Also served are homemade soups, salads, and filling omelets in the morning. ♦ Jewish deli ♦ M-F 7AM-6PM; Sa-Su 8AM-3PM. 2112 NE 65th St. 526.0525

THE ☙SANTA☙FE☙CAFE☙
F O O D S   O F   N E W   M E X I C O

35 The Santa Fe Cafe ★★★$ This is New Mexican cooking at its best. Blue-corn tortillas are used in many of the zingy, flavorful dishes. A longtime favorite is the artichoke ramekin appetizer, baked with green chiles and *kasseri* cheese. The *chiles rellenos* tart is outstanding. Try any of the dishes that come with the Santa Fe's green sauce. And the margaritas here have won newspaper polls as the best in the city. ♦ Southwestern ♦ M, Su 5-10PM; Tu-F 11AM-2PM, 5-10PM; Sa 11AM-10PM. 2255 NE 65th St. 524.7736. Also at: 5910 Phinney Ave North. 783.9755

36 Ravenna Park **Clarence Bagley,** a Seattle pioneer and local historian, complained in the early 20th century that this 52-acre park was "a dark, damp, dismal hole in the ground for which the city paid an outrageous price." Bagley must have been a sourpuss to cast such a poor light on this urban gem.

A creek bed once ran from **Green Lake** through this heavily wooded ravine and drained into **Lake Washington.** History buffs say the area was home to an invigorating mineral springs and a magnificent stand of trees—giant evergreens 30 to 60 feet in diameter. It so impressed a realtor named **William W. Beck,** who bought it as part of a 300-acre tract, that he named it after the parklike Italian town of Ravenna. Beck also named the largest trees after famous people—**Teddy Roosevelt** and **Robert E. Lee** among them—and charged visitors 25 cents a head to enter his sanctuary. The city coveted his land and eventually acquired it through condemnation in 1911. But it promptly destroyed much of the park's grandeur by lowering Green Lake and cutting off the creek, then constructing an underground drainage system and toppling the great trees Beck had so admired, to be sold as cordwood.

Today, the park is minus its virgin timber, but it still feels like a small piece of wilderness within city limits. It boasts two large playgrounds on either end (in Lower Ravenna Park and in Cowen Park), joined together by a natural ravine and small creek. Quiet and unsculpted, this ravine sometimes seems imbued with magic (one writer called it a hobbit's realm) as it follows **Ravenna Creek** through steeply sloped brush- and fern-covered forestland. A wide trail here provides a 20-minute walk for families and a shorter but still soothing escape for runners during the daytime. Come night, however, transients may use the park, so be cautious. ♦ Between NE 55th and 62nd Sts, Ravenna Blvd NE, and 25th Ave NE

37 Lower Ravenna Park Walking east of the main park, the ravine empties into a broad field and baseball diamond. Above it, you'll come across a small playfield, playground, and tennis courts with full sun exposure. Keep walking up the hill and wind through a series of small, serene meadows where you can picnic at tables, read in solitude, or just listen to the many songbirds. Go farther, and you'll dead-end at a larger meadow that has a covered barbecue pit area. ♦ 20th Ave NE and NE 58th St

38 Ravenna Boulevard Designed by the **Olmsted Brothers** to be part of their chain of Seattle parks linked by boulevards, this once marked the Ravenna neighborhood's northern boundary. Now, the wide, grassy, tree-lined strip is a favorite for runners. ♦ Between 25th Ave NE and Green Lake

39 Burke-Gilman Trail This beloved, 12.5-mile recreational route runs along an abandoned **Burlington Northern** railbed. More than a million people bike, jog, or walk here each year. When an out-of-town millionaire tried in the late 1980s to buy a section of trail and derail the Burke-Gilman's expansion, townsfolk raised such a ruckus that he was lucky not to have been tarred and feathered. The scenic Burke-Gilman hugs **Lake Union** and then crawls east and north, virtually through the backyards of lakefront homes, until it reaches Kenmore's **Logboom Park** at the northern tip of **Lake Washington.** One caveat: 70 percent of trail users are bicyclists, so walkers should take extra care.

40 University Village Yes, it's a shopping mall, but this one won't "mall" you to death with its stale-aired enclosure. Several large stores anchor the complex, and more than 60 independent shops sell clothes, gift items, and home furnishings. Brick walkways, a fountain, and a casual pace suited to browsing help cut back on shopper's frenzy. **Caldwell's** (522.7531) carries ethnic and decorative home accessories such as New England crafts; Mexican folk art; African pots; and wicker tables, chairs, baskets, and boxes. **VIVA** (525.8482) and **Marlee** (522.6562) are popular for their exclusive women's apparel. **Teri's Toybox** (526.7147) sells kids' playthings and games. The deli **Pasta and Co.** (523.8594) offers tempting appetizers and salads; try the marinated chicken breasts, tortellini, or Chinese vermicelli.
♦ 25th Ave NE and NE 45th St. 523.0622

C.R. Roberts
Newspaper Columnist, Tacoma's *Morning News Tribune*

The best thing about Seattle (with the exception of **Pike Place Market**) is **Tacoma,** a city that's a 45-minute drive to the south, uncurdled by tourist popularity and civic pretension.

Shirley Collins
President, Sur La Table

Botticelli Cafe on Stewart Street—for Italian sodas, espresso, and a variety of grilled sandwiches.

Fran's Chocolates on East Madison Street—chocolates (handmade) and candy bars that are divine, especially the gold bar.

DeLaurenti's Specialty Foods on First Avenue in Pike Place Market—an enormous selection of fine food products from Italy.

Pike Place Market from May to December—the heart and soul of Seattle.

Sur La Table—according to the *Atlantic* magazine, the best kitchen equipment store in the country is in Pike Place Market.

Charles R. Cross
Editor, *The Rocket*

Seattle is a city of views. Watch the sun go down from the bluffs at **Discovery Park** and you'll discover Seattle's most romantic spot and maybe see me smooching with my sweetie after we've taken a long run. Other great views can be found at the **Volunteer Park** water tower, on Queen Anne Hill's **Highland Drive,** and on **Alki Beach** in West Seattle, where you get the best view of the city itself.

People in Seattle like to hang out, so if you want to fit in here, put on a flannel shirt and a baseball cap, ride a bike somewhere, and stay put for a few hours reading the paper and drinking coffee. My favorite restaurants for eating while hanging out include the **Hi-Spot Cafe, Julia's, Spot Bagel Bakery, Panko's, Sunlight Cafe,** and **Sala Thai,** most of which are in the Wallingford district.

Less than 10 feet from my office window in downtown Seattle, the monorail whizzes by every five minutes taking riders on the trip between **Westlake Center** and **Seattle Center.** Like much in Seattle, the monorail's weirdness has just become part of my life. I do notice the **Space Needle** through my window and I still love this ultimate monument to kitsch. This is what the future was supposed to look like? And I still love to take the trip to the top, but I never have been able to afford to actually eat at the revolving restaurant, which is, legend says, outrageously overpriced.

A lot of the Seattle experience is about getting stuck, since people move as slowly as slugs here and Seattle culture these days means "slacker" culture. Everyone just likes to hang out in espresso bars and cafes all day. You can even get an espresso at McDonald's and Burger King! I prefer Seattle's original espresso houses where you'll get ambience with your *latte,* such as the **Uptown Espresso** bar on Queen Anne Boulevard, **Espresso Express** on 15th Avenue NE, and **Cafe Septième** in the Belltown district.

When I do go into downtown it's hard to pass up the many wonders of **Pike Place Market** or the funky ambience of **Belltown** with the **2-11 Billiard Club,** the **Crocodile Cafe,** and other hip haunts. And you can't live in Seattle or visit the city these days without stopping at the rock 'n' roll night spots. Check out **Pioneer Square** and **Ballard** for blues, or go to the **Howell Street** area in downtown to visit any of the cutting-edge clubs there.

Anytime you're in Seattle you'll drink enough espresso to stay up all night. That's the real secret to the grunge sound of groups such as **Nirvana, Pearl Jam,** and **Soundgarden.** They're so wired on caffeine they have to grow their hair long, wear flannel shirts, and bang their heads around to stop their brains from exploding from a *latte* overdose. Now if these bands would only drink decaf, the Seattle sound would once again mean Scandinavian folk songs!

MERCER ISLAND

Lake
Washington

Luther
Burbank
Park

N. Mercer Wy.
I-90/Sunset Hwy.

Seward
Park

Stabbert
Emerly
Park

Ellis
Park

Groveland
Park

Island
Crest
Park

Pioneer
Park

Clarke
Beach
Park

For nos. 12-45,
see pg. 192

For nos. 46-75,
see pg. 201

Lake Washington Blvd.

Street labels:

SE 22nd St.
60th Ave. SE
SE 27th St.
SE 28th St.
W. Mercer Wy.
N. Mercer Wy.
SE 22nd St.
SE 24th St.
72nd Ave. SE
SE 27th St.
SE 29th St.
SE 32nd St.
SE 34th St.
74th Ave. SE
SE 36th St.
76th Ave. SE
SE 37th St.
SE 40th St.
SE 24th St.
SE 26th St.
Island Crest Wy.
80th Ave. SE
84th Ave. SE
SE 32nd St.
SE 34th St.
88th Ave. SE
SE 36th St.
90th Pl. SE
97th Ave. SE
SE 40th St.
96th Ave. SE
92nd Ave. SE
86th Ave. SE
SE 42nd St.
90th Ave. SE
92nd Ave. SE
93rd
SE 44th St.
88th Ave. SE
91st Ave. SE
SE 47th St.
SE 48th St.
E. Mercer Wy.
SE 53rd Pl.
SE 53rd Pl.
SE 57th
80th Ave. SE
SE 58th St.
SE 61st St.
SE 62nd St.
SE 63rd St.
SE 67th St.
80th Ave. SE
82nd Ave. SE
84th Ave. SE
SE 68th St.
SE 71st St.
SE 72nd St.
92nd Ave. SE
SE 72nd Pl.
78th Ave. SE
SE 78th St.
Island Crest Wy.
SE 80th St.
W. Mercer Wy.
E. Mercer Wy.
100th Ave. SE
104th Ave. SE

N

km 1/2 1
ml 1/4 1/2

Eastside

Places separated from other places by water—Venice, Valhalla, the New World—have traditionally held a certain allure. True to form, the suburban communities nestled on the near-east side of **Lake Washington**—principally **Mercer Island**, **Bellevue**, and **Kirkland**—always have been and probably always will be somebody's dreamland, though their aloofness was long ago breached by the construction of two floating bridges from Seattle.

Pioneer **Peter Kirk** set out in the 1880s to build the "Pittsburgh of the West" on the forested slopes above **Moss Bay**, an industrial capital of belching steel- and ironworks that never materialized (although another industry, coal, took hold just east of here). Before the first bridge was built across the lake, real estate baron **James Ditty** laid out a plan in 1928 for an Eastside utopia that included blimps traveling to downtown Seattle and huge observation towers in the midst of Mercer Island; boiled clean of its utopian ideals, Ditty's vision became instead the Bellevue of today. An advertisement from the 1940s solicited interest in the Eastside from Seattleites with the slogan "15 Minutes to Your Home in the Country." It seems a cruel joke now, when even a fairly athletic slug might outpace the heavy rush-hour traffic across the lake.

But people are still trying to make something of the Eastside, something bigger than it is in the eyes of many residents of Seattle: a conspicuously consuming, status-obsessed community that swears by its BMWs. Thousands of new singles and families are drawn here by the quality of life (including the fairly safe schools) and by booming high-tech industries (computer giant **Microsoft** and cellular phone purveyor **McCaw Communications** among them). Developers are, for better or worse, changing the face of the area in an effort to accommodate growth, while preservation-minded citizens strive to save a few really old buildings on the Eastside for future generations.

Neighborhood strip malls and well-groomed suburban lawns characterize the Eastside of today. Its treasures are hidden behind bands of neon color and billowed awnings. And though the Eastside currently represents the fourth-largest urban area in Washington state, it grew up as a bedroom community for Seattleites and is still very much ruled by the automobile. Only a few enclaves, such as **Beaux Arts Village**, southwest of downtown Bellevue, have escaped the rule of the road. Founded in 1908 as a rustic artists' commune (and for a while it was a nudists' colony), this lovely residential hideaway is still woven with streets barely wide enough for two cars to pass.

The look and attitude of the Eastside varies greatly from one district to the next. Mercer Island is primarily residential, bisected at its north end by Interstate 90. It boasts only a small commercial zone and is a leisurely ride for bicyclists. Kirkland offers the finest urban strolls, with a few buildings that have been preserved from Peter Kirk's time, and Bellevue is the most citified of the three districts. With businesses set back from the street in retail and office valleys, Bellevue is the legacy of one of the Eastside's most successful dreamers, **Kemper Freeman, Sr.**, who believed businesses that provided parking in front of their buildings would flourish. A rare Bellevue exception is **Main Street** in "Old Bellevue," an area just off the downtown core that resembles compact Kirkland, with many of its shops and restaurants just a few feet off the street, and parking harder to come by.

Aside from some obvious sites in Kirkland, historic buildings are in short supply throughout the Eastside, partly because of the area's relatively recent settlement (until the 20th century it was known mostly for farms and a whaling-fleet dock on Bellevue's **Meydenbauer Bay**), and partly because the value of its first structures was not recognized in the furor of slapdash post-World War II development. Much of the architecture of the past 40 years has failed to consider the Eastside's potential; many of the structures raised here were clearly second class. But that's changing. Several award-winning multiuse projects, such as **Carillon Point** and **Bellevue Place**, have taken great steps in making huge complexes accessible to the public and compatible with the Northwest environment. And city planners hope that the buildings going up today will represent them well into posterity . . . kind of a new concept around here.

1 Calkin's Landing The name actually should be spelled *Calkins* Landing (without an apostrophe), since it's titled after **Charles Cicero Calkins,** a lawyer from Illinois who had long ago abandoned the bar to become an entrepreneur, real-estate gambler, and Mercer Island's best-remembered dreamer. Arriving in Seattle in 1887 and determined that **Lake Washington's** only isle should shed its scratchy pioneer roots to become an ordered haven from the strictures of urban existence, Calkins raised a three-story hotel just up the hill from the present-day landing. It must have been a magical sight, an architectural amalgam of American railroad station and Swiss chalet, with dormers, turrets, and chimneys punctuating its tile roof, and broad, elegant porches skirting its lower levels. The grounds boasted mazes, promenades, a huge greenhouse with 635 varieties of roses, and 25 fountains, one with a 60-foot-wide bowl. A bathhouse held 100 boats and 28 dressing rooms for bathers, as well as a complete system of Turkish baths. The **Hotel Calkins** was to be the centerpiece of a new, nonindustrial community called **East Seattle**—Puget Sound's version of Newport, Rhode Island. Hoping to start a trend, the developer built a lavish home for himself on the north tip of what is now **Luther Burbank Park.**

But misfortune put an end to Calkins' schemes. Within a few years of each other, his daughter died, his wife divorced him, and the national depression of 1893 ripped away his financing. Calkins' mansion and later his hotel burned to their foundations. The developer set out in despair for southern California, where he again tried (and failed) to make his fortune in gold mining before he died in 1948 at the age of 98. It is sad and cruel that the only thing remaining of the elegance Calkins brought to Mercer Island is a mispunctuated sign on this tiny wedge of lawn and sand, where his hotel once had a dock. ♦ South of I-90, at 60th Ave SE and SE 28th St

2 Roanoke Inn $ Bartenders are generally versed in the colorful history of Mercer Island's longest-operating business. They'll explain how this joint was a general store when it opened in 1916; how there was once a pinball machine here that would pay off in quarters; and how this used to be a popular drinking spot for city swells. Those were the good old days, back when a ferry still connected the top of Mercer Island with Seattle, before I-90 took all the Roanoke's drive-by business away and left it baby-sitting a dead-end route to a dark old pier. Present owner **Hal Reeck's** stepfather was known to pack pistols into this place and fire them at inconvenient times, blowing holes in various walls and pieces of furniture.

Today most of the action here takes place between toothpaste commercials, on a TV screen, and many of the patrons even wear ties. But much of the tavern's classic atmosphere endures. A giant fireplace rests opposite the front door, gold trophies elbowing each other for room upon its mantel. Beer paraphernalia crowds the walls—everything from little statues of wild game (courtesy of the **Olympia Brewery**) to backlit photos of bathing-suited beauties plugging Coors. There's a dingy pool room in the back, but it's too cramped for anyone to properly wield a cue. During warm months the place to be is on the tav's long front porch, swapping tall tales and watching Lake Washington capture moonbeams.

The Roanoke stocks a minuscule selection of craft beers; most pours are of Henry Weinhard, Rainier, and Strohs. Yet if you insist, there are seltzers and wine coolers available, too. Food selections run to burgers, oyster stew, and taco salads. Although taverns like this are often renowned for their chili, the Roanoke's version comes from a can and is all but inedible. Perhaps the best time to visit is on Thursdays, for the weekly spaghetti feed. ♦ M-Sa 11AM-2AM; Su noon-10PM. 1825 72nd Ave SE. 232.0800

"Seattle is a moisturizing pad disguised as a city."

Jerry Seinfeld, comedian

Restaurants/Clubs: Red
Shops/ ♣ Outdoors: Green

Hotels: Blue
Sights/Culture: Black

3 Cafe Italia ★$$ Formerly called **Subito,** this airy and cheerful trattoria offers few real surprises but generally avoids Suburban Bland Disease. Try the chianti chicken. ♦ Italian ♦ Tu-Th 11:30AM-3PM, 5-9PM; F 11:30AM-3PM, 5-10PM; Sa-Su 5-10PM. 2448 76th Ave SE. 232.9009

4 Oh Chocolate! Tempting confections (including more than a dozen varieties of truffles) are handmade on the premises. ♦ M-Th, Sa 11AM-6PM; F 11AM-7PM. 2703 76th Ave SE. 232.4974

5 Finders A tiny, crowded store, Finders is chockablock with gift ideas: toys, handmade crafts, and quilts. ♦ M-Sa 10AM-6PM. 7607 SE 27th St. 236.1110

6 Thai on Mercer $ Roast lamb and the halibut with tamarind sauce are commend-able at this consistently excellent restaurant. Sit back and enjoy the restful, inviting ambience and the well-prepared, well-presented food. ♦ Thai ♦ M-F 11:30AM-2PM, 5-10PM; Sa-Su 5-10PM. 7691 SE 27th St. 236.9990

6 The French Pastry Place This tiny, cheerful, sunny spot in the center of Mercer Island's business district is good for *lattes* and—what else?—a French pastry before or after a morning stroll or afternoon bike ride. Owners **Jean-Claude Ferré** and **LeeAnn Belarde** make all the baked goods on the premises. There are always plenty of leftover newspapers around if you don't feel like schmoozing with the regulars. Smoking is prohibited. ♦ French bakery ♦ M-Th 7AM-6:30PM; F 7AM-7PM; Sa 8AM-5PM; Su 9AM-3PM. 7695 SE 27th St. 236.1727

7 Riley's For many years, this eclectic gift shop—named in honor of its owner, **James Crosby,** a longtime Mercer Island resident—was *the* place on the island to find that special something. Crosby is now retired, but the tradition he started lives on—thanks to **Gloria Riley,** a former employee, now owner. She also operates a similar store in the **Market Square** building. The emphasis is on such thoughtful items as elegant household goods, soaps, clothing, and greeting cards. ♦ M-Sa 10AM-5:30PM. 7811 SE 27th St. 232.0833

8 Alpenland Delicatessen ★$ This well-stocked deli offers generous sandwiches and other treats for eat-in or take-out lunches and picnics. ♦ Deli ♦ M-Sa 10AM-6PM. 2707 78th Ave SE. 232.4780

9 Mercer Island Cyclery There are no bicycle rentals here (or anywhere else on the island, for that matter). But you can rent rollerblades at the Cyclery, and the staff will also sell you equipment or make competent repairs on your bike. ♦ M, W, F 10AM-7PM; Sa 10AM-6PM; Su 11AM-5PM. 2827 80th Ave SE. 232.3443

10 Island Books An excellent general bookstore, Island Books has a large stock and a friendly staff made up of genuine readers. The spacious back room is devoted to kid's lit; there's also a huge playhouse and enough toys to keep any number of small-sized nonreaders occupied. This being the Seattle area, an espresso stand—the ever-popular **Espresso Sam's**—sits just inside the bookstore door. ♦ M-W, F-Sa 10AM-6PM; Th 10AM-8PM. 3014 78th Ave SE. 232.6920

11 Pon Proem Restaurant ★$ Here you'll find a colorful, cool decor and well-prepared Thai food. Try the chicken with cashews or fresh ginger. ♦ Thai ♦ M-Th 11:30AM-3PM, 5-9:30PM; F-Sa 5-10PM; Su 5-9PM. 3039 78th Ave SE. 236.8424

12 Red Lion Hotel $$ Some say the addition of this mammoth first-class hotel to Bellevue's hospitality trade in 1982 marked the city's coming of age as a business destination. Indeed, its 353 rooms and meeting space for 1,400 people seemed superfluous only for a short time. All rooms have balconies, and executive suites come with complimentary Continental breakfast, hors d'oeuvres, and a newspaper delivered to your room. ♦ 300 112th Ave SE. 455.1300, 800/547.8010; fax 455.0466

Within the Red Lion Hotel:

Misty's ★$$$$ Tableside cooking is what's best here. Indulge in the pleasure of watching your scampi flambé, steak Diane, or Caesar salad materialize right in front of you. ♦ Northwestern/Continental ♦ M-Th 11AM-2PM, 5-9PM; F-Sa 11AM-2PM, 5-10PM; Su 10AM-2PM, 5:30-9PM. 455.1300

13 Bellevue Hilton $$ The comfortable rooms are all decorated in soft color tones, with cable TV and movies available. But it's the other amenities that win this place most of its plaudits. Three vans will haul you around at no charge within a five-mile radius, which is ample reach for Bellevue's main attractions. There's an indoor pool, sauna, and Jacuzzi when the weather's no good. And security here is fabulous; women are actually walked to their cars. Substantial savings on business and weekend stays can be had by calling ahead and asking for the **Hilton Plan.** ♦ 100 112th Ave NE. 455.3330; 800/235.4458; fax 451.2473

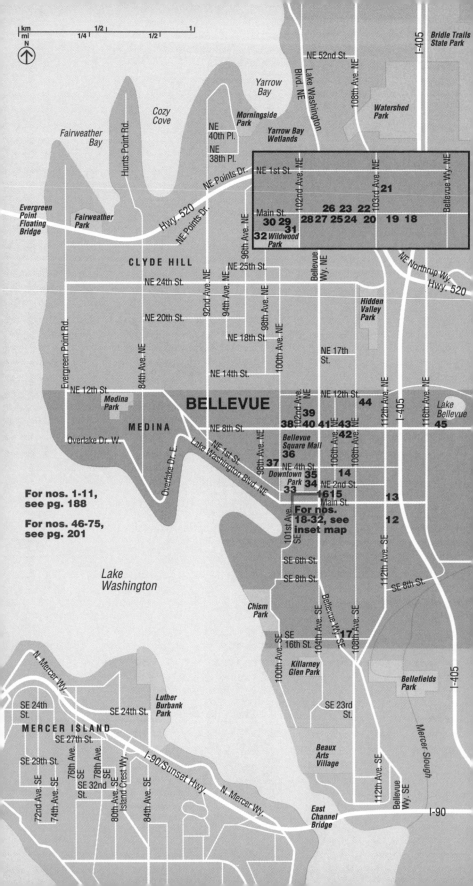

Within the Bellevue Hilton:

Sam's Bar and Grill $$ Northwestern and Continental cuisine are served in a low-key setting just across the breezeway from the hotel's front door. The chicken Dijon sautéed with onions and shallots is a good choice, as are the clam and salmon chowders. ♦ Northwestern/Continental ♦ Daily 6AM-11PM. 455.3330

14 Spazzo ★★$$ Spazzo is Italian slang for "a good time," in case you wondered. The **Schwartz Brothers,** who also own **Daniel's Broiler** and **Cucina! Cucina!,** have recently changed the name and the flavor of one of Bellevue's favorite dining spots; for years this was **Benjamin's,** the Eastside's premier penthouse restaurant. The view from the ninth floor of the **Key Bank Building** hasn't changed, but the cuisine now includes dishes from Greece, Turkey, and Northern Africa. Try the spit-roasted leg of lamb with preserved lemons and a roasted garlic and mint sauce. A *tapas* bar, purveying very affordable appetizers, stays open until 1AM. ♦ Old World Eclectic ♦ 11AM-11PM. 10655 NE Fourth St. Reservations for lunch only. 454.8255

15 Pogacha ★★$ Named for the distinctive Yugoslavian bread crust that makes pizzas served here so unusual, affordable Pogacha quickly became an Eastside favorite. The crunchy-yet-soft bread is made fresh daily and served in three dimensions: dinner-roll sized, medium size for sandwiches, and the hefty pizza-size disks that most resemble commercial Boboli crusts. The best pizza is topped with goat cheese, sun-dried tomatoes, and spinach. Owner **Helen Kranjcevich Brocard** also serves chicken and lamb dishes, and has a wine list containing about 30 selections. ♦ Pizza ♦ M 11:30AM-2:30PM; Tu-Th 11:30AM-2:30PM, 5:30-9PM; F 11:30AM-2:30PM, 5:30-10PM; Sa 5:30-10PM. 119 106th Ave NE. 455.5670

16 Rubato Records Bellevue's best-loved platter pawnshop carries 10,000 used compact discs, an expansive collection of 45s, and thousands of actual record albums. ♦ M-Sa 11AM-9PM; Su noon-5PM. 136 105th Ave NE. 455.9417

16 Giuseppe's ★$$ Like a rare plant that grows in dark, waterless clefts, this Italian restaurant and lounge thrives despite its basement strip-mall location in the shadow of a colossal hardware store. Try the veal cognac. ♦ Italian ♦ M-Sa 5-11PM. Lounge open M-Sa until 2AM. 144 105th Ave NE. 454.6868

17 Chace's Pancake Corral $ If you like a hearty stack o' cakes served with a smile at the crack of dawn, this friendly, that's-what-neighbors-are-for flapjack and coffee stop is worth the detour. It's the only place of its kind left in Bellevue. Owner **Bill Chace** quit counting birthdays at age 82 and still takes time to sit down with the customers, whether he knows them or not. A favorite here is banana pancakes with coconut syrup, but if you want to play the field, try the Joe Adams assortment. Joe was a customer who could never make up his mind whether to have buttermilk, buckwheat, potato, or strawberry pancakes, so Chace came up with this satisfying sampler. ♦ American ♦ M-W, F 5:45AM-2:30PM; Th 5:45AM-2:30PM, 5-8PM; Sa 6AM-3PM; Su 6:30AM-3PM. 1606 Bellevue Way SE. 454.8888

18 Stamp Gallery Proprietor **John Kardos,** a Hungarian transplant, has been here for 20 years. He specializes in European issues but has one of the Seattle area's largest collections of stamps from all over the world. ♦ Tu-Sa 10AM-5PM. 10335 Main St. 455.3781

19 Toy's Cafe ★$ Good Chinese food at an irresistible price has made this a neighborhood institution for decades. It's never been fancy, but the service is quick and courteous, and there's a pot of hot tea set at each table. Combos are the way to go here; sample three or four foods for not much more than each would cost separately. ♦ Chinese/Takeout ♦ Tu-Th 11:30AM-9:30PM; F 11:30AM-10PM; Sa 3:30-10PM; Su 3:30-9:30PM. 10311 Main St. 454.8815

20 Bellevue Barber Shop Nothing has changed since your dad was a kid and your grandfather brought him into a place just like this to get his ears lowered. The **Russel** family has been passing the good word and giving no-frills haircuts for 46 years. Their collection of **Bellevue High School** yearbooks, which you're welcome to peruse, predates the shop's 1926 building by two years. Opinions are plentiful and free; haircuts are $10, which includes being finished up with a straight razor. ♦ Tu-F 8AM-6PM; Sa 8AM-5PM. 10251 Main St. 455.0980

21 Azalea's Fountain Court ★★$$$$ Northwestern cuisine with French overtones flourishes in a somewhat preciously overdone space that's gaining a reputation for romantic atmosphere and good service. Fresh seafood is the chef's forté, especially the crab cakes, local mussels, and the baked salmon with an Albert sauce. Smoking is prohibited. ♦ Northwestern ♦ M-Sa 5:30-10PM. 22 103rd Ave NE. 451.0426

22 La Cocina del Puerco $ In this cafeteria-style restaurant you pay for food—hand-made tortillas and generous helpings—not for the overhead of fancy furnishings. The purely functional folding metal chairs and rickety card tables will drive the long-legged to madness. On the other hand, there are enough piñatas, posters, and other paraphernalia on the walls and ceiling to make you feel you've gotten tangled up in a Cinco de Mayo parade. Try the *chiles rellenos*. ♦ Mexican ♦ M-Sa 11:30AM-9PM; Su 1-9PM. 10246 Main St. 455.1151

23 Christmas House This year-round ornament and gift shop has expanded to include three buildings (two are in the back alley) carrying an ever-larger selection of knickknacks, bric-a-brac, baubles, bangles, and gewgaws to stuff every stocking and every space on the yule-bush. Quantity is more apparent than quality, but don't miss the traditional linden-wood carvings from the German Erzgebirge and several sizes of the hand-painted Fontanini nativity figures. ♦ M-Sa 10AM-5:30PM, Su noon-5PM Jan-Oct; M-Sa 10AM-9PM, Su noon-5PM Nov-Dec. 10230 Main St. 455.4225

24 Cuttysark
The shop's blinding assortment of brass goods salvaged from old ships can keep the nautically curious busy for a long time: coat hooks, portholes, soap dishes, lanterns, binnacles,  telegraphs, telescopes, and more. There are also thousands of non-brass items, including flags, books, paintings, charts, and ship models. The gent who launched this mainstay of Old Bellevue—a real English character—sold it in 1990, but by good fortune the new owner is a friendly man who has seen the value of keeping things largely as they were. ♦ M-F 9:30AM-5:30PM; Sa 9:30AM-5PM. 10235 Main St. 453.1265

25 Main Street Kids Book Company The very best thing you can do for your children is turn them loose in this marvelously stocked bookstore and let their magnets go to work. Even adults will be fascinated by the things illustrators are doing these days, but if not, there are books on parenting in the back. Ask the owner why his favorite book is most often **Peter Catalanotto's** *Dylan's Day Out*. ♦ M-Sa 9:30AM-5:30PM. 10217 Main Street. 455.8814

25 Dilly Dally The sign on the door—"Open til 5:30 or until the cow comes in"—typifies the spirit of this country craft store, and refers to **Lavender Blue,** a wooden cow on wheels that hangs out on the sidewalk during business hours. This mascot was ticketed for being an illegal sign, but owner **Nadine Lukoff** took her cow to court and won. Look closely; though of a predictable ilk—baskets, cards, boxes of cookies—most of Lukoff's stock can't be found anywhere else in the Northwest. ♦ M-Sa 10AM-5:30PM. 10217 Main St. 454.1518

26 Ross and Co. **Ross Bendixen** has been bending metal in this neighborhood for 25 years, specializing in custom-designed iron-and-steel furniture. His dynamic wall sculptures have become a hallmark of Old Bellevue. ♦ M-F 9AM-5PM; Sa 10AM-4PM. 10220 Main St. 455.4111

27 Fortnum's on Olde Main ★$ This place has gone through some identity crises in its time. Not long ago its decor—flying boats, mallards, and hunting dogs—betrayed the Yankee palate of then-owner **Captain Jackson Hughes.** But it has since returned to the ownership of the **Bahm** family, which owned it before Hughes. There's now a European cafe theme to the place. The menu is noticeably health oriented; fruits and vegetables dominate, though there are several good sandwiches for carnivores. Three-course prix-fixe dinners are served on Friday night, including a soup (wild mushroom, if you're lucky), a salad, and a selection of entrées that might include roast pork tenderloin with a culture-defying Oriental salsa. Floral print tablecloths and sponge-dappled walls have added some elegance to the Captain's old bucket. ♦ Continental ♦ M-Th, Sa 8:30AM-3:30PM; F 8:30AM-8:30PM. 10213 Main St. 455.2033

28 Oriental Interiors The shop specializes in rosewood furniture from China, but the building in which it's housed is equally interesting. Ostentatiously named the **City of Paris,** it was built as Bellevue's first bank, which became a casualty of the Depression as soon as it opened. The structure once housed Bellevue's first library as well as the first offices of the *Bellevue American* newspaper, now the daily *Journal American*. ♦ M-Sa 10AM-6PM; Su noon-5PM. 10203 Main St. 637.0860

29 ECCO—The Collection This particular
ECCO (others can be found in downtown and
in the U District) carries only **Liz Claiborne,**
women's sportswear known for being
comfortable, durable, and lately a shade
overpriced. The **Seattle Espresso** cart
outside on the corner is a favorite with
locals. ♦ M-Sa 10AM-6PM; Su 11AM-5PM.
10149 Main St. 453.5791. Also at: Rainier
Square. 622.4147; 2654 NE University
Village Mall. 524.6954

30 Bloomingals "Sportswear for fun" is the
slogan intended to draw women who shun
trends and want distinctive designs from
New York and San Francisco. The selection
used to be funkier but is still worth checking
out. ♦ M-Sa 10AM-6PM; Su 11AM-5PM.
10133 Main St. 451.2880

31 Old Bellevue Public Market Hidden
behind Bloomingals and the Liz Claiborne
shop is an old wood-frame house, built as a
residence by a veteran of the Civil War. The
men who later built the two shops in front of
it thoughtfully agreed to leave space between
them so the vintage house might remain
useful. It was the **Merchant's Cafe** for many
years; whalers from ships wintering in
Meydenbauer Bay boarded upstairs. Now it
operates as part of a public market, where
owner **Gene Hayes** sells mostly antiques and
crafts. An ardent historian and antique
collector, Hayes is struggling to revive
interest in some of Bellevue's oldest
buildings. Look quickly: the landlord has
development on his mind. ♦ Sa-Su 10AM-
6PM. 105 102nd Ave SE. 451.4419

32 Wildwood Park This little lawn surrounded by trees is all that's left of a park that
once reached west to what is now the
Meydenbauer Yacht Club. In the first years
of the 20th century Seattleites crossed Lake
Washington on a ferry to picnic on the grass
here, dance in a pavilion, and mess about in
boats—specifically, canoes. On big
occasions the dynamo from the ferry was
removed after the last run and used to light
the dance floor. ♦ 260 101st Ave SE

33 Bellevue Downtown Park An art history
professor at Yale University who helped
judge the park's design competition raved
about this civic effort as one of the most
significant of the century. At a total cost of
$20 million, the City of Bellevue purchased
nearly four blocks of prime downtown real
estate and set it aside (ostensibly forever) as
sacred, idle space, dedicated to daydreams
and dawdling. From the park, a proper study
can be made of downtown Bellevue's
skyscraper growth during the late 20th
century. The two blue ones most in evidence
to the east, **Security Pacific Plaza** (10620
NE Eighth Street) and **One Bellevue Center**
(411 108th Avenue NE), were built during

the '80s as bookends to anticipated heavy
development along 108th Avenue NE (alas,
the "books" themselves never materialized).
Depending on the sky, they can become
beacons of fire or disappear altogether. The
copper-toned **Koll Center** (500 108th Avenue
NE), at 27 stories Bellevue's tallest building,
incorporates multiple angles and sides on a
common center to suggest one building
exploding out of another. All three reflective
glass structures were designed by Seattle
architect **Gerald Geron.**

There are no recreational facilities here, no
programmed use of the site. What is here is
a low waterfall and a hypnotic canal crossed
by charming little bridges reminiscent of
those in Belgium or Vienna, as well as heaps
and heaps of grass. Perhaps the leveling of
two of Bellevue's oldest grade schools for
this park will prove forgivable (the
foundation of one remains as a topographic
attraction), as people take refuge not far
from the madding crowd. A stone marker
and four elms planted in 1926 in memory
of three World War I soldiers were left
undisturbed. By the way, at last check,
the city still hadn't figured out a more formal
name for this greensward. Send any and
all suggestions to city hall. ♦ 10201 NE
Fourth St

34 Games and Gizmos The back half of this
store is dedicated to role-playing games of
the Dungeons and Dragons sort, but up front
you'll find all your old favorites—tiddledy-
winks, chess, Twister. There are some
interesting cribbage and backgammon
boards, and plenty of brainteasing puzzles
for those who've mastered the Rubik's cube.
The floor is checkered black and white, of
course. ♦ M-Th 10AM-6PM; F 10AM-9PM;
Sa 10AM-7PM; Su 11AM-6PM. 211 Bellevue
Way NE. 462.1569

34 Psycho 5 Die-hard superheroes *Thor* and
Spiderman rub elbows with *Spawn, Ren and
Stimpy,* and Japanese animated creations
such as *Youngblood* in this comic-book,
video, and card shop. The owner knows his
stuff and relates to kids on their own level,
enthusing about soon-to-be-released comic
issues or a rare Steve Largent football card.
♦ M-Th 10:30AM-6:30PM; F-Sa 11AM-
7PM; Su noon-5PM. 221 Bellevue Way NE.
462.2869

Restaurants/Clubs: Red	**Hotels:** Blue
Shops/ 🌳 Outdoors: Green	**Sights/Culture:** Black

195

35 DeLaurenti's Specialty Foods A familiar name from Seattle's **Pike Place Market,** this is also one of the relative oldies in downtown Bellevue. The Italian and international food market is finally putting in a sandwich and espresso bar, so you can try its patés, salads, cheeses, meats, and fresh breads on the spot. Walk it off among the shelves of imported olives, olive oils, pastas, beans, ground semolina, basmati rice, teas, jams, and cookies. ♦ M-Sa 9AM-6PM. 317 Bellevue Way NE. 454.7155. Also at: Economy Market, Pike Place Market. 622.0141

36 Bellevue Square Mall Bellevue's quick growth from a berry patch to a major city can arguably be attributed to the efforts of **Kemper Freeman, Sr.,** who built the original Bellevue Square here at the end of World War II. His son **Kemper Freeman, Jr.,** constructed the present version in 1980, covering and filling in the spaces between anchor stores. About a third of Bellevue's retail business is conducted under this roof, which has skylights along its entire length to lend the mall below an ambience that architects **Cober-Slater** hoped would suggest a narrow European street. Fica trees planted right into the ground beneath the floor support this effect, as do the indoor clock tower (with a late 19th-century bell and movement salvaged from Mississippi's Winona County Courthouse) and the "pop out" storefronts and blade signs protruding into the mall. The usual heavyweights can be found here: **Nordstrom, J.C. Penney,** and **Bon Marché.** The **Bellevue Art Museum** is uniquely housed on the mall's third floor at the top of a glass elevator. ♦ NE Eighth St (between 100th Ave NE and Bellevue Way NE). 454.8096

Within Bellevue Square Mall:

The Nature Company You'll feel you've stepped into an expensive green rain forest when you enter this very green gallery of pricey gadgets, learning devices, and offbeat entertainments—globe puzzles; fish ties and bird shirts; books; telescopes; beeswax crayons; polished geodes; birdhouses; posters; children's science kits; tapes and CDs of bird songs, wolf talk, and ocean sounds; tea; Saturn holographs and life-size inflatable Emperor penguins. In a bind for some quartz? The Nature Company has it in four colors. ♦ M-Sa 9:30AM-9:30PM; Su 11AM-6PM. First floor. 450.0448. Also at: 2001 Western Ave. 443.1608

Kenneth Biehm Art Gallery Dalí and Matisse prints vie for wall space with limited editions by Michel Delacroix and Jiang. The leaning is toward big, busy, and bright, but the gallery has presented a collection of

small monochrome sketches and engravings by Rembrandt, two of which are part of the inventory here. ♦ M-Sa 9:30AM-9:30PM; Su 11AM-6PM. First floor. 454.0222

The Body Shop This international chain of soap and lotion shops is politically active all over the world, sponsoring such projects as an orphanage in Romania and the David Maybury Lewis public television series "Millennium." Founder **Anita Roddick** is even now beating the bushes of Third World countries for nature-friendly products that indigenous peoples can make and sell in a program called "Trade Not Aid," which has yielded several items already—paper from Nepal, acacia footsie rollers from southern India, and Brazil-nut oil from the Kayapo Indians of South America. High prices separate the dedicated from the curious, but if you don't buy here you can still register to vote. ♦ M-Sa 9:30AM-9:30PM; Su 11AM-6PM. First floor. 637.9535

Cellophane Square Anyone who knows the funky used records, tapes, and CDs store in Seattle's University District will be happy to know that the posh mall location hasn't altered the bottom line. The selection of new and used music is as good as ever. ♦ M-Sa 9:30AM-9:30PM; Su 11AM-6PM. First floor. 454.5059. Also at: 1311 NE 42nd St. 634.2280

Northwest Discovery About 70 percent of the jewelry and decorations sold here are by Northwest artists. The store is not jammed with merchandise, so vases by Bremerton glassblowers **Scott** and **Linda Curry** and wall designs by Seattle tile-maker **Paul Lewing** look a lot like they would in your home. Don't miss the Swedish door harps, and for fun, ask to see how the wine butler works. ♦ M-Sa 9:30AM-9:30PM; Su 11AM-6PM. First floor. 454.1676

Lucca's

Lucca's Pasta Bar $ An anomaly among mall-space dining choices, this small cafe somehow radiates cheerfulness. Bright, clean, judiciously decorated with tinted photographs of Venice and Rome, and staffed by a youthful crew who seem genuinely glad to see you, Lucca's is realized potential. The focaccia with a Caesar salad is actually quite good for a quickish lunch. Of course, they serve espresso. ♦ Italian ♦ M-Sa 9:30AM-9:30PM; Su 11AM-6PM. First floor. 451.2278

Restaurants/Clubs: Red	Hotels: Blue
Shops/ ♠ Outdoors: Green	**Sights/Culture:** Black

The
Bombay
Company

The Bombay Company The home of a retired English colonel could not be more stuffed with fox-hunt paintings, cricket tables, Italian leather decanters, and solid-brass lamps. Queen Anne and other reproductions are mostly of cherry or birch with mahogany finish, many adapted to pull their functional weight in today's world by housing files, VCRs, or cassette tapes. ♦ M-Sa 9:30AM-9:30PM; Su 11AM-6PM. Second floor. 455.8544

Pendleton In the 1800s the Bishop family began making wool blankets for Native Americans in Pendleton, Oregon. The wool is still cleaned, dyed, spun,

and woven at Washougal on the Columbia River, and all garments are made in America. The Chief Joseph blanket is the same pattern that has been made and sold by Pendleton since the 1920s. ♦ M-Sa 9:30AM-9:30PM; Su 11AM-6PM. Second floor. 453.9040. Also at: 1313 Fourth Ave. 682.4430

Port Chatham Smoked Seafood A handwritten note from **Julia Child** on the wall calls the salmon here the best she's ever had. Whether cold-smoked or kippered, the Alaskan king salmon and other seafoods prepared in Ballard and sold in this shop can travel with you in a box. You'll also find wild capers and caviar for sale here. ♦ M-Sa 9:30AM-9:30PM; Su 11AM-6PM. Second floor. 453.2441

Excalibur The quantity of sharp edges alone makes this shop an intrigue: kitchen cutlery by such household names as Henckel, Mundial, and Forschner; reproduction Viking and Samurai swords by Marta of Spain; Buck and Victorinox pocket and hunting knives. There are even battle-axes, just in case you've been looking for one since you first read about King Arthur and the Knights of the Round Table. ♦ M-Sa 9:30AM-9:30PM; Su 11AM-6PM. Second floor. 451.2514

Mrs. Field's Cookies Treat yourself after an afternoon's mall walking. Pick any semi-sweet chocolate variety. ♦ M-Sa 9:30AM-9:30PM; Su 11AM-6PM. Second floor. 454.1790

37 La Residence Suite Hotel $ This small, family-owned inn is undergoing an extensive face-lift in an effort to woo business travelers. Views, unfortunately, are mostly of the Bellevue Square Parking Garage, but elegant rosewood and leather furnishings, a friendly and hardworking staff, and complimentary fax service make it an attractive choice right on the edge of the Bellevue business district. Corporate rates are available. ♦ 475 100th Ave NE. 455.1475, 800/800.1993; fax 455.4692

38 Veneto's Grab a paper from the newsstand across the hall and indulge in a good espresso. ♦ Daily 6:30AM-9PM. 10116 NE Eighth St. 451.8323

38 Mr. "J" Kitchen Gourmet Everything you need to operate your kitchen—and much that you don't—is available at this **Bellevue Village** shop. Hanging baskets, skillets, and giant utensils form an almost junglelike upper canopy. Bins full of things such as citrus peelers, honey dippers, butter spreaders, and poultry lifters are constantly restocked so that no peg or shelf space is empty. An electric pepper grinder with a light (for poorly lit romantic dinners?), a crumb box with a removable trivet, a tripod-mounted solid-brass cork extractor, and a marble rolling pin can be found near more familiar Waterford crystal and Henckel cutlery. ♦ M-Sa 9:30AM-6PM; Su 11AM-5PM. 10116 NE Eighth St. 455.2270

39 University Book Store The **University District** original has been so successful that it was inevitable a branch would open on the Eastside. The selections of specialty literature, such as mysteries or science fiction, pale against those found at the older main store. But the Bellevue outlet contains two packed aisles of volumes about cooking, nutrition, and international cuisines. Browse to your heart's (and stomach's) content. ♦ M-F 10AM-9PM; Sa 10AM-6PM; Su 11AM-5PM. 990 102nd Ave NE. 646.3300. Also at: 4326 University Way NE. 634.3400

40 Starbucks Along with some of the best espresso made in the Seattle area, Starbucks sells everything for the home *latte* junkie—except the water, and there are even filters here for that. ♦ Coffeehouse ♦ M-F 6AM-9PM; Sa 7AM-8PM; Su 7:30AM-7PM. 10214 NE Eighth St. 454.0191

40 Silberman/Brown Stationers Owner **Sue Silberman** sums up the selection of new and antique pens, inkwells, and letter openers with a smile and a quip: "There's nothing in here you *need*." Items like a one-in-500 Lorenzo di Medici sterling-silver fountain pen ($1,500) make this more of a gift shop for the executive who has everything than a stationery store, so don't run in here for a package of three-ring notebook paper. ♦ M-F 10AM-5:30PM; Sa 10AM-5PM. 10220 NE Eighth St. 455.3663

41 Bellevue Place
Kemper Freeman, Jr.'s, high-rise complex was the first multiuse project of such magnitude in the Northwest. Nonetheless, as architecture it is only mediocre. The complex includes the **Seafirst Building,** the **MGM Building,** and the glass-domed **Wintergarten,** linking the towers. ♦ 10500 NE Eighth Ave. 453.5634

Within Bellevue Place:

St. Michael's Alley Named after the famous London back street where the intelligentsia and literati hung out during the 17th century, this espresso shop and bookseller, wedged into an awkward space on the first floor of the **Seafirst Building,** has captured the work force's coffee-break and last-minute-gift market. The two or three shelves of new and old book titles (perhaps 1,300 of them, total) are there mainly to whet the appetite; the owners are happy to order and gift wrap. ♦ M-Th, Sa 7AM-6PM; F 7AM-9PM. Seafirst Bldg, First floor. 453.9456

Daniel's Broiler ★★$$$$ Simultaneously chic in appearance (dark woods, onyx tabletops, etc.) and simple in many of its meal preparations, Daniel's is an ideal location for impressing people. Its 21st-floor setting in the **Seafirst Building** provides Bellevue's best dining views. A specialty is the "veal Daniel's"—tenderloin sautéed with wild mushrooms, olives, garlic, herbs, and stock. And twice (in 1987 and 1990) Daniel's has served the best bowl in the **Puget Sound Chowder Off.**

Live piano music is offered Tuesday through Saturday nights, with a jazz trio playing here on Sundays and a jazz guitarist on the deck Monday nights. The stylish bar is frequented by designer-suited men and women who might have done a lot of deep-breathing exercises to squeeze into their outfits. ♦ American ♦ M-Th 11:30AM-2PM, 5:30-10PM; F 11:30AM-2PM, 5:30-11PM; Sa 5:30-11PM; Su 5-10PM. Bar open M-Th 11:30AM-midnight; F 11:30AM-1:30AM; Sa 5PM-1:30AM; Su 5-11PM. Seafirst Bldg, 21st floor. 462.4662

Cucina! Cucina! ★★$$ Bicycles hanging at odd angles from the ceiling reflect the spirit of the after-work crowd that keeps this Italian hot spot going. As an appetizer, try the focaccia bread. If you're staying for dinner your choices range from pizzas and pastas to seafood, soups, salads, and more. The veal scaloppine sautéed with fresh sage, prosciutto, pine nuts, and garlic is a specialty. ♦ Italian ♦ M-Th 11:30AM-11PM; F-Sa 11:30AM-midnight; Su 11:30AM-10PM. Bar open daily until 1AM. MGM Bldg. First floor. 637.1177. Also at: 901 Fairview Ave North. 447.2782

41 Hyatt Regency at Bellevue Place $$$ The 382 rooms here are the most centrally located in Bellevue. Appointments are classy without being suburban ostentatious. Best choices are those rooms located high up on the south side (the hotel claims 24 stories). On the uppermost floors (the 23rd and 24th), the Regency Club is a "hotel within a hotel"—exclusive service and without argument the most spectacular views on the Eastside. ♦ 900 Bellevue Way NE. 462.1234, 800/233.1234; fax 451.3017

Within the Hyatt Regency at Bellevue Place:

Eques ★★$$$ Northwestern cuisine—especially seafood—finds an elegant venue among paintings and stone sculptures celebrating the noblest of creatures. The natural wood of the Hyatt's first floor and private alcoves make this a great place to relax. The braided baby coho salmon and petrale sole in a pesto hollandaise is sure to please. Service, however, is often less than exemplary. ♦ Northwestern ♦ Daily 6:30AM-3PM; 5:30-10:30PM. 451.3012

42 Tower Books The fire marshal must make special dispensation for this book-jammed store that's an even better resource for bibliophiles than Tower's other location on Lower Queen Anne. Especially generous are the mystery and science fiction sections. ♦ Daily 9AM-midnight. 10635 NE Eighth St. 451.1110. Also at: 20 Mercer St. 283.6333

Thinker TOYS

43 Thinker Toys A large, imaginatively decorated shop chock-full with toys, games, and puzzles designed not only to entertain children but to challenge them. Besides the popular construction sets by Lego, Brio, Erector, and Playmobile, you'll find fingerprint kits, world-map placemats, and chemistry sets. There are also plenty of squirt guns and bouncing rubber balls. ♦ M-F 10AM-9PM; Sa 10AM-6PM; Su noon-5PM. 10680 NE Eighth St. 453.0051

MUSEUM of DOLL ART

44 Rosalie Whyel Museum of Doll Art This Victorian-style museum was built slightly oversized to make visitors feel a little . . . well, doll-like. The exhibits contain all original antiques and collectibles from Whyel's collection, not reproductions. There's everything from ivory Eskimo dolls to "Mix and Match" Barbie gift sets. ♦ Admission; children 4 and under free when accompanied by a paying adult; annual passes and memberships available. M-W, F-Sa 10AM-5PM; Th 10AM-8PM; Su 1-5PM. 1116 108th Ave NE. 455.1116

45 The Pumphouse In a car-oriented place such as the Eastside, the qualification "neighborhood joint" should have more to do with camaraderie and familiarity than convenient location. Aggressively non-glitzy, the Pumphouse tavern is the closest thing Bellevue has to "Cheers." Burgers are large and juicy (order the bacon-and-cheese version), and potato skins are stuffed with green onions, melted cheese, and sour cream. ♦ M-F 7AM-midnight; Sa 10AM-midnight. 11802 NE Eighth St. 455.4110

46 Carillon Point The six bells (carillons) mounted on columns in the center of this office and hotel complex were forged in France and chime every half hour, lending the atmosphere of a European plaza on a small scale. The public dock, ample parking, and waterfront paths make the place accessible by boat, car, and foot, and the low-rise mixed-use buildings do not contend with the wooded hillside to the east. This bulge in the shoreline started out as the **Lake Washington Shipyards** and later became the training grounds for the **Seattle Seahawks** football team; the new buildings are occupied by the world headquarters of such firms as **McCaw Cellular Communications** and **Univar,** and the street level includes a healthy handful of retail shops and restaurants, including the inevitable **Starbucks.** Lots of parking is available, mostly underground. ♦ Off Lake Washington Blvd (near 102nd Ave NE, South of Houghton Beach Park). 889.2477

At Carillon Point:

Toppers Specializing in English floral design, Toppers uses as a base such Northwest natives as salal and huckleberry, importing flowers from all over the world to go with them. The florist shop doubles as an art gallery, presenting glassworks ranging from a $12 vase to a $1,200 **Dale Chihuly** sculpture. ♦ M-Sa 9AM-5PM; irregularly extended summer hours. 1260 Carillon Point. 889.9311

Hannigan/Adams Frank Hannigan is not only a goldsmith but a designer who lives and breathes his art. Though an avowed constructivist, he will make whatever you can dream up. Partner **Beth Adams'** more organic, sculpted pieces complement Hannigan's Bauhaus designs, and if you like the classic Tiffany's look, they can do that, too. You won't find any couches, coffee tables, or catalogues here—everything is made in the tiny workshop. The prices are realistic. ♦ M-Sa 11AM-6PM. 1230 Carillon Point. 889.9450

Yarrow Bay Grill and Beach Cafe ★$$$ One small staff and kitchen create sophisticated dishes for both the restaurant upstairs and the lower outdoor deck, where yups chill after work. The Alaskan king salmon steamed in saki and ginger and topped with a shiitake-pickled-ginger butter is a good choice in the Grill. If you're tired of fish, this is also a good opportunity to get your teeth into a 12-ounce New York steak topped with a green-peppercorn brandy sauce. Downstairs in the Beach Cafe, order a gin-and-tonic, one of the appetizerlike meals (ravioli stuffed with three cheeses is a good choice, as is the zesty bowl of Cajun popcorn shrimp), and sit back comfortably on the deck to watch the sun set upon Seattle. Only when you can no longer see through your fashionable dark glasses are you allowed to remove them. ♦ Seafood/Italian ♦ Grill M-F 11:30AM-2:30PM, 5:30-10PM; Sa-Su 5:30-10PM. Cafe M-Th, Su 11AM-10PM; F-Sa 11AM-11PM. Reservations recommended for the Grill. 889.9052

Woodmark Hotel $$ A bright atrium flanked by a curved staircase and filled with piano music welcomes you to the only hotel on the shores of Lake Washington. All 100 rooms and suites have TVs and VCRs, and most boast balconies with views westward. Guests with a business agenda will appreciate boardrooms with marble tabletops and leather swivel chairs, and banquet rooms to accommodate 250 people. For the insomniac with an appetite, a "Raid the Pantry" program offers complimentary late-night snacks. If you really want to impress yourself, stay in the **Woodmark Suite,** a 1,456-square-foot apartment with two balconies and a fireplace enjoyed by the likes of **Paul McCartney, Arnold Palmer,** and **Harry Connick, Jr.** Expensive but satisfying meals are available at the **Carillon Room** (★$$$$), where the salmon fillet comes with some of the best crab cakes to be found in these parts. ◆ 1200 Carillon Point. 822.3700, 800/822.3700

47 **Marsh Estate** Well-imbedded in the high-ticket residential park called **Marsh Commons** sits an elegant 1929 Tudor-style home (illustrated below) that is anything but common. It was erected by one **Louis Schuster Marsh,** born in Wisconsin in 1892 to a harness maker and carpenter who moved his family to the Seattle area in 1904. In later years Louis Marsh studied engineering at the University of Washington, taking time out only to care for his mother, who had been stricken with tuberculosis and had to be kept in a quarantine tent next to their home. After she died in 1916 (her ashes are buried in a rose garden behind Marsh Mansion), he went to work for **William Boeing's** airplane company, becoming that outfit's chief metallurgist.

"It was due to him that Boeing started manufacturing all-metal fuselages," says Boeing archivist **Marilyn Phipps.** But it was due to Boeing stock that Louis Marsh made a small fortune. So just over 10 years after joining the company, Marsh commissioned the Seattle architectural firm of **Edwin J. Ivey,** known for creating expensive abodes

in the Highlands neighborhood north of Seattle, to build his family a home reflecting his success. It's been said that much if not most of the design work was done by Ivey's partner at the time, **Elizabeth Ayer,** the first woman graduate of UW's architecture program and the first female architect licensed in Washington state. The finished estate included a series of waterfalls, tremendous hand-carved beams in the living and dining rooms, a darkroom in the basement, a pistol range, and an extensive wine cellar. A weathervane on the rooftop features the likeness of Marsh, an avid golfer, dressed in his sporting knickers.

Although the mansion is most interesting for its architectural attributes, its owners have recently instituted a schedule of small public tea services. ◆ Tea seatings Tu-F 11:30AM, 12:30PM, 1:30PM, 2:30PM. 6604 Lake Washington Blvd NE, across from Marsh Park. Reservations recommended. 827.7773

48 **Shamiana** ★★★$$ The weekend after *Seattle Times* columnist **John Hinterberger** named Shamiana one of his 10 best restaurants in the Seattle area, the place was packed and actually ran short of food. (Even now, it's best to come on week-nights, when the crowds are smaller.) Shamiana serves a westernized derivation of traditional Indian fare, mixing in Northwest ingredients and toning down spices somewhat for tender American palates. Still, the results are pleasing and safe for diners searching for a slightly exotic gustatory experience. The lunchtime buffet provides a sampling of many dishes, including cardamom-flavored lamb curry; meltingly tender velvet butter chicken, cumin-scented, in a tomato and cream sauce; potatoes studded with crushed peanuts; and a smooth *dal* of pureed lentils.

Marsh Estate

COURTESY OF THE KIRKLAND HERITAGE SOCIETY

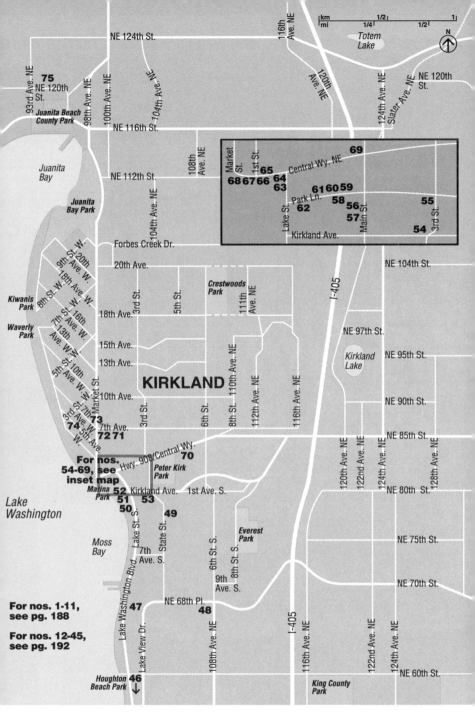

At dinner, try the intensely flavored pork Vindaloo, marinated in vinegar, ginger, and chili. By the way, the restaurant's moniker is borrowed from the name used for the colorful tents that hang bannerlike from Shamiana's ceiling. ♦ Indian ♦ M-Th 11AM-2:30PM, 5-9:30PM; F 11AM-2:30PM, 5-10PM; Sa 5-10PM; Su 5-9:30PM. 10724 NE 68th St. Reservations for 6 or more only. 827.4902

Microsoft Corporation chairman Bill Gates, who lives on the east side of Lake Washington, may be one of the wealthiest people in America (with a net worth, based on his stock holdings, of at least $7 billion), but he's not the only one enriched by his Seattle-area company. According to one Wall Street research firm, some 2,200 Microsoft employees—almost one in five—are millionaires.

Green's Funeral Home

COURTESY OF KIRKLAND HERITAGE SOCIETY

49 Green's Funeral Home Clark Nettleton, once the publisher of the *Seattle Post-Intelligencer,* built this Southern colonial home (pictured above) as a residence in 1914. It became a funeral home in 1931, and has been in the Green family since 1936. ♦ 400 State St

50 Third Floor Fish Cafe ★★$$$ Just yards from Anthony's is this classy upbeat upstart, with dangling fish mobiles to make you feel at home. The views are as good as any on Moss Bay, and thoughtful entrées such as grilled sea scallops with cider butter, apple-onion relish, and walnuts are complemented by some of the best appetizers and desserts around. Service here is consistently efficient. **Kathy Casey,** the wunderkind who made her reputation originally at **Fuller's** restaurant in downtown, created this cafe's concept. ♦ Seafood ♦ M-F 11:30AM-10PM; Sa 5-10PM. 205 Lake St. Reservations recommended. 822.3553

50 Anthony's Homeport ★★$$$ Some people come here for the sunset view over Lake Washington, but even if this first of many Anthony's branches were located in an underground parking garage it would be worth a visit just for the sautéed scallops, grilled salmon, and oysters. Try the pear crisp for dessert. For views, the next-best Anthony's choice is on Shilshole Bay, in Ballard. ♦ Seafood ♦ M-Th 4:30-10PM; F-Sa 4:30-11PM; Su 9AM-2PM, 3:30-10PM. Moss Bay Marina, Lake St South. Reservations recommended. 822.0225. Also at: 6135 Seaview Ave NW. 783.0780; Des Moines Marina, Des Moines. 824.1947; Edmonds Marina, Edmonds. 771.4400; Homeport Marina, Kirkland. 822.0225

51 Gunnar Nordstrom Gallery Contemporary original prints and paintings by international and local abstract expressionists are found at this gallery. Featured are **Robert Motherwell's** works, **James Rizzi's** 3-D paper constructions, and prints by **Toko Shinoda,** the 80-year-old grande dame of Japanese abstract expressionism. ♦ Tu-Su 11AM-6PM; some special summer hours. 127 Lake St South. 827.2822

52 Davinci's Flying Pizza and Pasta ★$ By day the bar is a quiet sports pub and the restaurant's garage-door front is opened to create a relaxing sidewalk cafe. But at night, the dance floor becomes a quasar of Kirkland nightlife, where the Eastside's young and vapid come to fluoresce. Mannequin parts spin from the ceiling among neon planets. Inventive poultry and seafood pizzas are available in the bar, but if you're really hungry try the restaurant, where the pasta is a savory alternative. The Straw and Hay—fettuccine tossed with ham and peas sautéed in garlic cream sauce—is particularly good. ♦ M-Th, Su 11:30AM-10PM; F-Sa 11:30AM-1AM. Bar open M-F 4PM-2AM; Sa-Su noon-2AM. 89 Kirkland Ave. 889.9000

52 Kirkland Clock Captain **John Anderson,** who ran ferries and steamboats on Lake Washington for more than 40 years, gave this handsome pedestaled timepiece to the City of Kirkland in 1935. ♦ Lake St South and Kirkland Ave

Restaurants/Clubs: Red   **Hotels:** Blue
Shops/ 🌳 Outdoors: Green   **Sights/Culture:** Black

**53 Danish-Swedish
Antiques** The country
furniture carried here is
mostly unpainted pine
and turn-of-the-century
antiques imported from
Sweden and Denmark by
Scandinavian owners **Ib**
and **Alaina Knoblauch.**
Here and there among
the many armoires—
increasingly popular as
entertainment centers—

are china cabinets, washstands with marble
tops, some porcelain accessories, and a few
Mora clocks with hand-painted faces. ♦ M-F
10AM-6PM; Sa 10AM-5PM; Su noon-5PM.
207 Kirkland Ave. 822.7899

53 Charing Cross The proprietors have done a
good job of infusing their inventory of
imported European gifts, mostly from
England, with personality and a kind of warm
elegance that is repeated in their treatment of
every visitor to the shop. What you buy in
here will likely be in the family for a while.
Though there are many new gifts, the
highlights are some centuries-old sterling-
silver saltcellars, antique mourning pins, a set
of crystal knife rests, old bookplates and
music sheets, and a collection of very small
clocks. ♦ M-F 10AM-6PM; Sa 10AM-5PM;
Su noon-5PM. 211 Kirkland Ave. 827.1385

54 Avoir Gallery One of Kirkland's first art
galleries and certainly its narrowest, the Avoir
is squeezed into a sliver of an old downtown
building (shown above). **Scott Fitzgerald,**
who bought the concern in 1992 from original
owners **Betty** and **Diane Charouhas,** has
continued their program of traditional,
contemporary, and three-dimensional works
by established local artists such as **Take
Hama** and **Marilyn Schultzky.** He has,
however, added a museum-quality framing
service. ♦ Tu-F 10AM-8PM; Sa 11AM-5PM;
Su noon-5PM. 216 Kirkland Ave. 827.8349

55 Old Heritage Place Seventy-two dealers
are represented under this one roof, each
occupying a small space jammed with relics
from yesteryear. The rub is that the dealers
are not present, so there's no one to answer
your questions about the old banjo or
bookshelf or set of fine china that catches

your eye. You're on your own—great if you
know just what you're looking for and don't
like sales pressure. ♦ M-Sa 10AM-5:30PM;
Su 11AM-5PM. 151 Third St. 828.4993

56 Renaissance Proprietor **Christine White**
has searched the world over for remarkable
yet affordable wines. A 1990 Caliterra
Cabernet Sauvignon, for example, from the
Maipo Valley in the Chilean Andes, goes for
less than $7. Tenute Marchese, a Chianti
Classico Reserva by the famous Antinori
family of Tuscany, can be had for less than
$25. White believes that exploring the world
of wine, for the beginner and the connoisseur
alike, should be fun rather than intimidating.
The only airs put on here are the smells of
European-style breads delivered still warm
from Seattle's **Grand Central Bakery** in
Pioneer Square. ♦ Tu-F 11AM-7PM; Sa
11AM-6PM. 117 Main St. 822.7678

57 Coyote Coffee Company $ Technically,
this is a retail store, not a restaurant, which is
why there are only three tables inside. Coyote
Coffee Company sells Michaelo's coffee, a
full-flavored espresso that doesn't leave a
bitter aftertaste. But there are also a few
sandwiches, salads, and desserts. Try the
zufolo—ambitiously seasoned Italian bread
with provolone cheese, salami, tomato, green
pepper, onion, and sweet basil—served, if
you're lucky enough to come on the right
day, with a delicious tabbouleh. Leave room
for the hazelnut chocolate mousse. The
shop's extra space is given over to pottery,
masks, paintings, prints, and basketry by
local artists. ♦ Coffeehouse ♦ M-F 6AM-8PM;
Sa 8AM-8PM. 111 Main St. 827.2507

58 Parklane Gallery Of the 13 shops on
Kirkland's regular **Gallery Walk** circuit (held
on the second Thursday night of every other
month), only this one is a co-op, owned and
operated by the artists represented. Among
the regular painting selections are **Loreita
Richards'** depictions of Native Americans and
some powerful Vietnam images by **Norm
Bergsma.** ♦ Tu-Th 11AM-7PM; F-Sa
11AM-9PM; Su noon-5PM. 145 Park Lane.
827.1462

59 The Norsemen This Scandinavian gift shop is loaded with things like baby bibs that say "Li'l Norsk" and wooden plaques declaring "It's a Blessing To Be Finnish." What the store lacks in class is perhaps made up for in variety. Sweatshirts, books, crackers, shelves of dolls and Swedish crystal, and even open-faced sandwiches are all for sale. It's the kind of place you'd need if you were throwing a party for Scandinavians. ♦ M-F 10AM-6PM; Sa 10AM-5PM. 140 Park Lane. 822.8715

60 Moss Bay Gallery Traditional Northwest and Southwest paintings by a variety of artists are featured. New owner **Rod Ingham** plans to handle more maritime art and has, accordingly, secured Kirkland's exclusive dealership of Alaskan marine artist **Rie Muñoz.** ♦ M-Th 10AM-6PM; F 10AM-7PM; Sa 10AM-5PM; Su noon-5PM. 128-A Park Lane. 822.3630

61 Ristorante Paradiso ★★$$ Sardinian **Fabrizio Loi's** Mediterranean cafe has a terrific location on Kirkland's most charming street, and in good weather several tables materialize on the sidewalk outside. Inside or out, the cioppino—mussels, scallops, shrimp, clams, and the fish of the day served in a marinara sauce with homemade croutons—is a mouth-engaging specialty, as is the *vitello scampi,* veal pounded thin and wrapped around tender sage shrimp with butter, garlic, and a white-wine-and-lemon sauce. The wonderful, soft bread is made fresh at least twice a day. ♦ Mediterranean ♦ M-Sa 11AM-2:30PM; Su 5-10:30PM. 120 Park Lane. 889.8601

61 Cass Contemporary Art A large, museumlike space offers a contemplative atmosphere in which every painting in the gallery shares the viewer's consciousness. **Keith Haring's** jittery stencil figures frolic next to abstracts by **Jasper Johns, Claes Oldenburg,** and **Andy Warhol.** Too many of these are untitled, for obvious reasons, but there are some real rippers, like *Colossal Flashlight in Place of Hoover Dam.* ♦ M-Sa 10AM-7PM; Su noon-6PM. 120 Park Lane. 889.8899

62 Wood 'n' You Some of the artists represented in this gallery—**Steve Hanks, Bev Doolittle,** and their imitators—can be found in others galleries nearby. **Ken Ledbetter's** elegant handcrafted picture frames of teak, koa, purple heart, and other exotic hardwoods cannot. ♦ M-Th 10AM-6PM; F 10AM-9PM; Sa 10AM-5PM; Su noon-5PM. 107 Park Lane. 827.6835

63 Alfi News This is the kind of newsstand and used-books outlet the Eastside needs desperately. It's a little disorganized, but that goes well with the rumpled atmosphere that makes so many bookworms feel at home. In a show of literati pride, the poetry journals are displayed up front, while the gun mags are nearly entombed beneath a stairwell. Complimentary espresso is served with $10 purchase. ♦ M-Th 9AM-10PM; F-Sa 9AM-11PM; Su 9AM-9PM. 113 Lake St South. 827.6486

64 Triple J Cafe $ Unless you can dislocate your lower jaw, you'll have trouble getting your mouth around one of the huge sandwiches at this tiny lunch joint owned by brothers **Jim, Jeff,** and **Jason Harnasch.** Split the meat loaf, the veggie, or the turkey and cranberry with a friend. Or enjoy an espresso and homemade muffins while you ponder the local artists' paintings featured on the walls. Believe it or not, this space has been a restaurant of one type or another since 1953. ♦ American ♦ M-F 6AM-3:30PM; Sa-Su 8AM-3:30PM. 101 Central Way NE. 822.7319

65 Ballard Furniture You may find it hard to accept that none of the pieces here is an antique. Twice as deep as it looks from the sidewalk, this second venture of a successful Seattle store is packed with reproductions and antique-looking originals. You'll see the distinctive hand-painted corners of the venerable Hitchcock line, as well as some of Lexington's hard-to-find solid cherry pieces. The earth-friendly accessories are by **Robert Beauchamp,** who uses only fallen trees for his ducks and other woodcrafts. Ask to sit in the Amish rocker made of steamed hickory boughs. ♦ M-W, F-Sa 10AM-6PM; Th 10AM-8PM; Su noon-5PM. 108 Central Way NE. 827.3331

66 Kirkland Roaster and Ale House ★$$ This dazzling place has lots of glass and brass and a nine-foot-high vertical spit. Roasted meats, including lamb and ham, are the specialty here, though the Roaster also serves a hearty bowl of clam chowder. And there are 19 draught beers on tap. It's generally crowded and noisy on Friday and Saturday nights. ♦ American ♦ Daily 11:30AM-10PM. 111 Central Way NE. 827.4400

67 Hale's Ales Brewery In the past decade, the Northwest has seen the rise of a strong microbrewery craft, including this distinctive Eastside business. Hale's doesn't officially give tours, being a small operation in a tight space, but staffers have been known to let the odd passerby in for a closer look when time allows. If the brewery is hopping, go next door to the Kirkland Roaster and Ale House, where six of their ales are on tap. ♦ 109 Central Way NE. 827.4359

68 Trickle Down—A Yuppie Pawn Shop
This new business is based on the realization that while young urban professionals may have it all, they may also be willing to hock a lot of it for cash on hand. The result is a store full of high-end used goods such as computers, espresso machines, radar equipment, sailboards, and riding lawn mowers, as well as the usual watches and cameras. Unlike a lot of urban pawnshops, this is a safe place to browse. It doesn't buy weapons. ♦ M-Sa 9:30AM-5:30PM. 107 Central Way NE. 827.9438

69 Cousins ★$ Plenty of natural light shows off the high ceilings and Art Deco interior of this family-run deli. The blintzes are great for breakfast, served in homemade crêpes. For lunch, try their cheese-steak sandwich, roast beef simmered in au jus, topped with onions, mushrooms, bell peppers, and melted Swiss, and served on a long French roll. The matzo-ball soup also comes highly recommended. ♦ European deli ♦ M-F 7AM-3PM; Sa-Su 7AM-2:30PM. 140 Central Way NE. 822.1076

70 Parkplace Unlike **Bellevue Square,** which does a third of Bellevue's retail business, the blissfully uncovered retail center does not monopolize Kirkland shopping but figures more as a larger sibling in a family of generally creative and accessible shops. Built in 1982, Parkplace stood with nearly 80 percent of its retail space empty for three years, when a face-lift and new property managers boosted business. Now all 150,000 square feet are leased. The complex also includes a five-story office tower with a clock on the top. Nestled among the 45 shops and restaurants here are the **Parkplace Theater** (with six screens), a health club, and, needless to say, a **Starbucks** coffee shop. ♦ 401 Park Pl

Within Parkplace:

The Wallflower The new owners are replacing the country stock with a rich Victorian inventory, but rural craft is still represented by elaborate arrangements of flowers on antique wood-frame windows. A good place to find unusual gifts, The Wallflower specializes in laces and linens. ♦ M-F 10AM-8PM; Sa 10AM-6PM; Su 11AM-5PM. 827.5337

Restaurants/Clubs: Red   Hotels: Blue
Shops/ 🌳 Outdoors: Green   **Sights/Culture:** Black

Pinocchio's Toys Stuffed with puzzles, games, things that snap together, things that come apart, and things that just sit there waiting for parents to trip over them, this toy shop looks like a kid's dream closet. In the midst of all this are some noteworthy collectibles, including hand-painted Russian *matruschkas* (stacking dolls) and airbrushed, limited-edition nutcrackers. The owners quit this business once but couldn't stay away for long. ♦ M-Th 10AM-8PM; F 10AM-9:30PM; Sa 10AM-6PM; Su 11AM-5PM. 827.1100

City Thai ★$ This is a small, quiet, and surprisingly elegant restaurant where owner **Joe Suwanvichit** takes much care with the presentation of food. For beginners, the *phad thai* makes a great introduction to an often daunting cuisine. Also tasty are the City Thai Chicken and the City Thai Beef, the latter cooked with carrots, potatoes, and roasted peanuts and served in a spicy curry with coconut milk. Cooks will be happy to turn down the temperature in any of their hot dishes. ♦ Thai ♦ M-Sa 11AM-10PM; Su 4PM-9PM. 827.2875

COURTESY OF THE KIRKLAND HERITAGE SOCIETY

71 Dr. Trueblood/Creger Home In 1907 this slender wood-frame house (pictured above) was bought by Kirkland's first physician, **Dr. Barclay Trueblood.** The now-quiet street in front of the house led out to the mill site on **Rose Hill** and was once the busiest avenue in Kirkland. ♦ 127 Seventh Ave West

Peter Kirk Building

COURTESY OF THE KIRKLAND HERITAGE SOCIETY

72 Peter Kirk Building Kirk's dream for a commercial community began to materialize with the construction of this handsome 1891 brick edifice (illustrated above), one of the first built by the **Kirkland Land and Improvement Company.** Their offices occupied the second floor above a large mercantile and drugstore. Refurbished by the **Creative Arts League,** it now houses the **Kirkland Arts Center,** which holds classes and presents shows in all media. ♦ Arts Center Tu-F 10AM-6PM; Sa 11AM-4PM. 620 Market St. 822.7161

73 Joshua Sears Building In 1891 Boston millionaire **Joshua M. Sears** built this two-story brick triangle in what was then the center of town. It was to be the official bank of the **Great Western Iron and Steel Works.** The steel mill never produced so much as an ingot, and the bank failed without ever opening. The beautiful brick arches inside were covered up when the building's interior was divided into apartments in the 1940s. They were rediscovered by developer **Lloyd Powell** and his wife when they bought the place in 1982 and went at it with $800,000 and a trowel. The restoration won the Powells numerous awards, including *Metropolitan Home* magazine's "Home of the Year," and was featured on the "This Old House" TV show. ♦ 701 Market St

74 The Bucklin Home The **Kirkland Land and Improvement Co.** built this wood-frame house (pictured below, at right) in 1889, and in 1904 it was bought by **Harry Thompkins,** who started a successful shipyard at what is now **Carillon Point.** This house was nearly condemned after a fire in 1975, but the Bucklin family was allowed to buy it with the promise that they would restore it. Renovations began with beams and other lumber salvaged from—of all places—the old shipyard. ♦ 202 Fifth Ave West

75 Cafe Juanita ★★★$$ It used to be that you couldn't get into this restaurant without either a reservation months in advance or a personal letter from the Pope. That was back in the late 1970s, when good Italian food wasn't as easy to procure as it is today. But as the trendoids moved on, room opened up again for local guests, and owner **Peter Dow** could sit back a little and keep closer watch on his kitchen. Dow is a cautious steward of his menu, rotating in some of his favorite specials without losing any tried-and-true successes. That means the *spiedini misti* you order this week—two skewers of lamb and Italian sausages, roasted with onions and green peppers—will probably always be on the menu. Dow also offers about 250 Italian wines, as well as three varieties produced under his own Cavatappi label: a Sauvignon blanc, a small amount of Cabernet Sauvignon, and a dark red, potent, and dry Maddalena—the only wine aged from Nebbiolo grapes in Washington state. ♦ Italian ♦ 9702 NE 120th Pl. Reservations recommended. 823.1505

Restaurants/Clubs: Red   **Hotels:** Blue
Shops/ 🌳 Outdoors: Green   **Sights/Culture:** Black

Sippin' Suds

Although Seattle's first brewery opened in the early 1860s at Fourth Avenue and Yesler Way, it was the microbrewery boom of the 1980s that earned this town its membership among beer-loving cities. As locals and other Americans became more interested in both food and drink, they discovered that a whole world of flavorful brews existed beyond the familiar domestic labels.

Ethnic restaurants had a lot to do with the influx of European beers, matching the stoutness and flavor of those products to their diverse menus. So, too, did **Jack McAuliffe,** who'd become acquainted with Scottish ales while he was stationed with the U.S. Navy in Britain and returned to the states to open the **New Albion Brewing Company** in Sonoma, California. Though New Albion was financially tapped out by 1983, it inspired beer lovers up and down the West Coast to try their hands at the microbrewery biz.

In 1982 veteran brewmeister **Bert Grant** started producing a dense and pungent Scottish ale at his **Yakima Brewing & Malting Company,** southeast of Seattle, in Yakima. At about the same time, the **Redhook Ale Brewery** began churning forth a fruity, Belgian-style ale at its plant in the Ballard neighborhood. Since then, Redhook has moved into headquarters in Fremont, introduced its more successful Ballard Bitter and other complex brews, and happily refined its original Redhook Ale. It is now the city's largest boutique beer maker, defying the traditional definition of a "microbrewery" as one producing fewer than 10,000 barrels a year. Other competitors have followed enthusiastically, from **Hale's Ales** (with breweries in Kirkland and Spokane, Washington) to **Maritime Pacific Brewing Company** of Seattle and **Roslyn Brewing Company**

in nearby Roslyn, a town that serves as the set for the make-believe Cicely, Alaska, of "Northern Exposure" fame.

It is the rare Seattle bar or tavern today that doesn't boast at least a few full-bodied microbrews on tap. You can also find a number of brewpubs, where beer is produced fresh on the premises. Brewpubs offer a wonderful opportunity to sample such unusual concoctions as ales spiced with oregano, barley wines, a variety of wheat beers, and seasonally produced extra-dense porters crafted to help your body ward off winter chills. A few Seattle-area brewpubs worth bellying up to:

Big Time Brewery, 4133 University Way NE, University District, 545.4509.

Maritime Pacific Brewery Company, 1514 NW Leary Way, Ballard, 782.6181.

Pacific Northwest Brewing Company, 322 Occidental Avenue South, Pioneer Square, 621.7002.

Pike Place Brewery, 1432 Western Avenue, Pike Place Market, 622.3373.

Trolleyman Pub at **Redhook Ale Brewery,** 3400 Phinney Avenue North, Fremont, 548.8000.

Although **Hale's Ales** doesn't have its own brewpub, it is located right next to and dispenses its beers directly through the Eastside's pleasant **Kirkland Roaster & Ale House,** 1111 Central Way, 827.4400.

If you haven't a friend or acquaintance to help you navigate the maze of microbrewery offerings available here, consult **Bart Becker's** spirited book, *Seattle Brews: The Insider's Guide to Neighborhood Alehouses, Brewpubs, and Bars* (1992; Alaska Northwest).

The Bucklin Home

COURTESY OF THE KIRKLAND HERITAGE SOCIETY

Bests

David Michael Buerge
Writer/Historian/Museum Critic

Seattle has its seasons. The loveliest? Smoldering fall. The most "Seattle"? Gray, rainy winter, when the city can be very cozy. What to do on those rainy days? Eat, drink, and be merry (or read) with someone you love.

Forget breakfast. For lunch, try a "steakbomb" at **Chicago Red Hots** (heaven to the palate, hell to the cardiovascular system) in North Seattle, a Burgermaster combo at the **Burgermaster** drive-in on Aurora Avenue North, or a Dick's deluxe burger (with extra onions) at any **Dick's** drive-in.

Seattle is bibliophile heaven. Don't fail to visit **Shorey Books** for used books, **Beatty Books** for rare ones, as well as the **Fillipi Book & Record Shop** and the **University Book Store.** While on University Way, try the avgolemono soup and the souvlakia plate at **The Continental Pastry Shop** while watching student and street life pass by.

Later on, try something light at **Ernie's Bar & Grill** in the **Edgewater Inn** on Pier 67. Or, a dozen Wescott's on the half shell and a whisky neat at **Shucker's** in the **Four Seasons Olympic Hotel.** The **Rainier Club** has the best Cobb salad in town. Try a gin Alexander at **Merchant's Cafe,** Seattle's oldest restaurant, dinner at **Hiram's-At-The-Locks** in the early evening, a cup of coffee on the flying bridge of a **Washington State Ferry** entering Elliott Bay at sunset, or a late-night meal of bouillabaisse at **Thirteen Coins.** During the Christmas shopping season, sip hot eggnog from **Nordstrom** while taking an evening ride in a horse-drawn carriage through the shopping district.

For fun with children, visit the **Woodland Park Zoo,** where the animals live in lovely, authentic settings.

Have a picnic lunch at the **Hiram M. Chittenden Locks,** featuring heavy maritime traffic, a delightful botanical garden, a museum, and a fish ladder with viewing ports to glimpse the salmon. You might want to build a winter fire on **Alki Beach** and roast marshmallows. While in West Seattle, if the weather is dry, take a walk in **Schmitz Park,** one of the last stretches of virgin forest around these parts. Shop for toys at **Magic Mouse** toys. Learn about Seattle's Nordic legacy at the **Nordic Heritage Museum** in Ballard, its Asian heritage at the **Wing Luke Asian Museum** in the International District, and **Boeing's** origins at the **Museum of Flight.** Also, you can't miss with any play put on by the **Seattle Children's Theatre.**

Finally, Seattle's best-kept secret—the Oriental temple-observatory atop **Smith Tower,** the city's loveliest building. On rainy winter evenings you can have the whole majestic place to yourself and your beloved. If the piano is still there, play Chopin's Prelude in D-flat Major—the "Raindrop Prelude," of course!

Kenneth A. Gouldthorpe
Editor/Publisher/Foreign Correspondent Emeritus; Freelance Writer, Pacific Publishing Associates

Seattle is a city of sights and sounds and uncanny beauty, where the ease of living and the quality of life are paramount considerations. It's a city that doesn't really understand what conspicuous consumption is all about, and it's home to a community that uses its parks and waterways on a daily basis, patronizes the arts like Easterners, yet tends to live a low-key, suburban existence.

What do I like about Seattle?

The balcony of **Ray's Boathouse** on a summer evening, with the Sound below me and the sun setting behind the mountains on the Olympic Peninsula.

Gorging at Sunday brunch in the **Georgian Room** of the **Four Seasons Olympic Hotel.**

Pike Place Market, for its superlative Washington seafood; its seasonal fruits, vegetables, and berries; and for the innovative originals you can find at the crafts stalls. Watching everyone ooh and aah as the fish vendors sling 30-pound salmons at each other when they make a sale.

A pint glass of superb ale from any of the Seattle or Washington microbreweries.

Visiting the **Chateau Ste. Michelle** winery in nearby Woodinville—it's like a quick trip to France.

Getting out of town and up into the **Cascades,** which takes less than an hour.

Starting my day by looking at the mountains and **Puget Sound** from the living room of my home and wondering how a place can be so consistently beautiful.

Taking my kids to the **Seattle Children's Theatre,** where I watch them as much as I watch the excellent productions.

Going to the **Pacific Northwest Ballet's** *Nutcracker* at Christmastime.

Inhaling those glorious smells at **Larsen Brothers Danish Bakery** and buying pastries and doughnuts for the kids' Friday night treat.

Seattleites going slightly berserk at the first signs of sun after the winter gray—and watching them do rain dances if the sun shines too consistently.

The lack of rental limousines and Rolls Royces.

People-watching at the ballet or the symphony and at opening nights, where garments run the gamut from T-shirts and jeans to tuxedos and nobody feels out of place.

Eating smoked salmon (cold-smoked, kippered, or lightly broiled) and barbecuing my own, straight from the Sound.

The purse seiners who fish a hundred yards or so from the house when the salmon are running.

I love never wearing a raincoat in the rain and going into a fine restaurant without a tie. I also love Thursday nights at SAM, the new downtown **Seattle Art Museum** (when hours of operation are extended well into the evening).

And after years of living all over the world, I love knowing, at last, that I belong here.

Jean Godden
City Columnist, *Seattle Times*

Seattle has been discovered recently, a minor misfortune for a city with bashful ways, rooted in ancestral Scandinavian ("vant to be alone") and Asian backgrounds. But once the locals overcome their native shyness, they're friendly enough to direct you to some favorite spots and pastimes. Chief among them:

Pike Place Market is the city's heartbeat. Founded in 1907 as a farmers' market, it's now a National Historic District teeming with 250 permanent businesses, nearly 100 farmers, and 200 artists and craftspeople. Where else could you buy wild mushrooms, fresh inkfish, a beaded dress from the 1930s, 38 kinds of doughnuts, and a Seattle Rain Festival T-shirt?

A walk along the **Waterfront** is de rigueur even on a blustery day when a salty breeze blows off Elliott Bay. You can see freighters from afar, visit the **Seattle Aquarium,** cruise the harbor on the *Goodtime* ships, and—when hunger strikes—buy a cup of steaming clam chowder from one of several sidewalk cafes.

Much of Seattle's shopping area surrounds **Westlake Park,** an urban triangle where civic events and political rallies are staged. Don't miss the **Bon Marché,** the city's biggest department store, or **Nordstrom,** the apparel chain's flagship store. A monorail station on the third floor of the nearby **Westlake Center** shopping complex will speed you to **Seattle Center,** home of the highly educational **Pacific Science Center** and the **Space Needle,** the kitschy symbol of the city.

The **Pacific First Centre** (at Fifth Avenue and Pike Street) is Seattle's downtown living room. When fatigue strikes, seek out the second-level lobby and sink into one of the leather chairs. The lobby has a world-class display of Pilchuck glass. Near the Fifth Avenue entry, there's a **Starbucks** kiosk where you can order the city's favorite drink: a double tall *latte* with a half inch of foam.

Not to be missed is the new **Seattle Art Museum;** a 48-foot-tall statue titled *Hammering Man* stands in front of the building. The highly controversial *Hammering Man* soundlessly pounds the back of his hand two-and-a-half times a minute. Permanent art museum exhibitions include North Coast Indian art and works from Africa and Pacific Rim countries.

The **Hiram M. Chittenden Locks** is second in size only to the Panama Canal in the Western Hemisphere. The locks serve as a marine elevator, boosting ships from the saltwater of Shilshole Bay to the freshwater of the Lake Washington Ship Canal. Stroll across the locks for a view of salmon swimming past a glass-sided fish ladder.

Woodland Park Zoo is world famous for its naturalistic exhibits, which include a marshland, a tropical forest, an African savanna, and the Southeast Asian elephant exhibit.

Go to dinner at a restaurant on **Shilshole Bay (Ray's Boathouse, Anthony's Homeport, Hiram's At The Locks)** where you can dine on seafood and watch as tiny tugs sail past pulling giant barges and the sun sets slowly behind the **Olympic Mountains.**

Charles Johnson
Author/Professor of English, University of Washington

The **Broadway** restaurant on Capitol Hill, a genuine people's place in a section of the city that feels like Berkeley, California, in the 1960s. If you're lucky, you might find a seat beside playwright August Wilson as he works and watches all manner of humanity pass by outside the window.

The **San Juan Islands**—especially **Orcas** and **Shaw**—in the summer. In addition to seeing fantastic marine life, you'll find air out there that is so clean you'll want to bottle it and take it home.

Poetry and fiction readings at **The Elliott Bay Book Company** (there's a reading almost every evening), which is something of a literary clearinghouse for Seattle, complete with a downstairs cafe for artistic types to chat over coffee and enough books upstairs to make a bibliophile's eyes go steamy with joy.

Henry Art Gallery on the University of Washington campus—a must-see if you're interested in the visual arts.

Seattle Repertory Theatre—easily the most exciting place for plays (new and old) in the Northwest.

Seattle Center, site of the World's Fair in the 1960s, is for me the '90s version of Coney Island but far classier, with the **Space Needle** rising from the grounds like a flying saucer (the restaurant up there turns a full circle every hour and gives a breathtaking view of the city).

Pioneer Square, particularly the ferry docks a few blocks west, where even a lubber like me can suck in enough salty air and the sound of gulls to imagine myself—Walter Mitty-fashion—about to board a frigate and flee all life's constraints on shore.

The **Meditation Room** at Sea-Tac Airport, which is the only one of its kind in the country. Zazen before you strap in? This idea appeals to me.

Pike Place Market—a *true* open-air market, much like a cornucopia of produce, fish, and fruit nestled between high-end shops and art galleries; the last time I was there three singers were crooning outside, Temptations-style, free of charge for a crowd of close to a hundred people.

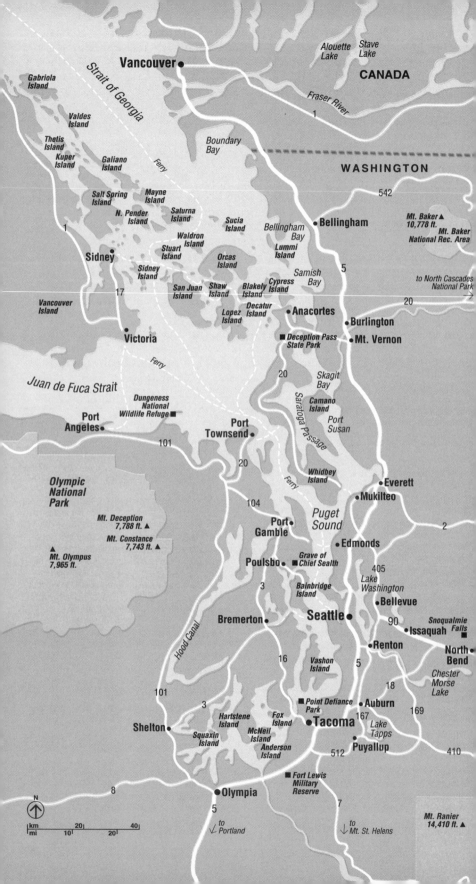

Day Trips

National magazines that have recently taken a shine to Seattle tend to view it as a single, remote destination rather than as a jumping-off point for explorations of nearby vineyards, villages, and volcanoes. That's unfortunate. First, because Seattle proper is not unlimited in its attractions; after four or five days here, travelers may start to feel somewhat edgy, a little trapped, worried that there isn't anything more to do than revisit Pike Place Market, Pioneer Square, and the Space Needle. Second, Seattlecentrism shortchanges the area's many virtues.

Within three hours of the city are rustic retreats in the **San Juan Islands,** ceremonial wine-grape crushings on the east side of **Lake Washington,** ski slopes, exotic summer gardens, and bird refuges. Architecture lovers will want to head south for a look at Washington state's impressive capital complex at **Olympia,** while cityphiles should venture north into two of Canada's most interesting urban areas. **Victoria** is the modest but growing island-bound capital of British Columbia, providing a wealth of history in a cozy, shop-laden English atmosphere. By contrast, **Vancouver,** just across the Strait of Georgia from Victoria, is Canada's third-largest metropolis (after Montreal and Toronto). **Rudyard Kipling,** seduced by the Vancouver area's beauty, proclaimed in his *Letters of Travel* that "such a land is good for an energetic man . . . it is also not bad for the loafer."

And then there's **Mount St. Helens,** to the south of Seattle, which caught the world's attention when it violently blew its stack in 1980. Although the state of Oregon tries to claim St. Helens as its own (it is physically closer to the city of Portland than to Seattle), the now-decimated peak remains one of Washington's prime draws.

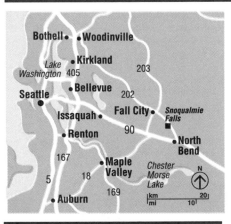

Eastside Wine Country

Seattleites tend to turn up their noses at the youthful suburbs east of town, but that's where the greatest number of wineries can be found. Begin at the **Paul Thomas Winery** (1717 136th Place NE, Bellevue; 747.1008), launched on the reputation of Thomas' fruit wines but now best known for its production of Cabernet Sauvignons and Chardonnays. **Covey Run at Moss Bay** (107 Central Way, Kirkland; 828.3848)—a tasting room for the larger Covey Run operation in Zillah, Washington—offers samplings of Merlots and Johannisberg Rieslings, as well as more unusual varietals, such as Aligoté. One of the Eastside's pioneer wineries, **Columbia,** has relocated from Bellevue to a quainter country location that offers picnic grounds (14030 NE 145th Street,

Woodinville; 488.2776). Try winemaker **David Lake's** Cabernets and Chardonnays.

Finally, drop by **Chateau Ste. Michelle** (14111 NE 145th Street, Woodinville; 488.1133), which is just across the street from Columbia Winery. Extensive grounds are open to picnickers, and classical concerts are held in an amphitheater during the warm months. If you have time, tote your wineglass on a tour of the two-acre garden behind the grounds' historic **Stimson Mansion.** Timber magnate **Frederick S. Stimson** arrived in Seattle in 1889, bought 206 acres of prime agricultural land on the Sammamish River, and built **Hollywood Farm,** a state-of-the-art dairy and poultry ranch, anchored by the manse. Around 1910 he hired famed landscape designers **Frederick Law Olmsted, Jr.,** and his adopted brother **John Charles Olmsted** to plan a garden, bordered by trees and shrubs, that would be filled with exotic plants. The formal results are still maintained today.

For a regularly updated guide to Washington's wine-touring opportunities, look up **Chuck Hill's** *Northwest Winery Guide* (published by Speed Graphics); it provides a brief history of each winery and tasting tips.

Heading back to Seattle after a full day of tapping the grape, take a detour from the Lake Washington floating bridges in favor of Highway 522 or Bothell Way, and stop for a sumptuous French dinner at **Gerard's Relais de Lyon** (★★★★$$$$). Owner/chef **Gerard Parrat,** a student and follower of famous French foodmeister **Paul Bocuse,** has been running this restaurant for more than 16 years. His cuisine remains firmly rooted in his Lyonnaise heritage.

Presentations might be considered a trifle fancy (imagine a terrine with slivers of artichoke heart, squab breast, and rare foie gras embedded in aspic), but some offerings should not be missed (the lobster bisque, for instance). Parrat's tangy Grand Marnier soufflé, made with one of Bocuse's recipes, is especially popular. Prices are astonishingly modest, with most appetizers available for less than $10, main dishes for not much more than $20, and the 10-course menu degustation priced at just $55 per person (for a minimum of two people). Only the wine-list selections have received criticism as limited and too costly; you may be particularly sensitive to this after a day in the wine country. ♦ French ♦ Tu-Su 5-9:30PM. 17121 Bothell Way NE, Bothell. Reservations recommended; 485.7600.

Difficult to get into but no less reliable a restaurant is **The Herbfarm** (★★★★$$$$) in Fall City, about 30 minutes east of Seattle. **Ron Zimmerman,** one of the founders of the old Early Winters outdoors equipment company, returned to his family farm after that business went kaput. He hired **Carrie Van Dyck,** who managed public relations for Early Winters, to help him promote the farm's products. The partners married and literally grew the farm from an herb nursery into a restaurant high on the local pecking order. Their exceptional salads—mixtures of spinach leaves, fennel, arugula, flower petals, and more (up to 35 ingredients)—are legendary. Prix-fixe meals (six courses at lunch, nine at dinner) based on fresh seasonal components (often including seafood) have an instructional quality to them; you don't just *consume* at these tables, you study how Zimmerman and his chefs have orchestrated a lunch or dinner for maximum impact and pleasure. Meals begin with a lively tour of the grounds, with Zimmerman nipping off leaves for you to rub and smell. After that, you're far more aware of the flowers and herbs in what you taste.

Unfortunately, getting a chance to eat here is no easy task; the restaurant, with places for only 32 people, is normally booked up months in advance. Seatings are only held once each day on Fridays, Saturdays, and Sundays. That could mean lunch or dinner, depending on Zimmerman's whim. (Generally, however, two weekends each month are reserved for lunch and two for dinner.) The restaurant takes six months of advance bookings on two days each year—on a Wednesday in early April and again on a Wednesday in mid-August. (Dates vary, so call ahead.) About 25 percent of the seating, however, is kept open until a week before serving. So if you call at 1PM on a Friday to check the following week's availability, chances are you could get in. A store at the farm sells herbs and other fine foodstuffs. ♦ Northwestern ♦ Lunches are served at noon; dinners may be served anytime from 7PM to 8PM, depending on the month. Store daily 10AM-5PM; closed in March. 32804 Issaquah-Fall City Rd, Fall City. Reservations required; 784.2222.

Seattle boasts more than 300 parks and playgrounds, for a combined 5,000 acres of parkland.

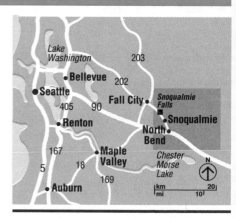

Land of "Twin Peaks"

King County's eastern cantons won international fame a few years ago when Washington native and filmmaker **David Lynch** chose to shoot his unsettlingly kinky TV series, "Twin Peaks" (and later a prequel motion picture, *Twin Peaks: Fire Walk with Me*), in the small towns of **North Bend** and **Snoqualmie.** The series was unusual for its tension-building background music of slow jazz and finger snapping, and its population of local characters, each weirder or lustier than the last. The mystery of young **Laura Palmer's** murder kept fans on the edge of their seats for two seasons and left those small Washington towns with a popularity founded on familiar exteriors and, as Lynch's FBI agent **Dale Cooper** would put it, damn fine cups of coffee.

Begin your leap into "Lynchville" by taking Interstate 90 from Bellevue to Exit 27. Follow the signs to Snoqualmie, then through the north end of town to **Snoqualmie Falls** (pictured at right); or take highways 908 and 202 from Kirkland to reach the falls by a more scenic route. This 270-foot cascade, a prominent background from "Twin Peaks," was renamed White Tail Falls for the show. It's *the* place to bring out-of-town guests. City folks and other tourists have been coming here to gawk since the late 19th century. A lookout point on a bluff to one side of the falls was improved and expanded not long ago, but crowds mount quickly on weekends, everybody equipped with cameras; arrive early if you hope to beat the stampede.

COURTESY OF THE SNOQUALMIE FALLS RESERVATION PROJECT

The Snoqualmie Indians have viewed this as a sacred site for centuries, and they've been struggling in more recent years to maintain its natural appearance. The tribe has not had a happy relationship with Puget

Power, the hydroelectric company that owns the land surrounding the falls and regulates how much water passes over its lip. The two parties are at an impasse regarding Puget Power's plans to expand its commercial and recreational facilities here. Information panels at the overlook outline these additions and renovations, which include consideration for fisheries, wetlands, and even flood prevention; the Snoqualmies are mentioned only in relation to the discovery of the falls by whites. Ironically, Puget Power's buildings at the falls are now protected as historic landmarks, while the Snoqualmies have no legal means to protect the actual falls.

The world's first underground electric generator, built in 1898, lies 270 feet deep in a chamber excavated from solid basaltic rock behind the falls. From the lookout point, you can see the opening of the tailrace, a 450-foot-long tunnel where water diverted through the turbines rejoins the river at the base of the falls. A one-mile round-trip trail will take you down for a closer look and a faceful of spray.

Perched at the very edge of the gorge is **The Salish Lodge,** otherwise known to Twin Peakers as the Great Northern Hotel. Formerly the Snoqualmie Falls Lodge, the landmark was remodeled in the late 1980s. A country feel was retained, but the place has lost its ingratiating weathered look. The **Salish Lodge Dining Room** (★★$$$) is famous for its front-row view of the falls and its six-course Country Breakfast: a platter of fruit accompanied by the Eye Opener (fresh-squeezed orange juice blended with lime juice, honey, and egg, and topped with grated nutmeg), an assortment of bran and fruit muffins baked every half hour and served with honey butter, old-fashioned rolled oats with cream and brown sugar, and the main course of apple-pork sausage, smoked bacon, and a grilled ham steak with your choice of egg preparations, plus hash browns, and sourdough biscuits—buttressed by a stack of whole-wheat buttermilk flapjacks. Bring a change of belts. The wine list is legendary. Sommelier **Randy Austin** says that at last count there were 725 labels available on the roster, including an 1882 Madeira Verdeljo ($250). Don't worry if you're not an expert oenophile; Austin has always been very helpful in educating the hotel's restaurant patrons about novel or arcane vintages to match their meals. ◆ Daily 7-11AM, 11:30AM-3PM, 5-10PM. Highway 202. Reservations recommended; 206/888.2556 (a long-distance call from Seattle).

Leaving the falls, backtrack through the town of Snoqualmie. Train buffs shouldn't miss the historical museum and a steam ride at the **Puget Sound and Snoqualmie Valley Railway,** which runs an hour and a half between Snoqualmie and **North Bend** on weekends from April through October (free for children under the age of 3; 746.4025). Follow signs from there into North Bend. This town is sprinkled with Swiss chalet-style shops and restaurants and loomed over by **Mount Si,** a colossal alp that seems to have wandered out of the Cascades and resettled here for a long nap. Named in honor of local homesteader **Josiah "Uncle Si" Merritt,** the mountain was featured ominously in a shot used for commercial breaks in the "Twin Peaks" series. (No, Si has no twin; rumor has it that Lynch's title alluded to the frontal engineering of his female costars rather than to a geological anomaly of his setting.) With a trailhead that starts just outside of town (drive south on North Bend Way, turn left on Mount Si Road and continue for about two and a half miles, watching for the trail sign) and a sweeping view of the Snoqualmie Valley, Si is a popular hike; on weekends the four-and-a-half-mile trail, though strenuous, is crowded with nature lovers. Just one caution: Don't forget to keep track of time; many people have spent miserable nights lost in these woods because they didn't allow enough time to hike back before dark. And the Haystack, a knob of bare rock at Si's top, is officially off limits. Views from there may be panoramic, but sudden sidewinds and updrafts can pick off even the most macho sightseers like ripe fruit.

Finish your "Peaks" experience at the **Mar T Cafe** ($), the show's pseudonymous Double R Diner. Has this place been adversely affected by stardom? Judge for yourself. A banner outside proclaims it "Home of Twin Peaks Pies." Peaks paraphernalia—T-shirts, autographed photos, a map matching real and fictitious place names—are all available by the cash register. And thanks to repeated mentions on Lynch's show, instead of the 30 cherry pies it used to sell in a week, this joint now peddles 30 a day. (Slices—$2.50 apiece—are available daily after 11AM; it's best heated and without ice cream.) But the large horseshoe bar ringed by shiny stools and the booths flanked by wood paneling are still the same as they were before fame came calling, and the ice-cream machine still hums like a diesel engine. ◆ Daily 5:30AM-8PM. 137 North Bend Way; 206/888.1221 (a long-distance call from Seattle).

"The Emerald City" has long proved an uncomfortable nickname for Seattle. Residents here don't relish its pie-in-the-sky associations with *The Wonderful Wizard of Oz* or the fact that other, less ambitious towns—such as Eugene, Oregon—have co-opted the cognomen as their own. But efforts to improve upon "The Emerald City" have so far failed. *Seattle Weekly* took nickname suggestions in the 1970s and wound up favoring "Lady Gray," a depressing allusion to the city's frequent cloud cover. "Jet City" has been mentioned a few times, but its link to the ups and downs of the Boeing Company (which contributed to Seattle's near financial collapse in the early 1970s) makes it an unlikely replacement. Any other suggestions?

Seattle's Wet Set

Turn over a rock at **Golden Gardens** park on Shilshole Bay and you have a good chance of encountering *Pachygrapsus crassipes,* the lined shore crab. You may only have a minute to extend greetings, however, before this inch-long green creature scurries off sideways in search of a new hideout. Don't bother giving chase. Plenty of other charming, if equally reclusive, animals can be found along this sandy stretch of land.

Puget Sound is inhabited by several thousand marine species. Most are small-bodied invertebrates (oysters, clams, urchins, crabs, anemones, and squids), but some are certifiable giants, thriving on this briny soup's ample food supply and fairly mild oceanic climate. Less than a hundred feet off the Golden Gardens shore, for instance, lurks *Octopus dofleini,* the world's largest octopus, a mottled red Schwarzenegger of a cephalopod with an arm span extending 25 feet. A bit farther out, on the Sound's silty bottom, rests the 10-pound geoduck (pronounced GOO-ee-duck), a mega-mollusk that qualifies as the world's largest burrowing clam.

Like the secretive shore crab *Pachygrapsus,* many local invertebrates are beach dwellers, occupying cozy niches in what scientists call the intertidal zone—that thin strip of earth bathed by ocean tides. To survive under such transitional conditions, many animals have radically changed their looks and behaviors. For example, the small colonial sea anemone, *Anthopleura,* resembles a plant more than an animal, while the limpet (a tiny, rock-hugging cousin of the snail) could very easily pass for a smooth stone.

On the rocky beaches (such as in **Mukilteo,** 20 miles north of Seattle), fish and invertebrates hide in the cracks and crevices between boulders or among the kelp and other seaweeds that grow abundantly at the water's edge. Sandy shores (like those at Golden Gardens or the city of **Edmonds,** another short excursion north of Seattle) are usually featureless plains that merge into eelgrass beds—underwater meadows that offer food and shelter to anything that lives on or near the bottom. Both beach types make fine destinations for intertidal explorers.

To get better acquainted with this curious, often colorful, community of the sea, visit the **Seattle Aquarium,** at Pier 59 on the city's Waterfront, where you'll meet all local beach dwellers face-to-face. Afterward pick up a good

field guide to intertidal life, either **Gloria Snively's** *Exploring Seashore Life in British Columbia, Washington, and Oregon* (1978, The Writing Works) or *Seashore Life of the Northern Pacific Coast,* by **Eugene Kozloff** (1983, University of Washington Press). And finally, procure a local tide table, available from larger bookstores in the city. Tidepooling requires taking advantage of two brief windows of opportunity, periods of approximately four to six hours each day, when the tides ebb and the intertidal zone is most accessible to exploration. Exactly how long and how wide these windows swing varies daily. But in the summer the lowest tides generally occur around midday. As winter approaches they fall between 9PM and midnight, making tidepooling a more difficult enterprise but no less rewarding as long as you have a flashlight in hand.

Don't presume, however, that only cold-blooded creatures will be joining you at the beach. A vast array of waterfowl and shorebirds also visit Seattle's coastline. Several of these, including the diminutive Bonaparte's gull, travel thousands of miles from central Alaska just to winter in the Emerald City. Others, such as the western and glaucous-winged gull, prefer the year-round comfort of urban beaches, piers, and marinas over life on the road. Regardless of their summer plans, all arrive at the local seashores with one thing in mind: the seafood smorgasbord that's uncovered with every out-going tide.

A pair of binoculars might help you espy some warm-blooded mammals—particularly harbor seals and California sea lions. Still farther from shore swim the area's sleek black-and-white killer whales (like the one pictured below), highly intelligent and surprisingly swift hunters of salmon, cod, halibut, and hake. Killer whales (or orcas) are actually more closely related to dolphins than to whales, and they spend their entire lives in extended family groupings called pods. (For an excellent background on these mammals, read Sasquatch Books' 1990 *Field Guide to the Orca,* by **David G. Gordon** and **Chuck Flaherty.**) Members of some of these tight-knit clans periodically stray from their homes in the **San Juan Islands** and venture south into Puget Sound. If you've never glimpsed a whale spouting or breaching in the wild, this is a good place to try your luck, although prepare yourself to wait patiently for that first sign of one of Moby Dick's great cousins.

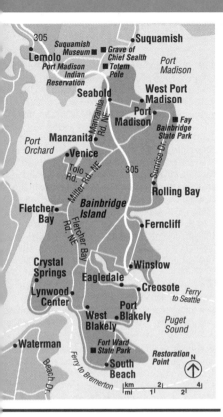

Bainbridge Island

For many years, Bainbridge—about 35 minutes west of Seattle by ferry—was considered a haven for hippies and others whose supreme desire was to drop away from public attention. Things didn't quite work out that way, though. Over the years threats to build a bridge across Puget Sound have come to naught. But as Seattle grew, well-to-do residents who didn't fancy moving to Bellevue, Kirkland, or some other Eastside 'burb, turned in this direction instead.

Bainbridge has enjoyed some interesting history. In the late 19th century the island's southern end sported a couple of saloons, a giant mill that could cut 500,000 board feet a day over two 10-hour shifts, and the 75-room **Bainbridge Hotel.** (All have since disappeared.) In the early 20th century the island figured briefly into the well-publicized and often comic escape of Butch Cassidy cohort **Harry Tracy** from a maximum-security prison in Oregon. (Officials ultimately forced Tracy to kill himself.) Most of that colorful heritage is gone, leaving a fairly peaceful, still heavily wooded escape—perfect for baby boomers . . . and for day-trippers.

The Bainbridge-bound ferry leaves from **Colman Dock/Pier 52** on the Seattle Waterfront. (Ferries depart every 40 to 60 minutes on weekends, from just after 6AM until slightly after 2AM; the last weekend return ferry leaves Bainbridge at about 1:15AM; call 464.6000 for more information.) You arrive at the hamlet of **Winslow,** home to a small Saturday farmer's market (held mid-spring through

fall at **Winslow Green,** on the corner of Madison Avenue and Winslow Way), plus a couple of cafes and a small but interesting bookstore.

If it's early when you exit the ferry, stop in at the **Streamliner Diner** (★$), a small island institution. Breakfasts are best here; just ask any of the people waiting in line outside for a table. (The first-come first-served problem is especially acute on weekends.) Try the omelets, the buttermilk waffles, or the Potatoes Deluxe, a stir-fry of diced spuds, lots of onions, and fresh veggies, all beneath a generous meltdown of cheese. ♦ M-F 7AM-3PM; Sa-Su 8AM-2:30PM. 397 Winslow Way, Winslow; 842.8595.

Once sated, roar west along Highway 305 to the **Bainbridge Island Winery,** only seven acres in size but with a reputation that's grown substantially since 1981, when owners **Gerard** and **Joan Bentryn** started this place. Vintages are styled in the German fashion, low in alcohol with some residual sweetness. The flagship wine is Müller-Thurgau, but **Corbet Clark,** in his book *American Wines of the Northwest,* gives raves as well to the "surprising" Siegerrebe, "a cross of Gewürztraminer with Madeleine Angevine, itself an old French cross." The Bentryns also produce a strong-selling strawberry wine. ♦ W-Su noon-5PM. 682 Hwy 305, Winslow; 842.9463.

The 150 acres of **Bloedel Reserve,** still farther to the west, were once the estate of a Canadian lumbering family. But since the 1980s these woodlands and gardens have been open to the public, with trails that give you a good look at exotic plant life imported from around the globe. Bring binoculars; birds enjoy a refuge here. Only 150 guests are allowed in each day, so make your reservations early. ♦ Admission. W-Su 10AM-4PM. 7521 NE Dolphin Dr (Hwy 305 at Agate Pass). Reservations required; 842.7631.

Finally, cross the bridge onto the Kitsap Peninsula at Agate Pass and turn left onto Sandy Pass Road to find the **Suquamish Museum**. The museum does a good job reciting local history in a manner sympathetic to the perspective of Puget Sound's Salish tribe. The life of **Chief Sealth** (after whom Seattle was named, see page 82) is illuminated through both displays and photographs. ♦ Admission. Daily 10AM-5PM June-Sept; F-Su 11AM-4PM Oct-May. Special arrangements also may be made during the week by calling 24 hours in advance, Oct through May; ask for Marilyn Jones; 206/598.3311 (a long-distance call from Seattle).

Chief Sealth's burial site can be found nearby, next to **St. Peter's Catholic Mission Church** in the Kitsap village of Suquamish. It's hard to miss the leader's tomb because it's marked with a pair of long canoes mounted atop poles.

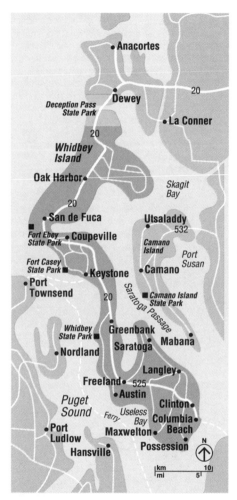

Whidbey Island

Thanks to the U.S. Supreme Court, Whidbey Island—a 50-mile snake of soil northwest of Seattle—is the longest island in the United States. (The court declared that challenger Long Island is a mere peninsula.) But it's thanks to ambitious hoteliers that Whidbey's natural beauty and easygoing charm may soon be run over in the rush to attract tourists.

The island is reached via a 20-minute ferry ride from the town of **Mukilteo,** 20 miles north of Seattle. (Ferries leave every half-hour on weekends, from about 6AM until 1AM; the last weekend return ferry leaves Whidbey at about 12:30AM. Call 464.6400 for specific rates.) The boat lets you off in the town of **Clinton,** from which you can pick up Highway 525.

Follow the highway for three miles, then take the detour east to **Langley.** This tiny town maintains a distinctly quaint air; it may be rivaled only by La Conner, Washington, in the number of curio shops it sprouts annually. Yet Langley seems especially susceptible to the blandishments of the tourist industry. It already claims a glut in its number of high-priced but small-occupancy "boutique hotels," which sell themselves on expansive views of **Saratoga Passage** and the **Cascade Mountains,** not on amenities such as swimming pools and putting greens.

Several fine restaurants draw day-trippers from the mainland. Try the Middle Eastern **Cafe Langley** (★★$$), where the crab cakes and *hummus* should not be missed. ♦ M, W-Th, Su 11AM-2PM, 5-8:30PM; Tu 5-8:30PM; F-Sa 11AM-2PM, 5-9PM. 113 First St; 206/221.3090 (a long-distance call from Seattle). Or sample owner/chef **Steve Nogal's** transporting five-course prix-fixe weekend dinners at the **Inn at Langley** (★★★$$$$), which concentrate on Northwest preparations and fare—from seafood to fresh vegetables. There's one seating a night, three nights a week. ♦ F-Sa 7PM; Su 6PM Memorial Day-Labor Day. 400 First St; 206/221.3033 (long distance from Seattle).

More such civilizing amenities are being planned for Whidbey, causing a local backlash and even some doubt among Seattleites who liked the island before it became popular. The time to see this place is now, before it's too late. On your agenda should be: a visit to the **Meerkeek Rhododendron Gardens,** 53 acres covered with some 2,000 varieties of Washington's official state flower (admission; W-Su 9AM-6PM; 15-1/2 miles north of the ferry on Highway 525 to Resort Road; 206/321.6682); a walk around the gorge at **Deception Pass** near Oak Harbor, with its 2,300 acres of forests and beaches; and, perhaps, an excursion up-island to **Fort Casey,** decommissioned but still boasting its old gun mounts and some dramatic outlooks (open daily 24 hours; three miles south of Coupeville on Admiralty Inlet; 206/678.4519, long distance from Seattle).

Get a better sense of Whidbey's heritage at the free-admission **Island County Historical Museum,** which is full of old photographs and Native American artifacts. ♦ Daily 11AM-4PM May-Oct; Sa-Su 11AM-4PM April. Alexander and Front Sts, Coupeville. 206/678.3310 (long distance from Seattle).

The term "flying saucer" was first used after Civil Air Pilot Kenneth Arnold, who was searching on 24 June 1947 for a military plane that had gone down near Mount Rainier, spotted instead a formation of nine brilliant, boomerang-shaped objects flying from Rainier toward Mount Adams. Asked to describe his odd encounter, Arnold compared the flight of his bogeys to an undulating kite tail or a "saucer skipping across the water." Thus was born one of the most popular unsolved mysteries of the 20th century.

As the sun finally withers from the sky, stop by the **Captain Whidbey Inn.** This 1907 madrona log lodge (pictured above) was once most reachable by steamship from Seattle. Now you can wheel up here in just a few hours for dinner or drinks on a terrific deck overlooking **Penn Cove,** where some of this region's finest mussels are harvested. ♦ Daily 6-9PM. Bar is open M-Th 5:30-10PM; F 4-10PM; Sa-Su noon-10PM. 2072 W. Captain Whidbey Inn Rd, Coupeville; 206/678.4097 (a long-distance call from Seattle).

San Juan Islands

There are 743 islands in the San Juan archipelago, but you can only see about 170 of them during high tide. Sixty of these are populated, most are privately owned (a few by single hermits), and the vast majority are unreachable except by private craft.

Kenmore Air (486.8400) offers scheduled floatplane service from Seattle to the San Juans. But certainly the most relaxing means of travel to the four largest islands here—Lopez, Shaw, Orcas, and San Juan (with an international spur on to Sidney, British Columbia)—is by ferry.

Washington State Ferries bound for the islands leave from the town of **Anacortes,** 78 miles north of Seattle (take Exit 230 from Interstate 5 and head 20 miles west to the terminal). During summer months 17 daily ferry departures from Anacortes are scheduled; there are fewer available between Labor Day and Memorial Day. Return schedules vary per island. (Call 464.6400 for schedules and rates.) The wait for space on ferry car decks can be long, so bring reading material; folks have spent two or more hours in line during the summer tourist crush. But if you begin early (the first sailing of the day varies slightly each quarter but is around 6AM), you'll improve your chances of getting on when you want.

It takes approximately an hour and a half to sail from Anacortes directly to **Friday Harbor,** on **San Juan,** the farthest you can go by ferry amongst these islands. You may want, however, to slow the pace of your journey by getting off and on the boat periodically to tour the four principal isles. In between, the boats provide huge picture windows for ample viewing of madrona-forested hills and narrow beaches. Eagles, gulls, and other able aviators are frequently seen, as are small fishing craft. Weather here tends to be milder than in Seattle, as the islands snuggle into the "rain shadow" of the Olympic Mountains to the west.

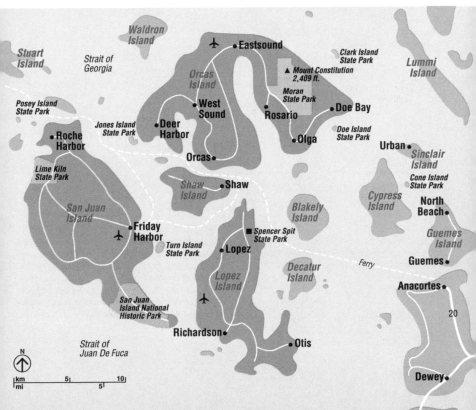

Flat, pastoral **Lopez** (about 45 minutes by ferry from Anacortes) provides the easiest bicycling on the islands, a 30-mile jaunt past sheep and cattle pastures that can be handled even by younger family members. Ride down to the island's southwest corner and **Shark Reef Preserve** to observe seals barking and flopping about. Lopez village (known for its strong grapevine of information and its liberal politics) barely makes it on the map, boasting a small but interesting **Lopez Island Historical Museum** (F-Su noon-4PM May-Sept; 206/468.2049) and a bakery, **Holly B's** (468.2133).

All four islands can claim parks, but underpopulated **Shaw Island**—dominated by three orders of Catholic nuns (one member of which always comes down to meet the ferry)—offers very little else in the way of traveler amenities.

At 57 square miles, horseshoe-shaped **Orcas** (an hour and 20 minutes by ferry from Anacortes) is the largest of these islands. Generally hilly (but okay for bike riding), it's dominated by 2,409-foot **Mount Constitution,** on top of which is an old stone lookout that offers views of everything between Mount Rainier and Vancouver, B.C. Drive up this peak or get a better feel for the island by huffing to it on foot through 4,934-acre **Moran State Park,** overlooking the island's eastern end. The town of **Eastsound,** maybe 10 miles north from the ferry landing, is slowly being transformed into a mini-Carmel, with bookstores, art galleries, and restaurants. On Saturdays, from April through October, local artisans and growers gather at a farmer's market on the grounds of the modest **Orcas Island Historical Museum.** Also in Eastsound is **Bilbo's Festivo** (★★$), a restaurant that combines mud walls with Navajo weavings and food influenced by New Mexican, Mexican, and Spanish cooking styles. Mesquite-grilled dinners of sirloin tips and local fish are excellent, but so are the burritos. The best seating is in the courtyard, where you can enjoy the quiet of early evening and where it's not unheard of for patrons to begin sing-alongs. ◆ Mexican ◆ M-F 5-9PM, Sa-Su 4:30-9PM mid Sept-May; M-F noon-2:30PM, 5-9PM, Sa-Su 4:30-9PM. N. Beach Rd and A St; 206/376.4728 (a long-distance call from Seattle). **Christina's** (★★★$$$$) is more romantic, a walk-up collection of small rooms with a dining porch that overlooks the water. Fare runs mostly to satisfying preparations of local seafood (including halibut and oysters), along with some red meats such as lamb. ◆ Seafood ◆ Daily 5-10PM May-Sept; M, Th-Su 5:30-10PM mid Feb-Apr; closed Jan through mid-Feb. N. Beach Rd and Horseshoe Way. Reservations recommended; 206/376.4904 (long distance from Seattle).

About 15 minutes from the ferry landing and three miles beyond Eastsound is **Rosario Resort.** A glistening white mansion on the waterfront, Rosario was built at the turn of the century by a former Seattle mayor and zillionaire boat-builder named **Robert Moran,** who left the city in 1904—after his doctor told him he had but six months to live. (As it turns out, Moran avoided the Reaper for 37 more years.) This resort is a wonderful place to hang out in good weather, inviting guests to drink buckets of margaritas by the pool and finish off lunch with a soothing afternoon massage. Meals in the dining room (including an almost-overwhelming Sunday brunch) are acceptable but not outstanding. Historical programs, including an organ concert and a history of the estate, are available Tuesday through Saturday at 9PM (with some expanded summer schedules). ◆ M-Th, Su 7:30AM-2PM, 6-9PM; F-Sa 7:30AM-2PM, 6-10PM. Horseshoe Way, on the east side of Orcas; 206/376.2222 (a long-distance call from Seattle).

The most populated of the islands is **San Juan.** This was the site of a particularly bizarre border dispute, the comic **Pig War** of 1859, a time when the British and the Americans shared an uneasy joint occupation of this island. The war was set off by an American farmer who shot and killed a pig that had been rooting in his garden. Turns out the porker belonged to the British **Hudson's Bay Company.** When the Brits sought to arrest the offending farmer, American infantry soldiers stepped in under the command of **General George Pickett** (who'd later enter the history books for his Civil War charge at Gettysburg). Tempers and armaments escalated, until **U.S. President James Buchanan** finally dispatched **General Winfield Scott** to negotiate a temporary truce. Joint occupation of San Juan Island continued until 1871, when none other than **Kaiser Wilhelm I** of Germany was asked to settle the border dispute. He drew the Canadian-U.S. border to the west of the island, through **Haro Strait,** thereby ceding San Juan to the Americans. You can visit the national historic sites of **American Camp** and **British Camp.** To reach the former, follow Cattle Point Road about six miles from the town of Friday Harbor toward the island's southeast tip. The nattier British Camp is about 12 miles farther, located off West Valley Road.

Before or after taking in the old British installation, stop at **Lime Kiln State Park,** which reputedly provides some of the best whale-watching opportunities in Washington state; posted signs will help you distinguish one species from another. (Premier viewing season is from late spring through early fall.) The **Friday Harbor Whale Museum** in town is a warehouselike structure stuffed with gray whale baleen, cetacean skeletons, and information about orcas and dolphins. Also look to the museum for information about whale-watching excursions. ◆ Admission. Daily 10AM-5PM June-Sept; daily 11AM-4PM Oct-May. 62 First St; 206/378.4710 (long distance from Seattle).

An unusual aspect of the San Juans' beauty is that much of it is fairly new, reclaimed from previous devastation. As the 19th century became the 20th, the air here was muddied with noxious fumes from lime kilns operating on San Juan Island. Roche Harbor, on the north end of San Juan, once hosted some of the busiest kilns—not to mention a steam-belching railroad and lumberyards. Today the harbor's focal point is the **Hotel de Haro,** built in 1886 by **John Stafford McMillin,** a Tacoma lawyer and owner of the old Roche Harbor Lime and Cement

Company here. McMillin built the hotel so his business clients (as well as a few other distinguished guests, including **Teddy Roosevelt**) might have a proper place to stay nearby. Worth visiting—if only for its Stephen Kingish oddity—is a mausoleum, tucked amidst a stand of Douglas firs about half a mile from the inn. The seven-pillared monument contains a round table and six chairs in its middle, each representing a member of McMillin's family. After a roam in the woods, stop on the hotel's deck, overlooking Roche Harbor, for a cold beer and to watch great blue herons coast forlornly over the evergreens.

Victoria, British Columbia

Extend your ferry journey through the San Juans to the **Vancouver Island** town of **Sidney,** convenient by either car or bus to the *veddy, veddy* English capital of British Columbia: Victoria. This city right on the southern tip of Vancouver Island is also reachable by seaplane from **Kenmore Air** (486.8400) and by way of the **Victoria Clipper's** passenger-only jet-propelled catamarans, which leave from Pier 69 on the Seattle Waterfront. (Two to four daily catamaran departures are scheduled, with tour frequency highest from June through September. The trip lasts

two-and-a-half hours. Board early for the best seats on the upper deck. Fares vary according to the time of year. 448.5000.)

Author **Rudyard Kipling** went a bit overboard when he described Victoria in the early 20th century. "To realize Victoria," he wrote, "you must take all that the eye admires in Bournemouth, Torquay, the Isle of Wight, the Happy Valley at Hong Kong, the Doon, Sorrento, and Camp's Bay—add reminiscences of the Thousand Islands and arrange the whole around the Bay of Naples with some Himalayas for the background." But things are changing here. Rapidly. Finally shedding its reputation as a retirement camp to the world, Victoria has attracted some innovative shops and restaurants, and downtown sidewalks no longer roll up after 10PM.

For a historical institution of its size, the **Royal British Columbia Museum** is wonderfully innovative. Dioramas record the extinction of woolly mammoths and the rise of Victorian storefronts, with the area's Native American heritage well represented.
♦ Admission. Daily 9:30AM-7PM May-Labor Day; daily 10AM-5:30PM Labor Day-April. 675 Belleville St; 604/387.3701. Just across Government Street reclines the imposing neo-Gothic **Parliament Building,** outlined in lights at night for a fairy-tale sort of atmosphere. (Free tours daily, every 20

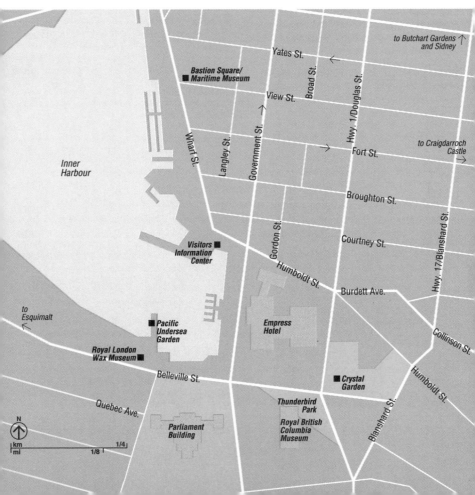

minutes May-Labor Day; M-F once an hour Labor Day-April. 604/387.3046.) A block north on Government Street is the **Empress Hotel** ($$$), opened in 1908 by the Canadian Pacific Railway and host to such luminaries as **Winston Churchill, John Wayne,** and **Richard Nixon** (he and his wife honeymooned here). There was talk in the mid-1960s of razing this grand dowager; instead, Canadian Pacific dumped $45 million into her restoration. The money has paid off. A pavilion has been added to one side of the old entrance, leaving the original lobby for high tea every afternoon (reservations required, 604/384.8111). Several luxury attic rooms have been opened, offering magnificent perspectives over Inner Harbour. The elegant **Palm Court** and **Crystal Ballroom** have been polished up, and a refurbished conservatory at the hotel's back connects it with the new **Victoria Conference Centre.**

Continue still farther north on Government Street to downtown's central shopping district. Here you'll find English suits at **George Straith Ltd.;** engulfing Cowichan sweaters at **Sasquatch Trading Co., Ltd.; Munro's Books,** a 1909 bank reformed wonderfully into the city's best and classiest bookstore; **E.A. Morris Tobacconist, Ltd.,** providing a floor-to-ceiling humidor, along with a broad selection of pipes and related products; **Murchie's Tea and Coffee,** redolent with the scents of buttery pastries and hot drinks; and the Dickensian treasure box of **Roger's Chocolates and English Sweet Shop,** full with chocolate creams, almond brittle, and marzipan bars. **Bastion Square,** between Yates and Fort streets, contains sidewalk restaurants, a maritime museum, and what is reportedly the location of Victoria's old gallows.

East of downtown is **Craigdarroch Castle,** a spooky climb of stone mounted above the city by coal tycoon **Robert Dunsmuir,** who built this estate in the late 19th century, hoping it would entice his Scottish wife into the frontier hinterlands of British Columbia. Tours are available daily. ♦ Admission. Daily 9AM-9PM mid-June to Labor Day; 10AM-5PM Labor Day to mid-June. 1050 Joan Crescent; 604/592.5323. For a relaxing lunch break, stop at **Spinnaker's Brew Pub,** in the nearby **Esquimalt** community, for a giant burger, some fresh flavorful beer, and a soothing view back toward Victoria. ♦ Daily 7AM-10PM. Pub open daily 11AM-11PM. 308 Catherine St; 604/386.2739.

On your way out of town, back to Sidney for either the Anacortes ferry or the B.C. boat to Vancouver, stop at **Butchart Gardens,** 50 acres of aggressively manicured property, suffused with flowers and impressive deep rock bays. If you still haven't eaten, light meals are available at the Gardens' entrance, and concerts are held here during the summer months. ♦ Admission. Daily 9AM-11PM July-Aug; daily 9AM-9PM June-Sept; daily 9AM-4PM Oct-Feb; daily 9AM-5PM Mar-May. Thirteen miles north of Victoria, off Hwy 17 at Brentwood; 604/652.4422.

Vancouver, British Columbia

A little more than 200 years after **Captain George Vancouver** sailed into nearby **Burrard Inlet** in 1792 to proclaim the area's beauty and claim it on behalf of England, Vancouver has become a city to rival Seattle for civic and cultural amenities (as well as for inner-city traffic).

Hong Kongese, fleeing 1997 Chinese control of their island nation, are migrating here in droves, building what are called "monster houses" to hold the families that follow in their paths. Meanwhile, the American Northwest endeavors to co-opt the city into an economic confederation that would take full advantage of the Canada-U.S. free-trade agreement. Seattle has already extended its grasp north, opening not one but *two* chic **Starbucks** coffee shops, kitty-corner from each other at Robson and Thurlow streets, and a proposal is afloat to build a bullet train between Burrard Inlet and Portland, Oregon. Dining trends are tripping over one another to infiltrate this city, with Italian joints especially ubiquitous. But don't hold that against **Villa Del Lupo** (★★$$), where chef **Julio Gonzalez,** along with partners **Vince** and **Mike Piccolo,** has created an exceptional restaurant in an old house near the **Queen Elizabeth Theatre.** Order the pungent, herby focaccia or the delicate mushroom mousse. Lamb shanks come in an incredibly rich heap, sauced with cinnamon, tomato, lemon, and red wine. Service can be a tad slow. ♦ Italian ♦ Daily 5:30-11PM. 869 Hamilton St; 604/688.7436. At **Le Coq D'or** (★★$$), owner **Bruno Born** has successfully shed his Italian past (he used to own **Zeppo's**) to create an artsy French bistro. Ask for lobster bisque with sherry and crème fraîche to begin, followed by veal medaillons with shiitake and morel mushrooms. Finish with crème brûlée. ♦ French ♦ Tu-F 11:30AM-3PM, 5:30-10PM; Sa-Su 9AM-4PM, 5-10:30PM. 3205 W. Broadway; 604/733.0035.

Perfect for walking is **Stanley Park,** a great peninsular greensward northwest of downtown, offering swimming beaches, more Northwest totem poles, and a zoo. At the urban core, try **Robson Street,** which provides as much of a character study as it does the opportunity to drain away in an afternoon every dollar you'd reserved for a week's worth of sight-seeing. People flock by the thousands to the stretch between Jervis and Granville streets on a sunny summer afternoon to browse for linens and modernist lamps, or to circle vulturelike around shoe stores until they finally settle on the brown lace-ups. Farther east along Robson Street, there's an obvious evolution from the terminally hip shops of the baby boom set to the pillared **Vancouver Art Gallery,** a former courthouse designed by Canadian architect **Francis Rattenbury,** who is also responsible for the Empress Hotel and Parliament Buildings in Victoria. (Admission. M, W, F-Sa 10AM-5PM; Th 10AM-9PM; Su noon-5PM. 750 Hornby St; 604/682.4668). Then it's on to big-ticket department stores such as **Eaton's** and **Pacific Centre,** where the distinct background theme is of plastic slapping confidently against countertops.

Granville Island Public Market, a former warehouse district on the south shore of False Creek, is thick with shops selling fresh produce, Southwestern art, and the makings for beaded bracelets. Stop by the market area's **Granville Island Brewing Co.** for excellent local craft beers, including the Lord Granville Natural Pale Ale. Unless you arrive early on a Saturday or Sunday, count on being bruised at least a little by the masses who descend upon this place at any hint of sunshine. ♦ Tours daily 2PM; 604/666.6477.

More endearing—for its eclecticism and richness of architectural fenestration—is **Gastown,** what used to be the center of Vancouver when it was known as Granville (or "Luck-Lucky" to the local Indians) and before a fire in 1886 leveled much of the then-wooden city. Just as Seattleites have given new purpose to many of their old buildings, Vancouver

residents have preserved much of their heritage in this district on Burrard Inlet. The huge brick-and-terracotta **Canadian Pacific Railway Station** on West Cordova has been refurbished as a terminus for the **SkyTrain** system that links downtown Vancouver with the community of New Westminster. Several turn-of-the-century edifices have been connected with a skylight as **Sinclair Centre,** a vast hive of card shops and art outlets. Others have been divided with ethnic restaurants and furniture outlets, giving some visitors the feeling that Gastown has turned too commercial.

An easy escape when that feeling comes over you is to **Chinatown,** just to the east. Misanthropes should deftly avoid this area along Pender and Hastings streets, where the quantity of human flesh per square inch can be alarming on weekend grocery shopping days. But for others, Chinatown bears the ambience of foreign territory seemingly risen from familiar land.

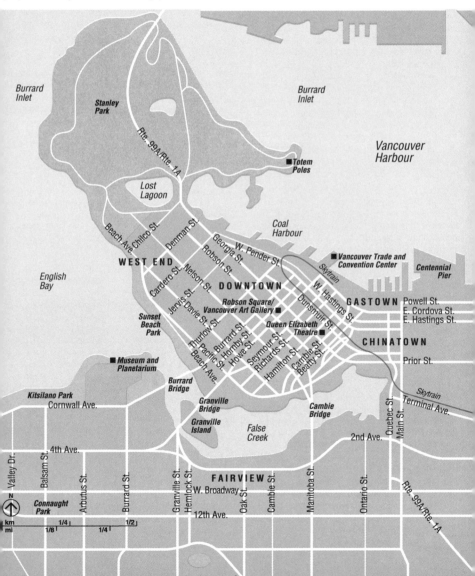

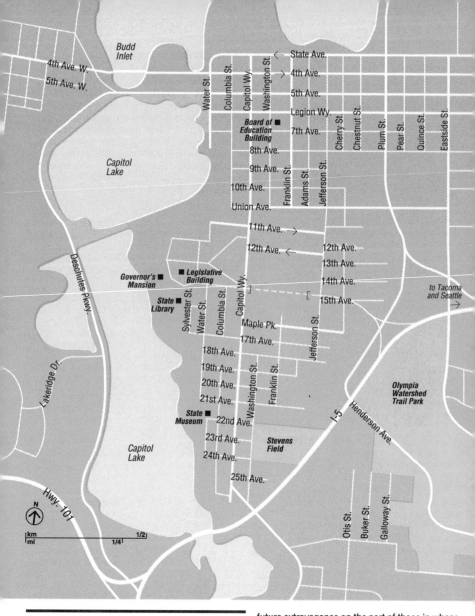

Olympia Capitol

In 1928 **Governor Roland E. Hartley** fumed publicly over $7 million that had been spent (with approval from his predecessor) to finally create a magnificent Olympia capitol complex for Washington state. Even on the day before state executives were to move into their new **Legislative Building** (illustrated at right), an occasion on which another public servant might have pontificated at length about how the monumental center symbolized the maturity and prosperity of his state, Hartley couldn't resist launching a few last darts at Washington's profligate lawmakers. "Today is an epochal day," he told reporters, "but it brings no joy to the heart of the taxpayer." Hartley worked himself into a bluster, the newspaper drudges scribbling wildly. "May the new building be a deterrent, rather than an incentive, to

future extravagance on the part of those in whose hands the business affairs of the state are entrusted." And he didn't stop there. After the complex's dedication, Hartley loaded some of the new capitol's "sumptuous furnishings"—including a few $47.50 spittoons—into an automobile and paraded them about the state to prove that his opponents in Olympia wouldn't hesitate to spend the taxpayers' hard-earned income. That the governor had made sure his own office in the Legislative Building would be the most sumptuous of all was not a subject touched on in his fulminations. Perched over **Budd Inlet,** at the southern tip of Puget Sound, Olympia shares the mediocrity of other small state capitols. But it's worth dropping in on, if only for the legislative campus and a couple of other sights.

Washington had talked since 1892 about raising a permanent statehouse. In 1893 it had even launched a nationwide competition to select an architect for the project. From 186 submissions, the commission chose **Ernest Flagg** of New York City, a young relation of shipping-and-railroad-magnate **Cornelius Vanderbilt** and a graduate of the Ecole des Beaux-Arts in Paris. Flagg planned a compact, heavily ornamented structure with a short dome and Corinthian columns running the length of its entry facade. Unfortunately, income from government land grants that was supposed to pay for Flagg's scheme fell short and construction on the building had to be halted soon after its foundations were laid. In 1901 the state approved instead the purchase of downtown Olympia's lordly old **Thurston County Courthouse** (now the **Board of Education Building**) as the temporary residence for Washington state government.

Forces didn't gear up to launch another capitol design competition until 1911. More money was available this go-around, but competition organizers insisted that Flagg's foundation should be integrated into any new conception, probably as the base for one of several buildings on a government campus. Flagg naturally assumed that his original commission was still in effect; in the years since 1893, he'd enhanced his bona fides by developing Manhattan's Singer Building and the Corcoran Art Gallery in Washington, DC. But the selection committee chose instead a couple of virtual unknowns: architects **Walter Wilder** and **Harry White.** Both had labored for a time with the famous New York firm of **McKim, Mead & White,** and in fact their plan for Washington's capitol owed an obvious debt to the work of that firm's late principal, **Stanford White,** who had created the Rhode Island capitol in the early 1890s, before being fatally shot by a jealous husband in 1906.

Wilder and White's initial Roman Classical Revival design called for a Legislative Building surrounded by five office structures, one of which would replace the 1908 brick **Governor's Mansion,** as well as an arrangement of stairs and landings descending to Budd Inlet and a grand promenade stretching into downtown, with a new railroad station at its terminus. Budget limitations doomed some embellishments, but results were nonetheless impressive. In Olympia, architecture historians **Henry-Russell Hitchcock** and

Legislative Building

William Seale wrote in their seminal work *Temples of Democracy: The State Capitols of the U.S.A.,* "the American renaissance in state capitol building reached its climax."

At the time of its raising, the Legislative Building's dome was the fourth tallest in the world—287 feet from the base—sliding into order behind those of St. Peter's of Rome (408 feet), St. Paul's Cathedral in London (319 feet), and the U.S. Capitol (307 feet). A massive Tiffany chandelier was hung inside its Alaskan marble rotunda. Other components are less ostentatious. Stairs leading to the north-side main entrance offer an imposing approach but pass beneath a largely unadorned pediment. The building presents colonnades on all four elevations, but most are fairly plain-looking. Wilder and White concentrated much of their decoration along the roofline, giving that an anthemion cresting, and at the east and west ends of the building where gables are fringed with dentilled cornices.

A face-lift in 1986, directed by **Barnett Schorr Architects** of Seattle, scrubbed Mount St. Helens' ash from the dome's exterior. Polish and color—including 48 rosettes and false-gold flourishes on column capitals—now brighten the rotunda's interior. Architecture and history enthusiasts should not miss an opportunity to visit. ♦ Free guided tours M-F 9AM-4:30PM; Sa-Su 10AM-4PM. Capitol Way (between 11th and 16th Aves); 206/586.8687.

Also worth seeing on the eight-acre campus are: the **State Library Building,** a more contemporary colonnaded edifice, designed in 1959 by noted architect **Paul Thiry** and containing Northwest art by **Mark Tobey** and **Kenneth Callahan,** as well as a collection of published works by Northwest authors; the **Governor's Mansion,** a Georgian Revival-style relic designed in 1908 by **Ambrose J. Russell** and **Everett P. Babcock,** who created other manses and some churches around Puget Sound (free guided tours W 1-2:30PM; call 586.8687 for reservations); and the Spanish-style **State Capitol Museum,** formerly the home of banker **Clarence J. Lord,** now containing old logging photos, Native American baskets, and more (Tu-F 10AM-4PM; Sa-Su noon-4PM; 211 W 21st Ave; 206/753.2580).

Not far away is the **Board of Education Building** and former **Thurston County Courthouse,** once home to Washington state's government. Architect **W.A. Ritchie,** armed with only a

correspondent's education in architecture from the U.S. Treasury Department, created this and other grand county courthouses in Spokane and Port Townsend. The imposing Olympia building blends massive stone archways nicely with rounded tower bases in a Romanesque Revival whole. There was originally a polygonal central tower on this structure, adding to its authoritative image, but that was destroyed by fire in 1928. A compatible west wing dates from 1905, when the courthouse began doubling as Olympia's city hall. Restoration has made this a most inviting structure. ♦ Franklin to Washington Sts, Legion Way to Seventh Ave.

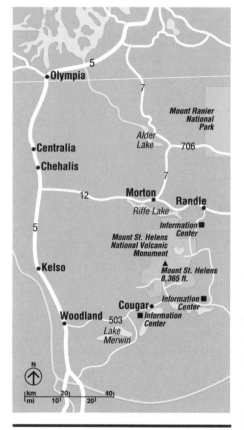

Mount St. Helens

It's something of a stretch to make this a day trip; with the mountain a good two hours south of Seattle, you may be justified in scheduling an overnight stay at one of the small towns along Interstate 5—especially if you intend to scale the broken peak.

Many mountains are taller than Mount St. Helens, the summit now 8,365 feet above sea level (before its May 1980 eruption, this peak was more than 1,300 feet higher), but the novelty of poking about what was very recently an active volcano can hardly be beat. Over the years, plants and wildlife have been returning to these slopes, and so have people. St. Helens is now a national volcanic monument, attracting more than 600,000 people every year.

Pack a lunch and start your study at the $5.3 million stone-and-timber **Visitors Center** (take Exit 49 off I-5 and head about five miles east on Highway 504 to **Castle Rock**). Here you'll see records of the devastation, notes on the deaths caused by the blast (at least 57), and photos of the ash and gases that spewed when four billion cubic yards of mountain were displaced (enough to provide each person on earth with one ton of ash). Children will love the walk-through volcano.

For a good view of the blast's results (a crater two miles across and half a mile deep), head to the northeast side. Take the I-5 turnoff east to Highway 12 and the town of **Randle** (about 49 miles from the turnoff). On the way, about three miles west of **Morton,** is a viewpoint where you can get a pretty good look into the crater. Fill your gas tank in Randle, as there are no stations between here and **Windy Ridge,** and then head east on Route 25; 10 miles along, there's an information station where you can ask questions before finally reaching Windy Ridge through miles of forest. Windy Ridge is about four miles north of Mount St. Helens—an unforgettable perspective, indeed. Climb a log-and-gravel path from there for still-better views of the mountain and what has become of **Spirit Lake,** once a popular vacation spot. It's so quiet up here it's hard to imagine that in 1980 this place echoed with a sound equivalent to 400 million tons of TNT exploding.

The mountain reopened to climbers in 1987, but all of them must be registered. (Steep fines are levied against hotdoggers.) The peak season is from 15 May through 31 October, when only 110 climbers are allowed up to the crater's lip each day. Permits may be obtained in advance from the Forest Service (write to Mount St. Helens National Monument, Route 1, Box 369, Amboy, Washington 98601; or call 206/247.5473). Seventy spaces are filled in advance for any one day, but 40 additional spaces are available only on what is essentially a first-come first-served basis. Interested parties must put their names on a list at **Jack's Restaurant and Sporting Goods** (Route 503, 23 miles east of Woodland and six miles from Cougar) the day before they hope to scale the mountain. At 6PM every day, those names are called in order until all 40 spaces are filled. (Unfortunately, each person can carry 12 people on his or her permit, so spaces often go quickly.) During the off-season (15 November to 15 May), climbers must still register at Jack's, but no advance permits are offered. Most climbers head up **Monitor Ridge** on the south face, a steep trek that may take seven to 10 hours round-trip. (Other routes are also available; ask for maps from the Forest Service.) It's a dusty climb during most of the summer, after the snow has melted, so you'll want to wear high boots or gaiters to keep the ash out of your socks. Also, don't wear contact lenses, as the ash can worm its way between them and your eyes. Bring plenty of water and energy food, and leave your dog behind because the glasslike ash can do serious damage to its paws.

Local Heroes

By ample justification and sometimes by the slimmest opportunity, people like to associate their hometown with one-time inhabitants who've gone on to fame and, perhaps, fortune. Seattle has an ample gallery of favorite sons and daughters.

Cartoonist **Hank Ketcham**, creator of the comic strip "Dennis the Menace," was born in Seattle in 1920. He based the character (whose first newspaper appearance was in 1951) on his son Dennis, who, at four and a half years of age, drove his mother—Ketcham's first wife, Alice—to label him a "menace." Ketcham now lives in California.

Stripper and burlesque queen **Gypsy Rose Lee** (née Rose Louise Hovick) was born in Seattle in 1914.

Martial artist **Bruce Lee,** perhaps most familiar from his movies (including *Enter the Dragon*) and his role as Kato on the old "Green Hornet" TV series, lived for four years in Seattle and attended the University of Washington. Although he was in Hong Kong when he died in 1973, he is buried in **Lake View Cemetery** on Seattle's Capitol Hill.

Barney Clark, the first person to receive a permanently implanted artificial heart, was a retired dentist from Des Moines, Washington, just south of Seattle. He lived on the device for a remarkable 112 days.

Red-headed funnywoman **Lynda Barry** was born in 1956 in Seattle's south end. Her first cartoons were published by the University of Washington's *Daily* in 1976, which led her to work at the now-defunct *Seattle Sun* and later to fame as a regular contributor to *Esquire* and as a novelist (*The Good Times Are Killing Me*).

Reclusive novelist **Thomas Pynchon** worked as a technical writer at Boeing from 2 February 1960 until 13 September 1962.

Betty MacDonald, who captured Washington farm life as never before in her novel *The Egg and I* (and later in the old "Ma and Pa Kettle" films, inspired by the book), moved from Colorado to Seattle in 1917 and died here in 1958.

Seattle native **Alice B. Toklas**—cook, author, and companion of writer **Gertrude Stein**—graduated at the turn of the century from the University of Washington with a degree in music.

Elizabeth Julesberg, the woman responsible for the "Dick and Jane" childhood readers, lived in Seattle for many years and died here in 1985.

Although efficiency expert and entrepreneur **James Emmet Casey** was born in Nevada, in 1907 he and three partners founded the **American Messenger Service** in a tiny basement under a sidewalk in Pioneer Square. Casey's creation grew to become today's **United Parcel Service.** The original Seattle office location is still marked at the corner of Second Avenue and South Main Street by a pleasant waterfall garden.

Eccentric poet **Theodore Roethke** taught at the University of Washington from 1947 until his death in 1963.

Herman Brix, a star football player and trackman at the University of Washington, took off for California, changed his name to **Bruce Bennett,** and became one of the first in a long string of Hollywood Tarzans.

President **Franklin D. Roosevelt's** daughter, **Anna,** was married to John Boettinger, publisher of the *Seattle Post-Intelligencer* in the late 1930s. As a result, **Eleanor Roosevelt** was a frequent guest at the Boettinger's Magnolia Bluff home, and FDR twice visited the Puget Sound area during World War II.

Tough-guy character actor **Howard Duff** was born in nearby Bremerton in 1917 but was reared in Seattle. He attended Roosevelt High School and worked as a window trimmer at the Bon Marché department store in the 1930s before heading off to Hollywood.

Frances Farmer, born in Seattle in 1914, graduated from West Seattle High School in 1931 with honors for her writing, debating, and leadership skills. She showed her feisty spirit early, winning a national award in 1930 for an essay she wrote on the death of God. She was later discovered by a film producer while traveling in the Soviet Union, during a trip she had earned by peddling subscriptions to a leftist Seattle paper. She went on to star next to Tyrone Power, Cary Grant, and Walter Brennan, before she was finally committed (by her own mother, who thought she'd gone crazy with alcohol) to Western State Hospital in Steilacoom. After discovering religion, Farmer was released and worked for several years as a maid in Seattle's **Olympic Hotel.** She made her comeback on television in 1957, and was the focus of the 1983 **Jessica Lange** movie, *Frances.*

Guitarist **Jimi Hendrix** was born in Seattle General Hospital in 1942 and reared in the primarily black **Central District.** Starmaker Chas Chandler, of the rock group the Animals, first heard Hendrix in 1966. He took Hendrix to London and launched a cultish career of music that burned brightly during the Summer of Love and only died out in 1970 when Hendrix himself perished from a barbiturate overdose. The rocker is buried at **Evergreen Memorial Cemetery** in Renton, just east of Seattle.

Gregory "Pappy" Boyington, whose exploits as a World War II flying ace were heralded in the TV series "Baa Baa Black Sheep" (starring Robert Conrad), was born in Idaho in 1912 but graduated from the University of Washington. He died in 1988.

Poet **Richard Hugo** may be most famous for the years he taught and wrote in Montana, but he was born in 1923 in White Center, just south of Seattle, and died of leukemia in Seattle in 1982.

Miss West Seattle of 1954 was aspiring actress Diane Friesen, who later changed her name to **Dyan Cannon.**

Born in Seattle in 1910, **Ted Jones** was a Boeing Company employee (he hung wings on B-17s) before he launched the modern hydroplane in 1950.

Essayist and novelist **E.B. White** landed in Seattle in 1922, four years before he enjoyed his first fame with the *New Yorker* and long before he penned *Charlotte's Web.* He arrived from Manhattan in a Model T he'd dubbed "Hotspur" and settled quickly into a job as the first full-time columnist for the *Seattle Times,* writing a sometimes-humorous anecdotal "Personal Column." Nine months later the Seattle daily fired him, saying it was "no reflection on [his] ability."

The late dance choreographer **Robert Joffrey** was born Abdullah Jaffa Anver Bey Kahn in Seattle in 1930. **Mark Morris,** a more controversial but no less well known choreographer, was born in Seattle in 1956 and attended Mount Baker's Franklin High School.

Renowned jazz singer **Diane Shuur** and **Kenny G,** the saxophonist **President Bill Clinton** calls his favorite musician, got their starts in Seattle.

Current residents of the Seattle area include:

Harry Anderson, the bumbling magician/judge from TV's "Night Court."

Novelist **Pete Dexter** (*Paris Trout, Brotherly Love*), who lives on Whidbey Island.

Software entrepreneur **Bill Gates,** the boss and brains at computer giant **Microsoft,** born in Seattle in 1955. Gates attended preppy Lakeside School, where fellow students thought him a bit absentminded.

Mark Helprin, famous for his collection *Ellis Island and Other Stories* but also more recently for his novel *A Soldier of the Great War.*

Charles Johnson, author of the National Book Award-winning *Middle Passage.*

Gary Larson, whose "The Far Side" cartoons are syndicated in more than 700 newspapers. Larson was born here in 1950.

Peg Phillips, who plays Ruth-Ann on TV's "Northern Exposure."

Tom Robbins, author of *Even Cowgirls Get the Blues* and many other novels, who lives in La Conner, a slow-paced town to the northwest.

Jim Whittaker, who in 1963 became the first American to surmount Mount Everest. Whittaker lives in West Seattle, about three miles from where he was born in 1929.

Wildlife photographer **Art Wolfe,** who lives in West Seattle.

Ann and **Nancy Wilson,** better known as the rock music duo **Heart.**

Tim Girvin
Designer, Tim Girvin Design, Inc.

Being a lucky person, I live in one of the nicer neighborhoods of the city, **Queen Anne.** Many of the homes date from the late 1800s to the early 20th century, and are arrayed throughout Queen Anne Hill, adjacent to and overlooking the city. **Highland Drive** here is a particularly spectacular loop with views out to the Sound; it makes an excellent running route with vistas of both the Cascade and the Olympic mountains.

The **Washington Park Arboretum** in the fall is a blaze of brilliantly colored deciduous trees from around the world; nestled inside is the **Japanese Tea Garden,** with its own traditionally crafted teahouse. A walk is particularly evocative when it's misty.

A couple of blocks from my office is **Pike Place Market.** An early morning stroll here is especially intriguing as the musicians get tuned up, the produce brokers arrange their stock, and the vendors array their wares, haggle for space, and converse. Down the way is the **Athenian Inn,** where you can have a schooner of beer at 6AM along with their motley crew or, for the more health conscious, a hearty breakfast.

Below the market is **Wild Ginger** (for Far Eastern *satay*) on Western Avenue. Straight down at the bottom of the hill on Western Avenue is **Al Boc-calino,** a lively celebration of Italian food, style, manner, and service.

North of Seattle, a windy ferry cruise from **Anacortes** to the **San Juan Islands** can be a wonderful voyage (however, avoid the ferry in the summer at all costs). Out on the coast, in the off-season, visit **Lake Quinault.** Farther west you'll find the long beaches at **Kalaloch.** During the winter, huge white castles of ocean foam called "spume" drift off the shore.

Design types should drop by **Peter Miller Books** on First Avenue. Afterward, you can walk across the street to the **Virginia Inn,** a tavern with lots of art on the walls and a doorway to the burgeoning arts community of **Belltown.**

For performance art, go to **On the Boards.** And **The Weathered Wall,** after 10:30PM, is a great club.

Killer squash games at the **Seattle Club** under Grand Master **Yusuf Khan.** Take your racquet and try to get a court!

A run to West Seattle brings you to **Lincoln Park,** for a shoreline walk of the Sound and a daily view of the ferries as they make their way out of Elliott Bay to Bremerton as well as Vashon and Bainbridge islands—a rather inefficient method of transportation but a wonderful visual service.

Forty-five minutes out of Seattle, the **Cascades** beckon with simple hikes or brisk strolls into the coniferous forests. I recommend **Lake Talapus,** the **Denny Creek Falls,** the **McClennan Butte** path, and a couple of walks on the railway lines (south and high on the hills, now in disuse) that one can see from Interstate 90.

Farther north of the Cascades on the **Loop Highway,** an extraordinary drive in the fall, are the **Big Four Ice Caves.** You can hike across a boardwalk path through a swamp and up the hills to massive openings in the side of a glacier, where a shower of icy water pours down in the mystic blue interior. Across the way is **Index Mountain,** the center point of the planet for some of the more difficult rock climbing—just watching is an adventure. And check out **Wallace Falls** nearby.

Fred Bassetti
Architect/Bassetti, Norton, Metler, Rekevics

A hundred years ago Bourke Cockran told the young Winston Churchill, "What the people want is the truth. That is the exciting thing. Tell the simple truth." Where do you find the truth in Seattle?

Start at the alley between Second and Third avenues at Lenora Street and go south two blocks to Stewart Street. (Don't do this at night unless you have an unusual taste for adventure.) Note the brick paving and brick-arched windows, old signs and hobo messages, shipping docks, steel ladder fire escapes, back doors, human-scale spaces, and old pipes and wires. Everything has the ring of truth.

Turn right two blocks to Post Alley, which leads north to shops and restaurants and south to the heart of **Pike Place Market.** Do you want haggis, kippers, fennel honey, fried burdocks, Bolivian shrimp soup, or a hundred varieties of spice? There must be 98 restaurants in the market. I go to the **Athenian Inn** for Greek, Dalmatian, Italian, Portuguese, or American food and a superb harbor view, and to **Campagne** for unvarying quality.

Walk to the offbeat **Waterfront** on the south end of downtown, passing through Seattle's oldest district, **Pioneer Square,** on the way. Our only street with fine old buildings on each side is **Occidental Avenue,** between Main and Jackson streets. Stop for a world-class *latte* at **Torrefazione Italia.** A half-block north and west you can pick up a picnic lunch at my wife's **Grand Central Bakery** (which has the best bread in town, according to a *Seattle Weekly* poll). Go through the lofty **Grand Central Arcade** to First Avenue, north to Washington Street, and one block left to the beginning of the Waterfront. Note the ornate iron pergola at the public boat landing there.

From the end of the boat landing, you get an unusual view of Seattle's dramatic skyline. Walk south past shipping container yards and the backs of old brick buildings. You will come, after a few blocks, to the railroad yards and the **Coast Guard Museum;** continue a block or so farther on and, at Massachusetts Street, turn right to the water's edge. I like to sit here on a chunk of broken concrete, munch my sandwich, admire the gigantic orange loading cranes and oceangoing ships nearby, look for floating logs and birds, and let calm take over.

Fishermen's Terminal in Ballard, where hundreds of fishing boats (purse seiners and trollers mainly) moor for the winter. Walk out on the docks to look at the high-tech fishing nets and to explore. **Chinook's** restaurant, on the main quay, is famous for its fish and unique wild-blackberry cobbler.

From here go north across the **Ballard Bridge** and turn right. If you walk or bicycle to Fremont, which is about a mile and a half to the east along the ship canal, you will experience a working waterfront with all manner of industrial activity.

At the north end of the Fremont Bridge, Seattle's most beloved sculpture, *People Waiting for the Interurban* by **Richard Beyer,** invites endless "dressing up" by uninhibited citizens. Another work of genius is *The Black Sun* at Volunteer Park by **Isamu Noguchi.**

Houseboats, almost unique to Seattle, are *real* houses on floats. They line the east and part of the west side of Lake Union and the west side of Portage Bay, across the water from the University of Washington. They are becoming gentrified, so look for the unimproved ones that used to sell for $700.

In this general area, at the south end of Lake Union (Seattle's in-town lake), is the **Center for Wooden Boats,** a much-valued keeper of tradition. Take time to visit the famous old salt-codfish schooner *Wawona* next door.

Bourke Cockran would feel right at home in any of these places.

Trevor Logan
Former Proprietor, The Gaslight Inn

Highland Drive overlook of Elliott Bay and downtown Seattle.

Broadway on **Capitol Hill.**

The most beautiful, romantic bed-and-breakfast in the West—**The Gaslight Inn.**

Of course, **Pike Place Market** and **Rainier Square.**

Washington Park Arboretum.

The sand dunes at **Fort Lawton.**

Ferry rides to **Winslow,** on **Bainbridge Island.**

Georgina's Pizza.

Elliott Bay Book Company.

The Two Bells Tavern—the best little hamburger joint in Seattle.

Sixty percent of the airline jets operating outside of the former Soviet Union were manufactured by Boeing. They transport 675 million passengers each year—that's 12 percent of the planet's population.

According to the *Washington Almanac,* if Puget Sound's coastline could be stretched from end to end, it would reach from Seattle to Chicago, a distance of 2,031 miles.

History

Archaeological evidence points to the existence of humans in western Washington as far back as 12,000 years ago. Native Americans living in this area were part of the Northwest Coast culture, which thrived from Oregon to southern Alaska. These people were not like the great tribes found elsewhere in North America. In fact, they weren't organized as tribes at all, but instead gathered in small villages of family-sized clans. Like the pioneers who would later invade the Pacific Northwest, the Native Americans who lived here alone for centuries were fiercely independent. Men became leaders not through any inheritance, but by dint of their abilities. They governed their fishing and gathering societies by example rather than might. Warfare was rare among these villages, and the land was bountiful, with plenty for all. What raids were made on other native groups may have had more to do with procuring slaves than territorial or clan rivalries.

Today's **King County** was populated by natives of the **Coast Salish** group. They averaged just under five and a half feet in height, and the men had more facial hair than was common among North American Indians. Pressure boards were often applied in infancy to flatten their foreheads. They were fine woodworkers, if somewhat less given to ceremonial carving than their counterparts in what is now British Columbia, using mostly red cedar in their canoes, their often-conical hats, and their long, narrow houses. Their culture grew up around rivers, and each enclave had a slightly different subdialect (which would later frustrate whites trying to negotiate treaties). Storytelling was a rich tradition among these people, and provided an important historical record.

Bustling downtown Seattle was once land belonging to the **Duwamish** people. (The **Suquamish,** who were led in the mid-19th century by **Chief Sealth,** lived on the west side of Puget Sound and claimed all the islands between.) After King County's **Indian War** of 1855-56, which wasn't precipitated by the Duwamish but tainted them nonetheless, these people were forced onto reservation lands on the western shore of Puget Sound. But over the next decade they drifted back to their old village sites near Seattle and were employed as laborers. Government promises to award them their own reservation were not kept. Once one of the largest Native American groups on Puget Sound, numbering in the thousands, today there are only several hundred Duwamish still inhabiting King County.

1775

Spanish explorer **Bruno Heceta** sends a boat ashore south of today's **Cape Flattery,** a headland at the entrance to the **Strait of Juan de Fuca.** The crew is captured and killed by Native Americans.

1778

British **Captain James Cook,** on his third round-the-globe tour, discovers Cape Flattery; however, he plies north rather than east, so he misses Puget Sound completely.

M. BLUM

circa 1786

Sealth, son of **Schweabe,** chief of the Suquamish and Scholitza Indians, and a future chief himself, is born on **Blake Island,** in western Puget Sound.

1790

The Spanish establish the first white settlement at **Neah Bay,** on the northwest Washington coast.

In the same year Spanish explorer **Manuel Quimper** sails deep into the Strait of Juan de Fuca, encountering and naming some of the **San Juan Islands.**

1792

After circumnavigating **Vancouver Island** in southwestern British Columbia, English **Captain George Vancouver** and his second lieutenant, **Peter Puget,** launch two separate explorations of the "inland sea," which Vancouver names Puget Sound.

1803

President Thomas Jefferson dispatches **Meriwether Lewis** and **William Clark** west to the mouth of the **Columbia River,** which they reach in 1805. Other Yankees are encouraged to follow.

1821

The **Florida Treaty** transfers all rights to territory north of the 42nd parallel to the United States. Britain's **Hudson's Bay Company (HBC),** however, still claims sole rights to the **Oregon Territory,** especially property north of the Columbia River, including present-day Washington state.

1845

In defiance of HBC hegemony, Yankees begin spilling north across the Columbia River.

1846

Finally yielding to U.S. pressure, Great Britain agrees to cede lands south of the 49th parallel (today's U.S.-Canada border) to the Yankees.

1850

The **Donation Land Law** encourages settlement of America's western territories by awarding 320 acres to every white or "half-breed" who will occupy and farm the land for at least four consecutive years. Another 320 acres are given to any couple married by 1 December 1851.

1851

On 13 November, seven months after leaving Illinois, Seattle founder **David Denny** and his party of 23 arrive at **Alki Point** aboard the ship *Exact.* Soon after, the families begin relocating to the east side of **Elliott Bay** for its thicker forests and deeper harbor.

1852

Pioneer **Dr. David Swinton ("Doc") Maynard** from Ohio arrives at Elliott Bay and befriends **Indian Chief Sealth.** When he and other city founders decide that their settlement's informal moniker, **Duwamps,** is

too inelegant, Maynard suggests "Seattle," a spin on the good chief's name that's easier to pronounce than the guttural Salish original.

Henry Yesler comes later in the year to build Seattle's first steam sawmill. Yesler's initial location is in **West Seattle,** but other pioneers convince him to build instead on Elliott Bay. The strip of land over which he drags his felled trees becomes known as "Skid Road."

The **Oregon Territorial Legislature,** meeting at the beginning of the year, carves King County from the eastern banks of Puget Sound. Seattle, though still not fully platted, becomes the county seat.

1853

President Millard Fillmore signs the act creating **Washington Territory.**

1855

Tensions between whites and Native Americans precipitate King County's so-called **Indian War.** The American battle sloop *Decatur,* sailing from Honolulu to protect Seattle settlers, rains cannonballs and grapeshot into forests beyond Third Avenue where invaders might be hiding. Natives retaliate by burning nearly every building in the county. After a final skirmish in March 1856, first **Territorial Governor Isaac Stevens** encourages punishment of warring Indians and the banishment of others to reservations.

1861

Washington's **Territorial University** (which is later named the **University of Washington**) is built where downtown's **Four Seasons Olympic Hotel** now stands.

1863

Seattle's first newspaper, the *Gazette,* rolls off its homemade presses. It will publish irregularly for the next three years.

1864

Asa Mercer, a three-year Seattle resident and the Territorial University's first president, travels to New England, where he convinces 11 young women (remembered by history texts as the **Mercer Girls** and by television audiences as the inspiration for "Here Come the Brides") to return with him as wives for very lonely Seattle men. Appreciative bachelors thereafter elect Mercer as their territorial senator, without even expecting him to campaign.

1866

Chief Sealth, who had somehow persuaded his people to stay out of the Indian War, dies at the Port Madison Reservation in Kitsap County.

1867

Former San Franciscan **Samuel Maxwell** founds the *Weekly Intelligencer,* which becomes a daily in 1876 and merges with the failing *Post* five years later to form what is known today as the *Seattle Post-Intelligencer.*

History

1869

The territorial legislature grants Seattle a city charter. City population: 1,107.

1870

Seattle's first grade school is erected.

1872

Representatives of the **Northern Pacific Railroad** visit Puget Sound to discuss the location of the railway's western terminus. To the shock of Seattleites, **Tacoma** is selected.

1878

German immigrant **Andrew Hemrich** founds a small brewery in south Seattle. He calls his beer **Rainier.**

1879

The city's first big fire destroys a number of wooden structures bordering the Waterfront, including **Yesler's Mill.**

1882

Seattle gets a taste of vigilantism after a pair of thieves try to hold up popular merchant **George B. Reynolds** at the corner of Third Avenue and Madison Street. When Reynolds reaches for his pistol, one of his assailants shoots him through the chest. Four hours later patrols find the thieves—**James Sullivan** and **William Howard**—hiding in a haystack. During a court hearing the next morning, an angered crowd of men seizes the suspects, drags them outside, and hangs them from a tree near what is now **Pioneer Place Park.** Still not satisfied, the vigilantes also storm the local jail, grab a man accused of killing a police officer, and hang him, too.

1883

Business baron **Henry Villard,** newly elected president of the Northern Pacific Railroad, agrees to link Seattle by rail with Tacoma and Portland, Oregon. But shortly after that, financial problems force Villard's resignation and closure of the Seattle extension.

1885

Violence erupts again when Seattleites hold an anti-Chinese congress and demand that local Asians leave western Washington. A similar declaration is made in Tacoma, which quickly puts its Chinese on trains headed for Portland. Seattle's Chinese don't depart so easily. After 197 of them are shipped to San Francisco, martial law is declared and U.S. troops halt the forced exodus.

1889

In mid-summer the **Great Seattle Fire** destroys 30 city blocks in what is now the historical **Pioneer Square** area.

On 11 November Washington becomes the 42nd state of the Union.

1892

Reginald H. Thomson is appointed city engineer and begins a 20-year regrading program that will drastically change Seattle's topography.

1893

The first train traveling **James J. Hill's** new **Great Northern Railroad** line reaches Seattle from St. Paul, Minnesota. Hill goes on to create the country's first trade and passenger services, between Puget Sound and the Orient.

1896

Bombastic former Midwestern publisher **Alden J. Blethen** buys the ailing *Press-Times* newspaper and re-creates it as the *Seattle Daily Times.*

1897

The steamship *Portland* arrives in Seattle with a ton of gold from Alaska, beginning a well-publicized and profitable rush through this city of men bound for the **Klondike.**

1898

Hundreds of thousands of men are processed through a new 640-acre U.S. Army base on **Magnolia Bluff,** bound for the **Spanish-American War.** The outpost is later named **Fort Lawton,** honoring a general killed in a Philippines skirmish.

1900

Illinois lumberman **Frederick Weyerhaeuser,** escaping diminishing timber reserves in the Midwest to land at Puget Sound, assembles a partnership to buy 900,000 forested acres in Washington and Oregon from the Northern Pacific Railroad. **The Weyerhaeuser Company** will dominate Northwest lumbering throughout the century.

Population of Seattle: 80,761—double what it was just 10 years before.

1907

Pike Place Market opens.

1908

William Boeing, the son of a wealthy Michigan timber baron, moves to Seattle after several years of running an independent timber operation in Grays Harbor in south Puget Sound.

1909

Seattle holds its first world's fair: the **Alaska-Yukon-Pacific Exposition.** After its close, the **Olmsted Brothers,** famed landscapers from Massachusetts, replan the fairgrounds as today's **University of Washington** campus.

1910

Washington's constitution is amended to allow women the vote, about 10 years before most other states do so.

The U.S. Congress authorizes construction of a ship canal linking **Lake Washington** with Puget Sound, and ground is broken for the first lock within a year.

Bill Boeing attends an air meet in California, where he becomes fascinated with the art of flying.

1914

As Europe comes to a boil with **World War I**, a barge loaded with dynamite for shipping to Russia explodes in Elliott Bay. Sabotage is suspected but never confirmed.

1916

Bill Boeing, along with navy officer **G. Conrad Westervelt,** founds an airplane enterprise on the **Duwamish River**—the beginnings of today's wealthy **Boeing Company.**

In **Everett,** just north of Seattle, labor conflicts between members of the **Industrial Workers of the World ("Wobblies")** and lumber companies lead to the so-called **Everett Massacre,** during which at least seven men are killed and 31 others are wounded by rifle fire.

Washingtonians vote to make the sale and consumption of alcoholic beverages unlawful—four years before national **Prohibition** begins.

1917

In April, **President Woodrow Wilson** engages the United States in World War I. A month later, the **Lake Washington Ship Canal** opens and U.S. Navy training craft begin docking off the University of Washington campus.

1918

The nation's influenza epidemic hits Seattle hard, killing 252 people out of every 100,000. Public assemblages are prohibited, and the local health department orders citizens to wear flu masks. The ban on congregation is lifted on 11 November, the day after the war's armistice is signed and a national holiday, so Seattleites can celebrate with each other.

1919

Three years after the Everett Massacre, Seattle hosts the nation's first general strike. Sixty thousand organized workers walk off their jobs in protest of the growing power of capitalists. The city lies tense and quiet for several days, until strikers agree to return to work. Unlike the protest in Everett, no blood is shed here.

1920

The **Volstead Act (Prohibition)** is passed by Congress, turning the nation dry and opening a wealth of opportunity for Seattle rumrunners.

1926

Bertha Landes is elected mayor of Seattle. She is the first woman to hold such an exalted post in a major U.S. city.

1929

New York stock markets crash in late October. As with so many other trends since, it takes several months for the **Great Depression** to reach Seattle.

1931

Huge shantytowns spring up near the Waterfront to house Seattle's many unemployed, mostly men. Officials try to burn out these **Hoovervilles,** but they always sprout anew.

1934

Longshoremen in Seattle, San Francisco, and elsewhere are idled for 98 days by the Pacific Coast waterfront strike. Strikebreakers are tossed into Elliott Bay or killed. **Mayor Charles Smith** fires his police chief for being too lenient with protesters, and orders a crowd of 2,000 strikers clubbed before the strike is settled.

1940

The **Lacey V. Murrow Floating Bridge** opens, connecting Seattle with its eastern suburbs.

1941

After the bombing of Hawaii's Pearl Harbor, the United States enters **World War II.** Boeing Company, the **Puget Sound Naval Shipyard** in nearby Bremerton, and other area manufacturers kick into high gear to feed the war machine. The U.S. Navy assumes control of Puget Sound shipping, and Seattle becomes a major Army transport center.

1942

Fearful of spies and saboteurs, the **Western Defense Command** orders that Japanese people living in Seattle and elsewhere on the coast be interned. Asians from **Bainbridge Island** are the first ones sent to detainment camps in Idaho.

1945

The atom-bombing of Hiroshima and Nagasaki ends the war with Japan. Victory celebrations are cooled, however, by news of peacetime economic declines, especially at Boeing, where annual sales drop from $600 million to $14 million.

1949

The worst earthquake recorded in Seattle history (measuring 7.2 on the Richter scale) strikes in mid-April.

1962

Seattle's second world's fair, the **Century 21 Exposition,** opens to six months of tremendous success.

1963

Proposals to level **Pike Place Market** in favor of high-rise rookeries prompt an aggressive preservation campaign.

1965

Efforts begin to revitalize **Pioneer Square,** the city's original but deteriorating downtown.

1967

National unrest reaches Seattle when the University of Washington's **Black Student Union** takes control of the university administration building. Protests against the **Vietnam War** begin citywide.

Looking for something to leaven tensions, Seattle advertising exec **David Stern** creates the now-ubiquitous **Happy Face** symbol.

1968

The city launches its **Forward Thrust Program** for improvements that include a new domed stadium, new parks, and street repairs. However, a plan to reduce traffic congestion by constructing light-rail train lines radiating from downtown into the 'burbs fails at the voting booth; federal matching funds go instead to Atlanta, Georgia, which builds its own popular rail system.

City population: 587,000—seven times what it was at the turn of the century.

1970

Boeing, suffering after demand for its jets fails to measure up to estimates, lays off 65,000 workers over the next two years—two-thirds of its work force. Unemployment in the city leaps 12 percent as a result. Despair grows and a billboard proclaims "Will the Last Person in Seattle Please Turn Out the Lights?"

1971

The **Starbucks** coffee company is founded. Its name comes from the java-dependent first mate in Herman Melville's novel, *Pequod.*

1974

A seven-acre historic district is created to save Pike Place Market.

1975

Harper's magazine names Seattle the country's most livable city.

1980

Mount St. Helens explodes a hundred miles south of Seattle, sprinkling King County with ash.

IBM execs meet with **Bill Gates,** a 25-year-old techie and co-inventor (with **Paul Allen**) of the computer language BASIC, whom IBM hopes will help create the software needed for a first generation of personal computers.

1983

The International District's **Wah Mee Club,** a gambling parlor, becomes a nightmare zone when three young hoods murder 13 witnesses in a holdup the worst robbery-related mass murder in U.S. history.

Citing financial woes, the *Seattle Post-Intelligencer* wins a joint-operating agreement with its rival, the *Seattle Times.*

The **Washington Public Power Supply System** (not-so-fondly nicknamed "Whoops") defaults on its $7 billion debt, ending hopes for cheap nuclear power in Washington and causing a tremendous ripple effect through Seattle financial circles.

1985

Aldus Corporation, an all-but-unknown Seattle computer software company, ships its first product, **PageMaker,** and creates a catchphrase to describe its operation: **desktop publishing.**

1986

Microsoft, Bill Gates' growing computer software company, offers its stock to the public. The value will go up 1,200 percent in just six years.

1989

Voters who are upset by a plague of new skyscrapers and construction-clogged streets in Seattle approve a cap on the height and bulk of downtown buildings.

The *New York Times* proclaims that Seattle is the nation's espresso capital.

Well-off Oregonians and Californians move to Seattle in hordes, creating a bizarre seller's market for real estate that drives local home shoppers out of town.

1990

The **Lacey V. Murrow Floating Bridge** sinks into Lake Washington.

1992

Race rioting in Los Angeles spills over into laid-back Seattle, where vandals and arsonists control city streets for most of a week.

After 60 years, **Longacres** horse track is shut down; Boeing plans to raze it in favor of a flight-training center.

1993

Boeing announces production cutbacks and massive layoffs, causing a tidal wave of doubt over Seattle's fiscal future.

Fire investigators capture a serial arsonist who may have set most of 125 suspicious blazes reported in King and Snohomish counties.

The deaths of at least two children are traced to a deadly bacteria in hamburgers served in Seattle by the **Jack in the Box** fast-food chain.

Bests

Donald E. Carlson
Architect/King County Arts Commissioner/
Urban Enthusiast

Having chef/owner **Bruce Naftaly** make a special dish at **Le Gourmand** restaurant in Ballard.

Visiting any **Larry's Market.**

Going to a movie at **Seven Gables Theaters.**

Renting a kayak and taking a scenic loop around **Lake Union.**

Going to the **Seattle Opera.**

Wining and dining on **The Pink Door** restaurant's outdoor deck.

A run around **Green Lake** on a warm day.

Renting a canoe at the **University of Washington** and canoeing through the **Washington Park Arboretum.**

Standing underneath the fish skylight at the **Seattle Aquarium.**

Talking to Louie and Marv at **DeLaurenti's Specialty Foods,** and to Frank and Roger at **Frank's Quality Produce,** both in **Pike Place Market.**

Viewing the art-glass exhibit in the **Pacific First Centre** at Fifth Avenue and Pike Street.

Browsing through **Peter Miller Books** and "shooting the shit" with Peter.

Taking our pet geoduck to obedience school.

Eating sushi at **Nikko**—especially the shrimp heads and monkfish livers.

Breakfast in the **Georgian Room** at the **Four Seasons Olympic Hotel.**

Attending **First Thursday** at the art galleries in **Pioneer Square.**

Greg Kucera
Owner, Greg Kucera Gallery

Spend an intimate, quiet evening dining at **Chez Shea** overlooking Pike Place Market and Elliott Bay. It's a small, elegant restaurant with a seasonal prix-fixe menu featuring the kind of dishes one can never talk one's mate into fixing—better to go out and have a romantic candlelit supper.

At the other end of the spectrum is **Ho-Ho Seafood,** in the International District. This Chinese restaurant specializes in a dish of steamed shrimp served in a chile and scallion soy sauce—and it's ambrosia, time after time.

Other favorite bites to eat include *kasu* cod (marinated in sake leftovers) at **Aoki,** on Broadway; fried calamari at **Adriatica,** overlooking Lake Union; grilled sweetbreads in mustard sauce at **Maximilien-in-the-Market** and pork gypsy at **Labuznik,** both in the Pike Place Market area.

My favorite bit of architecture is the old **Federal Court House** at Fifth Avenue and Madison Street. It's a wonderful lesson in rhythm, repetition, and, above all else, restraint. A few of the newer buildings could take a lesson.

The best views of the **Space Needle** are experienced while heading south on the Aurora Bridge or east on Olympic Boulevard near Kinnear Park. In either instance the top section of the Space Needle appears for only a few seconds and, at first glance, looks like an alien spacecraft hovering above the trees; it's a shocking illusion that is scary only the first time and is amusing thereafter . . . depending on the state of your inquiring mind.

Don't miss **Second Avenue,** which has become a "public-art street." Beginning with a view of **Jonathan Borofsky's** *Hammering Man* at the **Seattle Art Museum** and continuing south on Second Avenue toward **Pioneer Square,** one can see large-scale public sculpture by such notables as **Manuel Neri, Isamu Noguchi, Beverly Pepper,** and **Anne** and **Patrick Poirier.** Other major works by **Robert Irwin** and **Henry Moore** are nearby on Third and Fourth avenues, respectively.

Additional concentrations of public art can be seen in **Seattle Center,** the **Downtown Bus Tunnel** (especially in the Westlake Station downtown), the **Washington State Convention and Trade Center,** and **Sea-Tac Airport.** The airport includes large works by luminaries **Louise Nevelson, Robert Rauschenberg,** and **Frank Stella,** as well as Northwest artists such as **Ross Palmer Beecher, Francis Celentano, Robert Maki,** and **Alden Mason;** looking at all the art is a great way to kill time while waiting for a delayed flight.

Seattle is blessed with several fine Asian antique dealers. My favorites are **Kagedo** (for textiles and bronzes), **Crane Gallery** (for Peking glass), **Marvel on Madison** (for Imari), and **Honeychurch Antiques** (for porcelain and screens). All can be found in the downtown area.

On the first Thursday of each month, the Pioneer Square and downtown galleries open their new exhibitions in unison between 6PM and 8PM. While the **First Thursday** gallery walk no longer holds the same thrill for me (I've hosted more than a hundred of them in the past nine years), it's a great crowd-pleaser for art collectors and art enthusiasts.

Bushell's Auctions has public auctions every Tuesday of consigned material, mostly furniture and collectibles. The occasional find proves that one person's junk is another's treasure.

Seattle's location in the Pacific Northwest puts it closer to the Orient than any other port in the United States. It's nearly 300 nautical miles closer to Japan than San Francisco, and 600 miles closer than Los Angeles.

The Main Events

Seattle residents, ever the aspiring extroverts, love to party. Inspiration may come from occasions as noble and mystical as the return of salmon to Northwest spawning grounds or as ignominious as the approach of fall and winter rain showers. Calendars in this area weigh heavily with annual fests, sporting events, and artsy convocations. Some of the most popular year-round celebrations include:

January

Chinese New Year The **International District** comes alive with fairs, dragon-dense parades, and cultural displays. Festivities celebrating the symbolic expulsion of demons used to last a month, but West Coast Chinese have whittled their events down to about a week. Seattle's is held in either January or February, depending on the lunar calendar. Call 623.8171 for more information.

February

Fat Tuesday Pioneer Square jiggles with jazz, rock, and Cajun melodies, plus a waiter/waitress race and a wild (by local standards) parade, as Seattle presents its own week-long spin on Mardi Gras. Free outdoor events begin the week before Lent. For details, call 623.1162.

Northwest Flower and Garden Show This veritable Eden of horticulture seems to grow each year, feeding Seattle's much-written-about fondness for gardening. Hundreds of demonstration plots, supply sales booths, statuary displays, and lectures by landscapers and gardening writers round out the schedule. The event takes place at the **Convention and Trade Center;** admission is charged. For information, call 789.5333.

March

St. Patrick's Day Downtown resounds with bagpipe music and the beat of dancing feet as an annual parade follows a special green stripe painted down Fourth Avenue, from City Hall to Westlake Center. Meanwhile, the popular and not too intimidating four-mile **St. Patrick's Day Dash** leaves from **Jake O'Shaughnessey's** restaurant (at 100 Mercer Street), bound for the Kingdome. Call 623.0340 for more about the parade. Registration is required for the race; call 763.3333.

Whirligig An indoor carnival for children, Whirligig features puppet performances, music, juggling, and even yo-yo instruction. Rides (only 25 cents apiece) include a giant slide. The fun takes place at the **Center House** in the **Seattle Center;** call 864.7225.

April

Daffodil Festival The warm-up act for Skagit Valley's Tulip Festival later in the month, this half-century-old tradition includes a parade of flower-bedecked private boats along with some Navy craft at **Tacoma** and a giant floral parade that marches through four towns—Tacoma, Puyallup, Summer, and Orting—all in one day. The mid-April event is totally free; 206/627.6176 (a long-distance call from Seattle).

Skagit Valley Tulip Festival It is not always easy to gauge precisely when the 1,500 acres of tulip fields north of Seattle will bloom, but it's guaranteed that thousands of Washingtonians will rush to see them when they do. Because Skagit Valley roads are regularly jammed during this time with squealing rubberneckers, the best plan of action is to find a bicycle and ride casually between the fields, perhaps purchasing a few brilliant bunches along the way. Capitalizing on the floral draw, the adjacent town of **Mount Vernon** celebrates tulip season with parades and a street fair. And **La Conner** almost explodes at the seams as tourists finish off their visit with a stroll through that burg's many small shops. Salmon barbecues, pancake feeds, and formal bike tours may also be on the docket. Watch newspapers for the official blooming announcement. The tulip fields are located outside of **Mount Vernon,** 60 miles north of Seattle on Interstate 5. Call 206/428.8547 (a long-distance call from Seattle) for further details.

May

Northwest Folklife Festival With booths offering handmade crafts, banjo players in torn jeans, gospel performances, storytelling sessions, and clog-dancing exhibitions, this free four-day hootenanny wanna-be—said to be the country's largest folk fest—strives to show that Seattle hasn't sold out completely to glitz. Like most major functions at **Seattle Center,** it's dominated by food booths. Attendees are asked to help defray administrative costs by purchasing commemorative event pins. The festival is held every Memorial Day weekend; 684.7200.

Opening Day of Yachting Season This is a big deal in a city that claims one boat for every 12 people. There's a ceremonial regatta held on **Lake Union,** races to showcase the talents of the University of Washington rowing team, and lots of Sunday sailors just trying to steer clear of collisions on **Lake Washington.** Call the **Seattle Yacht Club** for more about this free event; 325.1000.

Pike Place Market Festival One of the city's most boisterous neighborhood hooplas, this free festival offers live-music stages, plenty of food and drink, clowns, and an activities area set aside specifically for children. It's held every Memorial Day weekend at Pike Place Market; for details, call 587.0351.

Poulsbo Viking Fest Break out your horned helmets and help celebrate the Scandinavian heritage of Puget Sound's most deliberately Norwegian village. Expect live music, traditional dancing, and a group of iron-stomached guests engaging in a *lutefisk*-eating contest. The event is free and it's held in Poulsbo, on the Kitsap Peninsula, 12 miles northwest of Winslow (Bainbridge Island) on Highway 305; call 206/779.4848 (long distance from Seattle) for further information.

Seattle International Film Festival Founded in 1976, this is supposed to be the best-attended film festival in North America, offering more than 140 new works from around the world at several Seattle theaters. (Showings usually continue into June.) Series tickets are very popular and go on sale in January. Call 324.9996 for information.

University Street Fair Fed by a colorful cross section of University of Washington students and well woven with curious arts and crafts booths, this free two-day street party, begun in 1969, is always worth a look. There are lots of mimes, musicians, and street eats, plus great people-watching. It's usually held the third weekend in May on University Way NE. For more about the fair, call 527.2567.

June

Fire Festival More than a century after its **Great Fire of 1889,** which completely flattened downtown, the city can commemorate that blaze without pangs of loss. Fire equipment parades along **First Avenue,** live entertainment heats up **Occidental Park,** and historical exhibits teach the dangers of pyromania. **Pioneer Square** marks the center of activity; call 623.1162.

Fremont Arts and Crafts Fair Fremonsters show up by the thousands for this eclectic neighborhood celebration featuring not only food and crafts booths but live-music stages and plenty of independent performers. It takes place at **North 34th Street,** just north of the Fremont Bridge. For more about the fair, call 548.8376.

Mainly Mozart Festival The **Seattle Symphony** schedules three weeks of concerts honoring the genius of **Amadeus Mozart** and other 18th-century composers. Admission is charged and performances take place at the University of Washington's **Meany Theater.** For schedules, call 443.4740.

Out to Lunch Summer is officially declared when the sounds of midday concerts (from jazz to calypso) begin resounding from downtown's canyonlands. The series is free and usually continues through early September. Call 623.0340 for specific locations.

Seattle-to-Portland Bicycle Rally (STP) Since 1979, thousands of cyclists have departed from the **Kingdome** on the annual STP, a 200-mile pedalthon through the valleys, forests, and farmlands of western Washington on the way to Portland, Oregon. Riders complete this "Tour de Northwest" in one or two days, depending on their exercise history and/or their threshold of masochism (facilities halfway through the course are available to overnighters). Sponsored by the **Cascade Bicycle Club,** registration is first-come first-served, with a limit of 10,000 riders. For registration materials, send a 9"x12" envelope with 75 cents postage to STP, c/o Cascade Bicycle Club, P.O. Box 31299, Seattle, WA 98103. For further details, call 522.2453.

July

Bite of Seattle Here's yet another shameless opportunity to eat yourself silly in public, as 50 or more local restaurants serve their specialties from open-air booths. Don't forget the Tums. This food fest takes place at the **Seattle Center;** 232.2982.

King County Fair Enjoy five days of rodeoing, ax-throwing contests, and music headliners at the state's oldest county fair beginning the third Wednesday in July. The King County Fairgrounds are in **Enumclaw,** just 42 miles southeast of Seattle; take Interstate 5 south to the Auburn exit, then Highway 104. For more about this event, call 206/825.7777 (a long-distance call from Seattle).

Mercer Island Summer Celebration Booths display arts and crafts, jugglers perform, children are invited to participate in distracting building projects (one year, they constructed a small bridge), and Saturday night swings with a live band beside the dance floor. This event takes place the second weekend of July at various venues in the Mercer Island central business district; call 236.2545.

Olympic Music Festival The **Philadelphia String Quartet** (confusingly, based in Seattle since 1966) joins other musicians in a 10-weekend series of chamber-music performances, held in a turn-of-the-century barn on the nearby Olympic Peninsula from June through September. Bring blankets for sitting and keeping warm. Admission is charged and the festival is held in **Quilcene,** on the west side of Puget Sound, 11 miles west of the Hood Canal Bridge on Highway 104. Call 527.8839.

Pacific Northwest Arts and Crafts Fair Bellevue upstages Seattle with this half-century-old exhibition of performing arts, crafts displays, and a juried show of visual arts at the **Bellevue Art Museum** in Bellevue Square. It's free and takes place the last weekend of July. Bellevue Square is at NE Eighth Street and Bellevue Way NE in Bellevue. Call 454.4900.

San Juan Island Dixieland Jazz Festival Ferries chugging to San Juan Island are especially full when Dixieland lovers swarm toward one of this area's finest summer musical events. The three-day festival offers bands from around the country; in previous years, Igor's Country Jazz Band (from Colorado), Black Dogs (Florida), and Hot Frogs (Australia) have all taken turns here. Performances are in both the town of **Friday Harbor** and at nearby **Roche Harbor,** with a band-filled shuttle boat running betwixt the two. Warning: Lodging reservations can be hard to find in the San Juan Islands during this time (late July), so call *very* early to score a room. Three- or individual-day passes are available. San Juan Island is northwest of Seattle by ferry. Call 206/378.5509 (a long-distance call from Seattle) for more about the festival.

Seafair Before Seattle became a politically correct kind of town, the **Seafair Pirates**—a horde of brawny, hard-drinking guys who dressed up once a year like **Blackbeard's** minions and kidnapped (at least temporarily) prominent Seattleites—were a colorful aspect of the local summer celebration scene. Now they're often considered kitschy. Some humorless critics even say these buccaneers are too frightening for children. Sheesh! What's a pirate to do? The rest of Seafair, at least, maintains the flavor and support it has enjoyed since 1950. Milk carton boat races on **Green Lake,** a torchlight parade, hydroplane races on **Lake Washington,** and a fly-over by the acrobatic **Blue Angels** are all on the schedule. Just give a wide berth to those dudes with their cutlasses. This event is mostly free and it's held from the third weekend of July through the first Sunday in August at various venues. Call 728.0123.

August

Evergreen State Fair Animal shows, stock-car races, a chili cook-off, totem-pole carving, and cow-milking contests are all part of this 11-day show-and-tell in the backwoods hamlet of **Monroe,** 30 miles northeast of Seattle. The fair takes place from late August through Labor Day and there is an admission charge. For further details, call 206/794.7832 (long distance from Seattle).

Gig Harbor Jazz Festival Jazz and blues mix at this musical weekend celebration, which in the past has attracted such notables as Robert Cray and Diane Shuur. Concerts are given on a natural, grassy amphitheater at Gig Harbor, 47 miles southwest of Seattle. Admission is charged; call 206/627.1504 (long distance from Seattle).

Seattle International Music Festival The schedule includes master classes and open rehearsals, as well as chamber-music concerts. Violinist **Dmitry Sitkovetsky,** director of the Finnish music festival Korsholm, also directs this series. Performances are at **Meany Hall,** on the University of Washington campus, as well as at the **Chateau Ste. Michelle Winery** in Woodinville and other city venues. Admission is charged; 233.0993.

September

Bumbershoot Seattle's premier entertainment event, playfully taking its name from a British term for umbrella, is a four-day extravaganza of music, art shows, literary readings, and food, food, food. **Seattle Center** fills with crafts booths, fortune tellers, balloon artists, and the riffs of nationally known musicologists. Admission is charged and it's held Labor Day weekend; 684.7200.

The Great Northwest Microbrewery Invitational Sample the breadth of this region's primo craft brews. Admission is charged and the pouring takes place at the **Seattle Center;** call 684.7200.

Leavenworth Autumn Leaf Festival The Cascade Mountains village of Leavenworth, 150 miles east of Seattle, applauds the color shift of deciduous trees with a schedule of Bavarian music, lots of Germanic foodstuffs, and a parade. New England expats shouldn't miss this free event; it's held the last weekend in September. Call 509/548.5807.

Western Washington Fair Most folks just call this country fest the **Puyallup Fair,** as in the slogan "Do the Puyallup" (for out-of-towners, that's *pew-AL-up*). For 17 days, children can stuff themselves silly on cotton candy and then try to hold it all down as they bump along on carnival rides. Adults watch rodeos, livestock shows, and well-known country-and-western musicians. The smells of livestock and

the grunts of pigs abound. The fair takes place at the Puyallup Fairgrounds, 35 miles south of Seattle off Interstate 5. For more information, call 841.5045.

October

St. Demetrios Greek Festival Lovers of bouzouki music and gyro sandwiches take note. This partially covered ethnic tribute to Rain City's 10,000-plus Greek descendants, held at **St. Demetrios Church,** thrives on dancing, heaped plates of Athenian cuisine, wonderfully sticky baklava, and arts and crafts exhibits. Long lines form at the food booths, so come early. Admission is charged; 325.4347.

Issaquah Salmon Days This free two-day event, held the first weekend of October, commemorates the annual return of the Northwest's premier sporting fish to its spawning grounds with a parade, salmon bake, hydroplane races on **Sammamish Lake,** and live entertainment. Pony rides and face painting are a favorite for children. Events are held all over Issaquah, 15 miles east of Seattle on Interstate 90; call 392.0661.

November

KING 5 Winterfest A free five-week holiday jamboree, the Winterfest offers entertainment for children, a tent-enclosed ice rink, an official tree-lighting ceremony, and, of course, a jolly old St. Nicholas. Sponsored by local KING-TV, it's held from late November through early January at the **Seattle Center.** Call 684.7200.

December

Christmas Ship The Christmas Ship sails over **Elliott Bay** and **Lake Washington,** sparkling with colorful lights and adding a festive spirit to Seattle's holiday season. Bonfires are set up on local beaches to watch the crafts' passage. For site information, call 684.4075.

The Messiah This is one of very few American performances of Handel's celebrated work to employ authentic instrumentation. Call early (323.1040) for reservations, as tickets always sell out. The performances are held from early- to mid-December at **St. Mark's Cathedral.**

The Nutcracker The **Pacific Northwest Ballet's** rendering of this classic fairy tale might be only vaguely recognizable to Russian Tsar Nicholas II, for whom Tchaikovsky first staged his ballet in 1892. Seattle artist **Maurice Sendak's** set designs help make this performance both more whimsical and more memorable than its competitors. Tickets go on sale in October; 547.5900.

New Year's Eve at the Space Needle As many as 20,000 chilled and damp celebrants huddle on three levels of the Needle (on the observation deck, in the Space Needle Restaurant, and at the Skyline level) to offer toasts and kisses. Local bands hold forth at the tower's base. As midnight approaches, one of the elevators climbs the Needle, finally lighting a 12-foot-high set of numbers that heralds the beginning of the new year. Admission is charged to the Needle. For more details, call 443.2100.

Index

Bold page numbers indicate main references.

Hotels

The hotels listed below are grouped according to their price ratings; they are also listed in the main index. The hotel price ratings reflect the base price of a standard room for two people for one night during the peak season.

$$$$ Big Bucks ($250 and up)
 $$$ Expensive ($175-$250)
  $$ Reasonable ($100-$175)
   $ The Price Is Right (less
       than $100)

$$$$

$$$

ACCESS® Travel Diary

Page	Entry #	Notes

ACCESS® Travel Diary

Page	Entry #	Notes

ACCESS® Travel Diary

Page	Entry #	Notes

ACCESS® Travel Diary

Page	Entry #	Notes

Credits

Writer/Researcher
J. Kingston Pierce

Contributors
Heather Doran Barbieri
John Doerper
Matthew Fleagle
Nick Gallo
David George Gordon
David Hooper

Jodi Pintler Pierce
Jeff Pike
Giselle Smith
Charles Smyth
Adam Woog

ACCESS®PRESS

Editorial Director
Rebecca Forée

Project Editor
Lisa Zuniga

Staff Editor
Karin Mullen

Assistant Editor
Erika Lenkert

Contributing Editors
Margie Lee
Antonia Moore

Proofreaders
Suzanne Samuel
Annelise Zamula

Word Processor
Jerry Stanton

Design Director
Ann Kook

Project Designer
Cherylonda Fitzgerald

Designers
Carrē Furukawa
Claudia A. Goulette
Kitti Homme

Maps
Michael Blum
Kitti Homme
Patti Keelin

Illustrations
Michael Blum

Special Thanks
Mona Behan
Sherrod Blankner
Clifford N. Carlsen III
Dave Cowan
Cullen Curtiss
Carol Ann Smallwood

Printing and Otabind
Webcom Limited

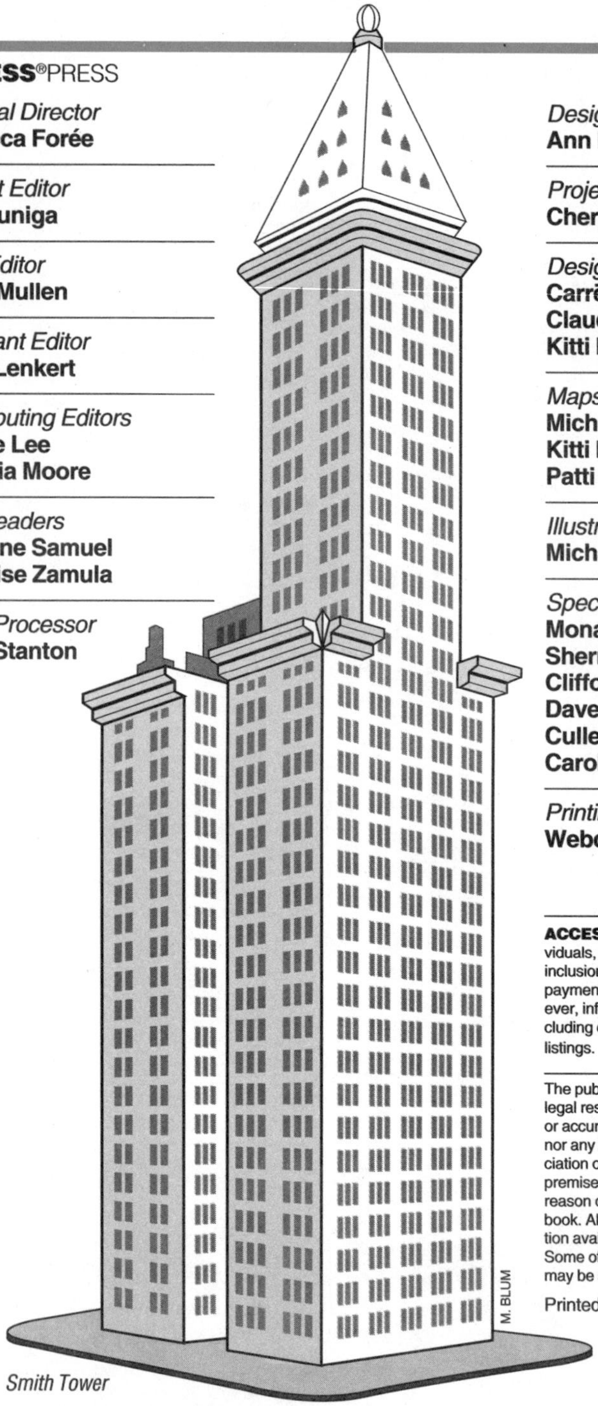

M. BLUM

Smith Tower